Human
Exceptionality

Human Exceptionality

Society, School, and Family

MICHAEL L. HARDMAN
University of Utah

CLIFFORD J. DREW
University of Utah

M. WINSTON EGAN
University of Utah

Allyn and Bacon, Inc.
Boston • London • Sydney • Toronto

DEDICATION

To our families: Terry, Robert, Jeffrey, Joel, and Camille Hardman; Laurie, Douglas, and Stephen Drew; Linda, Daniel, Amy, Mary Ann, and Marcia Egan

Series Editor: Jeffery W. Johnston

All photographs by John Telford

Library of Congress Cataloging in Publication Data

Hardman, Michael L.
  Human exceptionality.

  Bibliography: p.
  Includes index.
   1. Handicapped. 2. Exceptional children. 3. Individualism.
4. Handicapped—Services for. 5. Exceptional children—Services for.
6. Deviant behavior—Labeling theory. I. Drew, Clifford J., 1943–   . II. Egan, M. Winston. III. Title.
HV1568.H37 1984   362   83-17919
ISBN 0-205-08100-2

Printed in the United States of America
10 9 8 7 6 5 4 3 2   89 88 87 86 85 84

Contents

Foreword

What if it happened to you? What if you suddenly became the parent, brother, sister, uncle, or aunt of an "exceptional" child? And what if there were no warnings of this unexpected but not unusual event? What would you do?

That was the situation I faced fifteen years ago when my mentally retarded son was born. Like every other parent-to-be, I expected Jay to be normal, and I had a well-conceived notion of what I meant by normal. We all entertain the assumption and hopes that our children will be normal. But what if our assumptions are ill-founded and our hopes misplaced? What if it happens to us?

My world turned upside down when Jay was born. His birth was my personal Yorktown: When Cornwallis surrendered to Washington at Yorktown, the world turned upside down for the British and colonists alike. And Jay's life has been to me what Gandhi's was to India: a time when the persistent challenging of our old ways of life caused people to reform, to begin new ways of life.

What do we do when our world turns upside down? One major step we should take is to become educated, take instruction, learn cognitively those lessons we will come to know emotionally, and begin to adjust our rational selves to our emotional selves. How do we do that?

If the book you are about to read had been available to me at that time, some physician, psychologist, social worker, nurse, or parent of a handicapped child would have referred me to it, and between the shock waves of adjusting to my new reality, I would have read it and tried to learn from it. More than that, I would have kept it as one of my constant companions for use over the years. Why would I have wanted this book as my first reading in exceptionality, and why would it have been so useful over the years? Those reasons will apply to you both as a student and as a prospective professional, and to you or your friends or family, if it ever happens to you or them.

The principal reason is that this book is both educational and instructive. It is educational in the classic sense of "leading, drawing, bringing" a person from one stage of knowledge to another. In this sense, this book draws readers out of their cognitive and attitudinal status quo and impels them to a different one, to one that results in more acquired knowledge (raw learning) and a heightened sensitivity to the relative differences between the normal person and the exceptional person. And this book is instructive in the classic sense of "piling upon, putting in order, erecting" a new knowledge base. Most of us have some prior knowledge of exceptionality. We know people who are gifted and talented, who are physically or mentally disabled, or who are aged. The authors of this book add significantly to our store of knowledge about exceptional people.

Another important reason for reading and rereading this book is its reliance on and use of published research on exceptionality. While the book does not purport to be an exhaustive review of the literature on any given topic, it comes as close to that as it can and still remain consistent with its purpose of being an introductory textbook. It will therefore be useful to you as your career develops.

A third reason this book will be useful to you both now and later is its breadth. Introductory textbooks in special education typically do not address such major social issues as the exceptional person's family or the aging process as experienced by normal and exceptional people, but this book does. Nor do introductory textbooks start out educating and instructing by totally immersing the reader in the cultural and interdisciplinary aspects of exceptionality. This book, however, does just that: It submerges the reader in the indisputable fact that cultural expectations define both normalcy and exceptionality, and it moves from this proposition to a focus on the individual—on the *person* with a learning disability instead of on a learning-disabled person, on the *person* who experiences retardation instead of on a retardate, on the *person* who fits cultural and statistical constructs of normalcy instead of on a normate. What is more, this book forces the future educator to confront both the contributions and the limitations of one's own discipline (education) as well as those of functionally related disciplines (medicine, psychology, social work, anthropology, and law). Finally, this book identifies the major principles that guide special education and demonstrates that these are not new, but long-standing, principles; it brings one's professional history alive by making it relevant to current practices.

You will find that this book is accurate, reliable, and sensitive to the myriad of nuances about "exceptionality," about *that condition that we let ourselves be influenced by when we confront the unexpected.* So read and enjoy, and as you do, remember: *The most tragic limitations are those we place on ourselves.* The authors' perspective is that *we can remove self-imposed limitations, and in doing so, we can remove the limitations that others experience.* That is the ultimate test of the worth of this exceptional book.

H. Rutherford Turnbull, III
Professor and Chairman, Special Education
Courtesy Professor, Law
The University of Kansas
Lawrence, Kansas

Preface

What does the word *normal* mean to you? What do such terms as exceptional, deviant, disordered, disabled, or handicapped mean, and why are they used to describe human beings? Some labels, such as mentally retarded or deaf, are more familiar to you than others. Who or what influenced your knowledge and attitudes about these labels and the people behind them? It is likely that you were influenced most by life experiences and not by formal training. You may have a family member, friend, or casual acquaintance who is exceptional in some way. It may be that you are a person with exceptional characteristics. Then again, you may be approaching a study of human exceptionality with little or no background on the topic. You will find that a study of human exceptionality is a study of being human. Perhaps you will come to understand yourself better in the process.

Our goal is to introduce you to persons characterized as exceptional and stimulate you to examine the area of human services further. In Section I, we will discuss the methods often used to label human beings. We will look at some of the reasons we label and the effect labeling may have on a person. Our discussion will include an examination of the labeling process from the perspectives of several professions. We conclude this section with a historical review of people and events that have helped shape our present understanding of human differences.

Sections II through V provide an overview of each area of exceptionality, including definitions, characteristics, causation, prevalence, and intervention strategies. Section II focuses on learning and behavior disorders. This section deviates somewhat from some of the other introductory texts written in this area in that the framework for the discussion is a symptom-severity approach (mild, moderate, and severe/profound). You will be introduced to some of the current thinking on generic definitions (sometimes referred to as cross-categorical or noncategorical definitions), as well as to the traditional descriptors of mental retardation, behavior disorders, and learning disabilities. Section III examines speech and language disorders, hearing disorders, and visual disorders. The focus of Section IV is physical and health disorders. Section V discusses the definitions and intervention strategies for persons who possess extraordinary gifts and talents.

The introduction to human exceptionality ends with a section on the family unit and issues related to adulthood. The chapter on family perspectives discusses the effects that an exceptional child might have on the family. This chapter examines relationships between parents and professionals and explores the types of community resources that should be available to families with exceptional children. The final chapter in this volume is concerned with adulthood and the aging process. It examines some of the physical, intellectual, and behavioral characteristics of adults, as well as factors related to employment and use of leisure time.

The field of human exceptionality is relatively young and unexplored. For those seeking careers in human services, we hope this book will serve as a guidepost for future exploration. If after reading this volume you are excited and encouraged to study further in this area, then we have met our primary goal.

We wish to thank our colleagues and students at the University of Utah for their invaluable feedback on various chapters within this text. Our special thanks to Dr. Grant Bitter and Dr. Joan Wolf for their insightful critique of the chapters on hearing disorders and on the gifted and talented.

To Ellen Chandler, Ginger Danielsen, and Karen Wiley we express our appreciation for typing and retyping the manuscript and for genuinely caring about the quality of the finished product.

We are indebted to Sue Canavan and Jeff Johnston for the many hours they spent assisting us in bringing this manuscript to fruition. Without their support, patience, and understanding we could not have completed this project.

To John Telford, whose photographs appear throughout this book, special thanks for bringing life to our work.

Finally, to our colleagues around the country, who contributed their professional expertise to the early versions and final drafts of this manuscript and gave constructive criticisms that shaped our work, we hope this volume meets your expectations.

MLH
CJD
MWE

Human Exceptionality

SECTION I

Introduction

In this section we will establish a pattern that will serve as a foundation for the remainder of the book. We will discuss the concept of normalcy and its relevance to such labels as *disordered, deviant, disabled, pathological, abnormal, handicapped, and exceptional.* The labels we use to define and classify human exceptionality will be analyzed from the perspectives of several fields of study, including medicine, psychology, sociology, anthropology, and education. In addition, we will explore the historical foundations for human-service models and their relationship to the development of assessment techniques and treatment procedures for the person with exceptional characteristics. The following topical guidelines are intended to provide some focus for your reading of the two chapters in this section:

1. *Normal* is a relative term that is usually defined within the context of the culture.

2. There are several purposes for, and methods of, labeling human differences.

3. Research on the effects of labeling has been contradictory. We do know that not all labels are permanent or negative.

4. The terminology used to describe human differences may vary considerably, depending on the perspective of the professional in a given field of study.

5. Current practices in the treatment and education of exceptional individuals have been shaped by notable professionals across several fields of study.

6. Human service models of the twentieth century have been on a continuum ranging from segregation in institutions to integration in the community.

7. The doctrine of the least restrictive environment dictates that people with exceptional characteristics receive services in an environment that is commensurate with their developmental needs.

8. In order to meet the mandate of the least restrictive environment, comprehensive services within a community must be developed or adapted, in addition to those already existing in more restricted settings.

9. Medical services that focus on prevention as well as direct health care are an important component of community-based services to exceptional people.

10. Exceptional individuals must have access to social services within the community, including mental health centers, alternative living arrangements, transportation, barrier-free facilities, employment, and leisure activities.

11. Successful integration depends on the availability of appropriate educational services.

12. The rights of handicapped students to a free and appropriate public education have been reaffirmed by state and national legislation as well as by the judicial system.

CHAPTER ONE

Understanding Human Differences

Whether your career goals lie in the field of education, the behavioral and social sciences, medicine, or law, it is important that you view the exceptional individual from a broader perspective than that projected by a single profession. In this chapter we will introduce you to the study of human exceptionality through the viewpoints of several fields. Exceptional people live and function in many contexts. Obviously, their differences affect them as they try to adjust within their environment, but the differences also have a significant impact on their families and on society at large.

Exceptional individuals have more characteristics that are similar to those of normal people than they have distinguishing characteristics. Although exceptionality is sometimes described as a human problem, we prefer to characterize it as being human. Exceptionality may present certain problems, but it should not be viewed as always being difficult to understand or to deal with.

Peter is twelve years old and has an intelligence quotient of 110, 20/20 vision, and no measurable hearing loss. He is physically active and healthy with no serious medical problems. Academically, Peter is at approximately the seventh grade level in all basic subjects in school. Emotionally, he has developed appropriate family and peer relations for a child of his chronological age.

Is Peter normal? We can say that Peter meets the basic medical, educational, and social criteria of normalcy within his immediate environment. But what is normal, and how are the criteria for normalcy determined?

Normal is a relative term, and concepts of normalcy are defined within the context of the individual's culture. Normalcy will change as the culture changes. Normal may be described as the average physical and behavioral characteristics of individuals within a given social structure. A range of normalcy defines how much difference will be tolerated before a single individual is no longer accepted as normal.

Every society develops official and unofficial procedures to define what is normal. Within any given social order, the vast majority of individuals will fall within the range of accepted physical and behavioral criteria. There are, however, individuals who exhibit differences that do not meet the cultural expectations of normalcy. These differences can be exhibited in a number of ways. They may be physical, such as blindness or an inability to walk. They can also be overt behaviors, as seen in the child who is a discipline problem, or the child who does not learn the same way or at the same rate as his or her age-mates.

How does society deal with these human differences? Everyone is in some way different from everyone else. Therefore it is not a matter of merely being different; it is a matter of the type and extent of the difference. To describe the nature of significant difference, a society creates descriptors to identify individuals who differ from the accepted norm. This process is called *labeling*.

LABELING HUMAN DIFFERENCES

The purpose of a label is to describe, identify, and distinguish. The physician may label to distinguish the sick from the healthy; a sociologist labels to set the socially deviant apart from the culture core; and educators and psychologists label to identify students with learning, physical, or behavioral differences who need specialized instructional service. Labels have certain things in common. They are intended to indicate those who meet the acceptable standard for normalcy and those who do not. The labeling process is complex, and the variables are numerous. Labels are only rough approximations and consequently do not have comparable effects. Some are permanent; others are temporary. Some are positive; others are negative.

Labels categorize people on the basis of a cultural standard. A society establishes criteria that are easily exceeded by some but cannot be met by others.

SCHOOL DISTRICT
.DUCATION PROGRAM - IEP

TESTS UTILIZED   CLASSIFICATION Educably Mentally Ret

CTUAL ASSESS. WISC-R

ONAL ASSESS. Woodcock Johnson

BEHAVIORAL/ADAPTIVE ASSESS. AAMD

SPEECH/LANGUAGE ASSESS. Fisher-Logman

R (WHERE APPLICABLE) NA

STON within normal limits HEARING within normal limits

CLASSROOM OBSERVATION DONE

DATE: BY WHOM

STRENGTHS: (INDICATE PRESENT LEVEL OF FUNCTIONING)

Gets along well with peers
Has mastered self-help skills
Excellent parental support
Exhibits appropriate hygiene

LIMITATIONS: (INDICATE PRESENT LEVEL OF FUNCTIONING)

Labeling is the act of classifying children by one or more common characteristics.

Those in positions of power determine what is to be valued, tolerated, or sanctioned. For example, a society may value creativity, innovation, and imagination, and an individual with these attributes will therefore be valued by the larger group and rewarded with positive labels, such as bright, intelligent, or gifted. However, the individual whose creativity and innovation drastically exceed the limits of societal conformity may be branded with negative labels, such as radical, extremist, or rebel. There may be a fine line between the application of a positive or a negative label. The distinction is relative, dependent on the criteria established by the culture. In a pluralistic culture, the same label may be valued by one segment of the culture and devalued by another. The value of a label has been the subject of debate for many years. For example, Roos (1982) indicated that the label "mentally retarded" has been a mixed blessing. This label has been the basis for developing and providing services to people, but it has also promoted stereotyping and exclusion. We will discuss this issue later in the chapter.

Who Labels?

The impact of a label on any human being is also related to the source of the label. "The labeler may be a stranger, a significant other (individual whose opinions an individual cares about such as a spouse, close friend, or employer), an official labeler such as police, a psychiatrist or the individual himself or herself" (Feldman, 1978, p. 280). The source of the label is an important factor in determining the outcome of the labeling process.

Official labelers are sanctioned by the social majority to identify individuals who may be external to a societal standard. The criminal justice system, including the arresting officer, jury, and court judge, labels a person who commits a crime as a criminal. The criminal may be incarcerated in a penal institution and is consequently labeled a convict. The label is sanctioned within the social system, and the criminal is now readily identifiable. The social label will usually change our perception of the individual and in turn change the individual's self-concept. Additional examples of official labelers include medical personnel and behavioral and social scientists.

Whereas official labelers have the sanction of the social majority, unofficial labelers may have a much narrower impact. The unofficial labeler is usually some significant other, such as family, friends, teachers, or peers, and the applied label is meaningful only to this restricted group. The unofficial label may be expressed in a number of ways. One form of expression is derogatory slang terms, such as stupid, cripple, fat, or crazy. Some unofficial labels reflect more favorably on the individual. These include such terms as witty, smart, or cool. Other labels, such as ambitious or conformist, are left more to individual interpretation. It is important to note, however, that although the unofficial label may be initially restricted to the immediate peer group, the label may generalize beyond what was originally intended, to the point where it is

Educators label children after collecting different types of data.

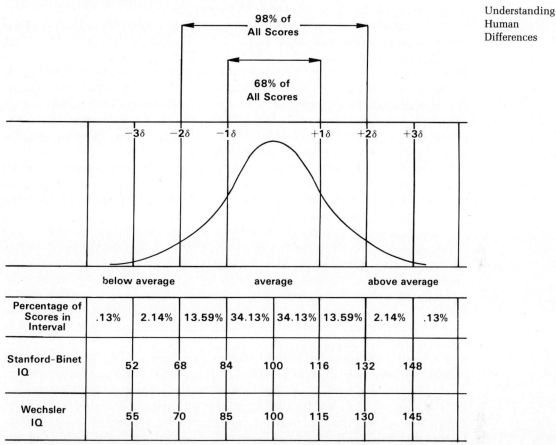

Percentage of Scores in Interval	.13%	2.14%	13.59%	34.13%	34.13%	13.59%	2.14%	.13%
Stanford–Binet IQ		52	68	84	100	116	132	148
Wechsler IQ		55	70	85	100	115	130	145

recognized by the larger society and eventually becomes official. This is also how new or extended meaning can be given to an old label.

Methods of Labeling

Significant physical and behavioral differences are found in every society, but infrequently. The vast majority of individuals within any given culture will conform to the established standards. "Conformity—people behaving as their cultural rules would have them behave—has been recognized by virtually everyone in social science as the dominant fact of life everywhere" (Edgerton, 1976, p. 3). For the most part, people look the way they are expected to look, behave the way they are expected to behave, and learn the way they are expected to learn. When an individual deviates substantially from the expectations, a number of methods can be used to describe the nature and extent of the differences.

Statistical relativity. The approach to labeling known as **statistical relativity** is consistent with the developmental view of human growth. "The developmental view . . . is based upon an understanding of normal intellectual, emotional, and physical development and what constitutes deviations in the course of normal development" (Wyne & O'Connor, 1979, p. 5). Human differences are the result of an interaction of biological and environmental factors. To understand these differences, we must first establish what is normal development. According to the developmental view, normal development can be explained statistically. We observe large numbers of individuals and look for those characteristics that occur most frequently at a specific chronological age level. For example, the average child with a chronological age of three months should be able to follow a moving object visually. *Average* is a statistical term based on observations of the behavior of three-month-old infants. An individual child's growth pattern is then compared to the group average. Differences in development (advanced or delayed) are labeled accordingly.

Application of the statistical approach to labeling may be seen in the measurement of intelligence. A person's intelligence may be measured by his or her score on a test intended to measure this hypothetical construct. The person's score is compared to the statistical average of age-mates who have taken the same test. The statistical average for intelligence tests is generally set at 100. Psychologists use a mathematical procedure to determine the extent to which an individual's score deviates from this average. This measurement is called a **standard deviation.** McConnell (1977) suggested, "When all is said and done the standard deviation is little more than a fairly accurate way of measuring percentages" (p. 24). Figure 1-1 illustrates that if a standard deviation of 15 points is used (Wechsler Intelligence Scales), approximately 68 percent of all scores will fall within plus or minus one standard deviation from the mean (a range of 85 to 115). Two standard deviations from the mean (a range of 70 to 130) will account for 98 percent of all scores. Normalcy on an intelligence test is defined by how far one deviates from the arithmetic average. Generally, you are considered normal if your score is within one standard deviation from the mean, because most persons (68 percent) will score within this range. If you score between one and two standard deviations from the mean, you have deviated more than would be expected for the majority of the population, and the differences, particularly if you are below the average, are now more readily identifiable. A score that is more than two standard deviations from the mean is considered to be significantly different (Grossman, 1977). On the lower end of the continuum, the label that is affixed may be mentally retarded; on the upper end, the label may be genius or gifted. Whatever the label, a score that is more than two standard deviations from the mean indicates that the performance is different from 98 percent of the population. (See Box 1-1.) Society will make a value judgment as to the importance of the difference.

Cultural Relativity. The approach to labeling known as **cultural relativity** defines normalcy according to the standards established by a specific social structure. Whereas the statistical approach measures only the frequency of behavior to define deviance, cultural definitions suggest that deviance can also be explained by examining the values inherent within the given culture. What constitutes a significant difference will change over time, from culture to culture, and among the various social classes within a culture. A label is applied as a result of a cultural response to the characteristics of the person. Therefore behavior reflects the culture, and the culture influences the behavior. Edgerton (1976) stated that people everywhere follow cultural rules, even though the rules are often arbitrary and vary dramatically from one society to the next.

The idea that human beings are the product of their culture has received its greatest thrust from anthropology. This discipline has emphasized "the diverse and arbitrary nature of man's rules about dress, food, sex, religion, etiquette, marriage, politics " (Edgerton, 1976, p. 8). The human infant is born so flexible that it is possible for most people to adjust within nearly any environment. Therefore the values of the culture are paramount in labeling human differences. From the cultural viewpoint, it is difficult to explain physical and behavioral difference statistically, because cultures and the various status symbols within the culture are fluid. Normalcy is in a continuous pattern of change within cultures. (See Box 1-2.)

Individual or Internal Relativity. Another dimension of the labeling process is the perception of the labeled individual in relationship to the labeler. This

BOX 1-1 STATISTICAL RELATIVITY

An example of the statistical method for defining normalcy can be seen in the process we call a census. A census is simply a frequency count, and from it we are able to state statistical facts about who or what is normal or typical. One of the most detailed examinations of any large population is the census of the United States, which is conducted every ten years. Shiels (1983) reported on what the 1980 census said about the changing face of the American family:

The statistics speak for themselves. The average American household, for instance, is steadily dwindling in size: of the 83.5 million in existence in 1980, more than one in five consisted of one person living alone; at the same time, the proportion of households composed of six or more individuals has dropped from 10.6 percent of the total

in 1970 to just over 5 percent today. Family households (related individuals living together) have grown by only 19 percent since 1970, while nonfamily households (made up of unrelated or single people) are up by 89 percent and now represent more than one-quarter of the total. Even the family households themselves have changed. The number of people who live in families headed by a man or woman without a spouse soared from 21.7 million in 1970 to 35 million today, largely because of the rising divorce rate and the increasing incidence of out-of-wedlock births. One out of every eight children—and nearly half of all black youngsters—now lives in a single-parent home.*

type of labeling is known as **individual** or **internal relativity.** The perceptions may not be consonant. It is possible for an individual to engage in a self-labeling process that is not recognized by the external environment. Self-imposed labels are a reflection of how individuals perceive themselves in the social order, though those perceptions may not be consistent with the societal view. The self-imposed label may remain internalized or eventually be recognized within society. The reverse of this process may also occur: The culture uses a label to identify a person, but the cultural label is never internalized or accepted by that person. (See Box 1-3.)

BOX 1-2 CULTURAL RELATIVITY

The diversity of cultural norms and values has been emphasized by anthropologist Ruth Benedict. In her work *Patterns of Culture* (1934), she suggests that the only way to understand cultural processes is to study the emotions and values that have become institutionalized within a specific culture. Benedict compares the dominant values of several cultures in order to highlight the importance of cultural relativism. The contrast between the Plains Indians and the Pueblo Indians of North America exemplifies the diversification of cultural values.

	Plains Indians	**Pueblo Indians**
Fasting	Fasting is a way to obtain visions.	Fasting is a means of preparing for ritual activity.
Torture	Self-torture is used for visions and protection.	Self-torture is absent.
Dancing	Dancing is employed to induce ecstatic states and is often wild.	Dancing is monotonous and is intended to promote crop growth.
Initiative	Value is placed on the self-reliant person of initiative who wins honor and prestige.	The ideal person is mild-mannered and tries not to stand out from the crowd
Death	Death promotes uninhibited grief, and mourning is prolonged and involves self-torture.	Death promotes sorrow, but little is made of the event.
War	The war hero is honored and envied.	The war hero must be purified of the impurities brought about by killing.
Suicide	Men often vow suicide if they have been failures or shamed.	Tales about suicide cannot be taken seriously.

Source: Adapted from John J. Collins, *Anthropology: Culture, Society, and Evolution,* © 1975, p. 214. Reprinted by permission of Prentice-Hall, Inc., Englewood Cliffs, N.J.

Research on the effects of labeling has been contradictory. We do know that not all labels have permanent effects (Feldman, 1978.) In addition, the effect of being labeled is not always the same from person to person. Rogers and Buffalo (1974) discussed several possible reactions to a societal label. These reactions range on a continuum from acceptance to rejection. At one end of this continuum the individual acknowledges or accepts the label, essentially agreeing with the larger group's perception. At the other end of the continuum, the individual totally rejects the label and actively seeks to have it removed. Between these two extremes are a variety of other reactions, for example: avoiding the label by escaping from the situation; using the deviant label to change a liability into an asset (as do boxers who are paid to channel their hostility into a controlled situation); or modifying the label by transforming it into more

BOX 1-3 INDIVIDUAL RELATIVITY

Thomas Alva Edison is an example of an individual who was labeled as intellectually slow during his childhood but never internalized the label. On the contrary, Edison totally rejected the label and sought throughout his life to have it removed. The following excerpts from Edison biographies provide us with insight on Thomas Edison as a young boy.

Alva appears to have been a perplexing problem for which Sam was unable to find a solution. The boy's active, inquisitive mind led him into places and predicaments a less vigorous mentality would not have considered. His great curiosity, his continuous flow of questions, caused many people, including his father, to think the boy was of low mentality. It appears that in those days a boy who asked countless questions was considered stupid. Apparently his father—a frequent target of the constant flow of puzzling questions—maintained a similar opinion of him. Perhaps this opinion was confirmed when, following his father's frequent "I don't know," the boy began countering with "Why don't you know?"*(Frost, 1969, p. 23)

Tom Edison caught scarlet fever and it was not until 1855, at the age of eight and a *half, that he began attending the white school house. Here he showed what has almost become a sign of genius: after only three months he returned home in tears, reporting that the teacher had described him as "addled." This was in fact no cause for alarm. Leonardo da Vinci, Hans Anderson and Niels Bohr were all singled out in their youth as cases of retarded development; Newton was considered a dunce; the teacher of Sir Humphry Davy commented, "While he was with me I could not discern the faculties by which he was so much distinguished"; and Einstein's headmaster was to warn that the boy "would never make a success of anything." As youths, all had one characteristic in common: each was an individualist, saw no need to explain himself and was thus listed among the odd men out.** (Clark, 1977, p. 9)*

*Source: Reprinted, by permission of the publisher, from L. A. Frost, *The Thomas A. Edison Album* (Seattle: Superior Publishing Co., 1969), p. 23.

** Source: Reprinted by permission from R. S. Clark, *Edison: The Man Who Made the Future* (New York: G. P Putnam's Sons, 1977), p. 9

acceptable terminology (such as social drinker in place of alcoholic). Although empirical studies have not been able to verify these specific outcomes, investigators have demonstrated that individual reactions to a cultural label are extremely diverse (Feldman, 1978; Gould, 1969; Schur, 1971; Thorsell & Klemke, 1971).

However, investigators have been unable to draw consistent conclusions about the influence of the label on the behavior of the labeled person (often because of design weaknesses in the studies). Is there a cause-and-effect relationship? Does labeling create differences? Rosenthal and Jacobsen (1968) examined this question in a well-known study involving intelligence. A group intelligence test was administered to elementary-age schoolchildren. Teachers were informed that this test was an effective method for determining intellectual potential. The teachers were then provided with a list of children (20 percent of the sample) and told that on the basis of the intelligence test these children had the greatest potential for intellectual growth. The list was, in fact, composed of children who had been randomly selected from the entire elementary school population. The test was administered again later in the school year, and the children who had been identified to the teachers as having the greatest potential scored significantly higher than the rest of the children in the school. Rosenthal and Jacobsen concluded that teacher expectations contributed to the differences in scores. The effect is often referred to as the **self-fulfilling prophecy**—or a person will become what he or she is labeled. Merton (1978) described the phenomenon as a "false definition of a situation evoking a new behavior which makes the originally false conception come true" (p. 67).

The research of Rosenthal and Jacobsen contains many methodological flaws and has not been consistently reproduced (Snow, 1969; Thorndike, 1968). Becker (1974) suggested that the theory is without foundation when viewed in relation to everyday experience. "It would seem foolish to propose that stick-up men stick up people simply because someone has labeled them stick-up men, or that everything a homosexual does results from someone having called him homosexual" (p. 42). Becker's position is supported in the literature (Keogh & Levitt, 1976; MacMillan & Becker, 1977). MacMillan, Jones, and Aloia (1974) suggested: "No evidence has been found of a direct relationship between self-concept and labeling. . . . And the methodological problems inherent in the vast majority of these studies render their findings difficult to interpret" (p. 246).

Teacher bias as a function of negative labels has been a focus of investigation in recent years. Foster, Ysseldyke, and Reese (1975) studied the expectations of special education teacher trainees relative to children labeled emotionally disturbed. They found that the trainees held preconceived negative stereotyped expectancies concerning these children. Ysseldyke and Foster (1978), in a study of elementary school teachers, reported that negative labels (e.g., emotionally disturbed and learning disabled) "generated initial negative stereotypes, which were retained in the observance of behaviors inconsistent with the labels" (p. 615).

Given the fact that the research on the effects of labeling has been contradictory, are there any logical arguments for continuing to use labels? Some reasons for retaining labeling have been proposed:

1. Funding of social services and educational programs are based on labeling. In other words, no label, no money.
2. Labeling helps professionals communicate effectively with one another and provides a common criterion for assessing research findings.
3. Abolishing the present labels will result in the evolution of different labels. A new label will always be there to replace the old one.
4. Labeling helps the public identify with the specific needs of a population. The public is able to differentiate more clearly between various categories of individuals (e.g., the needs of the blind in contrast to those of the mentally retarded).

The above rationale warrants further analysis. The first reason for continuing a label is based on present bureaucratic structure and is simply founded in tradition. We do it this way because this is the way we have always done it. However, when viewing the first reason in relation to the fourth reason, we gain a little more perspective on this logic. The justification is now extended to the historical reaction of a sympathetic general public. Monies are obtained because the public can identify and relate to specific categorical labels. This premise is based on the belief that public attitude is inalterable. For many years the public has developed conditioned responses to various social labels. Consequently, society reacts more to stereotyped group characteristics than to the needs of individual human beings. Although it has been argued that categorizing people on the basis of general characteristics ensures that services will be made available, this labeling process has not guaranteed that the quality of the service will meet the needs of the individual.

The second reason for retaining labels suggests that labeling helps professionals communicate about which populations need medical, social, or educational services. The emphasis is again on the kinds of people, or group identification, instead of on individuals. The professionals' perceptions of human differences seem to mirror the terminology of their specific disciplines. Is it possible that each discipline is using completely different terminology to describe the same person? Such terms as abnormal, deviant, pathological, disabled, disordered, and handicapped are common to specific fields of study. (We will discuss this in more depth later in this chapter.) Consequently, the argument that there is a common language within the research is not valid when viewed across professions. Professionals can facilitate services to the individual by developing communication systems that employ a common language and concentrate on individual characteristics.

The third reason for retaining labels argues that abolishing old labels will simply result in new ones. We need *some* labeling process in order to communicate the nature of human differences. Definitions and classification systems are developed to determine the parameters of the label and to distinguish one label from another, one person from another. However, classification systems may promote stereotyping, which is then maintained in social interaction. Scheff (1975), analyzing the term *insanity*, explained:

> Reaffirmation of the stereotype of insanity occurs not only in the mass media, but also in ordinary conversation, in jokes, anecdotes and even in conventional phrases. Such phrases as "Are you crazy?" or "It would be a madhouse," "It's driving me out of my mind," or "It's driving me distracted," and hundreds of others occur frequently in informal conversations. In this usage insanity itself is seldom the topic of conversation; the phrases are so much a part of ordinary language that only the person who considers each word carefully can eliminate them from his speech. Through verbal usages the stereotypes of insanity are a relatively permanent part of the social structure. (P. 276)

Two other effects of labeling must be addressed at this point: (1) the person and the label may become one and the same and (2) the environment can become a major criterion for labeling the individual.

Separating the Person and the Label. People are **learning disordered** because they are significantly subaverage in learning performance compared to other people of comparable chronological age. People are **behavior disordered** because they cannot take care of themselves, are unable to function in society, and are a threat to themselves and the people around them. The above statements show how general criteria can be used to label a person as learning disordered or behavior disordered. The statements appear to focus on the behavior of the individuals rather than the individuals themselves. Once a label is affixed, however, the person and the label may become inseparable. Instead of saying that Ruth does not possess age-appropriate intellectual or socialization abilities, we say that Ruth is a retardate. We lose sight of the fact that Ruth is a human being, with a few exceptional characteristics. If we fail to treat Ruth as a person with special needs, rather than as a label, we are doing an injustice not only to Ruth but to everyone else.

Environmental Bias. Labeling may also promote the misconception that human differences can be accurately categorized by determining a person's position or status within the environment. People are labeled on the basis of how we perceive them in the social structure. This is referred to as **environmental bias.** For example:

1. If you are in a mental hospital, you must be insane.
2. If you are in a state institution for the mentally retarded, you must be retarded.
3. If you are in a special education class, you must be handicapped.

There are two obvious weaknesses in the above premises. First, it has been stressed throughout this chapter that normalcy is a relative term and that what is viewed as normal in one context may be perceived differently in another.

Second, the environment in which we view the person will influence our perception of that person.

Rosenhan (1973) investigated environmental influence on human perception by having himself and seven other sane individuals admitted to a number of state mental hospitals across the country. Once the experimenters were in the mental hospital, the only way they could get out was to act normally and convince the staff they were mentally healthy. The question was whether the staff would catch them at their game and perceive them as healthy people instead of as mentally ill patients. Rosenhan reported that the pseudopatients were never detected by the hospital staff. Throughout their hospital stay, these patients were incorrectly labeled and treated as schizophrenics. Rosenhan's investigation demonstrates that the professionals' perception of normalcy can be biased by the environment in which their observations are made. The merits of the Rosenhan study have been widely debated in the scientific community since its original publication in 1973, but there has been no attempt to reproduce Rosenhan's findings. In an interview (Greenberg, 1981) Rosenhan said, "The first canon of science is that if you don't like the data, if you think there's something wrong you **replicate** it. . . . I think people are much more willing to talk about it than replicate it, not merely because replication is difficult, but because deep down in their hearts they believe the data will stand up. Those are very solid data." (P. 4)

THE STUDY OF HUMAN DIFFERENCES

At this point we will define constructs within the fields of medicine, psychology, sociology, anthropology, and education as they relate to various aspects of human differences. There are many differences in background, interests, and biases that distinguish one profession from another. In fact, these professions have developed separate communication systems that reflect each field's orientation to the study of human difference.

Medicine

The medical model has two dimensions: normal and pathological. *Normality* is defined as the absence of biological symptoms; *pathology* as the alterations of the organism produced by disease. The majority of human beings are nonpathological, but little attempt is made to differentiate superior or above-average levels of biological status. The emphasis is on defining the nature of the disease and its pathological effect on the organism. Disease is a state of ill health that interferes with or destroys the integrity of the organism.

The medical model, often referred to as the disease model, focuses primarily on biological aberrations. People are diagnosed as pathological if they exhibit biological symptoms that are contrary to physical norms. Normal, on the other hand, is defined only by the absence of biological symptoms. The model is universal (within Western cultures) and does not have values that are culturally relative. Mercer (1979) explained:

> When the medical practitioner diagnoses the physical state of the patient, the diagnosis is a value judgement about the current state of the organism. This evaluation is based on a universal value consensus that health is better than illness, that a nonsymptomatic condition is better than having symptoms of pathology. The medical model is not culture bound. Because the biological organism of the human species responds in similar fashion to physical trauma and disease processes regardless of its cultural milieu, assessment within the medical model need not take cultural factors into account. (P. 43)

The Diagnosis of Pathology. When diagnosing the problem, the physician carefully follows a definite pattern of procedures that include questioning the patient and obtaining a history, a physical examination, laboratory studies, and in some cases surgical exploration. The physician's diagnosis focuses on the deficits of the organism. The person who exhibits the deficit is labeled the *patient*, and the deficits are then described as the *patient's disease*. Because the medical model measures deficits, and not the absence thereof, the presence of pathological symptoms is described as a *positive diagnosis*. If the patient has no symptoms, the diagnosis is *negative*. In other words, negative is good and positive is bad. The code of the medical profession stresses that it is much worse for a physician to allow a sick person to go untreated (false negative) than it is to treat a well one (false positive).

Psychology

Modern psychology is most succinctly defined as the science of human and animal behavior, the study of overt acts and mental events of an organism that can be observed and/or evaluated. Broadly viewed, psychology is concerned with every detectable action of an individual. Behavior is the focus of psychology, and when the behavior of the organism does not meet the criteria of normalcy, it is labeled *abnormal*.

One cannot live in society without encountering the dynamics of abnormal behavior. The media are replete with incidents of murder, suicide, sexual aberrations, burglary, robbery, embezzlement, child abuse, and other incidents that display human behavioral disorders. The orientation of the media to the sensational aspects of abnormal behavior is shown by the media's emphasis on extreme cases. Nevertheless, these cases represent a point in the continuum of personal maladjustment that exists in our society. This continuum ranges from behaviors that are slightly deviant or eccentric (still within the confines of normal human experience), to *neuroses* (a partial disorganization characterized by combinations of anxieties, compulsions, obsessions, and phobias), to **psychosis** (a serious disorder resulting in loss of contact with reality and characterized by delusions, hallucinations, or illusions).

Assessment of abnormal behavior. The study of human psychological disturbance is historically founded in philosophy and religion. Until the Middle Ages, psychological disturbances were believed to be a result of divine intervention. The disturbed, or mad, person had made a pact with the devil, and the psychological affliction was a result of divine punishment. Psychological disturbances were a function of devils, witches, or demons residing within the person. During the sixteenth and seventeenth centuries, individuals with psychological disturbances continued to be viewed as mad persons, fools, and public threats who had to be ostracized from society. As medical technology expanded in the eighteenth century, the influence of theology began to diminish. Abnormal behavior was viewed as the result of physical disease, this view gave rise to the medical model.

Under the medical model, abnormal behavior is described in terms of the interrelationship of psychological, physiological, and social dysfunction. The disturbed individual is ill as opposed to healthy; thus the origin of the terms *mental illness* and *mental health*. A person with mental illness can then be described as a patient, and in many cases can be sent to a hospital to be cured.

Throughout the first half of the twentieth century, the medical model was considered the most logical and most scientific approach to understanding human psychological differences. Goldenberg (1977) indicated:

> (1) It has laid to rest all of the myths giving demonological explanations of disordered behavior. (2) It has made more acceptable to the public the humane view that psychologically disturbed people are sick, are not always fully accountable for their behavior, and deserve prompt and kind treatment, just as though they were physically ill. (3) It has opened up the area of mental illness as a legitimate research topic, utilizing the talents and techniques of physicians, psychologists, geneticists, biochemists, and others to ferret out the causes of psychological disorders. (4) It has offered hope in the form of treatment and rehabilitation programs for mental illness. (5) It has led to scientific discoveries such as general paresis (which is caused by a syphilitic infection that penetrates the brain and causes neurological deterioration and ultimately psychosis), offering hope that continued scientific exploration might lead to the discovery of treatable biological bases for still other psychological disorders. (P. 27)

In the latter part of the twentieth century, however, several critics have emerged to challenge the conceptual basis of the medical model (Cowen, 1973; Laing, 1967; Szasz, 1961). These critics view psychological disturbances more as a result of the interaction of the individual within the environment than as a disease within the individual. This cultural relativity model theorizes that social and environmental stress, in combination with the individual's inability to cope, leads to psychological disturbances. According to these critics, abnormal behavior is a social problem and therefore should be examined within the context of both psychology and sociology.

Sociology

Psychology and sociology are similar in that both disciplines are concerned with the study of human behavior. Sociology is defined as the science of social behavior, whereas psychology emphasizes the person as a separate being. Social interaction is only one aspect of behavior. As a scientific discipline, sociology is concerned primarily with modern cultures: group behavior, societal institutions, and intergroup relationships. It is concerned with examining the individual in relation to the physical and social environment. When individuals meet the social norms of the group, they are considered normal. When individuals are unable to adapt to social roles or to establish appropriate interpersonal relationships, their behaviors are labeled *deviant*. Unlike medical pathology, social deviance cannot be defined in universal terms. Instead, it is defined within the context of the culture and in any way the culture chooses to define it. "Group norms can establish almost any form of behavior, from the most innocent to the most harmful, as deviant. By the same token, norms can even 'purify' and legitimatize destructive behavior, such as waging war, gouging the public, and economic depredations, as not only acceptable, but even highly honorific" (Dinitz, Dynes & Clarke, 1975, pp. 3-4).

Assessment of Social Deviance. The cultural relativity model is based on several assumptions:

1. Normal behavior meets societal, cultural, or group expectations. Deviance is defined as a violation of social norms.
2. Social deviance is not necessarily an illness. Failure to conform to societal norms does not imply that the individual has pathological or biological deficits.
3. Each culture will determine the range of behaviors that will be defined as normal or deviant. These norms will be enforced by the social system. Those people with the greatest power within the social system can impose their criteria for normalcy on the less powerful.
4. Social deviance may be caused by the interaction of several factors, including genetic makeup and individual experiences within the social environment.

Anthropology

Anthropology is the science that deals with the origins, physical and cultural development, racial characteristics, social customs, and beliefs of humans. Physical anthropology is concerned with the physical structure of human beings and the evolution of that structure. Cultural anthropology primarily, although not exclusively, focuses upon the races, physical and mental characteristics, customs, and social relationships of nonliterate and, to a lesser extent, literate cultures. As a discipline, anthropology concentrates on the behavioral patterns that distinguish people in one society from those in another.

Edgerton (1976) explained that the role of anthropology in the development of a perspective on social deviance has been indirect but important:

It has been indirect in the sense that, unlike sociologists and psychologists, anthropologists have written very little about "deviant behavior"; it has been important, nonetheless, because what anthropologists have written about culture and human deviance has been most influential. This influence begins with the study of culture. That human behavior is highly patterned, that it reflects "culture," is a major contribution of anthropology. (Edgerton, 1976, p. 8)

Anthropological studies have demonstrated that various patterns of social structure breed different types of social deviance. Psychological disturbances and socially deviant behaviors considerably different from those found in Western society have been identified in a number of other cultures. Anthropology has been an important factor in helping psychology and sociology remove the biases of **ethnocentrism** and become more objective in their analyses of human differences.

Education

The educational process is founded on the interaction of three developmental domains: the cognitive domain, the affective domain, and the psychomotor domain. The cognitive domain is concerned with the acquisition of knowledge. Reasoning, thinking, and problem-solving abilities are important components of this domain. The affective domain focuses on behaviors that develop as a result of the individual's interaction with others in the environment. Feelings, emotions, attitudes, and socialization skills are components of this domain. The psychomotor domain reflects the relationship between mental processes and motor movements. This domain includes both gross (large-muscle) and fine (small-muscle) motor development.

As children progress through formal schooling, it is anticipated that they will learn and behave according to the expectations of the educational system, which is a product of cultural norms (as in the statistical and cultural definitions of normal discussed earlier in this chapter). Most children will move through the system in about the same way, requiring the same level of service, and within similar time frames. The public schools are entrenched in "education for the masses"—the greatest good for the greatest number. In other words, education seems to be aimed primarily at those students who meet the definition of normal.

Children and youths who do not meet educational expectations of normalcy are labeled according to the type and extent of their deviation. They are provided services and resources that are different from those required for the normal population. These differences in educational service patterns are reflected in the numerous terms used to describe these students: special, disabled, disordered, handicapped, exceptional.

Historically, special is the most widely used educational descriptor for students with differences. It is also used extensively to describe the nature of the educational services these students will require. Special is defined as unusual,

Schools have made noticeable improvement in meeting the needs of exceptional learners.

peculiar, unique, and distinctive. A special person has physical and behavioral characteristics that will differentiate that person from the normal peer group, and therefore establish the need for special education services. As an educational label, *special* has traditionally communicated a feeling of isolation or separatism. In fact, special education services have in the past been based on a segregation model within the field of education. Examples of this are the separate training programs in higher education, separate classrooms in public schools, and in some cases, separate school buildings. Many individuals with significant differences were not merely separated from regular education; they were excluded from all public education services. The concept of separatism and exclusion will be discussed more thoroughly in Chapter 2.

Other terms that describe physical and behavioral differences include *disorder, disability,* and *handicap.* Although these terms are often used synonymously, their definitions are not always consonant. A **disorder** is the broadest of the three terms and refers to a general malfunction of mental, physical, or psychological processes. It is defined as a disturbance in normal functioning. A **disability** is more specific than a disorder and results from a loss of physical functioning (loss of sight, hearing, legs, arms) or difficulties in learning and social adjustment that significantly interfere with normal growth and development. A disability is an internal problem beyond the control of the individual, whereas a **handicap** is a limitation imposed on the individual by the environment and by the person's capacity to deal with that limitation. For example, a person who is confined to a wheelchair has a physical disability, the inability to ambulate. The individual is dependent on the wheelchair for mobility, and the wheelchair is there to expand the person's life space. When the physical environment will not accommodate the wheelchair (e.g., a building without ramps, accessible only by stairs), the person's disability becomes a handicap. In this case the physical environment handicapped the individual. Historically, many children with physical and behavioral differences have been educationally handicapped because they have been excluded from schools, imposing a limitation on their opportunities for growth and development.

As an educational label, **handicapped** has a narrow focus and a negative connotation. In this context the word literally means "cap in hand" and originates from a time when the disabled begged in the streets in order to survive (Avoiding Handicapist Stereotypes, 1977, p. 1). The term *handicapped* is consistent with the medical model because it categorizes as handicapped only those individuals who are deficient in or lack ability. From such a perspective, people who exceed established norms are not identified for additional educational services. The term **exceptional** is much more comprehensive than *handicapped* and refers to any individual whose physical or behavioral performance deviates so substantially from the norm, either higher or lower, that additional educational and other services may be necessary to meet the individual's needs. An exceptional person is not necessarily a handicapped person.

CATEGORIZING PERSONS WITH EXCEPTIONAL CHARACTERISTICS

Persons with exceptional characteristics are identified for additional educational, social, or medical services on the basis of physical and behavioral characteristics that are inconsistent with the norm. These differences may be described as:

1. Having learning and behavioral disorders
2. Having speech and language disorders
3. Having sensory disorders
4. Having physical and other health disorders
5. Being gifted or talented

Learning and behavior disorders have traditionally been divided into three discrete categorical labels: mental retardation, behavior disorders (emotional disturbance), and specific learning disabilities.

Mental retardation refers to significantly subaverage general intellectual functioning existing concurrently with deficits in adaptive behavior and manifested during the developmental period (Grossman, 1977, p. 11).

Seriously **emotionally disturbed** is defined as a condition exhibiting one or more of the following characteristics over a long period of time and to a marked degree, which adversely affects education performance: (*a*) an inability to learn that cannot be explained by intellectual, sensory, or health factors, (*b*) an inability to build or maintain satisfactory interpersonal relationships with peers and teachers, (*c*) inappropriate behavior or feelings under normal circumstances, (*d*) a general pervasive mood of unhappiness or depression, (*e*) a tendency to develop physical symptoms or fears associated with personal or school problems (U.S. Department of Health, Education, and Welfare, 1977, p. 42478).

A specific **learning disability** is a disorder in one or more of the basic psychological processes involved in understanding or in using language, spoken or written, that may manifest itself in an imperfect ability to listen, think, speak, read, write, spell, or do mathematical calculations. The term includes such conditions as perceptual handicaps, brain injury, minimal brain dysfunction, dyslexia and developmental aphasia. The term does not include children who have learning problems that are primarily the result of visual, hearing, or motor handicaps, of mental retardation, of emotional disturbances, or of environmental, cultural, or economic disadvantage (U.S. Department of Health, Education, and Welfare, 1977, p. 42478).

Although traditionally viewed as mutually exclusive, these categories include descriptors in the areas of capacity, achievement, and socialization abilities which overlap from one label to the other. Educational methodologies based on these categorical labels have their roots substantially founded on the principles of the medical model. Such a model implies that there are specific and distinct causes of the learning and behavioral differences (known or unknown) and that these causes result in specific and distinct learning and behavioral characteristics of the labeled populations. This assumption, in turn, implies that educational programming should be based on these distinct categorical population characteristics. However, educational practice has not provided strong support for the distinctiveness of learning and behavioral characteristics for this exceptional population, at least to the degree suggested by traditional categories. It has become increasingly evident that individuals exhibiting mild and moderate learning and behavioral disabilities are often more alike than different.

Speech and language disorders is a generic term that describes an individual's difficulty in communicating effectively in the social environment. **Speech disorders** may be classified into three general areas: (1) articulation disabilities, (2) fluency disabilities, and (3) voice disorders (Meyen, 1978). **Articulation disabilities** include such problems as omissions, substitutions, additions, and distortion of sounds. **Fluency disabilities** are described as repetitions, prolongation of sounds, hesitations, impediments in the flow of speech, and interjections. **Voice disorders** involve abnormal acoustical qualities in speech. **Language disorders** are defined as "problems in comprehending, expressing or otherwise functionally utilizing spoken language. Often such difficulties portend or accompany academic difficulties in the areas of reading, writing and mathematics" (Meyen, 1978, p. 395).

Sensory disorders are defined as differences in vision and hearing that will affect educational performance. A **visual disorder** can be described as blindness or partial loss of sight.

> A person shall be considered blind whose central visual acuity does not exceed 20/200 in the better eye with correcting lenses or whose visual acuity, if better than 20/200, has a limit in the central field of vision to such a degree that its widest diameter subtends an angle of no greater than twenty degrees. (Connor, Hoover, Horton, Sands, Sternfeld & Wolinsky, 1975, p. 240)

The partially sighted are defined as: "persons with a visual acuity greater than 20/200 but not greater than 20/70 in the better eye after correction" (National Society for the Prevention of Blindness, 1966, p. 10). A **hearing disorder** may be described as deafness or being hard-of-hearing.

> A deaf person is one whose hearing disability precludes successful processing of linguistic information through audition, with or without a hearing aid. A hard-of-hearing person is one who, generally with the use of a hearing aid, has residual hearing sufficient to enable successful processing of linguistic information through audition. (Report of the Ad Hoc Committee to Define Deaf and Hard-of-Hearing, 1975, p. 509)

Physical and other health disorders may be defined as "permanent, temporary or intermittent medical disabilities that require modifications in curriculum and instructional strategies. . . . The [person's] physical limitations are often the basis of functional retardation as well as sensory, perceptual and conceptual deficits" (Wald, 1971, p. 95).

Gifted and talented individuals are described as possessing extraordinary cognitive abilities and being capable of superior performance in an educational program.

> Giftedness consists of an interaction among three basic clusters of human traits—these clusters being above-average general abilities, high levels of task commitment, and high levels of creativity. Gifted and talented children are those possessing or capable of developing this composite set of traits and applying them to any potentially valuable area of human performance. Children who manifest or are capable of developing an interaction among the three clusters require a wide variety of educational opportunities and services that are not ordinarily provided through regular instructional programs. (Renzulli, 1978, p. 261)

SUMMARY

Normal is a relative term used to describe the average physical and behavioral characteristics of individuals within a given culture. Most people within any social order will meet the accepted criteria for normalcy. For those who do not, we affix various labels to describe the nature of their differences. These labels may be official and sanctioned by society, or unoffical and restricted to a person's immediate peer group. Whether the label is official or unofficial, its purpose is to distinguish one person from another.

A number of approaches can be used to label differences. In the statistical approach, large numbers of individuals are observed so that the characteristics that occur most can be counted. From this count, an arithmetic average is established. Persons who do not substantially deviate from this average will meet the criteria for normalcy. The cultural approach, while recognizing that frequency of behavior is a means of establishing what is normal, also examines the values inherent within the culture. The application of a label is the result of a cultural response to the characteristics of the person. In addition to statistical and cultural labeling, a label may be self-imposed as a reflection of how individuals perceive themselves in the social order. The reverse of this can also occur: A label may be affixed by society but never internalized by the individual.

Research on the effects of labeling has been contradictory. We do know that the effects will vary from person to person and may be temporary or permanent. Reactions to a label are on a continuum from acceptance to rejection and include such varied responses as avoidance, escape, or modification of the label. One effect of labeling is known as the self-fulfilling prophecy, that is, a person will become what he or she is labeled. This controversial phenomenon has been examined by several investigators in recent years. Two other possible effects of labeling are the inability of society to separate the person from the label, and the influence of the environment on our perception of a person.

Describing or labeling human differences is not just an exercise in semantics. Labels are an integral part of our language. They communicate the concept of human difference and are based on theoretical models, definitions, and intervention systems that reflect a specific intent. The medical model focuses on biological deficits within an organism, differentiating physical health from organic pathology or disease. Psychology draws from both medicine and sociology to distinguish normal from abnormal behaviors. Sociology and anthropology are based on the relationshop of an individual to the referent group. Norms are established in relation to the culture, and labels distinguish conformity from social deviance.

Educational technology relies heavily on all these conceptual models to apply knowledge obtained through the physical and behavioral sciences. Traditionally, the knowledge base for education has been oriented to medical, psychological and social definitions of normal, but recently the concept of education in the public schools has been redefined to include populations that do not meet the standards of normalcy. This new definition is not restricted to a student's educational program in the public schools, which would be far too narrow an application. A person with physical and behavioral differences must be viewed in the context of his or her environment: the family, the school, and the society.

1. Discuss the differences between official and unofficial labels.
2. What are three approaches that can be used to describe the nature and extent of human differences?
3. The effect of a label will differ from person to person. Discuss several possible reactions to receiving a societal label.
4. Discuss how the environment can influence our perceptions of people with differences.
5. Discuss the two dimensions of the medical model.
6. What assumptions does the cultural relativity model make?
7. What role has the field of anthropology played in the study of human differences?
8. Distinguish between the educational descriptors *handicapped* and *exceptional*.
9. What five general descriptors can be used to categorize persons with exceptional characteristics?

CHAPTER TWO

A History of Human Services

The 1980s are witness to the implementation and expansion of services for persons with exceptional characteristics. In the 1970s we witnessed some of the most significant legal, technological, and attitudinal changes in the treatment of exceptional persons in the history of this country. Our present-day reaffirmation of the rights of exceptional people is the result of a centuries-long evolutionary process. Present-day concepts are actually the products of seeds planted centuries ago. Some of these seeds have yielded humane, healthy, and productive human service models. In some cases, however, the seeds were destructive of the needs and rights of exceptional people.

History is a valuable resource that can help us determine which human service models are appropriate for the exceptional individual in today's society. We can learn from those who have preceded us.

INDIVIDUALIZING TREATMENT AND EDUCATION

We must go back at least two centuries to find the first documented attempts to personalize a treatment program to the needs of exceptional individuals. During the seventeenth and eighteenth centuries, many professionals contributed to the understanding of human differences. Jean-Marc Itard (1775–1838) epitomizes the orientation of professionals during this period, and his work can be easily recognized in our modern medical, psychological, and educational intervention models.

Itard Revisited

In 1799 Jean-Marc Itard, a young physician and authority on diseases of the ear and the education of the deaf, was working for the National Institute of Deaf-mutes in Paris. Although he was a physician trained in the general notions of the medical model, Itard believed that the environment in conjunction with physiological stimulation could contribute to the learning potential of any human being. Itard was influenced by the earlier work of Philippe Pinel and John Locke, who revolutionized society's perception of deviance from the demonological and superstitious beliefs of the Middle Ages to an understanding of the deviant person as physically and mentally "sick." Locke attempted to distinguish idiocy from insanity, and Pinel, Itard's mentor, advocated that people characterized as insane or idiots needed to be treated humanely. However, Pinel's teachings emphasized that such individuals were essentially incurable and that any treatment to remedy their physiological disabilities would be fruitless. Locke's philisophy was contrary to that of Pinel. Locke described the mind as a blank slate that could be opened to all kinds of sensory input. The polar positions of Pinel and Locke represent the classic "nature versus nurture" controversy: What is the role of heredity as opposed to environmental influence?

Itard put the theories of Pinel and Locke to a test in his work with Victor, the wild boy of Aveyron. Victor was a young boy of twelve when found in the woods by hunters. He had not developed any language, and his behavior was virtually uncontrollable, described as savage or animal-like. Ignoring Pinel's diagnosis that the child was a hopeless and incurable idiot, Itard took responsibility for Victor and put him through a program of sensory stimulation intended to make him normal. After five years Victor had developed some verbal language and had become more socialized once he had become more accustomed to his new environment. But Itard described his work as a failure because Victor was not normal. Nevertheless, history has recognized Itard's contributions as among the most visible landmarks in the development of education and treatment for the exceptional individual. Itard's contributions include:

1. *A developmental approach to instruction.* The intervention is based on the interaction of biological/genetic characteristics and the physical environment.

In order to initiate treatment effectively, the professional must clearly identify where in the normal developmental sequence the individual is functioning.

2. *Individualized instruction.* The intervention is based on assessment of the needs, characteristics, and functioning level of the individual.
3. *Sensory stimulation.* The intervention is directed toward the remediation of deficits in the basic sensory systems: vision, hearing, touch, kinesthesis, smell, and taste.
4. *Systematic instruction.* The intervention begins with tasks the child is capable of performing and then gradually builds to more complex learning. The sequence builds from concrete or real objects to more abstract concepts or ideas.
5. *The functional life curriculum.* The intervention is directed toward the development of independent living skills within the individual's immediate environment. All content areas (e.g., self-care, motor, language, academic) are intended to assist individuals who have disabilities to function independently.

Itard's work was the cornerstone of early nineteenth-century treatment programs. His ideas about appropriate treatment were continued and expanded on by such individuals as Edouard Seguin, Thomas Hopkins Gallaudet, Samuel Gridley Howe, and Maria Montessori. Their contributions, along with those of other notable physicians and educators of this period, are highlighted in Table 2-1.

The treatment programs of the nineteenth century reconceptualized society's view of persons with exceptional characteristics. Superstitious beliefs, demonology, and the mystical explanations of earlier centuries were replaced by a more scientific approach to treatment, which was founded on the medical model. Although Itard and Seguin had demonstrated that positive changes in the development of the individual were possible, they had not been able to "cure" insanity and idiocy. These conditions continued to be viewed by most medical professionals as diseases; individuals exhibiting such symptoms were described as sick.

The late nineteenth and early twentieth century also saw a new school of thought focusing on the science of the mind. Modern psychology, as we know it today, is about one hundred years old and has its roots in the scientific studies of Wilhelm Wundt (1832–1920) and William James (1842–1910). In 1879 Wundt defined psychology as the science of conscious experience. The definition was founded on the complex principles of introspection—looking into oneself to analyze experiences. James expanded Wundt's conceptions of conscious experience in his treatise *The Principles of Psychology* (1890) to include learning, motivation, and emotions. In 1913 John B. Watson (1878–1958) shifted the subject matter of psychology from conscious experience to observable behavior and redefined psychology as the science of behavior. The field of psychology was no longer concerned merely with instincts; it also emphasized learned human behavior. Today psychology is concerned with both observable behavior and mental events.

Table 2-1/ Contributions of Physicians and Educators Concerned with Treatment of Exceptional Individuals (Seventeenth Through Nineteenth Centuries)

	Profession	*Major Contributions*
John Locke (1632–1704)	English philosopher	Distinguished between idiocy (mental retardation) and insanity (mental illness) (1690). Advocated the idea that there is no basic human nature, that our minds at birth are a blank slate.
Philippe Pinel (1742–1826)	French physician	Classified mental illness as a disease. Advocated humane treatment for the mentally ill.
Jean-Marc Itard (1775–1838)	French physician/educator	Believed that idiocy could be treated through educational intervention (1799). Advocated individualized intervention, sensory stimulation, systematic instruction.
Thomas Hopkins Gallaudet (1787–1851)	American minister/educator	Established first American residential school for the deaf (1817).
Samuel Gridley Howe (1801–1876)	American physician/educator	Involved in education of the blind and the deaf. Founded the Perkins Institute for the Blind (1832). As a social reformer, advocated public financial support for education and treatment of exceptional populations.
Dorothea Dix (1802–1887)	American educator	As a social reformer, secured reforms in U.S. mental institutions, making them professionally administered hospitals for the "sick" rather than punishment-oriented facilities (prisons).
Louis Braille (1809–1852)	French educator	Developed a system of reading and writing for the blind (1834).
Eduoard Seguin (1812–1880)	French physician/educator	Developed physiological method of treatment: intervention through sensory motor development. Established first school for the intellectually retarded in Paris (1837). Helped establish first residential facility for the retarded in the U.S. (1854).

Table 2-1 (continued)

33
A History of
Human Services

	Profession	*Major Contributions*
Maria Montessori (1870–1952)	Italian physician/educator	Involved in education of the mentally retarded. Developed theory and curricula for early-childhood education of normal and exceptional populations.

Watson Revisited

In 1920 John B. Watson demonstrated in an experiment with an eleven-month-old boy named Albert that abnormal behavior patterns were not necessarily internal to the organism, as theorized in the medical model (Watson and Rayner, 1920). He showed that abnormal behavior could be learned through the interaction of the individual with environmental stimuli. Albert, when initially exposed to a gentle white rat, showed no fear of the animal. He saw the animal as a toy and played with it freely. Watson then introduced a loud, terrifying noise directly behind Albert each time the rat was presented. After a period of time the boy became frightened by the sight of any furry white object, even though the loud noise was not present. Albert had learned to fear rats through conditioning.

Conditioning is the process in which new objects or situations come to elicit responses elicited by other stimuli. Watson's research on conditioning was based on the earlier work of the Russian physiologist Ivan Pavlov (1849–1936), who demonstrated that a bond could be established between a stimulus and a response where no bond had existed before. Watson believed that Pavlov had discovered some critical characteristics of learning through his work with animals, and he applied these principles to his research with humans. Watson's behavioral approach radically altered the emphasis on the internally diseased organism and focused primarily on the environmental determinants of deviance. His extreme position on environmental determinism is summarized in a statement he made in 1925:

> Give me a dozen healthy infants, well-formed, and my own specified world to bring them up and I'll guarantee to take any one at random and train him to become any type of specialist I might select—doctor, lawyer, artist, merchant, and yes, even beggar and thief, regardless of talents, penchants, tendencies, abilities, vocations, and race of his ancestors. (Watson, 1925, p. 218)

A recent examination of some of Watson's work suggests that it has not been reproduced consistently and that interpretations by others may contain significant errors (Samelson, 1980).

At the time Watson was influencing the development of American psychology, several other schools of thought were emerging in Europe, including

Gestalt psychology and dynamic psychology. In 1938 an American psychologist, B. F. Skinner, published his book *The Behavior of Organisms*, outlining the principles of operant voluntary behavior through studies on the effects of water and food reinforcement on the behavior of rats. In a later book, *Science and Human Behavior* (1953), Skinner described how principles of operant behavior influence the everyday lives of human beings. The contributions some of these twentieth-century psychologists have made to our understanding of human differences are highlighted in Table 2-2.

Table 2-2/ Contributions of Psychologists Concerned with Treatment of Exceptional Individuals (Late Nineteenth Through Early Twentieth Century)

	Profession	*Major Contributions*
Wilhelm Wundt (1832–1920)	German psychologist trained in physics, physiology, and philosophy	Defined psychology as the science of conscious experience. Developed system of psychology known as structuralism: discovering the structure or anatomy of conscious experience (what and how something happens). Established first laboratory for the scientific study of psychology (1879).
William James (1842–1910)	American psychologist	Extended study of psychology beyond conscious experience to a functional and applied psychology (functionalism: why something happens). Published *Principles of Psychology* in the U.S. (1890).
Sigmund Freud (1856–1939)	Viennese physician	Concerned with motivation and dynamics of personality. Saw mental life is more than consciousness, that there is an underlying force labeled the unconscious. As the father of psychoanalysis, developed a theory of personality, a philosophical view of human nature, and a method of treating disturbed individuals. Constructed a vocabulary of the mind (e.g., the id, ego and superego). Published basic ideas on psychoanalysis in *Die Traumdeutung.*
Ivan Pavlov (1849–1936)	Russian physiologist	Discovered a technique called "classical conditioning", the

Table 2-2 (continued)

35

A History of
Human Services

	Profession	*Major Contributions*
		principle that a neutral stimulus paired with a stimulus that already evokes a response will eventually evoke a response by itself. In Russian, published results of his studies on classical conditioning.
The Gestaltists (1912): Wolfgang Köhler Kurt Koffka Max Wertheimer	German psychologists	Responsible for what is known as Gestalt psychology: Behavior cannot be divided into discrete elements. Components must be brought together and examined as a pattern or whole; the whole is greater than the sum of its parts.
John B. Watson (1878–1958)	American psychologist	Shifted study of psychology away from conscious experience orientation of structuralists and fundamentalists to the study of observable behavior. Advocated that psychology be studied in a rigorous, objective, and experimental manner. Advocated that virtually all human behavior is learned. Changed the course of American psychology with paper on behaviorism (1913).
B. F. Skinner (1904–)	American psychologist	Described the basic principles of operant behavior and their influence on people. Advocated an interpretation of behavioral principles which led to a treatment approach commonly referred to as behavior modification.

SEGREGATION OR INTEGRATION? HUMAN SERVICES IN THE TWENTIETH CENTURY

The early twentieth century was marked by contrasts in the treatment of exceptional individuals. On the positive side, the scientific method was applied to the measurement of mental capacity (e.g., the Binet-Simon Intelligence Test,

1905). Services that had been denied to exceptional individuals for centuries were now more readily available. Special classes in urban public schools were established for the more mildly retarded, and for deaf and blind children on a limited basis. The intervention models of the European countries were generating new ideas about the care and education of exceptional people. Gearheart (1980) suggested that "programs in the United States which had started behind those in Europe were on their way to catching up or even forging ahead as the nineteenth century came to a close" (p. 8). As the twentieth century began, public sentiment was aroused and more federal, state, and local monies were being channeled into human services.

By contrast, there was at the same time a more negative perspective in the early twentieth century. Mental illness and mental retardation were viewed primarily as physiological **aberrations.** An increased emphasis on the study of eugenics promoted fears that the mentally and morally defective were defiling the race: "We must come to recognize feeble-mindedness, idiocy, imbecility, and insanity as largely communicable conditions or diseases, just as the ordinary physician recognizes smallpox, diptheria, etc., as communicable"(Sprattling, 1912; cited in Wolfensberger, 1975).

One of the first professionals of this period to theorize that inferior intelligence was hereditary was the American psychologist Henry Herbert Goddard. Director of the research laboratory of the Training School for the feebleminded (retarded) in Vineland, New Jersey, Goddard analyzed **genealogical** tables of school residents to determine the extent of feeblemindedness in their families. These case studies were based on interviews with relatives, observations of family behavior, and questioning of school residents about their family histories.

Goddard's notoriety extended beyond that of his colleagues and into the public domain with the publication of *The Kallikak Family: A Study in the Heredity of Feeblemindedness* (1912). Goddard traced the family tree of Deborah Kallikak, a Vineland School resident, back approximately four generations to the period of the revolutionary war. He claimed to have located 480 descendants. The study concluded, "Thirty-six have been illegitimate. There have been thirty-three sexually immoral persons, mostly prostitutes. There have been twenty-four confirmed alcoholics. There have been three epileptics. Eighty-two died in infancy. Three were criminal, eight kept houses of ill fame. . . ." (Goddard, 1912, p. 18).

Goddard attempted to convince the scientific and lay community that these results showed feeblemindedness to be hereditary, transmitted from generation to generation. He later hypothesized in his treatise *Feeblemindedness: Its Causes and Consequences* (1914) that there was an irrefutable link between intelligence and social deviation: The less intelligence people have, the less responsible they are for their actions. Therefore, less intelligent people are more likely to exhibit socially deviant or unacceptable behavior. Goddard's definition of social deviates included criminals, alcoholics, the sexually immoral, mongoloids, epileptics, the mentally ill, and the feebleminded. Goddard's thesis was widely accepted by American and European psychologists in the 1920s and 1930s, although it is no longer accepted by contemporary professionals in psychology or sociology (Suchar, 1978).

The eugenics theory, as espoused by Goddard and others, did establish strong social movements aimed at segregating various exceptional populations from society. The watchwords of the period were: (1) prevent the spread of social deviance and (2) protect society from the defective individual through segregation.

Social Segregation

Many professionals (Barr, 1915; Fernald, 1915; Johnson, 1908) supported Goddard's theory that mental and moral deviance were hereditary and that intellectual deficiencies were primarily fixed and incurable. The outcome of this theorizing was a widespread movement toward selective breeding and the overall prevention of defective individuals. This end brought about an extended period of alarm and fear of, as well as an indictment against, many exceptional people. In the latter half of this century we have come to recognize that hereditary factors play a less significant role in the causes of mental and social deviance than was once theorized, especially when compared to maternal health and sociocultural factors (Wolfensberger, 1975).

The focus of early twentieth-century preventive measures was the passage of state legislation that prohibited "mental and social deviates" from marrying. Eventually such legislation was expanded to include asexualization, or unsexing of the individual. Compulsory surgical sterilization became widespread, and laws were passed throughout the nation in an effort to reduce the number of deviates. Karier (1973) estimated that over 8,500 persons were sterilized in twenty-one states between 1907 and 1928. Sterilization laws in some states contained provisions for sterilizing not only the mentally retarded but also epileptics, the sexually promiscuous, and criminals.

Parallel to the passage of such laws was the movement to segregate deviant populations. Fernald (1915) viewed segregation as a strict separation of the sexes that would prevent further spread of deviance. The rationale was to protect society from the deviant, and the deviant from society. The result was the removal of large numbers of individuals from the community into an isolated, special-care facility whose sole purpose was the care and maintenance of the deviant person. These facilities became widely known as "institutions."

The Meaning of An Institution

An **institution** is defined as an establishment or facility governed by a collection of principles or fundamental rules. It is an organization having a social, educational, or religious purpose. The purpose may be to diagnose a problem; to correct, remediate, or rehabilitate; to care for and maintain; or to punish. Goffman (1975) identified five principal types of institutions:

1. Institutions for persons who are "incapable" and "harmless": the blind, aged, and orphaned

2. Institutions for persons who are "incapable" and who unintentionally pose a threat to the community: mental hospitals, TB sanitariums
3. Institutions for persons who intentionally endanger the community: prisons, jails, prisoner-of-war camps, concentration camps
4. Institutions established for some instrumental task: army barracks, boarding schools, work campuses
5. Institutions that are retreats from the secular world: abbeys, monasteries, convents, and cloisters. (P. 409–10)

Institutions for deviant populations have been subsumed under many different labels: "school," "hospital," "colony," "prison," and "asylum." The term "institution" did not originate with the facilities of early twentieth-century America. Asylums prominent in many parts of Europe in the seventeenth century were used to segregate, dehumanize, and punish moral defectives. Through the work of Pinel in France and Benjamin Rush, the father of American psychiatry, there began in the last half of the eighteenth century an era of humanitarian reform that encompassed the principles of moral treatment.

The early nineteenth century brought a period of optimism concerning the treatment and eventual cure of insanity and idiocy. Hope eventually eroded into despair in the latter half of the century, and with the **eugenics** movement, institutions began to move from treatment programs to merely care and maintenance. The educational and rehabilitative emphasis of the nineteenth century, which had focused on returning the individual to society, degenerated into terminal placement. Many professionals were convinced that it was necessary to segregate large numbers of mental and social deviates.

This influx of individuals into publicly funded institutions changed the character of these facilities and created financial dilemmas. Legislative appropriations were limited, and the emphasis was on providing care for the greatest number with the least amount of funds. Institutions became more and more concerned with social control. In order to manage large numbers of individuals with a limited financial base, institutions had to establish rigid rules and regulations. In many cases, these rules stripped away the individuals' identity and forced them into group regimentation. For example, individuals could have no personal possessions. They were forced to wear the institutional wardrobe and were given an identification tag and number.

These institutions, whether they were described as mental hospitals, state prisons, or colonies for the mentally retarded, shared a number of characteristics:

1. All aspects of life are conducted in the same place and under the same single authority.
2. Each phase of the member's daily activity is carried on in the immediate company of a large batch of others, all of whom are treated alike and required to do the same thing together.
3. All phases of the day's activities are tightly scheduled, . . . the whole sequence of activities being imposed from above by a system of explicit formal rulings and a body of officials.

4. Social mobility between the two strata is grossly restricted; social distance is typically great and often formally prescribed.
5. There exists a work ideology which the institution may define as treatment, rehabilitation, punishment, etc.
6. There exists a system of rewards and punishments which takes in the total life situation of the "inmate."
7. There exists a "mortification" or "stripping" process, where "desocialization" or "disculturation" takes place and "resocialization" begins. (Goffman, 1975, p. 410)

Several factors together changed the institution of the early twentieth century from a facility for moral and therapeutic treatment to one of custodial care. These included crowded conditions and the lack of a qualified professional staff. By the early 1920s, all states had hospitals for the mentally ill, and the numbers of large, isolated residential facilities for the mentally retarded were growing rapidly. For the most part, these facilities remained largely custodial and were characterized by locked living units, barred windows, and high walls surrounding the facility. Organized treatment programs declined, and "terminal" uncured patients accumulated. This forced even more expansion and the erection of new buildings. In addition, public and professional pessimism concerning the value of treatment programs meant diminishing funds for mental health care.

This alarming situation remained unchanged for nearly five decades and declined even further during the depression years of the 1930s and 1940s, when funds and human resources were in short supply (Goldenberg, 1977). In the early 1950s, the United States moved into an era of economic prosperity. By this time there were more than 500,000 persons committed to mental hospitals throughout the nation, and comparable numbers in institutions for the mentally retarded.

In the early 1950s, the first attempts to reform mental hospitals were initiated by the American Psychiatric Association, which led efforts to inspect and rate the nation's three hundred mental hospitals and called attention to the lack of therapeutic intervention and deplorable living conditions. In 1950, parents of the mentally retarded began to mobilize, and the National Association for Retarded Children (currently the Association for Retarded Citizens—USA) was founded. The purpose of this association is "to promote the general welfare of the mentally retarded of all ages everywhere: at home, in the communities, in institutions, and in public, private, and religious schools" (*Residential services: Position statements of the ARC*, 1976, p. 3).

Over the next two decades (1950–1970), the philosophy regarding segregation underwent some important changes. This period of reform ran parallel to the civil rights movement's concern with racial discrimination and school desegregation. Institutional practices were severely criticized by some professionals (Blatt & Kaplan, 1966), and the general public became aware that many state-operated institutions were oriented to minimal custodial care without any provision for treatment and habilitation. Parents and professionals coordinated their efforts and demanded that appropriate treatment be made available to residents of state institutions. Legal action was taken, and several suits were brought against states for operating inadequate facilities.

The Right to Treatment in an Institution

Several court cases of the past two decades have been significant in reforming state institutions for the mentally retarded and mentally ill. In the case of *Wyatt v. Stickney* (1972), a U.S. district court ruled that the patients at Bryce Hospital in the state of Alabama were being deprived of their right to individual treatment that would give them a realistic opportunity for **habilitation.** The court described the institutional facilities as human warehouses steeped in an atmosphere of psychological and physical deprivation. It further specified that the state must make changes to ensure a therapeutic environment. It was stipulated that:

1. Patients have a right to privacy and dignity.
2. Patients have a right to manage their own affairs, including marriage, divorce, and voting privileges.
3. Patients have a right to have visitors, to make telephone calls, and to receive confidential mail.
4. Patients have a right to be free from physical restraint and isolation.
5. Patients have a right to wear their own clothes and to keep personal possessions.
6. Patients have a right to an adequate medical program. Medication may not be used as punishment or for staff convenience and may not be used as a substitute for a full therapeutic program.
7. Patients engaged in labor comparable to work of hospital employees have a right to monetary compensation.
8. Patients must not be subjected to experimental research without informed consent.

Although the court's decision was specific only to Alabama, the federal government has compelled many states to comply with standards comparable to those handed down in *Wyatt v. Stickney* if they are receiving federal financial assistance.

The *Wyatt* decision was followed by another landmark decision in *O'Connor v. Donaldsen* (1975): The U.S. Supreme Court ruled that a state cannot confine persons labeled as mentally ill against their will and without treatment if they are not dangerous and if they are capable of surviving on their own or with the help of willing family members and friends. This judgment upheld the idea that involuntarily confined patients have a right to be treated or released.

In 1981 the U.S. Supreme Court in *Pennhurst State School and Hospital v. Halderman* handed down a major decision on the right to treatment in state institutions. *Pennhurst* began as a suit on behalf of the residents of a Pennsylvania state institution (Pennhurst School), alleging inhumane and dangerous conditions, unnecessary physical restraints, and lack of habilitative programs.

In 1979 the U.S. Court of Appeals in the third circuit affirmed the right of every mentally retarded person to receive habilitative care in the least restrictive environment (a concept discussed later in this chapter). However, the Supreme Court reversed this decision and found that current law does not create substantive rights to treatment in the **least restrictive environment.** Current law does no more than establish a national policy to improve treatment of the mentally retarded and to provide financial incentives to induce states to do so. It does not require states to expend their financial resources to provide specific kinds of treatment.

In 1982 the rights of mentally retarded persons in state institutions were again considered by the Supreme Court in *Youngberg v. Romeo.* In this case, the court dealt with the question of whether physical restraint or lack of safe conditions in a state institution was a violation of **due process.** The court held that appropriate training for the mentally retarded person is necessary to ensure safety and freedom from restraint. Although the decision is significant because it is the first time the Supreme Court has found that retarded persons in institutions have a right to treatment, the decision was limited only to safety and freedom from restraint. The larger issue of a general constitutional right to treatment has yet to be considered by the Supreme Court.

The Effects of Institutionalization

Not all institutions are alike. Investigations by Balla (1976), Blatt, Ozolins & McNally (1979), Butterfield (1967), and Zigler (1973) showed that present-day institutions continue to range from dehumanizing warehouses that have a deleterious effect on the cognitive and physiological development of the resident, to facilities that through systematic treatment and a noninstitutional atmosphere bring about positive behavioral changes. The latter type of institution attempts to normalize the environment of the individual by providing homelike living arrangements. Such efforts may include private or semiprivate bedrooms; family dining facilities; nonstandardization of furniture arrangements; choice of clothing and hairstyles; encouraging individual possessions; access to everyday risks (e.g., hot water, electrical applicances); individualized educational or therapeutic programs; and vocational opportunities corresponding to the individual's capabilities. Investigators have reported that the most harmful aspect of institutionalization is related to a restrictive regimen with little regard for individual needs or desires.

What constitutes a good institution continues to be a matter of legal and moral debate. Objective criteria have not been agreed on by parents or professionals. We do know that the original rationale for the social-segregation model in the early twentieth century is not valid. Institutional accomplishments of the past eighty years can be summed up in a few rather negative statements. Residential schools became isolated asylums concerned more with social management and regimentation than with education or treatment. The large state hospital or institution in many cases became places where residents were subject to physical abuse and emotional neglect (Blatt, Ozolins & McNally,

1979; Blatt & Kaplan, 1967; *O'Connor v. Donaldsen*, 1975; *Wyatt v. Stickney*, 1972). The civil rights of individuals were often ignored. In addition, the segregation model, originally intended to stop the spread of deviance, did not prevent mental or social problems as some early twentieth-century professionals predicted. Menolascino, McGee, and Casey (1982) discussed the need for alternatives beyond the institutional model:

> There is abundant information and research data available to support the contention that: (1) prolonged institutionalization has destructive developmental consequences . . . (2) appropriate community-based residential settings are generally more beneficial than institutional placements . . . and (3) mentally retarded individuals with a wide spectrum of disabilities—including the severely and profoundly retarded—can be successfully served in community-based settings. (P. 65)

Social Integration: Defining the Least Restrictive Alternative

The doctrine of the **least restrictive environment,** or **least restrictive alternative (LRE or LRA)** dictates that persons with exceptional characteristics receive services in an environment that is consistent with individual developmental needs. The doctrine is a legal concept applied to court cases where there is a conflict between personal liberties and government interests. The judgments in these court cases have progressively clarified the basis for the application of the LRE doctrine to social, medical, and educational services. The following position statements are intended to help define the concept's parameters.

There must be available a continuum of services capable of meeting an individual's developmental needs. The more restricted the continuum, the greater the probability that gaps will exist, thus forcing individuals into inappropriate environments. This position is contrary to the segregation models, where institutionalization was a routine placement of many individuals. The result of segregated services was a failure to develop community-based alternatives.

The least restrictive environment is defined by the developmental needs of the individual and not by the range of services available. Every effort should be made to expand environmental alternatives to meet the needs. If the needs of a person do not match the service patterns available, then the services must be altered in order to accommodate the individual. This position also emphasizes that a setting defined as "restrictive," such as a state hospital or institution, should be available only if the developmental needs of certain individuals warrant such a placement.

The LRE concept establishes that all environmental alternatives are fluid. Placement in any social or educational service pattern is not terminal or irreversible but must be continuously reassessed. This position reaffirms that individuals are not to be placed and then forgotten. The literature is replete with documentation of people who were placed in environments such as hospitals and institutions and never reevaluated for a less restrictive placement.

In order to meet the intent of the LRE doctrine, there must be an ongoing evaluation of individual growth. This process can be accomplished only through the interaction of the individual, parents, and professionals. This approach provides for a comprehensive evaluation, including medical, social, and educational factors.

Developing Community Resources

The intent of the LRE concept is to have available to the individual with exceptional characteristics comprehensive services within or as close as possible to family and community life, for example, educational programs, public transportation, meals in a restaurant, or freedom to take part in religious activities. In addition, the exceptional individual should be able to purchase additional services: dental examinations, medical treatment, life insurance, and so on. (Kenowitz, Gallaher & Edgar, 1977) The purpose of such services is to allow the person an opportunity to achieve community integration. In order to accomplish community integration, three factors should be taken into account: (1) the developmental level of the individual, (2) the ability of the individual with appropriate training to adapt to societal expectations, and (3) the ability and willingness of the society to adapt to and accommodate the individual with differences.

The developmental level of the person is an important component in the integration process. A misconception concerning the term *development* is found in the notion that it is defined solely on the basis of intellectual functioning and remains static throughout life. Wyne and O'Connor (1979) outlined the basic assumptions of development as follows:

Development refers to change in an individual's ability or capacity in any one or combination of three interacting domains—physical, emotional and intellectual. . . .

Development is continuous; it takes place during the entire life span of an individual from birth to death. . . .

Development is dependent upon adaptation to the individual's environment. In turn, adaptation is dependent upon learning. Even the most basic life-sustaining behaviors are learned. . . . Adaptation is the interrelationship between development and learning. Development occurs as the individual learns to adapt to the physical, intellectual and social environments. (P. 10–11)

Services within the community must be able to accommodate those who vary in different degrees from the established developmental norms. These services should reinforce those qualities in people with differences that have been internalized by society as normal.

The above assumptions are consistent with the principle of **normalization.** This principle, initially defined and developed in the Scandanavian countries, has been refined for application in the United States. Wolfensberger (1977) described the principle as "utilization of means which are as culturally normative as possible, in order to establish and/or maintain personal behaviors and characteristics which are as culturally normative as possible" (p. 306). The principle of normalization emphasizes the need to utilize existing community services appropriately to the fullest extent, while developing and implementing adaptive systems in medicine, social services, and education that will facilitate successful integration.

Medical Services. Appropriate medical care is an essential component of community-based service to exceptional people. The physician's role ranges from diagnostician and prognosticator to family adviser and friend. In many cases, the physician is the first professional parents will have contact with concerning their child's disability. This is particularly true when the child's problem is identifiable immediately after birth or during early childhood. The physician diagnoses the problem and communicates with the parents regarding medical prognosis and recommendations for treatment. Based on the medical information available, the physician and the parents reach a decision concerning proper medical intervention. The proposed intervention may, however, affect the child psychologically and/or educationally. For example, the physician may recommend that a child be committed to a state institution because of severe medical abnormalities. Such a recommendation often does not take into account the resources available to the child in the community or the child's psychological or educational prognosis for habilitation. Hardman and Drew (1980)

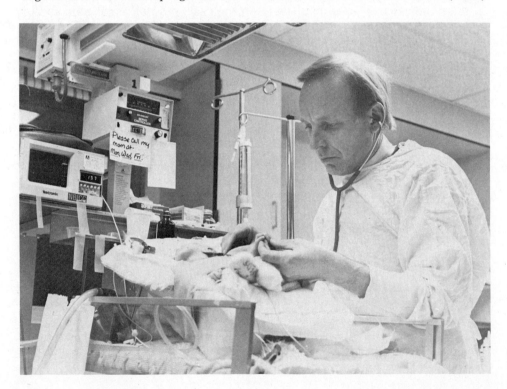

The role of a physician is multidimensional.

suggested that the physician often does not provide parents with enough information to make a well-informed decision. Physicians should not assume responsibility for being the only counseling resource to parents. They should be aware of additional resources within the community, including other parents, social workers, mental health professionals, and educators. The physician's role as counselor should be confined to medical matters and should not extend beyond the knowledge of the profession.

Medical services are often taken for granted simply because medicine is a readily available service for the majority of people. This is not true for many exceptional populations. It is not uncommon for a pediatrician to suggest that parents seek treatment elsewhere for their exceptional child. The physician is saying "I am not willing to treat your child" or "I am not equipped to treat your child." In either case, the physician may be frustrating the parents by not referring them to an appropriate medical specialist. This referral need be only for medical problems beyond the scope of the pediatrician's knowledge. What about the willingness of the physician to treat disabled patients for common illnesses, such as a cold, the flu, or a sore throat? In a survey conducted by Kenowitz, Gallaher, and Edgar (1977), eighteen pediatricians in the Seattle area were contacted concerning their willingness to treat a disabled child with a severe cold. Approximately 56 percent of the pediatricians were either unwilling or hesitant to treat the child. In addition, 39 percent referred the parents to the local child development and mental retardation center—a totally inappropriate agency, given that the medical problem was the common cold.

It is unfair to describe community medical professionals as unresponsive to the needs of exceptional populations. On the contrary, medical technology has prevented many disabilities and enhanced the quality of life for persons in institutions as well as in the community. The issue here is with the delivery of medical services within the community on a daily basis. In order to provide comprehensive medical services to a disabled population within a community structure, several things must be taken into consideration:

1. The physician in community practice (general practioners, pediatricians, etc.) must receive more medical training in the medical, psychological, and educational aspects of exceptional populations.
2. Physicians must be more willing to treat disabled patients for common illnesses where the treatment is irrelevant to the patient's disability.
3. Physicians need not become specialists in specific areas of disability, but they must have enough knowledge to refer the patient to an appropriate specialist when necessary.
4. Physicians must not extend their counseling role beyond medical matters, but must be aware of, and willing to refer the patient to, other community resources.

Thus, in some respects the medical profession must restrict its role, whereas in other respects it must be more willing to assume the proper role and responsibility. The medical profession must continue to support physician specialists and other allied health personnel who are well equipped to work with disabled populations. These specialized health professionals include geneticists and genetic counselors, physical and occupational therapists, public health nurses, and nutritional and dietary personnel.

Social Services. Integration of exceptional populations into the community structure depends on the accessibility of existing social/psychological services as well as on continual development of new alternatives. These necessary social services include community mental health centers, access to public buildings and transportation, community living alternatives, recreation and leisure-time activities, and employment opportunities.

Community mental health centers provide psychological services and early-intervention programs in a local setting. Such centers have provisions for both inpatient and outpatient care. Services provided by the centers include psychological evaluation, intensive treatment programs, and referrals to other agencies when appropriate. There are also provisions for crisis intervention on a twenty-four-hour-a-day basis, and rehabilitation services to help people restore physical, social, or vocational functioning.

Access to adequate housing and barrier-free facilities is essential for the integration of persons with physical disabilities into the community. A barrier-free environment may mean renovating some community facilities and incorporating barrier-free designs in new buildings and public transportation. For those in wheelchairs or on crutches, entrance ramps to and within public

Services provided by a mental health specialist may be very helpful to parents of a handicapped child.

buildings, accessibility to public telephones, vending machines, and restrooms, and lifts for public transportation vehicles would be needed. Community residential alternatives can be viewed on a continuum from placement in a large multipurpose insititution to living independently in a private home. Available living environments may include specialized care centers in addition to nursing, boarding, group-home, and foster-home placements.

Recreation and leisure-time opportunities within the community vary substantially according to age and the severity of the individual's disability. These services will also vary from community to community in terms of financial support and continuity of programs over time. Kenowitz et al. (1977) conducted a survey of parents of Down's syndrome children (six to twelve years of age) and found that the families did not have access to such services as dance and music lessons, tumbling, swimming, or scouting. All these services were available for other children within the community, however. Similar problems exist for adolescents and adults with exceptional characteristics. Many have not been able to adapt to the community because they could not use leisure time constructively. Adult populations may do little with their leisure time beyond watching television. Recreational programs must be developed to assist individuals in developing worthwhile leisure-time activities and a more satisfying lifestyle. Therapeutic recreation is a profession concerned specifically with this goal, using recreation to help people adapt their physical, emotional, or social characteristics to take advantage of leisure-time activities more independently in a community setting.

Employment opportunities within the community include a range from regular competitive employment to sheltered workshops in a segregated facility. The "right to work" creed is applicable to every disabled individual. Community employment alternatives consistent with a broad range of ability levels are necessary components of the community-service model.

Reaching the goal of appropriate community services will require modification of the public attitude and policy concerning the rights of individuals with exceptional characteristics. One piece of legislation, presently the most influential civil rights policy statement concerning persons with disabilities, is Public Law 93-112, Section 504 of the Vocational Rehabilitation Act of 1973:

> No otherwise qualified handicapped individual in the United States shall, solely by reason of his handicap, be excluded from the participation in, be denied the benefits of, or be subjected to discrimination under any program or activity receiving federal financial assistance.

Should a state be in violation of Section 504, it may lose federal funds dispersed throughout various state programs. More important, however, is the clear mandate in the law that the civil rights of the exceptional individual may not be abridged.

Educational Services. Successful integration of exceptional persons into a community setting depends on access to education and training. Today the

The educational rights of the handicapped have been affirmed by recent state and federal legislation.

rights of disabled students to a free and appropriate public education have been mandated by state and national legislation. Because much of this legislation and the courts excluded gifted and talented students, the more narrowly defined term "handicapped" is used. However, the movement toward appropriate education for *all* exceptional students is gaining momentum. As a result, the system is faced with the challenge of educating a diverse population of individual students. This means greater emphasis on precise and individualized instruction, effective use of professionals in several disciplines (e.g., psychologists, social workers, medical personnel) in assessment and programming, and a more clearly defined role for the educator. In order to understand more clearly why education will have an expanded role in the 1980s, we must first review the history of special education services in this century.

EDUCATING THE EXCEPTIONAL STUDENT IN THE PUBLIC SCHOOLS

A Beginning: 1900–1920

The education of exceptional children in the United States began in the early 1800s with the work of Itard, Seguin, Howe, and others. These efforts consisted of programs that were usually separate from the public schools. Many

instructional programs took place in segregated residential schools and were
concerned with educating the visually disordered, the hearing disordered, the
mentally retarded, and the emotionally disturbed. At first, the objective of these
programs was to return the individual to a more normalized environment,
including the public schools. This objective was never realized. By 1900,
segregation became the watchword, and many residential schools became
institutions for custodial care. Some facilities, particularly those for persons
with visual and hearing disorders, maintained an educational orientation.

The public schools of the early 1900s were not prepared for the
nontraditional learner. Education was defined by the basics: reading, writing,
and arithmetic. Any child who deviated from the established sequence, rate,
or process of learning either dropped out of school by choice or was excluded.
The emphasis for most students was on learning the basics and then leaving
school. Although laws requiring parents to keep their children in school until
a specified age had been in effect since the mid-1850s, fewer than 10 percent
of the school-age population graduated from high school in the early 1900s.
Today over 70 percent of the high school students in this country earn a diploma.
It is easy to see why mandatory education for exceptional individuals was not
an educational priority of the early twentieth-century.

Nevertheless, by 1910 several urban areas across the nation had made
some provisions for mentally retarded children in the schools. Public school
programs were not mandated by law. Local school officials could choose who
would and would not be served. The majority of these early special education
services were for learners with mild disorders. These school services closely
paralleled the larger social segregation model. Disabled students, although
located in the same facility as their regular education peers, were completely
separate from them. Special education meant segregated education. However,
the child's deviation from the norm could not be too substantial or the student
would be removed from the system entirely. Consequently, there was a need
to develop an assessment tool that could determine the intellectual characteristics
common to the majority of school-age children. This tool could be used to
identify children whose abilities were inferior to those of other children of the
same chronological age.

The result was an individual test of intelligence developed by Alfred Binet
and Theodore Simon (1905). The test was first used in the schools of France
to predict how well a student would function in school. In 1908 it was translated
into English by Henry Goddard for use in his studies of the Kallikak family.
In 1916 the Binet-Simon Scales (revised and standardized by Lewis Terman at
Stanford University) were published as the Stanford-Binet Intelligence Scale.
This test, along with numerous other scales, provided a means of identifying
children who deviated significantly from the average in intellectual capability,
at least as far as what the test measured. Intelligence scales have been recognized
as positive forces for identifying children who need additional educational
services, but they have also been used as a means of excluding children who
deviated too far from the norm and did not fit into any of the educational
programs available in the public schools.

Maintaining the Status Quo: 1920–1960

From 1920 to 1960 the availability of public school programs for exceptional children continued to be sporadic and selective. Some states, such as New York, New Jersey, and Massachusetts, enacted mandatory education for the mildly (educable) retarded. However, most states only *allowed* for special education; they did not *require* that the services be made available. Services to children with mild emotional disorders (discipline problems) were initiated in the early 1930s, but the residential center or mental hospital continued to be the only alternative for individuals with more severe emotional problems.

Special classes for children with physical disabilities were also started in the 1930s. These programs were for children with crippling conditions, heart defects, and other health-related problems that interfered with the ability to participate in regular education programs. Separate schools became very popular for these children during the late 1950s. These schools were specially equipped to accommodate the needs of the physically disabled, including elevators, ramps, and modified doors, toilets, and desks.

The preponderance of exceptional children receiving mandatory special education services in the 1980s, had they been born before 1960, would have remained in the regular classroom with no special education program. These children would have attended public schools as long as the discrepancy between the expected or normal learning rate, and their individual learning capabilities, was tolerable to the classroom teacher. When these nontraditional learners were no longer able to keep up with the required sequence for learning, they became school dropouts. For children with mild disorders, it may have taken several years for the discrepancy to be sufficient for exclusion to be the only alternative. However, for the more severely disordered child, a significant discrepancy was evident by the time the child reached school age. These children were seldom even considered for public education. In addition, gifted and talented children were not considered for special services, because they exceeded the norm. No attempt was made to identify or provide additional education for students on the basis of how far above the standard they were; gifted children were simply part of the majority of children referred to as normal.

An Era of Self-Examination: 1960–1970

During the late 1950s there was an increase in the number of public school classes for mildly retarded and emotionally disturbed children, but these classes continued to promote the traditional segregation model. Children were educated in an environment that isolated them from normal peers. The validity of these segregated special classes became an important issue in the field of education. Several studies (Ainsworth, 1959; Baldwin, 1958; Cassidy & Stanton, 1959; Johnson, 1961; Jordan 1959; Thurstone, 1959) examined the efficacy of special classes for mildly retarded children, comparing retarded students receiving their education in a special class with a retarded population that remained in the regular class without special education services. Johnson (1962) summarized

this research and suggested that there were no differences in academic achievement between retarded learners in special or regular education classes, although the retarded child's social adjustment was not harmed by the special class program. Dunn (1968) again cited the efficacy research and declared that most special classes for the mildly retarded could not be justified and should be abolished. He stated:

> In my view, much of our past and present practices are morally and educationally wrong. We have been living at the mercy of general educators who have referred their problem children to us. And we have been generally ill prepared and ineffective in educating these children. Let us stop being pressured into continuing and expanding a special education program that we know now to be undesirable for many of the children we are dedicated to serve. (P.5)

Although several authors in recent years (MacMillan & Becker, 1977; Robinson & Robinson, 1976) have suggested that many of the efficacy studies were poorly designed, these studies had already resulted in a movement toward an expansion of services in the public schools beyond the special class. One outcome of this expansion was a model where a child could remain in the regular class program for at least some portion of the school day, receiving special education when and where it was needed. This concept became widely known as **mainstreaming.**

The 1960s was a period for other major changes in the field of special education. First, the federal government took on an expanded role in the education of exceptional children. The passage of Public Law 88-164 in 1963 expanded university teacher-preparation programs in the areas of mental retardation, hearing, speech and language, and visual disorders, and the emotionally disturbed and physically disabled. Public Law 89-813 recognized special education within the federal bureaucracy and created the Bureau of Education for the Handicapped (BEH)* in the U.S. Office of Education (Department of Health, Education, and Welfare). The BEH became the clearinghouse for special education on a federal level. It provided grants to universities and colleges for the preparation of special education personnel. In addition, research and demonstration projects were funded nationwide to establish a research base for the education of disabled students in the public schools. Thus the BEH became the broker for direct financial aid to states seeking to establish special education services on a local level.

The 1960s also saw the advent of a new special education category: specific learning disabilities. This category of exceptionality emerged in response to a need to identify and classify children who required special education services but did not fit the existing categorical criteria for mental retardation or emotionally disabled. This population was not significantly impaired in their in-

---

*In May 1980, the BEH became the Office of Special Education and Rehabilitative Services in the newly established Department of Education.

tellectual functioning, nor did they exhibit behavioral deviance that met the criteria for emotional disabling conditions. However, their achievement in school-related subject areas, particularly reading and mathematics, was so far below the norm for their age-group that some type of additional service was required beyond the regular education program.

Reaffirming the Right to Education: 1970 to the Present

The 1970's are often described as a decade of revolution in the field of special education. Many of the landmark cases in the right to education for handicapped students were brought before the courts during this period. In addition, there were enacted major pieces of state and federal legislation that reaffirmed the handicapped individual's right to a free public education. What is often overlooked is that the rights of handicapped individuals came to the public forum as a part of a larger social issue: the civil rights of all minority populations in the United States. The civil rights movement of the 1950s and 1960s awakened the public to the issues of discrimination in employment, housing, access to public facilities (e.g., restaurants, transportation), and public education.

Education was reaffirmed as a right and not a privilege by the U.S. Supreme Court in the case of *Brown v. Topeka, Kansas, Board of Education* in 1954. In its decision the court ruled that education must be made available to everyone on an equal basis. A unanimous Supreme Court stated:

> In these days, it is doubtful that any child may reasonably be expected to succeed in life if he is denied the opportunity of an education.
> Such an opportunity, where the state has undertaken to provide it, is a right which must be made available to all on equal terms.

This decision set a major precedent for the education of exceptional children in the United States. Although the court specifically mandated that segregation of students on the basis of race was unconstitutional, the intent was that every child has a right to an education. Unfortunately, it was nearly twenty years before the federal courts were confronted directly with the issue of a free and appropriate education for exceptional children.

In 1971 the Pennsylvania Association for Retarded Citizens filed a class-action suit on behalf of retarded children living in Pennsylvania who were presently excluded from public education on the basis of intellectual deficiency (*Pennsylvania Association for Retarded Citizens v. Commonwealth of Pennsylvania, 1971*). The suit charged that more than 50,000 retarded children in the state were being denied their right to a free public education. The plaintiffs claimed that retarded children can learn if the educational program is adjusted to meet their individual needs. The central issue was whether public school programs should be required to accommodate the intellectually different child. The court rendered a consent agreement in May 1972 and upheld the claims of the plaintiffs. The court ordered Pennsylvania schools to provide a free public education to all retarded children (ages six to twenty-one) commensurate with their individual learning needs. In addition, preschool education was to be provided for retarded children if the local school district was providing it for other children.

Later that same year, the case of *Mills v. District of Columbia* (1972) expanded the Pennsylvania decision to include all handicapped children. The court, in a judgment against the District of Columbia, cited the *Brown* case as well as the equal protection and due process clauses of the Fourteenth Amendment.

> No State shall make or enforce any law which shall abridge the privileges or immunities of citizens of the United States; nor shall any State deprive any person of life, liberty, or property, without due process of law; nor deny to any person within its jurisdiction the equal protection of the laws. (U.S. Constitution, Amendment 14, Section 1)

District of Columbia schools were ordered to provide a free and appropriate education to every school-age disabled child. The court further noted that when regular public school assignment was not appropriate, alternative educational services must be made available. And lack of finances could not be used as an excuse to exclude exceptional children.

Thus, the right of exceptional children to an education was reaffirmed under the Constitution of the United States. The Pennsylvania and *Mills* cases served as catalysts for several court cases and pieces of legislation in the years that followed. Table 2-3 summarizes precedents that were established in the court cases and legislation from 1954 to 1975. By 1975 the legal revolution in the education of exceptional children was reaching its peak. Finally, the Congress of the United States, influenced by the efforts of parents and professionals alike, saw a need to bring together the various pieces of state and federal legislation into one comprehensive national public law. The Education of All Handicapped Children Act, Public Law 94-142, was passed by an overwhelming majority of the House and the Senate and signed into law by President Gerald Ford in May 1975.

Public Law (P.L.) 94-142 was intended to make available free and appropriate public education for all disabled children in the United States. One important purpose of the law was to provide monetary incentive to the various states to assist them in initiating appropriate educational services for exceptional children. Each state, in order to receive this federal aid, was required to comply with the provisions of the law. In effect, this means that P.L. 94-142 went beyond a simple mandate to serve exceptional children; it described how these children were to be educated. The law provided for:

1. Nondiscriminatory and multidisciplinary assessment of educational needs
2. Parental involvement in developing the child's educational program
3. Education in an environment suited to individual needs
4. An individualized education program (IEP)

Nondiscriminatory and Multidisciplinary Assessment. Several provisions related to the use of nondiscriminatory testing procedures in labeling and place-

Table 2-3/ Major Court Cases and Federal Legislation Focusing on the Right to Education for Handicapped Individuals (1954–1975)

Court Case/Legislation	Precedent
Brown v. Topeka, Kansas, Board of Education (1954)	Segregation of students by race held unconstitutional.
	Education is a right that must be available to all on equal terms.
Hobsen v. Hansen (1969)	The doctrine of equal educational opportunity is a part of the law of due process, and denying an equal educational opportunity is a violation of the Constitution.
	Placement of children in educational tracks based on performance on standardized tests is unconstitutional and discriminates against poor and minority children.
Diana v. California State Board of Education (1970)	Children tested for potential placement in a special education program must be assessed in their native or primary language.
	Children cannot be placed in special education classes on the basis of culturally biased tests.
Pennsylvania Association for Retarded Citizens v. Commonwealth of Pennsylvania (1971)	Pennsylvania schools must provide a free public education to all school-age retarded children.
Mills v. Board of Education of the District of Columbia (1972)	Declared exclusion of handicapped individuals from free appropriate public education is a violation of the due process and equal protection clause of the Fourteenth Amendment to the Constitution.
	Public schools in the District of Columbia must provide a free education to all handicapped children regardless of their functioning level or ability to adapt to the present educational system.
Public Law 93-112, Vocational Rehabilitation Act of 1973, Section 504 (1973)	Handicapped individuals cannot be excluded from the participation in, be denied benefits of, or be subjected to discrimination under any program or activity receiving federal financial assistance.
Public Law 93-380, Educational Amendments Act (1974)	Financial aid authorized to the states for the implementation of programs for exceptional children, including the gifted and talented.
	Due process requirements (procedural safeguards) established to protect rights of handicapped children and their families in special education placement decisions.
Public Law 94-142, Education for all Handicapped Children Act (1975)	A free and appropriate public education must be provided for all handicapped children in the U.S.

ment of children for special education services have been incorporated into P.L. 94-142. Many of these procedural requirements are an extension of prior court actions concerned with nonbiased assessment. These cases brought visibility to certain abuses inherent within traditional testing methods and provided a means to rectify this discrimination. The safeguards included:

1. The testing of children in their native or primary language whenever possible
2. The use of evaluation procedures selected and administered to prevent cultural or racial discrimination
3. The use of assessment tools validated for the purpose for which they are being used
4. Assessment by a multidisciplinary team utilizing several pieces of information to formulate a placement decision

Disabled students have too often been placed in special education programs on the basis of inadequate data and/or assessment information of questionable validity. Placement decisions have often been made using only a single score (e.g., intelligence quotient) from a standardized test or on the basis of a single professional's judgment. One result of these procedures has been a disproportionate number of ethnic minority children and children from lower socio-economic backgrounds being placed in special eduction programs.

Parent Involvement in the Educational Process. P.L. 94-142 delineates the role of parents in the education of their children. According to rules and regulations of the law (*Federal Register*, August 1977), parents have the right to:

1. Consent in writing before the child is initially evaluated
2. Consent in writing before the child is initially placed in a special education program
3. Request an independent education evaluation if they feel the school's evaluation is inappropriate
4. Request an evaluation at public expense if a due-process hearing decision is that the public agency's evaluation was inappropriate
5. Participate on the committee that considers the evaluation, placement, and programming of the child
6. Inspect and review educational records and challenge information believed to be inaccurate, misleading, or in violation of the privacy or other rights of the child
7. Request a copy of information from their child's educational record
8. Request a hearing concerning the school's proposal or refusal to initiate or change the identification, evaluation, or placement of the child, or the provision of a free appropriate public education

These procedural safeguards protect the child and family from decisions that could adversely affect their lives. In addition, families can be more secure in the knowledge that every reasonable attempt is being made to educate their child appropriately.

Education in the Least Restrictive Environment. All children have the right to learn in an environment consistent with their academic, social, and physical needs. Historically, special education services have been restricted to the isolated special class or special school. The efficacy research of the 1960s (discussed earlier in this chapter), in conjunction with a desire on the part of many to provide education for exceptional children as close to the norm as possible, brought about an expansion of this service-delivery model. The expanded continuum-of-services model was visually depicted by Deno in 1970. An adaptation of this continuum-of-services model may be found in Figure 2-1.

Figure 2-1/ Educational Service Options for Exceptional Students

Prevalence	Level	Educational Delivery System	Professional Responsibility
About 88% of all school-age students receive their education through level I or II. (Gifted and talented students are usually served here.)	I	Students placed in regular classroom with no additional or specialized assistance.	
	II	Students placed in regular classroom with consultative specialist providing assistance to classroom teacher. Child remains in regular class for entire school day.	Regular education has primary responsibility for child's educational program. Special education is a support service designed to facilitate the child's success in the educational mainstream.
About 6% of all school-age students receive their education through level III.	III	Students placed in regular classroom for majority of school day. Students attend special education resource room for specialized instruction in deficit areas.	
About 6% of all school-age students receive their education through levels IV–VII.	IV	Students placed in special education class for majority of day. Students attend regular class in subject areas consonant with their capabilities.	
	V	Students placed in full-time special education class in regular education school.	Special education has primary responsibility for child's educational program.
	VI	Students are placed in a separate special school for handicapped children, i.e., a residential facility.	
	VII	Students are educated through a homebound or hospital instructional program.	

Placement in a more restricted educational environment

As depicted in Figure 2-1, placement at Level I means that the student remains in the regular classroom with no additional support services. At this level, the adaptations necessary for a given student should be handled by the classroom teacher. Consequently, success of the student depends on a teacher who has skills in developing and adapting curricula to meet individual needs. A student placed at Level II also remains in the regular classroom, but consultive services are available to both the teacher and student. These services may be provided by a variety of professionals, including special educators, speech and language specialists, behavior specialists, physical education specialists, occupational therapists, physical therapists, school psychologists, and social workers. Services may range from assisting a teacher in the use of tests or modification of curriculum, to direct instruction with students in the classroom setting. Approximately 88 percent of all students in public school settings will be educated at Levels I and II.

The student who is placed at Level III continues in the regular classroom for a majority of the school day but also attends a "resource room" for specialized instruction. A resource-room program is under the direction of a qualified special educator, and the amount of time a student spends in the resource room varies according to student need. The approximate range of time is from as little as thirty minutes to as much as three hours a day. Instruction in a resource room is intended to reinforce or supplement the student's work in the regular classroom. The student receives necessary assistance to ensure his or her placement with the regular education peer group. About 6 percent of all school-age children are served in a resource-room setting. It is the most widely used public school setting for students labeled as handicapped. For Levels I, II, and III, the primary responsibility for the students' education lies with the regular class teacher. Consultive services, including special education, are intended to support the student's regular class placement.

Students placed at Level IV are in a special education classroom for the majority of the school day. At this level, there are provisions for a student to be integrated with regular education peers, whenever possible and consistent with the student's learning capabilities. For more moderately to severely disordered populations, this integration is usually for nonacademic subject areas. Level V placement involves full-time participation in a special education class. The student is not integrated with regular education students for formalized instructional activities. However, some level of integration may take place at recess periods, lunch assemblies, field trips, or during tutoring experiences. Placement at Level VI involves completely removing a student from the regular education facility to a classroom in a separate facility specifically for disabled students. These facilities include special day schools where students return home each day, as well as institutions or clinics where the educational program is one aspect of a twenty-four-hour-a-day comprehensive treatment program. Some students, because of the severity of their disorder, are unable to attend any school program and must receive service through a homebound or hospital program (Level VII). Placement at Level VII generally indicates a need for an itinerant teacher who visits the incapacitated student on a regular basis to provide tutorial assistance. Some students with chronic conditions may be placed at this level indefinitely, whereas others are served while recuperating from a short-term illness.

An Individualized Education Program. Every child possesses some characteristics that are unique and unlike those of other children. Education has rhetorically recognized these differences for many years but has not completely come to terms with the structure of an **individualized education program.** P.L. 94-142 provided a vehicle for the development of an education program based on multidisciplinary assessment and designed to meet the individual needs of the exceptional student. This vehicle is referred to in the law as an Individualized Education Program (**IEP**). Abeson and Weintraub (1977) explained this program as follows:

> The term individualized education program conveys important concepts that need to be specified. *Individualized* means that the program must be addressed to the educational needs of a single child rather than a class or group of children. *Education* means that the program is limited to those elements of the child's education that are specifically special education and related services as defined by the Act. *Program* means that the individualized education program is a statement of what will actually be provided to the child, as distinct from a plan that provides guidelines from which a program must subsequently be developed. (P. 5)

The IEP process provides an opportunity for parents and professionals to join together in the planning, implementing, and evaluating of a child's educational experience. The result should be more continuity in the delivery of educational services for exceptional children on a daily as well as an annual basis. It should also allow for the development of a more effective communication system between school personnel and the home. An IEP form is shown in Figure 2-2. This form is merely an example. However, all IEP forms contain some common elements: (1) a child's present level of performance, (2) statement of annual goals, (3) short-term instructional objectives, (4) related services, (5) percent of time in regular education, (6) beginning and ending dates for special education services, and (7) annual evaluation.

The special education placement process—referral for services through summative evaluation—is depicted in Figure 2-3. This flowchart summarizes the important procedures necessary to provide an appropriate education to an exceptional child.

It would be easy for us to be complacent in the 1980s. In our lifetime we have seen substantial political and judicial responses to discrimination against people with handicaps, and the result has been widespread litigation and legislation—literally a social revolution concerned with the rights of these people in our society. In the decade to come, we could sit back, dwell on our recent accomplishments, and tell ourselves that legal mandates will protect the person with differences from all forms of discrimination. In reality, the difficult challenge lies ahead. Our social and educational responsibility appears promising on paper, and the idea of paper compliance is already operational. However, beyond legal enforcement of the rights of persons with disabilities is a need to understand these individuals as human beings, not just social or educational labels. The successful integration of this population into our social system is dependent not only on legal mandates but also on the development of a positive public attitude. This does not necessarily come from legislation. To have a pervasive impact, positive attitude results from knowledge about individuals as students in our public schools, as family members, and as consumers within society. The remainder of this volume will examine these issues in several contexts.

Figure 2-2/ Sample Individualized Education Program Form

School District
Responsible _____

Date(s) of Meeting: _____

_____

Student _____
        (name or number)

_____

Current
Placement _____

Eligibility
Certified _____
        (date)

Period of Individualized Education Program

_____ to _____

Persons Present	Relationship to Child

Curriculum Areas* Requiring Special Education and Related Services	Present Level(s) of Performance	Annual Goals	Short-Term Objectives	Time Required	Objectives Attained (Dates)
Area 1					
Area 2					

*If more space is required, use an additonal sheet.

Figure 2-2 (continued)

A. List any special instructional material or media necessary to implement this individualized education program.

Special Education and Related Services Recommended	Personnel Responsible (Name and Title)	Date Services Begin	Duration
Curriculum Area 1			
Curriculum Area 2			

Student name or number _____

B. Describe the extent to which the child will participate in regular education programs.

_____

_____

_____

_____

C. Recommended type of placement: _____

   (include physical education)   _____

D. Provide justification for the type of educational placement.

_____

_____

_____

_____

E. Actual placement: _____

   _____

F. List the criteria, evaluating procedures, and schedule for determining whether the short term objectives are met.

Figure 2-2 (continued)

61
A History of
Human Services

Short-Term Objectives	Objective Criteria	Education Procedures	Schedule

Date of parental acceptance/rejection _____

Signature _____

Signature _____

Reprinted by permission fron *A Primer on Individualized Education Programs for Handicapped Children,* ed. Scottie Torres (Reston, Va.: Foundation for Exceptional Children, 1977), pp. 54–56. Available from the Foundation for Exceptional Children, 1920 Association Drive, Reston, Va. 22091. Publication Cost: $4.95

Figure 2-3/ /The Special Education Placement Process

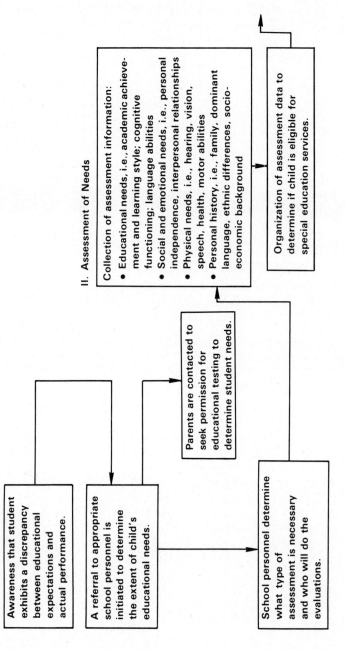

I. Referral for Services

Awareness that student exhibits a discrepancy between educational expectations and actual performance.

A referral to appropriate school personnel is initiated to determine the extent of child's educational needs.

Parents are contacted to seek permission for educational testing to determine student needs.

School personnel determine what type of assessment is necessary and who will do the evaluations.

II. Assessment of Needs

Collection of assessment information:

- Educational needs, i.e., academic achievement and learning style; cognitive functioning; language abilities
- Social and emotional needs, i.e., personal independence, interpersonal relationships
- Physical needs, i.e., hearing, vision, speech, health, motor abilities
- Personal history, i.e., family, dominant language, ethnic differences, socioeconomic background

Organization of assessment data to determine if child is eligible for special education services.

Figure 2-3 (continued)

III. Planning the Educational Program

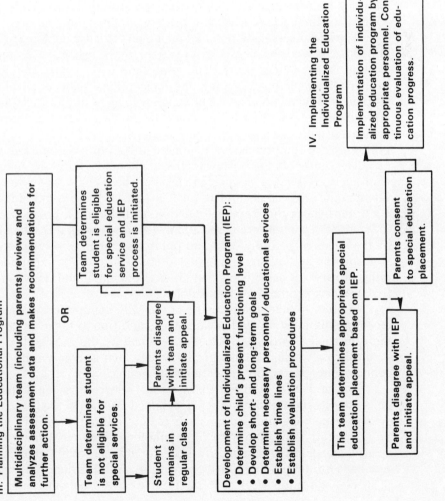

Multidisciplinary team (including parents) reviews and analyzes assessment data and makes recommendations for further action.

OR

Team determines student is not eligible for special services.

Team determines student is eligible for special education service and IEP process is initiated.

Parents disagree with team and initiate appeal.

Student remains in regular class.

Development of Individualized Education Program (IEP):
• Determine child's present functioning level
• Develop short- and long-term goals
• Determine necessary personnel/educational services
• Establish time lines
• Establish evaluation procedures

The team determines appropriate special education placement based on IEP.

Parents disagree with IEP and initiate appeal.

Parents consent to special education placement.

IV. Implementing the Individualized Education Program

Implementation of individualized education program by appropriate personnel. Continuous evaluation of education progress.

V. Evaluation of Student Program

Team determines student is no longer in need of special education services. Special Education Services are terminated.

Summative evaluation of student's IEP conducted at least annually to determine effectiveness of IEP and develop future goals for the child.

Special education services are continued and IEP is revised.

63

₰ SUMMARY

Many professionals have contributed to the understanding and treatment of people with exceptional characteristics. Pinel, Locke, Itard, Seguin, Howe, Montessori, Braille, Gallaudet, Binet, and Watson are but a few who over the past three centuries have influenced the educational and treatment approaches of the 1980s.

Human-service models in this century have run the gamut from segregation in hospitals and institutions to integration in community and educational settings. The social-segregation model of the early twentieth century was an outgrowth of the theory that mental and moral deviance was hereditary and incurable. Legislation during this period was aimed at controlling deviancce through the passage of marriage and sterilization laws. Segregated institutions became a primary service model in order to protect society from the deviant individual and the deviant individual from society. However, many of these facilities became human warehouses for custodial care with overcrowded conditions, unqualified staff, and inadequate financial support.

The social-segregation model remained virtually unchanged until parents and other advocates began to organize in the early 1950s and challenge institutional practices. In the late 1960s and early 1970s, the courts became involved in an attempt to reaffirm the constitutional rights of people warehoused without treatment programs. Today we recognize that not all institutions are alike. Some of these facilities continue to be isolated asylums concerned primarily with management and regimentation; others have adopted a philosophy of comprehensive treatment and a more normalized environment.

The concept of the least restrictive environment (LRE) expanded the narrow continuum of service advocated through the social-segregation model. The intent of the LRE is that services must be consistent with individual need. This doctrine dictates that services must be available on a broad continuum that includes both community-based and institutional programs. The LRE is defined by the needs of an individual and not by the range of services available. The concept stresses that environmental alternatives must be expanded to meet the range of needs. It establishes that all environmental alternatives are fluid, and that none are terminal or irreversible.

In order to meet the mandate of the LRE, comprehensive services within a community must be made available, in addition to those already existing in more restricted settings. Such services include the availability of necessary medical care, social/psychological services such as community mental health centers, and appropriate educational programs.

The models for delivery of educational services to exceptional populations are a microcosm of those in the larger social system. In the early 1900s, public schools were not geared to the needs of nontraditional learners, and there was no mandatory education for this population. There were some public school special education programs available for learners with more mild learning problems but few, if any, for those with severe disorders. The real expansion of special education services in public schools did not emerge until the 1950s, when there was a significant increase in classes for the mildly retarded and

the emotionally disturbed. During the 1960s and 1970s the role of the federal government expanded greatly, culminating in the passage of Public Law 94-142 (the Education for All Handicapped Children Act). Public Law 94-142 emphasized 1) parent involvement in the child's education program, 2) education in the least restrictive environment, and 3) an individualized education program for every handicapped child.

⸎ REVIEW QUESTIONS

1. What major contributions to the development of individualized treatment programs did Itard make?
2. Discuss some of the contributions of modern psychology to our understanding of human differences.
3. Why is the early twentieth century described as a "period of marked contrasts" in the treatment of exceptional persons?
4. Define "institution," and describe the principal types of total institutions.
5. What have the courts found regarding a person's right to treatment in an institution?
6. Discuss the concept of the least restrictive environment.
7. Discuss the types of community services that must be available to ensure compliance with the least restrictive environment concept.
8. Why are the 1970s described as a decade of revolution in the field of special education?
9. Why are the Pennsylvania and *Mills* cases significant to the education of persons with disabilities?
10. Describe the major provisions of the Education for All Handicapped Children Act (P.L. 94-142).

SECTION II

Learning and Behavior Disorders

Our study of areas of exceptionality begins with people who exhibit learning and behavior disorders. In this section we will introduce some of the current trends and established practices regarding definitions and intervention strategies for this population. Chapter 3 gives an overview of definitions and classification concepts. Several parameters that can be used to classify persons with learning and behavior disorders are discussed. One such parameter is symptom severity: the degree to which an individual deviates from an established norm (e.g., mild, moderate, severe, and profound). Each of the remaining three chapters in this section are organized according to a symptom-severity classification approach. In Chapter 4 we examine mild disorders, where deficits are manifested primarily in the educational environment and the student may need only limited instructional support to remain in the regular education setting. Moderate learning and behavior disorders are discussed in Chapter 5. At this level of functioning, the deficits are evident in both social and educational environments. Substantially altered patterns of intervention must be available to assist persons with moderate learning and behavior disorders in adjusting to environmental demands. Chapter 6 examines

definitions and intervention strategies for people who exhibit severe and profound/multiple disorders. These individuals may be impaired in nearly every facet of life. They have deficits that transcend the characteristics of a single handicapping condition; most have significant multiple impairments.

In addition to using a symptom-severity approach as a framework for our discussion of people with learning and behavior disorders, we will discuss this population using two different perspectives on definition. You will be introduced to a generic (cross-categorical, noncategorical) approach to defining learning and behavior disorders, as well as to the more familiar categorical descriptors of mental retardation, behavior disorders, and learning disabilities. The following are topical guidelines for Section II:

1. Learning and behaviors may be categorized on several parameters (bases).
2. Traditional classification approaches for learning and behavior disorders use the descriptors *mental retardation*, *behavior disorders*, and *learning disabilities*.
3. Generic classification approaches represent a different approach to catego-

rization of learning and behavior disorders.

4. Generic approaches use a symptom-severity parameter for classification and include the descriptors *mild, moderate, severe,* and *profound.*

5. The problems encountered by individuals with mild learning and behavior disorders occur primarily within the school setting.

6. People with mild learning and behavior disorders share a variety of academic and behavioral characteristics that transcend traditional approaches to classification.

7. Students with mild learning and behavior disorders are unable to meet the academic or behavior standards of the regular education classroom without specialized support services.

8. The collaboration of the regular classroom teacher and support-service personnel is essential in creating an adaptive fit between the demands of the school environment and the needs of students with mild learning and behavior disorders.

9. Individuals with moderate learning and behavior disorders exhibit deficits in several environmental settings (e.g., home, community, and school). They will need more medical, social, and educational services than mildly disordered individuals.

10. The traditional categories of mental retardation, behavior disorders, and learning disabilities are more distinct at the moderate level of functioning.

11. Intervention strategies for people with moderate learning and behavior disorders may include medical therapy and psychological services as well as specialized educational programs.

12. The needs of students with moderate learning and behavior disorders dictate a more restricted educational environment under the direction of a special education teacher.

13. People with severe and profound/multiple disorders may have deficits in nearly every area of functioning.

14. The serious nature of severe and profound/multiple disorders necessitates the services of several professions in order to meet the diverse needs of the individual.

15. For the vast majority of people with severe and profound/multiple disorders, deficits are evident at birth and require immediate intervention.

16. Severe and profound/multiple disorders may be caused by several factors, e.g., chromosomal abnormalities, drugs, infections, trauma, and accidents.

17. The field of medicine has two important functions in relation to severe and profound/multiple disorders: prevention and direct health care.

18. A lifelong social support system, including alternative living arrangements and vocational and recreational services, may be needed to meet the needs of those with severe and profound/multiple disorders.

19. Educational services for individuals with severe and profound/multiple disorders focus on advancing the person to the next highest level of functioning regardless of how developmentally delayed the person may be.

CHAPTER THREE

Definitions and Classification Systems for Learning and Behavior Disorders

Parameters of Definition/Classification Concepts
Traditional Classification Approaches
   Mental Retardation
   Behavior Disorders
   Learning Disabilities
Generic Classification Approaches:

A Different Perspective
   Mild Learning and Behavior Disorders
   Moderate Learning and Behavior Disorders
   Severe and Profound/Multiple Disorders

Definitions and classifications of learning and behavior disorders have taken many forms over the years. In some cases the different systems came about because of the variety of disciplines involved in research and treatment. In others, the different systems have emerged because of varying purposes for classification.

Regardless of the definition or classification system employed, it is possible to examine learning and behavior disorders in terms of the parameters, or bases, on which behaviors are categorized. This provides us with a tool for viewing different definition and classification processes.

Labels and classification systems are products of the human mind. Humans are born with a variety of physiological and psychological differences and are then categorized and labeled according to systems developed by other humans. The labels, and the influences they have, vary greatly depending on the perspective of the labeler, which may be shaped by cultural and/or professional background. Lay people, as well as medical, psychological, educational, and other professional personnel, may have very different views of human status and conditions.

This chapter will examine a variety of definition and classification concepts associated with learning and behavior disorders. The discussion will address the traditional categorical classifications (mental retardation, behavior disorders, learning disabilities) as well as generic approaches that may intersect and include more than one of the traditional categories. Generic and traditional approaches represent conceptual alternatives with respect to classification of

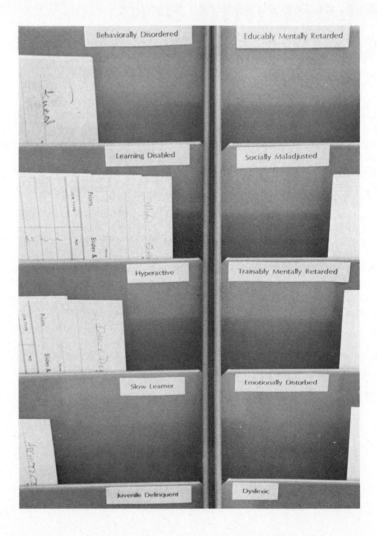

Classification categories for the handicapped are numerous.

exceptionalities. While both approaches are useful in certain instances, neither, singly, serves the broad range of learning and behavior differences adequately. The distinctions and blends of approaches discussed in this chapter are based on research and current theory related to human exceptionality.

71

Definitions and
Classification
Systems for
Learning and
Behavior
Disorders

Parameters of Definition/ Classification Concepts

There are many different ways to define and categorize human conditions. Individuals may be viewed differently if we are focusing on their social behavior as opposed to their work productivity, their weight versus physical fitness, and so on. Such variations in perspective may be due to a number of factors, such as one's disciplinary background, cultural heritage, and personal convictions. However, a common thread does run through these differences. In each case there are certain parameters on which a behavior is categorized. *Parameter* in this context refers to the basis or bases used for classification.

Chinn, Drew, and Logan (1979) identified several **classification parameters** in the area of mental retardation. They noted that "although used with varying frequency, six general parameters for classification seem evident: (1) symptom severity, (2) symptom etiology, (3) syndrome description, (4) adaptive behavior, (5) educability expectations, and (6) behavioral manifestations" (p. 15). These parameters, with minor conceptual modifications, can also be useful in classifying the broader population of learning- and behavior-disordered individuals.

Symptom severity refers to the degree of deviation from the norm (e.g., an individual with an IQ of 30 is classified differently from someone with an IQ of 55; likewise, a classification difference would exist between an individual with an IQ of 100 and one with an IQ of 150). Symptom severity has commonly been used in the field of mental retardation, although it has not been the only parameter employed in this area.

Etiology refers to the cause of exceptionality. In most cases the cause remains speculation, for a single cause cannot be actually determined. The etiology parameter has been a source of considerable theorizing in nearly every area of exceptionality and thus has appeared in a variety of traditional categorical systems.

The **description of syndromes** has probably been used most frequently by the medical profession to designate different types of exceptionality. Often the term applied to a condition is derived from the name of a pioneer scientist studying it (e.g., Down's syndrome). In other cases, a syndrome label may involve technical terminology related to the nature of the condition (e.g., neurofibromatosis). Syndrome descriptions have also been used in several traditional categories.

Adaptive behavior is basically viewed in terms of one's ability to be socially appropriate and personally responsible. A person's adaptive-behavior level significantly influences his or her ability to associate with others successfully. This ability (or relative lack of it) is often a problem for those with significant behavioral differences and has consequently been associated with a variety of categorical systems.

Educability expectation is a parameter that is essentially self-explanatory. It represents a prediction of expected educational achievement and may involve a grade-level expectation or predicted achievement in behavioral terms (e.g., learning primarily limited to self-help skills). This parameter has been employed in every area of exceptionality.

Behavioral manifestation is a classification parameter that has been used in a number of ways and in the context of many different disorders. This parameter focuses on the areas and levels of observable performance. It has been employed in a flexible fashion in most classification systems and has overlapped into some of the other parameter areas.

A given classification or definition is like a single photograph of a person. What is recorded represents only a given behavior at a particular time and in a particular set of circumstances. Parameters of classification provide us with a powerful tool for analyzing various category systems. Some parameters are present in one or two systems, whereas others are used to a degree in several. The parameters are important because they allow us to view exceptionality across differing classification perspectives. This is useful for those studying human exceptionality, if order is to emerge from the overall examination of differences. We will make repeated reference to parameters of classification as we continue. Figure 3-1 presents a graphic representation of classification parameters and the manner in which they may converge to result in a diagnosis of exceptionality. This type of conceptualization could easily be modified so that parameters are added or deleted, depending on the condition.

TRADITIONAL CLASSIFICATION APPROACHES

One cannot begin an examination of traditional categories without noting what is considered traditional and how it came to be viewed in that manner. Today's society changes so rapidly that it tests one's cognitive capacity to stay abreast. For example, professionals entering the field of learning and behavior disorders only ten years ago may find that many of the latest and most revolutionary ideas of that decade are now passé. Consequently, what we present as traditional categories may be questioned by some and are likely to be viewed differently in the future.

Traditional categories of learning and behavior disorders include mental retardation, behavior disorders (also termed emotional and social disturbances), and learning disabilities. Each of these categories has classification systems aimed at further discrimination of individual conditions. Often a given category will include several parameters for classification.

Mental Retardation

Mental retardation has been studied for many decades and by a variety of disciplines. Consequently the field involves several classification systems and

Figure 3-1/ Parameters of Classification   **73**

Definitions and
Classification
Systems for
Learning and
Behavior
Disorders

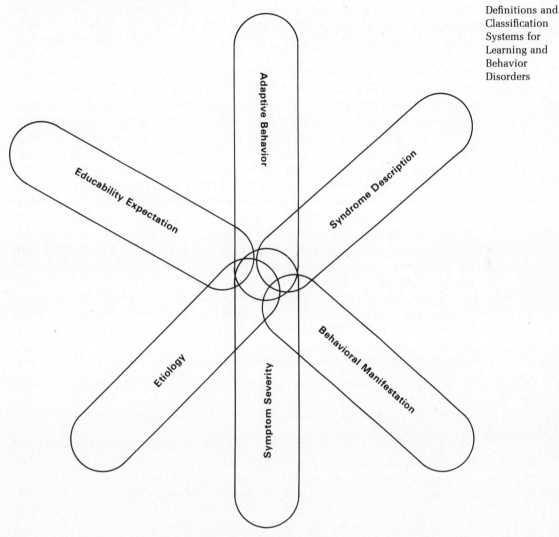

multiple parameters. Perhaps the most widely accepted scientific definition is that of the American Association on Mental Deficiency (AAMD), an interdisciplinary organization. The AAMD definition states that "mental retardation refers to significantly subaverage general intellectual functioning existing concurrently with deficits in adaptive behavior, and manifested during the developmental period" (Grossman, 1977, p. 11). The essential features of this definition have also been adopted by the American Psychiatric Association (*Diagnostic and Statistical Manual of Mental Disorders, 1980*).

Symptom severity has served as a classification parameter in mental retardation for many years in terms of measured intelligence. Four levels of intelligence are used to group mentally retarded individuals according to AAMD standards: (1) mild—IQ 52 to 67; (2) moderate—IQ 36 to 51; (3) Severe—IQ 20 to 35; and (4) profound—IQ 19 or below. The American Psychiatric Association employs the same four severity classifications and uses basically the same IQ groupings. The above IQ levels are based on measurements from the Stanford-Binet intelligence scales and are somewhat flexible since it is generally accepted that there may be about five IQ points of error (either inflated or depressed) in any score obtained. The AAMD symptom-severity categories classify individuals as retarded (in terms of IQ) when their scores fall two standard deviations or more below the mean. Each severity category represents an additional standard deviation (SD) of deficit below the mean (i.e., moderate level, -3 SD; severe level, -4 SD).

Adaptive behavior is also used as a classification parameter in mental retardation and is defined in terms of personal independence and social responsibility. This parameter overlaps with symptom severity because it is typically viewed in terms of the degree of *maladaptation*. Adaptive behavior is also examined from a developmental perspective, since what is acceptable behavior for a youngster differs from behavior appropriate for an adult. The AAMD definition of "developmental period" is the "time between birth and the 18th birthday" (Grossman, 1977, p. 11).

Etiology has been prominent in the field of mental retardation, as it has in other areas of exceptionality. The etiological classification scheme in mental retardation has also been referred to as a medical classification because it emerged primarily from the field of medicine. The AAMD (Grossman, 1977) etiological classification includes ten categories:

1. Mental retardation following infection and intoxication (e.g., syphilis, rubella)
2. Mental retardation following trauma or physical agent (e.g., injury during birth, prenatal injury)
3. Mental retardation with nutritional or metabolic disorders (e.g., PKU, thyroid dysfunction)
4. Mental retardation associated with gross postnatal brain disease (e.g., tuberous sclerosis, Sturge-Weber-Dimitri disease)
5. Mental retardation associated with diseases and conditions resulting from unknown prenatal influences (e.g., hydrocephalus)
6. Mental retardation associated with chromosomal abnormality (e.g., Down's syndrome)
7. Mental retardation associated with gestational disorders (e.g., prematurity)
8. Mental retardation following psychiatric disorders (e.g., autism)
9. Mental retardation associated with environmental influences (e.g., sensory deprivation, social disadvantage)
10. Mental retardation associated with other conditions (e.g., unknown causes or such known causes as blindness or deafness

Syndrome descriptions have been widely used in mental retardation. This parameter overlaps with the above etiology categories and has also been used primarily by the medical profession. Typically, syndrome labels represent specific conditions that are classified within broader etiological categories. For example, under "gross postnatal brain disease" we find such syndromes as neurofibromatosis (also known as von Reklinghausen's disease), tuberous sclerosis, and Huntington's chorea. Under "mental retardation associated with unknown prenatal influence" we find anencephaly, hydrocephalus, and Apert's syndrome. Many different syndromes or clinical types have been identified in mental retardation. Readers interested in detailed study of mental retardation syndromes can consult volumes focusing on these disorders (e.g., Carter, 1975, 1978; Gellis & Feingold, 1968; Lemeshow, 1982).

Educability expectation has been employed in mental retardation for many years. This parameter also overlaps with symptom severity. The specific categories used vary greatly, depending on the locale and source consulted. Frequently this type of system specifies a label, an approximate IQ range, and a statement of predicted achievement. For example, Chinn et al. (1979) identified four levels as follows:

1. Dull-normal, *IQ 75 to about 90: "Capable of competing in school in most areas except in the strictly academic areas where performance is below average . . . "
2. Educable, IQ 50 to about 75: "Second to fifth-grade achievement in school academic areas . . . "
3. Trainable, IQ 20 to 49: "Learning primarily in the area of self-help skills, very limited achievement in areas considered academic . . . "
4. Custodial, IQ below 20: "Usually unable to achieve even sufficient skills to care for basic needs . . . "(P. 23)

Other achievement statements focused on social adjustment and expected occupational performance. Consequently, this classification parameter also intersects with adaptive behavior.

Behavioral manifestation has also been used as a parameter of classification in mental retardation. This perspective has emerged largely from behavioral psychology and differs considerably from other categorical approaches. For the most part, it employs descriptions (often quite detailed and precise) of an individual's performance or skills. Less concern is evident in terms of grouping individuals than treating deficit skills. In addition, little attention (often none) is given to causation.

Behavior Disorders

Like mental retardation, behavior disorders have been recognized and studied for a long time. As a result, the terminology, definition, and classification systems have varied considerably. Behavioral deviance necessarily has a referent in normal behavior, or that which is viewed as accepted by society. Thus any "definition of behavioral *disorder* or emotional *disturbance* is unavoidably a

---

* This classification level is used very infrequently because it is inconsistent with the IQ levels established by the AAMD definition.

Behavior disor-
ders can affect
learning and
cause great
frustration.

subjective matter'' (Kauffman, 1981, p. 14; emphasis in the original). The federal regulations for Public Law 94-142 employs the following definitional language for the label *seriously emotionally disturbed:*

> The term [seriously emotionally disturbed] means a condition exhibiting one or more of the following characteristics over a long period of time and to a marked degree, which adversely affects education performance:
>
> (a) An inability to learn which cannot be explained by intellectual, sensory, or health factors
>
> (b) An inability to build or maintain satisfactory interpersonal relationships with peers and teachers
>
> (c) Inappropriate types of behavior or feelings under normal circumstances
>
> (d) A general pervasive mood of unhappiness or depression
>
> or
>
> (e) A tendency to develop physical symptoms or fears associated with personal or school problems
>
> The term also includes children who are schizophrenic or autistic. The term does not include children who are socially maladjusted, unless it is determined that they are seriously emotionally disturbed. (U. S. Department of Health, Education, and Welfare, 1977, p. 42478).

The area of behavior disorders is broad and includes many different conditions, so it is not surprising that several classification approaches have been employed. Some systems use varying classification parameters. For example, the American Psychiatric Association's *Diagnostic and Statistical Manual of Mental Disorders* (DSM III, 1980) lists the following disorders typically first evident during infancy, childhood, or adolescence:

77

Definitions and
Classification
Systems for
Learning and
Behavior
Disorders

1. Mental retardation (DSM III is an extremely broad classification scheme that includes the full range of disorders)
2. Attention deficit disorders (including such symptoms as hyperactivity, which we will see again in the learning disabilities area)
3. Anxiety disorders of childhood or adolescence.
4. Other disorders of infancy, childhood, or adolescence (e.g., schizoid disorders)
5. Eating disorders (e.g., anorexia nervosa, bulimia)
6. Stereotyped movement disorders (e.g., tics, Tourette's disease)
7. Other disorders with physical manifestations (e.g., stuttering, which we will discuss later as a speech disorder; enuresis, encopresis, and sleep disorders)

These categories are the first point of reference for clinicians using DSM III. If an appropriate diagnosis cannot be determined from this list, further classification is possible from DSM III using the list of organic mental disorders, which includes:

1. Dementias arising in the senium and presenium (e.g., senility with delusions or depression)
2. Substance-use disorders (e.g., disorders induced by drugs or alcohol)
3. Schizophrenic disorders
4. Paranoid disorders
5. Affective disorders (e.g., manic, depressive)
6. Anxiety disorders (e.g., phobias, obsessions)
7. Somatoform disorders (e.g., hypochondria)
8. Dissociative disorders (e.g., psychogenic amnesia)
9. Psychosexual disorders (e.g., sexual fetish, masochism, atypical sex drive)
10. Adjustment disorders (e.g., depression, anxiety)

We have not listed all the DSM III classifications, but we have provided a sample. Even with the limited listing, it is clear that several parameters of classification are employed. DSM III uses symptom severity in determining whether or not a given disorder is acute or chronic, and severity also comes into play in terms of transient or malingering conditions. Etiology is also a parameter that plays a prominent role in certain disorders (but not in all). Adaptive behavior underlies the basic scheme of DSM III, and syndrome description is evident in several types of conditions. Behavioral manifestation is nearly a constant in terms of the clinical descriptions made during diagnosis. Thus the DSM III system for viewing behavior disorders employs five of the six classification parameters we have discussed.

Earlier we noted that behavior disorders are defined and classified in the context of normal behavior. A precise notion of normality is not simple to derive, however. Clarizio and McCoy (1976) indicated that although there is no acceptable definition of normality, there are specific components every definition must include. They suggested that the following must be taken into account:

1. The child's developmental level (since what is required as normal at one age might well be viewed as abnormal at another)
2. The child's culture or subculture
3. Allowances for individuality
4. A multidimensional approach (i.e., the definition must take into account how the child functions in various representative areas of development)

Rhodes (1967) combined the concepts of *normal* and *behavioral deviance* by discussing these terms in the context of behavioral prohibitions and sanctions in the culture. When certain individuals create a disturbance in an environment by departing from the cultural standards for acceptable behavior, they draw unfavorable attention to themselves and force the imposition of sanctions. Individuals who violate cultural specifications to the degree that exhibited behavior consistently evokes disturbed reactions in those around them are deemed as being the most disturbed. So once again we encounter the use of symptom severity in viewing those with disorders. Behavior disorders involve several classification parameters that often overlap (e.g., adaptive-behavior disturbance in combination with severity or etiology). For a more complete examination of the traditional classification systems employed in behavior disorders, the reader can examine volumes focusing on this area (e.g., Kauffman, 1981).

Learning Disabilities

Perhaps more than any other traditional disorder category, the category of learning disabilities has generated controversy, confusion, and polarization among contemporary professionals. Prior to the 1960s, educational services for the learning disabled were virtually nonexistent. Many children presently identified as exhibiting specific learning disabilities were earlier labeled as *remedial learners, emotionally handicapped,* or even *mentally retarded*—if they received any additional instructional support at all. Today learning disabilities has become the largest single program for exceptional children in many schools. Although a relatively new discipline, its growth rate is unparalleled by any other area in special education.

Definitions associated with learning disabilities have not reflected any consistency within or among professional disciplines. This may be the result of the field's unique evolution, its highly accelerated growth pattern, and its strong interdisciplinary nature. During the field's embryonic period, several disciplines (including medicine, psychology, speech/language, and education) contributed to the confusion associated with inconsistent use of terminology. Education coined the phrase *specific learning disabilities*; psychology used

79

Definitions and
Classification
Systems for
Learning and
Behavior
Disorders

Learning disabili-
ties are evi-
denced in a
variety of ways.

such terms as *perceptual disorders* and **hyperkinetic** behavior; speech and
language employed the terms **aphasia** and **dyslexia;** and medicine used such
labels as *brain damage, minimal brain dysfunction, brain injury,* and
impairment. Brain injury (Strauss & Lehtinen, 1947), **minimal brain dysfunction**
(Clements, 1966), and *learning disabilities* (Kirk, 1963) are among the more
commonly used terms.

A brain-injured child was described as having an organic impairment that
would result in perceptual problems, thinking disorders, and emotional
instability. A child with minimal brain dysfunction manifested similar problems,
but in addition there was evidence of language, memory, motor, and impulse-
control difficulties. Clements' definition of minimal brain dysfunction
characterized the individual as average or above average in intelligence in order
to distinguish the disorder from mental retardation.

Kirk (1963) introduced the phrase *specific learning disabilities,* and his
original conceptual model remains essentially intact today. Learning disabilities
is presently defined by delays or deviations in the basic academic subjects (e.g.,
arithmetic, reading, spelling, writing), as well as speech and language problems.
In addition, these disability areas cannot be attributed to mental retardation,
sensory deficits, or emotional disturbance. It has become common practice in
educational circles to describe learning-disabled individuals on the basis of
what they are not. For example, although they have a number of problems,
they are not retarded, not emotionally disturbed, or not deaf. *Learning disabilities*
is a general educational term—an umbrella label—that includes a variety of
different disorder conditions (Gelfand, Jenson & Drew, 1982).

The most widely used definition of learning disabilities was developed by the National Advisory Committee on Handicapped Children (1968) of the U.S. Office of Education. This committee developed a definition similar in concept to Kirk's (1963) definition. The Office of Education definition was initially incorporated in Public Law 91-320, the Learning Disabilities Act of 1969, and was employed heavily in Public Law 94-142, the Education of All Handicapped Children Act of 1975. The definition in P.L. 94-142 reads as follows:

> "Specific learning disability" means a disorder in one or more of the basic psychological processes involved in understanding or in using language, spoken or written, which may manifest itself in an imperfect ability to listen, think, speak, read, write, spell, or to do mathematical calculations. The term includes such conditions as perceptual handicaps, brain injury, minimal brain dysfunction, dyslexia, and developmental aphasia. The term does not include children who have learning problems which are primarily the result of visual, hearing, or motor handicaps, of mental retardation, of emotional disturbance, or of environmental, cultural, or economic disadvantage. (U.S. Congress Education of All Handicapped Children Act, 1975, Section 5(b) (4))

Individuals who might be labeled *learning disabled* represent a complex constellation of behaviors and conditions. However, the learning disabled have not formally been classified into differing categories within the broad label. (In fact, learning disabilities has generally been viewed as a "mild" disorder, despite the fact that clinicians have observed differing severity of symptoms for years.) Although they have not been placed in any classification scheme, learning-disabled individuals have often been described in the context of the classification parameters we mentioned earlier. For example, the DSM III (1980) uses the label **attention deficit disorder** with qualifying subcategories of (1) with hyperactivity, (2) without hyperactivity, and (3) residual type (used for adults). Here we see the use of syndrome description, behavioral manifestation, and the implication of adaptive behavior as classification parameters operating in an overlapping fashion.

Learning disabled children have also been viewed from other perspectives. For example, the original federal rules and regulations published to clarify P.L. 94-142 provided additional information. According to these rules and regulations, any criterion for classifying a child as learning disabled must be based on the already existing *severe* discrepancy between capacity and achievement. The determination for placement was based on:

1. Whether a child does not achieve commensurate with his or her age and ability when provided with appropriate educational experiences
2. Whether the child has a *severe* discrepancy between achievement and intellectual ability in one or more of seven areas relating to communication skills and mathematical abilities (U.S. Department of Health, Education, and Welfare, 1977, p. 65082)

The person's learning disability must be determined on an individual basis, and the severe discrepancy between achievement and intellectual ability must be in one or more of the following areas:

1. Oral expression
2. Listening comprehension
3. Written expression
4. Basic reading skill
5. Reading comprehension
6. Mathematical calculation
7. Mathematical reasoning
(U.S. Department of Health, Education, and Welfare, 1977, p. 65083)

81
Definitions and
Classification
Systems for
Learning and
Behavior
Disorders

The intended meaning of the term *severe discrepancy* is presently open for debate among professionals. There is a notion here that coincides with symptom severity as a classification parameter, although it has not been specified in terms of measurement. What is an acceptable percentage of discrepancy between a child's achievement and expected grade level—25 percent? 35 percent? 50 percent? Bateman (1965) first introduced the discrepancy concept as an added dimension to the definition of learning disabilities. She defined learning-disabled children as "those who manifest an educationally significant discrepancy between their estimated intellectual potential and actual level of performance related to basic [learning processes]" (p. 220). Here we see an educability-expectation parameter involved in the area of learning disabilities, but once again there is considerable vagueness regarding what is required for labeling in terms of measurement.

GENERIC CLASSIFICATION APPROACHES: A DIFFERENT PERSPECTIVE

The debate regarding categorical versus generic definitions and classifications of learning and behavior disorders has gained considerable attention in the field of education over the past ten years. Some professionals have maintained that the traditional categories of mental retardation, behavior disorders, and learning disabilities do not clearly define or adequately differentiate the needs of exceptional students in the classroom (Hallahan & Kauffman, 1976; Hardman, 1981; Laycock, 1980; Lilly, 1979). Others have suggested that generic labels are nonfunctional and that the individual categories are more relevant to educational programming (Becker, 1978; Keogh, Becker, Kukic & Kukic, 1972).

Many psychologists and educators have attempted to break away from the traditional categories. In large part, efforts to date have been unsuccessful. Some approaches have represented little more than semantic exercises that utilized different terms but remained within the same conceptual framework. Others have been dramatically different but have accomplished little except to fuel a polarized debate between advocates of generic and traditional classification schemes. Little serious effort has been given to a careful examination of the bases or parameters employed for classification and to the circumstances under which they may be functional or nonfunctional. Wholesale elimination of traditional categories may be as ineffective as clinging to them tenaciously without exploring their usefulness.

Determining which parameters of classification are useful has been a continuing problem for those working with people who have learning and behavior disorders. For example, the role of etiology has long been a problem for both practitioners and researchers. Historically, etiology has figured prominently in many facets of working with exceptional populations and has often been involved in definitions, as we have seen. The use of causation has frequently been characterized as reflecting the medical model, even though actual medical diagnosis may not have been involved. As we proceed, you will find that the etiology parameter is considered functional and useful in certain circumstances and not in others. This is also true for other classification parameters.

Mild Learning and Behavior Disorders

A generic conceptualization of disorder conditions based on symptom severity has not been widely utilized. The notion of mild versus more severe levels of problems has not even been consistent across traditional categorical areas. For example, the classification system used by the American Association on Mental Deficiency has used symptom severity for many years. On the other hand, learning disability definitions have largely overlooked this type of thinking. In fact, learning disabilities, as a category, has often been viewed as being totally a mild disorder, even in the face of clinical impressions to the contrary. It is our view that learning disabilities can be conceptualized using a symptom-severity parameter that ranges from the mild to more severe.

The notion of **mild learning and behavior disorders** presupposes a generic symptom-severity framework regardless of specific behavioral attributes that may be shared or discrepant between conditions. Our effort to conceptualize the mildly disordered in a noncategorical fashion requires that the traditional categories be viewed within an umbrella model of symptom severity. It also requires that accommodation be made for the shared and discrepant behavioral attributes of the population being addressed. Given these requirements, we find that the following definition provides a generic framework for mild learning and behavior disorders:

Individuals with mild learning and behavior disorders exhibit academic and/or social-interpersonal performance deficits that generally become evident in a school-related setting and make it necessary for the individuals to receive additional support services beyond those typically offered in a regular education setting. However, it is assumed that a mildly disordered student would remain in the regular education setting for the majority of the school day. The severity of the performance deficit for this population ranges from one to two standard deviations below the interindividual and/or intraindividual mean on the measure(s) being recorded.

This definition is necessarily broad, which is to be expected given the breadth of the population under consideration. Certain points in this definition need examination to clarify meaning.

The phrase *"academic and/or social-interpersonal performance deficits"* is necessary because these are generally shared attributes of this population. It is not uncommon to find mildly disordered students who are lower in academic ability also exhibiting aberrant behavioral patterns, or vice versa. The definition allows for the independent occurrence of an academic deficit or behavior deviance, but it also suggests that if both disorders occur in a parallel fashion they are included within the single definition. It is assumed that an individual functioning at this level will generally be able to adapt to the social environment outside the classroom setting. Problems that do emerge are not likely to be serious enough to cause a referral on behavior alone.

Causality is not an issue in this definition, because etiology for the mildly disordered population is largely unknown and is often undeterminable. This is not intended to suggest that research should be curtailed or that etiology should not be dealt with when it can be determined. In most cases, however, causation is not important with regard to treatment for mild learning and behavior disorders.

In large part, the performance deficits of mildy disordered individuals become evident in school-related settings. Problems may well occur in other settings, but the most pronounced difficulties clearly relate to the structured environment of formal schooling. This has led to certain characterizations such as the "six-hour retardate" (President's Committee on Mental Retardation, 1969; MacMillan, Meyers & Morrison, 1980). (This notion arose from observations that certain youngsters appeared "retarded" only during the six hours a day they were in school.)

The phrase *"on the measure(s) being recorded"* is necessarily broad because of the variety of specific attributes required for assessment. Depending on the problem that resulted in a referral, the attributes may include one or more of several measures, such as adaptive behavior, academic achievement, and intellectual functioning. This provides the flexibility to use standardized instruments, more informal assessments, and behavioral checklists (e.g., observation), as well as systems of assessment that combine several types of measures.

Use of the phrase *"one to two standard deviations below the interindividual and/or intraindividual mean"* involves the one to two standard deviation deficit and specifies severity level. This differs somewhat from certain trends in more traditional categories. For example, in 1973 the AAMD moved to two standard deviations as the upper limit on IQ and essentially declassified as mentally retarded all individuals functioning between that level and the mean. The current approach would permit such individuals to receive services as mildly learning disordered, but it avoids using the label retardation, which has such a negative connotation. Even though the AAMD has ceased viewing mental retardation as unchangeable, the general connotation of the label is one of permanence and social stigma. The current definition is meant to emphasize present functional performance, which may well be rectified by specific intervention techniques. It is the authors' contention that the term "mild learning and behavior disorders" is broad enough that it is unlikely to become a diagnostic term, but it can be used in a number of ways that are functional for intervention purposes, as will be examined more fully in Chapter 4. Educators and psychologists would therefore be required to focus more directly on a functional description of the problem behavior than has historically been the case where labels became diagnostic entities. Table 3-1 compares the current scheme with that of the AAMD and the educational classifications in terms of mental retardation. It should be noted that this table addresses symptom severity only with regard to IQ.

An individual's performance may be described statistically by comparing him or her with others of the same chronological age (interindividual differences), or the person may be described in terms of an analysis of his or her own individual strengths and weaknesses (intraindividual differences) (Kirk, 1972). Thus the phrase "**interindividual** and/or **intraindividual** mean" is used. An interindividual assessment is often referred to as a **norm-referenced** or standardized measure of student abilities, because the individual is compared to a larger group where a mean or average score has been determined. The

Table 3-1/ Comparison of Classification Schemes for Mental Retardation

Deviation from Mean on Standardized Test of Intelligence	Generic Classification Scheme	American Association on Mental Deficiency Classification Scheme (Grossman, 1977)	Educational Classification Scheme
1 SD*	Mild learning and behavior disorders	(No classification term for individuals functioning at this level)	Dull-normal (This term currently not commonly used)
2 SD	Moderate learning and behavior disorders (includes moderate mental retardation)	Mild mental retardation	Educable mentally retarded
3 SD		Moderate mental retardation	Trainable mentally retarded
4 SD	Severe and profound/multiple disorders (includes severe and profound mental retardation)	Severe mental retardation	Custodial
5 SD		Profound mental retardation	Custodial

* SD = Standard deviation

larger group may be a nationwide sample of students (e.g., standardized intelligence tests), or it may be as small as a measure of the student in comparison to classmates. This form of assessment establishes students' academic or behavioral status within the environment in which they are expected to succeed. Intraindividual assessment does not compare the student to other students, but analyzes the student's individual strengths and weaknesses. As with interindividual assessment, a mean or average is determined. However, the average is calculated on several of the *individual's* performance areas (e.g., giving letter sounds, recognizing common word parts, sound blending). Then each area of performance is compared to the individual's average, in addition to an assessment of differences between performance areas. Depending on the nature of the problem, one may need to view the child on an interindividual basis, an intraindividual basis, or both. Strong cases have been made that effective programming, particularly where a return to the regular classroom is anticipated, cannot be accomplished without attention to both (Drew, Freston & Logan, 1972). The use of average performance (means) does not restrict this definition to standardized tests where means have been established through norms. Such an anchor point can easily be determined using behavior checklists and precision teaching techniques on both inter- and intraindividual bases. The basic premise of this part of the definition is that a functional analysis of the individual's performance areas will be made.

85

Definitions and
Classification
Systems for
Learning and
Behavior
Disorders

Moderate Learning and Behavior Disorders

The discussion of mild learning and behavior disorders emphasized shared attributes among traditional categories. As we move to cases with greater deviance, traditional categories become more distinct, and individuals with various deviant characteristics are more different from one another than before. Certain behavioral characteristics remain shared by individuals with different primary diagnoses. However, the identification of a primary disabling condition (and distinguishing it from secondary or accompanying characteristics) is much more easily accomplished at this level than at the level of mild disorders.

Despite greater reliance on traditional diagnostic categories, the notion of a generic deviance model still holds. In this context the definition of **moderate learning and behavior disorders** is as follows:

An individual with moderate learning or behavior disorders exhibits intellectual, academic, and/or social-interpersonal performance deficits that range between two and three standard deviations below the interindividual and/or intraindividual mean on the measure(s) being recorded. These performance deficits are not limited to any given setting but are typically evident in the broad spectrum of environmental settings. Etiology(ies) of the problem(s) may be identified in some cases but typically cannot be pinpointed precisely. Individuals with functional disorders at this level will require substantially altered patterns of service and treatment and may need modified environmental accommodations.

As with the definition of mild learning and behavior disorders, this definition is broad, which is to be expected in view of the breadth of the population under consideration. However, this definition represents a generic framework consistent with that provided for mild learning and behavior differences. As we proceed, and in later chapters, it will become evident that more discrete labels and specific conditions must be examined. However, certain points enmeshed in this generic definition must be further examined.

The phrase *"intellectual, academic, and/or social-interpersonal performance deficits"* is clearly more expansive in the parameters of performance than the mildly disordered definition presented earlier. The term *intellectual* has been added because with this population when an intellectual deficit is involved it is far more evident and pronounced than at the level of mild disorders. (Some individuals with mild learning and behavior disorders may exhibit learning or achievement difficulties that would suggest intellectual deficits, but still do not evidence sufficient deviations in measured intelligence for it to be considered a primary problem.) The other terms appear for a second time but are viewed differently from the mildly disordered primarily in terms of deficit severity (greater) and the environment in which a performance problem may be apparent (deficits being evident in a broader range of environments than in the case of mildly disordered individuals). As before, difficulties may be exhibited in more than one area of functioning, but with this population, multiple performance deficits are more frequently evident and more serious than with the mildly disordered. However, the primary disabling condition is also more easily identified than with mildly disordered individuals. In addition, because of the severity of problems, causes are more likely to be identifiable.

This definition relies heavily on the symptom-severity framework. One important part of the current definition involves the severity terminology, which indicated problems that *"range between two and three standard deviations below the interindividual and/or intraindividual mean on the measure(s) being recorded."* The subsequent qualifying statements in this definition also indicate that other matters, such as etiology, may be identifiable as we encounter more severe disabilities.

Severe and Profound/Multiple Disorders

Having described mild and moderate learning and behavior disorders, we will now turn to **severe and profound/multiple disorders.** The focus here has changed with the use of the term *multiple* and the elimination of the phrase *learning and behavior.* The reason for this is that when we move to this level of functioning, we almost always encounter individuals with multiple disorders and problems that extend far beyond the learning and behavior arenas. Our generic definition is as follows:

Individuals with severe and profound/multiple disorders exhibit physical, sensory, intellectual, and/or social-interpersonal performance deficits that range beyond three standard deviations below the interindividual and/or intraindividual mean on the measure(s) being recorded. These deficits are not limited

87

Definitions and
Classification
Systems for
Learning and
Behavior
Disorders

to any given setting but are evident in all environmental settings and often involve deficits in several areas of performance. Etiologies are more likely to be identifiable at this level of functioning, but exact cause(s) may be unknown in a large number of cases. Individuals with functional disorders at this level will require significantly altered environments with regard to care, treatment, and accommodation.

This definition provides a generic framework consistent with those definitions presented earlier. However, important definitional changes at this level of functioning involve several points.

We have already noted that the term *multiple* has been added to this definition and that individuals functioning at this level almost always evidence disorders in more than one performance area. The possibility of multiple disorders was not excluded from the mild and moderate populations, although it was not specifically stated in the definitions. Inclusion of the term *multiple* in the definition here is meant to emphasize how often multiple problems occur at the severe-disorder level and the seriousness of the multiple problems. Further emphasis is added by the phrase *"often involve deficits in several areas of performance."*

The parameters of performance have once again been altered to include physical and sensory areas not evident in the previous definitions. These areas have also been incorporated in the severe definitional statement for emphasis. Certainly individuals functioning at higher levels may evidence some problems in these areas, as we shall see in later chapters. At the severe disorder level, however, physical and/or sensory deficits tend to be more frequent and pronounced than in the case of less extreme disorders.

The symptom severity has increased in this definition, moving to *"beyond three standard deviations below the interindividual and/or intraindividual mean on the measure(s) being recorded."* This statement is self-explanatory, although a point regarding the handicap impact needs reemphasizing here. The reader will note that we have focused on the term *disorder* and carefully avoided *handicap* in most of this discussion. The reason for this is simply that the two notions are not synonymous. For example, one may have a severe visual deficit (i.e., be blind) but not be severely *handicapped* because of accommodations in the environment, special mobility training, and special instructional technology. Thus in certain circumstances a disorder may be severe while the handicap impact is much less pronounced.

The symptom-severity classification parameter is centrally present in all three of the preceding definitions. However, the other parameters vary greatly with regard to their importance in each definition. Etiology is not prominent at the mild or moderate level, but it becomes somewhat more evident at the severe-profound level. Educability is not addressed in the traditional expectation manner, although reference to educational or treatment settings and alterations are cited. Adaptive behavior and behavioral manifestations are present both in terms of measures and in terms of potential settings in which deviance is likely to be evident. Syndrome description plays no major role in these generic definitions. However, clinicians will be inclined to use certain traditional syndrome descriptions when characterizing some individual dis-

orders under the moderate and severe-profound categories. Classification parameters can be appropriately employed in a variable fashion—when they are
functional.

⚘ SUMMARY

Learning and behavior disorders have been classified in a variety of ways over
the years. In part, variation in classification has been a result of the use of
different bases, or ways of viewing a disorder. One discipline may view a
mentally retarded person in terms of what caused the retardation, another
discipline might categorize that individual in terms of expected educational
achievement. Bases for categorization can be referred to as parameters of
classification. A paramenter of classification might be a factor such as symptom
severity, where a person would be categorized according to the degree to which
he or she deviated from the norm on a given measure.

Parameters of classification have varied in a number of ways. For example,
the field of mental retardation has employed symptom severity, syndrome
description, adaptive behavior, educational expectation, etiology, and behavioral
manifestation as classification parameters. Other areas of study have used some
of these. Parameters of classification should be employed when they are
functional, and in a logical manner, which has not always been the case.

We have discussed some of the traditional definitions and classification
systems associated with mental retardation, learning disabilities, and behavior
disorders. In addition, learning and behavior disorders were examined from a
more generic point of view that emphasizes mild, moderate, and severe-profound
descriptions. The parameters of classification can be compared both in terms
of the traditional categories and in terms of the generic approach.

⚘ REVIEW QUESTIONS

1. What are parameters of classification, and how are they used with exceptional
   individuals?
2. Which parameters of classification have been used in mental retardation?
   Discuss the manner in which they have been employed.
3. Several factors have contributed to definitional problems in the area of
   learning disabilities. What are they and how have they caused difficulties?
4. What are the arguments on each side of the categorical versus generic
   conceptualizations of human exceptionality?
5. Discuss the environments in which difficulties are typically evident for
   individuals with (a) mild learning and behavior disorders, (b) moderate
   learning or behavior disorders, and (c) severe and profound/multiple
   disorders.
6. Discuss the intervention setting appropriate for individuals with (a) mild
   learning and behavior disorders, (b) moderate learning or behavior disorders,
   and (c) severe and profound/multiple disorders.

CHAPTER FOUR

Mild Learning and Behavior Disorders

Every educator has been confronted with students who exhibit mild learning and behavior problems. The significance of such problems depends on a number of factors. From the school's standpoint, the problem is often viewed in terms of its effect on the student's academic achievement and teacher performance, as well as any negative effect on the student's classmates, which may be evident (or anticipated). The reality is that if the student functions outside the limits of academic or behavioral norms, it is likely that his or her performance will be considered a problem that requires intervention beyond that offered to age-mates.

Marilyn is nine years old and in her second month of fourth grade at Willowbrook Elementary School. Her classroom teacher describes her as a slow learner and a poorly motivated student. Marilyn is unable to cope with the behavioral or academic requirements of the classroom without assistance beyond that required for the other students. She has a reading vocabulary that is beginning third-grade level and consistently struggles with reading-comprehension activities. In math she is still attempting to master basic subtraction facts but is proficient in number identification and single-digit addition. Marilyn has communicated to her parents and teacher the frustrations she is encountering at school and that she sees school as a negative aspect of her life. Her teacher confirms this negative attitude and states that Marilyn has difficulty completing assigned tasks and is often reprimanded for daydreaming or visiting with classmates at inappropriate times. Marilyn was recently referred to the school psychologist for an interindividual analysis of her educational skills. These standardized tests described Marilyn as functioning more than one standard deviation below the mean on an individual test of intelligence (IQ 83); achievement-test scores ranged from the end of second-grade level in reading to third grade, first month, in math; and language expression and reception were below the average of students in her classroom.

Marilyn is a student with learning and behavior problems. She has remained in the regular classroom environment with no additional educational services

Marilyn

since she was six years old. While Marilyn's academic and behavioral performance in the classroom deviates enough to require some additional instruction programming beyond her classmates, it is anticipated that once these services are available she can remain in the regular classroom. Marilyn exhibits a *mild* learning and behavior disorder. The problems of children with mild learning and behavior disorders become most evident in school; there is a negligible effect on behavior outside the instructional setting. Consequently, as these individuals move into adulthood the learning and behavior disordered classification is usually no longer applicable if adequate special services have been provided during the school years.

The framework for this chapter is the generic definition of mild learning and behavior disorders presented in Chapter 3 (see page 82). This definition emphasizes the breadth of this population and allows for considerable flexibility in identifying and providing educational support services. This generic definition stresses that the primary reason for identifying this population is to enhance their opportunities for success in the regular education classroom. In order to deal with the variety of characteristics exhibited by these students, the definiton purposely does not limit the areas for assessment. Depending on the problem that has resulted in a referral, assessment may include several measures, such as adaptive behavior, academic achievement, and cognitive functioning. This provides the professional with the flexibility of using whatever assessment tools are necessary to determine the extent of the academic or behavioral deficits and to make recommendations for educational intervention. The definition is meant to emphasize *present* functional deficits that may well be rectified through educational intervention. Educators and psychologists will have to focus more directly on functional descriptions of the problem behavior than has been the case where categorical labels became diagnostic entities.

TRADITIONAL CLASSIFICATION SYSTEMS

Before we discuss the generic classification of mild learning and behavior disorders, it is necessary to place the population in a more traditional perspective within the field of education. We will briefly examine the descriptive labels that are often employed in the field: mental retardation, behavior disorders, and specific learning disabilities.

The label *mental retardation*, as defined by the American Association on Mental Deficiency (AAMD), is not applicable in the context of this chapter. The current AAMD definition describes a mentally retarded person as functioning two or more standard deviations below the mean on a standardized test of intelligence, with deficits in adaptive behavior (Grossman, 1977). We are focusing on children and youth who score between one and two standard deviations below the mean. However, the current AAMD definition is a revision of an earlier one (Heber, 1961), which included this higher functioning population. The revised AAMD definition removed the label of retardation from all individuals with IQs between 70 and 85 (Wechsler Intelligence Scales). Burton Blatt, in an interview with Jordan (1973), commented on this change:

> This committee has cured more mental retardation than all clinicians and scientists since the beginning of time! They reduced the incidence, or the theoretical incidence, or the psychometric incidence, from 16 percent to 3 percent. Just by changing the definition! Well, you can't do this with leprosy, you can't do this with syphilis, and you can't do this with pregnancy. You can't do it with any objective disease. But you can do it with mental retardation. (Pp. 223-24)

The 1961 AAMD definition classified as *borderline* individuals who were functioning between one and two standard deviations below the mean. Educators often labeled these children *dull-normal* or *slow learners*. Slow learner was commonly used to describe a child who although capable of learning some fundamental academic skills was unable to learn at the same rate as classmates.

Students with mild behavior disorders are often sanctioned within the regular education classroom because they do not *consistently* meet established behavioral norms. Their behavior will violate standards in one set of circumstances and be accepted in another. This acceptance or rejection will depend on the range of tolerance within the environment. The student has problems relating consistently to peers and authority figures (e.g., parents and teachers) and is unable to function appropriately in school-related activities (i.e., academically oriented tasks). Eventually this individual will exhibit an overall pervasive mood of discontent and begin to withdraw from anything in school that might bring more failure. School is viewed as being unrelated to individual needs and personally unrewarding. Pate (1963) suggested that the student's observable behavior is so inappropriate that the regular class placement without some level of additional support service is disrupting to the peer group, places undue pressure on the classroom teacher, and contributes further to the disturbance of the student. However, the tolerance level for this disruptive behavior will vary from teacher to teacher. It is not uncommon to find a child described as *disturbed* when placed with one classroom teacher and perfectly within the limits of acceptable behavior when interacting with another. Therefore, as classification systems are applied to children with mild behavior disorders, it is necessary to focus directly on the observable behaviors of the child in the given situation rather than on generalized nonfunctional terminology.

Several authors have suggested that students with mild behavior disorders be grouped on the basis of the most appropriate educational environment (Hardman, 1981; Kauffman, 1977; Kelly, Bullock & Dykes, 1977). Kauffman indicated that students with mild behavior disorders can be taught in the regular classroom as long as adequate support services are available to the classroom teacher. He proposed a definition of behavior disorders based on placement in the appropriate educational environment. Kelly et al. stated that students with mild behavior disorders "can be helped adequately by the regular classroom teacher and/or other school resource personnel through periodic counseling and/or short term individual attention and instruction" (p. 10). Whether the student will remain in the regular classroom will depend on the severity of the observed deviant behavior.

The student's behavior disorder must be accurately assessed in relation to the requirements of the classroom situation. Mild behavior problems may be classified as behavior excesses (acting out, aggression), behavior deficits (withdrawal), problems related to consistent attendance (high rates of absenteeism), and difficulties in interpersonal relationships (socialization skills, communication patterns). The severity of the exhibited behaviors may be examined from several perspectives. First, utilizing a statistical approach, it is necessary to determine whether any discrepancy exists between the student's chronological age and actual behavioral characteristics. This is important in determining the student's status in relationship to a norm. The statistical approach will provide information concerning how much the individual deviates from the established standard and whether the deviation is significant (Is there a basis for concern?). In addition to determining whether the behaviors are age-appropriate, professionals must analyze the frequency of the problem behavior(s). How often do these behaviors occur, and under what circumstances? Are these inappropriate behaviors related to specific activities or individuals? Do these problems continue even after someone intervenes? The professional should assess the influence of these behaviors on classmates, teachers, and the family unit. The individual's interaction and eventual adaptation or maladjustment to the parameters of environmental influence will ultimately determine the degree of the problem, enabling the distinction between mild, moderate, severe, and profound disorders.

Although specific learning disabilities has been characterized by many professionals as a mild disorder (Idol-Maestas, Lloyd & Lilly, 1981; Ysseldyke & Algozzine, 1979), there has been little attempt within the field to validate this premise empirically. Harber (1981) reported that the research in the area of learning disabilities has failed to identify subgroups within this heterogeneous population. In a review of the research in learning disabilities, Kavale and Nye (1981) suggested that "the LD [learning disabilities] research literature is marked by ambiguities and confusion about the criteria to be used for LD classification" (p. 383).

Recently there have been attempts to attend to the issue of symptom severity (Deloach, Earl, Brown, Poplin & Warner, 1981; Larsen, 1978; Torgesen & Dice, 1980; Weller, 1980). Weller proposed a model that consolidates criteria from several sources as a means of identifying severity level. The model utilizes functional/adaptive ability criteria to differentiate students with mild disorders from those with more severe problems. It focuses on a variety of skill areas, including the effect of the problem on other abilities (e.g., social skills) and alteration of future life needs. Deloach et al. (1981) suggested that the differences between mildly and severely disabled populations may be determined through the perceptions of teachers in the field. Using a questionnaire format, they analyzed the clinical judgment of 223 teachers of learning disabilities regarding the characteristics of elementary and secondary students. Results of this study indicated that these teachers viewed students with learning disabilities as a heterogeneous group functioning at differing levels of severity. These functioning levels ranged from students viewed as non–learning disabled to those with severe disabilities. The teachers indicated that approximately 30 percent of the students in their classrooms had learning problems that they did not attribute to learning disabilities. This finding is consistent with the contention that many students currently being served as learning disabled are being inappropriately referred. Larsen (1978) commented on this phenonomen:

> It is . . . likely that the large number of students who are referred for mild to moderate underachievement are simply unmotivated, poorly taught, come from home environments where scholastic success is not highly valued, or are dull-normal in intelligence. For all intents and purposes, these students should not automatically be considered as learning-disabled, since there is little evidence that placement in special education will improve their academic functioning. (P. 7)

Deloach et al. (1981) also found that approximately 20 percent of the students in classes for the learning disabled were functioning at a level that warranted classification as *severe learning disabled*. They reported that the most significant factors in distinguishing mild problems from severe problems were the need of students with severe learning disabilities for individualized instruction, the necessity for alternative curricular approaches for severely disabled students, and a significant discrepancy between a student's score on intelligence scales and grade-level functioning as measured by achievement tests.

CHILDREN AND YOUTH WITH MILD LEARNING AND BEHAVIOR DISORDERS

Characteristics

Individuals with mild learning and behavior disorders share a variety of characteristics that cut across the more traditional categorical definitions. Although special education has consistently endeavored to preserve categorical purity, many professionals indicate that when the child's actual performance in the classroom is examined, there is considerable overlap, particularly at the mild severity level (Balow, 1978; Hardman, 1981; Laycock, 1980; Lilly, 1979; Wang, 1981).

The discrepant characteristics of individuals with mild learning and behavior disorders have been overemphasized by many professionals, leaving the general public with a narrow and often inaccurate perception of this population. However, emerging educational methodologies have begun to stress the imporance of the learning environment and material content as well as individual learner and teacher styles. These methodologies serve to broaden the considerations given in educational programming to include attention to the curricular approach rather than a focus on the generalized characteristics of a special education category. Hardman (1981) indicated that educational

programming has been based more on definitional expectations according to categorical label than on the individual student's actual task performance. This educational phenomenon is illustrated in Table 4-1, which compares expectations according to traditonal categorical definitions with the actual performance of students within the given categorical area.

Laycock (1980) suggested that there is real danger in adhering strictly to the categorical approach at the mild severity level, because it implies that each category is homogeneous. An examination of individuals with mild learning and behavior disorders reveals that this is not the case.

> The term mental retardation, for example, is currently applied to hundreds of different syndromes. Likewise, learning disabilities and emotional disturbance are generic or global terms covering a variety of specific problems. It is misleading to use the labels as though all children within the category exhibit common attributes. . . . In addition to variance within categories, there is also overlap between categories. Human beings cannot be pigeon-holed as neatly as definitions would lead us to believe. (Laycock, 1980, p. 53)

Students with mild learning and behavior disorders are often defined and categorized primarily by exclusion—by what they are not. The specific-learning-disabled child is usually defined as one who is not intellectually inferior, even though children of varying intellectual functioning levels may exhibit specific learning disabilities (Hammill, 1976).

Mental age is another factor that must be considered when comparing lower-IQ individuals to individuals defined as learning disabled or behavior disordered. The concept of mental age was initially developed by Binet and Simon (1905) to express a student's intellectual development compared to students of comparable chronological age. For example, if a child has a chronological age of nine and a mental age of approximately nine, the child's intellectual development is described as normal. The lower the mental age in comparison to the chronological age, the greater the intellectual deficit. A growing body of literature suggests that when mental age is equivalent, differences between school-age mentally retarded and nonretarded subjects are minimal or nonexistent (Cantor & Ryan, 1962; Drew, 1969; Girardeau & Ellis, 1962; Ring & Palermo, 1969).

When comparing mild behavior-disordered and learning-disabled populations, intelligence is considered a common attribute. By definition, these two categories involve individuals who are normal in intelligence. The differences between mild behavior disorders and specific learning disabilities have been explained more in terms of social-adjustment differences and learner characteristics. However, learning-disabled individuals may also exhibit secondary behavioral disorders. In addition, mild behavior-disordered populations may also have learning difficulties comparable to those exhibited by individuals defined as learning disabled (Hallahan & Kauffman, 1976; Wallace & McLoughlin, 1975).

The performance of students in the classroom also suggests that behavior problems are not specific to any one intellectual functioning level. It is well known, both clinically and from the scientific literature, that individuals with

Table 4-1/ Capacity, Achievement, and Social Performance by Special Education Categorical Area

	Definitial Expectation	*Actual Performance*
Capacity (Intelligence)	*Mild Behavior Disorders:* Average or above-average performance on intelligence tests.	*Mild Behavior Disorders:* Behavior problems occur in all ranges of intelligence, e.g., mentally retarded range.
	Learning Disabilities: Average or above-average performance on intelligence tests.	*Learning Disabilities:* Specific learning disabilities occur in all ranges of intelligence, e.g., mentally retarded range.
	Mild Mental Retardation: Low potential—significantly subaverage (two standard deviations below the mean) performance on intelligence tests.	*Mild Mental Retardation:* Mental retardation is limited by definition to IQ below 70. Definition excludes children whose IQ is *between* one and two standard deviations below the mean (IQ 70-85).
Achievement (Academic Learning)	*Mild Behavior Disorders:* Definitions do not generally include low achievement as a criterion.	*Mild Behavior Disorders:* Low achievement can be secondary effect of behavior disorders (behavior problems interfere with academic learning).
	Learning Disabilities: Low achievement is an integral part of the learning disabilities (LD) definitional concept. Child will perform at least one or two years below grade level.	*Learning Disabilities:* Child performs at least one or two years below grade level.
	Mental Retardation: Low intelligence indicates poor academic potential.	*Mental Retardation:* Mildly retarded child performs at least one or two years below grade level.
Social skills (Adaptive behavior)	*Behavior Disorders:* Child will be deficient in socialization and classroom adaptation skills.	*Behavioral Disorders:* Child is deficient in socialization and classroom adaptation skills.
	Learning Disabilities: Social deficits are not included in LD definitional structure.	*Learning Disabilities:* Poor performance in social and adaptive behavior may be secondary effect of learning problems.

Table 4-1 (Continued)

	Definital Expectation	Actual Performance
	Mental Retardation: Adaptive behavior skills are an integral part of mental retardation definition.	*Mental Retardation:* IQ continues to be *major* factor for categorization. Social deficits are not necessarily correlated with poor performance on intelligence tests.

Source: Reprinted, by permission of the publisher, from M. L. Hardman, "Learner Characteristics of Students with Mild Learning and Behavior Differences," in M. L. Hardman, M. W. Egan, and E. D. Landau, *The Exceptional Student in the Regular Classroom* (Dubuque, Iowa: William C. Brown Co., 1981), p. 60.

intellectual deficits also exhibit a considerable amount of behavior that is socially and interpersonally maladaptive (Drew, 1971; Eyman & Call, 1977; Richardson, 1978; Johnson & Morasky, 1977). Problems in social adjustment must therefore be viewed as a characteristic that is shared to a considerable degree.

One factor that has long been viewed as characteristic of the learning-disabled population is variability between areas of functioning. General descriptions of learning disabilities have often emphasized great intraindividual differences between skill areas (Johnson & Morasky, 1977). Frequently this variability in aptitude patterns has been used as a distinguishing characteristic between learning-disabled and mentally retarded populations. Typically, individuals thought to be retarded are expected to exhibit a rather flat or consistent profile of abilities as contrasted with the pronounced intraindividual variability associated with learning disabilities. As with other attributes, however, intraindividual variability does not seem to be the sole domain of students with learning disabilities. Several authors have strongly indicated that intraindividual variability can occur for students with mental retardation and behavior disorders (Dunn, 1973; Hallahan & Kauffman, 1976; Hammill, Leigh, McNutt & Larsen, 1981; O'Grady, 1974).

Our discussion has emphasized a considerable commonality of behavioral attributes between traditional categories at the mild level. This does not negate the fact that differences do exist between the traditional categories, especially in terms of overall ability, rate of learning, and attention to task. It does, however, stress that the traditional labels are not useful in the development of an educational program for students with mild learning and behavior disorders. Our effort to conceptualize mild disorders in a generic fashion requires that the traditional categories be viewed within an umbrella model of symptom severity. It also requires that accommodation be made for the shared and discrepant behavioral characteristics of students with mild learning and behavior disorders.

Causation

The cause(s) of mild learning and behavior disorders is largely unknown. Because so many factors can interact and contribute to these learning and behavior differences, it may not be possible to determine cause. However, we do know that individuals exhibiting mild learning and behavior disorders are not usually characterized by physical or sensory deficits. These are individuals whose problems are primarily educationally related. They are not easily identified as disordered once they are outside the educational environment. Laycock (1980) indicated, "It is not until the child enters school and cannot meet age or grade expectations that a disability is actually identified" (p. 51).

Numerous etiological factors have been associated with learning and behavior disorders, for example, diverse cultural backgrounds, socioeconomic differences, and poor teaching. Mercer and Lewis (1979) confirmed that students whose cultural backgrounds were different from the dominant core culture, and whose socioeconomic status was on the lower end of the continuum, were more likely to be initially identified and labeled as having a disability by the public education system. These authors also indicated that the same population was not viewed by the community as deviant outside the school setting.

Several authors (Engelmann, 1977; Haring, 1978; Lovitt, 1978) have indicated that poor teaching may be a primary reason for many of the school-related problems exhibited by students with mild learning and behavior disorders.

> Perhaps 90 percent or more of the children who are labeled "learning disabled" exhibit a disability not because of anything wrong with their perception, synapses, or memory, but because they have been seriously mistaught. Learning disabilities are made, not born. (Engelmann, 1977, pp. 46-47)

Haring suggested that we need to examine more closely the way teachers are educated in university preparation programs and the effectiveness with which they are applying what they have been taught. Are teachers utilizing the appropriate procedures, methods, and materials necessary to ensure maximum growth and development in their students?

Several other factors are associated with mild learning and behavior disorders, for example, high absenteeism during the early school years or differing value systems within the home concerning the importance of school. Some factors are more internal to the individual, such as poor motivation or inadequate memory and retention skills. The list goes on and on, but the issues of causality remain unresolved. L'Abate and Curtis (1975) explained:

> Determining the causes of borderline deficits may become a futile, academic exercise and an indication of unresolved authority and power struggles among those who are interested in exceptionalities in children. Ultimately, regardless of the exceptionality's origin and nature, the special educator should work to cultivate the child's assets and to minimize his liabilities. (P. 63)

Prevalence

To understand the magnitude of mild learning and behavior disorders, it is important to describe the frequency of occurrence for these problems in the public schools. Two terms are commonly used in the research to describe frequency of occurrence: **prevalence** and **incidence.** Several authors have suggested that the literature in special education has ignored the distinction between these two terms (Marozas, May & Lehman, 1980; Gelfand, Jensen & Drew, 1982). Although the two terms have been used interchangeably, the difference between them is substantial. For the purposes of this text, we will define *prevalence* as the number of persons in any given population who exhibit a condition or problem at a specific point in time. *Incidence,* on the other hand, refers to the number of new cases of a condition that have been identified within a specific period of time. "Simply stated, incidence means new and prevalence means all" (Marozas et al., 1980, p. 230).

The necessity of establishing prevalence figures is based on a number of administrative factors in the delivery of educational services to students who need intervention beyond that generally offered in the regular educational classroom. One reason the schools need to establish prevalence figures is that they must identify the approximate number of students who will require special education services so that federal and state dollars can be allocated according to the needs of each categorical area (e.g., mental retardation, specific learning disabilities, visually disabled). This is one of the reasons for maintaining the more traditional categorical label. Briefly stated, it says that if you do not label the deviance the money will not reach the right child. Estimates of prevalence assist the schools in planning and funding educational services based on the monies available. Prevalence figures also provide information concerning the extent to which the schools are adequately providing service to their exceptional population. (Is there a discrepancy between estimated prevalence figures and the number of children receiving service?) Consequently, students are labeled categorically, and financial resources are dependent on these designated categorizations. In order to establish limits on the number of students who are to receive financial assistance through the federal government under P.L. 94-142, a ceiling has been established for those who qualify as exceptional under the law. The maximum percentage of students between the ages of three and twenty-one who may be labeled as handicapped is 12 percent.

Despite the administrative rationale for establishing categorical prevalence, there are problems associated with this practice. It is extremely difficult to obtain accurate estimates of prevalence. In addition, there are no practical means available to count heads in order to establish prevalence figures. The Census Bureau does not gather statistics on the areas of exceptionality and the endeavor is far too expensive to be undertaken privately. Even if we had the resources to count every exceptional person, the difficulties in agreeing on one acceptable definition for each categorical area might be insurmountable. For example, estimated prevalence figures for individuals with behavior disorders will vary considerably, depending on the agency or person defining the population, the instrument used in evaluating the problem, and the reasons for attempting to estimate the prevalence (Balow, 1979; Reinert, 1976). This variance in prevalence estimates has been consistently documented for each traditional categorical area discussed in this chapter. Therefore it is essential to remember that prevalence estimates depend on several fluid factors. Prevalence estimates for the traditional categories of mental retardation (one to two standard deviations below the mean on an intelligence test), behavior disorders, and specific learning disabilities may be found in Table 4-2.

Whether a student is labeled *handicapped* (as defined by federal or state regulation) will depend on the level of educational intervention the individual requires. This decision is best handled by a multidisciplinary team responsible for determining the most appropriate educational program and environment for the student within the confines of the given culture and geographical area. Depending on federal and state funding patterns, this team must generally work within the parameters of the 12 percent prevalence figure established for services to the disabled under P.L. 94-142 (see Chapter 2). Returning to our def-

Table 4-2/ Prevalence Estimates for Traditional Categories at the Mild Severity Level

	Percentage of General Population	Description of Severity
Mental Retardation		
Terman (1916)	14%	Borderline and moron
Wechsler (1958)	14%	Borderline and moron
Heber (1961)	13.5%	Borderline and mild
Behavior Disorders		
Wickman (1928)	42%	Mild adjustment problems
Rogers (1942)	33%	Mild emotional disturbance
Bower (1960)	10%	Handicapped by their emotions
Stennett (1966)	5-10%	Adjustment difficulties of sufficient severity to warrant professional intervention
Glidewell & Swallow (1968)	35%	Some adjustment problems
	10%	Adjustment problems that require professional assistance
Specific Learning Disabilities		
Newbrough & Kelly (1962)	14%	Two years below grade level
National Advisory Committee on Handicapped Children (1968)	1-3%	Specific learning disabilities
Myklebust & Boshes (1969)	3-5%	Learning disabilities; significant discrepancy between achievement and expectancy for child
Kass & Myklebust (1969) Commission on Emotional and Learning Disorders in Children (1970)	3-5%	Learning disabilities
	1.6%	Learning disabilities
Meier (1971)	15%	Two years or more below grade expectancy
Dunn (1973)	1-2%	Major specific learning disabilities

inition of mild learning and behavior disorders, this means that not all these mildly involved students would qualify for special education services or be labeled handicapped under this law. Given the 12 percent ceiling, we estimate that about 6 percent of the school-age population would qualify for funds under the description "mild learning and behavior disorders." This means that an additional 7 percent of the school-age population will need additional educational services and be considered mild learning and behavior disordered, but will not qualify for money targeted for students with disabilities. The above figures are based on the estimate that approximately 13 percent of all individuals will fall between one and two standard deviations below the mean. See Figure 1-1 (page 9).

INTERVENTION STRATEGIES

Students with mild learning and behavior disorders have been characterized as being unable to meet the academic or behavior standards of the regular education environment. While the deviation is substantial enough to require some level of instructional programming beyond their classmates, it is anticipated that such students will remain in the regular classroom for the greater part, if not all, of their school lives. These individuals will stand out as discipline problems, slow learners, and poorly motivated students. Beyond the classroom, however, these negative attributes are not evident as much, and the individual appears to have a better adaptive fit. Cassell (1976) described adaptive fitting as a dynamic and continous process of negotiation between an individual and the environment intended to secure mutual coexistence. The individual is expected to modify his or her behavior to meet the standards of the system, and the system, when confronted with the unique attributes of the individual, is also expected to make the appropriate adjustments. Adaptive fitting aptly describes the attempts of students with mild learning and behavior disorders to meet the expectations of various learning environments. These individuals have found that the requirements for survival within public education are beyond their adaptive capabilities and that the system is not able to accommodate their academic or behavioral differences. The result is the development of negative attitudes toward the educational environment. Buchanan and Wolf (1981) explained:

> Imagine what it would be like to be in an environment which gives you nothing but negative feedback most of the time—a place you hate, activities which are difficult and at which you frequently fail, a setting in which the other people involved emphasize your negative qualities—your inability to do something or your lack of knowledge. How would you feel about entering that environment six hours a day, five days a week, approximately 180 days a year for many years to come? (P. 119)

Wang (1981) developed a program for students with mild learning and behavior disorders that is based on the concept of adaptive fitting. The purpose of this

Adaptive Learning Environments Program is to implement a classroom structure that can adapt to individual differences while teaching students with
learning and behavior problems to develop self-management skills. These management skills would help them profit from their school experiences. The specific components of this adaptive fitting program include:

1. A series of highly structured and hierarchically organized curricula for academic skills development
2. An exploratory learning component that includes a variety of learning options
3. A classroom management system designed specifically to teach students
   self-management skills
4. A family involvement program that attempts to reinforce the integration of
   school and home experiences
5. A multi-age and team-teaching organization that increases flexibility.
   (P. 205)

For years the regular classroom teacher has had to assist students with
learning and behavior problems without any effective support systems. This
need no longer be the case. The emergence of collaborative efforts between the
classroom teacher and the myriad of specialists available within public education represents a major breakthrough in the education of individuals with
mild learning and behavior disorders.

Coordinating Educational Services

There are two models of collaboration available within the public schools
designed to enhance the student's educational opportunities within the
mainstream: the consulting-teacher model and the resource-room teacher model.
Each of these views the regular classroom teacher as being primarily responsible
for the education of the student. The services provided through each of the
collaborative models is intended to support the regular education curriculum.

The Consulting Teacher Model. The regular classroom teacher, particularly
at the elementary level, is expected to teach nearly every school-related subject
area. The elementary classroom teacher is responsible for teaching the basic
subjects, including reading, writing, and arithmetic. In addition, the teacher is
supposed to be developing within the student an appreciation for the arts, good
citizenship, and maintenance of a sound physical body. The teacher is trained
as a generalist, acquiring general knowledge of every subject area. When regular
classroom teachers are confronted with instructional problems that are beyond
their experience and previous training, however, the result is often frustration
for the teacher and failure for the student. Given the present structure of public
education (e.g., class size), it is unrealistic and unnecessary for classroom teachers
to become specialists in every school subject.

Many school districts offer support to classroom teachers through
professionals who have extensive background in specific curriculum areas.
These include specialists in reading, arithmetic, language, motor development,

The consulting
teacher assists
the regular class-
room teacher in
serving children
with learning
difficulties.

or the arts. These professionals are usually referred to as *consulting teachers*, although the terms *curriculum specialist, master teacher*, and *itinerant teacher* may also be used. These professionals all have the responsibility of providing support to regular classroom teachers and their students. They may assist the teacher in further defining and refining the nature of a student's problem and may recommend appropriate assessment devices and intervention strategies. Reynolds and Birch (1982) explained that the consulting-teacher model has several important features, including the training and support of regular classroom teachers in their own backyard and the emphasis on modifying the regular education environment to accommodate exceptional students, rather than having these individuals removed to separate settings. In a class of thirty students, approximately one or two of these youngsters would make it necessary for the classroom teacher to utilize the services of a consulting teacher.

The Resource-Room Teacher Model. In the resource-room teacher model, the student receives specialized instruction in a classroom that is separate from the regular education setting but still within the same school building. While still receiving the majority of instruction in their regular education classroom, students with learning and behavior difficulties come to the resource room for short period(s) during the day to supplement their school curricula. The resource room is not intended to be a study hall, where students come to do their homework or spend time catching up on other classwork. This room is under the direction of a qualified special education teacher whose role is to provide individualized instruction in academic or behavioral areas that are negatively affecting the student's chances for success in the educational mainstream. The resource-room teacher in collaboration with an educational team, including the students' regular classroom teacher, identifies high-risk skill areas and then develops and implements instruction intended to increase proficiency to a level where the student is competitive with classmates.

The resource-room model represents a major change in the delivery of educational services to exceptional populations. Prior to its introduction, educational alternatives for exceptional students were limited to (1) placement in a regular education classroom without any additional or instructional assistance, (2) segregation in a special education setting for the school day, or (3) exclusion from public education. Research on the efficacy of special classes, in addition to recently altered views concerning the concept of least restrictive environment (LRE), have presented strong influences for change.

It can be anticipated that approximately one or two students in a classroom of thirty, or about 6 percent of the school-age population, will need the additional instructional services offered through the resource-room program. In many states, because a student is receiving direct special education services, there is a requirement that the individual be labeled as exceptional in order to fund the resource-room program through federal and state special education funds. Therefore, in order to adhere to the concept of the least restrictive environment and the definition of mild learning and behavior disorders, students receiving instruction through the resource-room program, by definition, have learning or behavior problems that require assistance beyond that offered through the consulting-teacher model. Although the problems are still of a mild nature, these students require their instructional assistance in a more restricted setting than the regular classroom.

The resource-room model has some important features that differ from traditional special education role patterns. It allows students to remain with age-mates for the majority of the school day, while removing a great deal of the stigma associated with segregated special education classrooms (Jenkins & Mayhall, 1977). It also provides support to the regular classroom teacher, who although realizing that these students have potential for success in the regular classroom, finds it extremely difficult to provide the appropriate individualized instruction to one or two students (Wiederholt, Hammill & Brown, 1978).

The Role of the Regular Classroom Teacher

Today's classroom teachers are confronted with the challenge of educating all students for the complex demands of our society. They are at the same time faced with an increased responsibility to meet the needs of certain students who require additional instructional support in order to succeed in school. The integration of exceptional students into a regular education classroom may be met with frustration, anger, or refusal on the part of teachers. These reactions are symptomatic of the confusion surrounding the term *mainstreaming*. Mainstreaming, in many educational circles, has been synonymous with dumping, that is, returning the exceptional student to regular education without any support service to the classroom teacher and at the expense of other students in the class. We oppose this practice and suggest that students with learning and behavior disorders be placed in regular classes only when the following conditions have been fulfilled:

1. The exceptional student has been appropriately assessed by a multi-disciplinary team of professionals, and the regular classroom has been determined to be the least restrictive environment
2. The classroom teacher has been adequately trained in how to meet the learning and behavioral needs of the exceptional student
3. Appropriate support personnel and instructional materials are readily available to the teacher

All these factors must be present if the student is to have a reasonable chance for success.

A multidisciplinary approach to assessment and educational planning is not only sound educational practice but also a legal mandate for disabled children receiving services under federal legislation (see Chapter 2). Swanson

The multidisciplinary team plays a critical role in the identification, diagnosis and placement process.

and Willis (1979) defined the team approach as an opportunity for various professionals to

> evaluate, collaborate, and cooperate with each other in planning the provision of appropriate services for an exceptional child. The team may include any combination of the following—or other needed— professionals: educators (special, regular, administrative), medical personnel, psychologists and/or psychometrists, social workers, speech pathologists, physical therapists, vocational rehabilitation specialists. Parents are also very important and necessary contributors to the team. (P. 13)

The educational program of the exceptional student is developed utilizing data accrued by this multidisciplinary team. The role(s) of each professional in relation to program-planning, intervention, and evaluation of program effectiveness should be clearly delineated in the student's educational plan. In the case of students with mild learning and behavior disorders, the regular classroom teacher has the primary responsibility for implementing the appropriate educational program, with consulting or resource-room teachers providing the necessary support.

In order to meet the needs of exceptional students and to function as an informed team member, regular teachers must receive expanded training at the preservice level. The National Advisory Council on Education Professions Development (1976) suggested that regular classroom teachers need to understand how a disorder affects a student's ability to acquire academic skills or cope socially in the educational environment. Teachers need to be able to recognize learning and behavioral problems and to prescribe and implement individualized programs. They must develop an understanding of mainstreaming and be aware of the kind of assistance support personnel available to them can give.

An Instructional Decision-making Model

Learning is a continual process of adaptation for students with mild learning and behavior disorders as they attempt to cope with the demands of school. These students learn to adapt to the limited time constraints placed on them by the educational system. They do not learn as quickly or as efficiently as their classmates and are constantly fighting a battle against failure. They must somehow learn to deal with a curriculum that is rigid and allows little room for learning or behavior differences. They must also be able to adapt to a teaching process that may be oriented to the majority of students within the classroom and is not based on individualized assessment of needs or personalized instruction. In spite of major obstacles, however, these students can learn not only to survive in the regular education environment but also to develop personal/ social and academic skills that will orient them to striving for success rather than to fighting failure. Success can be achieved only if the teacher remains flexible, adapting to meet the needs of these students.

An educational team plays an important role in creating the adaptive fit between the school environment and student needs. This team makes critical decisions concerning educational goals and objectives, the appropriate curricula, and the least restrictive environmental alternatives. The magnitude of these decisions is illustrated in Figure 4-1, a three-dimensional model for instructional decision-making.

Several curricular approaches can be used in teaching children with mild learning and behavior disorders. The major approach may be termed "the learning of basic skils," which stresses that the student must learn a specified set of skills that are sequenced, each a prerequisite to the next step. This process can be exemplified by briefly analyzing the foundation approach to teaching reading. Hansen and Eaton (1978) defined the reading process as "a blend of many separate skills working in harmony. If one skill or cluster of skills is missing, the entire process breaks down and the child is unable to read or comprehend" (p. 41). The teaching of basic reading skills can be divided into three phases: (1) the development of readiness skills (e.g., left to right sequencing, visual and auditory discrimination skills, memory skills), (2) word-recognition or decoding skills (breaking the code and correctly identifying the abstract symbols in sequence), and (3) reading comprehension (giving symbols meaning). The basic-skills approach, whether it be in reading or any other content area, lays the groundwork for further development and higher levels of functioning. However,

Figure 4-1/ An Instructional Decision-making Model

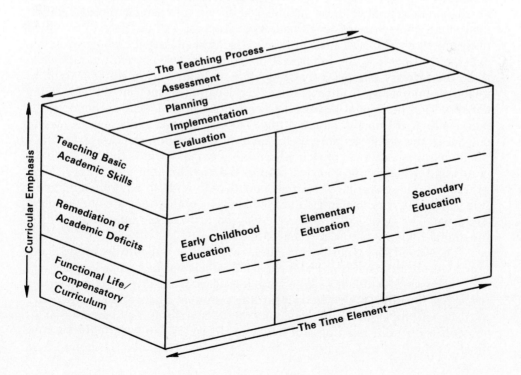

not all children learn basic skills within the time-frame dictated by the schools.

Educators have available to them several alternatives that will assist students who do not learn in the traditional way or within the specified time-frame. One alternative is to remediate the gaps in the student's repertoire of skills. The remediation approach identifies the specific gaps by determining what skills the student does or does not have and then locating appropriate materials and instructional approaches to correct the problem. This approach focuses on "changing the learner in some way so that he or she may more effectively relate to the educational program as it is provided and administered for all students" (Marsh, Gearheart & Gearheart, 1978, p. 85). Gaps in information may be the result either of poor teaching or of lack of ability on the part of the student. Therefore it is doubtful that the learner's behavior can be changed by repeating that which resulted in failure (e.g., asking the student to try harder). Teaching must be more systematic and precise if these deficits are to be remediated.

Another alternative for educators is to teach basic skills using a functional life/compensatory curriculum. This approach teaches only those skills that would facilitate the student's accommodation to society. "The focus is on changing the learning environment or the academic requirements so that the student may learn in spite of a fundamental weakness or deficiency" (Marsh et al., p. 85). Content areas within a functional life/compensatory curriculum might include daily living skills (e.g., self-care, consumer financing, community travel), personal-social skills (e.g., learning socially responsible behaviors), communication skills, or occupational/vocational skills. This approach is based on the premise that if these practical skills are not taught through formal instruction, they will not be learned. Most students will not need to be taught these functional skills because they have already been learned through everyday experience. However, the functional life/compensatory curriculum may need to be the primary emphasis for students who cannot learn through basic or remedial approaches to instruction. This does not mean that students being taught with a functional-life approach are not learning basic academic skills (i.e., reading, arithmetic, handwriting). These academic skills may be taught, but not in the same sequence as in the basic-skills approach. For example, a functional-life reading approach would initially teach words that are high-use words and necessary for survival within the environment (e.g., danger, exit, restrooms). These words are paired immediately with an environmental cue. It is possible to combine curricular approaches, because they are not mutually exclusive. The basic-skills approach may be utilized in conjunction with a functional-life orientation in some skill areas.

The eductional team is confronted with some difficult decisions about how to teach and what is to be taught. These decisions must take into account such factors as the student's age and previous learning history, and the available resources. In addition, decisions regarding a student's educational experience must be encompassed within the constraints of time. It may be true that all students with mild learning and behavior disorders can eventually learn as much as their normal classmates, but time in the classroom is limited, and decisions have to be made concerning how to use the available time efficiently. Figure 4-1, a curricular decision-making model (see page 109), illustrates that the time factor can be separated into three educational dimensions: the early childhood, elementary years, and secondary years. The curricular emphasis is different for each dimension.

The young preschool-age child with a mild disorder may exhibit subtle developmental discrepancies in comparison to age-mates, but parents may not identify these discrepancies as significant enough to seek intervention. Even if parents are concerned and seek help for their child prior to school age, they may be confronted with professionals who are apathetic toward early childhood education. Lerner (1976) indicated that some educators are concerned that early-childhood programs may actually create rather than remedy problems, since the child may not be mature enough to cope with the pressures of structured learning in an educational environment. This maturation philosophy has been ingrained into educators and parents. Simply stated, it says wait for the child to reach a point of maturation where he or she may be ready to learn certain skills. Unfortunately, this philosophy has kept many children out of the public schools for years while waiting for them to mature. The antithesis of the maturation philosophy is the prevention of further learning and behavior problems through intervention. Project Head Start, initially funded as a federal preschool program for disadvantaged students, represents a prevention program the purpose of which is to identify and instruct high-risk children prior to their entering public school. Although Head Start programs did not generate the results that were initially anticipated (the virtual elimination of school-adjustment problems for the disadvantaged student), it did represent a beginning. The rationale for early education is widely accepted in the field of special education and is part of the mandate of the Education for All Handicapped Children Act. Early-childhood education programs for children with mild learning and behavior disorders would focus on the development of communication skills, social interaction, and readiness for formal instruction.

The elementary school years are a time when the emphasis is on learning academic and socialization skills. For most children these skills are learned quickly and eventually become tools that expand the child's knowledge in all content areas. However, the student with mild learning and behavior disorders may still be struggling with basic academics and appropriate social skills long after his or her peers have become proficient in these areas.

Secondary-school educators will also have to determine the appropriate curricular emphasis for the student, based on the academic level the student has attained during the elementary years. The adolescent may have acquired enough foundation skills to function successfully in other content areas, such as social studies, algebra, history, and chemistry, or the primary instructional emphasis may have to be on career education and vocational training. These areas of emphasis are not mutually exclusive, however, and the intervention may also be a combination of both academic and vocational skills training. Sitlington (1979) illustrated the components of a career education/vocational training program for adolescents. See Figure 4-2.

Figure 4-2/ Components of a Career Education/Vocational Training Program for Adolescents

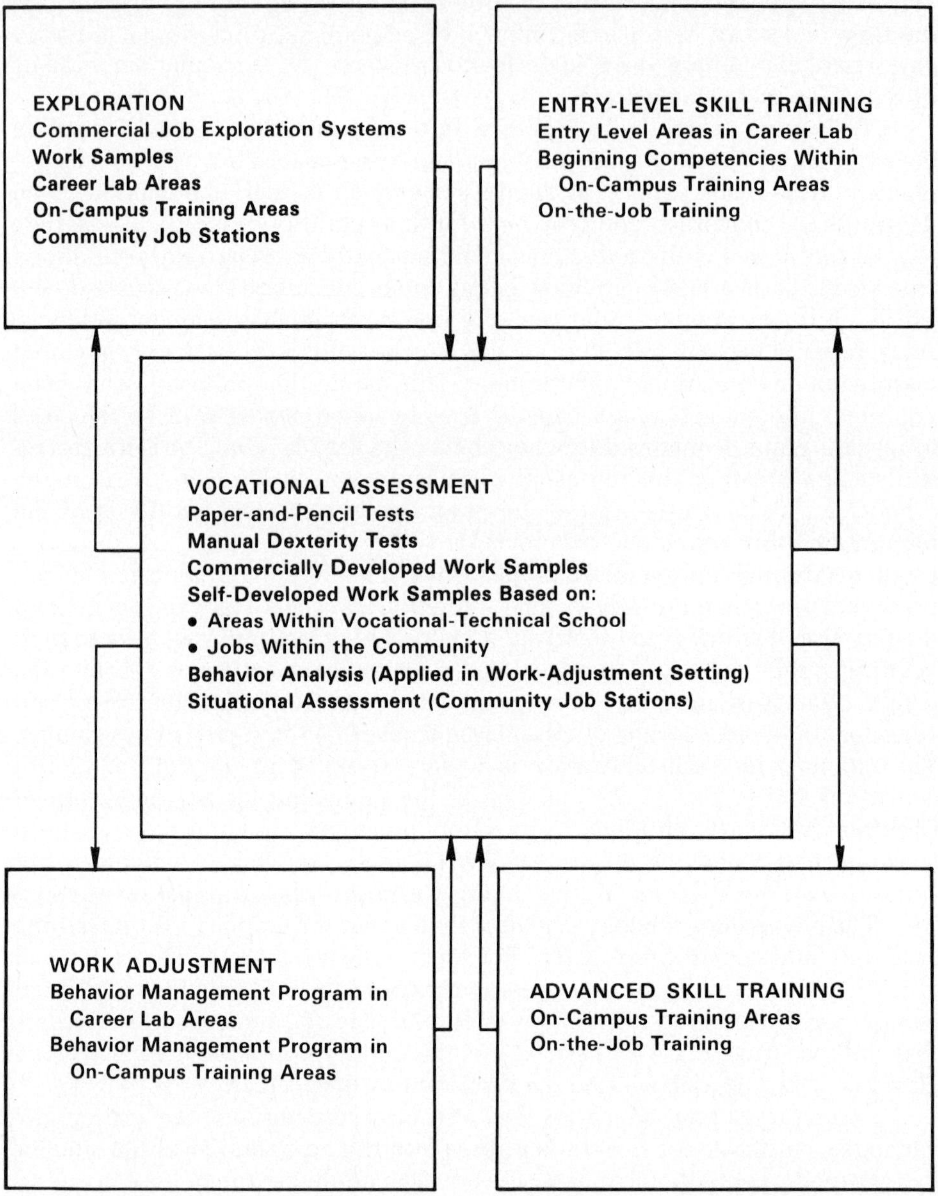

EXPLORATION
Commercial Job Exploration Systems
Work Samples
Career Lab Areas
On-Campus Training Areas
Community Job Stations

ENTRY-LEVEL SKILL TRAINING
Entry Level Areas in Career Lab
Beginning Competencies Within
  On-Campus Training Areas
On-the-Job Training

VOCATIONAL ASSESSMENT
Paper-and-Pencil Tests
Manual Dexterity Tests
Commercially Developed Work Samples
Self-Developed Work Samples Based on:
● Areas Within Vocational-Technical School
● Jobs Within the Community
Behavior Analysis (Applied in Work-Adjustment Setting)
Situational Assessment (Community Job Stations)

WORK ADJUSTMENT
Behavior Management Program in
  Career Lab Areas
Behavior Management Program in
  On-Campus Training Areas

ADVANCED SKILL TRAINING
On-Campus Training Areas
On-the-Job Training

Source: Reprinted from P. L. Sitlington, "Vocational Assessment and Training of the Handi-capped," *Focus on Exceptional Children,* 1979, *12*(4), 10. Copyright © Love Publishing Co. Used by permission.

Individuals with mild learning and behavior disorders have been described as casualties of an educational system that has been unable to meet their academic or social needs. These students have traditionally been classified as having borderline mental retardation, mild behavior disorders, and specific learning disabilities. The more informal (unofficial) labels include slow learner, discipline problem, or poorly motivated student. The causes of mild learning and behavior disorders are generally unknown, but these problems are closely associated with diverse cultural backgrounds, socioeconomic differences, or poor teaching. The traditional categories have emphasized the discrepant characteristics of these students even when actual performance in the classroom suggests a considerable overlap from category to category in both academic and behavioral skills.

A generic conceptualization of mild learning and behavior disorders describes these students as functioning at approximately one to two standard deviations below the mean on measures of inter- and intraindividual differences. Approximately 13 percent of all school-age children have mild learning and behavior problems.

The specialized instructional support systems for these students are designed to enhance their development in the regular education program. Two primary models of support are the consulting teacher and resource-room teacher. While the regular classroom teacher has primary responsibility for the education of the student, these support personnel collaborate with the teacher and assist in the modification of the student's program in the assessed deficit areas.

Success in regular education depends on an adaptive fit between the demands of the school and the needs and ability of each student. Several factors must be considered in this adaptive process, including the development of appropriate goals and objectives, modification of curriculum (e.g., basic skills, remediation, functional life/compensatory skills), and an analysis of the time available to meet the objectives.

REVIEW QUESTIONS

1. Why are students with mild learning and behavior disorders described as casualties of the educational system?
2. Discuss some of the characteristics shared by students with mild learning and behavior disorders.
3. Discuss factors (e.g., diverse cultural background, socioeconomic conditions, poor teaching) associated with causes of mild learning and behavior disorders.
4. Why is it necessary to establish prevalence figures for students with mild learning and behavior disorders? Would all students with such disorders be considered "handicapped" using state and federal prevalence guidelines?
5. Discuss "adaptive fitting" as it applies to students with mild learning and behavior disorders in an educational setting.

6. Discuss the purpose of consulting-teacher and resource-room teacher services for students with mild learning and behavior disorders. How do these service models differ in their approach to assisting the child in the regular classroom?

7. What is the role of the regular classroom teacher in providing educational services to students with mild learning and behavior disorders?

8. Compare and contrast three curricular approaches (basic skills, remediation, functional/compensatory) that can be used in teaching students with mild learning and behavior disorders.

CHAPTER FIVE

Moderate Learning and Behavior Disorders

Moderate Learning Disorders: An Examination of Characteristics
   Mental Retardation

Behavior Disorders
Learning Disabilities
Intervention Strategies

Problems more serious than those already discussed face the professional working with individuals who exhibit moderate learning and behavior disorders. The differences are more pronounced, the difficulties are more pervasive, and the treatment requires more extensive inter-vention than with mild disorders. Individuals with moderate learning and behavior disorders are also more likely to be viewed in terms of traditional categories, such as mental retardation, behavior disorders, and learning disabilities.

In this chaper we will continue our examination of learning and behavior disorders as we focus on people whose differences from the norm are more pronounced. The generic definition of moderate learning and behavior disorders presented in Chapter 3 (see page 87) provides the framework for our discussion. The performance deficits of this population are between two and three standard deviations (SDs) below the mean on the measures recorded and will be evidenced in several environmental settings (e.g., home, community, and school). Individuals functioning at this level will require substantial services in excess of those required for the more mildly disordered population.

The primary distinguishing characteristics associated with the traditional categories of mental retardation, behavior disorders, and learning disabilities become more distinct at the moderate level of functioning. It is true that many people who have moderate learning disorders also manifest behavioral problems, and vice versa, but in many cases moderate disorders can be assessed with regard to which may be the primary difficulty and which is the secondary or concomitant problem (something not as easily accomplished with those who are in the mild range of problem severity).

While adhering to the parameters of the generic definition, our discussion will examine moderate learning and behavior disorders utilizing the categories of mental retardation, behavior disorders, and learning disabilities.

MODERATE LEARNING AND BEHAVIOR DISORDERS: AN EXAMINATION OF CHARACTERISTICS

Mental Retardation

Tim developed considerably more slowly than his older brother, which caused some concern for his parents. Although he is six years old, his functioning in many areas is much like that of a child one or two years younger. He does interact with other children his age in play activities, but if the game becomes complex or involves more than one or two children, he tends to withdraw. Tim has learned the required self-help skills for his age level, including dressing, feeding, and personal hygiene. The family became concerned about Tim's hearing because of slow speech development, but this was judged to be normal when he was tested. The audiologist referred the family to a psychologist for further evaluation. Although the audiologist said nothing specific, Tim's responses during the hearing test led her to suspect an overall developmental delay. The psychologist conducted a series of observations and administered a standardized intelligence test. The test scores indicated that Tim's IQ was about 60, which placed him between two and three standard deviations below the mean of 100. Observations suggested that his socialization skills were also below that expected for a child his age. With both these areas showing such deficits, the next and delicate task was to talk with the parents. Tim seemed to be functioning in a manner that suggested mental retardation.

Tim

Much of Tim's progress will depend on the environment he lives in and the education he receives. Academically, he may be expected to achieve somewhere between the second- and fifth-grade levels. As he grows older, he may be able to achieve partial independence occupationally and socially within the community. Most likely, Tim will need some support from his family or other agencies. Individuals with mental retardation functioning at the moderate severity level would score between 55 and 69 on the Wechsler IQ Scales, and between 4 and 19 on the Adaptive Behavior Inventory for Children **(ABIC).** This latter measure is part of the System of Multicultural Pluralistic Assessment **(SOMPA)** (Mercer & Lewis, 1977). The ABIC is mentioned in this example because standard deviations were presented in the original standardization data, whereas other measures of adaptive behavior have not provided such information. Clearly other measures, both in terms of IQ and adaptive behavior, may result in different score ranges for the moderate level of severity. However, the common denominator remains the two-to-three standard deviation range (or similar measure of dispersion if standard deviations are not available or cannot be obtained). These deficit scores would be necessary on both IQ and adaptive behavior measures. An individual with a score below two standard deviations on only one measure would be likely to be functioning at the mild level of severity. A person who scored between one to two standard deviations on both measures would be viewed as functioning in the mild range. In all cases, clinical judgment is important when we are assessing human behavior. No definition or classification system will (or should) replace this essential assessment component, although it can provide guidelines for such judgments.

Our conceptualization of moderate mental retardation is consistent with the AAMD definitional criteria for the condition of mental retardation (see page 75), but it is inconsistent with the AAMD's symptom-severity classification system. The AAMD classification describes individuals functioning between two and three standard deviations below the mean as mildly retarded. The phrase *mildly retarded* has been used synonymously with the public school classification of *educable mentally retarded* (EMR). Regardless of the terminology employed, we contend that the problems encountered by and the range of services needed for persons functioning at this severity level are too significant to be labeled "mild." Several authors have indicated that students in the public schools who are functioning at this severity level will require more intensive instruction than can be provided in the regular classroom (even when special education support services are available) (Gottleib, 1981; MacMillan & Borthwick, 1980; Myers, 1976). These students will require specialized programming and curricula for the majority of their school day. MacMillan and Borthwick have suggested that the students labeled as educable mentally retarded in today's schools are more disabled than students under the same classification in the 1960s and early 1970s. This is because during the 1960s and early 1970s most EMR students were in the 70-to-85 IQ range (between 1 and 2 SDs below the mean) (MacMillan, Meyers & Morrison, 1980). Gottleib (1981) indicated that presently "the category of EMR appears to be reserved for the lower end of the EMR IQ range, usually for children having an IQ of about 65 or lower" (p. 124).

Many moderately retarded children are not identified until they enter school at the age of five or six. This is because the child may not exhibit severe physical anomalies that are readily identifiable during the early childhood years. Nevertheless, the preschool child with moderate mental retardation will exhibit one- or two-year delays, particularly in the development of socialization skills and academic readiness. As the child enters school, these developmental lags become more apparent in the classroom environment. During the early primary grades it is not uncommon for the child's intellectual and social differences to be attributed to immaturity. However, by third grade the school will generally realize the need for specialized intervention beyond the regular class. Unfortunately, schools have often lost valuable instruction time by not intervening when the problem was first suspected.

Research on the educational achievement of children with moderate mental retardation has suggested that there will be significant deficits in the areas of reading and mathematics. As early as 1940, Kirk indicated that children with IQs between two and three standard deviations below the mean would read anywhere from first- to fourth-grade level. A more recent investigation (Carter, 1975) indicated that school-age students with moderate mental retardation have poor reading mechanics and comprehension when compared to the norm. In fact, most read below their own mental-age level. Arithmetic skills are also deficient for these children, although the performance may be more consonant with their mental age. These children may be able to learn basic computations but be unable to apply concepts appropriately.

There appears to be no significant differences in the development of gross motor skills for individuals with moderate mental retardation when compared to their normal peers (Rarick & Dobbins, 1972). However, research on physical fitness indicates that this population is typically inferior to nonretarded peers of the same chronological age. In the area of physical health, little data are available on this population, but because many of these children come from lower socioeconomic backgrounds, a higher prevalence of health-related problems is expected (Logan & Rose, 1982).

The learning and memory capabilities of people with retardation are clearly deficient compared to the norm. These individuals have difficulty focusing on relevant stimuli in a learning situation (Mercer & Snell, 1977); are deficient in the development of learning sets (Denny, 1964); have inefficient rehearsal strategies that interfere with long-term memory abilities (Frank & Rabinovitch, 1974); are unable to benefit from incidental learning cues in their environment (Hardman & Drew, 1975); and do not effectively transfer knowledge to new tasks or situations (Stephens, 1972). The adaptive functioning (social competence) skills of this population are also deficient. In general, these individuals have lower self-images (Zigler, Balla & Watson, 1972), greater expectancy for failure (Zigler & Balla, 1981), and difficulties in establishing positive peer relationships (Stager & Young, 1981).

Causation. Etiology has historically played a prominent role in the literature on mental retardation. In fact, etiology has been one basis for classification in mental retardation by the AAMD (Grossman, 1977), the American Psychiatric Association (*Diagnostic and Statistical Manual of Mental Disorders,* 1980), and the World Health Organization (*International Classification,* 1967). The AAMD classifies mental retardation in terms of ten categories of etiology (see Chapter 3, page 76).

For the population described in this chapter as moderately retarded, etiology is not generally identifiable. In fact, the cause of the problem can be identified in only 15 to 25 percent of all cases (Zigler, 1978). The etiology of moderate mental retardation is primarily linked to categories nine and ten in the AAMD scheme, although there may be some overlap into the other eight categories. (For purposes of discussion, etiological categories one through eight will be presented in more depth in Chapter 6 of this volume.) There are a significant number of children within this category who come from lower socioeconomic families and different cultural backgrounds. MacMillan (1982) explained:

> The highest prevalence . . . occurs among people referred to as "culturally deprived," "culturally different," "culturally disadvantaged," or some other term that connotes adverse economic and living conditions. Children of high risk are those who live in slums and, frequently, who are members of certain ethnic minority groups. In these high-risk groups there is poor medical care for mother and child, a high rate of broken families, and little value for education or motivation to achieve. (Pp. 86-87)

Prevalence. It is generally estimated that from 1 to 3 percent of the total population have mental retardation (Grossman, 1977). The population functioning between two and three standard deviations below the mean comprises approximately 90 percent of this estimated prevalence. Therefore, based on a 3 percent prevalence estimate, approximately 2.5 percent of the general population would be classified at this level of functioning.

Behavior Disorders

John was a very disruptive student who had been referred numerous times to a variety of public school and community agencies. From the time he was in the second grade until he reached fifth grade, he had been in constant trouble, not only with his parents but also with his teachers and neighbors. A review of his school history showed that he had been described as obnoxious, a holy terror, and downright sneaky. In terms of his academic performance, he had not done well either. He was considerably below the level of his classmates in all subjects except for art and physical education. In creative activities, particularly artwork, he did extremely well.

His most obvious problem was his behavior. He was extremely noncompliant. He did things when he felt like doing them, regardless of setting or rules. He had few if any close friends. He was regularly involved in fights and teasing. The school utilized all its available resources and personnel to assist John and his family in dealing with their problem, but these efforts were to no avail. His misbehavior was not limited solely to school environments. Children in his neighborhood avoided him, and his family had a difficult time relating to him. During the middle of John's elementary school years his mother and father were divorced. John's father maintained custody of the children (two younger sisters and John). Within a year John's father remarried. The new mother made sincere attempts to become John's friend, but that friendship never materialized to any significant degree. Over time, John and his stepmother became bitter enemies. With the demise of his family relationships and lack of any substantive success in school, his already dismal school record became worse. He was eventually referred at the beginning of the fifth grade for placement in a self-contained class for behaviorally disordered students. The placement was finalized during the seventh week of school.

John now regularly attends this class. It is hoped that he will not need to be removed from his home for placement in a residential facility. His parents feel that this class will be helpful to them as well as John. They also will be involved in some ongoing therapy provided by the local mental health agency while John is placed in this program. With considerable effort on the parent's part and the treatment staff within the school, John may be back in the regular class within eighteen to twenty months.

Youngsters in ever-increasing numbers are being identified as behaviorally disordered. They are also diagnosed as needing some professional support services, depending on the severity or nature of the problems. Kauffman (1977) developed a definition of behavior disorders which incorporated three levels of severity. He defined behavior disorders in the following manner:

> Children with behavioral disorders are those who chronically and markedly respond to their environment in socially unacceptable and/or personally unsatisfying ways, but who can be taught more socially acceptable and personally gratifying behavior. Children with mild and moderate behavior disorders can be taught effectively with their normal peers (if their teachers receive appropriate consultive help) or in a special resource or self-contained class with reasonable hope of quick reintegration with their normal peers. Children with severe and profound behavior disorders require intensive and prolonged intervention and must be taught at home, in a special class, special school, or residential institutions. (P. 23)

The levels of severity as described by Kauffman compare favorably with the deviation notion discussed earlier in the generic definition of moderate learning and behavior disorders. Children who deviate "chronically or markedly" are likely to be served in special schools, residential centers, clinics, or hospitals. On the other hand, those who deviate less chronically or markedly are served in less restrictive environments such as regular classrooms, resource rooms, or self-contained special classes.

A variety of classification schemes have been developed to describe the relative severity of behavior disorders. The American Psychiatric Association (*Diagnostic and Statistical Manual,* 1980) subdivided behavior problems into several major categories. These categories are discussed in Chapter 3 of this volume (page 79). As one might expect, these categories are medically oriented and tailored for medical or psychiatric child-care professionals. Other systems (e.g., Ackerson, 1942; Hewitt & Jenkins, 1946; Quay, 1972; 1975) are primarily dimensional approaches; categories are based on dimensions of behaviors. Researchers identify clusters of behaviors that are highly interrelated. Clusters are then given names that broadly describe the behaviors characteristic of each dimension. These dimensions are generally identified as (1) **conduct disorders,** (2) **personality disorders,** and (3) **disorders associated with immaturity and inadequacy.** Children exhibiting conduct disorders are disobedient, show destructive tendencies, and explode into temper tantrums. Those diagnosed as having a personality disorder may be overly anxious, extremely shy or self-conscious, or unusually sad much of the time. In the immaturity category, we find children who are exceptionally clumsy, socially inadequate, or easily flustered. We all experience some or all of these traits from time to time. However, individuals who would be considered as having a disorder deviate from the norm to the point that the behaviors or emotions could be described as being acute or chronic. Compared to the American Psychological Association (APA) classification scheme, the dimensional approach is more limited in scope, but it has been empirically derived and consequently is more appealing to some professionals. Neither system provides much information regarding causes, treatment, or cures.

The behavioral characteristics of individuals functioning at a moderate level of severity are identified more easily than those associated with a mild disorder. Gropper, Kress, Hughes, and Pekich (1968) developed a number of criteria for quickly analyzing the severity of a child's behavior problems in a school setting (see Table 5-1). On closer examination of the criteria developed

Table 5-1/ Criteria for Classifying Problem Behavior

Description of Criteria	Normal	Problem	Referable
Intensity How disruptive of the child's other activities is the problem behavior?	*NONDISRUPTIVE* Behavior does *not* interfere with the child's other activities.	*DISRUPTIVE* Behavior interferes with the child's other activities.	*EXTREMELY DISRUPTIVE* Behavior completely disrupts child's other activities.
Appropriateness Is the behavior a reasonable response to the situation?	*REASONABLE* Response is acceptable or expected for the situation.	*INAPPROPRIATE* Response is undesirable for the situation.	*EXCESSIVE* Response is out of proportion to the situation.
Duration How long does the behavior episode last?	*SHORT-LIVED* Episode lasts only a short time (short time within a class period).	*MODERATELY LONG* Episode extends over a longer period (some carry over from one class to the next).	*LONG-LASTING* Episodes are long-lasting (greater part of a day).
Frequency How often does the behavior occur?	*INFREQUENT* Behavior usually is not repeated (rarely repeated in a day; rarely repeated on other days).	*FREQUENT* Behavior is repeated (may be repeated several times a day; may be repeated on several days).	*HABITUAL* Behavior happens all the time (repeated often during day; repeated on many days).
Specificity/ generality In how many types of situations does the behavior occur?	*OCCURS IN SPECIFIC SITUATION* Behavior occurs in specific type of situation.	*OCCURS IN SEVERAL SITUATIONS* Behavior occurs in more than one type of situation.	*OCCURS IN MANY SITUATIONS* Behavior occurs in many types of situations.
Manageability How easily does the behavior respond to management efforts?	*EASILY MANAGED* Responds readily to management efforts.	*DIFFICULT TO MANAGE* Inconsistent or slow response to management efforts.	*CANNOT BE MANAGED* Does not respond to management efforts.
Assessability of circumstances How easily can the circumstances that produced the behavior be identified?	*EASILY ASSESSED* Easy to identify situation or condition producing behavior.	*DIFFICULT TO ASSESS* Situation or condition producing behavior difficult to identify.	*CANNOT BE ASSESSED* Cannot identify situation or condition producing behavior.

Table 5-1 (Continued)

Description of Criteria	Normal	Problem	Referable
Comparison with maturity level of class How close to the norm of the class is the problem behavior?	**NO DEVIATION FROM LEVEL OF CLASS** Behavior is par for the group.	**BELOW LEVEL OF CLASS** Behavior is below the group level.	**CONSIDERABLY BELOW LEVEL OF CLASS** Behavior is considerably below the group level.
Number of problem behaviors exhibited	Rarely more than one.	Usually more than one.	Usually many and varied.
Acceptance by peers Does the child have difficulty being accepted by peers?	**ACCEPTED** Is accepted by peers.	**HAS DIFFICULTY GETTING ALONG** May have difficulty with particular individuals.	**NOT ACCEPTED** Unaccepted by group.

Source: Reprinted, by permission, from G. Gropper, G. Kress, R. Hughes, and J. Pekich, "Training Teachers to Recognize and Manage Social and Emotional Problems in the Classroom," *Journal of Teacher Education,* 1968, *19,* 481.

by Gropper et al., we can see how the descriptors beneath the "referable" column provide a means for selecting the children who may have a moderate to severe behavior disorder. These descriptors also correspond closely to the generic definition of moderate learning and behavior disorders presented earlier. Behaviors at the moderate level of severity are characterized by several factors:

1. The behaviors are generally excessive, disruptive, and inappropriate (in some instances, however, it is not the excessiveness of behaviors, but a lack of behaviors, that causes concern).
2. The behaviors exhibited do not compare favorably with those manifested by normal children.
3. The behaviors are generally unacceptable to the child, his or her normal peers, or adults.
4. The number of problem behaviors exhibited is comparatively high.
5. The problem behaviors interfere with the child's expected performance relative to chronological age (in terms of school, home, or the community).
6. The intellectual capacity and academic achievement of behaviorally disordered students are generally below average. (Kauffman, 1977)

One might surmise from the discussion thus far that almost any behavior or class of behaviors exhibited (or not exhibited) to an extreme degree may qualify an individual for referral and eventual diagnosis of behavior disorders. Generally the behaviors of greatest concern to professionals fall under the descriptive categories delineated by Kauffman. These are: (1) hyperactivity, (2) distractibility, (3) impulsivity, (4) aggression, (5) withdrawal, (6) immaturity, (7) inadequacy, and (8) deficiencies in moral development. Within and across each of these categories are subcategories that deal with such behaviors as

Hyperactivity is a
common prob-
lem among
young children.

juvenile delinquency, habit disorders (e.g., **enuresis, encopresis**), **school phobia, elective mutism,** and others. Some of the problem behaviors cited within
the subcategories cannot be treated only by significantly altering the child's
school environment or placement. In the case of encopresis (soiling), the parents
may consult a behavioral psychologist or psychiatrist to resolve the problem.
School personnel may be involved only in a tangential fashion.

Newcomer (1980) presented a severity scheme for classifying behavior
disorders which contains some important parameters of evaluation (see Table
5-2). One of these parameters involves an "insight index," which relates to the
child's awareness or understanding of his or her behavioral problems. Is the
child aware of the behavioral deviance, and does he or she understand the
reasons for the behavior and the impact of the behavior (on self, family, and
others)? Another parameter of similar importance is the "conscious control"
dimension, which relates to whether the child makes an attempt to control
the behavior deviance and the degree to which such attempts are successful
(or whether the behavior is totally out of control). These parameters (and others)

Table 5-2/ Criteria for Determining Degree of Disturbance

	Degree of Disturbance		
Criteria	Mild	Moderate	Severe
Precipitating events	Highly stressful	Moderately stressful	Not stressful
Destructiveness	Not destructive	Occasionally destructive	Usually destructive
Maturational appropriateness	Behavior typical for age	Some behavior untypical for age	Behavior too young or too old
Personal functioning	Cares for own needs	Usually cares for own needs	Unable to care for own needs
Social functioning	Usually able to relate to others	Usually unable to relate to others	Not able to relate to others
Reality index	Usually sees events as they are	Occasionally sees events as they are	Little contact with reality
Insight index	Aware of behavior	Usually aware of behavior	Usually not aware of behavior
Conscious control	Usually can control behavior	Occasionally can control behavior	Little control over behavior
Social responsiveness	Usually acts appropriately	Occasionally acts appropriately	Rarely acts appropriately

Source: From Phyllis L. Newcomer, *Understanding and Teaching Emotionally Disturbed Children*, p. 111. Copyright © 1980 by Allyn and Bacon, Inc. Reprinted with permission.

are particularly helpful to professionals and parents who are responsible for referring a student for further evaluation.

A variety of techniques have been utilized to identify children with behavior disorders. These techniques closely parallel the theoretical framework or philosophical perspective of the evaluator. Usually the actual diagnosis of the behavioral problems is preceded by a set of screening procedures. The screening is done using a behavior checklist or a variety of sociometric devices (e.g., peer ratings) and teacher rating scales. Bower and Lambert (1962) developed an extensive process for conducting in-school screening. Others (e.g., Burks, 1977; Long, Fagan & Stevens, 1971; Spivack & Spotts, 1966: Spivack, Spotts & Haimes, 1967; Spivack & Swift, 1967; Walker, 1976) have also developed rating scales for use in screening children with suspected behavior disorders. Some of these rating scales provide measures of standard deviation that are particularly well suited to the generic definitional criteria for classifying children with moderate learning and behavior disorders. For example, the Walker Problem Behavior Identification Checklist (Walker, 1976) provides five scales that describe various types of problem behaviors (acting out, withdrawal, distractibility, disturbed peer relations, and immaturity). Each of these scales can be scored on the student's deviation from the mean on a Profile Analysis Chart (see Figure 5-1). For instance, a student who receives a rating of 3 on the acting-out scale would be considered average or normal in terms of aggressive behavior. In contrast, a student with a rating of 16 on this scale would be seriously considered for referral and intervention, since such a score would

Figure 5-1/ Profile Analysis Chart

Profile Analysis Chart (PAC)

T-Score	Scale 1 Acting-out Male	Scale 1 Acting-out Female	Scale 2 Withdrawal Male	Scale 2 Withdrawal Female	Scale 3 Distractibility Male	Scale 3 Distractibility Female	Scale 4 Disturbed Peer Relations Male	Scale 4 Disturbed Peer Relations Female	Scale 5 Immaturity Male	Scale 5 Immaturity Female	T-Score
Over 110		20-26						7-11			—
110		19									110
—						13				10	—
—		18									—
105		17									105
—						12		6		9	—
100		16									100
—		15				11					—
95									10	8	95
—		14				10		5			—
90	26	13		14					9		90
—	25									7	—
—	24	12	14	13		9					—
85	23								8		85
—	22	11	13	12			11	4		6	—
—	21		12	11		8					—
80	20	10					10				80
—	19		11	10		7	9			5	—
—	18	9		9	13		8	3	6		75
75	17		10			6					75
—	16	8	9		12				5	4	—
70	15	7	8	8	11	5	7				70
—	14			7	10						—
—	13	6	7				6	2	4	3	—
65	12		6	6	9	4	5				65
—	11	5									—
—	10			5	8				3		—
60	9	4	5		7	3	4			2	60
—	8	3	4	4	6		3	1	2		—
—	7			3						1	55
55	6	2	3		5	2	2		1		55
—	5			2	4						—
—	4	1	2			1	1				50
50	3		1	1	3						50
—	2	0			2	0	0	0	0	0	—
45	1		0	0	1						45
—	0										—
X	3.20	1.05	1.59	1.59	3.77	1.33	1.18	.35	.76	.52	X
S.D.	5.70	2.98	3.32	3.08	3.74	2.05	3.01	1.08	1.99	1.64	S.D.

fall beyond two standard deviations on this measure. The same rating system would apply to the other scales. Ratings below the level of a "50 T-Score" would be considered average. However, those above a "70 T-Score" would be considered candidates for the moderately to severely disturbed designation.

Spivack et al. (1966; 1967) have also developed a number of rating scales for evaluating the behaviors of children and youths which can be summarized using profiles. An example drawn from the Devereaux Child Behavior (DCB) Rating Scale (Spivack & Spotts, 1966) illustrates their approach to reporting scores in standard-deviation units. The ratings on this instrument are accomplished in a straightforward fashion. The rater is given a listing of various descriptive statements, such as the following:

Compared to normal children, *how often does the child* . . .

Item 8: Have a fixed facial expression that lacks feeling?

Item 16: Appear completely inactive and lethargic?

Item 32: Have a blank stare or faraway look in his eyes?

Item 34: Daydream?

Item 35: Look unhappy, sad, and unsmiling?

Item 53: Look happy, smiling, and cheerful?

The majority of these items (8, 16, 32, 34, and 35) are rated according to a five-point scale (1—never; 2—rarely; 3—occasionally; 4—often; 5—very frequently). Item 53 is rated in an inverse fashion because of the manner in which the question is stated. Let us assume that a youngster received a rating of 5 on each of the first five items mentioned (8, 16, 32, 34, and 35) and a total score of 30. Such a score would fall just beyond two standard deviations from the mean on the behavioral factor labeled "emotional detachment." Again this score, combined with the other behavior factor scores, would provide measures of the degree of deviation between the rated child and normal children. As such, these measures and attendant scores may be very helpful to teachers, parents, or child-care workers who must find a means to quantify their perceptions regarding a child's behavior problems.

Behavioral-analysis techniques may also be utilized to make comparisons between children and youths suspected of manifesting serious behavioral problems. One such technique is direct observation. Using this method, a well-trained observer can count and record a variety of behaviors that may be of concern to the teacher, parent, or other interested party while at the same time monitoring these behaviors in a number of other randomly selected students. For example, assume that John is a student of concern to us. In fact, we are seriously thinking about referring him, but we want to be sure he is truly excessive in his behaviors, particularly aggressive behaviors. We decide to select hitting and other related well-defined target behaviors as our focus of observation. Using an interval observation method, we observe John and five other male students for a week. At the end of the week, our data are summarized in Table 5-3. If we were to obtain the standard deviation for this set of numbers, we would find that 17 instances of John's aggressive behavior fall well beyond two standard deviations above the mean. These data would be helpful in rendering a referral decision, but alone they would not be sufficient. The data do, however, illustrate the potential usefulness of actual recordings of behavioral instances and events for referral and other diagnostic evaluations.

Table 5-3/ Summary of Aggressive Behavior

Student	No. of Aggressive Behaviors from Oct. 6 to Oct. 11
John	17
Steve	1
Dan	2
Mike	0
Fred	2
Stan	1

Screening is conducted to identify youngsters who deviate significantly in their inter-intrapersonal learning and social behaviors in a variety of settings and circumstances. In this regard, Gropper et al. (1968) developed criteria for educators and others called on to make referral decisions (see Table 5-1).

Once the screening process has been concluded, specialists and/or consultants (e.g., psychologists, special educators, social workers, psychiatrists) complete an in-depth assessment of the child's academic and social-emotional strengths and weaknesses in various environmental settings (e.g., classroom, home, playground). The personnel may (1) analyze classroom and playground interactions with peers and teachers using behavioral-analysis techniques (i.e., observations with frequency counts of various types of behaviors or interactions); (2) administer various tests to evaluate personality, achievement, and intellectual factors; (3) interview the parents and the child; (4) observe the child at home; and/or (5) apply an array of other assessment procedures. Many of the assessment devices utilized, particularly the projective and personality inventories, do not provide information that reliably differentiates disordered individuals from nondisordered individuals. Likewise, information gained from these devices cannot be readily translated into specific programming for individuals with behavior disorders. Of greatest promise at this point are behavioral-analysis techniques, which provide a concrete means for evaluating present problem behaviors and intervention effects.

Causation. Many philosophers, physicians, theologians, and others have attempted to explain why people behave as they do. Historically, disturbed and other deviant populations were described as being possessed by evil spirits. It was presumed that the presence of evil spirits within these individuals made them behave the way they did. The treatment of choice at that time was religious in nature. Later, Sigmund Freud and others promoted the notion that behavior could be explained in terms of subconscious phenomena or early traumatic experiences. More recently, some theorists have attributed disordered behaviors to inappropriate learning or complex interactions that take place between individuals and environments. From a biological perspective, others have suggested that aberrant behaviors are caused by certain biochemical substances, brain abnormalities or injuries, or chromosomal irregularity.

With such a wealth of etiological explanations, it is easy to see why the field of behavior disorders has often been characterized as confused or disturbed itself. However, the variety of theoretical frameworks and perspectives does

provide the clinician with choices for explaining the presence of certain behavior. As we encountered in other disorder areas, the varying theoretical
perspectives also result in a certain amount of professional bickering. Many
times such professional arguing is not productive and causes considerable
consternation on the part of consumers of services. In this regard it may be
productive for professionals to become "technical eclecticists" who are able to
utilize the best of each theoretical explanation to assist individuals with problems. Kauffman (1977) stated, "The first or ultimate cause of behavior disorders
almost always remains unknown. . . . The focus of the special educators concern
should be on those contributing factors that can be altered by the teacher" (p.
263). Kauffman's statement is also appropriate for other professionals who are
anxious to help children with behavior disorders. Table 5-4 provides an
overview of etiologies and causal factors associated with various theoretical
frameworks.

The biological framework explains behavior disorders as a function of
inherited or otherwise inherent conditions within the body, or injury to the
central nervous system. The symptoms or behavior problems presumably surface as a function of some physical abnormality or disease.

Psychological processes, predispositions or instincts, and early traumatic
experiences explain behavior disorders from a psychoanalytic perspective. The

Table 5-4/ Etiologies and Causal Factors Associated with Behavior Disorders

Theoretical Framework	Etiologies/Causal Factors
Biological	Genetic inheritance Biochemical abnormalities Neurological abnormalities Injury to the central nervous system
Psychoanalytical	Psychological processes Functioning of the mind: id, ego, and superego Inherited predispositions (instinctual processes) Early-childhood experiences
Behavioral	Environmental events 1. Failure to learn adaptive behaviors 2. Learning of maladaptive behaviors 3. Developing maladaptive behaviors as a result of stressful environment circumstances (Coleman, 1972)
Phenomenological	Faulty learning about one's self Misuse of defense mechanisms Feelings, thoughts, and events Emanating from the "self"
Sociological/ecological	Role assignment (labeling) Cultural transmission Social disorganization Distorted communication Differential association Negative interactions and transactions with others

psychological processes are basically unconscious, unobservable events that occur in the mind among the well-known psychic constructs of the id (the drives component), the ego (the reality component), and the superego (the conscience component). As one gains insight regarding psychic conflicts by means of psychotherapy, one is supposedly able gradually to eliminate or to solve the problem behaviors. For children, this process theoretically occurs through play therapy, in which inner conflicts are revealed and subsequently resolved through parent therapy and therapeutic play experiences with understanding adults.

The behavioristic approach to understanding behavioral disorders focuses on aspects of the environment that produce or reward the behaviors of concern. Both adults and children are given an opportunity to learn new adaptive behaviors. Gradually, aberrant behaviors are eliminated or replaced by more appropriate behaviors.

From a phenomenological point of view, abnormal behaviors arise from feelings, thoughts, and past events tied to a person's self-perceptions or self-concepts. The faulty perceptions or feelings cause individuals to behave in ways that are counterproductive to self-fulfillment or self-actualization. Therapy associated with this approach is centered on helping people develop satisfactory perceptions and behaviors consonant with self-selected values.

The sociological/ecological model is by far the most encompassing. Based on this model, aberrant behaviors are presumed to be caused by a variety of interactions and transactions with other people. For some, the aberrant behaviors are taught as a part of one's culture. For others, the deviant behaviors are a function of labeling. Individuals labeled as juvenile delinquents, acccording to this perspective, gradually adopt the delinquency label and the behaviors associated with the label. In addition, others who are aware of the label begin to treat labeled people as if they were truly delinquent (see Chapter 1, page 20). Such treatment theoretically promotes the delinquent behavior. Another source of aberrant behavior associated with this model is differential association. This source of deviance is closely related to the cultural-transmission explanation of deviance: People exhibit behavior problems in an attempt to conform to the wishes and expectations of a group they wish to join or maintain affiliation with. Finally, the sociological/ecological perspective views the presence of aberrant behavior in an individual as a function of a variety of interactions and transactions that are derived from a broad array of environmental settings.

Each of these models contributes different information regarding the causes of behavioral disorders. As mentioned earlier, we are rarely able to isolate the exact cause of a child's behavior disorders, but we do have an understanding of many conditions and factors that contribute to disordered behavior.

Prevalence. Estimates of the prevalence of behavior disorders vary greatly from one source to the next. Schultz, Hirshoren, Manton, and Henderson (1971) found prevalence figures ranging from 0.05 percent to 15.0 percent. The U.S. Office of Education (1975) estimated that 2 percent of the children in the country have behavior disorders. Bower (1969) suggested that about 10 percent of the children in an average class setting will require some assistance in resolving behavior problems.

Kelly, Bullock, and Dykes (1977) provided some prevalence figures from an educational perspective which were cast in a severity framework. They employed three classifications: mild, moderate, and severe. Approximately 20 percent of the students in this study were identified by their teachers as exhibiting behavior disorders. Among these youngsters, 12.6 percent were judged to be mildly disordered, 5.6 percent were classified in the moderate category, and 2.2 percent were put in the severe category.

Approximately 3 percent of the children and youths in the United States are referred and processed as juvenile delinquents (Federal Bureau of Investigation, 1979). A significant percentage (about 18 percent) of the juvenile delinquents initially identified return as chronic serious offenders (Wolfgang, Figlio & Sellin, 1972). These prevalence figures are also subject to many of the problems generally associated with prevalence precision.

The most conservative prevalence estimates for moderate behavior disorders range from about 0.5 percent to 1.5 or 2.5 percent. However, until advancements are made in articulating an operational definition of behavior disorders and completing studies that are methodologically sound, the prevalence figures cited in this section will be subject to error and controversy. At present, they are the best estimates available and will remain such until the proper measures have been taken to correct definitional and methodological problems of the past research.

Finally, behavior disorders are not a randomly distributed phenomenon. Referral rates for very young children (preschool through the primary grades) are quite low (Redick, 1973). By contrast, the rate increases dramatically during the preadolescent and adolescent years (Morse, Cutler & Fink, 1964). Clarizio and McCoy (1976) suggested that these differences in rates between young and older children may be a function of referral policies rather than age itself. With regard to delinquency, arrest rates rise rapidly during the junior high period until about age seventeen, at which time they gradually begin to taper off (Kvaraceus, 1966).

Behavior disorders are also not equally distributed between the sexes. Males outnumber females at least two to one in exhibiting behavior disorders (Kelly, Bullock & Dykes, 1977). However, the ratio of males and females becomes more nearly equal as they reach the young adult years. Delinquency is primarily a male phenomenon, although the ratio of female to male delinquents appears to be changing (females increasing) (Clarizio & McCoy, 1976).

Learning Disabilities

Michelle's difficulties in learning fundamental tool skills were evident from the time she entered school. Although her intelligence score was well within the normal range, she had been unable to master the foundation skills in reading, was a poor speller, and had deficits in hand-

writing and gross motor development. Each year her teachers reported that she was capable of doing the work required but that her problems with visual perception interfered with her performance. Michelle was unable to align words on a page, reversed numbers and letters, wrote words from the bottom to the top of the page, and read from right to left. Now, at the age of fourteen, Michelle is facing high school with reading skills that are over four years behind grade level. Her reading vocabulary is comparable to that of a third- or fourth-grader, but she has great difficulty using reading as a tool for learning. A tape recorder is one of her most valuable possessions. It allows her to sit comfortably through lectures, knowing she does not have to fumble with taking notes. She can play back the discussion over and over to get the necessary information. Michelle performs much better in the area of math, especially when she is required to do computations where little reading is involved. Most of Michelle's early school experiences have been in a regular classroom with resource-room assistance. As she moved into the middle grades, however, the educational team in her school recommended that she receive a more extensive special education program in a self-contained classroom. This recommendation was based on some serious problems in maintaining positive peer relationships as well as her inconsistent performance in academic subjects.

Until recently, the literature in education had virtually ignored the notion of symptom severity as it related to definitions and concepts of learning disabilities. The most influential definition was developed by the National Advisory Committee on Handicapped Children (1968) and later incorporated into Public Law 94-142 with only minor changes (see Chapter 3, page 82). Although this definition is the most widely used and a part of federal law, there are other conceptualizations of this population. Learning disabilities has probably been defined in more different ways than any other type of disorder. In fact, Cruickshank (1972) noted that over forty different terms were in use to describe what were essentially the same behaviors. It is clear that, with regard to learning disabilities, there is no uniformly accepted definition.

The wide variety of terminology and definitions of learning disabilities emerged partly from the varying theoretical views of the problem. For example, perceptual-motor theorists (e.g., Cruickshank, Kephart, Getman, Barsh, Frostig) emphasized the interaction between the various channels of perception and motor activity. The perceptual motor theory of learning disabilities "examines the normal sequential development of motor patterns and motor generalizations and compares the motor development of children with learning problems of that of normal children" (Lerner, 1981, p. 192). However, *language disability theorists* (e.g., Orton, Hirsch, Myklebust, Kirk) concentrate on the child's deficiency in the reception or production of language. Language plays a critical role in learning, and "an intimate relationship exists between learning disabilities and deficits in language" (Lerner, 1981, p. 249).

On the basis of these two theories alone, it is clear that we are addressing very divergent views. Learning disabilities is a field that has many theoretical perspectives in terms of the nature of problems as well as causation and treatment. This becomes most perplexing when we ask how so many terms and theories can be used to describe the same behaviors. Some more recent literature has taken a different view of learning disabilities. Instead of focusing on the differing terminology, some have suggested that we are grouping many different specific disorders under one term. "Learning disabilities is a general educational term. . . . We contend that the term can be used only as a generalized referent and that it encompasses a variety of specific types of problems" (Gelfand, Jenson & Drew, 1982, p. 214). Benton and Pearl (1978) provided support for this notion by suggesting that even certain *types* of learning disabilities, specifically dyslexia, represent a collection of different disorders. In one sense this thinking is not surprising. It has long been acknowledged that the learning disabilities population is very heterogeneous. However, even in the face of this knowledge, professionals in the area have continued attempting to characterize people with learning disabilities as though they were a unitary entity. Such characterizations have typically taken on more of the theoretical or disciplinary perspective of the professional than an objective behavioral description of the individual being evaluated. Thus there has been a propensity to characterize the disorder rather than describe the characteristics of an individual with problems. Such characterizations will inevitably be in error with a population that represents an aggregate of various disorders.

The above problems have been manifested in the research focusing on this population. In a review of the learning disability research, Harber (1981) indicated: "There is a definite need for researchers to specify the parameters of the population under study. Currently, there is much variation in the characteristics which are equated with the classification of learning disabilities" (p. 379). She further suggested that the generalizability of such studies is in question and that replication is not possible.

As a response to P.L. 94-142's definition, which has been described as exclusionary and ambiguous (Cruickshank, 1977; Hammill, 1974), the National Joint Committee for Learning Disabilities proposed a new definition in 1981:

> Learning disabilities is a generic term that refers to a heterogeneous group of disorders manifested by significant difficulties in the acquisition and use of listening, speaking, reading, writing, reasoning or mathematical abilities. These disorders are intrinsic to the individual and presumed to be due to central nervous system dysfunction. Even though a learning disability may occur concomitantly with other handicapping conditions (e.g., sensory impairment, mental retardation, social and emotional disturbance) or environmental influences (e.g., cultural differences, insufficient/inappropriate instruction, psychogenic factors), it is not the direct result of those conditions or influences.

Hammill, Leigh, McNutt, and Larsen (1981) pointed out that "the purpose of the definition was to establish learning disabilities theoretically—not to set up specific operational criteria for identifying individual cases" (p. 339). This proposed definition is important to the present discussion for two reasons. First,

A child with
learning disabili-
ties may have
difficulty learn-
ing how to write
accurately and
legibly.

it describes *learning disabilities* as a generic term that refers to a heterogeneous group of disorders. Second, the individual with learning disabilities must manifest *significant* difficulties. The use of the word *significant* is an obvious attempt to remove the connotation of a mild problem. It should be noted that the same term is used in the AAMD definition of mental retardation: "*significantly* subaverage general intellectual functioning" (Grossman, 1977, emphasis added).

In our examination of learning disabilities, we will describe behavioral characteristics from differing theoretical views. Learning disabilities is a field whose empirical base is insufficient to select one perspective or to characterize the population, but it is important to provide examples of how an individual might be classified as learning disabled using different theories and perspectives. Hallahan and Kauffman suggested that five general areas are usually present in definitions of learning disabilities. They are "(1) academic retardation, (2) uneven development between different areas of functioning, (3) central nervous system dysfunction may or may not be present, (4) the learning problems are not due to environmental disadvantage, and (5) learning problems are not due to mental retardation or emotional disturbance" (1976, p. 20). Combinations of these and other behavioral characteristics have from time to time been represented in various theoretical views of learning disabilities. For example, the uneven development of skill areas (intraindividual discrepancies) has been prominently evident and debated in the literature during the past 10 years.

The divergent theoretical views and definitions associated with this population have resulted in a heterogeneous group of individuals being described as learning disabled. One perspective mentioned earlier in our discussion was language-disability theory. We will now examine a diagnostic procedure that has been widely used by theorists of this inclination. The Illinois Test of Psycholinguistic Abilities, popularly known as the ITPA (Kirk, McCarthy & Kirk, 1968), was developed to assess language functioning of children from about two and a half to ten years of age. The ITPA is a complicated instrument involving several subtests in such areas as auditory reception, visual reception, auditory association, visual association, verbal expression, manual expression, grammatical closure, visual closure, auditory memory, visual memory, auditory closure, and sound blending. Functional deficits in several of these areas have been characteristics attributed to learning disabled individuals at one time or another. It should be noted that Samuel Kirk, one of the authors of the ITPA, was a proponent of the idea that learning disabilities involved great unevenness in terms of intraindividual skills. Kirk stated: "One of the areas in which intraindividual differences are most dramatic and most relevant is that of learning disabilities. Here we find children who often appear quite normal in most respects but have marked disabilities in one area or another. We also find children who appear mentally retarded but have normal abilities in some areas" (1972, p. 41). The ITPA, with its many subtests, is designed from this perspective.

The ITPA has a scaled score mean of 36 and a standard deviation of 6. This is the case for the composite score as well as the subtests (Paraskevopoulos & Kirk, 1969). Scaling in this fashion permits the ITPA to be used for both inter- and intraindividual evaluation. According to the generic definition of moderate learning disorders presented earlier, there must exist an intraindividual discrepancy that is between two and three standard deviations. For example, if a child had a composite scaled mean of 29, scores on any subtest (e.g., visual closure, visual memory) that ranged between 11 and 17 would suggest moderate learning disabilities.

The ITPA has received widespread attention since its development. We have discussed it partly because of this popularity, but also as an example of the language theory related to learning disabilities. But this model has not been without its serious critics. Criticism has come from several fronts. From personnel in the field have come complaints about the cumbersome and lengthy administration, as well as the extensive training necessary for examiners to be qualified. In addition, serious questions have been raised regarding the ITPA's usefulness and validity (Hammill & Larsen, 1974; Newcomer & Hammill, 1975; Salvia & Ysseldyke, 1978; Silverstein, 1978). Such criticism is not uncommon in measurement fields, particularly when efforts involve disorders that lack conceptual clarity and a substantial empirical base, such as learning disabilities. This leads us to call once again for increased and continuing rigorous research in the area.

One of the definitional areas related to learning disabilities identified by Hallahan and Kauffman (1976) involved academic retardation. Academic retardation may occur for a number of reasons. A youngster may be academically slow because of limited intelligence (as in mental retardation), impaired vision or hearing, or any of a number of other factors. However, each of these areas mentioned is specifically eliminated as a part of the definition of learning disabilities. Thus we must look at the characteristics of a child who is academically retarded but not mentally retarded, visually impaired, or with reduced hearing. Academic retardation has been very prominent in the field of learning disabilities, although one may be tempted to label it a theoretical view. Certainly it has been very much involved in labeling individuals with learning disabilities by public schools and state agencies.

What does academic retardation mean in terms of learning disabilities? This seemingly simple question has presented great difficulties for workers in the field. The approaches to defining academic retardation for learning disabilities have been as variable as the theories regarding the disorder. In many cases, measurement and consequent identification of an individual as learning disabled have differed from state to state and even between school districts within a state. Despite this variability and confusion, we must examine academic retardation in learning disabilities because of its widespread use in school districts and agencies around the United States. Although many classification decisions are based on clinical judgments (by diagnosticians, teachers, and administrators), we will attempt to speak in statistical terms and outcomes from formal evaluations in concert with the generic definition/classification scheme. This is not intended to discount clinical judgment—we noted earlier that such assessment is vital to useful decisions. The problem here is simple. The parameters and influences related to clinical judgment are difficult to put on the printed page in a clear and precise fashion.

Academic retardation in learning disabilities describes a child's academic performance that is substantially below his or her potential. Several factors have led to confusion and variable application of this notion. For example, questions have often been raised regarding how one determines potential. Scores from intelligence tests have served this function, but arguments have continually surrounded such tests in general, and specifically the idea that measured intelligence represents potential. Aside from those arguments, considerable difficulty has been encountered in terms of what is meant by the qualifying statement "substantially below" (regarding the academic-potential discrepancy). We noted above that this has been interpreted and qualified in a highly variable fashion. There has been little agreement regarding how much of a discrepancy must exist for someone to be considered learning disabled.

There are several variations in quantifying a discrepancy between achievement and ability using an expectancy formula. An example of this method was used by Myklebust (1968) in an attempt to quantify academic deficits. Myklebust employed the concept of a learning quotient (LQ), which includes several components that he viewed as important in learning disabilities. The LQ is derived by first establishing an expectancy age from the following formula (Myklebust, 1968, p. 5).

$$\frac{\text{Mental Age} + \text{Life Age} + \text{Grade Age}}{3} = \text{Expectancy Age}$$

In this formula the mental age is obtained from evaluation of the individual using a standardized intelligence test. Life age represents the individual's

chronological age. Grade age represents the typical age of children who are in the grade in which the child being evaluated is enrolled. Once the expectancy age is obtained, the learning quotient can be derived by dividing that figure into the child's actual achievement level (in, say, arithmetic) and multiplying the outcome by 100. Thus the formula for the overall learning quotient is:

$$\text{Learning Quotient} = \frac{\text{Actual Achievement}}{\text{Expectancy Age}} \times 100$$

For example, suppose we have a girl with an expectancy age of 10 who has an arithmetic achievement level equivalent to children who are 9 years old (derived from an achievement test score and converted to an age equivalent). Her learning quotient on arithmetic would be 90 (9 ÷ 10 × 100).

We still have not addressed the question regarding the amount of achievement/ability discrepancy necessary for someone to be considered learning disabled. Myklebust had an idea regarding this as he developed the learning quotient. He was clearly basing much of his thinking on the ratio method of calculating IQ (a procedure no longer used today). He extended this analogy further in establishing an LQ figure necessary for identifying a learning disability. Myklebust stated his reasoning in the following manner:

> Although long experience with learning disabilities is lacking, our procedure is to follow the practice evolved in the study of intelligence. We employ the 10 percent level of differentiation. This procedure is logical

on the basis that we use 90 I.Q. as the "cut-off" point for average intelligence. If 90 percent of average is considered normal intellectually, then 90 percent of average should be the base-line in computing expectancy for learning. Accordingly, a Learning Quotient of 89 is taken as the "cut-off" point; a quotient of 89 or below constitutes the basis for classification as having a learning disability. (Myklebust, 1968, p. 6)

The reader should remember the date on this quotation—1968. We no longer use an IQ score of 90 as the benchmark for normal intellectual functioning. Furthermore, one could certainly argue with portions of the logic employed by Myklebust. The fact remains, however, that the notion of an achievement/ability discrepancy has been widely used for identifying learning disabilities in education. Myklebust provided a serious attempt to quantify this notion. Others (e.g., Algozzine, Forgnone, Mercer & Trifiletti, 1979; Harris, 1970; Kaluger & Kolson, 1969) have proposed similar formulas for ascertaining discrepancy between achievement and ability.

A third method for quantifying discrepancy is the use of standard scores. This method involves a comparison of standard scores (e.g., z scores, T scores) from an ability test with those on a test of academic achievement. There are several advantages to this method. "Such scores can be subjected to mathematical calculations and comparisons across tests, subject matter (subtests), as well as age or grade levels" (Cone & Wilson, 1981, p. 364).

Up to this point in our analysis of learning disabilities, we have discussed the uneven development of skill areas and discrepancy between academic achievement and ability. However, these represent the tip of the iceberg with respect to the characteristics that have been attributed to those labeled as learning disabled. Many and varied behavioral characteristics have been associated with such individuals. It is important to reiterate our view that *learning disabilities* is a generalized educational term representing an aggregation of many different disorders. In many cases, solid empirical evidence for certain characteristics of the learning disabled is scanty or even absent. A substantial amount of what is known about this population can be considered to represent primarily "clinical lore" (Bryan, 1974). This will become more evident as we proceed and discuss the learning disabled in terms of characteristics and causation.

Hyperactivity is a behavioral characteristic commonly associated with children who are labeled as learning disabled. Hyperactivity (also termed *hyperkinesis*) is typically thought of as a general excess of activity. Professionals working in the area of learning disabilities, particularly teachers, often mention hyperactivity first as they describe these children. Such children are typically depicted as fidgeting a great deal and being able to sit still for only a short time. Most descriptions involve the characterization of an overly active child.

Certain points need to be considered as we discuss hyperactivity in learning-disabled children. First, not all children who are learning disabled are hyperactive, and vice versa. This was highlighted by Rosenthal and Allen (1978) in a literature review when they sought to differentiate learning disabilities, hyperkinesis, and minimal brain dysfunction. They noted, "There is probably such a degree of overlap between these categories that perhaps half of the subjects in a learning disability study might also be labeled either minimally brain dysfunctional or hyperkinetic'' (p. 693). This should not be interpreted to mean that *half* the learning disabled are hyperactive. More correctly, this statement emphasizes the confusion regarding learning disabilities and how it relates to or is distinguishable from hyperkinesis. A second point warranting attention involves the notion that hyperkinesis is characterized as a general excess of activity. This idea may be more a function of stereotyped expectations than descriptions based on accurate observations. Research suggests that it may not be correct to view hyperkinesis as a general excess of activity. Evidence does indicate that hyperactive children have a higher level of activity than their normal peers in structured settings (which may be descriptive of certain classroom circumstances). However, more unstructured settings (e.g., play settings) seem to result in no differences between hyperactive children and other children (Baxley & LeBlanc, 1976; Whalen & Henker, 1976). This point will emerge again when we examine theories regarding causes of hyperactivity and treatment.

Learning disabilities have also been associated with **perceptual abnormalities.** Such problems have been conspicuous in the historical development of the field of learning disabilities, emerging largely from the early work of Goldstein (1936; 1939) and Werner and Strauss (1939; 1941). Interest in this perspective has declined over the years, although some have continued to place perception difficulties in a prominent position with respect to behavior and causation of learning disabilities (e.g., Cruickshank, 1972).

Perceptual difficulties in learning disabled persons represent a constellation of behavioral abnormalities rather than a single characteristic. Descriptions of these problems have included the visual, auditory, and **haptic** sensory systems (*haptic* referring to touch sensation and information transmitted to the individual through body movement and/or position). Visual-perception difficulties have been the area most associated with learning disabilities. It is important to remember that the classification of learning disabilities excludes impaired vision in the traditional sense. As we examine the visual-perception problems of learning disabled persons, we are discussing something distinctly different. Lerner (1981) described an example of the type of abnormality that we are addressing, and one that would seriously interfere with school performance. In this case the child may view a visual stimulus (such as a letter in the alphabet) in terms of unrelated parts rather than as an integrated pattern. Lerner stated that ''when asked to identify the capital letter 'A,' the child with perceptual disorders may perceive three unrelated lines rather than a meaningful whole'' (1981, p. 30). Clearly such a perception would result in performance problems in the school setting.

Visual perception problems may also emerge in terms of **figure-ground discrimination,** the process of distinguishing an object from its background. Most of us have little difficulty with figure-ground discrimination. However, certain children labeled as learning disabled are unable to accomplish such a task. Children with this type of problem may have difficulty focusing on a word or sentence in a page of a textbook. This would certainly result in difficulties in the school setting. This particular example also presents a good illustration of the theoretical problems in learning disabilities. A given behavior may be interpreted quite differently, depending on the research, theory, or disciplinary perspective being employed. The problem in our example *may* be a disorder of figure-ground discrimination, but it may also be representative of an attention deficit or memory problems. These areas have also been associated with difficulties encountered by learning disabled children. Thus the same abnormal behavior could be accounted for by several theories, and it should be noted that we have mentioned only a few. Confusion is clearly evident in the field of learning disabilities, but we are convinced that continued and more rigorous empirical research will clarify such issues.

Discrimination has also been involved in descriptions of learning disabled persons in areas other than figure-ground discrimination. Difficulties in **visual discrimination** have frequently been associated with learning disabilities. Individuals with such problems may be unable to distinguish one visual stimulus from another (e.g., words such as *sit* and *sat* or letters such as V and W). This may result in the reversal of such letters as *b* and *d*, which has often been noted in learning-disabled children. This type of error is common among young children and often causes great concern for parents, but most children develop normally and show relatively few reversal or rotation errors on visual images by about seven or eight years of age (Gibson, Gibson, Pick & Osser, 1962). The child who "continues to have difficulty and who even makes frequent errors on easily discriminable letters" should be viewed as a potential problem and perhaps given extra help (Hallahan & Kauffman, 1976, p. 81).

We also mentioned that perception problems have been associated with learning disabilities in terms of the auditory sensory system. Some children have been characterized as being unable to distinguish between the sounds of different words or syllables, or even to identify certain environmental sounds (e.g., the telephone) and differentiate those sounds from others. Such problems have been termed **auditory discrimination** deficits. Learning disabled persons have also been described as having difficulties in **auditory blending, auditory memory,** and **auditory association.** Those with blending problems may not be able to blend the parts of a word into an integrated whole as they pronounce it. Auditory-memory difficulties may result in an inability to recall information presented verbally. An auditory-association deficiency may cause the child to be unable to associate ideas or information presented verbally. Difficulties in these areas would create problems for a child with regard to school performance. Once again it is important to remember that children with hearing impairments, in the traditional sense, are excluded in definitions of learning disabilities.

As noted above, haptic perception problems have also been associated with learning disabilities. Such difficulties are thought to be relatively uncommon (Mercer, 1979), but theoretically they may be important in terms of some areas of school performance (Ayres, 1975; Wedell, 1973). For example, haptic perception may be important in handwriting, because tactile information is transmitted regarding the grasp of a pen or pencil. In addition, **kinesthetic** information is transmitted in terms of the movements of the hand and arm as one writes. Learning-disabled children have often been described by their teachers as having poor handwriting, with difficulties in spacing letters and staying on the lines of a piece of paper. (However, such problems could also be due to visual-perception abnormalities—another example of theoretical differences, confusion, and a lack of empirical evidence in the field of learning disabilities.)

It should be emphasized that not all individuals labeled as having learning disabilities exhibit behaviors suggesting perceptual problems. Widely varying configurations of deficits seem to be evident among individuals identified as learning disabled. We should also mention the relative lack of empirical evidence regarding perceptual problems in those labeled as learning disabled. In many cases the notion of "perceptual dysfunction" is represented more by clinical descriptions of teachers and other clinicians than by rigorous research. However, such "clinical lore" (Bryan, 1974) is widespread enough that it must be discussed in the learning disabilities area.

Many other characteristics have been attributed to the learning disabled. For example, teachers have long complained about poor memory in such children. In many cases the children seem to learn material on one day but cannot recall it the next day. Research on the memory of learning-disabled children has been scanty and the results have been inconclusive. Some evidence suggests that the learning disabled perform more poorly than normal children on memory tasks (e.g., Bauer, 1977), whereas other results indicate no differences (Swanson, 1979). Research in this area too needs increased effort to confirm, refute, or clarify clinical impressions.

Attention problems have also been prominently associated with learning disabilities. Such problems have most often been clinically characterized in terms of a short attention span. Parents and teachers frequently note that their learning-disabled children cannot sustain attention more than a very short time. Some evidence has supported the observation of a short attention span with these children (e.g., Sykes, Douglas & Morgenstern, 1973), but other research indicates that learning disabled children encounter difficulties in attending *selectively* (Hallahan, Kauffman & Ball, 1973; Pelham & Ross, 1977; Tarver, Hallahan, Kauffman & Ball, 1976). This type of problem results in an inability to focus on the task or information that is centrally important rather than that which is peripheral or irrelevant.

We have described several behavioral characteristics that have been attributed to individuals labeled as learning disabled. It is increasingly evident that learning disabilities represent a very heterogeneous set of problems and that many different specific syndromes are involved under this general label. We have examined some of the characteristics associated with learning disabilities, although we have provided only a selective overview.

Causation. Over the years, learning disabilities have generally been viewed as being caused by **neurological** damage or at least neurological abnormalities of some type. A large segment of the professionals within this field support this contention (Adelman, 1979; Gaddes, 1980; Hallahan & Cruickshank, 1973; Reid & Hresko, 1981; Wacker, 1982). Neurological involvement has even been specified as an identification criteria in numerous research studies focusing on learning disabilities (Kavale & Nye, 1981).

A variety of factors may result in neurological damage such as that associated with learning disabilities. Part of what was discussed in relation to mental retardation becomes relevant here as well. For example, damage may be inflicted on the neurological system at birth in a number of ways (such as abnormal fetal positioning during delivery or **anoxia.**) Infections might also result in neurological damage and learning disabilities. (Several such problems are examined in Chapter 6.) It must be remembered that neurological damage, as a cause of learning disabilities, must be largely inferred, since direct evidence is usually not available.

Genetic causation has also been implicated in the causation of learning disabilities. This is always a concern for parents with regard to all types of learning and behavior disorders. Some evidence is available that would suggest genetic influences. However, it is important to remember the uncertain empirical foundation regarding the entire field of learning disabilities. Most likely we are examining many different specific problems with multiple causes. Some researchers have obtained results that suggest a genetic linkage (e.g., Hallgren, 1950; Hermann, 1959). These findings must be interpreted cautiously, because of the well-known difficulties in separating the influences of heredity and environment (Gelfand et al., 1982). Environmental influences are often mentioned as a possible cause of learning disabilities. Such factors as diet inadequacies, food additives, radiation stress, fluorescent lighting, unshielded television tubes, smoking, drinking, and drug consumption are now only beginning to be investigated as possible links to learning disabilities. Research results in these areas remain inconclusive.

Prevalence. The problems of determining accurate figures regarding prevalence are exacerbated by the variety of definitions, theoretical views, and assessment procedures employed in learning disabilities. Wallace & McLoughlin (1979) have cited estimates ranging from 1 to 28 percent. The National Advisory Committee on Handicapped Children estimated that between 1 and 3 percent of all schoolchildren are learning disabled (1968).

The relative absence of empirical evidence is a problem that further compounds the difficulties in determining the prevalence of learning disabilities. Studies aimed at gathering such data have not been conducted in learning disabilities to the same degree that they have in other disorders (Bruininks, Glaman & Clark, 1971). However, some data have been collected. For example, Meier (1971) studied over three thousand second-grade children in the Rocky Mountain area and derived an estimated 15 percent prevalence figure. Myklebust and Boshes (1969) also conducted an investigation in which 2,767 schoolchildren were screened to identify underachievers. Their data indicated that 15 percent of this population could be considered underachievers, based on a learning quotient of 89 or below. However, when exclusionary criteria were applied to the underachievers (i.e., children with no serious deficits in emotional adjustment, vision, hearing, intelligence, or motor ability) half the group could not be classified as learning disabled (Myklebust, Bannochie & Killen, 1971). Thus these data resulted in 7.5 percent of the original sample being identified as learning disabled.

INTERVENTION STRATEGIES

There are several approaches to the treatment and education of individuals with moderate learning and behavior disorders. In the field of medicine, it is the role of the physician to diagnose abnormal or delayed development in the areas of language and behavior as well as motor functions. Richmond and Walzer (1973) viewed the pediatrician as responsible for diagnosing physical handicaps that may significantly affect learning and behavior; for interpreting medical findings to the family and other professionals; for referring the family to specialists when a child's condition exceeds the physician's knowledge base; and for specifying medical therapy for physical or emotional disorders.

An example of therapeutic intervention may be illustrated in the area of hyperactivity. On the surface, hyperactivity would lead one to believe that such children are overly aroused, that is, may be suffering from a greater-than-normal physiological arousal. Such notions led many to recommend instructional environments that had few distracting stimuli (i.e., "low-stimulus" or "stimulus-free" settings). However, one treatment often employed with hyperactive individuals presented some logical dilemmas for the overarousal theory. It has been common practice for many years to administer medication as a means of controlling hyperactivity. One type of medication often used is from the amphetamine family (frequently Ritalin). Amphetamines are known to increase activity in most people, yet they seem to decrease activity in hyperactive children. Thus the theoretical dilemma regarding arousal for such individuals presents itself (and adds to the mystique regarding these children).

More current thinking with respect to hyperactivity may provide the missing logic in terms of reactions to amphetamines. Some literature has suggested that hyperactive individuals may be plagued by abnormally *low* physiological arousal rather than being overly aroused (Satterfield & Dawson, 1971; Zentall, 1975). It has been hypothesized that the apparent high level of motor activity in hyperkinetic individuals may be "an attempt on the part of the patient to increase his **proprioceptive**" stimulation (Satterfield & Dawson, 1971, p. 196). Such a notion would explain the higher level of activity in certain circumstances, plus the apparent quieting effect of amphetamines. Hyperactive children may be receiving adequate stimulation on the playground but not in a structured instructional setting (which would be in concert with empirical evidence presented earlier). Further, such a theory would more logically explain the effect of amphetamines on hyperactive children. If amphetamines raise arousal in such individuals (as they do with most of us), they might not require extraordinary activity for an adequate level of stimulation. Future research is crucial in this area, because so much still remains unknown regarding medications and learning or behavior problems. For example, exactly which drug will be effective is seldom known until after treatment has begun. Wender stated, "It is impossible to predict beforehand to which medication a child will best respond." He further noted, "It may be necessary to try several drugs before the best one is found" (1973, p. 59). In addition, research has recently suggested that drug treatment may *not* result in academic improvement in the learning disabled (Rie, Rie, Stewart & Ambuel, 1976a, 1976b).

The physician's role in the intervention process extends far beyond drug therapy. As a care-giver, the physician is involved in physical management of the individual in terms of routine physical care, surgery, and treatment. Medical therapy, as a treatment alternative, can take many forms in addition to medication. These may include nutritional or dietary programs, dental services, and physical, occupational, or speech therapy. An example of dietary intervention may be found in the control of the disorder known as **phenylketonuria (PKU).** In this case the physician is involved in preventing or diminishing damage to the child by controlling the child's diet. PKU is a metabolic disorder where the infant cannot properly process phenylalanine, a substance prominent in milk. PKU can be diagnosed medically early, and mental retardation can actually be prevented if treatment is initiated within a few days after birth. Intervention involves a carefully controlled diet that restricts the phenylalanine content of what is ingested. If PKU remains untreated, the resulting mental retardation may be quite severe.

The educational needs of individuals with moderate learning and behavior warrant a more restricted instructional environment in comparison to mildly disordered populations. Students with moderate learning and behavior disorders will spend the majority, if not all, of their school lives in a special education classroom. (See Chapter 2, page 57, delivery-system levels IV and V.) This classroom provides students with a teacher specially trained to meet their needs, a smaller pupil-teacher ratio that enhances individualized instruction, and specialized materials and equipment. Much of what was discussed in Chapter 4 regarding instructional decision-making has relevance for the moderately disordered population. The teaching process does not change for this student, but there may be a stronger emphasis on remedial or functional/compensatory skills (see page 110) and social interaction training. Consequently, the role of the special education teacher is one of direct, primary service to students across a variety of subject areas. As a member of the educational team, the teacher is responsible for (1) identifying students whose needs dictate placement in a more structured educational environment; (2) consulting with other professionals in the development of goals and strategies to meet individual needs; (3) implementing a comprehensive educational program through the use of appropriate methods and materials; (4) continually evaluating the effectiveness of the educational program; and (5) modifying instructional approaches when necessary.

ȷ̂ SUMMARY

The traditional categories of mental retardation, learning disabilities, and behavior disorders are more distinct at the moderate severity level. People with mental retardation exhibit significant deficits in intellectual functioning and adaptive behavior skills. This population will have difficulty acquiring skills in reading and mathematics, but they are capable of achieving some mastery of these tool subjects. Research with mentally retarded individuals has suggested that their memory capabilities are deficient in comparison to the norm; they do not benefit as well from incidental cues in the environment; and they have inadequate transfer skills. Mentally retarded individuals may have lower self-images and therefore experience more problems establishing and maintaining positive peer relationships. The etiology of moderate mental retardation is not generally identifiable, although there is a positive relationship with lower socioeconomic status and differing cultural backgrounds.

Individuals with behavior disorders respond to their environment in socially unacceptable ways. Behavior problems may be identified as conduct disorders, personality disorders, and disorders associated with immaturity and inadequacy. Conduct disorders are characterized by disobedience, destructive tendencies, and temper tantrums. Personality disorders are characterized by overanxiousness, shyness, self-conscious behavior, and sadness. The category of immaturity and inadequacy includes such behaviors as clumsiness, social inadequacy, and low tolerance for frustration. Behavior problems at the moderate level of severity are generally excessive, disruptive, and inappropriate. They deviate substantially from those of normal peers. These problem behaviors interfere with the individual's ability to adapt to the home, school, or community environment. In general, this population is characterized as hyperactive, distractible, impulsive, aggressive, withdrawn, immature, inadequate, and deficient in moral development. Several techniques may be employed to identify behavior disorders. These include analysis of interactions with peers and adults; administration of personality, achievement, and intelligence tests; and interviews with child, family, and friends. The etiology of behavior disorders may be explained from a variety of theoretical frameworks. These explanations range from subconscious phenomena or early-childhood traumatic experiences, to biochemical imbalances, brain abnormalities, chromosomal irregularity, and observable environmental influences.

Intervention strategies for individuals with moderate behavior disorders often involve the physician and the prescription of medical therapy. This therapy may include the use of drugs, nutritional or dietary programs, dental services, and physical, occupational, or speech therapy. Educational intervention will require a more restricted educational placement and a special education teacher. This teacher, in conjunction with an educational team, is responsible for developing goals and instructional strategies to meet individual needs, implement the educational program, evaluate the program's effectiveness, and modify instructional approaches when necessary.

Learning disabilities is conceptualized in a variety of ways, depending on the theoretical perspective of the professional. The divergent views associated with this area have led to the use of inconsistent terminology and definitional structures. More recently, learning disabilities has been described as a generic term that represents a collection of heterogeneous disorders. Individuals with learning disabilities are characterized as having difficulty learning the basic tool subjects of reading, writing, and arithmetic. They are unable to receive auditory information or to express their thoughts in a way conducive to learning and retention. Other behavioral characteristics associated with learning disabilities include hyperactivity, perceptual abnormalities (of the visual, auditory, and haptic systems), and attentional problems. Individuals with learning disabilities may be described as exhibiting uneven development in the learning of skills areas. Children with learning disabilities may exhibit no problems learning skills in some areas but have marked disabilities in others. This population is also described as functioning substantially below their potential. There is a discrepancy between their ability as measured by a test of intelligence and their actual grade achievement. This discrepancy can be quantified in a number of ways, including grade-level deviations, expectancy formulas, standard-score comparisons, and regression analysis. The etiology of learning disabilities is often associated with some type of neurological abnormality. Neurological damage may be the result of such factors as genetic influence, infections, drugs, diet, smoking, or drinking, to name but a few. These factors are largely inferred, since direct evidence is not available.

REVIEW QUESTIONS

1. Discuss why the characteristics associated with traditional categories become more relevant with moderate learning and behavior disorders than with mild ones.
2. Compare the generic classification of moderate mental retardation with that of the AAMD in terms of symptom severity.
3. How could Kauffman's eight descriptive categories for behavior disorders serve as parameters of classification intersecting with symptom severity? How would this configuration appear if drawn like the parameter graphic in Figure 3-1 (page 75)?
4. Describe how the notion of uneven development in learning disabilities has been assessed in language.
5. Describe how one can quantify a moderate learning disability in terms of discrepancy in academic potential.
6. How do the intervention strategies and settings for moderate learning and behavior disorders differ from those for mild disorders?

CHAPTER SIX

Severe and Profound/ Multiple Disorders

Definitions and Classification Systems
    Categorical Descriptors
    Generic Definitions
    Causation
    Prevalence

Intervention Strategies
    Medical Services
    Social/Psychological Services
    Educational Services

People with severe and profound/multiple disorders may be impaired in nearly every facet of life. Some of these people will have severe intellectual, learning, and behavior disorders, others are physically disabled or sensory impaired. Most have disorders that transcend our ideas of single-handicapping categories; they have significant multiple problems. The needs of these people cannot be met by one profession. The nature of these disorders extends equally into the fields of medicine, psychology, and education. Since this population exhibits such diverse characteristics and involves several professional perspectives, it is not surprising that numerous definitions and intervention strategies have been employed to describe and treat these individuals.

Tony is nineteen years old, lives at home, and is dependent on his parents. His days are spent working in a sheltered vocational training program, where clients perform a number of vocationally related functions. Tony assembles small toys for a local company and is being trained to operate power tools for wood- and metal-cutting tasks. The pay he receives is minimal, and at present it is doubtful that Tony will ever contribute substantially to his own support. He will likely be dependent on either his family or society for some financial assistance. Tony is capable of caring for his own physical needs. He has learned to dress and feed himself. He understands the importance of personal grooming and has acquired appropriate hygiene skills. He is able to communicate many of his needs and wants verbally but is limited in his social language abilities. Tony has never learned to read, and his leisure hours are spent watching television or listening to the radio. He has virtually no social life outside the family unit.

Becky is a six-year-old who has significant delays in her intellectual, language, and motor development. These problems have been evident from birth. Her mother experienced a long, unusually difficult labor,

Tony

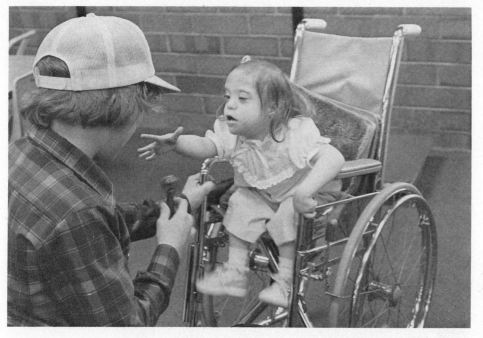

Becky

and Becky endured severe heart-rate dips (at times her heart rate was undetectable). During delivery, Becky suffered from birth asphyxiation and epileptic seizures. The attending physician described her as flacid (soft and limp) with abnormal muscle reflexes. Becky has not yet learned to walk, is not toilet trained, and has no means of communication with others in her environment. She lives at home and attends a special school during the day. Her educational program includes work with therapists to develop her gross motor abilities in order to enhance her mobility. Speech and language specialists are examining the possibility of teaching several alternative forms of communication (e.g., language boards, or manual or signing communication systems), because Becky has not developed any verbal skills. The special education staff is focusing on decreasing Becky's dependence on others by teaching some basic self-care skills such as feeding, toileting, and grooming. The medical and educational prognosis for Becky is unknown. The professional staff does not know what the ultimate long-term impact of this intervention will be, but they do know that Becky is learning.

Carl sits alone in his bedroom and stares blankly into space. As others move in and out, Carl does not speak to them or even acknowledge their presence. If any attempt is made by others to rearrange his environment, he may become hostile and seek to preserve the status quo; he will not tolerate any changes in his daily routine. Carl spends his time rocking back and forth while manipulating objects with his hands.

Carl

*He is thirty-one years old and has been in the hospital receiving ther-
apy for the past sixteen years.*

The above cases depict some of the characteristics associated with severe
and profound/multiple disorders. A generic definition of this area of exceptionality may be found in Chapter 3, page 88. The intent of this definition is
to provide a general framework for understanding the magnitude of disorders
exhibited by these individuals. While generic descriptors of this population
are being advocated by many professionals, some still prefer the categorical
approach (see Chapter 3, pages 83–84). We will examine descriptors from the
categorical perspective and the generic perspective.

DEFINITIONS AND CLASSIFICATION SYSTEMS

Categorical Descriptors

Mental Retardation.* Historically, definitions of severe and profound mental
retardation have been pejorative and nonfunctional. Many definitions

*The mentally regarded population discussed in this section includes those people classified by
the AAMD as moderately retarded, and by the educational system as trainable mentally retarded. A rationale for classification may be found in Chapter 5, page

emphasized routine care and maintenance rather than treatment and education. However, recent legislation (e.g., P.L. 94-142) and litigation (e.g., *Wyatt v. Stickney*) have opened new doors for mentally retarded people and put pressure on the professions to develop and implement treatment aimed at improving the quality of their lives.

An examination of the characteristics of individuals with severe and profound retardation reveals the significant nature of these disorders. The higher-functioning individuals within this classification are capable of developing skills that will allow some independence within their physical environment. These self-help skills include the ability to dress and feed themselves, to care for their personal health and grooming needs (e.g., toileting), and to develop safety habits that will allow them to move safely throughout their environment. These people have some means of communication. Most can develop verbal language skills, but some may be able to learn only manual communication. Their social-interaction skills are limited, however, making it difficult for them to relate spontaneously to others.

Contrast the above characteristics with those of the lowest functioning group in this classification, and the diverse nature of the population becomes clear. These individuals are dependent on others to maintain even their most basic life functions (e.g., feeding, toileting, dressing). They are incapable of self-maintenance and seldom develop functional communication skills. The significance of their disorders may require a lifetime of complete supervision, whether it be in a special-care facility (e.g., institution, nursing home, care center) or at home. In terms of treatment or educational intervention, the only thing we can realistically say about this group is that the long-term prognosis for habilitation is unknown. This does not mean that treatment beyond routine care and maintenance will not be fruitful. It simply means that, at present, we do not know. The extreme nature of these handicaps was the primary reason education excluded such individuals from the public schools for so long. Mori and Masters (1980) indicated that exclusion could be justified "on the basis of lack of resources, lack of facilities, and lack of trained personnel to provide an adequate educational experience for this population" (p. 17). Given the present emphasis on research and alternative intervention approaches with this population, the future may hold some answers and bring about a different outlook for these people.

We have briefly reviewed the general characteristics of two extreme groups within the classification of severe and profound mental retardation. Between these two extremes are persons who exhibit a wide range of physical, sensory, and social characteristics. Table 6-1 illustrates the range of characteristics based on an individual's deviation from the norm on a standardized test of intelligence.

Behavior Disorders. Persons who exhibit severe behavior disorders are often described as psychotic, crazy, or insane. *Psychotic* is a general term. It may be used to refer to any number of severe maladaptive behaviors or clusters of behaviors. In contrast, the terms **schizophrenic** and **sociopathic** refer to conditions that are subcategories of severe behavior disorders.

Table 6-1/ Physical, Sensory, and Social Characteristics of Individuals with Severe and Profound Mental Retardation

Characteristics	*Intellectual Deviation from the Norm[a]* (Amt. Below Mean on Standardized Test of Intelligence)		
	3 SDs	*4 SDs*	*5 SDs*
Physical Development			
Motor	—Gross and fine motor coordination is usually deficient. However, the individual is usually ambulatory and capable of independent mobility. —Perceptual-motor skills do exist, but are often deficient in comparison to norm (e.g., body awareness, sense of touch, eye-hand coordination).	—As many as 80% have significant motor difficulties (i.e., poor or non-ambulatory skills). Gross or fine motor skills may be present, but the individual may lack control, resulting in awkward or inept motor movement.	—Some gross motor development is evident, but fine motor skills are inept. —Individuals are usually nonambulatory and are not capable of independent mobility within the environment. —Perceptual-motor skills are often nonexistent.
Sensory	—The greater the intellectual deviation, the higher the incidence of compounding sensory losses (i.e., vision and hearing impairments). Individuals functioning from four to five SDs below the mean will generally exhibit multiple physical aberrations.		
Social characteristics			
Communication	—Most individuals are deficient in speech and language skills, but many develop language abilities that allow them some level of communication with others.	—Without exception, individuals will exhibit significant speech and language delays and deviations (e.g., lack of expressive and receptive language, poor articulation, and little, if any, spontaneous interaction).	—Individuals will not exhibit spontaneous communication patterns. Bizzare speech may be evident (e.g., echolalic speech, speech out of context [purposeless speech]). —Language abilities are grossly inadequate.
Self-help	—Individuals may lack self-help skills, but are capable of acquiring survival skills that will enhance their independence within the environment (e.g., feeding, toilet-training,	—Individuals lack basic self-help, survival skills. Habilitation is possible for very basic skills (e.g., feeding, toileting). However, many will remain somewhat dependent on others for	—Individuals will generally not profit from self-care training, except in very low-level skill areas (e.g., developmental skills for children under 6 months of age). —Individuals will

Table 6-1 (Continued)

151

Severe and
Profound/
Multiple
Disorders

Characteristics	Intellectual Deviation from the Norm[a] (Amt. Below Mean on Standardized Test of Intelligence)		
	3 SDs	*4 SDs*	*5 SDs*
	dressing, personal hygiene, functional academics [reading, arithmetic]).	everyday needs. —Individuals are generally not capable of learning functional academic skills.	require total care for a lifetime.

[a] The extreme nature of the disorders makes it difficult to measure IQ for individuals at the lower level of the intellectual continuum. Therefore the reader should be cautioned that IQ levels are only approximations, because many of these individuals are untestable on standardized measures of intelligence.

Individuals with severe behavior disorders behave in ways that are truly unusual and different. Moreover, the frequency of their problematic behaviors is also inordinately high. For example, a child may spend literally hours repetitively spinning an ashtray and watching it each time as it comes to rest on the floor. In addition, tremendous energy may be expended moving the hands rapidly in front of his or her face. Such self-stimulating behaviors greatly interfere with language and social development.

Various attempts have been made to define the nature of severe behavior disorders. Stainback and Stainback (1980) contrasted the characteristics of the mildly and severely disordered according to various definitional components (see Table 6-2). As illustrated in Table 6-2, severely disordered children differ significantly from the mildy disordered in a variety of intellectual, social, academic, and behavioral domains.

In some related research, Olson, Algozzine, and Schmid (1980) conducted a survey to determine the perceptions of teachers of behavior disordered children regarding the descriptors mild, moderate, and severe behavior disorders. The following statements regarding seriously disturbed children reflect the views of the majority surveyed:

1. A residential center is the best placement for most of these children.
2. These children are often classified as **autistic** or schizophrenic.
3. These children usually show no social interest in relating to others.
4. These children are most often multi-handicapped.
5. The problems of this group of children are more likely to be genetically or organically based. (Olson et al., p. 100)

The *Diagnostic and Statistical Manual* (DSM III, 1980) of the American Psychiatric Association identified several categories of adult, adolescent, and childhood disorders. Only the category *pervasive developmental disorders* refers directly to childhood conditions. Subsumed under this category are the conditions known as infantile autism and childhood onset pervasive developmental disorder. We will examine these two conditions in some detail.

Table 6-2/ Characteristics of Children Who Exhibit Maladaptive Behavior

Definition	Mildly Disturbed	Severely Disturbed	Comment
Intellectual or cognitive ability: as measured by a standardized intelligence test.	Average IQ score in low-normal or dull-normal range.	Average IQ in mentally retarded range.	Actual range for both groups is from retarded to gifted.
Achievement: as measured by achievement test scores predominately in reading and arithmetic.	Generally achieve at a lower level than their IQ level would imply. Children classified as conduct disordered or delinquents further behind than other categories.	Markedly deficient in academic areas. Generally function at basic levels in language, toileting, eating, rudimentary reading and math.	Both levels range the spectrum, but most are generally below average. Any seriously disturbed high achievers are usually erratic in responding.
Underselectivity: difficulty focusing on relevant stimuli and screening out irrelevant stimuli. *Overselectivity:* attention to limited aspects of a task, lacks ability to zero out.	Difficulty focusing on task at hand. Tend to be underselective.	Tend to be overselective. Often exhibit "gaze aversion," will not make or maintain eye contact.	Both levels as a group have attending problems; however, research indicates that the type of attending problem may be different depending on the seriousness of the emotional disturbance.
Hyperactivity: inability to modulate motor behavior in accordance with the demands of a situation. *Impulsivity:* quick, almost instantaneous response to stimulation.	Frequently exhibit hyperactivity and impulsivity.	Frequently exhibit hyperactivity and impulsivity.	Reflectivity, the tendency to look, think, and consider alternatives, is the reverse of impulsivity.
Withdrawal: includes withdrawal from human contact and/or general overall withdrawal of interest in the environment.	May consistently refrain from initiating conversation, refrain from play with others, or exhibit lack of concern or interest in the environment—shy, immature, wallflower, but not oblivious to surroundings.	May lack contact with reality and subsequently develop own world—often called autistic, schizophrenic, psychotic.	Depression is sometimes associated with withdrawal.
Physical aggression: destructive actions against self and other people and things. *Verbal aggression:* Includes yelling, cursing,	May be obnoxious, negative, oppositional, and/or generally nasty. Generally *not* violent, brutal, destructive, assaultive, or physically	May frequently, consistently over a long period of time, display aggressive behaviors of a serious nature.	"Normal" children also display aggressive behaviors, but usually less onerous and at a lower rate.

Table 6-2 (Continued)

Definition	Mildly Disturbed	Severely Disturbed	Comment
abusive language, threats and self-destructive statements.	damaging to others and self.		
Helplessness: does not appear to be interested in trying to do anything, does not set goals for self, often does not respond to assigned tasks.	May exhibit lack of joy and interest in life, fail to perform tasks previously exhibited, unwillingness to try, tends to give up quickly.	May be highly dependent, pessimistic, and suicidal; may be unable to perform basic life skills.	Teacher's task is to provide appropriate training that is based on the level the child is actually functioning.

Source: Reprinted, by permission of the authors and the publisher, from S. Stainback and W. Stainback, *Educating Children with Severe Maladaptive Behaviors* (New York: Grune & Stratton, 1980), pp. 26-27.

Autism, * as first introduced in the literature, referred to patients characterized by social withdrawal (Bleuler, 1911). Kanner (1943) expanded the definition to include several dimensions: (1) speech and language deficits, (2) a compulsion for maintaining sameness in various environmental settings, (3) bizarre repetitive motility patterns (e.g., flapping an ear, visual stimulation by rapid finger movement in front of the eyes), (4) intellectual discontinuity (islands of precocity accompanied by intellectual and adaptive retardation), and (5) severe problems in relating to others during spontaneous play. The diagnostic criteria for infantile autism presented in DSM III include (1) onset before thirty months of age, (2) lack of responsiveness to others, (3) gross deficits or deviations in language development (e.g., **echolalia**), (4) bizarre responses to various aspects of the environment, and (5) the absence of delusions, hallucinations, or incoherence. The long-term prognosis for individuals with autism is generally not positive. "One child in six makes an adequate social adjustment and is able to do some kind of regular work by adulthood; another one in six makes only fair adjustment; and two-thirds remain severely handicapped and unable to lead independent lives" (DSM III, 1980, p. 88).

Childhood onset pervasive developmental disorder is characterized by (1) gross impairment in social relationships, (2) sudden and excessive anxiety, (3) poor affect, (4) resistance to environmental change, (5) oddities of motor movement, (6) abnormal speech, (7) sensitivity to sensory stimuli, (8) self-mutilation, and (9) the absence of delusions and hallucinations (DSM III). This disorder is closely related to infantile autism. The primary difference between the two conditions is age of occurrence. The age of onset for this condition is after thirty months and before 12 years.

Another classification within DSM III is schizophrenic disorders. **Schizophrenia** is characterized by disturbances in thought, mood, and behavior. Persons with schizophrenia appear to be in their own fantasy world. They are not

---

*Although we discuss autism under the general category of behavior disorders, you should be aware that the National Society for Autistic Children views autism as a condition separate from severe emotional disturbance. It describes autism as a physiologically based brain or neurological disorder that results in severe learning problems.

interested in the usual activities that individuals of a comparable age would pursue. Their moods range from sheer excitement to utter apathy. Speech is likely to be limited and to reveal thinking that is incoherent. One of the most distinguishing characteristics of schizophrenia is the presence of hallucinations. These individuals may hear voices and/or experience delusions that are unrealistic. The DSM III diagnostic criteria for schizophrenic disorders include bizarre delusions without any basis in fact; persecutory, religious, somatic, or grandiose delusions; auditory hallucinations (hearing voices); incoherence; illogical thinking; and inappropriate speech. There is an overall deterioration in work, social relations, and self-care.

Learning Disabilities. Although there have been recent attempts to couch learning disabilities within the symptom-severity parameter for classification (National Joint Committee, 1981), there is still no clear distinction between mild, moderate, and severe disorders. The notion of learning disabilities as a moderate to severe disorder is discussed in Chapter 5, pages 131–141.

Multiple Disorders. The vast majority of persons with severe and profound disorders exhibit multiple problems. The nature of these problems may include a combination of any one or more of the several categories of exceptionality. However, mental retardation is a primary symptom in the greatest number of cases. Persons with profound retardation invariably suffer from significant physical and psychological disorders in addition to subaverage intellectual functioning (Hardman & Drew, 1977; Swanson & Willis, 1979; Van Etten, Arkell & Van Etten, 1980). Severely and profoundly retarded persons have a higher incidence of congenital heart disease, epilepsy, respiratory problems, diabetes, and metabolic disorders. They exhibit poor muscle tone and are often plagued with such conditions as spasticity, athetosis, and hypotonia (Mori & Masters, 1980). These people may also be inflicted with sensory impairments, including vision and hearing disorders.

The relationship between severe retardation and emotional disturbance has not been understood as clearly as that between retardation and physical disorders. In fact, there has been a great deal of confusion concerning the overlapping characteristics of these supposedly different populations. Characteristics of severely emotionally disturbed persons appear to be closely related to those of individuals with severe and profound retardation, but by definition the severely disturbed are not truly retarded. However, several studies have indicated that a significant relationship does exist (Bartak & Rutter, 1973; Lovaas, Koegel, Simmons & Long, 1973). Kauffman (1977), citing these investigations, explained:

> With the past several years data have been accumulated to indicate that IQs of most autistic and other psychotic children can be reliably and validly tested and that the majority of such children score in the moderately to mildly retarded range of intelligence. . . . Some psychotic children will have tested IQs in the severely to profoundly retarded

range, and a small number will achieve normal or above IQ scores. (P. 119)

There are also multiple disorders where mental retardation is not a primary symptom. One such disorder is deaf-blindness. The concomitant vision and hearing disorders exhibited by deaf-blind people result in severe communication deficits as well as developmental and educational difficulties. These multiple problems preclude placement in single-category programs for either the deaf or the blind and necessitate accommodation in highly specialized service centers.

As previously suggested, severe multiple disorders can include any combination of physical, psychological, intellectual, or sensory disorders. Some combinations are more prevalent than others, but there is an incidence of all combinations. The great number of possible combinations has presented some difficult labeling issues for professionals concerned with providing appropriate treatment programs for this heterogeneous population. Van Etten, Arkell, and Van Etten (1980) indicated:

> The variety of labels that have been used to designate the child with two or more severe disabilities has become a source of confusion to educators, resulting in complications in the planning and organization of special education programs. In particular, initial classification of such children has been especially troublesome to the schools. How, for example, should a child be labeled who is deaf, blind and functioning as mentally retarded? Where should such a child be placed educationally where there are special programs in each area? (P. 26)

Generic Definitions

Definitions based on a generic structure utilize the symptom-severity classification parameter (see page 73). The terms used to describe the population include *severely handicapped, profoundly handicapped,* or *severely multiply handicapped.* Note, however, that few generic definitions distinguish between severe and profound conditions. Justen and Brown (1977) conducted a survey of state departments of education and reported that there is little consensus on the distinction between definitions of severe and profound conditions. These conditions are often treated as a single category within the educational system.

Generic definitions of the severely handicapped may be based on a description of behavioral characteristics and/or the instructional needs of the individual. We will first examine those definitions that describe primarily behavioral characteristics. Sontag, Burke, and York (1973) developed a clear behavioral definition of the severely handicapped:

> Are not toilet trained; aggress toward others; do not attend to even the most pronounced social stimuli; self mutilate; ruminate; self stimulate; do not walk, speak, hear, or see; manifest durable and in-

tense temper tantrums; are not under even the rudimentary forms of
verbal control; do not imitate; manifest minimally controlled seizures;
and/or have extremely brittle medical existences. (P. 21)

Behavioral descriptors are also a major component of the definition formulated
by the U.S. Office of Education (1974):

Severely handicapped children may possess severe language or
perceptual-cognitive deprivations and evidence a number of abnormal
behaviors including failure to attend to even the most pronounced
social stimuli, self-mutilation, self-stimulation, manifestation of durable
and intense temper tantrums, and the absence of even the most rudimentary forms of verbal control. They may also have an extremely fragile physiological condition. (USOE, 1974, Section 121.2)

Although the above definitions attempt to describe the specific characteristics of the severely handicapped, they may be too precise. Professionals
will encounter problems of excessive inclusion or exclusion in attempting to
place children in educational programs if they employ these behaviorally oriented definitions. What if the child exhibits some, but not all, of the behavioral
characteristics used in the definition? For example, should a child be excluded
from programs for the severely handicapped because he or she self-stimulates,
ruminates, and is unable to walk but is toilet trained? Along the same line,
should a child be included within the category who is not toilet trained but
does walk, has developed limited communication, and socialization skills?

The second approach to defining the severely handicapped is to develop
the definition around the instructional needs of the student. Haring (1978)
proposed that definitions of the severely handicapped concentrate more on
instructional need and less on general, often stereotyped, population characteristics. "Basically, a person is severely handicapped if he cannot do even the
simplest things that other people can do and if excessive inappropriate behaviors interfere with his acceptance and functioning" (Haring, 1978, p. 199).
Brown and York (1974) presented a similar definition:

If students do not speak, follow directions, play with peers, control
their own behaviors, etc. they are severely handicapped in their ability
to function in society and need to be taught such skills. (P. 4)

Wilcox (1979) also supported a stronger emphasis on instructional need and
suggested that these definitions refer to an absolute level of functioning. "Definitions which reference absolute functioning levels, though admittedly arbitrary, do carry reasonable information regarding the probable content of
instruction and do allow for the removal of the label 'severely handicapped'
based on demonstrated student progress: as students acquire more skills, they
lose the label" (Wilcox, 1979, p. 139). The emphasis is on identifying severely
handicapped children on the basis of their developmental competence in comparison with normal children of a lower chronological age.

The multitude of characteristics exhibited by people with severe and profound disorders is mirrored by the numerous definitions associated with this population. A close analysis of definitional structures reveals a great deal of redundancy from one definition to another; all describe a population whose life needs cannot be met without substantial assistance from society. This population has been, and is likely to continue to be, dependent in some fashion on social support systems for a lifetime.

Causation

Multiple problems result from multiple causes. For the vast majority of this population, the problems are evident at birth. Birth defects may be the result of genetic or metabolic disorders, including chromosomal abnormalities, phenylketonuria, or **Rh incompatibility.** Birth defects may also be caused by drugs, smoking, or alcohol-related problems; poor maternal nutrition; infectious diseases (e.g., rubella); radiation exposure; venereal disease; or advanced maternal age. Severe and profound disorders can also be the result of factors that occur later in life, such as poisoning, accidents, malnutrition, physical and emotional neglect, and disease.

As the framework for our discussion on causes of severe and profound disorders, we will use the etiological classification system adopted by the American Association on Mental Deficiency (AAMD) (see Chapter 3, page 76). Although this system primarily addresses causes of mental retardation, it has specific relevance to the multiple factors associated with severe and profound disorders. This section will focus on categories 1 through 8 of the AAMD scheme. We will include an analysis of several conditions that do not necessarily result in severe or profound disorders (e.g., **Down's syndrome, hydrocephalus,** phenylketonuria). These conditions are presented in this chapter for discussion purposes only; they may *or may not* result in a severe or profound disorder. For example, persons with Down's syndrome, discussed in this section under chromosomal abnormalities, have measured intelligence ranging from near normal to profound retardation. Most persons with Down's syndrome have an intelligence quotient in the range of 40 to 65 (approximately two to four standard deviations below the mean on a test of general intelligence).

Our first etiological category involves infection and intoxication. Several types of maternal infections may result in fetal difficulties. In some cases the outcome is spontaneous abortion, in others it may be moderate or even severe defects in the baby. The probability of damage is particularly high if the infection occurs during the first three months of pregnancy, although defects of a less severe nature may result from maternal infection occurring later in the gestation period. Congenital rubella (German measles) is the type of infection that is perhaps most widely known. Rubella is a viral infection that causes a variety of problems, especially if the mother contracts the infection during the first trimester of pregnancy. Deafness is the most frequent outcome of congenital rubella. Other difficulties include mental retardation, blindness, cerebral palsy, cardiac problems, and seizures, as well as a variety of other neurological problems. Rubella represents a significant cause of mental retardation. Approximately 50 percent of the unborn babies will be affected if the mother contracts rubella during the first trimester (Cooper & Krugman, 1966).

Another infection associated with severe disorders is syphilis. Syphilis is caused by bacteria transmitted through sexual contact, and maternal infection with syphilis may cause serious problems for the fetus. The fetus is particularly likely to be affected if the maternal syphilis infection continues beyond the eighteenth week of pregnancy. (Successful treatment *may* prevent serious damage if it is implemented prior to the eighteenth week.) With syphilis, bacteria actually cross the placenta and infect the fetus. This results in damage to the tissue of the central nervous system as well as to the circulatory system. Congenital syphilis may result in spontaneous abortion or stillbirth. For the infant who survives the neonatal period, a variety of physical and cognitive problems will result.

Several prenatal infections may result in other severe disorders. For example, **toxoplasmosis** is a protozoan-caused infection carried by raw meat and fecal material. Evidence indicates that the damage of toxoplasmosis may be significant, with nearly 85 percent of surviving babies being mentally retarded and also having other problems such as blindness and convulsions (Sever, 1970). Toxoplasmosis is primarily a threat if the mother is exposed during pregnancy, whereas infection prior to conception seems to cause minimal danger to the fetus.

Intoxication, the second part of this etiological category, refers to disorders that occur when there is cerebral damage due to an excessive level of some toxic agent in the mother-fetus system. Excessive maternal use of drugs or alcohol, or exposure to certain industrial chemicals, may result in toxic agents in the mother's system that cause damage to the fetus. Similarly, the unborn baby may be seriously affected if incompatible blood types exist between the mother and fetus. The most widely known form of this problem is found when the mother's blood is Rh-negative while the fetus has Rh-positive blood. In this situation the mother's system may become sensitized to the incompatible blood type and produce defensive antibodies that damage the fetus. Sensitization most commonly happens during delivery, when the baby's Rh-positive blood may leak into the mother's circulatory system. Consequently, the first baby born to an Rh-negative mother is usually not in danger, since sensitization and antibody development has either not occurred or is not at a toxic level. (However, the first baby may be in grave danger if there has been an Rh-positive transfusion administered to the mother some time in the past.) Subsequent babies risk considerable prenatal damage if the mother has not received immediate medical treatment at the time of potential sensitization to deter the formation of antibodies. Fortunately, medical technology has advanced to a point that such treatment is typically available.

Infection or intoxication damage does not always occur during the prenatal period. We chose to discuss them here because the infections classified under the AAMD scheme are predominantly prenatal. Severe disorders may also occur as a result of postnatal infections and toxic excesses. For example, encephalitis may damage the central nervous system functioning following certain types of childhood infections (e.g., measles, mumps), as can certain toxic reaction incidents occurring after birth (e.g., lead poisoning, carbon-monoxide poisoning, drugs).

Another etiology category related to the prenatal period is disorders that are associated with chromosomal abnormality. Chromosomes are thread-like bodies that carry the genes that play an important role in determining inherited characteristics. Defects resulting from chromosomal abnormalities are typically dramatic, because the resulting damage is often severe and accompanied by visually evident abnormalities. Often the lay person has a stereotyped image of the disorders characterized by such aberrations and an inflated assessment of how frequently they occur. In the total population, genetically caused defects are relatively rare. Cell structure of the vast majority of humans is normal, and development proceeds without accident. Human body cells normally have forty-six chromosomes that are arranged in twenty-three pairs. Aberrations occurring in chromosomal arrangement, either before fertilization or during early cell division, may result in a variety of abnormal characteristics.

One of the most widely recognized types of mental retardation, **Down's syndrome,** results from chromosomal abnormality. Down's syndrome is a condition that results in facial and physical characteristics that are visibly distinctive. Facial features resemble those of Asians, which has resulted in use of the term *mongoloid* or *mongolism* (after the people of the Mongol empire, founded in the twelfth century by Genghis Khan. The Mongols had facial features marked by distinctive epicanthic eye folds, prominent cheekbones, straight black hair, and a small somewhat flattened nose). There are three different types of Down's syndrome, each resulting from a different chromosomal aberration.

The most common cause of Down's syndrome is **nondisjunction** (the chromosomal pairs do not separate properly as the sperm or egg cells are formed). Down's syndrome caused by nondisjunction is characterized by an extra chromosome at the twenty-first pair and thus is also known as "Trisomy 21." The person then has forty-seven chromosomes instead of forty-six. Figure 6-1 shows the configuration of chromosomes for a female with Down's syndrome of this type. The cell-division error occurs before fertilization, and the impact on the fetus is severe. Once the cell-division process is begun, all developing tissue carries the genetic makeup of those preceding cells.

Abnormal chromosome material in the twenty-first pair is also present in the second type of Down's syndrome, known as **translocation.** Translocation occurs when a portion of the chromosome breaks off from the twenty-first pair and fuses with material from another pair. In this condition, the person has forty-five chromosomes instead of the normal forty-six.

Mosaicism, the third type of Down's syndrome, is distinctly different from the other conditions because the chromosomal accident occurs after fertilization. Consequently the mosaic Down's fetus develops normally for a period of time before the cell division error appears. This individual thus has a mixed chromosomal configuration with some tissue being made up of normal cells and some made up of abnormal cells. Once again the affected cells often show abnormality in the twenty-first pair, but the important factor is the time when

Figure 6-1/ Chromosome Configuration of a Down's Syndrome Female with Trisomy 21.
The chromosomes in this figure are grouped (A-G) according to a standard system known as a
karyotype. A karyotype is a classification of photographed human chromosomes that is obtained
from a blood or skin sample.

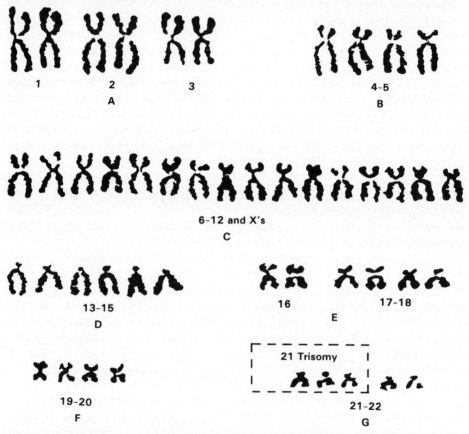

Source: Reprinted, by permission, from D. W. Smith and A. A. Wilson, *The Child with Down's Syndrome (Mongolism)* (Philadelphia: W. B. Saunders Co., 1973), p. 6.

the error occurred. The damage may be severe if the abnormality emerged very early in the embryo's development, because the proportion of cells affected in such a case will be much greater than if the error occurs later in the developmental cycle. In addition, the portion of the embryo that is developing most rapidly in the early gestation period includes the central nervous system. Individuals with mosaic Down's syndrome may vary greatly in terms of intellectual functioning from very mild to severe levels of impairment. The severity of deficit depends on the timing of the chromosomal error.

Down's syndrome has received widespread attention in literature and has been a favored topic in textbooks for many years. Part of this attention has come because of the apparent ability to identify a cause with some degree of certainty. The cause of such genetic errors became increasingly associated with maternal age, while paternal age was generally viewed as not influencing the incidence of Down's syndrome. Even recent literature cites the incidence of Down's syndrome in twenty-year-old mothers at 1 in 2,000 live births, whereas maternal age over forty-five is reported to be 1 in 20 (Miller & Erbe, 1978). Most literature has focused on nondisjunction as being most related to increasing maternal age (e.g., Linsjö, 1974; Mikkelsen & Stene, 1970). Translocation has been associated less with age, and seemingly in an inverse fashion. Translocation seems to occur in about 9 percent of Down's infants for mothers under thirty, and in 2 percent of Down's infants born to mothers over thirty. However, recent research has also begun to implicate paternal age, although results are somewhat conflicting. For example, studies in Denmark and Japan have indicated a dramatic increase in the incidence of Down's syndrome births with increased paternal age, over fifty-five (Matsunaga, Tonomura, Oishi & Kikuchi, 1978; Stene, Fischer, Stene, Mikkelsen & Peterson, 1977). However, Erickson (1978) did not obtain results supporting such a phenomenon in the United States. Thus as we examine causation in this syndrome, the evidence is somewhat uncertain. There seems little question that maternal age is related, but we must now also view the father's age as being potentially important in the chromosomal abnormalities associated with Down's syndrome (Abroms & Bennett, 1980).

While Down's syndrome is not the only result of chromosomal abnormalities, it is the most widely recognized. Our intent is to be illustrative rather than exhaustive. Readers interested in more complete information may wish to consult any of a number of volumes that focus solely on such topics (e.g., Carter, 1975).

Severe disorders may be caused prenatally by gestation disorders, another category in the AAMD scheme. The most typical problems in this category involve prematurity and low birth weight. In the former case we are generally referring to infants "delivered before 37 weeks from the first day of the last menstrual period" (Grossman, 1977, p. 66). Low birth weight is viewed in terms of babies that weigh 2,500 grams or less at birth. Prematurity and low birth rate often occur together.

Severe disorders are also caused by unknown prenatal influences. Some of the syndromes in this category are extremely severe with regard to the individual's level of functioning, but as suggested by the category label, etiology is not definitely known. One type of clinical syndrome in this category involves malformations of cerebral tissue. Perhaps the most dramatic of these malformations is known as anencephaly. Anencephaly is a condition where the individual has a partial or even complete absence of cerebral tissue. In some cases, portions of the brain appear to develop and then degenerate. The prognosis for such an individual is not very promising, and most do not survive beyond a few hours or days. Hydrocephalus is another type of syndrome that is categorized in the unknown prenatal influence class. Hydrocephalus is a condition where an excess of cerebrospinal fluid accumulates in the skull and results in potentially damaging pressure on cerebral tissue. Cerebrospinal fluid circulates in the central nervous system much as blood does in the circulatory system. As this process occurs, a certain amount of fluid is absorbed and is replaced by newly produced fluid. Hydrocephalus may occur when either the production system or the absorption system malfunctions (i.e., from either overproduction of cerebrospinal fluid or insufficient absorption). In either case, greater-than-normal amounts of fluid accumulate and create pressure on the brain. Hydrocephalus may or may not involve an enlarged head, depending on when the production or absorption imbalance occurs. If it is present at birth or shortly thereafter, the seams of the child's skull will not have grown closed and the pressure will result in an enlarged head. Hydrocephaly may result in varied intellectual functioning. If surgical intervention occurs early the damage may be slight, because the pressure has not been serious. If such intervention does not occur or is not undertaken early, the degree of mental retardation may range from moderate to severe.

We now come to the logical conclusion of gestation: the delivery or birth of a baby. Several factors during delivery that may result in severe disorders that would be classified under the AAMD category of trauma or physical agent. Although traumas or physical accidents may occur during the prenatal period (e.g., excessive radiation), we will focus on delivery problems.

The continuing supply of oxygen and nutrients to the baby is a critical factor during delivery. One threat to these processes involves the position of the fetus. Normal fetal position places the baby with the head toward the cervix and the face toward the mother's back. Certain other positions may result in fetal damage as delivery proceeds. One of these is known as a **breech presentation,** in which the buttocks, rather than the head, of the fetus are positioned toward the cervix. Thus, the baby would be delivered longitudinally backward with respect to what is normal. Figure 6-2 illustrates a breech position. The breech delivery can result in several difficulties that may cause disorders. First, because the head will exit last rather than first, it may be subjected to several

Figure 6-2/ Example of a Breech Fetal Position

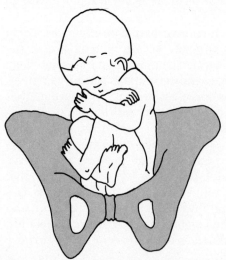

types of stress that would not occur if the delivery were normal. The labor contractions during the later stages of delivery are stronger and more rapid than during initial delivery. This means that the head is passing through the birth canal under more stress than it would normally have, and the pressure of the contractions has a direct impact on the fetal skull rather than on the buttocks as in a normal position. In addition, in a normally positioned delivery the head is molded gradually (with the less frequent and less intense contractions) as it passes through the pelvic girdle. In a breech position the molding may occur incompletely or in a sudden fashion, which may cause brain pressure and even mechanical damage to the cerebral tissue. This may be further exacerbated because the molding of the skull bones is done in a reverse fashion with regard to passage through the pelvic girdle.

The breech position may cause additional difficulties for the fetus. During the prenatal period the fetus obtains oxygen and nutrients through the umbilical cord. For the most part, the cord is constructed in a fashion that functions properly for normal delivery positions. During a normal birth presentation, the head of the fetus exits first, which provides a potential source of oxygen through the lungs even if the cord disengages. In a breech presentation the cord may not be long enough to remain attached while the head is expelled, or it may become pinched between the baby's body and the pelvic girdle. In either case the oxygen may be reduced or even eliminated for a period of time until the head is expelled and the lungs begin to function. If this occurs and continues for a significant period of time, the baby may be without oxygen to the point that damage to the brain ensues. Such a condition is known as *anoxia* (oxygen-deprived) and can result in serious difficulties.

Other abnormal positions can result in delivery problems and damage to the fetus. For example, the fetus may lie across the birth canal in what is known as a **transverse** position. In such cases the baby literally cannot exit through the birth canal, or if the baby does exit, severe damage may occur in a variety of forms. Figure 6-3 illustrates a transverse presentation and indicates the difficulties that would be encountered in delivery.

In some cases labor and delivery proceed so rapidly that the fetal skull does not have time to mold properly or in a sufficiently gentle fashion. The less intense labor that occurs early is very important both to the head of the baby and to the pelvic girdle of the mother. The pelvic joints (bony structures connected by tissue) actually stretch, further permitting passage of the baby and molding of the baby's skull. If these processes do not occur gradually, under the low intensity early labor, the cerebral tissue of the baby may be damaged. Such rapid births (generally less than two hours) are known as **precipitous births** and may result in mental retardation as well as other problems.

Abnormally long deliveries may also cause problems. A normal delivery generally involves about seven to twelve hours of labor. Some of the difficulties in such situations are similar to those of a precipitous birth. For example, if advanced labor, which is characterized by intense and frequent contractions, continues for a prolonged period, there is once again an abnormal amount of pressure placed on the skull of the baby. Such pressure over that period of time may result in mechanical damage to the tissue and blood vessels. The

Figure 6-3/ Example of a Transverse Presentation

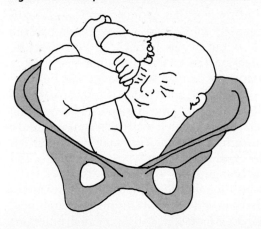

second type of problem that may occur with prolonged labor is separation of the placenta from the mother's supply system. As the placenta detaches, the oxygen supply is reduced or terminated, which may result in severe damage to the baby or even a stillbirth.

The first postnatal category of causation to be examined is disorders of metabolism or nutrition. As we begin this discussion, it will become evident that even the distinction of prenatal versus postnatal is somewhat flexible. Some disorders associated with the postnatal period may also emerge as causes prenatally. This is the case with our first metabolic disorder, phenylketonuria (PKU). Although PKU is primarily a problem in the postnatal infant, it may also present difficulties because of PKU problems that exist prenatally (e.g., if the mother is a carrier of PKU but does not have the fully developed condition).

PKU is an inherited metabolic disorder where the individual is not able to process phenylalanine properly. This presents a special problem with infants, since phenylalanine is a substance found in many foods ingested at this age (e.g., milk). The inability to process phenylalanine results in a toxic accumulation of substances that damage tissue in the central nervous system. If it is untreated or not treated promptly (mostly through dietary restrictions), PKU may cause varying degrees of mental retardation ranging from moderate to severe deficits. If treatment is promptly instituted, however, damage may be largely prevented or at least reduced to only mild deficits.

Milk also presents a problem for infants affected by another metabolic disorder, **galactosemia.** In this case, the youngster is unable properly to process lactose, which is the primary sugar in milk and is also found in other foods. If galactosemia remains untreated (e.g., if the infant continues on a milk diet) serious damage results, such as cataracts, heightened susceptibility to infection, and reduced intellectual functioning. Dietary control by eliminating milk and other foods containing lactose must be undertaken in a rigorous fashion. Galactosemia is a rare disease, and consequently the long-term effectiveness of treatment remains uncertain. However, there is evidence that treatment greatly reduces the severity of damage, although affected individuals who are treated still function intellectually somewhat below their unaffected siblings (Robinson & Robinson, 1976).

Severe disorders associated with gross postnatal brain disease is another etiological category. Our first example, **neurofibromatosis,** is an inherited disorder that results in multiple tumors in the skin, peripheral nerve tissue, and other areas such as the brain. Intellectual deficits do not occur in all cases, although Robinson and Robinson (1976) noted that mental retardation and epilepsy are evident in about 10 percent of the cases. The severity of mental retardation and other problems resulting from neurofibromatosis seem to relate to the location of tumors (e.g., in the cerebral tissue) and the size and growth of these tumors. Severe disorders due to gross prenatal brain disease occur with a variety of other conditions, including tuberous sclerosis (also involving tumors in the central nervous system tissue) and degeneration of cerebral white matter.

Severe behavior problems (psychiatric disorders under the AAMD scheme) have been attributed to both genetic and environmental factors. Some genetic researchers (Kanter, 1953; Slater, 1968) have suggested that there is an inherited predisposition toward schizophrenia. Other investigators (Heath, Krupp, Byers & Liljekvist, 1967; Hoffer, Osmond & Smythies, 1954) have postulated that schizophrenia is determined by biochemical abnormalities in the body. Still others (behaviorists, family theorists) have hypothesized that psychosis is a result of an abnormal relationship between the individual and the environment.

Although we have presented a number of possible causal factors for severe and profound disorders, you should be aware that etiology is unknown and undeterminable for many conditions. In addition, many severe conditions are due to the interaction of several etiological factors.

Prevalence

Individuals with severe and profound disorders constitute a very small percentage of the general population. Even if we consider the multitude of conditions, prevalence estimates generally range from no more than 0.1 to 1.0 percent. Approximately 4 out of every 1,000 persons are severely and profoundly handicapped where the primary symptom is mental retardation (falling more than three standard deviations below the mean on tests of intelligence). In addition, 2 to 4 out of every 10,000 children exhibit some form of severe behavior disorder.

INTERVENTION STRATEGIES

In order to meet the diverse needs of people with severe and profound disorders, several professions must be involved in the treatment and education process. Historically, medicine has played the greatest role in care and treatment, since many of these individuals were committed to state or private institutions. In the past these institutions have been oriented more to physical care and maintenance than to habilitative programs. However, as institutions broaden their treatment approaches and as community programs expand, the need for more appropriate social and educational services becomes apparent. Social services include the programs that are necessary to facilitate the individual's integration into the family unit as well as society in general. The term *education* must be redefined to go beyond the traditional academically oriented curricula and to include functional life programs that focus on survival skills. When working in harmony, the fields of medicine, the social services, and education form a network of professionals that provide the best means available to habilitate those with severe and profound disorders.

Medical Services

The field of medicine has two important functions in the treatment of severe and profound disorders. The first is preventive medicine, which is concerned with discovering new ways to prevent and control medical conditions frequently associated with severe and profound disorders. The second is direct medical care, which focuses on diagnosing the condition to prevent impairments from becoming disabilities, recommending the appropriate medical treatment, and maintaining a state of physical well-being.

Prevention. Prevention is a laudable goal for society, but some means to achieve this end may not meet with the same level of enthusiasm from all factions of society. The less controversial preventive measures are immunizations against disease, maternal nutritional habits during pregnancy, appropriate prenatal care, and screening for genetic disorders at birth.

Immunizations can protect family members from contracting serious illness and in addition guard against a woman's becoming ill during pregnancy. Diseases such as rubella, which may result in severe mental retardation, heart disease, or blindness, can be controlled through routine immunization programs. Improper nutritional habits during pregnancy may also contribute to fetal problems. Chinn, Drew, and Logan (1979) reported that "maternal malnutrition, which is usually a life-long state of inadequacy, has been implicated as exerting possible damaging influence on the fetus, particularly to the central nervous system" (p. 154). Poor nutritional habits are part of a much larger social problem: the lack of appropriate prenatal care during the gestation period. In 1976 the President's Committee on Mental Retardation reported that at least 30 percent of all expectant mothers do not see a physician during pregnancy. This happens despite the fact that ongoing prenatal assessment can monitor the health of the mother in such areas as diet, physical exercise, and state of mind. A medical history can alert the attending physician to any potential dangers for the mother or the unborn infant that may result from family genetics, prior trauma, or illness. The physician is able to monitor the health of the fetus, including heart rate, physical size, and position in the uterus. At the time of birth, several factors relevant to the infant's health can be assessed. A procedure known as Apgar Scoring evaluates the infant on heart rate, respiratory condition, muscle tone, reflex irritability, and color. This screening procedure alerts the medical staff to infants who may warrant closer monitoring and more in-depth assessments. Other screening procedures conducted in the medical laboratory within the first few days of life can detect anomalies that if not treated will eventually lead to mental retardation, psychological disorders, physical disabilities, or even death. The effects of disorders such as phenylketonuria and Rh incompatability can be substantially diminished if assessed at birth and treated immediately.

Other methods of prevention are more involved with issues of morality and ethics. These include genetic screening and counseling, and therapeutic abortion. **Genetic screening** is defined as "a search in a population for persons possessing certain genotypes that (1) are already associated with disease or predisposed to disease, (2) may lead to disease in their descendants, or (3) produce other variations not known to be associated with disease" (National Academy of Sciences, 1975, p. 9). Genetic screening may be conducted at various times in the family planning process or during pregnancy. When screening is conducted prior to conception, the purpose is to determine whether the parents are predisposed to genetic anomalies that could be inherited by their offspring. If screening takes place after conception, the purpose is to determine if the fetus has any genetic abnormalities. This can be accomplished through one of several medical procedures (e.g., amniocentesis, fetoscopy, ultrasound).

Once genetic screening has been completed, it is the responsibility of a counselor to inform parents of the results. Parents are then made more fully aware of potential outcomes and options. While the genetic counselor does not make decisions for the parents regarding family planning, he or she prepares the parents to exercise their rights. Hardman and Drew (1978) indicated:

> The genetic counselor must also be prepared to answer all questions openly and completely in order for the parent to become fully informed concerning the problem being faced. If the information provision and discussion approach are adhered to, the argument of discrimination and interference with individual rights is largely disarmed. (P. 392)

The primary outcome of genetic counseling can be viewed in terms of informing the parents concerning decisions they have to make about whether to (1) have children based on the probability of a genetic anomaly occurring or (2) abort a pregnancy if prenatal assessment indicates that the developing fetus has a genetic anomaly. The decision whether or not to abort involves a moral controversy that society has been trying to deal with for years. For example, if a Down's syndrome fetus is detected, what are the intervention options? Certainly one option involves continuing the pregnancy and making mental, physical, and fiscal preparations for the additional care that may be required by such an individual (both as a child and in the years beyond childhood). The other option is to undergo a pregnancy termination. Often termed a *"therapeutic abortion,"* it is an abortion nonetheless and presents ethical dilemmas for many people. These issues have begun to emerge in the literature on mental retardation (e.g., Chinn et al., 1979; Hardman & Drew, 1978; 1980), but they have long been a concern in the literature of other fields (e.g., Fletcher, 1975; Ramsey,

1973; Williams, 1966). In certain cases, the neonatal period presents some of the same dilemmas, but they are perhaps even more difficult from an ethical perspective (Burt, 1976; Diamond, 1977; Duff & Campbell, 1973; Fletcher, 1968; Horan & Mall, 1977; Robertson, 1975; Shaw, 1977). During the neonatal period, the issue is usually whether to withhold medical treatment from a defective newborn. This raises such ethical and moral questions as who makes these decisions; what are the circumstances under which the decisions are made; and what is the criterion used to determine that treatment is to be withheld.

Direct Health Care. Most severely and profoundly disordered people exhibit symptoms that are evident at birth. Consequently, a physician is usually the first professional to come in contact with this population. The physician's primary role is one of diagnostician, counselor, and care-giver. As diagnostician, the physician analyzes the nature and cause of pathology and then, based on the medical information available, counsels the family concerning prognosis. The physician's role as family counselor has been challenged by some professionals in the behavioral sciences and by parents, because such counseling often exceeds the medical domain. This concern reflects the opinion that medical personnel should deliberate only on medical matters and should recommend other resources such as educators, psychologists, social workers, clergy, or parent groups when dealing with issues external to medicine.

Social/Psychological Services

Social/psychological needs of people with severe and profound disorders extend into many aspects of the social system, such as the primary family unit, the extended family, the neighborhood, the educational environment, and larger community structures. Lifelong support services need to be available in order for the severely disordered person to succeed, or even survive. The necessary services may be classified into five general categories: (1) community support services, (2) family support services, (3) alternative living arrangements, (4) vocational services, and (5) leisure-time services. Figure 6-4 illustrates some of the services included within each of the general categories.

Educational Services

Education is a new concept as it relates to persons with severe and profound disorders. Historically, this population was defined as a noneducable by the public schools because they did not fit the programs offered by general education. Educational programs were built on a foundation of academic learning that emphasized reading, writing, and arithmetic. For persons with severe disorders, these are not high-priority need areas. Because these individuals did not meet the requirements of the program, they were excluded from it. Schools were not expected to adapt to the needs of the disordered individual—the individual was expected to adapt to the system.

Figure 6-4/ Classification of Community Service Needs

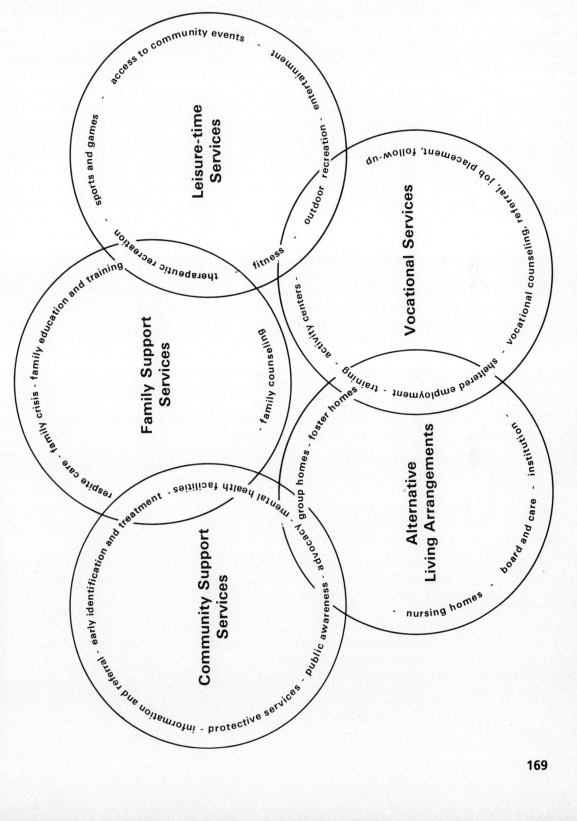

The schools, which excluded this population for so long, are now faced with a new challenge: appropriate education of the severely and profoundly disordered. Based on a new set of values, the concept of education has been redefined. No longer do the schools dictate a general curriculum emphasizing only academic learning. Instead, education is defined as advancing an individual to the next highest level of functioning, regardless of how developmentally delayed or deviant he or she may be. For those who are severely and profoundly disordered, their differences are substantial, and require services far beyond the scope of one discipline. Although educators have traditionally been autonomous in their classrooms, this practice cannot continue if the needs of these individuals are to be met. To gain a more in-depth perspective on the educational needs of this group, we will analyze the curriculum content areas that may be taught in the schools, the scope of educational services, and the instructional process.

The Curriculum Content Areas. Educational programming for people with severe and profound disorders focuses on decreasing dependence on others while concurrently teaching adaptation to the surrounding environment. People with severe and profound disorders exist for the most part in a very restricted environment consisting of the home or other alternative living arrangement (e.g., institution or community-care center), and the school, or sheltered vocational program. Their environment is restricted because they are unable to function without direct assistance from others. Therefore, the educational curriculum must concentrate on those functional skills that will improve their day-to-day existence.

The curriculum for severely and profoundly disordered individuals will generally include the following content areas:

1. Motor skills
2. Self-care skills
3. Social skills
4. Communication skills
5. Functional academic skills
6. Prevocational/vocational skills.

The development of motor skills is a fundamental component of the developmental process and a prerequisite to successful learning in other content areas, including self-care, social skills, and vocational skills. Bunker (1978) suggested:

> Human movement provides the basic psychomotor framework for development, for through movement all children discover critical elements about their bodies, their environment, and their social interactions. All young children must "move to learn and learn to move," and as they move, reach, touch and explore, they begin to develop a concept of their body. (p. 180)

Gross motor development is concerned with general mobility (i.e., interaction of the body with the environment). Gross motor skills are developed in a sequence ranging from movements that make balance possible, to higher-order locomotor patterns. Locomotor patterns are intended to move the person freely through the environment. Gross motor movements include head and neck control, rolling, body righting, sitting, creeping, crawling, standing, walking, running, jumping, and skipping. Fine motor development requires more precision and steadiness than the skills developed in the gross motor area. Fine motor skills include reaching, grasping, and the manipulation of objects. The development of fine motor skills is initially dependent on the ability of the child to "visually fix" on an object and "visually track" a moving target (Mori & Masters, 1980). Coordination of the eye and hand is an integral factor in many skill areas as well as in fine motor development. Eye-hand coordination is the basis for social/leisure-time activities and is essential to the development of object-control skills required in vocational situations.

The development of self-care skills is another important content area relevant to independence in the environment. Self-care areas include feeding, dressing, and personal-hygiene skills. Feeding skills range from finger-feeding, drinking from a cup, and proper table behaviors such as the use of utensils and napkins, to serving food and etiquette. Dressing skills include buttoning, zipping, buckling, lacing, and tying. Personal-hygiene skills also range on a continuum from rather primitive developmental skills to higher-level skills relevant to adult behavior. Low-level skills include toileting, face and hand-washing, bathing, toothbrushing, hair-combing, and shampooing. Skills associated with adolescent and adult years include skin care, shaving, hair-setting, use of deodorants and cosmetics, and menstrual hygiene.

Social-skills training is closely aligned with the self-care area in that it relates many of the self-care concepts to the development of good interpersonal relationships. Social-skills training emphasizes the importance of physical appearance, proper manners, apropriate use of leisure time, and sexual behavior. The area of social skills may also focus on the development of personality characteristics conducive to successful integration in society.

The ability to communicate with others is also essential to expanded opportunities for growth and development. Without communication there is no interaction. Communication systems for people with severe and profound disorders take three general forms: (1) verbal language, (2) manual communication (e.g., sign language, language boards), and (3) a combination of verbal and manual approaches. The approach employed will depend on what the individual is capable of. If he or she is able to develop the requisite skills for spoken language, everyday interactive skills will be greatly enhanced. Manual communication must be considered when a person is not able to develop verbal skills as an effective means of communication. The important factor is that the individual develop some form of communication.

A functional academic curriculum is intended to expand the individual's knowledge in daily living, recreation, and vocational areas. Functional academics are taught only when a person has acquired the prerequisite skills. Snell (1978) indicated:

> When working to "functionalize" learned skills, your [the classroom teacher] instructional materials need to be realistic; most workbooks, readers, commercial charts, flashcards, and dittoed worksheets are not practical because your students cannot relate the materials to the desired skills. Instead you will need materials such as newspapers, street signs, price tags from stores and movie tickets. You will be unable to remain within the four walls of your classroom if you expect your students to reach the goals of functional skill development. (P. 301)

Vocational training for those with severe and profound disorders has been fraught with problems because of a pessimistic attitude that professionals and the general public have about its effectiveness. Many vocational programs were no more than peonage, with no theoretical or conceptual basis for training. Today the negative philosophy about vocational training has largely been replaced by a commitment to the development of relevant vocational programs for this population, whether it be in sheltered or competitive employment settings (Gold, 1975; Peck, Apolloni & Cooke; 1981, Pomerantz & Marholin, 1977). As a content area, vocational preparation is essentially a composite of basic skills taught in other areas. These include communication, motor devel-

A sheltered workshop may prepare a student for employment in a commercial work setting.

opment, recreation, and self-care. Blue (1964) suggested that prevocational training should focus on gross and fine motor skills, perseverance, sustained performance, and response to motivation and rewards. Once these prerequisite skills have been learned, instruction can emphasize important work-adjustment skills, such as punctuality, task correction, responsibility, socialization, independence on the job, initiative, and safety.

The Scope of Educational Services. Education and training for people with severe and profound disorders is a lifetime process that begins at the time of onset of the disorder. In most cases, intervention will begin at birth and be carried through to the adult years. The importance of early intervention cannot be overstated. Hayden and McGinness (1977) stressed that "failure to provide a stimulating early environment leads not only to a continuation of the developmental status quo, but to actual atrophy of sensory abilities and to developmental regression" (p. 153).

Early intervention techniques, such as infant stimulation programs, focus on the acquisition of sensorimotor functions and intellectual development. This would involve learning simple reflex activity and equilibrium reactions. Subsequent intervention would then expand into all areas of human growth and development. Intervention based on normal patterns of growth is often referred to as the developmental approach, because it seeks to develop, remedy, or adapt learner skills based on the disordered individual's variation from what is considered to be normal. This progression of skills continues as the child ages chronologically, but the rate of progression is significantly different from the norm. For example, some profoundly retarded persons may never exceed a developmental age of 6 months. Others may develop to a functioning level that will enable them to live as adults with moderate levels of societal support and supervision.

Administrative Considerations. The special school has been a service-delivery option for children with severe and profound disorders for many years. Proponents of this option argue that these schools provide for (1) greater homogeneity in grouping and programming, (2) teacher specialization in such areas as art, language, physical education, and music, and (3) centralization of teaching materials, which will result in a more efficient use of programs available. In addition, some parents of severely disordered individuals believe that their children will be happier in a segregated environment that minimizes ridicule from others and risk of failure.

Critics of the segregated special schools suggest that these facilities are not consonant with the concept of the least restrictive environment. They argue that these schools offer little, if any, opportunity for interaction with normal peers and deprive the child with a severe and profound disorder of valuable learning and socialization experiences. Orelove and Hanley (1977) suggested that segregated facilities cannot be financially or ideologically justified. Public school administrators must plan to include this population in existing regular education facilities.

The Instructional Process. Teaching severely and profoundly disordered individuals is radically different from traditional educational approaches. At an elementary level, the traditional approach has always relied on the efforts of one teacher to conduct relevant assessments, implement the program in all content areas, and evaluate student progress. At the secondary level, the process is similar, except that teachers specialize in one or two content areas and then instruct large groups of students in their fields of specialization. Both these approaches have one important underlying factor in common: they use primarily the expertise and resources of a single discipline—education. Given the diverse needs of individuals with severe and profound disorders, the single-discipline orientation is an inefficient and ineffective approach to education. In fact, federal legislation now mandates that a team consisting of professionals from several disciplines assess the educational needs of exceptional children. The law also provides that services not usually defined as educational in nature must be made available if they assist a student in benefiting from a special education program. They are defined by law as *related services.*

> Related services means transportation, and such developmental, corrective, and other supportive services (including speech pathology and audiology, psychological services, physical and occupational therapy, recreation, and medical and counseling services) . . . as may be required to assist a handicapped child to benefit from special education, and includes the early identification and assessment of handicapping conditions in children. (U.S. Congress, Education for All Handicapped Children Act, 1975)

There are several perspectives on how to use the variety of professionals required. The three main approaches to the role of team members are (1) the multidisciplinary approach, (2) the interdisciplinary approach, and (3) the transdisciplinary approach. These approaches are conceptually different in the way they view the assessment, programming, and evaluation process.

The multidisciplinary approach involves the expertise of several professionals who usually work independently of one another. These professionals conduct independent assessments, write and implement separate program plans, and evaluate progress within the parameters of their own discipline. This process may be modified by having each of the professionals conduct an independent assessment and write separate program plans but then forward the data to one person (usually the educator), who alone would be responsible for implementing and evaluating the entire program.

The interdisciplinary approach represents a significant alteration in the process. During the assessment phase, team members do undertake independent assessments, but program development is carried out as a collaborative effort among professionals. A group decision is made about what areas are of greatest priority for the student. Based on these priorities, a program is developed and appropriate personnel are assigned to implement it. The student is viewed from several perspectives in order to ascertain the areas of need that must be met in the time available. One problem with the interdisciplinary approach, however, is that beyond the program-development phase, interaction among professionals often ceases, and no one person coordinates the efforts of the various professionals.

According to Hart (1977), the transdisciplinary approach is a response to the problems associated with the other two approaches. Figure 6-5 illustrates the transdisciplinary model. In this approach the critical concept is the introduction of a primary therapist. Hart indicated:

> A primary therapist is designated to deal with individual children. In an attempt to reduce the compartmentalization and fragmentizing of services to the child, one person is appointed for direct contact. This reduces the number of professionals involved in the direct care of the child. This approach may be similar to the preceding two in the initial evaluation and may use an interdisciplinary approach in making the initial plan for implementation. However, implementation is carried out by only one of the members in cooperation with the others. Each discipline then depends upon the others, supporting the efforts of the others, although being neither dominant nor parasitic. (Hart 1977, p. 393)

Regardless of what approach is used in the schools, the team process is the key to an appropriate treatment plan. Interaction among professionals in conjunction with input from parents forms the core to greater understanding and eventual long-term success.

SUMMARY

Persons with severe and profound disorders generally have multiple impairments that transcend the characteristics associated with a single disabling condition. The characteristics of people with mental retardation range from being able to develop skills that will facilitate independence within their environment, to being unable to care for themselves at all. The severely and profoundly retarded exhibit serious deficiencies in cognitive development, physical development, and communication skills. In addition, greater intellectual deficiency tends to result in a higher incidence of compounding sensory dysfunction.

People with behavior disorders can be discussed under two general categories: pervasive developmental disorders and schizophrenia. Pervasive developmental disorders include the conditions of infantile autism and childhood-onset pervasive developmental disorders. The primary difference between these two conditions is the age of onset. Infantile autism is defined as occurring prior to thirty months of age, and childhood-onset pervasive developmental disorder occurs after thirty months of age. Both conditions are characterized by deficits in language function, inadequate socialization skills, and resistance to change within the environment.

Generic definitions utilize the symptom-severity parameter of classification to describe this population. Generic descriptors include severely handicapped,

176

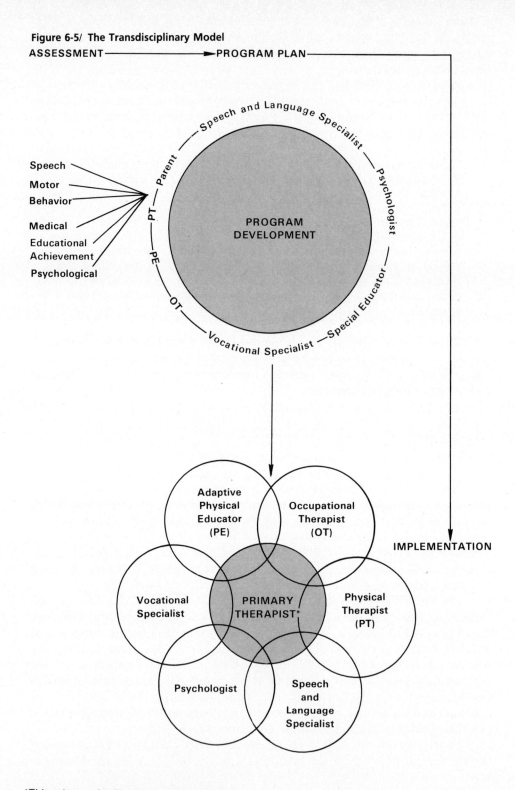

Figure 6-5/ The Transdisciplinary Model

ASSESSMENT ⟶ PROGRAM PLAN

Speech
Motor
Behavior
Medical
Educational
Achievement
Psychological

Parent — Speech and Language Specialist — Psychologist

PT

PE

OT

Vocational Specialist — Special Educator

PROGRAM DEVELOPMENT

IMPLEMENTATION

Adaptive Physical Educator (PE)

Occupational Therapist (OT)

Vocational Specialist

PRIMARY THERAPIST*

Physical Therapist (PT)

Psychologist

Speech and Language Specialist

*This role may be filled by a special educator.

profoundly handicapped, and severely multiply handicapped. Few definitions clearly distinguish between severe and profound conditions. Generic definitions may be based on (1) a description of behavioral characteristics and/or (2) the instructional needs of an individual.

There are many causes associated with severe and profound disorders. These causes include infections, intoxications, trauma, malnutrition, metabolic dysfunction, brain disease, diseases resulting from unknown prenatal influence, chromosomal abnormalities, gestational disorders, and psychiatric disorders. For many conditions, etiology is unknown and undeterminable.

The significance of severe and profound disorders dictates that this population be assisted through the resources of several professions, including medicine, the social services, and education. Intervention strategies must begin at the time of onset of the disorder, which in most cases is birth, and focus on decreasing the individual's dependence on others. Medical personnel are concerned with prevention and care of concomitant health problems. Mental health professionals provide for the social support systems essential to survival. Education concentrates on the development of communication, self-care, motor, and other functional life skills that will enhance opportunities for growth and development.

These individuals will learn as they live, so everything that is taught must be applicable to the routine of daily life. Even though we have little documentation of the long-term impact of treatment, professionals agree that this population can learn to develop meaningful skills that will expand their independence. We are only beginning to cope with the conceptual demands of working with this population. Therefore, some of the most significant challenges are ahead. What we learn will help us understand even more about human differences in general.

REVIEW QUESTIONS

1. Discuss the range of characteristics exhibited by persons with severe and profound mental retardation.
2. What characteristics are associated with childhood-onset pervasive developmental disorder and autism? What is the primary difference between these two conditions?
3. The majority of persons with severe and profound disorders have multiple problems. Discuss the categories of exceptionality (e.g., mental retardation, behavior disorders) that may be seen in combination for persons with severe multiple disorders.
4. Discuss the generic definitions of severe and profound disorders. How do these definitions differ from categorical approaches?
5. Discuss the eight etiological classifications associated with severe and profound disorders presented in this chapter.
6. Why is it necessary for professionals from several fields to be involved in the education and treatment of persons with severe and profound disorders?

7. What are two important functions of the field of medicine in the treatment of severe and profound disorders?
8. Why are professionals facing a new challenge in the education of children with severe and profound disorders?
9. Discuss six content areas that are generally included in the educational program of a severely disabled child.
10. Distinguish between the multidisciplinary, interdisciplinary, and trans-disciplinary approaches.

SECTION III

Communication and Sensory Disorders

Our study of human exceptionality now turns to communication and sensory disorders. In this section we will introduce you to several types of problems, including disorders of speech and language, hearing, and vision.

Communication is an extremely complex activity. Chapter 7 examines communication disorders in terms of two broad areas: speech and language. These areas are interrelated, and each involves components where disorders may pose serious difficulties. Causation may range from physiological abnormalities to a variety of learned behaviors and environmental influences. Abnormal speech or language can have a substantial impact on an individual's life, and treatment may be long and difficult.

Chapters 8 and 9 discuss hearing and vision disorders respectively. Both hearing and vision are extremely important sources of information and contribute greatly to human development. Most of us attach meaning to objects in our environment through vision and hearing and give labels to such objects by means of some form of communication. Thus the senses of hearing and vision are relatives of speech and language in the broad picture of human development. Disorders in either vision or hearing can have a serious impact on those so affected. Problems in either area can involve any number of physiological abnormalities. Intervention may include medical, psychological, and/or educational treatments that deviate from those typically provided for people without such difficulties. The following are topical guidelines for Section III:

1. Speech and language are both complex and interrelated. It is difficult to determine where one ends and another begins.
2. Speech and language disorders take many different forms and may be caused by a variety of physiological and/or environmental influences.
3. Speech and language disorders often have a serious impact on an individual's life.
4. Treatments of speech and language disorders are varied and may be lengthy, difficult, and have varied success rates.
5. Hearing disorders may have a serious impact on the development of individuals so affected in many different ways.
6. Hearing disorders may be caused by a wide variety of problems.

7. The fields of medicine, psychology, and education all play important roles in assisting those with hearing disorders.

8. Visual disorders may be categorized into blind and partially sighted subgroups. They may also be classified according to the anatomical site of the problem.

9. Visual disorders may have a variety of serious impacts on those so affected.

10. Intervention strategies for individuals with a visual disorder range from prevention to rehabilitation.

CHAPTER SEVEN

Speech and Language Disorders

Speech Disorders
    Comments on Assessment
    Prevalence
    Stuttering
    Delayed Speech

Articulation Disorders
Voice Disorders
Language Disorders
    Types of Language Disorders

Humans typically communicate with one another many times a day. Communication is one of the most complicated processes we undertake, and yet it is one we seldom think much about unless there is a problem. Speech and language represent two components of communication where we encounter disorders from time to time. Speech and language are highly interrelated, and problems in either area can have a significant impact on a person's daily life. Because of their complexity, precise determination of problem etiology is often perplexing and treatment may be difficult.

Communicating with others is one of the most complex activities that humans undertake. Most would agree that communication is extremely important to daily existence and societal progress. Certainly it has received a great deal of attention during the past twenty years. Many people have made considerable money writing books and building careers aimed at helping us "communicate." Communication has become a fashionable activity in which to be engaged. Problems between students and their elders during the 1960s were often attributed to a lack of meaningful dialogue—summarized in the catchword *communication*. Difficulties between youngsters and parents, supervisors and workers, husbands and wives, are all frequently attributed to communication problems. Sometimes it seems as though most of our difficulties could be solved if the adversaries received "communication treatments."

The above statements may appear cynical, and they probably are in one sense. We definitely believe that human communication is extremely important. However, we also agree with Hurt, Scott, and McCroskey (1978), who stated that "communication is merely a tool that helps us adapt to and change our environment" (p. 9). Communication is a tool of interchange between individuals, and part of that tool is speech and language.

Many authors treat **speech** and **language** as if they were synonymous terms. Distinctions are often ignored completely, or given only perfunctory attention. Although they are definitely related, *speech* and *language* are not synonymous. Kretschmer and Kretschmer (1978) stated:

> *Language may be expressed through speech, but not in all cases.*
> Speech is the audible production of language, the result of manipula-

Communication
is essential to
interpersonal
success.

tion of the vocal tract and oral musculature. Language, on the other hand, denotes the intended messages contained in the speaker's utterances. It is possible to have speech without language, as with parrots . . . , or language without speech, as with deaf persons who express language in a manual mode. (P. 1, emphasis in the original)

Communication is the broad concept; language is a part of communication. Speech is often thought of as a part of language, although, as noted above, language may exist without speech.

Speech, language, and communication represent concepts that are interrelated, and consequently it is difficult to determine where one ends and another begins. They are overlapping, but *communication* is generally viewed as the broader, umbrella concept, with language and speech being progressively more narrow. Figure 7-1 illustrates the interrelationship of speech, language, and communication in a simple model.

Figure 7-1/ Conceptual Model of Communication, Language and Speech

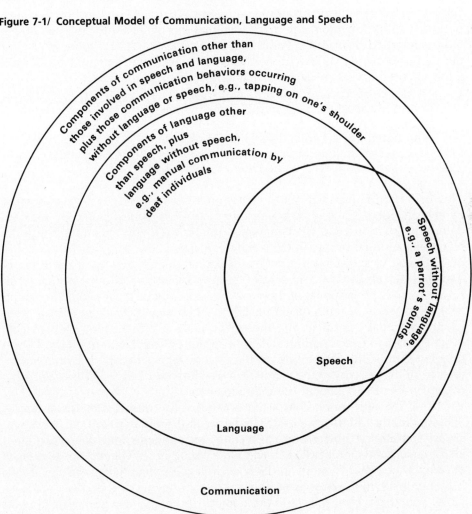

Language is generally viewed as including four major components: phonology, syntax, morphology, and semantics. **Phonology** represents the system of speech sounds that an individual utters. **Syntax** involves the "order and the way in which words and sequences of words are combined into phrases, clauses, and sentences" (Cole & Cole, 1981, p. 4). **Morphology** is concerned with the form and internal structure of words, that is, the transformations of words in terms of such areas as tense and number (e.g., plural). Such transformations involve prefixes, suffixes, and inflections. Syntax and morphology combine to form what we know as grammar. **Semantics** represents the "component of language most concerned with the meaning or understanding of language" (Cole & Cole, 1981, p. 8).

SPEECH DISORDERS

Definitions of **speech disorders** have varied greatly. Many authorities have proposed definitions, some quite detailed in terms of characteristics and others more general (Milisen, 1971; Perkins, 1971; Van Riper, 1972; Wood, 1971). For the purposes of this volume, a synthesis of major definitions will serve well. Such a synthesis was presented by Gelfand, Jenson, and Drew:

> Defective speech or a speech disorder (which are terms often used interchangeably) refers to speech behavior which is sufficiently deviant from normal or accepted speaking patterns that it attracts attention, interferes with communication, and adversely affects communication for either the speaker or the listener. (1982, p. 161)

This definition is broad in that it refers to a constellation of several specific speech disorders. Each of these specific conditions is designated by separate definitions that describe the behavior exhibited. We will encounter these descriptions and definitions in the following pages.

Speech is extremely important in contemporary society. It is no secret that speaking ability can add greatly to one's success or disappointment with regard to both professional and personal-social arenas. Most people are about average in terms of their speaking ability. They may envy those who are unusually articulate, but also pity those who have a difficult time with speech. What is it like to have a serious deficit in speech ability? Certainly it is different for each individual, depending on the circumstances in which he or she operates and the severity of the deficit. We can, however, catch a glimpse of what it may be like by looking at the following case.

The first portion of Doug's life was basically normal. He was an active and apparently intelligent child. His father and mother were both well educated—the father a professor in a university, the mother a nurse. Doug exhibited all the normal developmental behaviors of a young child. There was no evidence of serious abnormality in his initial speech development, but at the age of four his parents began to observe an unusual lack of fluency in his speech. Doug's father was the first to label the problem as **stuttering** and he began to work with Doug to correct it. Doug's mother was reluctant to attempt to solve the

problem on a family basis. She was inclined to seek professional assistance,
but was not successful in convincing Doug and his father to agree. The success
of the corrective program provided by the father was not great, and we pick
up Doug at age fourteen. (It should be noted that fluency problems often end
during childhood. Doug's case is not necessarily typical.) At this point Doug
is a stutterer, and this speech pattern results in some feelings of fear and
embarrassment, which have an impact on his lifestyle. In his diary he recounts
a day in his life this way:

> The best time of day is before I get out of bed because I don't have to
> talk. The only problem during this time is that I dread the rest of the
> day. I have to see my Mom and Dad at breakfast and say something—
> which will always end up in my stuttering; Dad trying to correct or
> help me; and Mom trying to anticipate what I am struggling to say.
> Since I have to go to breakfast, I try to wait until Dad has left for the
> office so that the number of people I have to deal with is reduced. This
> morning I was successful, but there was still Mom trying to please
> and asking what I wanted for breakfast. God, I wish that she would just
> put something in front of me. Even if it wasn't great it would be better
> than having to talk, and stutter. I asked for a hot roll this morning. I
> really wanted cereal but I knew that I would block on that, plus Mom
> would have asked why I didn't want something hot.

We've only taken a glimpse at Doug's day, but even that illustrated how
his abnormal speech affects his life. Doug carries some strong emotional reactions to his stuttering. The stuttering also significantly alters his behavior,
as indicated in the scenario presented above. It is easy to imagine the impact
it must have on his behavior in such settings as the classroom or social encounters with his peers (the home and parents should be much safer than these
other situations). Speech is so central to functioning in our society that disorders
in this area often have an incredible impact on individuals with such problems.
As children, they may be subject to ridicule by peers, begin to feel inadequate
in general, and suffer serious emotional distress. Such outcomes are illustrated
by the cartoon in Figure 7-2.

There are a variety of different speech disorders, and considerable diversity in terms of theoretical perspectives regarding causation and treatment. We
cannot thoroughly examine all the different speech problems in a book of this
type. Comprehensive volumes much longer than this one have focused primarily on this topic (e.g., Travis, 1971). We will, however, discuss several
speech disorders that represent the major problems in this area.

In the case of Doug, we encountered stuttering, one of the most widely
recognized speech disorders. Stuttering is characterized by a disruption of the
fluency, flow, or rhythm of speech. Wood (1971) defined stuttering as "a disturbance of rhythm and fluency of speech by an intermittent blocking, a convulsive repetition, or prolongation of sounds, syllables, words, phrases, or
posture of the speech organs" (p. 21). Stuttering is perhaps the most studied
of all speech disorders and has fascinated researchers for decades.

Figure 7-2/ Fluency Problems Often Cause Emotional Pain

"Even Birds Can Talk!"

Source: Charles Van Riper, *Speech Correction: Principles and Methods,* 5th ed. © 1972, p. 10.
Reprinted by permission of Prentice-Hall, Inc., Englewood Cliffs, N.J.

Delayed speech is another type of problem we will discuss. **Delayed speech** refers to a deficit in speaking proficiency where the individual performs like someone much younger. Wood (1971) defined delayed speech as "failure of speech to develop at the expected age; usually due to slow maturation, hearing impairment, brain injury, mental retardation, or emotional disturbance" (p. 11). Thus delayed speech may be evident for a variety of reasons; it may also take many forms, and treatment may vary accordingly.

Articulation disorders are by far the largest category of all speech problems. For most of those affected, the label *functional articulation disorders* is used. This term refers to articulation problems that are not due to "appreciable structural, physiological, or neurological basis in the speech mechanism or its supporting structures, but which can be accounted for by normal variations in the organism or by environmental or psychological factors" (Powers, 1971, p. 837). An **articulation disorder** is essentially an abnormality in the speech-sound production process which results in inaccurate or otherwise inappropriate execution of the speaking act (e.g., omissions or additions of certain sounds, distortion of sounds).

Voice disorders are another type of speech problem. In a general sense, a voice disorder is evident when individuals speak "habitually with a voice that differs in pitch, loudness, or quality from the voices of others of the same age and sex" in their cultural group (Moore, 1971, p. 535). These distinctions (e.g., age, sex, cultural group) will become important as we explore this topic. Such differences will also serve to reemphasize the fluid nature of normalcy standards.

Comments on Assessment

Because speech disorders occur in many different forms, many different methods are used to evaluate these problems. Recent work in speech disorders has emphasized the systematic assessment of performance differences by both formal and informal means (Hutchinson, Hanson & Mecham, 1979; Mecham & Willbrand, 1979). In some cases the evaluation procedures are published in a manual accompanying the assessment instrument. The manual contains information about arithmetic means and standard deviations, which makes it easy to describe speech disorders in terms of a systematic symptom-severity classification. However, it is a simple matter to calculate means and standard deviations when they are not available. These calculations provide a standard for determining the severity of speech disorders regardless of the assessment device used or type of problem. Examples of such conversions have been given before in the context of other disorders. Such a generalized systematic approach has not been employed in speech disorders but may warrant future attention.

Prevalence

We have already encountered the difficulties involved in prevalence estimates due to differences in definitions and data collection procedures. The field of speech disorders is no less vulnerable to this problem than any other field, and prevalence estimates vary considerably. The most typical prevalence figures cited for speech disorders indicate that between 7 and 10 percent of the population is affected (Emerick & Hatten, 1979). The American Speech-Language-Hearing Association suggested that 5 percent of the American population has a speech or language impairment. On a general basis, these figures do not deviate greatly from other estimates over the years (e.g., Perkins, 1971), but some data suggest substantial differences between geographic locales. Milisen (1971) reported studies indicating percentages ranging from 1 percent in Philadelphia to over 21 percent in Fresno, California. Clearly prevalence estimates vary substantially. These figures are further confounding when one views the overall 12 percent ceiling for services to the disabled noted in P.L. 94-142. Obviously some speech disorders of a milder nature will not be eligible for federally funded services.

The frequency with which speech problems occur diminishes in the population as age increases. Speech disorders are identified in about 12 to 15 percent of the children in kindergarten through grade four. For children in grades five through eight, the figure declines to about 4 to 5 percent. The latter rate remains somewhat constant after grade eight unless treatment intervenes (Milisen, 1971). Thus age and development serve to diminish speech disorders considerably, more so with certain types of problems than others, as we shall see.

Stuttering

From the perspective of lay people, stuttering is probably the most widely recognized type of speech problem. It is also one that is frequently studied by researchers in speech pathology. This recognition and interest is somewhat paradoxical, since stuttering occurs infrequently and has one of the lower prevalence rates when compared to other speech disorders (Milisen, 1971). For example, some estimates have indicated that articulation disorders occur in the United States nearly six times as often as stuttering problems. Likewise, communicative language disorders, including such problems as **aphasia,** occur nearly one and a half times as frequently as stuttering (Perkins, 1971). With this perspective of varying frequencies in mind, it is interesting that stuttering holds such prominence in most of our conceptualizations of speech disorders.

Part of the common view of stuttering probably comes from the nature of the behavior involved in the problem. Stuttering is typically defined as a disturbance in the rhythm and fluency of speech. These disturbances include periodic blocking, repetition, impediment, and/or prolonging of portions of the speech. These may involve certain sounds, syllables, words, or phrases, and they may differ from stutterer to stutterer. (The diary of Doug described some of his particular problems as he thought about asking for breakfast.) Such interruptions in the flow of speech are very evident to both the speaker and listener. They are perhaps more pronounced in terms of intruding on the communication act than other types of speech disorders. Furthermore, listeners often become quite uncomfortable and may try to assist the stuttering speaker with missing or incomplete words. This level of discomfort may be magnified by certain physical movements, gestures, or facial distortions that often accompany stuttering. All this may make the experience a very vivid and easily remembered one for the listener, which may account for part of the prominence of stuttering in the larger picture of speech disorders.

Parents frequently become concerned about stuttering as their young children are learning to talk. Most children exhibit a certain amount of fluency problems as they develop speech. These fluency problems involve disruptions in the rhythm and flow and include some or all of the behaviors described above (blocking, repetition, and prolonging of sounds, syllables, words, or phrases). Generally such speech patterns represent normal fluency problems during early speech development which diminish and cease as maturation progresses. However, these normal fluency problems have historically played an important role in some theories with respect to causation of stuttering.

Causation. Stuttering is a disorder that has fascinated behavioral scientists for many years. The search for a cause has led in many directions. One of the difficulties with these efforts has been that researchers were often seeking a *single* cause. Current thinking suggests that stuttering may have a variety of causes (Helm, Butler & Benson, 1977), and the search for a single cause has been largely discarded. Recent theories regarding the causes of stuttering seem to take three basic perspectives: (1) theories that view the disorder as an emotional problem; that is, stuttering as the outward manifestation of an emotional disturbance of some type; (2) theories that view stuttering as caused by a constitutional or neurological problem; and (3) theories that view stuttering as a learned behavior.

The field in general has begun to show a decreased interest in both the emotional and constitutional etiology theories of stuttering. The emotional-problem theory tends to be held predominantly by psychiatrists and certain counseling psychologists. Van Riper (1972) suggested that this may be "because their clinical practice brings them, not the garden variety of stutterers, but those with deep-seated emotional problems" (p. 253). Empirical research in this area is largely lacking, and the emotional-causation notion is quite difficult to study.

A few studies continue to appear investigating the constitutional-cause theory of stuttering. Some research has indicated that stutterers may have a cortical organization different from that of their counterparts with fluent speech (Cohen & Hanson, 1975), but the nature of such differences remains unclear and a matter for speculation. Certain results have suggested that stutterers and those with fluent speech use different sections of the brain to process material (Moore & Lang, 1977). Other evidence seems to indicate that stutterers may have cerebral-dominance problems to a greater degree than nonstutterers (i.e., they may have one hemisphere that does *not* dominate over the other in information-processing) (Brady & Berson, 1975; Sommers, Brady & Moore, 1975). Conversely, other researchers have obtained results that suggest cerebral-dominance difficulties do not significantly influence stuttering (Gruber & Powell, 1974; Slorach & Noeher, 1973). Thus as we view the evidence regarding constitutional causation, we find that some interest continues, but results are mixed.

A persistent theory over the years regarding causation of stuttering relates to learning. This line of reasoning views stuttering essentially as a learned behavior that emanates from the normal fluency problems evident in early speech development (Bloodstein, Alper & Zisk, 1975). A great deal of the current thinking and treatment seems to follow this logic. Descriptions of how one might learn to stutter abound, and a comprehensive presentation is beyond the scope of this text. Wendell Johnson described this perspective in 1941. It is presented in abridged form in Box 7-1. Although this is not a recent piece of writing, it is included because of the graphic manner in which the description was set forth.

There has been some interest in the notion that stuttering may be substantially influenced by heredity. This line of thinking has been approached from several perspectives, one of which is that it may be sex related. The logic of this theory has certain appeal on the surface, since males outnumber females about four to one in the stuttering population. Thus it is possible that the genetic material that determines an individual's sex may also carry material that contributes to stuttering under certain circumstances. However, this hypothesis is difficult to test and remains only speculation. Heredity has also been of interest because of the high incidence of stuttering within certain family lines as well as in research on twins (e.g., Sheehan & Costly, 1977). Once again, however, we are faced with the difficulty of separating heredity and environmental influence.

The cause of stuttering has been an elusive and perplexing matter for professionals working in speech pathology. Researchers and clinicians continue to seek such information, however, with the hope of identifying more effective treatment and prevention measures. The work of Perkins, Rudas, Johnson, and Bell (1976) represents an example of such work. These investigators studied subjects ranging in age from fourteen to sixty-seven. Their findings suggested that stuttering may be a function of voice coordination with articulation and respiration. One could easily view this in terms of physiological dysfunction, but it could also be placed in the theoretical perspective of learning (or a combination of the two). We will return to this notion as we discuss certain treatment procedures (e.g., Azrin & Nunn, 1974).

Intervention. A wide variety of treatment approaches have been employed with stutterers over the years with mixed results. Such varied techniques as play therapy, creative dramatics, parental counseling, and group counseling with parents have been useful in working with children who stutter. Even

---

BOX 7-1 AN OPEN LETTER TO THE MOTHER OF A STUTTERING CHILD

My dear Mrs. Smith:

I thoroughly appreciate your concern over the speech difficulty of Fred, your four-year-old boy. You say that he is in good health, that he is mentally alert, and is generally normal by any standards you know about. I note that you have been careful not to change his handedness, and that he is now generally right handed. But in spite of all this he stutters.

It will interest you to know that the majority of four-year-old stutterers just about fit that description. I want to say to you very nearly the same things I should say to the mothers of thousands of other "Freds." There are some stuttering children who are not like your boy, and their mothers need somewhat different advice. But the "Freds" make up the majority. . . .

First of all, I want to put you at ease if I can by stressing that the most recent studies have tended strongly to discredit the popular view, which perhaps you share, that stutterers are generally abnormal or inferior in some very fundamental sense. Concerning this point, I should like to make as clear a statement as possible—and I make it on the basis of over one hundred scientific studies of stuttering in older children and adults, and five recent in-vestigations involving over two hundred young children, stutterers and non-stutterers. . . .

We found, for example, that two-, three-, and four-year-olds—all the children of these ages in a large nursery school, somewhat better than average children by most standards—spoke, on the average, in such a way that one out of every four words figured in some kind of repetition! The whole word was repeated, or the first sound or syllable of it was repeated, or it was part of a repeated phrase. One out of four words was the average; about half of the children repeated more frequently than that. Another way to summarize the findings is to say that the average child makes 45 repetitions per thousand words. This was the average—the norm. . . .

Investigation seemed to show that a rose by any other name doesn't smell the same at all. If you call a child a stutterer you get one kind of speech—and personality—development, and if you call him a normal or superior speaker you get another kind of development—within limits but they seem to be rather wide limits.

I can illustrate what I mean by telling you briefly about two cases. The first case is that of Jimmy, who as a pupil in the grades was

psychotherapy has been used to treat some cases of stuttering, but success has been limited (Van Riper, 1972). The rhythm of speech has also been the focus of some therapy for stuttering. In some cases this approach has included the use of a metronome to establish a rhythm for the speaking act (e.g., Wohl, 1968). Relaxation therapy has also been employed, since tenseness has typically been a characteristic observed in stutterers (e.g., Gray, 1968). In all the techniques mentioned, the outcomes have been mixed, with some cases resulting in success and others being disappointing. It has not been uncommon for stutterers to undergo repeated treatments with various approaches. The inability of any treatment or treatments consistently to provide stutterers with fluid speech demonstrates that there is still need for research on this area.

A complete understanding of stuttering remains elusive. However, the treatment approaches have increasingly focused on direct behavioral therapy that attempts to teach the stutterer fluent speech patterns. Some of these

---

BOX 7-1 **(Continued)**

regarded as a superior speaker. He won a number of speaking contests and often served as chairman of small groups. Upon entering the ninth grade, he changed to another school. A "speech examiner" saw Jimmy twice during the one year he spent in that school. The first time she made a phonograph record of his speech. The second time she played the record for him, and after listening to it, told him he was a stutterer.

Now, if you have ever tried to speak into a phonograph recording machine you probably suspect what is true. Practically all children who have done this—in studies with which I am familiar—have shown a considerable number of hesitations, repetitions, broken sentences, etc. It is easy to see how the apparently untrained teacher misjudged Jimmy who was, after all, a superior speaker as ninth-graders go.

He took the diagnosis to heart, however. The teacher told him to speak slowly, to watch himself, and to try to control his speech. Jimmy's parents were quite upset. They looked upon Jimmy's speech as one of his chief talents, and they set about with a will to help him, reminding him of any little slip or hesitation. Jimmy became as self-conscious as the legendary centipede who has been told "how" to walk. He soon developed a quite serious case of stuttering—tense, jerky, hesitant, apprehensive speech.

The second case was Gene, a three-year-old boy. His father became concerned over the fact that now and then Gene repeated a sound or a word. Gene didn't seem to know he was doing it, and he wasn't the least bit tense about it. But the father consulted the family doctor and told him that Gene was stuttering. The doctor took his word for it. (Practically all stutterers are originally diagnosed by laymen—parents and teachers—and "experts" almost never challenge the diagnoses!) He told the father to have Gene take a deep breath before trying to speak. Within forty-eight hours Gene was practically speechless. The deep breath became a frantic gasping from which Gene looked out with wide-eyed, helpless bewilderment. . . .

Source: "An Open Letter to the Mother of a 'Stuttering' Child," by Wendell Johnson, Appendix VII, pp. 558-67, abridged, from *Speech Handicapped School Children*, revised edition, by Wendell Johnson, Spencer J. Brown, James F. Curtis, Clarence W. Edney, and Jacqueline Keaster. Copyright 1948, 1956, by Harper & Row, Publishers, Inc. by permission of the publisher.

procedures include providing knowledge regarding physiological status with direct instruction about correct speaking behaviors (e.g., Azrin & Nunn, 1974). Although continued research is essential, such treatment has been promising, as illustrated by the graphed data in Figure 7-3. Stuttering is a complex problem, and effective treatment is likely to be found in various combinations of therapies that are equally complex.

Delayed Speech

Children who do not evidence speaking proficiency characteristic of their age-group are usually diagnosed as having delayed speech. Two points require examination. First, it is important to remember that we are referring to extreme delays and reduced speaking competency, those that vastly exceed the normal

Figure 7-3/ Data Representing the Frequency of Stuttering for Fourteen Clients

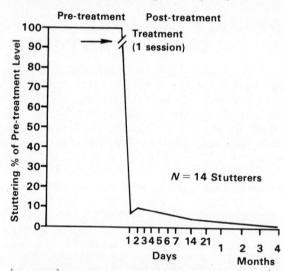

The graphed data for pre-treatment were obtained just prior to treatment. The frequency of stuttering after treatment was obtained from records maintained by the clients each day. Data points are expressed in terms of a percentage of individual client's pre-treatment status (thus the pre-treatment level is 100 percent). Pre-treatment frequencies ranged from 2 to 1,000 incidents per day (mean = 372 per day), and the number of years of stuttering ranged from 2 to 65 (mean = 24 years). Treatment occurred during a single two-hour session, designated by the slash mark at the arrow (follow-up assistance and encouragement was employed through telephone contacts). The treatment session involved an interview examining the inconvenience resulting from stuttering, plus training in several behavior-modification procedures aimed at reducing the problem. Fourteen clients are included in all the data through the first month; the fourth month includes eight clients. The data are given for each day of the first week, for each week of the first month, and monthly thereafter.

Source: Reprinted, by permission, from N. H. Azrin and R. G. Nunn, "A Rapid Method of Eliminating Stuttering by a Regulated Breathing Approach," *Behaviour Research and Therapy,* 1974, *12,* 279-86.

range of variation in performance. Second, we need to examine how delayed speech differs from other types of speech disorders. After all, one could contend that those who stutter or exhibit articulation disorders have reduced speaking proficiency.

Children with delayed speech may have few or no verbalizations that can be interpreted as conventional speech. Some communicate solely through physical gestures. Others may use a combination of gestures and vocal sounds that are not even close approximations of words. Still others may speak, but in a very limited manner, perhaps using single words (typically nouns without auxiliary words) and/or primitive sentences that are short or incomplete (Powers, 1971). Such communication behavior is normal for infants and very young children, but here we are referring to children who are well beyond the age at which they should be speaking in at least a partially fluent fashion.

The distinctions between delayed speech and other disorders is our second preliminary point. The differences between stuttering and delayed speech are clear from the behaviors described above and those mentioned earlier for stutterers, but distinctions between delayed speech and articulation disorders are not as clear at first. In fact, Van Riper (1972) noted that "delayed speech often approximates the pattern of a very severe articulation disorder, and some cases so diagnosed probably belong to this category" (pp. 48-49). Powers (1971) discussed delayed speech in the context of functional articulation disorders and distinguished it from infantile perseveration—both a form of immature

Gestural speech is common in very young children.

speech. Her description is helpful in terms of conceptualizing delayed speech, although she made it clear that we should not expect sharp and definitive distinctions. Powers examined this topic in the following manner:

> There are two general types of disorder which both fall within the broad category of speech immaturity. These are *delayed speech*, which is a more complex and profound disorder, and *infantile perseveration*. Delayed speech is the more inclusive of the two. Indeed, infantile perseveration can be thought of as the articulatory aspect of delayed speech, but there is no sharp distinction between the two. If a child's speech immaturity is confined largely to sound omissions and substitutions, if he has learned to rely mainly on speech as his means of communication, if there is considerable output of speech, if the onset of speech has been fairly typical, if he attempts sentences as well as words and phrases, his speech deviation can best be referred to as *infantile perseveration*. If, however, there has been little or no attempt at speech until past two years of age, if gestures and nonspeech vocalizations are used extensively, if speech is limited mainly to nouns, with little use of qualifying, connective, or auxiliary words, if vocabulary is meager, if single words are used for sentences or phrases, most speech clinicians would tend to call the disorder *delayed speech*. The distinction between *infantile perseveration* and *delayed speech* is thus both qualitative and quantitative, but there is considerable overlap between them in symptomatology. (1971, p. 843; emphasis in the original)

The prevalence of delayed speech seems particularly unclear, and estimates have varied so greatly that Milisen (1971) characterized them as meaningless. Further research is necessary for us to determine the extent of such problems more precisely.

Causation. As suggested above, cases of delayed speech may take a variety of forms, so it is not surprising that causation of these problems also varies greatly. Several types of environmental deprivation contribute to delayed speech. For example, partial or complete hearing loss may cause an individual to evidence serious delay (or absence) of speech development. Since the auditory stimulus and modeling is deficient, learning to speak is most difficult. The broader environment may also result in delayed speech for those with normal hearing. In some cases a child lives in a set of circumstances where there is little opportunity to learn speech (or some environments may actually interfere with the development of speech). Other problems may contribute to delayed speech, such as cerebral palsy and emotional disturbances (e.g., childhood schizophrenia, autism). Even less severe emotional problems may result in delayed speech, like negativism, which can be viewed as an emotional problem stemming from a relational difficulty (relational problems between parents and child).

Negativism is a set of behaviors that many of us observe in some form as children develop speech. There is a great deal of pressure on children during the period when they are normally developing their speaking skills. Parents (and others) expect them to go to bed when told, to control urination and defecation properly, and to learn appropriate eating skills—among many other things. The demands are great, and in some cases they may exceed a child's tolerance level with regard to performance. There are many ways to react when more is demanded than one is able to produce. Negativism resulting in delayed speech represents one of these reactions.

Refusal is one way children may react to excessive performance demands. In normal development, children occasionally do refuse to follow the directions of adults. One very effective area of refusal (on the part of the child) is speaking; the reprisal options on the part of parents are few and may be ineffective. As parents it is relatively simple to punish refusal misbehaviors when they involve such acts as refusing to go to bed or to clean up one's room. However, it is a different matter when parents deal with a refusal to talk or to learn to talk. It is not easy to force a child to talk through conventional punishment techniques. (In fact, the child may be able to communicate needs adequately using gestures, which further complicates the problem.)

Viewing the problem from another angle, there are other situations where children may be punished *for* talking. Parents may see a child's attempt to communicate as an irritant. It may be too loud or timed badly, while the adults are reading, watching television, or engaged in conversation (even more rules to learn at such a tender age).

From these descriptions we can see that some children might have delayed speech that represents environmentally controlled learning due to refusal or rebellion. Not speaking may be reinforced in some instances, and in others it may be a way of expressing refusal that is unlikely to result in punishment. Thus in some cases children may *not learn* to speak and in others they may *learn not* to speak. If such circumstances exist at the time a child would normally develop speech and they persist for a substantial length of time, seriously delayed speech may result.

We mentioned earlier that delayed speech may emerge from experience deprivation, where the environment either limits or hinders the opportunity to learn speech. Basic principles of learning suggest that when one is first learning a skill, the configuration of stimulus and reinforcement contingencies are important. A skill that is just beginning to develop is fragile. Stimuli and reinforcement must be reasonably consistent, appropriate, and properly timed. If such conditions do not exist, the skill development may be retarded or even negated. This does not mean that the environment (the home) must be an orchestrated language-development program. Most households involve sufficiently adequate approximations of appropriate contingencies to permit and promote speech learning.

Learning to speak is no different from learning other skills. Stimulus and reward contingencies must be structured so that the child can learn to speak, or seriously delayed speech may result. There are homes where conversation is abnormally infrequent. Parents may converse rarely with either each other or the child. In such a case, the child may have infrequent speech modeling and little reinforcement for speaking. The result may be delayed speech due to the relative paucity of contingencies that would promote learning to speak appropriately. It is also possible that verbal interchanges between parents reflects a strained relationship or emotional problems. The environment in such circumstances may be tense and troubled—involving threats, arguments, and shouting of an unpleasant nature. A child who is learning to speak in this type of situation may learn that speech is associated with unpleasant feelings or even punishment. Seriously delayed speech may result from these environmental circumstances. When such contingencies are combined with infrequent interchanges, the learning (not to speak and not learning to speak) may be particularly potent.

The environment we just described represents an unpleasant set of circumstances as well as one where learning speech may be impaired. One may have a great concern about the amount of love and caring in such a situation. But delayed speech can also occur in families where one would generally say there is great love and caring, at least with respect to observable behavior. In some environments there may be little need for a child to learn speech. Some parents are particularly concerned about satisfying all their child's needs or desires. Carrying this desire to the extreme, this superparent may anticipate the child's wants (e.g., toys, water, food) and provide for them even before the child makes a verbalized request. Such children may only gesture and their parents will respond (thus rewarding gestures and not shaping speech skills). Learning to speak is much more complex than making simple movements or facial grimaces, and speech learning is more exacting. If gesturing is rewarded, speaking will be less likely to be learned properly.

Our discussion indicates that delayed speech is a complex phenomenon. Causation is equally complicated—as complicated as the speech development process itself. The reader who is a new parent, or anticipating parenthood, should know that the vast majority of children learn to speak normally. Certainly parents should not become so self-conscious that they create a problem situation. If we conduct ourselves in normal fashion, our children will have normal speech. Extreme environments of any type (e.g., loving or unloving) can result in a variety of problems. Only on rare occasions are extreme environments appropriate for the development of speech.

Intervention. Treatment approaches for delayed speech are as varied as the causes. Whatever the cause, the effective treatment is one that will teach the child appropriate speaking proficiency for his or her age-group. In some cases, matters other than just defective learning must be considered in the treatment procedures (e.g., hearing impairments). Such cases may involve surgery and prosthetic appliances such as hearing aides, as well as specially designed instructional techniques aimed at teaching speech.

If delayed speech is caused primarily by defective learning (not accompanied by other difficulties), treatment may focus on the basic principles of learned behavior. In a general sense the stimulus and reinforcement patterns that contributed to delayed speech must be altered. The configuration of these contingencies must be rearranged so that appropriate speaking behaviors can be learned. This process sounds simple, but the identification and control of such contingencies may be complex. There has been some success with direct teaching interventions using applied behavior analysis (e.g., Bricker & Bricker, 1974; Sloane, Johnston & Harris, 1968). Further treatment research is needed to evaluate the relative effectiveness of differing procedures.

Earlier we discussed cases of delayed speech caused by a child's refusal to speak (negativism). Such behavior may seem like another speech disorder known as *elective mutism* (or voluntary mutism), but these two conditions are quite different. The electively mute child *does* have speaking abilities but chooses not to speak. This is distinguished from extreme speech delays, where the skills have not been acquired or, if so, only on a limited basis. Friedman and Kargan (1973) described the elective mute as "a child who does not speak, but who has no speech or language disorders . . . no physical defect of the speech mechanism . . . is not aphasic, nor . . . of sufficiently deficient general intelligence so as to be unable to formulate speech" (p. 249). Electively mute children generally do speak, but only in certain situations and/or in the presence of certain individuals. The causes of elective mutism may be similar to those examined with negativism. The configuration of stimulus, reinforcement, and punishment contingencies is typically different, however, resulting in the selective use of speaking abilities that have already been acquired. Treatment of elective mutism has generally involved behavioral procedures aimed at modifying the circumstances under which the child will talk (e.g., Bauermeister & Jemial, 1975; Colligan, Colligan & Dilliard, 1977; Griffith, Schnell, McNees, Bissinger & Huff, 1975; Van Der Kooy & Webster, 1975).

Articulation Disorders

Articulation disorders represent a prevalent type of speech disorder. Emerick and Hatten (1979) indicated that the majority of speech problems public school clinicians contend with involve articulation disorders. Van Riper (1972) estimated that articulation problems represent about 75 percent of the speech disorders encountered by such professionals. For the most part these difficulties are functional articulation disorders mentioned earlier—not disorders caused by a conspicuous physiological defect (Powers, 1971). However, a certain number of articulation disorders do not fit into the functional type and may be attributed to physiological abnormality. We will explore different causes later in this section.

There is controversy about the treatment of articulation disorders, due in part to the relatively large number of disorders that are functional in nature. In a substantial number of functional articulation disorder cases, a predictable developmental progression occurs. In such cases, articulation problems diminish and may even cease to exist as the child matures. This phenomenon has led many school administrators and parents to express reluctance regarding the treatment of functional articulation disorders in younger students. The argument is basically one of resources. If a significant proportion of articulation disorders are likely to be reduced by continued development, why expend precious (and increasingly strained) resources to correct them? The logic is obvious and has a certain amount of appeal, but, it can be applied only with caution. In general, improvement of articulation performance will continue until a child is about nine or ten years of age. If articulation problems persist beyond these ages, they are unlikely to improve unless intense intervention occurs. Further, the longer such difficulties are allowed to continue, the more difficult treatment becomes, and the probability of success is reduced (Milisen, 1971).

Causation. The causes of articulation disorders are varied. Some are caused by physical malformations, such as mouth, jaw, or teeth structures that are abnormal. In other cases, articulation disorders are the result of nerve injury or brain damage. Functional articulation disorders are generally viewed as being due to defective learning of the speaking act in one form or another (Hutchinson, Hanson & Mecham, 1979). As with other behavior problems, however, such categories of causation are not as distinct in practice as may be suggested by textbook discussion. There is definitely a blurring even between such broad types as functional and organic. Bloomer stated that "the correspondence between structure and function is imperfect because some speakers are capable of compensating for seemingly insurmountable handicaps of orofacial deformity, whereas other speakers whose structures are anatomically satisfactory reveal handicapping defects of function" (1971, p. 715). Thus some individuals who exhibit physical malformations that *should* result in articulation problems do not, and vice versa.

Despite this qualifying note, we will examine causation of articulation performance deficits in terms of two general categories: those that are due to physical oral malformations and those that are clearly functional because of the absence of physical deformity. These distinctions remain useful for instructional purposes, since it is the unusual individual who can overcome physical abnormality and articulate satisfactorily. Even with general types of causes there may be a variety of specific circumstances that result in articulation difficulties. We cannot examine all the possibilities in the limited space of this volume, so we will be selective in our discussion.

The physical abnormalities we will examine can be considered in terms of malformed structures of the oral cavity. (Other types of physical defects can affect articulation performances, such as an abnormal or absent larynx.) Speech formation involves many different physical structures that must be interfaced with learned muscle/tissue movements, auditory feedback, and a multitude of other factors. Although these coordinated functions are almost never perfect, they occur for most of us in an unbelievably successful manner (and one that most of us think little about). Malformed oral structures alter the manner in which coordinated movements must take place. With certain deformities, normal or accurate production of sounds is extremely difficult, if not impossible.

One oral malformation that most lay people are acquainted with is the **cleft palate** (often referred to by speech pathologists as "clefts of the lip or palate" or both). The cleft palate is a "fissure [gap] of the soft palate [a movable muscular sheet attached to the rear part of the hard palate which is the bony anterior part of the roof of the mouth] and roof of the mouth, sometimes extending through [the upper lip]" (Wood, 1971, p. 10). The roof of the mouth serves an important function in accurate sound production. There is a reduced division of the nasal and mouth cavities with a cleft palate, which influences the movement of air that is important in articulation performance. Clefts occur **congenitally** in about 1 out of every 750 births (Morris & Greulich, 1968) and may take any of several forms. Figure 7-4 shows a normal palate configuration (A) and unilateral and bilateral cleft palates (B and C). In the cases of the cleft palates, it is easy to see how articulation performance would be impaired. These problems are caused by developmental difficulties *in utero* and are often later corrected by surgery.

Dental structure plays a significant role in articulation performance. Because tongue and lips work together with the teeth in an intricate manner to form many sounds, dental abnormalities may result in serious articulation disorders. Some dental malformations are associated with cleft palates, as portrayed by parts B and C of Figure 7-4. A variety of dental deformities not associated with clefts often cause articulation difficulties. We can examine only a few of these conditions. The interested reader may wish to consult other sources for more complete information (e.g., Bloomer, 1971; Perkins, 1971).

Figure 7-4/ Normal and Cleft Palate Configurations

A

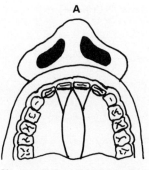

Normal Palate Configuration

B

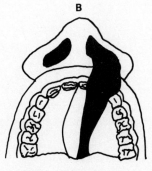

Unilateral Cleft Palate

C

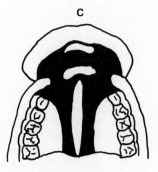

Bilateral Cleft Palate

The natural fitting-together of the teeth in upper and lower jaws is important to speech production. The general term used for referring to the closure and fitting-together of dental structures is **occlusion** or *dental occlusion*. When the fit is abnormal for some reason, such a condition is known as a *malocclusion*. The occlusion involves several factors, including the biting height of the teeth (when the jaws are closed), the alignment of teeth in upper and lower jaws, the nature of the curves in upper and lower jaws, and the positioning of individual teeth.

A normal occlusion (for adults) is portrayed in part A of Figure 7-5. The teeth of the upper jaw normally extend slightly beyond those of the lower jaw, and the bite overlap of those on top over those on the bottom is about one-third for the front teeth (incisors) when closed. This presents a normal configuration, and abnormalities take many forms. We will discuss only two here.

There are cases where the overbite of the top teeth is unusually large, that is, the normal amount of difference between the lower and upper dental structure is exaggerated. Such conditions may be due to the positioning of the upper and lower jaws. Part B of Figure 7-5 illustrates a malocclusion of this type where there is a misalignment of the jaw structures. Other malformations of dental patterns also result in articulation difficulties. In some cases we find nearly the opposite situation of the exaggerated upper jaw position. This is illustrated by part C of Figure 7-5 and is once again a jaw misalignment. (Both

Figure 7-5/ Normal and Abnormal Dental Occlusions

A

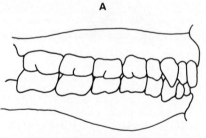

Normal Dental Occlusion

B   C

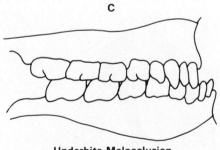

Overbite Malocclusion   **Underbite Malocclusion**

exaggerated overbites and underbites may also be the result of abnormal teeth positioning or angles as well as jaw misalignment.)

Functional articulation disorders are generally thought to be caused by faulty learning. In many cases the source or sources of defective learning in terms of speaking is difficult to identify (Hutchinson, Hanson & Mecham, 1979; Van Riper, 1972). Like other articulation problems, it has long been documented that those of a functional nature have many specific causes (Wintz, 1969). In some cases the existing stimulus and reinforcement contingencies may not be appropriate for shaping accurate articulation. It is not uncommon for unthinking adults to view the normal inaccuracies of speech in young children as cute or amusing. Consequently such baby talk may be reinforced in a powerful manner (e.g., asking the young child to say a particular word in the presence of grandparents or other guests). This can be incredibly rewarding for the young child, who is then on center stage and may be reinforced by laughter and/or physical affection such as hugs or kisses. Such potent rewards may result in misarticulations that linger long beyond the time when normal maturation would have them diminish or cease. It should be noted, however, that the influence of baby-talk interactions between parents and children has recently been seriously questioned (Cromer, 1981). In certain cases, parental reinforcement for accurate articulation may be unsystematic. Parents are busy in their daily routines, and encouraging their children to speak properly may not be high among their conscious ordering of personal priorities. However, if one considers the potential outcomes, it is clear that parents might be more cautious in this respect.

Defective learning can come from many sources. Parental modeling can result in articulation disorders. Some adults imitate the baby talk of young children when speaking to them. If parents, grandparents, or friends realized the potential results of such behavior, they would certainly alter the nature of verbal interchanges with young children. Modeling is a potent tool in shaping learned behavior.

Intervention. Treatment of articulation disorders takes many forms. Clearly the treatment for disorders due to physical abnormalities will be different from the treatment for disorders that are functional in nature. However, in many cases treatment may include a combination of procedures.

Considerable progress has been evident over the years with respect to surgical repair of cleft palates. Such techniques may involve several different procedures because of the dramatic nature of the structural defect as portrayed in Figure 7-4. Some procedures include bone grafts to the hard portion of the palate, as well as stretching and stitching together the fleshy tissue. As suggested by the drawings in Figure 7-4, surgery is also frequently necessary for the upper lip and nose structures, and dental corrective efforts may be undertaken as well. It may also be necessary to train or retrain the individual in terms of articulation, depending on the age of the patient at the time of surgery and the success of the surgical procedures. Continued development of the individual may result in later problems. Early correction has resulted in successful healing and speech for as many as 90 percent of treated cases (Converse, 1965), but the permanence of such results may be questionable in light of later growth spurts. The National Institute of Dental Research reported in 1967 that articulation problems emerged in 40 percent of the patients as a result of growth several years after cleft-palate surgery. Treatment for cleft-palate cases has also involved the use of prosthetic appliances, for instance an appliance that basically serves as the upper palate or at least covers the fissures. Such an appliance may be attached to the teeth to hold them in position and can be visualized in terms of the palate portion of many upper portions of artificial dentures. Readers interested in more details may wish to consult volumes examining such treatment more completely (e.g., Perkins, 1971, pp. 188-90).

Dental malformations (aside from those associated with clefts) are also often treated by means of procedures aimed at correcting the physical defect. Surgery may be undertaken to alter the jaw structure and alignment. In some cases, orthodontic treatment may involve the repositioning of teeth through extractions and pressure applied using braces. The use of prosthetic appliances may be required, such as full or partial artificial dentures. As in other types of problems, the articulation patient who has orthodontic treatment will often require treatment to learn proper speech performance (Bloomer, 1971).

Treatment of functional articulation disorders typically focuses on relearning the speaking act. Specific causation of the defective learning is difficult to identify precisely, but the basic assumption with such cases is that there was an inappropriate configuration of stimulus and reinforcement contingencies in the environment during the time that speech development occurred.

A speech clinician provides individualized treatment for students with speech or language disorders.

Treatment will attempt to rearrange those contingencies so that accurate artic- ulation can be learned. Several behavior-modification procedures have been employed successfully in treating functional articulation disorders (e.g., John- ston & Johnston, 1972; Mowrer, Baker & Schutz, 1968; Ryan, 1971; Wolfe & Irwin, 1975). In all cases, treatment techniques are complex.

Voice Disorders

Voice disorders involve unusual or abnormal acoustical qualities in the sounds made when a person speaks. All people have differing acoustical qualities in their voices. In the area of voice disorders, we are considering characteristics that are habitual and sufficiently different that they are noticeable and may divert a listener's attention from the content of a message.

Voice disorders have received relatively little attention compared to other speech problems. This lack of attention is due to several factors. First, voice normalcy or abnormality represents a great deal of subjective judgment. What is normal varies considerably according to the circumstances (e.g., football games, barroom conversation, seminar discussion) and geographical location (e.g., western, rural, New England, Deep South), as well as family environments, personality, and physical structure of the speech mechanism. Another factor contributing to the lack of attention to voice disorders is related to the acceptable ranges of normal voice. Most individuals have voices that are within our tolerance ranges of acceptable acoustic sound production. When we are discussing voice *disorders*, we are referring to extreme deviations from the norm. Finally, voice disorders have received relatively little attention from professionals in speech pathology. Knepflar (1976) noted, "I believe that voice problems constitute the most overlooked area in the diagnosis of communication disorders and that most training programs for speech pathologists are weaker in the area of voice than any other aspect of the field" (p. 14).

Despite the relative lack of attention, voice disorders are a significant problem within one area of speech dysfunction. Milisen (1971) reported widely varying prevalence figures for voice disorders ranging from 0.5 percent to 4.5 percent in the general population (varying greatly between populations of elementary, high school, and college students). He estimated that, in general, voice defects were present in about 1 percent of the total population. Milisen also noted that voice disorders "constitute between five and 15 percent of the defective-speech population" (1971, p. 628). These figures vary somewhat from those presented by Perkins (1971), who estimated that about one million people were affected by voice disorders. Based on Perkins' assumed population of 200 million, this would place the prevalence of voice disorders at 0.5 percent of the total population, which is at the lower end of results obtained in the prevalence studies reviewed by Milisen (1971). Both authors are cautious regarding the accuracy and usefulness of such figures.

The nature of voice disorders varies greatly. Earlier we encountered the general description of voice-disordered individuals as those who speak "habitually with a voice that differs in pitch, loudness, or quality from the voices of others of the same age and sex within [their cultural group]" (Moore, 1971, p. 535). This definition provides considerable latitude, but it also outlines the general parameters of voice disorders that are often discussed in the literature: pitch, loudness, and quality. Thus an individual with a voice disorder may exhibit a deviation in one or a combination of these factors that significantly interferes with communication. The interference occurs when the abnormal voice factor results in listener attention being focused on the sound rather than on the message being conveyed.

Hutchinson, Hanson, and Mecham described voice pitch:

An efficient, appropriate pitch is suited to the situation, the speaker's **laryngeal** structure and to the speech content. It allows for upward and downward inflections without undue strain or voice breaks. It varies within the sentence and within longer units of speech, according to meaning and emotions the speaker wishes to convey. It does not call undue attention to itself. (1979, p. 207)

The acoustic characteristics of voice quality include such factors as degree of nasality, "breathy" speech, and hoarse-sounding speech. As with the other parameters of voice, loudness is a subjective determination. The normal voice is not habitually characterized by excessive loudness or unusual softness. Loudness depends a great deal on the circumstances surrounding the communication.

Pitch disorders may take several forms. The voice may have an abnormally high or low pitch, it may be characterized by pitch breaks or a restricted pitch range, or it may be monotonal or monopitched. Many of us experienced pitch breaks as we progressed through adolescence. Although these are more commonly associated with young males, they also occur in females (Van Riper, 1972). Such pitch breaks are a normal part of development, but if they persist much beyond adolescence, they may signal laryngeal difficulties (Brewer, 1975). Abnormally high- or low-pitched voices may be due to a variety of problems. They may be learned through imitation (such as the young boy attempting to sound like his older brother or his father). They may also be learned from certain circumstances that the individual is in (e.g., those placed in positions of authority who perceive a lower voice pitch as necesssary to suggest the image of power). Organic conditions, such as hormone imbalance, may also result in abnormally high- or low-pitched voices.

Voice disorders involving loudness may likewise have varied causes. Excessively loud or soft voices may be learned either through imitation or through perceptions of the environment much like those mentioned for pitch disorders. Other cases of abnormal vocal intensity occur because the individual has not learned to monitor loudness. Beyond the learning difficulties, however, some intensity voice disorders occur because of organic problems. For example, abnormally low vocal intensity may result from such problems as paralysis of vocal cords, laryngeal trauma (e.g., larynx surgery for cancer, damage to the larynx through accident or disease), and pulmonary diseases (e.g., asthma, emphysema). Excessively loud speech may also occur as a result of such organic problems as hearing impairments and brain damage (Hutchinson et al., 1979).

Voice disorders having to do with quality-of-speech problems include such production deviances as abnormal nasality in the sound as well as hoarse and "breathy" speech. Abnormal nasality may take the form of a voice that sounds overly nasal (hypernasality) or a voice that evidences a reduced acoustic sound (denasality or hyponasality) that dulls the resonance of consonants. Hypernasality occurs "primarily because the back door to the nose fails to close sufficiently" (Van Riper, 1972, p. 154). Such conditions can be due to improper tissue movement in the speech mechanism, or they may result from such organic defects as an imperfectly repaired cleft palate. Excessive hypernasality may also be acquired through learning, as in the case of country music or speech that represents an extreme form of the hillbilly dialect. Denasality is a type of voice quality that we have all experienced when we have a severe head cold or hay fever. The sounds produced are congested and/or dulled, with reduced acoustic resonance. In some cases, however, denasality in voice production is the result of learning or abnormal physical structures rather than these more common problems, which most of us experience periodically.

Treatment of voice disorders varies from surgical intervention to prosthetic devices and behavior modification implemented to restructure learned speaking patterns that are abnormal. We cannot examine all the specific voice disorders, their causes, and their treatment in this discussion. The interested reader may wish to consult other volumes that focus specifically on speech problems (e.g., Hutchinson et al., 1979; Travis, 1971; Van Riper, 1972).

LANGUAGE DISORDERS

Language has assumed many forms throughout history. Certain early Native Americans communicated through a system of clucking sounds made with the tongue and teeth. Such sounds were also used in combination with hand signs and spoken language that often differed greatly between tribes. (These language systems have been described in historical documents. An excellent portrayal of such language differences is found in *Sacajawea* by A. L. Waldo, 1978.) Current definitions of language reflect the breadth necessary to encompass diverse communication systems, but they are also restrictive in that they focus on the components of language in contemporary society. For example, Lucas (1980) noted that language reflects "a system of symbols agreed upon by two or more people and governed by the linguistic properties inherent in phonology, syntax, morphology, and semantics" (p. 242).

Language disorders occur when there is a serious disruption of the language process. Such malfunction may occur in one or more of the components of language. Because language is one of the most complex sets of behaviors exhibited by humans, language disorders are complex. Language involves memory, learning, message reception and processing, and expressive skills. Thus an individual with a language disorder may have deficits in any of these areas, and it may be difficult to identify precisely the nature of the problem. In addition, language problems may arise in the form of language delays or language disorders. The term *language delay* is used when the normal rate of developmental progress is interrupted but the systematic sequence of development remains essentially intact. In this case, the acquisition of language is merely slowed. The term *language disorder* is different in that this term is used in the language literature "when the language acquisition is not systematic and/or sequential. . . . A language disordered child is not progressing systematically and sequentially in any aspect of rule-governed and purposive linguistic behavior" (Lucas, 1980, pp. 52, 54). We will use the term *language disorder* in a general sense and discuss several different types. Where evidence suggests that delay may be a major contributor, we will discuss it.

Types of Language Disorders

A review of the literature reveals a wide range of terminology used to describe the processes involved in language as well as disorders in those processes. One common approach is to view language disorders in terms of receptive and expressive problems. We will examine these broad categories, as well as aphasia, a problem that may occur in both children and adults.

Receptive language disorders result from difficulties in comprehending what others say. "Children with receptive language problems are often noticed when they fail to follow directions given by an adult. Often these children appear to be inattentive or may seem as though they do not hear or listen to directions" (Cole & Cole, 1981, p. 20). Individuals with receptive language disorders have great difficulty understanding the messages of others and may process only part of what is being said to them (in some cases, none of what is being said). Thus they have a substantial problem in language processing, which is basically half of language (the other part being language production). Wiig and Semel (1980) defined language processing as "the act of listening and interpreting spoken language" (p. 3).

Expressive language disorders are exhibited when individuals have difficulty in language production, "the act of formulating and using spoken language" (Wiig & Semel, 1980, p. 3). Those with expressive language disorders may have a limited vocabulary and rely on "the same core of words no matter what the situation" (Cole & Cole, 1981, p. 21). Expressive language disorders may appear as immature speech and often result in personal interaction difficulties.

Identifying the precise cause of different language disorders can be difficult. The answers are not clear regarding what contributes to normal language acquisition, exactly how those contributions occur, or how malfunctions influence language disorders. We do know that certain sensory and other physiological systems must be intact and developing normally for language processes to progress normally. For example, if the hearing system is seriously impaired (see Chapter 8), a language deficit may result. Likewise, serious brain damage might deter normal language functioning. Learning must also progress in a systematic and sequential fashion for language to develop appropriately. Language-learning is like other learning: it must be stimulated and reinforced in order for the behavior to be acquired and mastered.

As we examined other disorders, we encountered many of the physiological problems that may be causative factors in language difficulties. Neurological damage that may affect language functioning can occur prenatally, during birth, or later in life (even adulthood). For example, oxygen deprivation before or during birth may result in language disorders. Likewise, a mechanical injury at birth or an accident later in life can also cause language problems. Serious emotional disorders may be accompanied by language disturbances if the individual's perception of the world is substantially distorted.

Learning opportunities may be seriously deficient or otherwise disrupted and result in language disorders. As with speech, youngsters may not learn language because the environment is not conducive to such learning. Modeling in the home may be so infrequent that a child cannot learn language in a normal fashion. This might be the case in a family where no speaking occurred because the parents were deaf (even though the children had normal hearing). Such circumstances are rare, but when they occur a language delay is likely. The parents cannot model the language for their children, nor can they respond to and reinforce such behavior. It should be emphasized, however, that learning outcomes are variable. In situations that seem normal, we may find a child with serious language difficulty; in circumstances that seem dismal, we may find youngsters whose language facility is normal. Gelfand et al. (1982) cited an example involving four brothers with normal hearing who were born and raised by parents who were both deaf and had no spoken language facility. These boys seemed to develop language quite normally, although they cannot account for that development. They have distinguished themselves in various manners ranging from earning Ph.D.'s and M.D.'s (one holds both degrees) to becoming a millionaire through patented inventions.

The previous example represents a rare set of circumstances, but it is a good illustration of how variable and poorly understood language learning is. The assumption has long been that language-deprived environments place children at risk for exhibiting language delays or disorders. For example, it has been thought that language acquisition may be delayed when parents use baby talk in communicating with their young children. Such a view is based on the fundamental principles of learning theory that youngsters learn what is modeled and taught. There is little question that this perspective is sound with most skill acquisition. Many clinical reports of language problems would seem to uphold such a notion in this area, and research has also supported *certain* relationships between parental verbalizations and child language development (e.g., Newport, Gleitman & Gleitman, 1977). However, Cromer (1981) reviewed research on language acquisition and concluded that "most studies of baby talk fail to explain the acquisition of [language] structure" (p. 70). Thus the effects of parental modeling on child language development may not be as clear and simple as once thought.

The distinctions between speech and language problems are blurred, because they overlap so much as functions. Receptive and expressive language disorders are as intertwined as speech and language. When an individual does not express language well, is it because there is a receptive problem or an expressive problem? These cannot be separated cleanly, and thus causation is also not a topic that can be clearly divided into categories.

Treatment of language disorders must take into account the nature of the problem and the manner in which the individual is affected. Thus intervention is an individualized undertaking, just as with other types of disorders. Some causes are more easily identified than others and may or may not be remedied by mechanical or medical intervention. Other types of treatment basically involve instruction or language training. Cole and Cole (1981) outlined several sequential steps in effective language training:

1. Identifying the child
2. Assessing the child
3. Establishing the instructional objectives
4. Developing the language intervention program
5. Implementing the language intervention program
6. Reassessing the child
7. Reteaching if necessary. (P. 81).

Language-training programs are tailored to the individual's needs in terms of strengths and limitations. In fact, current terminology labels these as **individualized language plans (ILPs),** similar in concept to the individualized educational plans (IEPs) mandated by P.L. 94-142. These intervention plans include long-range goals (annual), a set of more short-range and specific behavioral objectives, a statement of resources to be used in achieving the objectives, a description of evaluation methods, dates the program was initiated and completed, and an evaluation of the individual's generalization of skills (Cole & Cole, 1981). Such language-training programs are based on learning theory and are aimed at systematic shaping or teaching of language skills. For young children such interventions often focus on beginning language stimulation. Such treatment is intended to emulate the conditions under which youngsters normally learn language, but the conditions are usually intensified and made more systematic (Weiss & Lillywhite, 1976). In many such cases, parents are trained and involved in the intervention.

Aphasia represents a type of language disorder that has been described in the literature for more than a century and a half. Although definitions have varied over time, they have employed strikingly consistent themes. For example, Wood (1971) noted that aphasia was the same as dysphasia and defined them as "partial or complete loss of the ability to speak or to comprehend the spoken word due to injury, disease, or maldevelopment of the brain" (p. 11). Wiig and Semel (1980) defined *aphasic* as "having an acquired language disorder caused by brain damage with complete or partial impairment of language comprehension, formulation and use" (p. 443). Thus definitions of aphasia commonly link the disorder to brain injury either through mechanical accidents or through other insults.

Over the years many different types of aphasia and/or conditions associated with aphasia have been identified and labeled (e.g., agnosia, paraphrasia, dysprosody). Aphasic language disturbances have also been classified in terms of receptive and expressive problems. All the aphasia sublabels cannot be listed or described here, and there is no widespread agreement regarding their distinctiveness or usefulness.

Aphasia may be present both in childhood and during the adult years. The term *developmental aphasia* has been widely used with affected children despite the long-standing connection of such problems with neurological damage. Studies have shown that aphasic children often begin to use words at age two or later, and phrases at age four (e.g., Morely, Court, Miller & Garside, 1955). The link between aphasia and neurological abnormalities in youngsters has been of continuing interest to researchers, with some evidence suggesting support. For example, Geschwind (1968) found significant differences in the sizes of the auditory cortex in aphasic's right and left hemispheres. Such findings have prompted continual investigation exploring the neurological makeup of aphasic children. Despite the numerous theories and assumptions, direct and objective evidence identifying neurological dysfunction in relation to aphasia has been difficult to acquire.

Adult aphasia has had as many varied definitions as childhood aphasia. Eisenson (1971a) suggested that there was likely to be more agreement between professionals with regard to identifying an aphasic individual than "agreement as to definitions of aphasia or to the *essence* of aphasic involvement" (p. 1220; emphasis in the original). According to Eisenson (1971a), the following observations are important in identifying aphasics:

1. At some stage in their involvement, persons designated as aphasic indicate impairment for intake of sequential verbal events as well as for verbal sequential output. Intake disturbances are often labeled as memory or attention span defects. Output sequential disturbances are manifest in syntactical defects for formulations that are appropriate and relatively specific to the situation.

2. On a probability basis, aphasic involvements are in general expressed in a reduced likelihood that a given linguistic formulation will be understood (appropriately evaluated), or produced (appropriately formulated) in kind and manner consistent with the situation (events associated with the linguistic formulation). In general, the more intellectual and abstract the expected linguistic reaction, the less likely it is that the reaction will occur. (P. 1220)

Eisenson's observations related to adult aphasics remind us of definitions encountered earlier. The only factor missing is the causation link to neurological malfunction. However, the assumption of brain damage is very much associated with aphasia during adulthood. The causes of such brain damage are diverse. A variety of physical traumas may result in aphasic involvement (e.g., automobile and industrial accidents, shooting incidents). Other factors, such as strokes, tumors, and diseases that affect brain tissue, may have the same result. In most cases, aphasic trauma seems to be associated with damage in the left hemisphere of the brain.

Many approaches have been used to remediate aphasia, but consistent and verifiable results have been slow to emerge. As with other disorders, remediation typically involves the development of an individual's profile of strengths and limitations. From such a profile an individualized treatment plan can be designed. Several questions or points immediately surface revolving around what to teach or to remediate first. On one dimension, Myklebust (1971) suggested that input problems should receive attention before output difficulties. He noted that "*input precedes output.* To use the spoken word meaningfully, the child must first be able to comprehend it" (p. 1214; emphasis in the original). Data remain forthcoming to support this assumption, but the logic appears sound. Another dimension asks whether teaching should focus on an individual's strengths or weak areas. This argument has been raised with respect to many disorders from time to time and remains largely unresolved. Nearly all clinicians have their own opinions or carry with them some personal formula for balancing the extremes. Cooper and Griffiths (1978) made an interesting point concerning this dilemma with aphasic children: Teaching exclusively to one's deficit areas may result in more failure experiences than are either necessary or helpful to the child's overall progress. Good clinical judgment needs to be exercised in balancing remediation attention to the aphasic child's strengths and weaknesses. And we are once again in need of scientific evidence.

Remediation for adult aphasics begins from a perspective different from that for children in that the task involves *relearning or reacquiring* language function. Views regarding treatment have varied over the years. Early approaches included the expectation that adult aphasics would exhibit spontaneous recovery if left alone. This approach has largely been replaced by a view that patients will be more likely to progress if direct therapeutic instruction is employed (Eisenson, 1971b).

Therapy for adult aphasics has some predictable similarities to treatment of children. Areas of strength and limitation must receive attention when an individualized remediation program is being planned. However, development of a profile of strengths and deficits may involve some areas different from those of children because of age differences. For example, Eisenson (1971b) noted three broad areas needing attention for most adult aphasics: "social, linguistic, and vocational readjustments" (p. 1253). Although children need attention beyond just language, these broad areas are likely to differ in terms of the amount of attention given (some not even being relevant, such as the vocational area), and the notion of readjustment differs substantially from initial skill acquisition. The individualized treatment program for adult aphasics will also have to involve evaluation, profile development, and teaching in specific behavioral areas within each of the broad domains. Such training should begin as soon as possible, depending on the patient's condition. Often a certain amount of spontaneous recovery occurs during the first six months after an event resulting in aphasic involvement. However, waiting beyond about two months to initiate treatment may not only be unnecessary but also seriously delay recovery to whatever degree may be possible.

♗ SUMMARY

Several types of speech and language disorders cause significant difficulties for those affected. Causes range from physiological abnormalities to a variety of learned behaviors. Some theories have also linked certain communication disorders to emotional or phychological problems. Regardless of specific causation, seriously abnormal speech or language functioning can have a substantial impact on an individual's life pattern and may also result in great emotional stress.

Stuttering is probably the most widely recognized speech disorder. It is characterized by serious disruptions in the flow of rhythm of speech. Delayed speech is another speech problem. A person with delayed speech exhibits speaking proficiency characteristic of someone much younger. A third type of speech problem involves disorders of articulation. Articulation disorders represent the largest category of speech defect, and prevalence varies greatly among age-groups. Articulation disorders present abnormalities in the speech-sound production process which result in inaccurate or inappropriate execution of the speaking act. Another category of speech problems is voice disorders, which are not common, but may cause the affected individual considerable difficulty. Voice disorders may include one or a combination of abnormalities in pitch, loudness, or quality of voice sound produced.

Language disorders are complex problems because they involve so many different but intertwined functions (e.g., learning, memory, message-processing, expression). Two broad areas of language difficulties are receptive language disorders and expressive language disorders. Individuals with receptive disorders have great difficulty understanding what others say or write to them and may process only part of a message. Those with expressive disorders encounter problems in language production. Aphasia is a type of language disorder that is related to neurological damage and malfunction. Treatment of all language disorders is based on an individualized profile of strengths and deficit areas.

♗ REVIEW QUESTIONS

1. How can a speech disorder influence a person's social life, emotional outlook, and career choices?
2. How might assessment of speech functioning be viewed with regard to symptom severity?

3. Describe your reactions when interacting with a stutterer. How do they differ your reactions to encounters with people who have other speech imperfections?

4. Describe your childhood home environment with respect to language usage (as well as you can recall). What features of that environment might have shaped your speech development?

5. Most of us have encountered a person with what might be considered a voice difference (if not a disorder). Describe what this person sounded like, and your reaction to the person.

6. Why may speech be viewed as a subset or part (but not all) of language?

7. How do *you* think the four sons with normal hearing born to deaf parents could develop normal language facility?

8. How does aphasia differ from other types of language dysfunction?

9. How does the treatment for adult aphasics differ from that for child aphasics?

CHAPTER EIGHT

Hearing Disorders

In a world that is often controlled by sound, the ability to hear and speak is a critical link in the development of human communication. Children who can hear learn to talk by being talked to. Our everyday communication systems would make little sense without sound. Telephones, loudspeakers, radios, stereos, and intercoms can become useless mediums in a world void of sound. Our sense of hearing is an important factor in the way we learn to perceive our world and in the way the world perceives us.

How difficult is it, then, for the person who cannot hear to adjust to a hearing world? In reality, the effects of a hearing loss are quite individual and may be related to several variables. In this chapter we will explore some of these factors.

Cindy is the oldest of three children. She was born with normal hearing, but at the age of eight she developed spinal meningitis. The disease resulted in a severe hearing loss in both ears. Cindy's parents worked diligently with her to retain the precious speech that had been acquired prior to the loss of hearing. Their work was reinforced through her educational experiences. Cindy spent the remainder of her elementary school years in a special school for children with hearing disorders, but as an adolescent she went on to her neighborhood high school, where she graduated with honors. She continued her education at the university level, receiving an undergraduate degree in philosophy and completing law school. Cindy is now a successful real-estate lawyer and is very active in civic and charitable endeavors. Her leisure time is spent oil-painting, reading history books, or relaxing on a local golf course.

Although Cindy is unable to hear a single word or experience the most rudimentary sound, her life is one of independence and fulfillment. In Cindy's case, as well as those of many people with a hearing disorder, the obstacles presented by the loss of hearing were not insurmountable.

People with a hearing disorder have been described as outsiders in a world "created and controlled by those who hear" (Higgins, 1980, p. 22). The term *outsider* implies that these people may be stigmatized by society, and if that is so, they must find some way to compensate. Higgins suggested that individuals with a hearing disorder may deal with the stigma in a number of ways. Some may try to adjust as much as possible to the demands of the hearing

Cindy

world. Others live a life of isolation, with few contacts with the hearing world.
Still others become a part of organized groups whose members share the common bond of a hearing loss.

THE AUDITORY PROCESS

Audition is defined as the act or sense of hearing. The auditory process involves the transmission of sound through the vibration of an object to a receiver. The process originates with a vibrator, such as a string, reed, membrane, or column of air, that causes a displacement of air particles. In order for a vibration to become sound, there must be a medium to carry it. Air is the most common carrier, but vibrations can also be carried by metal, water, or other substances. The displacement of air particles by the vibrator produces a pattern of circular waves that move away from the source. This movement is referred to as a sound wave and can be illustrated by imagining the ripples resulting from a pebble dropped in a pool of water. Sound waves are patterns of pressure that alternately push together, then pull apart in a spherical expansion. Sound waves are carried through a medium (e.g., air) to a receiver. The human ear is one of the most sensitive receivers there is; it is capable of being activated by incredibly small amounts of pressure. The ear is so sensitive that it can react to stimuli as slight as thermal acoustic pressure. O'Neill (1964) suggested: "If the structure of the ear allowed for any greater sensitivity, man would be bothered by the Brownian movements.* He could hear the coffee in his cup" (pp. 11-12).

The Human Ear

The ear is the mechanism through which sound is collected, processed, and transmitted to a specific area in the brain that decodes the sensations into a meaningful language. The anatomy of the hearing mechanism will be discussed in terms of the external, middle, and inner ears. These structures are illustrated in Figure 8-1.

The External Ear. The external ear consists of a cartilage structure on the side of the head called an auricle, or pinna, and an external ear canal referred to as the meatus. The auricle is the only outwardly visible part of the ear and is attached to the skull by three ligaments. The purpose of the auricle is to collect sound waves and funnel them into the meatus (ear canal). The meatus secretes a wax called cerumen, which protects the inner structures of the ear by trapping foreign materials and lubricating the canal and eardrum. The eardrum (tympanic membrane) is located at the inner end of the canal between the external and middle ear. This concave membrane is positioned in such a manner that when struck by sound waves it is able to vibrate freely.

The Middle Ear. The inner surface of the eardrum is located in the air-filled cavity of the middle ear. This surface consists of three small bones that form

*A Brownian movement is the irregular motion of microscopic particles suspended in liquids or gases. It results from the impact of molecules of the fluid surrounding the particles.

Figure 8-1/ The Structure of the Human Ear

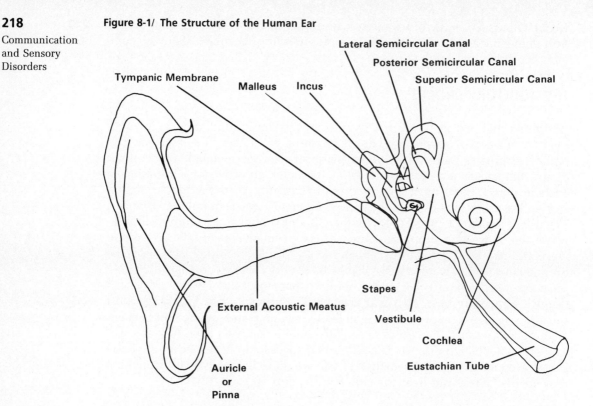

the **ossicular chain.** These bones are the malleus, incus, and stapes, often referred to as the hammer, anvil, and stirrup because each shape is similar to those common objects. These three bones transmit the vibrations from the external ear through the cavity of the middle ear to the inner ear.

The **eustachian tube** is a structure that extends between the throat and the middle ear cavity. Its purpose is to equalize the air pressure on the eardrum with that of the outside. This is accomplished by controlling the flow of air into the middle-ear cavity. Although air conduction is the primary avenue through which sound reaches the inner ear, it is possible for conduction to occur through the bones of the skull. Bone conduction appears comparable to air conduction in that the patterns of displacement produced in the inner ear are similar.

The Inner Ear. The inner ear is an organ consisting of a multitude of intricate passageways. This labyrinth, which is the best-protected organ in the human body, contains the **cochlea** and the vestibule, a central cavity where sound enters directly from the middle ear.

The cochlea lies horizontally in front of the vestibule, where it can be activated by movement in the ossicular chain. The cochlea is filled with fluid that is comparable in composition to cerebral spinal fluid. Within the cochlea is Corti's organ, a structure of highly specialized cells that translate vibration into nerve impulses that are sent directly to the brain.

The other major structure within the inner ear is the **vestibular mechanism,** containing the semicircular canals that control balance. The semicircular canals have enlarged portions at one end and are filled with fluid that responds to head movement. The vestibular mechanism integrates sensory input passing to the brain and assists the body in maintaining its equilibrium. Motion and gravity are detected through this mechanism, allowing the individual to differentiate whether sensory input is associated with body movement or is a function of the external environment.

HEARING DISORDERS: DEFINITIONS AND CONCEPTS

One approach to defining a hearing disorder is to measure the *degree* of the hearing loss. This is accomplished by assessing a person's sensitivity to loudness (sound intensity) and pitch (sound frequency). The unit used to measure sound intensity is the **decibel** (dB), and the range of human hearing is approximately 0 to 130 dBs. Sounds louder than 130 dBs are extremely painful to the ear. Table 8-1 illustrates various common environmental sounds and their measurable decibel level.

The frequency of sound is determined by measuring the number of cycles that vibrating molecules complete per second. The unit used to measure cycles per second is the **hertz** (Hz). The higher the frequency, the higher the Hz. The human ear can hear sounds ranging from 20 to approximately 15,000 Hz. The pitch of speech sounds is 300 to 4,000 Hz, whereas a piano keyboard would range from 27.5 to 4,186 Hz. Although it is possible for the human ear to hear sounds at the 15,000 Hz level, the vast majority of sounds in our environment range from 300 to 4,000 Hz.

Table 8-1/ Common Environmental Sounds with Estimated Decibel (dB) Level

Decibel Level (sound intensity)	
140 dB	Jet aircraft (80 feet from tail at takeoff)
130 dB	Jackhammer
120 dB	Loud thunder
110 dB	Live music
100 dB	Chain saw
90 dB	Street traffic
80 dB	Telephone ring
70 dB	Door slam
60 dB	Washing machine
50 dB	Conversational speech (40-60 dB)
40 dB	Electric typewriter
30 dB	Pencil writing
20 dB	Watch ticking
10 dB	Whisper
0 dB	Lowest threshold of hearing for the human ear

The degree of hearing loss, measured in decibel and hertz units, is ascertained by using a process known as audiometric evaluation. Audiometric evaluation can be conducted utilizing tones that are relatively free of external noise (pure tone audiometry) or spoken words, in which speech perception is measured (speech audiometry). An electronic device (**audiometer**) is used to detect a person's response to sound stimuli. A record (**audiogram**) is obtained from the audiometer that graphs the individual's threshold for hearing at various sound frequencies. Figure 8-2 illustrates a sample audiologic evaluation form.

Figure 8-2/ Sample Audiologic Evaluation Form

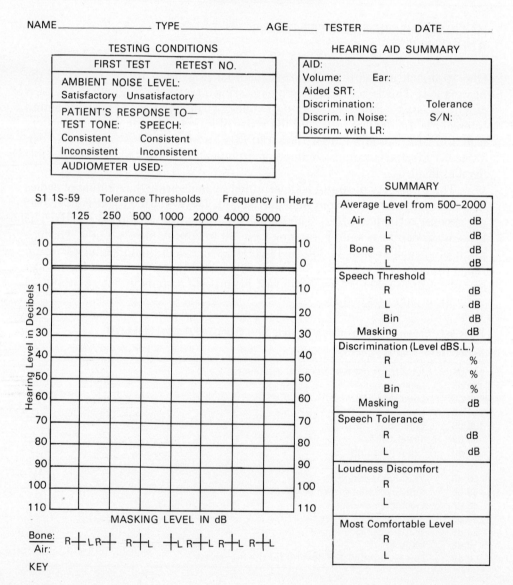

Figure 8–2/ Continued

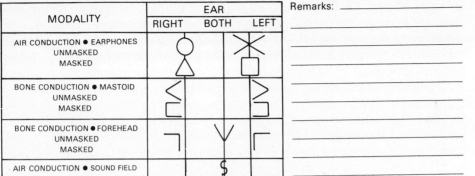

MODALITY	EAR			Remarks:
	RIGHT	BOTH	LEFT	
AIR CONDUCTION ● EARPHONES UNMASKED MASKED				
BONE CONDUCTION ● MASTOID UNMASKED MASKED				
BONE CONDUCTION ● FOREHEAD UNMASKED MASKED				
AIR CONDUCTION ● SOUND FIELD				

Reprinted, by permission, from J.H. Lovrinic, "Pure Tone and Speech Audiometry," in
R.W. Keith, ed., *Audiology for the Physician* (Baltimore: Williams & Wilkins, 1980), p. 19.
Copyright © 1980, the Williams & Wilkins Co., Baltimore.

The audiogram is located in the center portion of the form. On this audiogram, frequencies (Hz) are recorded along the horizontal axis; normal range is 500 to 2,000 Hz. The vertical axis records the amount of loss in decibels, ranging up to 110 dB loss. The form also includes a section describing test conditions, a hearing-aid summary, and an analysis of air and bone conduction tests.

In addition to measuring a person's sensitivity to loudness and pitch, there are two other factors in defining a hearing disorder: the age of onset and the anatomical site of the loss. A hearing disorder may be present at birth (congenital) or acquired at any time during one's life. The distinction between congenital and acquired disorders is an important one. The age of onset will be a critical variable in determining the type and extent of intervention necessary to minimize the effect of the individual's disorder. This is particularly true in relation to speech and language development and is reflected in the need to distinguish between pre- and postlingual disorders. Prelingual disorders are either present at birth or occur early in life prior to speech development. Postlingual disorders occur at an age following speech development. Sanders (1980) stressed:

> The age at which deafness occurs, and equally important, the age at which diagnosis is made and intervention procedures are begun, will have a crucial effect upon the child's subsequent pattern of cognitive development, communication, academic achievement, and social adaptation. The critical factor appears to be whether or not the hearing deficit occurs before the acquisition of verbal language, or at least before language learning processes have been activated. (P. 227)

The two primary types of hearing loss based on anatomical location are peripheral and central auditory problems. There are three types of peripheral hearing loss: conductive, sensorineural, and mixed. **Conductive hearing losses** result from poor conduction of sound along the passages leading to the sense organ (inner ear). The loss may result from a blockage in the external canal, as well as from an obstruction interfering with the movement of the ear-drum or ossicles. The overall effect is a reduction or loss of "loudness." A conductive loss can be offset by amplification (hearing aids) and medical intervention. Surgery has proven to be effective in reducing or even restoring a conductive loss.

Sensorineural hearing losses are a result of an abnormal sense organ and a damaged auditory nerve. A sensorineural loss may distort sound, affecting the clarity of human speech. At present, sensorineural losses cannot be treated adequately through medical intervention. A sensorineural loss is generally more severe than a conductive loss, and it is of greater duration. Losses greater than 70 dB are usually sensorineural and involve severe damage to the inner ear. One common way to determine whether a loss is conductive or sensorineural is to administer an air and bone conduction test. An individual with a con-ductive loss would be unable to hear a vibrating tuning fork held close to the ear, because air passages to the inner ear are blocked. However, if the same fork were applied to the skull, the person with a conductive loss may be able to hear it as well as someone with normal hearing. An individual with a sen-sorineural loss would not be able to hear the vibrating fork regardless of its placement. However, this test is not always accurate and must therefore be used with caution in distinguishing between conductive and sensorineural losses. Davis (1978a) suggested: "There are practical pitfalls. Some skulls and the skin and soft tissues over them do not conduct sound as well as others. . . . In general, the audiologist or otologist hesitates to conclude that he is dealing with sensory-neural hearing loss simply on the basis of finding poor hearing by bone conduction without supporting evidence" (pp. 93-94).

Mixed hearing loss (a combination of conductive and sensorineural prob-lems) may also be assessed through the use of an air and bone conduction test. In the case of a mixed loss, abnormalities will be evident in both tests. However, the more significant problems will appear on the air test.

Although most hearing loss is peripheral in nature, some problems do occur where there is no measurable peripheral loss. This type of loss is referred to as a central auditory disorder and occurs when there is a dysfunction in the cerebral cortex. The cerebral cortex is the outer layer of gray matter of the brain: it governs thought, reasoning, memory, sensation, and voluntary movement. Consequently, a central auditory problem is not a loss in the ability to hear sound but a disorder of symbolic processes, including auditory perception, discrimination, comprehension of sound, and language development (expres-sive and receptive).

CLASSIFICATION OF HEARING DISORDERS

Hearing disorders may be classified into two general subgroups: deaf and hard-of-hearing (or partially hearing). The term **deaf** is often overused and misunderstood. Although this term is commonly applied to a wide variety of hearing disorders, it should be used in a more precise fashion. Deafness, as defined by the Advisory Committee on the Education of the Deaf (1971), is a loss that is greater than 75 to 80 dB in the better ear. A deaf person is described as unable to recognize sound or the meaning of sound pressure waves (Delk, 1973). However, the degree of loss as measured on an audiometer should not be the sole criterion for defining deafness. Ross (1977) suggested that the term *deaf* be limited to those whose primary input is vision and who are precluded from understanding speech through the ear. Berg (1976) stated:

> The deaf child typically has profound or total loss of auditory sensitivity and very little or no auditory perception. Under the most ideal listening and hearing aid conditions, he either does not hear the speech signal or perceives so little of it that audition may not serve as the primary sensory modality for the acquisition of spoken language or for the monitoring of speech. (P. 5)

From an educational perspective, the above definition strongly implies that the sense of hearing cannot be used as a functional source for acquiring new knowledge.

For persons defined as **hard-of-hearing,** the sense of hearing is defective but remains somewhat functional:

> A hard-of-hearing person is one who, generally with the use of a hearing aid, has residual hearing sufficient to enable successful processing of linguistic information through audition. (Report of the Ad Hoc Committee to Define Deaf and Hard-of-Hearing, 1975, p. 509)

Berg (1976) suggested that what the person who is hard-of-hearing perceives at any given moment depends on several factors, including "hearing sensitivity, faintness of sound, distance between speaker and listener, noise background, language proficiency, past experience, environmental awareness, and corresponding lack of compensatory judgments" (p. 3).

The distinction between *deaf* and *hard-of-hearing,* based on the functional use of residual hearing, is not as clear as many traditional definitions would imply. New techniques in the development of hearing aids, as well as improved diagnostic procedures, have made it possible for many children labeled as deaf to use their hearing functionally under limited circumstances.

Hearing disorders may also be classified by means of a symptom-severity approach. Table 8-2 illustrates a symptom-severity classification system and presents information relative to a child's ability to understand speech patterns at the various severity levels. In addition, it highlights implications for educational placement. Karchmer, Milone, and Wolk (1979) advocated the use of a similar classification system as a means to analyze the degree of hearing loss in relation to educational placement. They described three categories of students with hearing impairments: "the group with less than severe hearing loss (≤ 70 dB), the group with severe loss (71-90 dB), and the group of students

Table 8-2/ Classification of Hearing Disorders

Average Hearing Loss in Better Ear as Measured in Decibels (dB) (ISO[a]) at 500–2,000 Hertz (Hz)	Severity Level	Effect on Ability to Understand Speech	Typical Classroom Setting and General Language Characteristics of Students with a Hearing Loss
0-25dB	Insignificant	No significant difficulty with faint or normal speech	Individual is likely to be fully integrated into regular education setting. Support services, if any, would be minimal.
25-40dB	Mild (hard-of-hearing)	Frequent difficulty with faint sounds; some difficulty with normal speech (conversations, groups)	Individual is likely to be integrated into regular education setting with support services available to develop/maintain speech and language. Hearing aid is recommended.
40-60dB	Moderate (hard-of-hearing)	Frequent difficulty with normal speech (conversations, groups); some difficulty with loud speech	Individual is likely to be placed in special class for the deaf during significant part of the day, but can be integrated for at least some portion of the day. Individual will exhibit language delays, articulation problems, and omission of consonants.
60-80dB	Severe (range includes hard-of-hearing and deaf)	Frequent difficulty with even loud speech; may have difficulty understanding even shouted or amplified speech	Individual is likely to be placed in special class with little or no integration into regular education setting. Even with amplification, person is unable to process ordinary conversational sound. Individual will likely have severe speech and language disorder.
80 dB or more	Profound (deaf)	Usually cannot understand even amplified speech	Individual is likely to be placed in special class or school for the deaf. Individual will have severe speech and language disorder or may have no oral speech.

[a] International Standards Organization

who are profoundly deaf (91 or greater dB)" (p. 98). This system collapses the
categories of insignificant, mild, and moderate disorders presented in Table 8-2 into a single combined group labeled "less than severe." Karchmer et al. (1979) suggested that there is strong empirical support for this combined group. According to a study by Jensema, Karchmer, and Trybus (1978), students with a loss of less than 70 dB share a wide variety of characteristics, including speech intelligibility. These authors further suggested that the less-than-severe group had characteristics significantly different from those of the severe and profound groups.

Classification systems based solely on the degree of loss should be utilized with a great deal of caution in determining appropriate intervention strategies for hearing-disordered individuals. These systems do not reflect the capabilities, background, or experiences of the individuals; they merely suggest parameters for measuring a physical defect in auditory function. Bitter (1981) suggested that professionals involved in the assessment process should be "very cautious in delimiting definitions of hearing impairment to avoid the mistake of inflexible classifications and stereotypes which include quantitative measurements in decibels or percentages" (p. 5). Many factors must be assessed in the process of determining the potential of individuals with a hearing loss. In addition to severity of loss, such factors as general intelligence, emotional stability, scope and quality of early education and training, and the family environment must also be considered.

CHARACTERISTICS

In this section we will examine some of the general characteristics associated with people with hearing disorders, including intelligence, speech and language skills, educational achievement, and social development. As we begin our discussion, it should be emphasized again that the effect of a hearing disorder on the learning or social adjustment of the individual is extremely varied. The influence may be far-reaching, as in the case of prelingual sensorineural deafness, or quite minimal, as in the case of a mild postlingual conductive disorder. Fortunately there has recently been increased emphasis on prevention, early detection, and intervention, which has resulted in a much-improved prognosis for the individual with a hearing disorder.

Intelligence

The intelligence of people with hearing disorders has been a subject of controversy for the better part of this century. Although intellectual functioning has been studied extensively, the validity of these investigations has been questioned by several authors (Davis, 1977; McConnell, 1973; Meadow, 1980). Early investigations (Pinter, Eisenson & Stanton, 1941) reported that hearing-disordered individuals scored in the low 90s when tested on standard IQ scales.

However, later reviews of the research (Meadow, 1980; Vernon, 1969; Vernon & Brown, 1964) suggested that hearing-disordered children had approximately the same distribution of IQ scores as hearing children, although the mean score was slightly lower. Meadow also indicated that the equal distribution of scores for hearing disordered and normal children occurred only when the intelligence test involved the use of nonverbal instructions and did not require oral responses from the student. Davis (1977) suggested that test developers and administrators have not fully accounted for the relationship between atypical linguistic development and performance on the IQ test. Meadow further stated: "Baseline data on language ability, spoken and signed, should be accumulated for deaf subjects and used in designing and administering test instruments, and in interpreting the test performance results" (p. 71).

A study conducted by Schlesinger and Meadow (1976) revealed that hearing children were superior to deaf children on three major tests of intellectual development. One striking find, however, was that the pattern of performance was consistent across the two populations. Deaf children, although attaining concepts at a later stage than normal, appear to learn them in approximately the same sequence as hearing children.

Speech and Language Skills

Speech and language skills are the areas of development most severely affected for those with a hearing disorder. Yet the effect of a hearing disorder on language development will vary considerably. For people with mild and moderate losses, the effect on speech and language may be minimal. Even for individuals born with a moderate loss, effective communication skills are possible because the voiced sounds of conversational speech remain audible. Although individuals with a moderate loss cannot hear unvoiced sounds and distant speech, language delays can be prevented if the hearing loss is diagnosed and treated early (Ling & Ling, 1978). The majority of people with a hearing disorder are able to use speech as the primary mode for language acquisition.

For the person who is congenitally deaf, most loud speech is inaudible, even with the use of the most sophisticated hearing aids. These people are unable to receive information through the speech process unless they have learned to lip (speech) read. Sound production of the deaf person is extremely low in intelligibility. Oyers and Frankmann (1975) reported significant articulation, voice quality, and tone-discrimination problems in deaf children. Jensema, Karchmer, and Trybus (1978) surveyed teachers of hearing-disordered children from across the nation, and more than 42 percent of the students were rated as having barely intelligible or unintelligible speech. In addition, the survey indicated that approximately 13 percent of these hearing disordered students would not even speak.

Persons who are congenitally deaf have a great deal of difficulty adequately communicating with the hearing world. In order to have any chance of overcoming this severe handicap, they must have access to early and extensive training in language production and comprehension. Ling and Ling (1978) indicated that "hearing impairment is a serious barrier to verbal learning, and with those whose hearing impairment is more than minimal, it can only be gained through deliberate programming" (p. 31).

Educational Achievement

The educational achievement of students with a hearing disorder may be significantly delayed in comparison to their hearing peers. It should come as no surprise that this population has considerable difficulty succeeding in a system that depends primarily on the spoken word and written language to transmit knowledge. Low achievement is characteristic of deaf students, who average three to four years below their age-appropriate grade level (Mandell & Fiscus, 1981). However, even students with mild to moderate losses achieve below expectations based on their performance on tests of cognitive ability.

Reading is the academic area most negatively affected. Brooks (1978) indicated that "despite dedicated and tireless efforts by educators of the deaf, early severe hearing loss persists as a promissory for reading failure" (p. 87). Wrightstone, Aronow, and Moskowitz (1963) administered the Metropolitan Achievement Test to over five thousand deaf students (ages ten to sixteen) with an average hearing loss of 84 dB. Their results indicated that the average reading level of this population did not exceed what most professionals consider to be "functional literacy" (approximately fourth-grade level). Poor reading achievement for hearing-disordered students has been well documented in the literature (Kodman, 1963; Ling, 1972; Trybus & Karchmer, 1977). "Even when subgroups of deaf children are examined and differences found among those with varying characteristics, the students performing at a higher level still do not score at levels equivalent to their hearing peers" (Meadow, 1980, p. 55).

The development of arithmetic-computation skills has also been investigated and found to be deficient for deaf students in comparison to the norm. Meadow (1980), in a review of recent studies focusing on academic achievement, reported that "the highest average achievement by any deaf age group on arithmetic computation was at grade level 6.7" (p. 72). In addition, several studies (Boothroyd, 1971; Heider & Heider, 1940) have investigated the written language utilized by deaf students. These investigations basically agree that, compared to the norm, the vocabulary of the deaf student is simple and limited. Written sentences are generally shorter and more rudimentary, resembling sentences of less mature hearing students.

Social Development

A hearing disorder results in modification of the individual's capacity to receive and process auditory stimuli. People with a hearing disorder receive a reduced amount of auditory information, which is also distorted, compared to the input received by those with normal hearing. Consequently, perceptions of auditory information are different from the norm. Sanders (1980) stated:

> The problem is not simply one involving a reduction of sensitivity to sound; it concerns the whole process of structuring an awareness and

understanding of things, events, people, and even self. The hearing-impaired child must develop his perceptions using an auditory system which distorts or even eliminates information that the normal developing child uses to build his understanding of the world. (P. 219)

Meadow (1980) reviewed the literature on social and psychological development in deaf children and reported that they appear to be less socially mature than hearing children. Delayed language acquisition may lead to more limited opportunities for social interaction. Deaf children may have more adjustment problems than their hearing counterparts. In spite of these findings, Meadow also suggested: "It would be a mistake to conclude that there is a single 'deaf personality type.' *There is much diversity among deaf people, and it is related to education, communication, and experience*" (pp. 96-97; emphasis added).

The generalization that individuals with a hearing disorder are socially immature has received some support in the literature (Altshuler, 1964; Meadow, 1976; Myklebust, 1960; Schlesinger, 1978), but there is little consensus regarding the reasons for the immaturity. Schlesinger posed these questions: "Does the absence of early auditory stimulation, feedback, and communication in itself create a propensity toward these behavioral and achievement patterns, or does early profound deafness elicit particular responses from parents, teachers, siblings, and friends that contribute to a particular set of cognitive and behavioral deficiencies?" (p. 158).

Social maladjustment patterns are also positively correlated with the severity of the loss and the type of impairment. The more severe the loss, the greater the potential for social isolation and resulting social maladjustment. In addition, those individuals with a sensorineural disorder will need more assistance in adapting to the social environment because of the difficulties encountered in processing and internalizing auditory information.

CAUSATION

A number of conditions may result in a hearing disorder. These conditions are generally classified as congenital factors or acquired factors. Our discussion will focus on these factors while highlighting etiological classifications according to anatomical site of loss (external, middle, or inner ear).

Congenital Factors

Konigsmark (1972) estimated that there are more than sixty types of hereditary hearing disorders. It has been reported that approximately 1 in every 2,000 infants has hereditary deafness (Proctor & Proctor, 1967). The cause of hereditary deafness has been directly linked to the patterns of Mendelian inheritance: autosomal dominant, autosomal recessive, X-linked recessive, and X-linked dominant. Autosomal recessive mutant genes are responsible for approximately 75 to 80 percent of hereditary deafness (Nance, 1976). Nance estimated that one in every eight people is a carrier of an autosomal-recessive mutant gene.

Autosomal-dominant and X-linked recessive mutant genes account for the remaining 20 to 25 percent of hereditary deafness. A study by Ries (1973) of over 41,000 students enrolled in programs for the deaf indicated that approximately 7 percent of this population had hereditary deafness. However, Vernon (1968) suggested that the incidence of hereditary deafness depended on the definition employed. In a study of children who either applied for or were admitted to the California School for the Deaf at Riverside, Vernon indicated that if the definition of hereditary deafness included only students with deaf parents, the incidence was 5.4 percent. If the definition was expanded to include students who had any history of deafness in their family, the incidence was 26 percent. This figure was inflated even more by Nance (1976), who estimated that 50 percent of all deafness is due to genetic factors.

One of the more common diseases that affect the sense of hearing is **otosclerosis.** The cause of this disease is unknown, but it is generally believed to be hereditary. Otosclerosis is characterized by the destruction of the capsular bone in the middle ear and the growth of a weblike bone that attaches to the stapes. The stapes is restricted and unable to function properly. Hearing disorders occur in about 15 percent of all cases of otosclerosis, and the incidence is twice as high for females as for males. Victims of otosclerosis suffer from high-pitched throbbing or ringing sounds know as tinnitus, a condition associated with disease of the inner ear.

Several conditions, athough not inherited, can result in a congenital sensorineural loss. The major cause of nongenetic congenital deafness is infection, of which prenatal rubella, cytomegalic inclusion disease, and toxoplasmosis are the most common.

The rubella epidemic of 1963–1965 dramatically increased the incidence of deafness in the United States. In a review of the literature on prenatal rubella, Abroms (1977) indicated that the disease caused approximately 10 percent of all congenital deafness. Hicks (1970) reported that in the population he investigated, 40 percent were deaf as a result of rubella. About 50 percent of all children with rubella have a severe hearing disorder. Most hearing disorders caused by rubella are sensorineural, although a small percentage may be mixed. In addition to hearing disorders in rubella children, it is not uncommon to find heart disease (50 percent), cataracts or glaucoma (40 percent), and psychomotor retardation (40 percent) (Abroms, 1977). Since the advent of rubella vaccine, the elimination of this disease has become a nationwide campaign, and the incidence of rubella has dramatically decreased.

Cytomegalic inclusion disease is a condition in newborns due to infection by cytomegalovirus (CMV); it is characterized by jaundice, microcephaly, hemolytic anemia, mental retardation, hepatosplenomegaly (enlargement of the liver and spleen), and hearing disorders. CMV infection is responsible for nervous system disease in about four thousand births a year in the United States (Hanshaw, 1970).

Congenital toxoplasmosis infection is due to the transmission of *Toxoplasma gondii* from an infected mother to an infant *in utero*. Jaundice and anemia are generally evident, but frequently the disease also results in central nervous system disorders (e.g., seizures, hydrocephalus, microcephaly). Approximately 17 percent of the infants born with this disease are deaf (Eichenwald, 1956).

Other factors associated with congenital sensorineural hearing disorders include maternal Rh-factor incompatability and the use of **ototoxic drugs.** Maternal Rh-factor incompatability can lead to multiple disabling conditions, including deafness. Fortunately, deafness as a result of Rh-factor problems is no longer common (Lim, 1977). With the advent of an anti-Rh gamma globulin (RhoGAM) in 1968, the incidence of Rh-factor incompatability has significantly decreased. If injected into the mother within the first seventy-two hours of birth, she will not produce antibodies that harm the unborn infant. However, as Moores (1978) pointed out, "all of this depends on good prenatal care, something that many mothers do not receive. The Rh factor remains a cause of deafness" (p. 90).

Ototoxic drugs as so labeled because of their deleterious effect on the sense of hearing. If these drugs are taken during pregnancy, the result may be a serious hearing disorder in the infant. Ototoxic drugs include neomycin, and streptomycin. Although rare, congenital sensorineural disorders can also be caused by congenital syphilis, maternal chickenpox, anoxia, and birth trauma.

A condition know as atresia is a major cause of congenital conductive disorders. **Congenital aural atresia** results when the external auditory canal is either malformed or completely absent at birth. A congenital malformation may lead to a blockage of the ear canal due to an accumulation of cerumen (wax). This wax hardens and blocks incoming sound waves from being transmitted to the middle ear.

Acquired Factors

The most common cause of hearing disorders in the postnatal period is infection, although it has also shown the most significant decrease in this century (Meadow, 1980). Postnatal infections, such as measles, mumps, influenza, typhoid fever, and scarlet fever, are all associated with hearing loss. **Meningitis,** an inflammation of the membranes that cover the brain and spinal cord, is a cause of postnatal deafness in school-age children. There are several types of meningitis, but the meningococcal variety is by far the most common. It is highly contagious and can be transmitted by contact. Loss of hearing, sight, paralysis, and brain damage are all complications of this disease. However, there has been a recent decrease in the incidence of meningitis due to the development of antibiotics and chemotherapy.

Another common problem that may result from postnatal infection is know as **otitis media,** an inflammation of the middle ear. This condition is the result of severe head colds and spreads from the eustachian tube to the middle ear. Otitis media has been found to be highly correlated with hearing problems. Olmstead, Alvarez, Moroney, and Eversden (1964) studied eighty-two children with acute otitis media and found that 77 percent had some degree of hearing loss within a six-month period following the illness. Of this population, 12 percent suffered a persistent loss.

Environmental factors, including extreme changes in air pressure caused by explosions, physical abuse of the cranial area, foreign objects, and hazardous noise are also factors that contribute to postnatal hearing disorders. Loud noise is rapidly becoming one of the major causes of hearing problems. All of us are being subjected to hazardous noise, such as jet engines or excessively loud music, more often than ever before. Glorig (1972) indicated that occupational noise is now the leading cause of sensorineural hearing loss. Other factors associated with acquired hearing disorders include the degenerative process in the ear as a result of aging, cerebral hemorrhages, allergies, and intercranial tumors.

PREVALENCE

It has been difficult to determine accurately the prevalence of hearing disorders in this country. The major problems with prevalence estimates appear to be (1) inconsistent definitional criteria and (2) methodological problems in the surveys utilized. Hoemann and Briga (1981) stated:

> Unfortunately, the various surveys that have been undertaken have used different criteria for defining terms, both for the severity of the loss and for the age of onset. Moreover, some of the samples have been biased in that they have underrepresented populations of lower socio-economic status, multiply handicapped groups, and racial and ethnic minorities. (P. 224)

Other factors must also be taken into consideration when analyzing investigations on prevalence. Did the study differentiate between unilateral and bilateral loss? From what population was the sample drawn? School-age? Prevocational? Adult? Total?

Perhaps the most comprehensive survey of prevalence was the National Census of the Deaf Population (NCDP) (Schein & Delk, 1974). The NCDP estimated that approximately 2 out of every 1,000 persons under the age of nineteen had a severe disorder that affected both ears (bilateral). This figure doubled the previous estimates of the U.S. Bureau of the Census in a survey conducted forty years earlier. The NCDP reported that the prevalence figure for all hearing impairments was 6.6 percent. This figure included everyone in the survey who responded that they had difficulty hearing in one or both ears. Table 8-3 illustrates the actual number and the rate per 100,000 for persons with a hearing disorder. Data are classified by the degree of the loss and the age of onset. These data translate to an estimated 13.4 million people in the United States who have a significant hearing loss, and of these, 1.8 million are defined as deaf. Based on the NCDP data, Shein and Delk (1974) indicated that "impairment of hearing is the single most prevalent chronic physical disability in the United States. More persons suffer a hearing defect than have visual impairments, heart disease, or other chronic disabilities" (p. 1).

Table 8-3/ Prevalence and Prevalence Rates for Hearing Impairments in the Civilian Noninstitutionalized Population, by Degree and Age at Onset: United States, 1971.

Degree	Age at Onset	No.	Rate per 100,000
All hearing impairments[a]	All ages	13,362,842	6,603
Significant bilateral[b]	All ages	6,548,842	3,236
Deafness	All ages	1,767,046	873
	Prevocational[c]	410,522	203
	Prelingual[d]	201,626	100

[a] Includes people who are deaf and those people described as hard-of-hearing.
[b] Includes people who have a significant hearing loss in both ears.
[c] Prior to 19 years of age.
[d] Prior to 3 years of age.
Source: Reprinted, by permission, from J. D. Schein, and M. T. Delk, *The Deaf Population in the United States* (Silver Spring, Md.: National Association of the Deaf, 1974), p. 16.

The Annual Survey of Hearing Impaired Children and Youth (1977–1978) reported on 54,080 students in nearly 700 special education programs across the United States (approximately 80 percent of the total population estimated to be in programs for the hearing impaired). Frequency and percent distributions for students in this survey are summarized by degree of loss in Table 8-4.

Table 8-4/ Frequency and Percent Distributions of Hearing Loss for Students (Annual Survey of Hearing Impaired Children and Youth, 1977–1978)

	Frequency (N)	Percent
Total number of students in Annual Survey	54,080	100.0
Number of students for whom audiological data were not reported or incomplete	2,818	5.2
Total known data (better-ear average)	51,262	100.0
Normal (less than 27 dB)	2,250	4.4
Mild (27-40 dB)	2,743	5.4
Moderate (41-55 dB)	4,536	8.8
Moderately severe (56-70 dB)	6,640	13.0
Severe (71-90 dB)	12,666	24.7
Profound (91 dB or greater)	22,427	43.7

Source: Reprinted, by permission, from M. Karchmer, M. Milone, and S. Wolk, "Educational Significance of Hearing Loss at Three Levels of Severity," *American Annals of the Deaf,* 1979, *124,* 97-109.

Gentile and McCarthy (1973) estimated that approximately 33 percent of the deaf population exhibit some type of disorder(s) in addition to a hearing loss. These additional disorders include visual problems, emotional disturbance, and perceptual motor deficits. Craig and Craig (1975) indicated that of the total population enrolled in schools or classes for the deaf in 1974, aproximately 21 percent had multiple disorders.

Finally, the NCDP reported that the critical period for acquiring deafness is age three. Based on the survey of prevocationally deaf children, "7 in 10 were deaf before 3, and almost 9 in 10 by age 5" (Schein & Delk, 1974, p. 115).

INTERVENTION STRATEGIES

Persons with a hearing disorder will require various levels of support from professionals, depending on the severity of the loss and the ability to adjust to the demands of the hearing world. In this section we will examine three principal areas of intervention: medical, social/psychological, and educational. Although these areas are discussed independently, the effective collaboration of professionals in these areas is absolutely necessary if the comprehensive needs of the individual are to be met.

Medical Services

Medicine plays a major role in the prevention, early detection, and remediation of hearing disorders. Several specialists in this field will be integrally involved in the intervention process. These include the genetics specialist, the **otologist,** the pediatrician, the family practitioner, and the neurosurgeon.

Prevention of hearing disorders is a primary concern of the genetics specialist. A significant number of hearing disorders are inherited or occur during prenatal, perinatal, and postnatal development. Consequently, the genetics specialist is an important link in preventing disorders through family counseling and prenatal screening. (A discussion of genetic screening and counseling may be found in Chapter 6 of this volume.)

Early detection of a hearing problem can prevent, or at least minimize, the impact of the disorder on the overall development of an individual. Generally, it is the responsibility of the pediatrician or family practitioner to be

Early testing for hearing problems is essential.

suspicious of a problem and to refer the family to an appropriate hearing specialist. Dipietro, Knight, and Sams (1981) suggested that the role of the physician is to "encourage early and accurate diagnostic testing whether the patient is an infant, a child, or an adult. Referral to specialists who can diagnose and treat hearing impairments and provide special services is almost always necessary" (p. 109). In order to meet their responsibilities, these physicians must be aware of family history, which requires listening carefully to the observations of parents. Since many hearing disorders may not be identified through family history, it is imperative that the physician also conduct a thorough physical examination of the child. The physician must be alert to any symptoms that indicate potential sensory loss.

An otologist is the medical specialist who is most concerned with the hearing organ and its diseases. Otology is a component of the larger specialty of diseases of the ear, nose and throat. The otologist, like the pediatrician, screens for potential hearing problems, but the process is much more specialized and exhaustive. Jaffe (1977) outlined a procedure to determine the etiology and extent of a hearing loss. This process involved an analysis of prenatal, perinatal, and postnatal history, in addition to past family history. Table 8-5 illustrates the list of topics that are included in this process. The otologist also conducts an extensive physical examination of the ear to identify syndromes that are associated with conductive or sensorineural loss. This information, in conjunction with family history, provides data regarding appropriate medical treatment. This treatment may involve medical therapy or surgical intervention. Common therapeutic procedures include monitoring aural hygiene (e.g. keeping the external ear free from wax); blowing out the ear (a process to remove mucus blocking the eustachian tube); and the use of antibiotics to treat infections. Surgical techniques may involve the cosmetic and functional restructuring of congenital malformations such as a deformed external ear or a closed external canal (atresia). Fenestration is the surgical creation of a new opening in the labyrinth of the ear to restore hearing. A stapedectomy is a surgical process conducted under a microscope whereby a fixed stapes is replaced with a prosthetic device capable of vibrating, thus permitting the transmission of sound waves. A myringoplasty is a surgical reconstruction of a perforated tympanic membrane (ear drum).

A cochlear implant is a relatively new surgical procedure that has great promise, but has yet to be thoroughly tested. The purpose of an implant is to restore hearing through electronic stimulation of the auditory nerve. Paparella and Davis (1978) indicated that:

> The objectives of the implant are, first, to provide a permanent indwelling prosthesis that can deliver electrical stimuli to whatever auditory nerve fibers remain in a deaf ear, and second, to provide selective stimulation, related to acoustic frequency, for different nerve fibers through several electrodes. (P. 177)

Prior to concluding our discussion of medical services, it is important to examine the relationship between otology and audiology. Audiology, the sci-

Table 8-5/ Sample Form for Taking Family and Past History to Detect Etiology of Hearing Loss
in Children

	Place ✓ where appropriate			
	YES	NO	UNCERTAIN	DESCRIBE
FAMILY HISTORY				
Were parents relatives before marriage?				
Family history of hearing loss				
Family history of kidney disease (Alport's)				
Family history of thyroid goiter (Pendred's)				
Family history of progressive blindness (retinitis pigmentosa)				
Family history of previous stillbirths or abortions				
PRENATAL HISTORY				
Drugs during pregnancy				
Ototoxic drugs (especially injectable antibiotics like gentamycin or kanamycin)				
Bleeding problems				
Anemia				
Toxemia				
Diabetes				
Rubella				
Cytomegalovirus				
Toxoplasmosis				
Herpes virus				
Syphilis				
Other infections, Specify ———				
General anesthetic				
High altitude exposure				
X-ray exposure				
PERINATAL HISTORY				
Mother				
Prolonged, difficult or precipitate labor				
Premature rupture of membranes				

Table 8–5 (Continued)

	Place √ where appropriate			
	YES	NO	UNCERTAIN	DESCRIBE
Hemorrhage, abruptio, or placenta previa				
Baby Low birth weight (under 1,500 grams)				
Low Apgar score				
Breathing problem at birth (cyanosis or hypoxia) with or without oxygen therapy				
Yellow jaundice (Rh incompatibility and others)				
Infections				
Ototoxic drugs (especially injectable antibiotics like gentamycin and kanamycin)				
Paralysis				
Convulsions				
Prolonged stay in incubator				
POSTNATAL HISTORY Ear infections without drainage				
Ear infections with drainage				
Cholesteatoma				
Lancing ear (myringotomy)				
Tubes				
Other ear surgery				
Ototoxic drugs (especially antibiotics by injection)				
POSTNATAL HISTORY Tonsillectomy and/or adenoidectomy				
Ear trauma				
Head trauma				
Meningitis				
Mumps				
Measles				

Table 8–5 (Continued)

237

Hearing
Disorders

	Place √ where appropriate			
	YES	**NO**	**UNCERTAIN**	**DESCRIBE**
Tuberculosis				
Poliomyelitis				
Scarlet fever				
Typhoid fever				
Severe infection				
Facial palsy (Bell's)				
Severe trouble breathing				
Sudden episodes of unconsciousness				
Gait, balance, or coordination disturbance				
Cerebral palsy				
Convulsions				
Visual difficulties, eye surgery				
Kidney disease				

Source: Reprinted, by permission of the publisher, from B. F. Jaffe, "History and Physical Examination for Evaluating Hearing Loss in Children," in B. F. Jaffe, Ed., *Hearing Loss in Children* (Baltimore: University Park Press, 1977), pp. 154-57.

ence of hearing, is the study of hearing disorders that cannot be improved through medical therapy or surgery. The otologist presents a biological perspective, whereas the audiologist emphasizes the sociological and educational impact of a hearing loss. Although audiologists are not trained in the field of medicine, these professionals interact constantly with otologists in order to provide a comprehensive assessment of hearing dysfunction. The audiologist is trained in audiometry, the measurement of hearing. Davis (1978b) stated that the purposes of audiometry are (1) to assist in medical diagnosis; (2) to provide an overall assessment of hearing to ascertain the need for support services; (3) to screen large populations and identify persons who should be referred for a more in-depth assessment; and (4) to detect changes in hearing that might have resulted from exposure to hazard (e.g., loud noises).

Another important function of the audiologist and otologist is to provide assistance regarding the selection and use of hearing aids. At one time or another, most people with a hearing disorder will wear a hearing aid. In a sample of hearing impaired children in the United States, Karchmer and Kirwin (1977), found that over 80 percent of this population wore an amplification device. They reported that almost 90 percent of all children with moderate or severe losses (41-90 dB) consistently used a hearing aid. Nonwearers were found in greatest proportion among those children with a profound loss. Even so, approximately 77 percent of this population used a hearing aid.

The audiologist
assesses the soci-
ological and psy-
chological impact
of a hearing loss.

Hearing aids are instruments used to make sounds louder, but they do not correct hearing. Butler (1981) indicated: "The hearing aid is like a public address system. It makes the sound louder, but the student does not hear all sounds even with the aid" (p. 167). Hearing aids have been used for centuries. The early acoustic aids included cupping one's hand behind the ear and the ear trumpet. Modern electroacoustic aids do not depend on the loudness of the human voice to amplify sound, but utilize batteries to increase volume. Electroacoustic aids come in two main types: body aids (strapped to the body) and behind-the-ear aids. These aids may be fitted monaurally (on one ear) or binaurally (on both ears). Although the quality of commercially available aids has improved dramatically in recent years, they do have distinct limitations. Niemoeller (1978) stated:

> No hearing aid can ever compensate for a hearing loss. Everyone who is thinking of getting a hearing aid should realize at the onset that there are limits to what any hearing aid can possibly do. . . . For example, an ear with sensorineural deafness may be unable to hear high tones no matter how much they are amplified. (P. 325)

It is the audiologist's responsibility to weigh all the factors involved (e.g., convenience, size, weight) in the selection and use of an aid for a client. The client should then be directed to a reputable hearing-aid dealer.

Social/Psychological Services

The social consequences of a hearing disorder are highly correlated with the severity of the impairment. For the deaf individual, social integration has been extremely difficult because societal views of deafness have reinforced social isolation. The belief that a deaf person is incompetent has been a predominant theme from the time of the early Hebrews and Romans, who deprived deaf persons of their civil rights, to twentieth-century America, where in some areas it is still difficult for deaf adults to obtain a driver's license, obtain adequate insurance coverage, and be gainfully employed. "With respect to employment, the deaf have been unemployed, underemployed, and likely to be passed over for promotion" (Higgins, 1980, p. 27). On the average, deaf adults earn approximately 20 percent less than hearing persons in the competitive market (Schein, 1979). The population that has had the greatest difficulty are those born congenitally deaf. The inability to hear and understand speech has often isolated these people into their own social subgroup: a deaf community. A deaf community is a group of people with "common interests, common language (sign language), and common culture" (Schein, 1979, p. 479). It is a society "largely made up of persons having an early, severe hearing impairment" (Schein, p. 479). Higgins (1980) indicated that membership in a deaf community is an achieved status, where the individual meets certain prerequisites, such as "(1) identification with the deaf world, (2) shared experiences that come to being hearing impaired, and (3) participation in the community's activities" (p. 38). The majority of deaf people do not seek membership in the deaf community, and an even smaller percentage of those defined as hard-of-hearing belong to this social subgroup.

Most persons with a hearing disorder seek community ties and desire social relationships with their hearing peers. They marry, raise a family, and hold a job. It is true that those who are deaf tend to marry other deaf persons. Schein and Delk (1974) reported that eight out of ten deaf marriages are between deaf partners. However, this phenomenon declines substantially for those who are postlingually deaf or hard-of-hearing. Even in marriages where both partners are deaf, only 12 percent of the offspring are deaf. Therefore, deaf parents are usually in a situation of presiding over a household of children whose hearing is normal.

The social life of most persons with a hearing disorder is generally no different from that of hearing persons. They participate in the arts, enjoy sports, and have leisure-time and recreation interests similar to those of their hearing peers. A segment of the deaf population is actively involved in organizations specifically intended to meet the needs of deaf people. The National Association for the Deaf (NAD), organized in 1880, is the preeminent organization in deaf society. The philosophy of the NAD is:

> All deaf persons have the right to life, liberty, and the pursuit of happiness and . . . this right must be evidenced in ways that meet the satisfaction of the deaf persons themselves rather than that of their teachers and parents, who do not live with the condition. (Schreiber, 1979, p. 565)

The NAD serves the deaf population in many capacities. Among its many contributions, the NAD publishes books on deafness, sponsors cultural activities, and lobbies around the country for legislation promoting the rights of deaf persons.

Another prominent organization is the Alexander Graham Bell Association for the Deaf. This association promotes the integration of persons with a hearing disorder into the social mainstream. The major thrust is the improvement of proficiency in speech communications. Fellendorf (1979) stated:

> Appropriate measures taken by skilled teachers and informed parents can lead many hearing-impaired children to intelligible communication, the key to normalized relationships with a hearing society. Intelligible speech is necessary for the integration of the hearing-impaired child into normal educational channels and eventually into the vocation of his or her choice. (P. 561)

The Alexander Graham Bell Association is a clearinghouse for information for deaf persons and their advocates. The association publishes widely in the areas of parent counseling, teaching methodology, speech-reading, and auditory training. In addition, it sponsors national and regional conferences focusing on a variety of issues pertinent to the social adjustment of deaf persons.

Because of the unique communication problems of persons with a hearing disorder, many are unable to benefit from mental health services in their community. Tucker (1981) indicated that most mental health professionals are unaware of the communication barriers that prevent this population from obtaining service. The President's Commission on Mental Health (Mental Health

The child with a hearing loss may profit from regular class placement if appropriate support services are provided.

Needs, 1978) reported that there were only about fifteen mental health service programs in the United States for persons with a hearing disorder.

Mental health professionals must be trained to work with the unique problems of hearing-disordered persons. These professionals should be working with parents as early as possible to assist the young child in adjusting to the imposed sensory limitation. As children with hearing disorders become older, counselors must be available to help them explore their feelings regarding the disorder and cope with the reactions of parents, family, and peers. Finally, it is extremely important for mental health personnel to realize that "each individual's disability will be unique" (Boulton, Cull & Hardy, 1974, p. 182).

Educational Services

In the United States, educational programs for hearing disordered children emerged in the early nineteenth century, and the residential school for the deaf was the primary model for educational service delivery. The residential school was a live-in facility where the student was segregated from the family environment. In the latter half of the nineteenth century, day schools were established, where a student lived with his or her family while receiving an education in a special school for the deaf. As the century drew to a close, some public schools established special classes for hearing-disordered children located within a regular education facility.

The residential school continued to be a model for educational services well into the twentieth century. However, with the introduction of electrical amplification, advances in medical treatment, and improved educational technology, more options became available within the public school system. Presently, educational programs for hearing-disordered students are on a continuum from the residential school to regular class placement with support services. Figure 8–3 illustrates the distribution of educational placement for hearing-impaired students according to severity of hearing loss (less than severe, severe, and profound; see pages 227–229).

The delivery of educational services to students with a hearing disorder is in the process of change. Yater (1977) suggested, "There is an increase in preschool education with an ever-increasing responsibility of public schools to provide or coordinate such services. . . . There is also a movement toward greater individualization of educational programming including greater use of auxiliary services and of the use of specific hearing specialists" (pp. 12-13). There is little disagreement among educators that the education of the child with a hearing disorder must begin at the time of the diagnosis. Earlier diagnosis raises the probability that the child will achieve to potential.

Educational goals for students with a hearing disorder are comparable to those of their hearing peers. Butler (1981) indicated: "The hearing-impaired student faces the same problems and adjustments in the classroom that every other student faces. Hearing-impaired students bring the same strengths and weaknesses and the same creativity" (p. 171). The most formidable problem for the educator is the student's communication deficits.

Figure 8–3/ Distribution of Hearing Loss by Type of Program

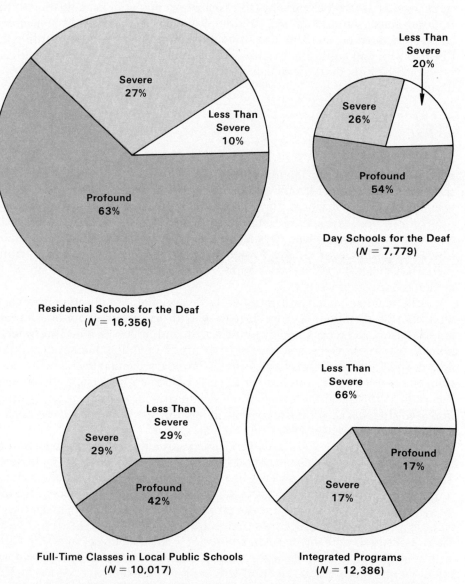

Distribution of Hearing Loss by Type of Program
(Annual Survey of Hearing Impaired Children and Youth, 1977-1978)

Severe
27%

Less Than
Severe
10%

Profound
63%

Residential Schools for the Deaf
(N = 16,356)

Less Than
Severe
20%

Severe
26%

Profound
54%

Day Schools for the Deaf
(N = 7,779)

Less Than
Severe
29%

Severe
29%

Profound
42%

Full-Time Classes in Local Public Schools
(N = 10,017)

Less Than
Severe
66%

Profound
17%

Severe
17%

Integrated Programs
(N = 12,386)

Reprinted, by permission, from M. Karchmer, M. Milone, and S. Wolk, "Educational Significance of Hearing Loss at Three Levels of Severity," *American Annals of the Deaf*, 1979, *124*, 97-109.

Teaching Communication Skills. There are four common approaches to teaching communication skills to students with a hearing disorder: auditory, oral, manual, and total communication. The auditory approach emphasizes the use of amplified sound and residual hearing to develop oral communication skills. The auditory channel is considered the primary avenue for language development, regardless of the severity or type of hearing loss. Students are strongly encouraged to learn normal speech production, and the use of manual communication (other than natural gestures) is discouraged. In addition to the common body-type and behind-the-ear hearing aids, the approach utilizes a variety of electroacoustic devices to enhance residual hearing:

> The CROS (controlateral routing of signals) type is for unilateral (one ear) losses. Sound is routed from the bad ear side of the head to the good ear side for input. . . . The desk-type trainer is larger than any of the wearable aids. It uses headphones or body-type aid receivers and is suitable for children with even losses of 90-110dB. . . . Hard wire systems rely on wires to interconnect teacher, microphone(s), amplifier, headphones, or body-type receivers of children. . . . Loop, magnetic induction systems employ a microphone wired to an amplifier. The signal is broadcast electromagnetically from a loop driven by the amplifier and is received by a coil in the body-type aids of children. . . . In the wireless, radio frequency system, the teacher wears a wireless microphone transmitter which broadcasts her speech signal by radio transmission. (Berg, 1976, pp. 66-67)

The oral approach to teaching communication skills also emphasizes the use of amplified sound and residual hearing to develop oral language. In addition to electroacoustical amplification, the teacher may employ speech-reading, reading and writing, and motokinesthetic speech training (feeling an individual's face and reproducing breath and voice patterns) (Downs, 1977). Speech-reading (sometimes referred to as lipreading) is the process of understanding another person's speech by watching lip movement and facial and body gestures. This skill is difficult to master, especially for the prelingually deaf person. It has been estimated that only about 4 percent of deaf adults are proficient speech readers (Pahz & Pahz, 1978). One problem with speech-reading is that many sounds are not distinguishable on the lips. In addition, the reader must attend carefully to every word spoken, a difficult task for preschool and primary-age children.

The oral approach is often combined with the auditory method and may be referred to as the auditory-oral, or aural-oral, method. Silverman, Lane, and Calvert (1978) suggested that all the above terms are "synonyms for the same fundamental method, or they designate variations within the same general framework" (p. 442). These authors coined the phrase *auditory global method* to describe any approach where the "primary, although not always exclusive, channel for speech and language development is auditory and . . . the input is fluent, connected speech" (p. 442).

The manual approach to teaching communication skills stresses the use of signs in teaching deaf children to communicate. The utilization of signs is based on the premise that many deaf children will be unable to develop oral language and consequently must have some means of communication. Manual communication systems are divided into two main categories: sign languages and sign systems.

Sign languages are a systematic and complex combination of hand movements that communicate whole words or complete thoughts rather than single letters of the alphabet. One of the most common sign languages is the American Sign Language (**Ameslan**). Ameslan has a vocabulary of about six thousand signs. Examples of Ameslan signs may be found in Figure 8–4. Ameslan is currently the most widely used sign language among many deaf adults because it is easy to master, and historically it has been the preferred mode of communication. Ameslan is a language, but it is not English. In fact, it is more similar to Chinese in that its signs represent concepts rather than single words (Fant, 1972).

Sign systems are different from sign languages in that they attempt to "create manual-visual equivalents to oral languages" (Mayberry, 1978, p. 407). Finger-spelling is a signing system that incorporates all twenty-six letters of the alphabet. Each letter is signed independently on one hand to form words. Figure 8–5 illustrates the manual alphabet. Finger-spelling, probably the oldest form of signing, has been relegated to more of a supplement to Ameslan. It is not uncommon to see a deaf adult using finger-spelling in a situation where there is no Ameslan sign for a word. The four sign systems used in the United States are Seeing Exact English, Signing Exact English, Linguistics of Visual English, and Signed Exact English. Today few educators rely solely on the manual system to teach communication skills. However, the sytem is in common use as a component of the fourth, combined approach to teaching communication skills, known as total communication.

Total communication, often described as a new concept in the teaching of communication skills to the hearing disordered, actually has roots that can be traced to the late 1800s. During this period, many professionals (e.g., Gallaudet; see Chapter 2) advocated an instructional system that employed every method possible to teach communication skills. This approach was known as the combined system or simultaneous method. The methodology of the early combined system was imprecise, and essentially any recognized approach to teaching communication was used as long as it included a manual component. The concept of total communication differs from the older combined system in several ways:

> For the most part the combined system usually began with two strikes against it—that is, with an oral failure and after critical learning periods had passed. A total communication approach starts at the beginning even before the child is emerging from his infancy. *More important, total communication is not a system, but a philosophy* that incorporates the combined system and the oral system and whatever else is necessary to put the child at the center of our attention. In some instances, it might not be appropriate to utilize such procedures as sign language; in many cases it would be appropriate. (Pahz & Pahz, 1978, p. 62; emphasis added)

Figure 8–4/ Examples of Ameslan Signs

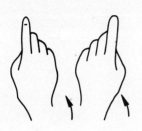

Come

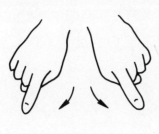

Go

Wrong

Drink

Right

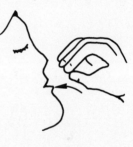

Eat

Thank you

Good

Chair and Sit

Figure 8–5/ The Manual Alphabet

The manual alphabet as the receiver sees it:

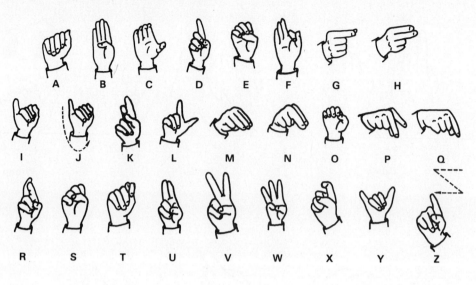

The manual alphabet as the sender sees it:

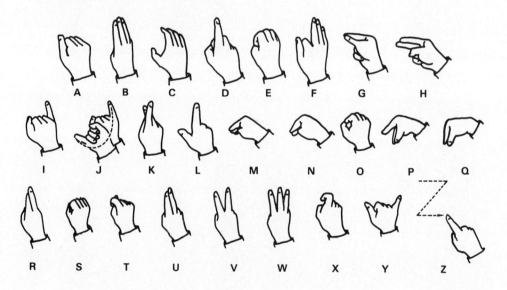

Total communication programs employ the use of residual hearing, amplification, speech-reading, speech-training, reading, and writing in combination with manual systems. A method that may be used as an aid to total communication but is not a necessary component of the approach is cued speech. Cued speech is intended to facilitate the development of oral communication by combining hand signals with speech-reading. Gestures provide additional information concerning sounds not identifiable by lipreading. The result is that an individual has access to all sounds in the English language through either the lips or the hands.

Telecommunication Devices. Educational and leisure-time opportunities for persons with a hearing disorder are being greatly expanded through such technological advances as closed-caption television and computer-assisted instruction. The close-captioning process translates the dialogue from a television program into captions (subtitles). These captions are then converted to electronic codes that can be inserted into the television picture on sets that are specially adapted with decoding devices. The process is called the line-21 system, because the caption is inserted into blank line 21 of the picture.

Captioning is not a new idea and was in fact first used on motion picture film in 1958. Currently, there are over sixty libraries in the United States that distribute captioned films for the deaf. Closed-captioning on television has experienced steady growth in a short period of time. The service has been available only since 1980. Caldwell (1981) indicated that during its first year of operation national programming was available at least thirty hours a week; more than seventy advertisers had committed to having specials and commercials captioned; and close-captioned videotapes for classroom instruction and

Closed caption TV programs for the deaf have increased steadily since 1980.

home entertainment were being introduced into the retail market. Caldwell (1981) stated:

> Evidence is mounting that closed captioning is far more than a techno-logical breakthrough; it is a sociological and psychological triumph as well. Hearing-impaired people of all ages are already enabled to com-municate more freely with their hearing peers as they share information and entertainment gleaned from the television screen. (pp. 629–30)

Computer-assisted instruction also offers an exciting dimension to learn-ing for persons with a hearing disorder. Through telephone lines, an individual can send and receive vast amounts of visual information that is stored in computer systems across the United States. Another recent technological de-velopment, the videodisc, combines the computer-assisted system and the tele-vision video display. The videodisc, which is a record-like platter, allows individuals to work with instructional material at their own pace and convenience.

⚡ SUMMARY

The ability to hear opens the door to comunication development and adds an important dimension to the way we perceive the world. For those with a hearing disorder, the development of communication skills is the most important factor in the life-adjustment process. The effect of the disorder on the educational and social adjustment of an individual will depend on a number of factors: the type and severity of loss, age of onset, intellectual capabilities, emotional sta-bility, and the availability and quality of medical, psychological, and educa-tional services.

The two primary types of hearing loss are peripheral and central auditory. A peripheral loss may be conductive (poor conduction of sound along passages to the sense organ), sensorineural (abnormal sense organ and damaged auditory nerve), or mixed (combination of conductive and sensorineural). A central auditory loss occurs when there is a dysfunction in the cerebral cortex of the brain.

Hearing disorders may be classified into two general subgroups: deaf and hard-of-hearing. Most persons with a hearing disorder are not deaf and maintain a functional level of residual hearing, particularly with electroacoustical am-plification. Hearing disorders may also be classified through the use of a symp-tom-severity approach (e.g., mild through profound disorders).

A review of the characteristics of hearing-disordered persons indicates that the population may exhibit socially immature behavior compared with hearing peers, have significant deficits in speech and language skills, and be consistently behind hearing peers in educational achievement. However, these characteristics are positively correlated with the severity of the hearing loss and the type of impairment.

Adequate support services to this population are essential if they are to achieve integration and gain independence in society. The fields of medicine, psychology, and education play critical roles in assisting the person with a hearing disorder. Medical personnel, from the geneticist to the family practitioner, are integrally involved in the prevention, detection, and remediation of a hearing problem. Medical treatment includes both therapeutic procedures and surgical techniques. Medicine is also responsible, in conjunction with audiology, for the selection and use of amplification devices.

The social and psychological adjustment for the hearing-disordered person is also dependent on a number of variables. Most persons with a hearing disorder are integrated into society and desire social ties with the hearing world. Others desire to be a part of a community of deaf people, where there are shared interests, language, and culture.

Educational services for this population are representative of the continuum available to most exceptional populations. Services range from regular class placement to live-in residential schools. The development of communication skills is a primary objective for students with a hearing disorder.

REVIEW QUESTIONS

1. Describe the basic functions of the external, middle, and inner ear.
2. How are sound intensity and sound frequency measured?
3. Distinguish between being deaf and being hard-of-hearing.
4. Discuss the effects of a hearing disorder on language development.
5. What are some factors associated with hereditary deafness?
6. Discuss environmental factors associated with an acquired hearing loss.
7. Why is early detection of a hearing loss so important?
8. Discuss four approaches to teaching communication skills to persons with a hearing disorder.

CHAPTER NINE

Visual Disorders

Through the visual process we observe the world around us and develop an appreciation for and a greater understanding of the physical environment. Vision is one of our most important sources for the acquisition and assimilation of knowledge, but we usually take our vision for granted. From the moment we wake up in the morning, our dependence on sight is obvious. We rely on our eyes to guide us around our surroundings, inform us through the written word, and give us pleasure and relaxation.

What if this precious sight were lost or impaired? How would our perceptions of the world change?

By the time Jamie was three months old it was evident that he was not responding to objects within his visual field. His parents became concerned and sought the help of a medical specialist. The ophthalmologist confirmed their suspicions: "Your child has a visual disorder caused by a congenital cataract." As a young child, Jamie learned what it meant to move through his world with limited vision. He stumbled and fell frequently as he attempted to orient himself to people and objects around him. On entering school, it was clear that Jamie would need assistance from a vision specialist, but he could still remain with his age-mates in a regular classroom setting. The vision specialist worked with Jamie and his teacher on basic adaptive techniques in the classroom, such as the elimination of unnecessary glare on table and books, the removal of objects that might impede mobility and learning, and the introduction of special lighting to enhance his residual vision. Jamie's visual disorder has not prevented him from pursuing career and leisure-time interests. He is currently a successful sales representative for a local department-store chain. His leisure time is spent hiking, enjoying a good novel, or attending college sporting events.

"Of all the ills and imperfections of humankind, blindness is the most universally dreaded" (Koestler, 1976, p. 1). The fear of losing one's sight is often nurtured by the belief that persons with a visual disorder are not able to live productive lives. Kirtley (1975) reviewed the literature on the attitudes of the sighted

Jamie

toward the blind and concluded that people with sight have little understanding of those without sight. Some people believe that the blind are likely to live a deprived socioeconomic and cultural existence. Bateman (1965) found that sighted children believed that their blind peers were incapable of learning many basic skills (e.g., time-telling) or enjoying leisure-time and recreational activities (e.g., swimming, television). Lowenfeld (1975) suggested that negative attitudes toward persons with a visual disorder set an unfavorable atmosphere for social understanding and integration. However, since the days of ancient Greece and the achievements of the blind poet and scholar Homer, there have been innumerable visually disordered persons who have made outstanding advances in the fields of science, music, literature, law, medicine, and the humanities. Table 9-1 highlights several individuals who, although blind or partially sighted, have made significant contributions to society.

THE VISUAL PROCESS

In a physical sense, vision is defined as the act of seeing with the eye. The physical components of the visual system include the eye, the visual center in the brain, and the **optic nerve,** which connects the eye to the visual center. The basic anatomy of the human eye is illustrated in Figure 9-1. The **cornea** is the external covering of the eye, and in the presence of light it reflects visual

Table 9-1/ Contributions of Notable Blind or Partially Sighted Persons

Name	Contributions
Homer	The first widely known European poet and scholar. His epic poems the *Iliad* and the *Odyssey* shaped contemporary thought concerning human dignity and honor.
Ludovigo Scapinelli (1585–1633)	Eminent Italian philologist and poet.
John Milton (1608–1674)	English poet and political writer. Although not blinded until the age of forty-four, his most notable works, *Paradise Lost, Paradise Regained*, and *Samson Agonistes*, were written after he lost his sight.
Nicholas Saunderson (1682–1739)	English mathematician and teacher. Professor of mathematics at Cambridge University. Invented the first arithmetic board for the blind.
William Hickling Prescott (1796–1859)	American writer and scholar. A renowned historian known for such works as *The History of the Conquest of Mexico* and *The History of the Conquest of Peru.*
Frederick Delius (1862–1934)	English composer. Created such works as *The Magic Fountain, Koanga*, and *Appalachia.*
Alec Templeton (1910–1963)	Pianist, composer, and radio performer.
Ray Charles (1932–)	Popular pianist, composer, bandleader, and singer.

Figure 9-1/ Basic Anatomy of the Human Eye

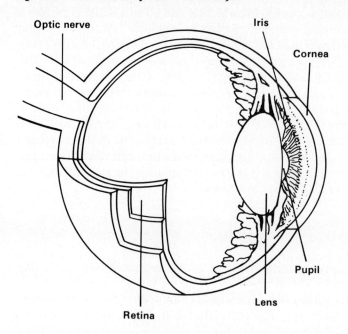

stimuli. These reflected light rays pass through the **pupil,** which is an opening in the **iris.** The pupil expands or contracts to control the amount of light entering the eye. The iris is the colored portion of the eye and consists of membranous tissue and muscles whose function is to adjust the size of the pupil. The lens focuses the light rays by changing their direction so they strike the **retina** directly. As in a camera lens, the lens of the eye reverses the image. The retina consists of light-sensitive cells that transmit the image to the brain by means of the optic nerve. Images from the retina remain upside down until they are flipped over in the visual center of the brain.

The visual process is a much more complex phenomenon than is shown by a description of the physical components of vision. Schrock (1978) proposed that vision be viewed in a much broader context. He described vision as "the result of the integration of a number of subskills that allow the individual to process and appropriately respond to the information contained in the light energy that reaches his eyes" (p. 31). Getman (1965) emphasized that vision is dependent on a number of subsystems, including (1) an antigravity process that allows the person to stand and move erect through the environment; (2) a centering subsystem that assists the person in locating objects in space relative to their own position; (3) an identification subsystem that integrates information from several sources and matches current visual experiences with past experiences; and (4) a speech-auditory system that matches vision with the language system of the individual, facilitating the development of a code that can be stored and more efficiently retrieved.

Vision is an important link to the physical world, helping us gain information beyond the range of other senses, while also helping us to integrate the information acquired primarily through hearing, touch, smell, or taste. The way we perceive visual stimuli will shape our interactions with, and reactions to, the environment, while providing a foundation for the development of a more complex learning structure.

VISUAL DISORDERS: DEFINITIONS AND CONCEPTS

Definitions of visual disorders usually employ two basic criteria: **visual acuity** and the field of vision. Visual acuity may be measured through the use of the **Snellen Test,** developed in 1862 by the Dutch ophthalmologist Herman Snellen. This visual screening test is used primarily to measure central distance vision. A person stands twenty feet from a letter or E chart and reads each symbol beginning with the top row. The different sizes for each symbol represent what a person with normal vision would see at the various distances indicated on the chart. The person's visual acuity is then indicated by the use of an index that refers to the distance at which an object can be recognized. The person with normal eyesight is defined as having 20/20 vision. If an individual is able to read only the first line of the chart, then his or her visual acuity would be described as 20/200. What this person reads at 20 feet a person with normal vision can read at 200 feet.

The Snellen Chart is limited in scope and must be used primarily as an initial screening device that is supplemented by more in-depth assessments, such as a thorough ophthalmological examination. Parents, physicians, school nurses, and educators must also carefully observe the child's behavior, and a complete history of any presenting symptoms of a visual disorder should be documented. These observable symptoms fall into three categories: appearance, behavior, and complaints. Table 9-2 describes some warning signs under these categories. The existence of symptoms does not necessarily mean a person has a visual disorder, but it does indicate that an appropriate specialist should be consulted for further examination.

The definition of blindness adopted by the American Medical Association in 1934 uses "limited field of vision" as a definitional criteria in addition to visual acuity. A person is considered blind if his or her field of vision is limited at its widest angle to 20 degrees or less (see Figure 9-2). A restricted field is also referred to as tunnel vision, pinhole vision, or tubular vision. A restricted field of vision severely limits a person's ability to participate in athletics, read, or drive a car.

Visual disorders may be divided into the general subgroups of *blind* and *partially sighted.* The word *blind* has many diverse meanings. In fact, there are over 150 citations for *blind* in Webster's Unabridged Dictionary. Definitions of blindness may be categorized using a medical-legal orientation or an educational orientation.

The medical-legal definition of blindness, adopted by the American Medical Association states:

A person shall be considered blind whose central visual acuity does not exceed 20/200 in the better eye with correcting lenses or whose

Table 9-2/ Observable Symptoms of Visual Disorders

Appearance
  Crossed eyes, or eyes not functioning together
  Swollen eyelids
  Red-rimmed, crusted eyelids
  Frequent sties
  Bloodshot eyes
  Pupils of different sizes
  Eyes in constant motion
Behavior
  Walks with extreme caution
  Blinks constantly
  Trips or stumbles frequently
  Rubs eyes frequently
  Is overly sensitive to light
  Tilts head; shuts or covers one eye when reading
  Frowns when trying to see distant objects
  Is unable to distinguish colors
  Fails to see objects in his peripheral (side) vision
  Holds reading material at an abnormal distance—either very close or at a great distance
  Distorts face when using concentrated vision
Complaints of
  Dizziness
  Frequent headaches
  Pain in the eyes
  Blurry letters or objects
  Double vision
  Burning or itching eyelids

Source: From R. H. Craig, and C. Howard, "Teaching Students with Visual Impairments," in M. L. Hardman, M. W. Egan, and E. D. Landau, eds., *What Will We Do in the Morning? The Exceptional Student in the Classroom,* p. 188. © 1981 Wm. C. Brown Company Publishers, Dubuque, Iowa. Reprinted by permission.

> visual acuity, if better than 20/200, has a limit in the central field of vision to such a degree that its widest diameter subtends an angle of no greater than twenty degrees. (Connor, Hoover, Horton, Sands, Sternfeld & Wolinsky, 1975, p. 240)

Most people considered legally blind have some light perception; only about 20 percent are totally without sight.

Educational definitions of blindness focus primarily on the student's ability to use vision as an avenue for learning. Taylor (1973) suggested that children who are unable to use their sight and who rely on the other senses should be considered "educationally blind." Craig and Howard (1981) indicated that educational blindness in its simplest form can be defined by whether the student must use braille when reading. Regardless of the definition used, the purpose in labeling a child "educationally blind" is to ensure an appropriate instructional program. This program must assist the blind student in utilizing other senses, including hearing or touch, as a means to succeed in a classroom setting.

A variety of terms may be used to describe levels of visual dysfunction, and this has created some confusion among professionals in various fields of

Figure 9-2/ The Field of Vision

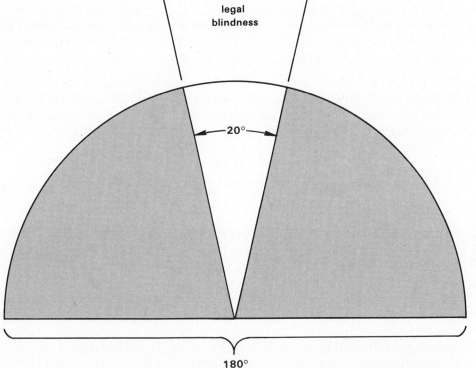

study. The rationale for the development of various definitions is directly related to their intended use. For example, in order to be eligible for income-tax exemptions or special assistance from the American Printing House for the Blind, individuals with a visual disorder must qualify under one of the two general subcategories: blind or partially sighted. The partially sighted are defined as "persons with a visual acuity greater than 20/200 but not greater than 20/70 in the better eye after correction" (National Society for the Prevention of Blindness, 1966, p. 10).

The field of education also distinguishes between blind and partially sighted in order to determine the level and extent of additional support services. The partially sighted are described as students who are able to use their vision as a primary source of learning. Suran and Rizzo (1979) suggested that "educational goals for the partially sighted child include maximal use of the child's functional residual vision by means of magnification, illumination, specialized teaching aids (such as large print books and posters), as well as exercises designed to increase visual efficiency" (p. 149). The position of these authors is contrary to the philosophy of sight conservation or sight-saving, which advocated the restricted use of the eye. Several studies conducted during the 1960s indicated that extended reliance on residual vision in conjunction with visual stimulation training actually improved a person's ability to use sight as an avenue for learning (Barraga, 1964; Ashcroft, 1966).

The distinction between *blind* and *partially sighted* has not significantly minimized the confusion relating to the terminology associated with visual problems. In an attempt to refine terminology and functionally group various levels of visual problems, Barraga (1976) proposed the following descriptors:

1. *Visual impairment:* A deviation in the structure and functioning of the eye.
2. *Visual handicap:* A visual impairment that interferes with optimal learning and achievement. Educational experiences, including teaching methodology, instructional programs, and the learning environment, must be modified to enhance growth.
3. *Low vision:* An impairment in distance vision. The individual *is* able to perceive objects at close range (e.g., a few inches or feet).
4. *Limited vision:* Sight is limited only under specific circumstances (e.g., low illumination).

Visual disorders may be classified according to the anatomical site of the problem. Anatomical disorders include impairment of the refractive structures of the eye, muscle anomalies in the visual system, and problems of the receptive structures of the eye.

Refractive problems are the most common type of visual disorders and occur when the refractive structures of the eye (i.e., cornea, aqueous humor, lens, vitreous fluid) fail to focus light rays properly on the retina. The four types of refractive problems are (1) hyperopia, or farsightedness; (2) myopia, or nearsightedness; (3) astigmatism, or blurred vision; and (4) cataracts.

Hyperopia occurs when the eyeball is excessively short (flat corneal structure), forcing the light rays to focus behind the retina. The person with hyperopia is able to visualize objects at a distance clearly but unable to see them at close range. This individual may require reading glasses.

Myopia occurs when the eyeball is excessively long (increased curvature of the corneal surface), forcing the light rays to focus on the plane in front of the retina. The person with myopia is able to view objects at close range clearly but unable to see them from any distance (e.g., 100 feet). Figure 9-3 diagrams the myopic and hyperopic eyeball and compares them to the normal human eye.

Astigmatism occurs when the surface of the cornea is uneven or the lens is structurally defective, preventing the light rays from converging at one point. The rays of light are refracted in different directions, and the visual images are unclear and distorted. Astigmatism may occur independently of or in conjunction with myopia or hyperopia.

Cataracts occur when the lens becomes opaque, resulting in severely distorted vision or total blindness. Surgical treatment for cataracts has advanced rapidly in recent years, preventing many serious visual problems.

Muscular defects of the visual system occur when the major muscles within the eye are inadequately developed or atrophy, resulting in a loss of control and an inability to maintain tension. People with muscle disorders are

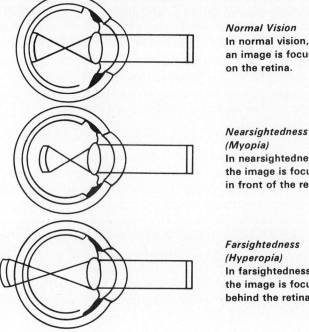

Normal Vision
In normal vision,
an image is focused
on the retina.

Nearsightedness
(Myopia)
In nearsightedness.
the image is focused
in front of the retina.

Farsightedness
(Hyperopia)
In farsightedness,
the image is focused
behind the retina.

unable to maintain their focus on a given object for even short periods of time. The three types of muscle disorders include nystagmus (uncontrolled rapid eye movements), strabismus (crossed eyes), and amblyopia (loss of vision due to muscle imbalance).

Nystagmus is a continuous, involuntary rapid movement of the eyeballs. The nystagmus pattern may be either circular or in a side-to-side sequence.

Strabismus occurs when the muscles of the eye are unable to pull equally and the eyes therefore cannot focus together on the same object. Internal strabismus occurs when the eyes are pulled inward toward the nose. External strabismus occurs when the eyes are pulled out toward the ears. The eyes may also shift on a vertical plane, but this is rare. Strabismus can be corrected through surgical intervention. Persons with strabismus often experience a phenomenon known as double vision. In order to correct the double vision and reduce the visual confusion, the brain attempts to suppress the image in one eye. As a result, the unused eye atrophies and loses its ability to see. This condition is know as **amblyopia.** Amblyopia can also be corrected by surgery, or by forcing the affected eye into focus by covering the unafffected eye.

Disorders associated with the receptive structures of the eye occur when there is a degeneration of, or damage to, the retina and the optic nerve. These disorders include optic atrophy, retinis pigmentosa, retinal detachment, retrolental fibroplasia, and glaucoma. **Optic atrophy** is a degenerative disease that results from deteriorating nerve fibers connecting the retina to the brain. **Ret-**

initis pigmentosa is a hereditary condition resulting from a break in the **choroid** (a vascular membrane containing pigment cells which lies between the retina and the sclera). The condition appears initially as nightblindness but eventually results in total blindness.

Retinal detachment is a condition that occurs when the retina is separated from the choroid and the sclera. This detachment may result from such disorders as glaucoma, retinal degeneration, or extreme myopia. In extreme myopia the eyeball becomes so long that the retina is actually pulled away from the eye tissue. Surgical treatment is possible, but it must be done immediately after the occurrence if sight is to be restored.

Until recently, **retrolental fibroplasia** was one of the most devastating eye disorders in young children. This disorder occurs when premature infants are administered too much oxygen. Scar tissue forms behind the lens of the eye and prevents light rays from reaching the retina. Retrolental fibroplasia gained widespread attention in the early 1940s with the advent of improved incubators for premature infants. These incubators substantially improved the concentration of oxygen available to an infant but resulted in a drastic increase in the number of visually disabled children. The disorder has also been associated with neurological, speech, and behavior problems in children and adolescents. Now that a cause-and-effect relationship has been established between increased oxygen levels and blindness, the number of infants affected by this disorder has been virtually eliminated.

CHARACTERISTICS

In this section we will examine general characteristics associated with orientation and mobility, perceptual-motor development, cognitive ability, speech and language skills, educational achievement, and social development. As we begin our discussion, we again emphasize that a disorder present at birth will have a more significant effect on the development of the individual than one that occurs later in life. Several investigators have confirmed that useful visual imagery disappeared if sight was lost prior to the age of five (Blank, 1958; Lowenfeld, 1980; Schlaegel, 1953; Toth, 1938). If sight was lost after the age of five, it is possible for the person to retain some visual frame of reference. This frame of reference may be maintained over a period of years, depending on the severity of the visual problem. Lowenfeld delineated six graduations of visual disorders according to their impact on the person's memory and sensory functions:

1. Total blindness, congenital or acquired before the age of five years
2. Total blindness, acquired after five years of age
3. Partial blindness, congenital
4. Partial blindness, acquired
5. Partial sight, congenital
6. Partial sight, acquired (1980, p. 260)

These categories are in order of the degree of influence on the individual. Total
blindness that occurs prior to age five has the greatest negative influence on overall functioning. However, these categories are merely generalities, and many people blind from birth or early childhood are able to achieve a functioning level consistent with sighted persons of equal ability.

Orientation and Mobility

A visual disorder may impair orientation and mobility in several ways. The individual may be unable to orient to other people or objects in the environment simply because he or she cannot see them. This lack of sight may prevent persons with a visual disorder from understanding their own relative position in space, and consequently they are unable to move in the right direction. They may develop a fear of getting injured and attempt to restrict their movements to protect themselves. In addition, parents and professionals may contribute to such fears by protecting them from everyday risk. Any unnecessary restrictions will hinder the individual's acquisition of independent mobility skills and create an atmosphere for lifelong dependence.

A visual disorder may also have an effect on fine motor coordination and interfere with the ability to manipulate objects. Poor eye-hand coordination interferes with learning how to use tools (e.g., eating utensils, toothbrush, knives, hammers, screwdrivers) necessary for everyday functioning and occupational efficiency. In order to prevent or remediate fine-motor problems, many people with visual disorders will require extensive training that must begin early and focus directly on experiences that will enhance opportunities for independent living.

Perceptual-Motor Development

Perceptual-motor development is essential to development locomotion skills, but it is also important in the development of cognition, language, socialization, and personality. In a comprehensive review of the literature, Warren (1977) reported that the blind child's perceptual discrimination abilities in such areas as texture, weight, and sound are comparable to those of sighted peers. However, the blind do not perform as well on more complex tasks of perception, including form identification, spatial relations, and perceptual-motor integration. An early visual experience prior to the onset of blindness or partial loss of sight may provide a child with some advantage in the acquisition of manipulatory and locomotor skills.

A popular notion regarding the perceptual abilities of persons with a visual disorder is that because of their diminished sight they develop greater capacity in the other sensory areas. This empirically invalid notion is known as sensory compensation. Telford and Sawrey (1981) reviewed the literature on sensory compensation and reported:

> Studies have consistently shown that persons with vision are either
> equal or superior to the blind in their ability to identify the direction or

distance of the source of a sound, to discriminate the relative intensities of tones, to recognize tactile forms, and to discriminate relative pressures, temperatures or weights, as well as in their acuteness of smell, taste, and the vibratory sense. . . . Any superiority of the blind in the perceptual areas is the result of increased attention to small cues and is a source of information and guidance. It is apparently not the result of a lowering of sensory thresholds. (P. 353)

Intelligence

For a child with a visual disorder, perceptions of the world may be based on input from senses other than vision. This is particularly true of the blind child, whose learning experiences are significantly restricted by the lack of vision (Zinkin, 1979). Consequently, everyday learning experiences that we take for granted are substantially diminished. Warren (1977) reviewed the literature on intellectual development and reported that blind children differ from their sighted peers in some areas. These areas ranged from understanding spatial concepts to a knowledge of the general properties of the world, as assessed by Piagetian tasks. Several investigators have confirmed that intellectual development and performance can be negatively affected by a visual disorder (Barraga, 1974; Lowenfeld, 1974; Scholl, 1974). However, the comparisons of sighted to sightless individuals on tests of intelligence may not be appropriate. The only fair way to compare the intellectual capabilities of sighted and blind children is on tasks where the visual disorder does not interfere with performance. Kirtley (1975) suggested that intellectual differences existing between the visually disordered and the sighted population may be attributed to a number of factors, including unfavorable home environment and neurological or physical handicaps. In addition, he stated, "There is no correlation of intelligence with the age at which sight has been lost" (p. 141).

Speech and Language Skills

For children with sight, speech and language development occurs primarily through the integration of visual experiences and the symbols of the spoken word. Depending on the degree of loss, children with visual disorders are again at a distinct disadvantage in developing speech and language skills because they are unable to visually associate the word with the object. This child cannot learn speech by visual imitation and must rely on hearing or touch for input. Consequently, speech may develop at a slower rate for those who are congenitally blind. Once these children have learned speech, however, it is typically fluent.

There is little evidence that children with a visual disorder are different from their sighted peers in overall language development. Warren (1977) reported, "The production and refinement of sounds, the acquisition of early vocabulary, and the acquisition of grammatical forms are not apparently different in important ways" (p. 244). However, the preschool-age visually disordered child may develop a phenomenon known as "verbalisms." Verbalisms are the excessive use of speech (wordiness), in which individuals use words that have little meaning to them.

Educational Achievement

The educational achievement of students with a visual disorder may be significantly delayed when compared to that of sighted age-mates (Lowenfeld, 1980). Ashcroft (1963) suggested that several variables may influence the academic performance of visually disordered students:

1. Late entry to school
2. Years of failure in unspecialized programs before placement in appropriate programs
3. Loss of time in school due to surgery or treatment for eye conditions or illness
4. Lack of opportunity for schooling
5. The slower rate of acquiring information from reading in braille, large type, or through auditory means. (P. 432)

The available literature over the past twenty years continues to support Ashcroft's contentions, although it is no longer true that many visually disordered students are excluded from public education. With the advent of federal legislation in the 1970s, public school programs for the visually disordered have dramatically expanded.

Although the number of public school programs for the visually disordered has been increasing, other variables, as described by Ashcroft, remain issues for further debate. On the average, blind children are two years older than sighted children in their same grade. Thus any direct comparisons of visually disordered students to sighted students would indicate significantly retarded academic growth. However, this age phenomenon may have resulted from entering school at a later age, absence from school due to medical problems associated with the eye, lack of appropriate school facilities, and use of braille. Kirtley (1975) suggested that touch reading is at least three times slower than visual reading. "Sole reliance on braille reading means a relatively slow acquisition of knowledge" (p. 142).

Social Development

The ability to adapt to the social environment depends on a number of factors, both hereditary and experiential. It is true that each of us experiences the world in his or her own way, but there are common bonds that give a foundation on which to build perceptions of the world around us. One such bond is vision. Without vision, perceptions about ourselves and those around us would be drastically different. For the person with a visual disorder, these differences in perception may result in some social/emotional difficulties. For example, visually disordered people are unable to imitate the physical mannerisms of others and therefore do not develop one very important component of a social communication system: body language. The subtleties of nonverbal communication may significantly alter the intended meaning of spoken words. A person's inability to develop a nonverbal communication system through the acquisition of visual cues will have profound consequences on interpersonal interactions, not only for the visually disordered person's reception or interpretation of verbal language, but also for what he or she expresses to others. The sighted person may misinterpret the intended meaning because visual cues are not consistent with the spoken word.

Social problems may also result from the exclusion of persons with a visual disorder form social activities that are integrally related to the use of vision (e.g., tennis, golf, card or board games, movies). These individuals are often excluded from such activities without a second thought, because they cannot see. This only serves to reinforce the mistaken idea that they do not want to participate and would not enjoy these activities. Exclusion of the visually impaired individual from social experiences is more often a product of the negative attitude of the public toward visual disorders than the person's lack of social adjustment skills.

Lowenfeld (1980) reviewed the literature on public attitudes toward blindness and concluded that although many studies supported the contention that the blind are perceived to be helpless and dependent, attitudes are changing. He further suggested that much of the information generated by research is inconclusive and that more in-depth studies are needed. Lowenfeld's optimism concerning the growth of a social consciousness in regard to the blind is certainly a welcome perception, but it is not entirely supported in the literature. The public in general, and more specifically those close to the visually disordered person, is a powerful influence on the individual's self-concept and social-interaction capabilities. Attitudes of the general public are not, at present, one of acceptance and integration. Willis, Groves, and Fuhrman (1979) suggested, "Visual disability may well be the most difficult exceptionality for sighted persons to accept" (p. 354). Jones, Gottfried, and Owens (1966) found that the blind were rated the lowest on a social-acceptance scale comparing twelve exceptional populations. Those with partial sight were more accepted by the public.

CAUSATION

Visual disorders may result from a multitude of circumstances. Fraser and Friedman (1967) classified causes of visual disorders in young children into four general areas: (1) genetically determined disorders, (2) prenatally acquired disorders, (3) perinatally acquired disorders, and (4) postnatally acquired disorders.

Genetically Determined Disorders

A number of genetic conditions may result in a visual disorder. These include **choroido-retinal degeneration** (a deterioration of the choroid and retina), **retinablastoma** (a malignant tumor in the retina), **pseudoglioma** (a nonmalignant intraocular disturbance resulting from the detachment of the retina), **optic atrophy** (loss of function of optic-nerve fibers), cataracts, myopia associated with retinal detachment, lesions of the cornea, abnormalities of the iris (i.e., coloboma, aniridia), **microphthalmus** (abnormally small eyeball), **anophthalmos** (absence of the eyeball), and **buphthalmos** (abnormal distention and enlargement of the eyeball). In addition, a visual disorder may be a result of other malformations. For example, hydrocephalus may lead to optic atrophy.

Prenatally Acquired Disorders

Several factors present during the prenatal period, such as the introduction of drugs into the fetal system or radiation, may result in a visual disorder. The most widely known causes of blindness in the fetus are infections. Fraser and Friedman indicated:

> Prenatal infections due to the virus of rubella, the protozoan of toxoplasmosis and the spirochete of syphilis may lead to blindness. Doubtless other infectious agents can lead to blindness in this way. For example, the possible role has been much discussed of the viruses of influenza, cytomegalic inclusion body disease, mumps and measles, but as of yet there is no unequivocal evidence incriminating these agents, either in this series or in general. (1968, p. 105)

Perinatally Acquired Disorders

The leading cause of blindness in children during the 1940s and 1950s was **retrolental fibroplasia (RLF).** The identification of RLF in premature infants represents one of the most tragic periods in the field of medicine. RLF, as originally described by Terry (1942), results from the administration of oxygen over prolonged periods of time to low-birth-weight infants. Medical researchers, however, did not learn of this association until the early 1950s. Lowenfeld (1980) reported: "In the peak years of this disease, some states reported that almost 80 percent of their preschool blind children had lost their sight as a result of RLF. It has been established that RLF caused blindness in more than 10,000 babies who have now reached adulthood" (p. 259).

Postnatally Acquired Disorders

Visual disorders occurring during the postnatal period may be due to several factors. Accidents, infections, inflammations, tumors, or vascular diseases are all associated with loss of sight during the first year of life. Although the majority of visual disorders occur prior to adolescence or adult years (approximately 60 percent occur before the age of one), some visual problems are associated with factors occurring during adulthood (e.g., injuries, disease, advanced age).

PREVALENCE

Prevalence is difficult to determine, since definitions of a visual disorder are not consistent from state to state. Reynolds and Birch (1982) indicated that at least 20 percent of the population have some visual problems, but most of these defects can be corrected to a level where they do not pose a handicap to the learning process. The figure of 0.1 percent is the most frequently cited prevalence figure for school-age children who meet the legal definitions of blindness and partially sighted. Based on population estimates, there are approximately 55,000 school-age visually disordered children, but that figure is simply an estimate and does not reflect the actual number of children in need of or receiving special education services in the schools. The American Printing House for the Blind (1979) provides data on the number of legally blind children registered annually by this agency. In 1977 the American Printing House registered 30,587 legally blind children. This figure does not include students whose visual acuity is better than 20/70.

Thousands of blind children born during the maternal rubella epidemic in 1963 and 1964 constituted a significant percentage of the enrollment in special education and residential schools for the blind in the mid-1970s. Maternal rubella is now essentially under control, since the introduction of a rubella vaccine, and RLF, another major etiological factor in the 1960s, has declined rapidly. However, a large percentage of blindness still has an unknown etiology. Lowenfeld (1980) suggested that this is proof that "our knowledge of causes of blindness is still far from satisfactory" (p. 259).

Thus far we have focused on prevalence figures as they relate to school-age children. Blindness also occurs as a function of increasing age. Ginsberg (1973–1974) indicated that 75 percent of all blind people living in the mid-1970s were over forty-five years old. Table 9-3 summarizes blindess rates in 1978 according to age-group.

INTERVENTION STRATEGIES

Individuals with a visual disorder will require specialized support services if they are to achieve independence in their school and community environment. These support systems range from medical prevention in early life to adult rehabilitation and education. The level of intervention will depend on the severity of the disorder and the availability of qualified professionals.

Medical Services

Prevention of visual disorders is essentially within the purview of the field of medicine and falls into several categories, including genetic screening and counseling, appropriate prenatal care, and early developmental assessment.

Since many causes of blindness are hereditary, it is important for the family to be aware of genetic services. One purpose of genetic screening is to identify those who are planning for a family and may possess certain detrimental genotypes that can be passed on to their descendants. Screening may also be conducted after conception in order to determine whether the unborn fetus possesses any genetic abnormalities. Following the screening, a genetic counselor informs the parents about the results of the tests, so that the family is able to make an informed decision.

Table 9–3/ Prevalence of Legal Blindness in Adults (Age 45 and Older), United States, 1978

Age	Rate per 100,000
45–64	246
65–74	636
75–84	1,512
85 +	3,003

Source: Reprinted, by permission, from National Society to Prevent Blindness, *Vision Problems in the U.S.* (New York: National Society to Prevent Blindness, 1980), "Data Analysis," p. 5.

Adequate prenatal care is another effective deterrent to visual problems. Parents must be made aware of the potential hazards associated with poor nutritional habits, the use of drugs, or exposure to radiation during pregnancy. One example of preventive care during this period is the use of antibiotics to treat various infections, such as influenza, measles, or syphilis, thus reducing the risk of infection to the unborn fetus.

Developmental screening is also a widely recognized means of prevention. Early screening of developmental problems enables the family physician to analyze several treatment alternatives and, when necessary, to refer the child to an appropriate specialist. The specialist conducts a more thorough evaluation of the child's developmental delays. Early visual screening, which also includes hearing, speech, motor, and psychological development should be a component of this general developmental assessment. Raikes (1979) described four periods during the early childhood years, when visual screening should routinely take place. She suggested that a complete medical examination be conducted at birth, which would include the general physiological condition of the newborn, a family history, and information concerning any problems during gestation or delivery. When observing the general condition of the baby immediately after birth "[the] eyes should be examined for damage, infection and congenital abnormalities" (Raikes, 1979, p. 2). At six weeks of age, visual screening should be a component of another general developmental assessment. This examination should include input from the parents concerning how their child is responding (e.g., smiling, fixing on the face). The physician should check eye movement, as well as search for any infection, crusting on the eyes, or epiphora (an overflow of tears from obstruction of the lacrimal ducts). The next examination should occur at about six months of age. A defensive blink should be present at this age, and eye movement should be full and conjugate. If there is any imbalance in eye movements, a more thorough examination should be conducted. Family history is extremely important, since in many cases there is a familial pattern. Between the ages of one and five, visual evaluation should be conducted at regular intervals. A particularly important period is the time just prior to the child's entering school. Visual problems must not go undetected as these youngsters attempt to cope with the new and complex demands of the educational environment.

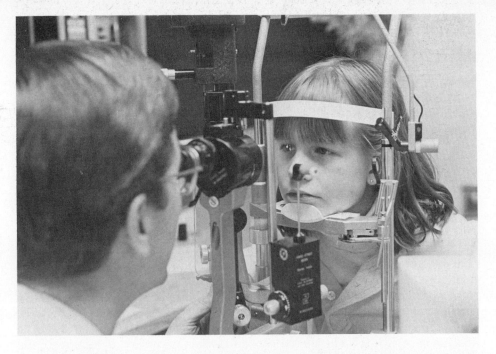

Visual examinations should be conducted regularly with children.

In addition to medicine's emphasis on prevention of visual disorders, this profession has made significant strides in the treatment of these problems. The nature of medical intervention will depend on the type and severity of the disorder. For the partially sighted, use of an optical aid can vastly improve their access to the visual world. Most of these aids are in the form of corrective glasses or contact lenses, which are designed to magnify the image on the retina. Some aids are able to improve muscle control within the eye, while others clarify the retinal image. Appropriate use of optical aids in conjunction with regular medical examinations will not only help correct existing visual problems but may also prevent further deterioration of existing vision.

Surgery and drug therapy have also played important roles in treating visual disorders. Treatment in these areas may range from the extremely complex surgical procedures associated with corneal transplants to the process known as **atropinization.** Atropinization is treatment for cataracts that involves washing out the eye with the alkaloid drug atropine, which will permanently dilate the pupil.

Social/Psychological Services

Some individuals with a visual disorder may have social adjustment problems, which include poor self-concept and general feelings of inferiority. So it is important for mental-health services to be available as early as possible in the person's life. These services may begin with infant stimulation programs and counseling for the family. As these children grow older, group counseling techniques may assist them in coping with feelings concerning blindness. In

addition, the individual may need some guidance in the area of human sexuality.
Limited vision may distort the perception of the physical body. Counseling will eventually extend into matters focusing on marriage, family, and adult relationships. For the visually disordered adult, special guidance may also be necessary in preparation for employment and independent living.

Social and psychological intervention must be expanded to include services for the elderly blind. Kirtley (1975) indicated that "problems usually associated with blindness (including prejudicial attitudes and discriminatory social practices) become greatly amplified with age" (p. 162). Rehabilitation may be extremely difficult to achieve in aged blind populations due to several factors, including loneliness, serious health problems, or lack of family assistance.

Educational Services

Historically, education of blind individuals was implemented primarily through specialized residential facilities. These segregated centers for the blind have traditionally been referred to as asylums, institutions, or schools. One of the first such facilities in the United States was the New England Asylum for the Blind, later named the Perkins School. This facility opened its doors in 1832 and was one of several Eastern schools that used treatment models borrowed from already well-established institutions for the blind in Europe. For the most part the early U.S. institutions operated as "closed" schools, where a blind person would live and learn in an environment that was essentially segregated from the core culture. These segregation policies went as far as separating blind males and females and allowing only a minimal level of closely supervised interaction. Lowenfeld (1975) suggested that the philosophy of the closed school was to retain blind people in "an environment that prepares them for future life but does not expose them to it" (p. 101).

More recently, some residential schools have advocated an "open" system of intervention, based on the philosophy that blind children should have every opportunity to gain the same kind of experiences that would be available if they were growing up in their own communities. Both open and closed residential facilities remain today as alternative intervention modes, but they are no longer the primary social or educational system for a blind person. The vast majority of blind and partially sighted individuals now live at home, attend local public schools, and interact within the community. However, in some instances a residential facility may still be an alternative, where the family may be unable to cope with a visually disordered child and where a separate (usually temporary) living arrangement is in the best interests of the child and the family.

Educational programs for students with a visual disorder are based on a principle of flexible placement. Myriad services are available for these students in the public schools, ranging from regular class placement with little or no assistance from specialists to segregated residential schools. Between these extremes of delivery systems, the public schools will generally offer several alternative classroom structures, including the use of a consulting teacher, resource rooms, part-time special classes, or full-time special classes. Placement of a visually disordered student into one of these delivery modes depends on the impact of the individual's disorder on overall educational achievement. Many visually disordered students are able to function successfully within regular education if the learning environment is adapted to meet their needs. Craig and Howard (1981) have suggested:

> Visually impaired children can listen, speak, think, and participate in many physical activities. Most of them can even see, though not as clearly as the other pupils. . . . Since the child's basic needs parallel those of sighted peers, the classroom teacher is capable of meeting them. Because one important avenue of sensory input is weak or absent, the mode of presentation of lessons must be altered occasionally, but not the content or the goal. The academic curriculum of the visually impaired child should match that of the sighted child. (P. 189)

Whether the student is to be integrated into the regular classroom or taught in a special class, a vision specialist must be available, either to support the regular classroom teacher or to provide direct instruction to the student. A vision specialist has received specialized training in the education of visually disordered students and holds professional certification in this area. This specialist and the rest of the educational support team must be knowledgeable concerning appropriate educational assessment techniques, specialized curriculum materials and teaching approaches, and the use of various communication media.

Assessment. In general, the educational assessment process is no different for visually disordered students than it is for their sighted peers. An educational team is interested in the cognitive ability, academic achievement, language skills, motor performance, and social/emotional functioning of the student. Assessment must also be focused specifically on how the visually disordered student utilizes any remaining vision (visual efficiency) in conjunction with other senses.

The nature and severity of the visual problem will determine the assessment instruments to be used. Some assessment instruments have been developed specifically for the visually disordered. Others are intended for sighted students, but have been adapted to visually disordered students. There are also instruments that have been developed for sighted students which are used in their original form with visually disordered students. Regardless of the instruments employed, educational assessment, in conjunction with medical and psychological data, must provide the diagnostic information that will ensure an appropriate educational experience for the student.

Curriculum Content Areas. The educational needs of students with a visual disorder are comparable to those of their sighted counterparts. In addition, many of the instructional methods currently used with sighted students are applicable with the visually disordered. However, it is important for the educator to be aware of certain content areas that are essential to the visually disordered student's success in the educational environment but are usually not a focal point for sighted students. These areas include mobility and orientation training, as well as acquisition of daily living skills.

The ability to move safely and efficiently through the environment enhances one's opportunities to learn more about the world and thus to be less dependent on others for survival. A lack of mobility restricts individuals with a visual disorder in nearly every aspect of their educational life. Such a student may be unable to orient to physical structures in the classroom (e.g., desks, chairs, aisles), hallways, restrooms, library, or cafeteria. Whereas a sighted person is able automatically to establish a relative position in space, the visually disordered person must be taught some means of compensating for a lack of visual input. This may be accomplished in a number of ways. Halliday and Kurzhals (1976) stressed that "orientation and mobility should be emphasized in every situation of the school program" (p. 15). It is important for blind or partially sighted students not only to learn the physical structure of their school but also to develop specific techniques that can be employed to orient them to unfamiliar surroundings. These techniques involve using the other senses. Although it is not true that the blind are able to hear better than sighted persons, they may be able to learn to use their hearing more effectively by focusing on subtle auditory cues that go unnoticed by sighted people. Efficient use of the auditory sense in conjunction with the other senses (including any remaining

Use of the long cane facilitates mobility.

vision) is an important key to independent travel for the visually disordered. Independent travel with a sighted companion but without the use of cane, guide dog, or electronic device is the most common form of travel for young school-age children. As these children grow older, they may be instructed in the use of a long cane. Guide dogs or electronic mobility devices may be appropriate for the adolescent or adult, whose need to travel independently will significantly increase with age. However, most electronic devices are still in an experimental stage, and the long-term functional use of these instruments is yet to be determined. A variety of electronic mobility devices are currently being studied. These devices do everything from enhancing hearing efficiency to detecting obstacles.

The acquisition of daily living skills is another curriculum area that is important to success in the classroom and independence in society. Most sighted people take for granted many routine events of the day, such as eating, dressing, bathing, or toileting. An individual with sight learns very early in life the tasks associated with perceptual-motor development, including grasping, lifting, balancing, pouring, and manipulating objects. These daily living tasks become more complex during the school years as a child learns personal hygiene, grooming, and social etiquette. Eventually, sighted individuals acquire many complex daily living skills that will contribute to their independence as adults. Cooking, cleaning, repairing, sewing, mowing, and trimming are all a part of the daily tasks associated with adult life and are learned from experiences that are usually not a part of an individual's formalized educational program. For someone with a visual disorder, however, routine daily living skills are not learned in the give-and-take of everyday experiences. In fact, the visually disordered child may be discouraged from developing self-help skills and protected from the challenges and risks of everyday life. Schools may then be faced with providing the child with appropriate experiences that will encourage independence. Several authors have suggested that training in self-help areas is vital to the child and should not be ignored by educators as something routinely learned as the youngster moves through life. Chapman (1978) indicated: "Systematic teaching is essential here although the child will need plenty of opportunities to find out for himself how to do things and do them the way that suits him best, as well as having guided help in mastering techniques" (p. 110).

Mobility training and the acquisition of daily living skills are components of an educational program that must also concentrate on the traditional curriculum areas. Particular emphasis must be placed on developing receptive and expressive language skills. Students with a visual disorder must learn to listen in order to understand the auditory world more clearly. Finely tuned receptive skills will contribute to the development of expressive language, which will allow these children to describe orally their perceptions of the world. Oral expression can then be expanded to include handwriting as a means of communication. The acquisition of social and instructional language skills will open the door to many areas, including mathematics and reading.

Abstract mathematical concepts may be difficult for blind students, who will probably require additional practice in learning to master symbols, number facts, and higher-level calculations. As these concepts become more complex, additional aids may be necessary to facilitate learning. Specially designed talking calculators, rulers, compasses, and the Cranmer abacus have been developed to assist the blind in this area.

Reading is another activity that can greatly expand the knowledge base for visually disordered individuals. For the partially sighted, various optical aids are available. These include video systems that magnify print, hand-held magnifiers, magnifiers attached to eyeglasses, and other telescopic aids. Another means to facilitate reading for partially sighted students is the use of large-print books. These books are generally available through the American Printing House for the Blind and come in several print sizes (see Figure 9-4). Other factors that must be considered in teaching reading to partially sighted students include adequate illumination and the reduction of glare.

Figure 9-4/ Illustrations of Large-Print Type

12 Point When darkness fell, the women began preparing a great heap of wood for the circle of ceremonial fires. Then Chanuka slipped into the river and swam silently

18 Point When darkness fell, the women preparing a great heap of wood circle of ceremonial fires. Then Ch slipped into the river and swam s

24 Point When darkness fell, th preparing a great heap circle of ceremonial fires slipped into the river an

Communication Media. For partially sighted students, the visual channel may remain a source of input. The use of optical aids in conjunction with auditory and tactile stimuli allows the individual an integrated sensory approach to learning. This approach is not possible for the blind student. A blind person does not have access to visual stimuli and must compensate for this loss through the use of tactile and auditory media. Through these media, blind children develop an understanding of themselves and the world around them. One facet of this developmental process is the acquisition of language, and one facet of language development is learning how to read.

The tactile sense represents a blind student's entry into the symbolic world of reading. Currently, the most widely used tactile medium for teaching blind people to read is the raised-line braille system. This system, which originated with the work of Louis Braille in 1829, is a code that utilizes a six-dot cell. There are sixty-three different alphabetical, numerical, and grammatical characters. In order to become a proficient braille reader, one must learn 263 different configurations (i.e., alphabet letters, punctuation marks, short-form words, contractions). As illustrated in Figure 9-5, braille is not a tactile reproduction of the standard English alphabet but a separate medium for reading and writing.

Although braille is still considered by some to be an efficient means for teaching reading and writing, it does have several disadvantages. Braille readers are two to three times slower than print readers, averaging about ninety words per minute in the upper elementary grades (Harley, Henderson & Truan, 1979). Braille writing, which is usually accomplished through the use of a slate and stylus, is tedious and slow (see Figure 9-6). Using this procedure, a student writes a mirror image of the reading code, moving from right to left. The writing process may be facilitated by using a braille writer, pictured in Figure 9-7. This hand-operated machine has six keys that correspond to each dot in the braille cell.

There are several other disadvantages to using braille. The reading material is extremely bulky, with each individual cell covering a quarter of an inch. A braille book may be as much as four times larger than a comparable print book and cost ten times as much. Finally, most braille books are published by the

Figure 9-5/ The Braille Alphabet

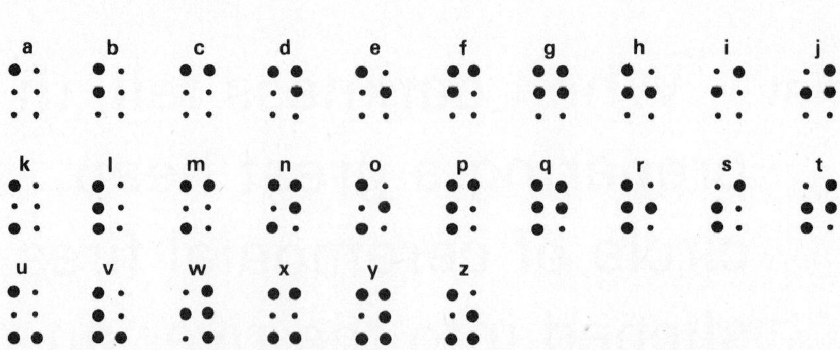

American Printing House for the Blind and thus are limited in their range of available topics.

A recent innovation for braille readers that may reduce some of the problems associated with the medium is the paperless brailler. This machine stores information on cassettes and then converts the material to braille cells, which are projected onto a screen. The paperless brailler is still in the experimental stage and will require years of research in order to determine its long-term feasibility. This machine is representative of the continuing research in the development of communication media for the blind. However, many newer systems do not incorporate braille as the media for communication. Although it is the most widely known tactile medium, braille is not functional for a large number of blind individuals. Since it requires tactile sensitivity, many aged blind persons or others with compounding illnesses (e.g., diabetes) are unable to use the system.

One of the most popular tactile devices that does not use the braille system is the optacon scanner (see Figure 9-8). Printed material is exposed to a camera and then reproduced on a finger pad, using a series of vibrating pins. These pins are tactile reproductions of the printed material. The optacon was developed by J. C. Bliss and became available commercially in 1971. There are currently over three thousand optacons in use worldwide. Although the optacon greatly expands a visually disordered person's access to the printed word, it too suffers from some of the same fundamental problems as the braille system. First, it still requires tactile sensitivity. Second, reading remains a slow, laborious process. Tobin and James (1974) reported that reading rate on the

Figure 9-7/ The Braille Writer

optacon after a short training session averaged only about ten words per minute, although some subjects were able to maintain forty words per minute for short time-spans. However, the training period for this study was from twelve to forty-eight hours of practice, and the investigators did not examine the effects of systematic and continuous use of the optacon on reading speed. Although the optacon is more than a decade old, much research remains to be done, and many improvements are currently being developed and field-tested (e.g., a self-contained hand-held model).

For many blind individuals, the tactile medium may not be the most functional or the most efficient means of acquiring information. Some blind people will have to rely solely on the auditory sense, while others are able to integrate tactile and auditory input. Specialized auditory media for the blind are becoming increasingly available. One recent example is the development

Figure 9-8/ An Optacon Scanner

277
Visual Disorders

of the Kurzweil Reading Machine (see Figure 9-9). This machine, developed by the Kurzweil Computer Products Company, was first introduced in 1975. It converts printed matter into synthetic speech at a rate of approximately 250 words per minute. Models are presently being field-tested nationwide. Other auditory aids that assist the blind include talking calculators, talking-book machines, record players, and audio tape recorders.

SUMMARY

For people with a visual disorder, perceptions of the world may be acquired primarily through other senses. The effect of the disorder on overall development is related to problem severity. The level of severity is usually defined through the measurement of visual acuity and the field of vision. Visual acuity is associated with central distance vision. The field of vision relates to measures of peripheral sight.

Figure 9-9/ The Kurzweil Reading Machine

Visual disorders may be classified according to two general subgroups: blind and partially sighted. Most individuals with a visual disorder are not totally blind and do retain some residual vision. Visual disorders may also be classified according to the anatomical site of the problem. Anatomical disorders include impairment of the refractive structures of the eye, muscle anomalies in the visual system, and problems of the receptive structures of the eye.

A review of characteristics of individuals with a visual disorder suggests that this population will have impaired orientation and mobility skills. There is also evidence of delayed educational achievement and social adaptation skills when this population is compared to their sighted age-mates. However, persons with a visual disorder will develop comparable language skills.

Intervention strategies for those with a visual disorder run the gambit from prevention to rehabilitation. The field of medicine must continue its efforts in genetic screening and counseling, appropriate prenatal care, and developmental assessment, while at the same time expanding its knowledge base in the medical treatment of blindness. Innovative surgery techniques and the use of drug therapy represent new horizons in the treatment of individuals with a visual disorder.

Social and psychological intervention must also be expanded to emphasize not only segregated living conditions but also independent community environments. Community-based mental health and vocational services are essential components in the successful integration of the visually disordered into society.

Educational opportunities for students with a visual disorder include several classroom and curricular options. Current educational services emphasize flexible placement alternatives that take into consideration the diverse educational and psychological needs of students.

ŝ REVIEW QUESTIONS

1. Briefly describe the anatomy of the human eye.
2. What is visual acuity?
3. Distinguish between definitions of blindness and partial sight.
4. Discuss classifications of visual disorders according to anatomical site of loss.
5. What effect does a visual disorder have on orientation and mobility and perceptual-motor development?
6. Discuss several factors that may result in a visual disorder if they occur during the prenatal, perinatal, or postnatal period.
7. Discuss the role of medical personnel in the prevention of visual disorders.
8. What currently available communication media can facilitate learning for persons with a visual disorder?

SECTION IV

Physical and Health Disorders

This section examines physical and health disorders. Individuals with physical impairments experience central nervous system problems or skeletal and muscular disorders. Health disorders include systemic disorders, stress-related problems, and life-endangering diseases, as well as other conditions that threaten an individual's well-being. Causation for both health and physical disorders ranges from physical and other trauma (e.g., accidents) to developmental and genetic abnormalities. Treatments are as variable as the conditions, and in some cases intervention means managing or controlling the problem rather than any "cure" in a literal sense. The following are topical guidelines for Section IV:

1. Physical disorders generally refer to impairments that interfere with one's mobility, coordination, learning, or personal adjustment.

2. A variety of medical, psychological, rehabilitation, and educational treatments may be employed with physical disorders, depending on the specific condition.

3. The impact a physical disorder may have on both the individual and his or her family may vary greatly depending on a number of factors.

4. Several types of health disorders or conditions may seriously interfere with an individual's functioning.

5. The impact of a health disorder may differ substantially depending on a variety of factors.

6. Interventions with health disorders often involve management or an ongoing control of the condition.

CHAPTER TEN

Physical Disorders

Central Nervous System Disorders
    Cerebral Palsy
    Epilepsy
    Spina Bifida
    Spinal Cord Injuries

Skeletal and Muscular Disorders
    Arthritis
    Amputations
    Muscular Dystrophy

Physical disorders such as cerebral palsy, epilepsy, spina bifida, and arthritis affect the lives and families of many people. The overall impact of these and other related conditions depends on the age of onset, the seriousness of the impairment, the visibility of the condition, family attitudes and support, and peer acceptance. Physical disorders frequently interfere with a person's capacity to speak to others, to move about independently, to engage in various activities, and to develop certain academic and social skills. Fortunately there has been some headway in making various environments more accessible. Moreover, technological advances in equipment and instructional apparatus have greatly enlarged the opportunities for people with physical disorders.

It was late August and very hot. Several of Rob's friends had joined him at the family cabin on the Washougal River outside Portland. This was the type of day that made the swimming hole the only place to be. Rob was a high school freshman, rather thin, and this year he had passed the magic 6-foot-4-inch mark that was so essential to his first love—basketball. He enjoyed basketball more than any other part of school. Right now, however, he was intent on the pool of water below him as the others cheered and shouted challenges for him to dive. He had jumped before, but swimming was not his strong suit, and a dive from here was something new.

Rob does not remember leaving the rock overhang or hitting the water. The next conscious act involved an attempt to respond to Jim's frantic cry for him to move his legs.

The doctors pounded him with small mallets, pricked him with pins. He could see them doing these things but could feel nothing. His spinal cord had been severed when he struck the large tree trunk below the surface of the water. Days later, after he had been transferred to the university hospital, he still could not believe that the damage was permanent. He kept telling himself that he would soon be up and moving around and that he would soon return to school.

More than two years elapsed before Rob returned to school. During that time he spent most of his time in the hospital, although he had some brief visits home. He underwent many tests, and the physical therapist worked with him daily. After two years Rob still could not move his legs, although he had some minimal control of his arms and legs. The physicians mentioned something about less severe damage to the upper part of the spinal cord but that it had been completely severed down lower. He had no bladder control and soiled his clothes without even knowing it.

Rob's buddies were no longer in the same classes, and some of them had graduated. Consequently, he had virtually no social life, which in some ways was all right with him, because he was embarrassed by his many problems associated with the accident. The physical problems were bad enough, but they were compounded by his emotional difficulties. The depression was chronic and severely hampered his life in nearly every way. He had difficulty studying and generally felt like a loser, something that he had never experienced before. Rob's saving grace was his family. They supported him strongly, obtaining counseling and participating in the sessions when necessary.

Rob made it. He still loves basketball and attends every game at the university, where he now teaches. He finished his schooling and was awarded a Ph.D. in psychology at the age of twenty-eight. Last year he was promoted to the rank of associate professor and received tenure based on his active research and teaching effectiveness. Certainly his life is different, but it is one that he is proud of. His goals have changed, but he has no remorse, because Rob realizes that most people's goals change from time to time.

A variety of physical and health disorders influence children, adolescents, and adults. The brief case study of Rob represents some of the problems encountered by individuals with physical disorders. Physically impaired individuals are characterized by central nervous system problems or skeletal and muscular disorders. For purposes of discussion, we have separated physical and health disorders into two chapters, the former being presented in this chapter and the latter examined in Chapter 11. As we have seen, such distinctions are often not clearly evident. Table 10–1 provides an overview of the disorders and conditions that will be reviewed in this chapter. First, it is important to review several terms used in the literature pertaining to both physical disorders and health disorders.

The term **impairment** refers to a physical deviation from what is typically viewed as physically normal. The impairment may be a structural, functional, developmental, or organizational deviation (Mullins, 1979). For example, an individual may be born with an incomplete arm (a structural deviation) or may have an organ that operates improperly (a functional deviation). A developmental deviation would be a condition in which some part of the physical growth process is not complete. For instance, a child's spine may not close completely, thereby creating a condition known as spina bifida. Organizational deviations occur when the sequence of growth processes occurs in an irregular fashion. An infant whose skull closes prematurely while the brain tissue is still growing would fall into this classification.

The term **disability** refers to a loss or limitation in physical function or difficulties in learning and social adjustment that significantly impact an individual's level of functioning. Simply stated, a disability is a description of what an individual cannot do because of a physical impairment (Mullins, 1979). For example, a child with paralysis of the legs will be unable to walk unassisted. A youngster with cerebral palsy may be unable to throw or catch a ball because of severe muscle contractions.

Table 10-1/ Physical Disorders and Conditions by Category

Central Nervous System Disorders
  Cerebral palsy
  Epilepsy
  Spina bifida
  Spinal cord injuries

Skeletal and Muscular Disorders
  Arthritis
  Amputations
  Muscular dystrophy

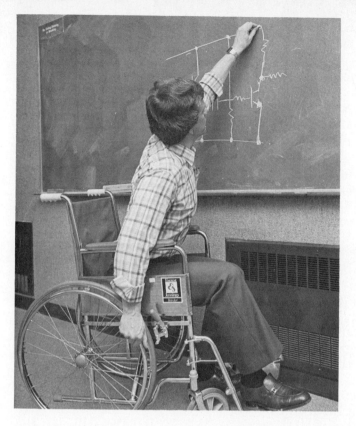

Rob

The term **handicap** has been defined in a variety of ways. According to Calhoun and Hawisher, (1979), "a handicap is a cumulative result of the obstacles that the disability imposes between the individual and his maximum functional level" (p. 4). Mullins defined a handicap as follows:

> Handicap, then, is not objective and measurable. It does not exist in the abstract. It is not a physical thing, like an impairment or even the relatively observable curtailment of function or behaviour that comprises a disability. A handicap is an experience. The action and reaction of the handicapped person's mind and body to the impairment and disability are part of that experience. The action and reaction of others in the environment are part of the experience.

> A handicap is the disadvantage imposed by impairment or disability, which the person experiences in his particular environment. The handicap depends on the physical and psychological characteristics of the person, on the culture, and specific circumstances in place and time, in which the handicapped person finds himself. (1979, p. 24)

It is clear that Mullins viewed a handicap as the outcome of a number of complex interactions and relationships. The seriousness of a handicap is relative in the sense that it is a function of the individual's perception. If one's environment has been supportive and personally rewarding, a handicap may be viewed by the individual more as an inconvenience than a severe hindrance. Conversely, if one's environment has been nonsupportive the handicap may be considerable and quite debilitating. Perceptions that disabled individuals have derived from their environments largely determine the magnitude of their handicap. Many physically disabled people do not view themselves as handicapped. People with such perceptions often behave and perform in a way that their impairments do not severely interfere with their careers or other activities. In this section we will use the term *physically and other health disordered* to describe individuals who may or may not be handicapped but who will definitely have physical or health impairments that cause disabilities.

Physical disorders generally refer to impairments that interfere with an individual's mobility, coordination, communication, learning, or personal adjustment. These impairments are usually diagnosed by physicians. Primary-care physicians (pediatricians or general practitioners) ordinarily refer children suspected of having serious physical impairments to other specialists. These specialists refine the diagnosis and recommend treatment. They are also responsible for determining the extent of an impairment and the consequences of the disability. A variety of medical and rehabilitation personnel may be involved in treatment, depending on the nature of the problem(s). As a youngster with physical disorders grows older, many different disciplines may be included in the total treatment program (e.g., psychology, education, vocational rehabilitation).

The overall impact of a physical disorder depends on several factors: (1) age of onset, (2) degree of disability, (3) visibility of the condition, (4) family and social support, (5) attitudes toward the individual, and (6) social status with peers (Lewandowski & Cruickshank, 1980). A child born with paralyzed legs is likely to be severely limited in the number and types of exploratory activities he or she can pursue. The growth and development derived from crawling around household furniture and other items will be missing to a certain extent. Likewise, the usual learning gained from being able to explore one's environment freely by walking, climbing, and running will be absent in varying degrees. Skill acquisition in the social domain may also be impeded, because the child may not have the same level of opportunity to interact with peers and learn from them as normal children.

In contrast, older youngsters who acquire paralysis in lower body extremities are faced with different problems. Such individuals must deal with a condition for which they have little or no preparation. By contrast, young children have never really known what it is like to use their legs freely for running, jumping, and walking. Such a child's adjustment to paralysis occurs more gradually, whereas those injured later in life must deal with the stark realities of the disparities between their preaccident and postaccident functioning. Also, those injured later may have already gleaned from their environment many of the basic academic and social skills necessary for successful participation in society. As noted above, the child with a congenital problem or one who is injured at a very young age must master these skills in a more restrictive environment.

In our case study, Rob had a very visible condition resulting from his accident. The presence of him in his wheelchair provoked a lot of attention when he returned to school. This attention, however, gradually subsided. The degree of his disability limited his mobility and some opportunities for socialization, but the disability had little, if any, impact on his ability to get an education. The support he received from his family played a major role in his becoming an active contributor to and participant in society. The attitude Rob developed about himself was extremely important to his success in becoming a highly skilled researcher and teacher. His disability, although psychologically painful at times, did not prevent him from succeeding and utilizing his abilities.

Physical disabilities often interfere with an individual's socialization and growth. Reduced physical mobility often prevents the person from participating in many of the social and physical activities available to those without disabilities. Architectural barriers in buildings, and transportation barriers, may cause difficulties in terms of both leisure activities and employment. Many physically disordered people are employable but have no means of transporting themselves to work. Although progress has been evident recently, many buildings remain inaccessible for those with physical disabilities.

The socialization goals of those with physical disorders are similar to those of their nondisabled peers. Disabled adolescents often anticipate and think about completing school, preparing for a career, courtship, marriage, and becoming a parent. All these goals and activities are influenced by the presence of a physical disorder, and most of these activities involve relationships with others.

It is worth noting in this regard that research on the interactions of able-bodied people with the physically disabled reveals several interesting findings. Able-bodied people in face-to-face interaction with disabled individuals tend to maintain more physical distance, terminate their conversations more quickly, feel less comfortable in terms of communication, display less variability in expressions, smile less, engage in less eye contact, and exhibit greater motor inhibition (Albrecht, 1976). All these factors have an immense impact on the communication process, the roles that people with physical disabilities assume, and the feedback they receive regarding their competency and adequacy.

Contemporary Western society tends to place great value on physical beauty and prowess, independence, and mobility. It is readily evident that these attributes and conditions are difficult for the individual with physical disabilities to achieve. However, with appropriate and comprehensive treatment, individuals with physical disorders can redefine their roles and pursuits and thereby achieve the independence and other goals needed for successful living. This notion was evident in our case study of Rob.

The major physical conditions can be subdivided into two areas: central nervous system disorders, and skeletal and muscular disorders. Included within the **central nervous systems disorders** are cerebral palsy, epilepsy, spina bifida and spinal cord injuries. Those conditions found within the skeletal and muscular disorders include arthritis, amputations, and muscular dystrophy.

Cerebral Palsy

The whole time I was growing up I had friends who were older than I, because kids my own age just never accepted me. I had braces on my legs until I was in the fourth grade. The kids were always making fun of me and being cruel. They would never let me join in games with them. I guess older kids tolerated me because they saw me as just a young kid hanging around with them. I was fat when I was younger, and because my cerebral palsy made it hard for me to go to the bathroom, I was always wetting my pants. That made things worse, because not only did I look terrible, I also smelled terrible.

My mother would get very upset when I wet my pants. She thought I did it because I was too lazy to go to the bathroom. It would get to the point where I was wetting my pants every day, and my mother would let it go for about a week and then she would explode. She was very hurt and angered by my problem, and she also was ashamed that I couldn't control myself better.

I had the same problem in school. My first-grade teacher ... wouldn't let me use the bathroom by myself. She used to claim that I couldn't walk down the stairs alone, which was completely untrue. This meant I didn't get a chance to use the bathroom all day, and by the time I got home I had already wet my pants.

When I was in school, I would start crying if any of the other children started talking about my braces or the way I walked. I spent most of my elementary school years in the back of the classroom crying. The kids didn't even have to say anything malicious; they only needed to mention that I was different to start me crying. I just couldn't cope with hearing about how different I was.

In the seventh grade, when I was 11, I had an operation on my bladder. I finally had some control over myself and stopped wetting my pants. That improved my self-image a lot. I also started going to a new school—it was like I was making a new start in life. I took theatre and music lessons, and learned how to handle a camera.

Theatre was the best thing that happened at that time. For the first time in my life, I started seeing myself as a person and not just a fat, crippled girl. When you are involved in theatre you have to be very honest with yourself. I had to start coping with and accepting the fact that I was different. Once I could admit this, I was on my way to becoming able to deal with other people's reactions to me.

I know that I will never be able to do things that take a lot of physical strength or endurance. I've tried dance, skiing, roller skating, baseball, football—almost everything you could think of. I can't do any of these things well, but it's very important to me that I've been willing to try them.

I'll always have my funny gait. It's really very slight and other people don't always notice it, but I do. And sometimes when I go to buy a dress, the hem will hang more on one side than the other because my body is slightly lopsided. I can start feeling very sorry for myself at times, but when I think how very far I've come since all that crying I used to do in the back of the room, I really feel very lucky.*(Education Development Center, 1975, pp. 58-59)

Definitions and Concepts.   Cruickshank (1976) defined **cerebral palsy** as a neurological syndrome evidenced by motor problems, general physical weakness, lack of coordination, and physical dysfunction. The syndrome is not contagious, progressive, or remittent. Its seriousness and overall impact can be very mild to very severe. A variety of classification schemes have been employed to describe the different types of cerebral palsy, but the two major schemes for classification focus respectively on the motor and topographical characteristics of the syndrome. The motor scheme emphasizes the type and nature of physiological involvement or impairment. The topographical scheme focuses on the various body parts or limbs that are affected.

Several categories of motor involvement have been identified, each varying according to the nature and extent of brain damage involved. They are:

1. *Spasticity.* An individual with spastic cerebral palsy experiences great difficulty in attempting to utilize muscles for movement. Involuntary contractions of the muscles take place as the individual attempts to stretch or use various muscle groups. Spasticity prevents the person from performing controlled voluntary motion.
2. *Athetosis.* An individual with **athetosis** is characterized by constant contorted twisting motions, particularly in the wrists and fingers. Facial contortions are also common. The continual movement and contraction of successive muscle groups prevents any well-controlled use of muscular motion.
3. *Ataxia.* An individual with **ataxia** experiences extreme difficulties in controlling both gross and fine motor movements. Problems related to balance, position in space, and directionality make coordinated movement extremely difficult if not impossible.
4. *Rigidity.* An individual with **rigidity** has one of the most severe and rare types of cerebral palsy. This condition is characterized by continuous and diffuse tension as the limbs are extended. Walking or movement of any type is extremely difficult.

---

* From *No Two Alike: Helping Children with Special Needs.* Copyright 1974, 1975. Used by permission of Education Development Center, Inc., 55 Chapel Street, Newton, Massachusetts 02160.

5. *Tremor.* An individual with **tremors** manifests motions that are constant, involuntary, and uncontrollable. The motions are of a rhythmic, alternating, or pendular pattern. They occur as a result of muscle contractions that are continually taking place.

6. *Atonia.* An individual with **atonia** has little if any muscle tone. The muscles fail to respond to stimulation. This condition is extremely rare in its true form.

7. *Mixed.* An individual with **mixed** cerebral palsy may manifest parts and combinations of all conditions reviewed to this point.

The topographical classification approach refers not only to designations given to individuals with cerebral palsy but also to those who have paralysis conditions that resulted from accidents or such neurological diseases as polio. The topographical classification system includes seven categories:

1. **Monoplegia,** which involves one limb
2. **Paraplegia,** which involves the legs only
3. **Hemiplegia,** which involves one side of the body in a lateral fashion
4. **Triplegia,** which involves three appendages or limbs, usually both legs and one arm
5. **Quadraplegia,** which involves all four limbs or extremities
6. **Diplegia,** which refers to a condition in which the legs are more involved than the arms
7. **Double hemiplegia,** which involves both halves of the body, with one side more involved than the other

Cerebral palsy is a complex and perplexing condition. The affected individual is likely to have mild to severe problems in nonmotor areas of functioning as well. These difficulties may include hearing deficits, speech and language impairments, intellectual deficits, visual impairments, and general perceptual problems. Because of the multifaceted nature of this condition, many people with cerebral palsy are considered to be multihandicapped. Thus cerebral palsy cannot be characterized by a set of homogeneous symptoms. It is a condition in which a variety of problems may be present in varying degrees of severity (Lewandowski & Cruickshank, 1980). For instance, 45 percent of those with cerebral palsy are considered to be mentally retarded. On the other hand, 35 percent are average to above average in intellectual ability, with the remaining percentage in the "borderline dull" range (Heilman, 1952). As with most disabilities, estimates vary greatly, depending on the sampling procedures and assessment techniques employed.

Causation and Prevalence. The causes of cerebral palsy are varied. Any condition that can adversely affect the brain may cause cerebral palsy. Chronic diseases, maternal infection, birth trauma, infections, and hemorrhaging may all be sources for this neurological/motor disorder.

The prevalence of cerebral palsy ranges from 1.7 per 1,000 to 6 per 1,000 (Friedman & MacQueen, 1971; Kurland, Kurtzke & Goldberg, 1973; Parker, 1979). These figures fluctuate as a function of several variables. Many children born with cerebral palsy or developing it later come from families who are unable to provide medical care. Consequently, many of these children do not become known to physicians or agencies that collect prevalence information.

The spasticity category accounts for approximately 50 percent of the cases of cerebral palsy (Batshaw & Perret, 1981). The most common type of cerebral palsy reported in children is the mixed type. The affected child may exhibit characteristics of athetoid, spastic, and possibly ataxic cerebral palsy. Less than 10 percent of the cases of cerebral palsy involve rigid and tremor conditions. As noted above, cerebral palsy is often accompanied by other conditions, such as learning disabilities and mental retardation. This overlap of conditions complicates the categorization process and affects prevalence figures reported.

Intervention.   A number of professionals are needed to diagnose and provide treatment for the multifaceted nature of cerebral palsy. The initial diagnosis of the condition generally occurs very early in life. Subsequent diagnosis of accompanying problems and deficits occurs in an ongoing fashion. The assessment process can often be quite difficult if a child's condition includes impairments that make it difficult or impossible for him or her to respond to test items. This is particularly true if the child's language and motor skills are greatly impaired. Some attempts have been made to adapt test items to evaluate the cerebral palsied more adequately (e.g., Haeussermann, 1952; Peters, 1964). These efforts have met with mixed results.

Treatment of cerebral palsy and its attendant conditions is best undertaken in a multidisciplinary fashion. Medical and motor aspects are handled by orthopedic personnel. Surgery may be necessary for treatment of muscle and tendon problems. Physical therapists provide training in muscle use, including how to utilize prosthetic and bracing devices effectively. Medical and physical therapy is aimed at achieving more controlled mobility and psychomotor behavior (Parker, 1979).

Professionals providing educational services must be aware that a student with cerebral palsy and his or her parents have dealt extensively with referral agencies, referral procedures, evaluations, and interventions and that the child's being able to attend school is a tremendous accomplishment. Students with cerebral palsy will often require daily physical therapy sessions. A physical therapist is responsible for developing the students' physical skills. Therapy includes techniques designed to strengthen muscles, to teach muscle relaxation, and to optimize the students' skills for ambulation, independent travel, and movement. Teachers need to be aware of the energy depletion that occurs as a function of these therapies and make appropriate accommodations to permit students time to recharge themselves for further academic activities. By maintaining regular communication and taking into account the effort involved, both the classroom teacher and the therapist can optimize the physical and academic growth of cerebral-palsied students.

Frequently students with cerebral palsy must wear braces that help prevent deformities and facilitate ambulation. Teachers should be aware of and have some understanding of the functions of braces and how they operate.

Teachers and classmates can occasionally help the student with braces in terms of unlocking or locking certain components, depending on the type of movement required. Braces may also cause sores or irritations, so teachers should be sensitive to complaints regarding brace problems and mention them to parents and school nurses. In some cases, cerebral-palsied students may require surgery when bracing and physical therapy have not been effective in preventing or correcting an existing or potential deformity. After surgery, students generally return to school with a cast. When arrangements are made for comfortable seating and means for toileting, they can again receive the benefits of attending school and participating in learning activities.

The location and type of educational treatment depends on an individual's unique learning needs. If the condition is accompanied by significant intellectual or other deficits, an individual may be served in one of several special education environments. If a child can be suitably served in a regular school environment, that too is a potential placement. As a rule, education and related services for cerebral-palsied students must be provided by a diverse team of medical and education professionals. These services generally span the entire time the student is in school.

Epilepsy

Mike was seventeen and had recurring moments of blankness and staring that bothered him. He had been seen by the doctors at the Family Practice Clinic, who referred him to a specialist. The specialist told Mike that he had something like "small" seizures (she actually mentioned petit mal seizures), but she couldn't tell him what caused them so Mike decided she didn't know what she was talking about. He became quite uncooperative with the medical personnel and was intent on concealing his condition. His school performance became erratic, and he often pretended to have completed an assignment when he had not. Further, Mike blamed others for his performance problems.

Mike's parents were quite protective. They would not allow him to stay home alone or to travel alone, even to school. They did not explain to Mike what his problem was, talking to medical personnel behind his back. Mike was aware of this behavior and was further frightened by all the mystery. He became increasingly secretive about his "spells," tried to hide the problems, and grew increasingly dependent on his parents.

Mike was also bothered by related conflicts generated by his condition. Although he was frightened and dependent on his parents, he wanted to be more independent, to be like his peers, to hold a job. He had participated in counseling sessions at school for some time, but he could not bring himself to admit openly that he had a problem, despite the fact that other students were able to talk about their disabilities. As he listened to them, Mike began to wonder whether he could also admit that he had difficulties, and if that would help him enter the world of his peers. Finally he mustered all his courage and nearly shouted to the group, "I have seizures too, small ones." At that point everyone turned to him, but with supportive looks rather than the ridicule he had expected. He began to cry, and then talked about his fears for the entire session.

That was a turning point for Mike. He began to cooperate with the medical personnel and soon was receiving treatment with excellent results. His seizures were dramatically reduced and his feelings about himself were greatly enhanced. Although Mike's parents remained apprehensive, he insisted on continuing treatment and getting a part-time job.

Mike is now successful in insurance sales, and his supervisor anticipates a promising career. Mike has come a long way from when we first met him at age seventeen.

Definitions and Concepts. The term **epilepsy** is used to describe a variety of disorders of brain function that are characterized by recurrent seizures. Seizures are clusters of behavior that occur in response to abnormal neurochemical activity in the brain. They typically have the effect of altering the individual's level of consciousness while simultaneously resulting in certain characteristic motor patterns. Several classification schemes have been employed to describe the various types of seizure disorders. The International League Against Epilepsy (Gastaut, 1970), in conjunction with other societies and organizations, recommended a clinical and electroencephalographical classification of epileptic seizures consisting of four major types of seizure descriptions: (1) partial seizures, wherein the neurochemical discharge in the brain is localized or focal; (2) generalized seizures, wherein the neurochemical discharge involves both sides or hemispheres of the brain or is not clearly localized; (3) unilateral or predominantly unilateral seizures, wherein the discharge is confined to one hemisphere of the brain; (4) unclassified seizures. We will, however, utilize Solomon and Plum's (1976) classification system, because it more graphically portrays the nature of epileptic seizures. The terms *neonatal, grand mal, petit mal, focal cerebral* (motor, sensory, and psychomotor) and *minor motor epilepsy* describe the different types of seizures.

Neonatal seizures, occurring in approximately 5 in 1,000 newborns, are frequently attributable to diffuse disturbances in the brain. Clonic movements (alternating contractions and relaxations of various muscles or muscle groups) in an extremity, pedaling or swimming motions, or unusual posturing of the infant may be strong indices of neonatal seizures. Such convulsive behaviors may represent the presence of serious underlying disease process that is emerging in the infant. It may, however, be clinically difficult to differentiate these behaviors from the typical movements and actions of young infants.

Grand mal seizures are often preceded by a warning signal known as an aura. The individual experiencing an aura senses a unique sound, odor, or physical sensation just prior to the onset of a seizure. In some instances the seizure is also signaled by a cry or other similar sound. With a loss of consciousness, the affected individual falls to the ground. This is the tonic phase of the seizure (see Figure 10-1). Initially, the trunk and head of the body become rigid. This rigidity is followed by involuntary muscle contractions (violent shaking) of the extremities, which is the clonic phase of the seizure (see Figure 10-1). Irregular breathing, blueness in the lips and face, increased salivation, loss of bladder and bowel control, and perspiration may occur to one degree or another. The nature, scope, frequency, and duration of grand mal seizures vary greatly from person to person. Such seizures may last as long as twenty minutes or less than one minute (Parker, 1979). One of the more dangerous aspects of grand mal seizures involves potential injury from falling and striking objects in the environment. In responding to a grand mal seizure, it is best for observers to ease the person to the floor if posssible, remove any dangerous objects from the immediate vicinity, place a soft pad under the person's head

Figure 10-1/ Tonic and Clonic Phases of a Grand Mal Seizure

Grand Mal Seizure, Tonic Phase

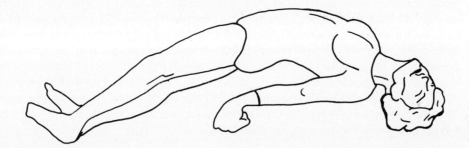

Grand Mal Seizure, Clonic Phase

(e.g., a coat or blanket), and allow the person to rest after the seizure has terminated. Following this type of seizure, a person may exhibit drowsiness, nausea, a headache, or combination of these symptoms. Such symptoms should be treated with appropriate rest, medication, or other therapeutic remedies. Each individual's seizure characteristics and attendant after-effects will vary along a number of dimensions and should be treated with this variability in mind.

Petit mal seizures often appear as a form of daydreaming. They are characterized by brief periods (moments or seconds) of inattention that may be accompanied by rapid eye-blinking or head-twitching. The individual's consciousness is altered in an almost imperceptible manner. People with this type of seizure disorder may experience these mini-seizures as often as one hundred times a day (Parker, 1979). Such inattentive behavior may be viewed as daydreaming by an insensitive teacher or work supervisor. The lapses in attention caused by this form of epilepsy can greatly hamper the individual's ability to respond properly to or profit from a teacher's lecture or discussion. Treatment and control of petit mal seizures is generally achieved through prescribed medication.

Focal seizures may be subdivided according to the following descriptors: motor seizures, sensory seizures, and psychomotor seizures. Hughlings Jackson, an English neurologist, was the first to describe the typical progression of a focal motor seizure. As a result, some refer to this type of seizure as a Jacksonian motor seizure. If the seizure emanates from a lesion (damaged area) in the motor cortex of the brain, which governs the hand, it will generally begin in the contralateral thumb (the thumb on the opposite side of the affected area of the brain). It will then progressively involve the whole hand, then move to the arm, face, and so on (see Figure 10-2). Jacksonian motor seizures may also begin in the corner of the mouth and eventually involve the entire face and other portions of the upper torso.

Figure 10-2/ Focal Seizure

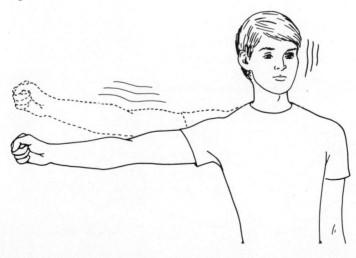

Sensory seizures refer to discharges from the brain that cause the individual to experience numbness or tingling in the affected extremity. Less frequently, the person may even feel a burning sensation in the hand that gradually moves to other parts of the body or remains localized. Visual hallucinations, auditory sensations, and feelings associated with vertigo may also be experienced by people who have sensory seizures.

Psychomotor seizures are characterized by inappropriate, purposeless behavior that the individual exhibits suddenly. Many of these types of seizures are preceded by a recognizable sensation, called an aura. Temper tantrums, lip-smacking, incoherent muttering, rubbing of the legs or arms, or any number of other repetitive behaviors can be involved in a psychomotor seizure (see Figure 10-3). As with other seizures, the individual has no recollection of the actual seizure events. Psychomotor seizures are generally brief, but they can last as long as twenty minutes. In treating this condition, particularly in adults, one should refrain from directly interfering with the accompanying behavior.

Minor motor seizures include myoclonic seizures (shocklike contractions involving parts of a muscle, an entire muscle, or groups of muscles), akinetic seizures, and infantile spasms. Myoclonic seizures may involve sudden brief limb- or trunk-muscle contractions that may occur singly or repetitively. Akinetic "drop attacks" are seizures that involve an absence or poverty of repetitive movements (see Figure 10-4). Occasional jerks of the body affect nearly every person at one time or another as they doze off to sleep, but recurring myoclonic seizures are very serious. They may in some instances be an uncomplicated or less intense form of grand mal epilepsy.

Figure 10-3/ Psychomotor Seizure

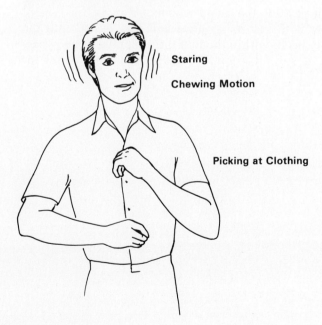

Staring

Chewing Motion

Picking at Clothing

Figure 10-4/ An Akinetic Seizure

Akinetic seizures generally occur in children during the preschool years. They may occur several times a day. Sometimes these seizures result in damage to a child's teeth or more serious craniofacial injury. Children affected by "drop attacks" often wear helmets in order to protect themselves from the sudden falls they experience.

Infantile spasms are characterized by flexor (flexor muscles govern the movement of various joints of the body) spasms of the arms, legs, and head (see Figure 10-5). Infantile spasms have also been described as "jackknife" seizures. As indicated in Figure 10-5, the infant who experiences this type of seizure becomes bowed over with his or her arms and legs pulled into the body. Such seizures generally begin within the first three months or two years of life. The spasms may last for several seconds or occur in clusters lasting for

Figure 10-5/ Infantile Spasms

several minutes. Some 90 percent of the infants with this seizure condition are mentally retarded.

Diagnosis of the various types of seizure disorders occurs in a number of fashions. As a rule, the actual medical diagnosis takes place after one or several seizure incidents have been observed in the person. "The peak ages of seizures occurrence are in the newborn period, in late infancy, and in early adolescence and preadolescence (from 9 to 15 years of age)" (Svoboda, 1979, p. 40). According to Rodin (1975), a "reliable informant" is absolutely essential in establishing an accurate diagnosis of epilepsy. Such an informant may provide valuable information regarding the nature, duration, and circumstances surrounding the seizures. The informant may also provide additional information about the child's or youth's development and medical history.

Causation and Prevalence. Exact causation of the various types of epilepsy remains unclear, but any condition that may adversely affect the brain and its functioning is a potential cause for seizure disorders (see Figures 10-6 and 10-7). In a similar fashion, precise reasons for the actual triggering of a seizure onset are also unknown. In selective instances, a seizure may be instigated by repetitive visual stimuli to which the seizure-prone individual attends. Seizures may also occur in normal individuals as a function of a fever, brain tumor, or disease condition.

Prevalence figures for epilepsy vary. This is a function of the social stigma associated with seizure disorders. Green (1980) has indicated that 7 percent of the childen under age five are affected by seizures. Almost 90 percent of all individuals who are epileptic experience their first seizure prior to their twentieth birthday (Solomon & Plum, 1976).

Figure 10-6/ Etiology Related to Age of Onset of Seizures

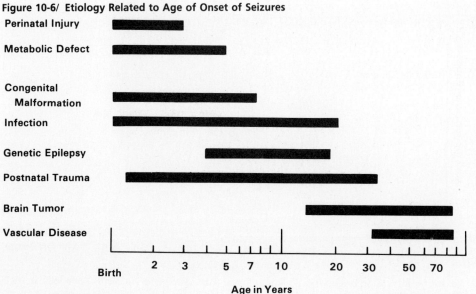

Source: From G.E. Solomon and F. Plum, *Clinical Management of Seizures* (Philadelphia: W.B. Saunders, 1976).

Prevalance estimates fluctuate according to the types of groups investigated and the time period selected for review. Children with cerebral palsy or moderate-to-severe mental retardation are much more likely to have seizure disorders than their normal counterparts. Also, adults who have reached the stage of senescence (sixty to eighty years of age and older) are much more likely to have problems with convulsions. With regard to various time periods, the prevalance of epilepsy caused by head injuries due to automobile accidents declined in the United States when the speed limit was reduced from 70 to 55 miles per hour. With the increased use of motorcycles for transportation, however, many youngsters and adults developed epilepsy as a function of head injuries obtained in motorcycle accidents.

The stigma associated with epilepsy also plays a role in the accuracy of prevalance estimates. Many parents are reluctant to reveal that someone in the family has epilepsy. Consequently, they often do not share this information with school and other officials responsible for collecting data concerning prevalence levels. This is also true of those who develop the condition. They may be reluctant to report it for fear that they will lose their jobs, be unable to retain their driver's license, or suffer social rejection.

The actual incidence (new cases) of epilepsy according to age and type of epilepsy is interesting. Infantile spasms peak during the middle part of the first year of life (see Figure 10-7). The peak periods for akinetic minor motor and petit mal seizures occur respectively during the third and seventh years of life. Grand mal epilepsy may emerge in individuals during almost any period in the life span, with gradual increase in incidence until about age fifteen.

Figure 10-7/ Incidence and Type of Epilepsy Related to Age of Onset

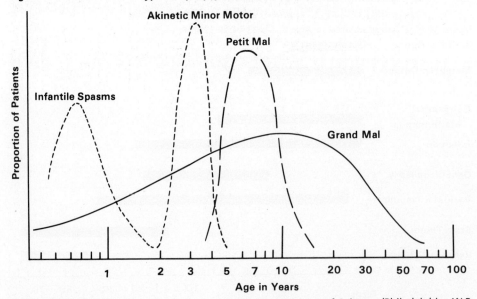

Source: From G.E. Solomon and F. Plum, *Clinical Management of Seizures* (Philadelphia: W.B. Saunders, 1976).

Thereafter the incidence for grand mal seizures declines precipitously to age seventy.

Intervention. Treatment of the various epileptic conditions takes a variety of forms. Once a referral has been made by a general practitioner, pediatrician, or internist, the patient is interviewed and examined by a neurologist. During the interview, the neurologist attempts to (1) identify potential causes for the condition, (2) determine the exact nature and extent of seizure difficulties, and (3) determine the circumstances and events surrounding each seizure incident. The interview is accompanied by a thorough neurological exam. The electroencephalograph is fundamental to the diagnostic process and assists the neurologist in assessing brain-wave activity. This instrument is also helpful in identifying potential structural abnormalities within the brain. It should be noted that many epilepsies are not detectable through electroencephalographic measures. However, utilizing information from the interview and results derived from neurological measures, the neurologist may be able to prescribe an effective treatment program for the epileptic individual. Many epilepsies can be successfully treated with careful medical management.

The primary medical treatment generally involves anticonvulsant drug therapy in conjunction with other physiological support therapies. According to the Epilepsy Foundation of America (1973), 50 percent of those with seizure disorders are able to achieve complete control of their seizures with anticonvulsant drugs. An additional 30 percent are able to obtain partial control—the instances and nature of seizures become fewer and often less severe as a result of medication. Parents, teachers, and other family members also play a critical role in observing and monitoring the ongoing effects of drug therapy. Careful monitoring of the individual's behavior in a variety of settings may prevent adverse drug effects and problems related to overdosage.

Various forms of biofeedback have recently been employed to help individuals deal with seizure conditions. Sophisticated equipment may be used to signal the epileptic immediately when he or she is producing a brain-wave pattern portraying calmness, relaxation, or other related states. Gradually the patient becomes capable of producing these relaxed brain-wave patterns through the feedback provided by the signaling device. This treatment approach is still in its infancy and is not fully substantiated by scientific research. It does, however, provide an approach to altering brain-functioning without the use of medication.

As with other neurological conditions, many individuals with seizure disorders also have serious accompanying problems, such as mental retardation, cerebral palsy, and emotional or psychological difficulties. Each individual with a seizure disorder must be treated with an array of medical, educational, social, and psychological strategies. Counseling may be helpful to some, while others may benefit from very specific career planning and vocational training. Special education is not generally required for children with convulsive disorders unless the seizures are characteristic of other more serious impairments that adversely affect their academic and social functioning. Seizure-disordered individuals need from others responses that are calm and free of stigmas. The efforts of various professionals and family members must be carefully orchestrated to provide affected individuals with an optimal chance to profit maximally from their abilities and talents. Personally tailored treatment is the key to success in treating people who have epilespy.

Spina Bifida

Kathy had experienced a difficult childhood. Now at the age of fourteen she was beginning to undergo the physical changes of early adolescence, although her social growth was substantially behind those of her age-mates. Kathy had always been somewhat different, but she had never been labeled handicapped. She walked with an ungainly gait and was quite uncoordinated. To her peers she seemed rather strange, and she was always slow in school. Things had grown worse for Kathy lately, in terms of social relations and academic performance.

Kathy was born in a logging camp in western Oregon. The delivery had been routine, but there were few medical services available in the small community. Many changes had transpired since that time. Her father had been promoted in the company, and the family now lived in Eugene, where the main company mill was located. Fortunately the family had more resources now, and Kathy's mother sought medical help for Kathy. The physician examined her and immediately referred them to a specialist at the University of Oregon Medical School in Portland.

The diagnosis explained a great deal but did not provide much guidance regarding treatment. Kathy was the victim of a partial spina bifida that had occurred very early in her development. The condition had not been diagnosed earlier because of the scarce medical services available in the remote logging camp. It had resulted in reduced physical ability and had also caused a mild level of mental retardation. There certainly was no cure now, at the age of fourteen, but at least Kathy's parents learned of some special programs that might help her grow academically as much as possible. There also seemed to be some possibility that physical problems could be alleviated to a certain degree through special help. Kathy was still a very sad young lady because of the ridicule and punishment she had received from her peers.

Definition and Concepts. Spina bifida is a birth defect of the nervous system. Until about the twelfth week of pregnancy, the backbone of a developing fetus remains open. If for some reason certain bones of the spinal column fail to close properly, a cleft or opening is formed. The abnormal opening may allow the contents of the spinal canal to flow between the bones that did not fully close. Spina bifida may or may not influence intellectual functioning, but it frequently involves some paralysis of various portions of the body, depending on the hidden location of the opening. There are two types of spina bifida: spina bifida occulta and spina bifida cystica.

Spina bifida occulta is a very mild condition in which an oblique slit is present in one or several of the vertebral structures. "It is 'occult' [hidden] in the sense that it may be evident only on radiological examination" (Stark, 1977, p. 9). Spina bifida occulta has little if any impact on the developing infant. However, the condition is occasionally accompanied by other neurological problems.

There are two subdivisions of **spina bifida cystica** (see Figure 10-8). They include **spina bifida meningocele** and **spina bifida myelomeningocele.** The meningocele is characterized by a protrusion that presents itself in the form of a tumor-like sack on the back of the infant. This sack contains spinal fluid but no nerve tissue. In contrast, the myelomeningocele does contain nerve tissue. It is also the most serious variety of spina bifida in that it generally includes, as a part of its debilitating effects, paralysis or partial paralysis of certain body areas, lack of bowel and bladder control, and mental retardation. There are two types of myelomeningocele: one in which the tumor-like sack is open, revealing

Figure 10-8/ Side and Top Views of a Normal Spine, Spina Bifida Occulta, and Spina Bifida Cystica

Spina Bifida Cystica

Normal Spine

Side View

Cord

Bone

Spina Bifida with
Meningocele

Spina Bifida Occulta

Abnormal
Opening in Bone

Spina Bifida with
Myelomeningocele

Figure 10-8/ Continued

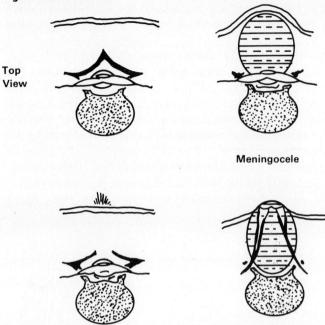

Top
View

Meningocele

Myelomeningocele

Stark, G.D. *Spina Bifida* (London, England: Blackwell Scientific Publication, 1977) p.5 (Top View)

the neural tissue, and one in which the sack is closed or covered with a combination of skin and membrane.

Research conducted by the National Institute of Neurological and Communicative Disorders and Stroke indicated that of those children with spina bifida who survive the first twenty-four hours after delivery, 20 percent will have moderate to severe mental retardation and 75 percent will have severe physical impairments. Those children born with a meningocele are likely to have normal intelligence. This is particularly true if the menigocele is not accompanied by any hydrocephalus (an abnormal amount of cerebrospinal fluid in the cranial cavity). Children with spina bifida occulta exhibit the normal range of intelligence. Children with myelomeningocele generally have IQs in low average to mildly retarded ranges (Calhoun & Hawisher, 1979). For affected children whose learning capacity is normal or above average, no special educational programming is required.

Causation and Prevalence. The exact cause of spina bifida is unknown. There is a slight tendency for the condition to run in families. It probably occurs as a function of certain prenatal factors interacting with genetic predispositions. It is also possible that certain agents taken in by the mother prior to or during the first few days of pregnancy may be responsible for the defect.

The prevalence figures for spina bifida (myelomeningocele and meningocele) vary markedly. The highest prevalence rate occurs in Ireland, with a figure exceeding 4 in 1,000 individuals. The lowest rate is found in tropical countries where the condition occurs in 0.5 in 1,000 individuals or less. In the United States, estimates are slightly greater than 1 in 1,000 live births (U.S. Department of Health and Human Services, 1981a). More females seem to develop the condition than males, with a ratio of about 3 to 1. Mullins (1979) reported that the prevalence of spina bifida in the United States is three times higher than that reported for the world population. Future research may provide answers regarding the reasons for these marked differences.

Intervention. It is now possible to identify babies with myelomeningocele before they are born by means of certain sophisticated instruments and techniques: ultrasonic scanning of the fetus to identify major defects late in pregnancy; fetoscopy, a moderately hazardous procedure to identify small defects; and amniocentesis, a procedure in which the level of alphafetoprotein (AFP) in the amnionic fluid is assessed. The presence of various concentrations of AFP is due to the opening in the spinal column.

A similar situation exists after the child with myelomeningocele is born. Depending on the nature of the lesion, its position on the spine, and the presence of other related conditions (e.g., hydrocephalus), the parents and the consulting physician will have to decide whether immediate medical action should be taken. Such decisions are extremely difficult, for they often entail problems and issues that are not easily or quickly resolved. The decision to undertake surgery is often made quickly if the problem is located very low on the infant's back and there is no presence of hydrocephalus. In cases where the myelomeningocele is relatively high on the spine and other conditions are present, such as meningitis, surgery may not be performed.

Children with spina bifida myelomeningocele have little if any bowel or bladder control. The lack of control is directly attributable to the paralysis caused by the malformation of the spinal cord. In addition, children with this condition will be paraplegic and have no sensation of temperature or pain in their legs. As these children mature, they can be trained to regulate their bowel movements through the use of suppositories. Once this training has been achieved, the individual no longer needs to worry about the problems associated with accidental soiling. Children may also be taught to use Credé's method, which involves a manual approach to eliminating urine.

Children with spina bifida myelomeningocele frequently have other orthopedic problems and complications (Mullins, 1979). Hip dislocations, contractures, and spinal defects are common among these children. With appropriate bracing, exercise, and conditioning, surgical intervention may be unnecessary. Fractures are also common among these children, and they often occur prior to birth without any significant trauma or insult to the bones involved. Such fractures are the result of reduced supply of blood to the bones. The bones become brittle through calcium leaching from surrounding tissues, a condition known as osteoporosis. Exercise in the form of standing and bearing weight is helpful in preventing this condition.

Physical therapists play a critical role in helping these children, particularly younger children, as they learn to cope with the paralysis caused by myelomeningocele. This paralysis limits the child's exploratory activities, which are critical to later learning and sensory-motor performance. With this in mind, many such children are fitted with a modified skateboard, which allows them to explore their surroundings. Utilizing the strength in their arms and hands, they may become quite adept at exploring their home environments. Gradually they graduate to leg braces, crutches, a wheelchair, or a combination of the three.

For the most part, children with spina bifida who have no signs of hydrocephalus have normal intelligence. Like other children, they may be average, below average, or above average in their intellectual performance. Consequently, they will receive education that is mainly similar to other students. Exceptions relate to the physical environment of the school and the coordinated support needed by these youngsters. The facilities within a school should be suited to the children's physical needs. Coat hooks, lockers, and water sources may need to be lowered to accommodate those who are confined to wheelchairs. Specialized seating and writing surfaces may be necessary.

There must be proper coordination and cooperation between parents, medical treatment teams, and teachers if these children are to master the problems associated with their condition. Such coordination is particularly critical during the early periods of school involvement, because it is during this time that they begin to master some of the problems associated with incontinence and mobility. Teachers may need to aid students in complying with their medication routines. It may be necessary to modify seating arrangements so that the students in wheelchairs are not always placed in the back of the room. Attention must also be directed at helping the student deal with new medical or hygenic devices that may be operating improperly. Later, as they progress through their schooling, they will need the help of counselors and career specialists in selecting and achieving goals commensurate with their abilities.

Spinal Cord Injuries

Eric was a freshman at Berkeley, just turned nineteen, and he enjoyed many of the things the other guys did, including cars, girls, booze, and pot. He didn't smoke a lot, nor did he drink that much. Eric might have a joint in the evening after class and a glass of wine now and then. He had grown fond of wine while he was at home. His parents represented the upper-middle-class sector of San Francisco, and they had a fine wine cellar. Pot was something that had been introduced into Eric's life outside the home. Some of his classmates smoked dope in high school, although he rarely had until enrolling in college.

One Friday evening Eric was driving across the Golden Gate Bridge with some of his friends, headed for Sausalito. There are a lot of questions in Eric's mind regarding what happened. It is not clear to him whether it was the early evening party or the young lady that was sitting next to him. Certainly he was not paying attention when the

*accident occurred. Eric was the only survivor. His three friends were
killed instantly, and the mother and baby in the other car had died the
next day. Often he wished he had died too. He might as well be dead,
he thought, as be in the condition that resulted from the fiery collision.
Eric's neck had been broken, and he was completely paralyzed. All
that was three years ago, but little had changed. He remained in the
rehabilitation center, depressed and with little hope of achieving all
the goals he had before.*

Definitions and Concepts. The spinal cord is the conduit through which the
brain transmits messages to various parts of the body. It is basically a cable of
nerve cells. The spinal cord controls both the motor and sensory functions of
various parts of the body in conjunction with peripheral nervous systems.
Without adequate pathways, the messages and sensations generated from the
nerve endings are not communicated. The spinal cord is enclosed by the spinal
column, which is made up of thirty-three vertebrae. These vertebrae, together
with the muscles attached to them, provide the protection for this invaluable
communication network. The spinal column is divided into several regions.
They include the cervical, thoracic, lumbar, sacral, and coccyx regions (see
Figure 10-9). The spinal cord is similarly divided into regions with the same
designations. Thirty-one identified spinal nerves are also attached to the spinal
cord. They find their way to other portions of the body between the vertebrae
of the spinal column.

  Spinal cord injury occurs when the spinal cord is traumatized or transected (i.e., cut). The cord can be traumatized from extreme extension or flexion
resulting from a fall, an automobile accident, or a sport injury. Transection of
the cord can also occur as a function of these types of accidents, although such
occurrences are extremely rare. Usually in such cases the cord is bruised or
otherwise injured. Within a short time after the injury the cord appears to swell,
and within hours hemorrhaging often occurs. Gradually a self-destructive process ensues in which the affected area slowly deteriorates and the damage
becomes irreversible.

  The overall impact of injury to an individual depends on the site and
nature of the insult, as illustrated in Figure 10-10. If the injury occurs in the
neck or upper back, resultant paralysis and effects will be much more extensive.
If the injury occurs in the lower back, paralysis will be confined to lower
extremities of the body. We can see from this information that spinal cord
injuries and their physical impact are similar to those derived from spina bifida
myelomeningocele. The terminology (paraplegia, quadraplegia, and hemiplegia) utilized to describe the impact is identical. It is worth noting however,
that the terms *paraplegia*, *quadraplegia*, and *hemiplegia* are global descriptions
of functioning and not precise enough to convey accurately the level of an
individual's functioning. For example, the degree of paralysis in two para-
plegics may be substantially different, depending on the location and nature
of the injury. In general, we can assume that the person with a spinal cord
injury will experience some level of paralysis from the point of the injury

Figure 10-9/ Spinal Column and Spinal Cord

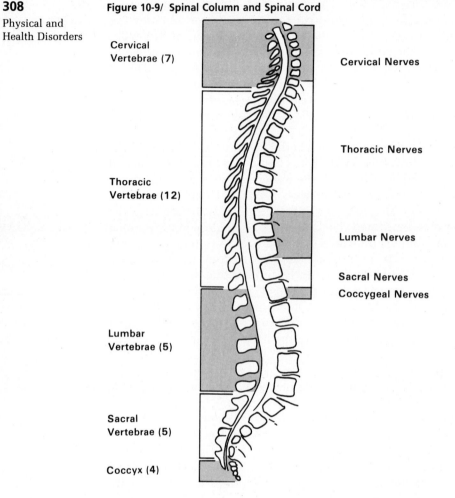

Cervical
Vertebrae (7)

Cervical Nerves

Thoracic Nerves

Thoracic
Vertebrae (12)

Lumbar Nerves

Sacral Nerves
Coccygeal Nerves

Lumbar
Vertebrae (5)

Sacral
Vertebrae (5)

Coccyx (4)

downward through the body. The amount of sensation lost and the degree of paralysis experienced by the individual depends on the amount of damage to the spinal cord and nerve roots at the point of insult.

The losses of voluntary movement and sensation are often staggering to the injured individual. Some quadraplegics are not able to move or to change their body position without the aid of an assistant or mechanical device. Even independent sitting is difficult for some quadraplegics. The paraplegic who has good use of one or both arms is able to compensate in part for paralysis of the lower extremity.

Injury to the spinal cord also affects other bodily systems. Bowel and bladder control are frequently lost. The individual may be incapable of perspiring in the affected areas due to sensorial loss, which seriously hinders the body's natural cooling system. The respiratory system may also be affected if the injury occurs in the cervical region. In such cases the individual may have to rely on a respirator or rocking bed for breathing assistance.

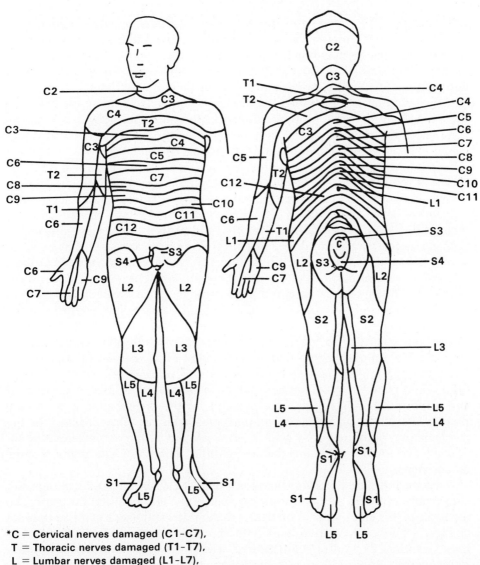

*C = Cervical nerves damaged (C1–C7),
 T = Thoracic nerves damaged (T1–T7),
 L = Lumbar nerves damaged (L1–L7),
 S = Sacral nerves damaged (S1–S5).

Causation and Incidence. While falls, accidents, and sport injuries can cause spinal cord injury, various diseases can also damage the spinal cord. Cancer, tumors, infections, abscesses of the spine, arthritis, multiple sclerosis, and poliomyelitis can all cause spinal cord injury. Motor vehicle accidents are responsible for approximately half of all spinal cord injuries (U.S. Department of Health and Human Services, 1981b). Some five to ten thousand new cases appear each year, 75 percent of which involve males. Individuals in the age-range from fifteen to thirty are most likely to incur such an injury (Howell, 1978).

Intervention. The immediate care rendered to a person with a spinal cord injury is critical. If proper procedures are not employed at this point, the impact of the injury can be magnified. Injured people who report a loss of sensation or movement should be lifted and transported with great care in a reclined or flat position. Ideally the individual should be taken immediately to a hospital emergency room, where skilled medical personnel can evaluate the extent of the damage and provide proper treatment. After an initial diagnosis has been completed, the injured person may be taken to an acute spinal cord injury center for the necessary medical and/or surgical treatment.

The first phase of treatment provided by a receiving hospital or specialized center is the management of shock. Quickly thereafter the individual is immobilized in order to prevent movement and further damage. As a rule, surgical procedures are not undertaken immediately. The major goal of medical treatment at this point is to stabilize the spine and prevent further complications. Catheterization may be employed to control urine flow, and steps may be taken to reduce hemorrhaging and swelling at the injury site. Traction may be utilized to stabilize certain portions of the spinal column and cord. Medical treatment of spinal cord injuries is long and often tedious. Once physicians have successfully stabilized the spine and treated any other medical conditions, the rehabilitation process proceeds at an accelerated pace. The individual is taught to use new muscles and to take advantage of any and all residual muscle strength. The injured person will also be taught to use certain orthopedic devices and equipment such as hand splints, braces, reachers, head sticks for typing, and plate guards. Together with an orthopedic specialist, occupational and physical therapists become responsible for the re-education and training process. Psychiatric and other support personnel are also engaged in the rehabilitation activities. The goal of all treatment is the achievement of independence to the maximum degree possible. This may take many months and/or years.

As the individual masters necessary self-care skills, other educational and career objectives are pursued with assistance of the rehabilitation team. The members of this team change constantly as the skills and needs of the individual change. Schooling for individuals with spinal cord injuries is similar to that for all children or adults. Modifications will be necessary in the school environment (providing grab bars near chalkboards, doors, and stairs; lowering towel dispensers; changing stall-door widths and swinging directions for doors; ordering adapted utensils; etc.), and the methods by which these individuals express the learning they have acquired may have to be altered. Note-takers may be necessary. The individual may use a tape recorder to verbally respond to test items or assignments. A typewriter may be employed to convey information if the individual has learned to use a head stick.

Vocationally and professionally, an individual with a spinal cord injury may need to be retrained or re-educated with assistance provided by vocational rehabilitation services. Some will have limitations that make it necessary for them to have full-time attendant care. Such care providers would assist with all the daily functions of bathing, grooming, dressing, shopping, and other activities. Recreational pursuits will also need to be changed. Many people who are limited to wheelchairs enjoy bowling, swimming, square-dancing, basketball and even golf. Since 1960, many wheelchair athletes have enjoyed participating in the Paraolympics. The adaptation process is often arduous and challenging, but with appropriate support the individual with a spinal cord injury can lead a fulfilling and meaningful life.

There are currently under way a number of innovative research projects that may have a profound influence on the treatment of spinal cord injuries. They include studies of the use of high doses of the various drugs to reduce swelling that occurs with spinal cord insult. Other investigators have experimented with localized cooling of spinal cord injuries to reduce swelling and to combat the onset of damage to other nerves. Attempts are also being made to utilize enzymes, hyperbaric oxygen (oxygen under pressure), and regeneration techniques to deal with spinal cord injuries. In the future, strategic placement of electrodes in paralyzed muscle tissue may restore functional movement to fingers, hands, wrists, and other appendages. Some research with animals has led scientists to believe that paralyzed individuals may eventually be able to stimulate the sacral nerve roots at the base of the spine electrically and thereby achieve bladder control. Such a control device would significantly lessen the number of paralyzed individuals who suffer from urinary-system dysfunctions and the number that die as a result of severe kidney damage (U.S. Department of Health and Human Services, 1981b).

Recreation is essential to the well being of all individuals.

SKELETAL AND MUSCULAR DISORDERS

Arthritis

Jane has been absent from school a great deal. When she does attend, she often complains about the pain that occurs as her arthritis episodes become acute. At other times, Jane feels fine and is able to participate in most of the school activities with her peers.

Jane despises her medication. It frequently causes side effects that are worse than the pain. Daytime rest periods help her cope with the rigors of her condition. Her academic achievement is well above average, and when her arthritis episodes subside she is a joy to be around.

Definition and Concepts. **Arthritis** is a disease typified by pain in and around the joints. Individuals of all ages can be affected by this condition. In children the condition is known as **juvenile rheumatoid arthritis** and manifests itself between eighteen months and four years of age. Arthritis in children is often preceded by a respiratory infection and can affect the entire body. Juvenile rheumatoid arthritis is frequently masked by symptoms characteristic of other disorders. Children who develop this condition are influenced by its presence in several significant fashions. They may miss a considerable amount of school,

The hands of a young person with severe arthritis.

as in the case of Jane. They may not be able to participate fully in many of the activities pursued by others during recesses or physical education periods. Fortunately, half of all children who have arthritis experience a complete remission of symptoms without serious side effects, and another one-quarter experience a complete remission with only limited crippling side effects. **Spondylitis of adolescence,** a form of rheumatoid arthritis, affects the entire body rather than isolated joints or areas. It is characterized by pain in the legs and lower back which results from swelling vertebrae of the back. It occurs during the teenage and young adult years and can be quite physically debilitating.

Causation and Prevalence. The exact causes of various arthritic conditions are not fully known. The initiating factors may be bacteria or viruses, but for reasons not completely understood, the body responds to these bacteria or viruses in a pathogenic (disease-producing) fashion. The actual pathogenic process is complicated and involves many complex interactions. Ultimately the critical components and fluids of the joints are altered, and the joints eventually become deformed. Spondylitis of adolescence appears to have some genetic basis, as it often tends to be a familial condition passed from generation to generation.

About 3 infants in 100,000 develop rheumatoid arthritis (Mullins, 1979). The Arthritis Foundation suggested that about 250,000 children are affected by this condition in the United States (1974). Many more females than males are affected, and the condition in children generally appears between the ages of one to four or nine to fourteen and may appear any time during adolescence.

Intervention. Anti-inflammatory drugs now make it possible for individuals with rheumatoid arthritis to reduce some of the pain associated with the condition. Frequently these medications cause side effects that may substantially influence the individual's academic, social, and behavioral performance. Teachers, parents, and health personnel need to be aware of these potential influences and respond with sensitivity.

Rheumatoid arthritis is a condition that often varies in intensity. During certain phases or time periods, affected individuals may have greater need for medication due to increased pain caused by inflammation. In addition, those with arthritis should be encouraged to participate in activities requiring the use of all joints to the degree possible. As with other impairments, educators or other care providers should avoid performing tasks for arthritic individuals that they can do for themselves. Overprotection on the part of others lessens the current and eventual effectiveness of the arthritic individual in dealing with the school and community and may lead to unnecessary dependency.

Amputations

Janet was born with congenital amputations. The thumb and one finger were missing from both hands. Existing fingers on both hands were considerably shorter than those of normal infants and slightly webbed.

Her right foot was a club foot and the left foot was composed of only a heel, which was about the size of a billiard ball. Everything else about Janet was very appealing. She had a friendly disposition and did virtually everything that normal children do during infancy and the toddler years.

When she was two, Janet underwent surgery in which the middle finger on both hands was removed. The surgeon also removed the webbing that interfered with her dexteriy. This operation made it possible for Janet to use her fingers as pincers. Two years later, the heel protruding from the left foot was surgically removed, and other orthopedic modifications were made in the ankle area. Since that time she has successfully used a series of prosthetic feet, which are held to the leg by suction. The design of each prosthetic foot was such that Janet only needed to slip her left leg into the prosthesis to be ready to go.

Janet is well-adjusted and doing well in school. She has successfully dealt with the obvious differences in her hands. Recently her younger sister, Susan, came home in tears because two of Susan's friends had said that they hated Susan. Janet tried to console her: "Now Susie, I used to be called 'freaky two fingers.' That's just kids. Don't worry about it."

Presently Janet is heavily involved in gymnastics and loves it. Her major complaint about life deals with her shoes. Because of her club foot, she must wear flat-soled shoes, or at least shoes with heels less than a quarter of an inch high. This is often perplexing, particularly because styles change so frequently. Overall she is very much a part of her peer environment and is now helping her sister deal with the challenges of normality.

Definitions and Concepts. There are two types of amputations: congenital and acquired. Congenital amputations are apparent at birth. They occur for a variety of reasons, which are not fully understood. As a normal fetus develops, tiny arm buds appear on the twenty-sixth day after conception. Shortly thereafter these buds begin to develop into the arm and hand components. At the end of the first month the fetus develops leg buds, which progress in a similar fashion. When a child is born with an amputation, it means that some portion of the budding process was terminated prematurely. Children may be born with minor congenital malformations or complete absences of limbs. Their adjustment to the condition is generally less traumatic than those who acquire an amputation later in life as teenagers or young adults. Children with congenital amputations also accept and respond more favorably to the use of prosthetic devices than those who experience amputations later on (acquired amputations).

Acquired amputations are generally the result of an injury or a therapeutic surgical procedure. Relatively few children have acquired amputations. Children who have cancer of the bone in an extremity may have to undergo surgery to remove the affected limb. Most acquired amputations occur as a function of accidents or injuries later in a child's life.

Adjusting to an amputation resulting from an accident or therapeutic surgery is extremely challenging. Many people following such incidents experience the loss of a limb in much the same way they would a death. They mourn and grieve the loss and gradually move through the stages necessary for adequate personal adjustment. They also often experience a condition in which pains or other sensations in the absent limb are perceived.

Causation and Prevalence. The causes of congenital amputations are not completely understood. Over the years we have become aware of a variety of drugs and substances that adversely affect the development of maturing fetuses. Thalidomide, quinine, aminoprotein, and Myleran have all been implicated regarding congenital amputations in children whose mothers used these substances during pregnancy. Certain genetic or inherited predispositions for congenital abnormalities in limbs have also been identified. The reasons for the actual triggering of these predispositions remains unknown, but the presence of certain agents, such as those mentioned, heightens the chances for birth defects. The same is true for the presence of the rubella virus.

Accurate prevalence figures are difficult to obtain. "Sampling techniques are notoriously inadequate" (Friedman, 1978b, p. 3). Females have far fewer amputations than males. The ratio of congenital to acquired amputations is two to one in children. Some 75 percent of the amputations in children age five to sixteen result from injuries and accidents. The other 25 percent are due to malignant diseases (Friedman, 1978b). Amputations are frequently performed surgically on accident victims in order to prevent further blood loss, which may be life threatening.

Intervention. As we have already noted, children born with congenital amputations generally have an easier time adjusting to the treatments and therapies provided by the orthopedic physician and occupational and physical therapists than do children, youths, and adults who acquire amputations later in their lives. Children with congenital amputations also adjust more readily to prosthetic equipment and feel less reluctant to utilize it in public settings. Utilization of various prostheses occurs in a developmental fashion. Young children born with incomplete legs may be provided with customized skateboards to assist them with crawling activities. Later they may be fitted with artificial legs tailored to their physical dimensions. As such children grow and develop, the prosthetic devices will be redesigned and modified according to their emerging physical needs. Maintenance and replacement of the devices is very costly. Fortunately some families have been aided in this endeavor by the Children's Bureau of the Department of Health, Education, and Welfare. Early encouragement of the use of prostheses is based on the notion that exposure and practice early in a child's life will significantly influence the skill with which the child will eventually perform and his or her acceptance of the process. Schooling for children with congenital amputations should proceed in a fashion commensurate with their intellectual capacity. As was the case with Janet, most children with congenital amputations will profit from education provided in normal school settings. The teacher's role in responding to students with both types of amputations is multifaceted. A child with a missing body part or parts often produces an avoidance reaction in others, particularly children. Teachers who display and encourage appropriate physical and social contact with the young amputee provide an excellent model for their students to imitate.

Individuals who acquire an amputation later in life (e.g., during their teen or adult years) generally experience a high level of shock, consternation, and adjustment problems. The first step in treatment is typically medical. The orthopedic surgeon has the responsibility for preparing the remaining stump for its eventual use in conjunction with a prosthetic device. Following the completion of surgical procedures, the second step of the treatment process is initiated. This step involves helping an individual cope with feelings and self-perceptions that emerge as a result of loss of a limb or limbs. The third step of the treatment process is rehabilitation. During this phase the orthopedic specialist, prosthetist, occupational therapist, physical therapist, and rehabilitation personnel work together to help amputees adjust to their condition and their prosthetic devices.

In the future, biomedical engineers, in conjunction with other health professionals, will have a profound effect on the lives of individuals with amputations. There are already available many devices that are activated by nothing more than the breath or eye movement of an amputee.

Muscular Dystrophy

It was December 15, 1977, a gloomy and rainy day in Seattle. Tom sat in his apartment waiting for his best friend to arrive. He had released his full-time attendant for the day, and the plans were carefully made for the afternoon. It was a depressing day. Tom had been chronically depressed for the past six months, and many factors had contributed to that depression.

Tom was twenty-eight years old and suffered from muscular dystrophy. He had lived in this apartment with his attendant for nearly two years now. He had no family, for his parents had been killed in an automobile accident in July 1974. The disease had rendered Tom quite helpless. For many people such problems would have been insurmountable, but Tom was a fighter. When he moved into the apartment he had accepted the situation, the need for an attendant, and the continuing pain, but he soon became unhappy with the existence. Soap operas on the television were not only ludicrous, they were boring. He decided that he had to do something more with his life, so he got a job as an operator for a telephone-answering service. Tom received calls for attorneys, physicians, and other professional people. It was a job he could do from the apartment, and the income really helped. But all that determination to help himself had led Tom to this afternoon of December 15,1977.

Tom's financial support had come largely from Social Security Disability (SSD) benefits, but when the agency discovered he was making nearly five hundred dollars a month, that support was terminated. It became impossible for Tom to continue paying both the rent and his attendant. This afternoon would take care of all that. The note remaining after the incident laid the blame for the tragedy in the lap of the Social Security agency. Tom could no longer deal with a society or a life that continually battered people, even when they fought to make themselves better and contribute to their life and that of others. The facts relating to the incident are few. It was declared to be a suicide, although there was some question regarding how Tom could have handled the weapon.*

Definition and Concepts. **Muscular dystrophy** is a term used to describe a variety of conditions. "Muscular dystrophies are a group of chronic inherited disorders characterized by progressive weakening and wasting of the voluntary skeletal muscles" (U.S. Department of Health and Human Services, 1980, p. 1). Each dystrophy condition varies in intensity and its manifestations. The seriousness of the various dystrophies is influenced by hereditary antecedents, the age of onset, the physical location and nature of onset, and the rate at which the condition progresses. Actual causes of muscular dystrophies are unknown, and there are no known cures for each of the various conditions. It affects the muscles of the hips, legs, shoulders, and arms. Afflicted individuals progressively lose their ability to walk and to use their arms and hands. The loss of ability is attributable to fatty tissue that gradually replaces the muscle tissue.

There are several types of muscular dystrophy, four of which will be mentioned in this section. The first, pseudohypertrophy, is found most frequently in males. It is also known as Duchenne muscular dystrophy. Limb-girdle muscular dystrophy represents a second type of muscular dystrophy. It typically manifests itself as muscle degeneration in the pelvic girdle, affecting the legs, or in the shoulder girdle, affecting the arms. Facioscapulohumeral muscular dystrophy affects muscles in the facial area, shoulders, and upper arms. Myotonic muscular dystrophy is initially characterized by weakness in the hands, feet, neck, and face.

Causation and Prevalence. The exact cause of muscular dystrophy remains unknown, but it is viewed as a hereditary disease. However, about one-third of the cases develop without any clear hereditary antecedents (Ferguson, 1975). The etiology of muscular dystrophy may be related to enzyme disturbances that subsequently affect muscle metabolism. About two hundred thousand people are affected by muscular dystrophies and other neuromuscular disor-

---

*This vignette is a fictionalized account of a true situation. It was changed for the purposes of the current volume in order to protect the privacy of those involved, both living and deceased.

ders. Some estimates indicate that about 4 in 1,000 people develop muscular dystrophy (Ferguson, 1975). One-third are between the ages of three and thirteen, and eight out of ten are males. Abnormalities in red blood cell membranes also suggest that the condition is a systemic disorder.

Diagnosis of muscular dystrophy is usually straight forward. An orthopedic specialist first completes a family history review and an orthopedic physical. The specialist observes the child's facial muscle pattern, gait, lifting performance, and rising from a supine position (lying on the back with the face upward). A series of other medical tests may be conducted. A biopsy (thin slice of muscle for microscopic review) may be taken from the muscle tissue. An electromyogram may be employed to measure the electrical activity in the impaired muscles. Serum enzyme tests may be used to assess the levels of certain enzymes that could be present in the body as a result of muscle deterioration. The diagnosis is completed and treatment is prescribed based on a synthesis of clinical observations and the information derived from medical tests.

Intervention. There is no known cure for muscular dystrophies. The focus of treatment is directed at maintaining or improving the individual's functioning, preserving his or her ambulatory independence as long as possible. The first phases of maintenance and prevention processes are handled by a physical therapist. The therapist is responsible for preventing or correcting (to the degree possible) contractures, which are a permanent shortening and thickening of muscle fiber. As the condition becomes more serious, treatment will generally include prescribing supportive devices such as walkers, braces, night splints, surgical corsets, and hospital beds. Eventually the individual with muscular dystrophy will be confined to a wheelchair, which should be tailored to the person's needs.

The individual with muscular dystrophy will frequently be given some type of medication. If the patient is receiving medication, parents and teachers will play an important role in observing any peculiar reactions that occur. As the condition advances, respiratory muscles are often affected, and the individual may be unable to cough strongly enough to expel mucus and phlegm. Any changes regarding the health status of a child should be reported immediately to the parents. Parents can then take appropriate preventive actions to forestall or avert an infection. People with muscular dystrophy should be encouraged to participate actively in all activities for which they have the skill. In fact, long periods of sitting should be avoided.

One of the major problems for the individual with muscular dystrophy is the appearance of contractures (permanent shortening of muscle fibers that induces decreased joint mobility), which seriously interfere with the individual's ability to walk or move in other manners. The best treatment for prevention of such contractures is physical therapy and the avoidance of classroom activities that involve prolonged periods without movement.

Education of individuals with muscular dystrophy may take place in a variety of settings, depending on the educational and physical needs of each student. Some are served in special classes for the physically disabled, others may be served in the regular classroom. Because of the progressive nature of muscular dystrophy, the life span for many afflicted individuals is relatively short. Consequently, parents, teachers, and others should prepare themselves (and the patient) as best they can for the advent of death. Several excellent books have been designed for this purpose (e.g., Barton, 1977; Gyulay, 1978; Kubler-Ross, 1975).

A variety of other muscular-skeletal disorders can affect a person's functioning and adaptation. These conditions include, but are not limited to, osteomyelitis (an inflammatory disease of the bone tissue); scoliosis (curvature of the spine which often causes severe pain), osteogenesis imperfecta (an inherited condition in which the bones are extremely brittle and easily broken); Legg-Calvé-Perthes disease (degeneration of the critical growth center of the top, round end of the thigh bone, which fits into the hip socket), and arthrogryposis (muscles of the limbs are absent at birth or are of diminished size or strength). For the most part, these and similar conditions do not necessarily require long-term placement in special education, but they do require medical intervention and treatment accompanied by periodic homebound or hospital instruction.

SUMMARY

Physical disorders generally have a considerable impact on the affected individual as well as on family members, friends, and others around them. Physical disorders may alter substantially the life and plans of the person affected. In many cases, however, the conditions can be successfully treated and/or managed through appropriate medical, social, and psychological intervention.

Cerebral palsy, a neurological dysfunction, has two major descriptive classifications: those focusing on the motor characteristics of the syndrome and those focusing on the topographical characteristics. A variety of causes have been identified, including birth trauma, maternal infection, and chronic infections. Treatment includes intervention from several disciplines.

Epilepsy is a general term representing several types of central nervous system disorders manifested by seizures. The precise causation of epilepsy remains unclear, although it is known that a variety of traumas to the brain may trigger the condition's emergence. Treatment typically involves medication to control the seizures.

Spina bifida, a birth defect of the nervous system, involves an abnormal process of prenatal development wherein the spinal cord fails to close properly. Causation is unknown, although heredity and certain substances ingested by the mother have been implicated. Treatment may include medical intervention through surgery.

Spinal cord injuries occur when the spinal cord is either traumatized or severed. Causation is related primarily to injury through traffic accidents, although sports and other injuries also contribute. Treatment generally involves medical intervention, but other disciplines are included in the continuing rehabilitation process.

Arthritis, skeletal and muscular disorder, is typified by pain in and around the joints. Causation of various arthritic conditions is not well understood, although certain bacteria and viruses have been implicated. Intervention often involves the administration of medication.

Amputations are of two general types: congenital and acquired. Congenital amputations, apparent at birth, represent developmental abnormalities. Acquired amputations are generally due to some injury or therapeutic surgery. Causation of congenital amputations varies and is not completely understood. A number of drugs have been identified as causing congenital amputations, and heredity may also play a part. Acquired amputations are caused by many different influences and/or incidents (e.g., injuries or surgery to correct problems or to save a person's life).

Muscular dystrophies are a group of disorders characterized by progressive weakening and wasting of the voluntary skeletal muscles. Approximately one-third of the cases of muscular dystrophy develop without any clear hereditary antecedents. In the remaining cases, the disorder appears to be hereditary. Unfortunately there is no known cure for the various dystrophies. Most treatment is directed at maintaining, improving, or preserving muscular functioning, particularly the ability to walk.

ŝ REVIEW QUESTIONS

1. Briefly discuss the critical factors that influence the overall adjustment of an individual with physical disorders.
2. Can one be disabled and yet not handicapped? In responding to this question, define in your own words the terms *disability, impairment,* and *handicap.*
3. Discuss the treatment challenges inherent in serving the educational needs of children with cerebral palsy.
4. Contrast the various types of seizures according to their characteristic features, and identify the procedures to be followed in responding to a grand mal seizure.
5. Identify the types of spina bifida and describe the impact each can have on the development of an infant.
6. Describe the critical aspects of the treatment process for someone who has experienced a serious spinal-cord injury.
7. Identify the differences between juvenile rheumatoid arthritis and spondylitis of adolescence.
8. Describe the impact of congenital versus acquired amputations.
9. Discuss the onset of problems that frequently occur with individuals who have muscular dystrophy. Identify the interventions that are generally applied in dealing with these problems.

CHAPTER ELEVEN

Health Disorders

Breathing is the most important thing in the world as you awaken at 2:30 in the morning. Your chest feels like someone is sitting on it, and you know there will be no more sleep tonight. Asthma is only one of many health problems that have significant impacts on people's lives. When a person's health severely restricts daily activities, what one can eat, or one's social contacts, the impact is significant. Most of us give little thought to our health on a daily basis, but for those with serious health disorders, their health status may represent the most significant factor in their lives.

Patty had always been the sick one in the family. As a diabetic, her childhood had been disrupted. Her physical development was delayed, and she was behind her peers in school because of frequent absences. Yet Patty achieved a great deal—for any youngster, let alone one with health problems. For the past five years, Patty had taken care of the family. When her mother died, Patty was only fifteen, but she assumed responsibility for most of the household chores and caring for her younger brother and sister.

Despite all Patty did for the family, she received little in return. Her brother and sister ridiculed her because she was "sick," and her father believed she would never be able to get a job or a husband. Patty basically held the same opinion about herself. Now at the age of twenty she had finally graduated from high school but had no goals for further education. Her aunt tried to convince Patty that a local vocational rehabilitation program would be exciting and good for her. Patty finally agreed, and her father reluctantly acquiesced.

The results were astonishing to all. It took time, but Patty began to believe in herself, dressed more attractively, performed well, and soon gained full-time employment outside the home. Patty has been gain-

Patty

A number of **health disorders** present serious problems for both youngsters and adults. These health disorders significantly alter not only the lives of those individuals who develop them but also the lives of the individual's family and others around them. In this chapter we will discuss various health disorders and conditions under the categories of systemic disorders, stress-related disorders, life-endangering diseases, and miscellaneous conditions.

The term *health disorders* refers to conditions or diseases that interfere with an individual's functioning. Not every condition discussed in this chapter is a disorder in the typical sense of the term. Some represent health conditions that can be more appropriately thought of as social problems (i.e., adolescent pregnancy, child abuse). However, like the other conditions, there is a substantial impact on the individual, family, and peers.

Unlike physical disorders, health disorders do not generally hinder the person's ability to move about in various settings. Architectural barriers do not seriously restrict the activities of the health disordered. The limitations are generally related to such conditions as reduced alertness and participation, fatigue, pain, fears, and stress. For example, a child with a heart condition may have to limit the amount of time spent in highly active games or team sports. In advanced stages, however, certain conditions seriously affect an individual's mobility.

The impact of a health disorder on an individual depends on such factors as (1) the seriousness of the condition, (2) the age at which the condition appears, (3) the support of the family and friends, (4) the quality of medical treatment provided, and (5) the nature of the condition (i.e., whether it is static or progressive). Referral and treatment processes for health disorders are similar to those employed for physical disorders. Primary-care physicians refer the affected individual to a specialist or several specialists for further diagnosis and/or treatment. Treatment for certain chronic health conditions can be lifelong.

The prevalence of social and psychological problems in children who have serious health disorders is somewhat higher than that of normal children (Pless, 1968; Sultz, Schesinger, Mosher & Feldman, 1972). A serious health problem seems to heighten an individual's chances for experiencing personal adjustment difficulties. The higher prevalence of emotional problems occurs as a function of several factors (Steinhauer, Mushin & Rae-Grant, 1974). For example, children with serious health disorders spend a considerable amount of time away from home receiving hospital care. Such hospitalization often hampers the development of relationships with siblings, parents, and peers (thus complicating the process of building friendships). Physical restriction may also be a factor. Many children with heart conditions must avoid becoming physically fatigued or stressed. Activity limitations exist in a variety of other health conditions, such as asthma and diabetes. It is easy to see how perplexed a child might become about not being able to participate with peers in physically demanding activities.

Diabetes

"Boy, your mom must be real mad at your sister. You got a Snickers and she only got an orange."

"Mom's not mad. It's just my sister is sugarless."

This is a cute response for a six-year-old, unaware of how wise his statement was. If a poll were taken of nondiabetics, the major fear of the disease would be the injection of insulin, but the quest to be "sugarless" is much more difficult.

"Sugarless" means a correct balance between food, exercise, sleep, and medication, not necessarily going without chocolate. For most, continual calculation of these items is overwhelming at first. It is important that the diabetic be aware of the harm that comes from not sticking to regimens, especially diet. Generally, the harm is not immediate, and years down the line when you suddenly can't see well enough to drive, or an ugly wound on your foot won't heal, it's a little late to wish you hadn't sneaked foods so much. On the other hand, sometimes it's difficult to ask for more food.

> At camp I was too afraid to say I needed fruit with my dinner and that
> the Lifesavers that were taken out of my suitcase were medicinal. As
> a result I went into a severe insulin reaction. This episode not only
> frightened the counselors and campers, but shouted to the others "I'm
> different from you!" which was hard for a thirteen-year-old.

Diabetes does not have to limit one's life. With discipline, patience, and honest communication management of the disease can increase awareness of good nutrition and health (Smith, 1982).

Definition and Concepts. "**Diabetes mellitus** is a disease characterized by abnormalities of the endocrine secretion of the pancreas, resulting in disordered metabolism of carbohydrates, fat, and protein and, in time, structural abnormalities in a variety of tissues" (Ellenberg, 1978, p. 353). Abnormal concentrations of sugar in the blood (hyperglycemia) and in the urine (glycosuria) prior to the discovery of insulin caused many individuals with this condition to experience diabetic ketoacidosis (insulin shock) and the progressive development of a coma or severe unconsciousness. However, the prevention and treatment of the accompanying conditions or complications (blindness, cardiovascular disease, and kidney disease) still pose tremendous challenges for the internist or diabetic specialist.

Juvenile diabetes is particularly challenging. Compared to adult diabetes, juvenile diabetes tends to be more severe. The disease in children progresses more quickly. Generally the symptoms are easily recognized. The child develops an unusual thirst for water and other liquids. The child's appetite also increases substantially, but listlessness and fatigue occur despite the increased food and liquid intake. Once the disease has been diagnosed, steps can be taken to prevent a diabetic coma, and treatment is provided for other ensuing conditions.

Adults who develop diabetes generally incur the disease between the ages of forty and fifty, with another increase in incidence occurring in the late seventies. They also experience complications from the disease, but the full onset of structural abnormalities does not occur as rapidly. Obesity is an outstanding characteristic of adults with diabetes. The vast majority of adult diabetics can control their condition by simply modifying their diet (Davidson, 1981; Podolsky, Krall & Bradley, 1980).

Causation and Prevalence. The causes of adult diabetes and juvenile diabetes remain obscure, although considerable research has been devoted to determining the biochemical mechanisms responsible for the onset. As with other disorders, an individual's environment and heredity both have an impact on the emergence and long-term nature of the condition. Juvenile diabetes appears to be more clearly linked to hereditary factors than the adult forms of the disease. The course of diabetes is greatly influenced by such factors as an individual's degree of obesity, level of personal stress, and the type of diet a prediabetic or diabetic maintains. The multifactorial etiology of diabetes is gradually becoming more clear through research efforts.

It is estimated that 5 percent of the U.S. population have diabetes (National Commission on Diabetes, 1975). The prevalence of diabetes has increased over 50 percent in the last decade. Some 50 percent of the children with juvenile diabetes will die within twenty-five years after the onset of the condition. Gorwitz, Howen, and Thompson (1976) conducted a survey of Michigan schoolchildren regarding the prevalence of diabetes. They found that 16 percent of the school-age children involved in their study had diabetes.

Intervention. Medical treatment of juvenile diabetes falls into two categories. Some physicians favor a very controlled chemical approach to treating the condition, while others favor a clinical approach. The regular intake of insulin is emphasized in both approaches. Insulin is absolutely essential for youngsters with juvenile diabetes.

Juvenile diabetes is a lifelong condition that can have a pronounced effect on an individual's behavior in a number of areas. The family is greatly affected by the presence of a youngster with diabetes. Not only must the family members cope with the medical expenses, but they must also assist the child in maintaining the prescribed regimen. The monitoring responsibility adds considerable stress to the diabetic's family routine.

Hypoglycemia associated with medical therapy frequently produces such effects as irritability, poor attention span, temper tantrums, and other related behaviors. Such behavior may be misinterpreted by school personnel or parents unless they have been adequately informed. Another factor that has a pronounced effect on the child is the limitation placed on various types of vigorous physical activity or exercise. If the exercise is regular and of the proper amount, rapid sugar depletion in the blood will not be a problem. An appropriate snack or candy before vigorous activity and thirty minutes after will lessen the chances of insulin shock.

Juvenile diabetics are confronted with many issues as they proceed through their schooling into adolescence and young adulthood. One involves the intensification of their disease and the emergence of other serious accompanying conditions. Adolescent diabetics must deal with the developmental challenges associated with this period, in addition to coping with the unique problems inherent in being a diabetic. As a rule, the adolescent period is one in which youngsters gradually become more autonomous and peer oriented. The controls of their parents and other family members are progressively replaced by those of the adolescent. Appropriate diet compliance, insulin, and activity management become increasingly the responsibility of the adolescent diabetic. The serious and often terminal nature of juvenile diabetes frequently presents an adolescent diabetic with perplexing questions. From one perspective, they would like to succeed in school, develop friendships, pursue a career, and eventually marry. From another perspective they realize that they may eventually lose their sight, develop arterial problems, and perhaps experience early death. Coping with these and other problems requires the skills of a variety of well-trained teachers, counselors, and other specialists. The treatment of juvenile diabetes is a long-term and multifaceted process.

Weight reduction is a crucial component of the treatment process of adult diabetics (Davidson, 1981). In fact, many adult diabetics can control their condition without medication by reducing their weight to normal levels for their height and build and adhering to an appropriate diet. However, some adults must take oral hypoglycemic agents in order to control their condition. Unfortunately the oral agents are not effective in children.

Cardiac Disorders

Stacey was born with a congenital heart condition. Openings in the heart wall were present at birth, allowing oxygenated and unoxygenated blood to mix. As a result, Stacey was cyanotic, blue in appearance. She was immediately placed on a respirator, and additional diagnostic assessments were undertaken to identify the cause of the cyanosis. After the physicians determined that her heart had some congenital defects, Stacey's parents were alerted and permission was obtained for surgery. Within a few hours of birth, Stacey underwent surgery to correct her heart problems. Stacey would have died in a few days if the condition had not been surgically corrected.

Since that time, Stacey has undergone a series of serious operations for other complications associated with her heart condition. Several electronic heart pacers have been implanted at various times. She has responded to hospitalization, surgery, and the frequent medical checkups with considerable courage. Although she has had recurring medical

problems, her schooling has proceeded in a normal fashion. She has
had to restrict her activity at recesses and during physical-education
periods, but she has taken creative dancing and enjoys sedentary activ-
ities such as reading and drawing.

Recently, at age eleven, Stacey's heart condition worsened and her life
has become somewhat tenuous. She now regularly experiences sei-
zures, and her circulation is often poor. The circulation problems cause
her legs to "fall asleep," as she describes it. Stacey's pediatric cardiol-
ogist, in conjunction with other medical specialists, is attempting to
resolve the present problems. Fortunately, Stacey has supportive par-
ents who have constantly encouraged and supported her.

Definitions and Concepts. Cardiovascular disease is a leading cause of death
in the United States. A basic understanding of the anatomy and functions of
the heart is a necessary preface to the identification and treatment of heart
disease. The heart in people of normal stature is about the size of an adult
closed fist (see Figure 11-1). It is located between the lungs just above the
diaphragm and stomach and weighs about half a pound. The heart is actually
a double, synchronized pump with chambers on each side of the septum (dividing wall). The "right heart" processes blood from the major veins and returns
it to the lungs through the pulmonary artery. Blood returning from the lungs
is processed by the "left heart" and is pumped to all parts of the body through
the aorta. Each chamber of the heart is subdivided into the atrium (upper
chamber) and ventricle (lower chamber). Between each chamber is found the
septum, or dividing wall. The flow of blood from one area to another is controlled by a number of valves. A normal adult heart beats about 100,800 times
in a twenty-four-hour period (Armington & Creighton, 1971). The entire blood
supply of an adult (about six quarts) passes through the complete cardiovascular
system in less than sixty seconds (Phibbs, 1979).

    There are four major types of **cardiac disorders:** (1) congenital heart dis-
ease, (2) rheumatic heart disease, (3) heart attacks, and (4) congestive heart
failure. We will limit our discussion primarily to the factors related to congenital and rheumatic heart disease. **Congenital heart disease** is usually detected immediately by medical personnel at birth. Infants with inborn anomalies
in heart structure or functioning, like Stacey, often display cyanosis (blueness
in appearance) or dyspnea (difficulty in breathing). The more common congenital heart defects involve openings in the wall of the atria (see Figure
11-2) or the ventricles, inappropriate operation of the pulmonary valves,
and excessive constriction of the major arterial channel. Recent advances in surgery, anesthesiology, and bioengineering have revolutionized the treatment of
both congenital and acquired heart conditions. The heart can now be surgically
repaired while a heart-lung machine carries on the individual's breathing and
heart fuctions. Heart valves can be repaired or replaced, and even the electrical
signal that triggers the pumping rhythm can be created with a pacemaker. The
number of infants who die of congenital heart disease has been dramatically
reduced as a result of these medical advances.

Figure 11-1/ Normal Heart
The arrows indicate the direction of blood flow through the four chambers and great vessels.
Adapted, by permission, from Clinical Education Aid No. 7, Ross Laboratories, Columbus, Ohio.

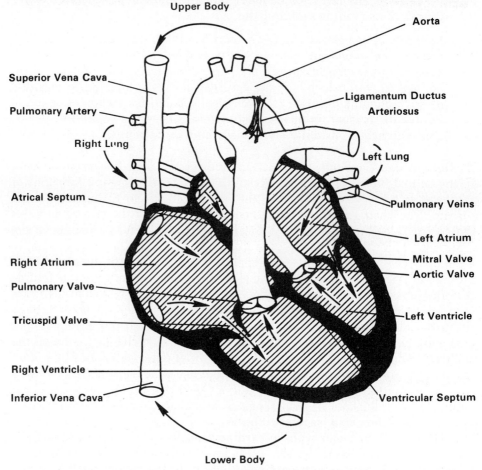

Rheumatic heart disease is a by-product of rheumatic fever. Although rheumatic fever affects the entire body, it has a pronounced impact on the heart and connective tissues of the body. The muscles, valves, and lining of the heart become inflamed and may be permanently damaged. About 33 percent of all individuals who have rheumatic fever suffer from residual side effects of heart damage. "Rheumatic fever licks the joints but bites the heart" was the way the French physician Laseque put it (Armington & Creighton, 1971, p. 43). If such damage is not corrected by surgery or other therapy, the person may experience a premature heart attack and early death.

Causation and Prevalence. Congenital heart conditions can be caused by a variety of factors. Certain drugs taken by the mother during critical periods of

Figure 11-2/ Atrial Septal Defect
Arrow indicates flow of blood from the left atrium (LA) to the right atrium (RA), thus over-
loading the right heart, pulmonary circulation, and left heart. Left to right shunt-no cyanosis.
Adapted, by permission, from Clinical Education Aid No. 7, Ross Laboratories, Columbus, Ohio.

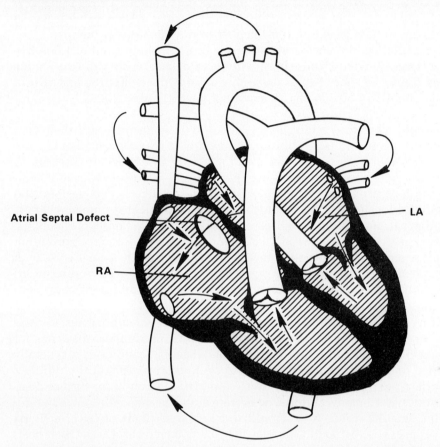

Atrial Septal Defect

LA

RA

prenatal development may damage the heart. The same is true with the presence
of rubella virus in the mother. During the fourth to twelfth weeks of gestation
the heart of the fetus is developing rapidly. If this developmental process is
interrupted by a virus or a drug, the fetal heart may be injured or incompletely
developed. Heart defects often run in families. In some instances the congenital
condition may be hereditary, or it may be a function of a genetic predisposition
that is triggered by certain environmental stimuli.

Rheumatic heart disease is an outcome of rheumatic fever. The fever is
caused by the streptococcus bacteria. The body, in response to the streptococcus
bacteria, develops antibodies to combat the invading bacterial substances (antigens). For reasons not yet understood, this interaction process between antibodies and antigens produces chronic inflammation in many areas of the body.
These attacks of inflammation are principally localized in the joints, heart, and
brain of the individual. The inflammation exhibits itself in tiny, microscopic

points that form in many tissues. These points of inflammation eventually heal, but the organ or tissue is left scarred. If scarring occurs along the vital edges of the heart valves, the result is a form of rheumatic heart disease. Such scarring generally has two effects. The valves may become stenotic or regurgitant. A stenotic valve is unable to open fully, whereas a regurgitant valve leaks, or allows blood to pass back into the chamber from which it was pumped.

Congenital heart defects are present in approximately 1 out of 1,000 live births. A large number of those born with heart defects at birth die during the first year of life. Of those babies remaining alive at the end of the first year of life, only about 1 in 30,000 has an abnormal heart (Walker, 1979).

Intervention. The ideal approach to dealing with congenital and rheumatic heart conditions would be prevention. Women who are pregnant should carefully restrict their diets, drug intake, and exposure to contagious diseases. In some instances, genetic counseling may provide prospective parents with helpful direction regarding potential risks of congenital defects. Youngsters who develop infections caused by streptococcus should be treated immediately using appropriate antibiotics. Such treatment will prevent the onset of rheumatic fever. For those who have already had rheumatic fever, secondary prevention programs should be employed to prevent or minimize a subsequent episode of the fever condition. The secondary prevention programs involve regular administrations of penicillin or sulfonamide. These medications prevent the conditions from recurring, if they are taken on a regular basis.

Heart disease in children is treated with a variety of approaches. Cardiac failures or other problems may be prevented with nonsurgical measures for may congenital heart conditions. Surgery for congenital conditions is generally postponed to reduce risk and to make the operation less technically difficult. Appropriate programs of rest and exercise prepare the child for further treatment. Fortunately many children with congenital heart conditions naturally sense the time at which they should rest or reduce their physical activity. Sedatives may be provided to enhance the beneficial effects of rest. Other heart medicines, such as digitalis, may also play a critical role in the maintenance process. It is the physician's task to monitor the child who may be at risk for heart failure or other complications. Regular examinations are vital for the infant or young child with cardiac problems.

Surgery for congenital heart conditions is generally corrective in nature. This is also true for rheumatic heart problems. Surgery is often postponed because of the risks involved. In many instances, however, the attending physicians may have no recourse but immediate surgical action.

Diagnosis of various heart defects is accomplished using a variety of techniques. An arteriographic examination may be performed for infants who are cyanotic (blue) because of a congenital heart condition. Other approaches (dyes, gases, and electrodes) are also used to identify different structural defects.

The child's age plays a significant role in the mortality rate. If a child is only a few days old, the mortality rate is very high, which is why most physicians wait for the child to grow and develop before initiating intensive surgery.

Mortality risks involved in corrective surgery for older children (ages six to twelve) range form 1 to 5 percent for most conditions.

Corrective surgery for rheumatic heart disease may involve repair or replacement of vital valves. Repair of the heart generally involves closing of abnormal openings in heart chamber walls or removal of extraneous tissue that prevents or interferes with blood flow. Valve replacement is a relatively common surgical procedure. Antibiotics, the heart-lung machine, and new surgical techniques have significantly reduced the number of deaths due to congenital heart malformations and rheumatic heart disease.

Both younger and older individuals who have experienced chronic cardiac problems must carefully select the physical activities they pursue. Rest and appropriate exercise are vital, particularly during convalescence. Teachers in cooperation with parents and the medical team should set realistic goals for a child recovering from a heart condition. The goals should be such that the child is not overly restricted. Often children develop counterproductive psychological attitudes during the postoperative period which may be detrimental to eventual performance in school. As these children progress through school, they should be provided with opportunities to match their skills and physical abilities with appropriate potential careers. Many students with cardiac conditions are eligible for vocational rehabilitation services provided in each state. The services provided by such state agencies may be very beneficial in helping students to select suitable careers and to receive medical assistance and support for technical or professional education.

STRESS–RELATED DISORDERS

Asthma

> I cannot say that my childhood experience of asthma itself left any particular mark, for I did not have it nearly as severely as do many child asthmatics. On the other hand, it undoubtedly contributed to the picture which my parents and others had of me as "delicate." . . . The effect of having asthma and other illnesses was to impair my physical confidence and to make me think of my body as a liability, a part of myself which I could not do without but which was liable to let me down and which was somehow inferior to those of other people. . . . Although I was for a time generally near the top of the class, by the time I was thirteen my performance deteriorated, and I did much less well throughout my school career than I should have. My impression is that many children who suffer a good deal of illness have the same experience. . . . From 1939 to 1969, however, I was almost free of asthma, although I continued to become wheezy to a very slight degree if I caught a cold, and always had a supply of ephedrine on hand to combat this. In 1969 asthma returned.

At first, I did not believe that I had asthma, thinking that my cough and wheeziness was the result of bronchitis. But it soon became obvious that infection was not the prime cause, and I had to learn to accept the fact that, after thirty years of almost complete freedom from the disease, I was once again "an asthmatic."

As is common enough, my symptoms fluctuated in severity during that autumn. Then, in December 1969, I had a really bad attack. It so happened that, through no fault of his, my general practitioner could not be reached for a considerable time. I was in bed, panting away, wholly absorbed in the question of how I could get enough air into my lungs, although by this time my breathing was out of voluntary control and had become purely automatic. I began to realize that this attack was not only the worst attack of asthma which I had ever had myself, it was the worst attack that I had even seen in anybody. . . . As time went on, and the attack showed no signs of subsiding, I suddenly realized that I was in danger. I remember thinking to myself, "If this goes on much longer, I might die." . . . I remember thinking, "It might go either way. I wonder which way it will go. Perhaps this is the end of my life."

When my doctor finally arrived, he was clearly more anxious than I was myself. Fortunately, he carried oxygen in his car, and I was soon finding some partial relief by breathing it. He also gave me an injection of cortisone, and telephoned to the chest specialist whom I had consulted to enquire whether there was anything else he could do.* (Storr, 1979, pp. 2-6)

Definitions and Concepts. **Asthma** is a "condition of altered dynamic state of respiratory passages due to the action of diverse stimuli resulting in airways obstruction of varying degree and duration, and reversible partially or completely, spontaneously or under treatment" (Kuzemko, 1980, p. 1). This chronic respiratory disorder is characterized not only by difficulty in breathing but also by excessive coughing, wheezing, and sputum. Other physiological and environmental factors are related to the condition. Some infants and children are allergic to certain substances, including various drugs, foods, inhalants, or bacteria. Certain tissue becomes sensitive under specified conditions and responds in a fairly predictable fashion. However, the emergence and presence of asthma cannot be explained by one etiological source. It is a condition with multiple antecedents and interacting agents (Pinkerton & Weaver, 1970). According to Pinkerton (1973), when the bronchus becomes labile or susceptible to change, a variety of psychological and physiological elements come together to produce an asthmatic attack. The severity and outcome of asthmatic episodes are greatly influenced by the interaction of these factors. A great deal of research has been focused on investigating the relationship between psychological prob-

*Source: Abridged from Asthma: The Facts *by Donald J. Lane and Anthony Storr. Copyright © Donald J. Lane and Anthony Storr 1979. By permission of Oxford University Press.*

lems and the presence of asthma (Ghory, 1972; Resh, 1970; Straker & Tamerin, 1974; Williams & McNicol, 1975). There appears to be a strong relationship between psychological problems and asthmatic episodes, but the nature of this relationship is not completely understood. As with juvenile diabetes and cystic fibrosis, asthma is a condition that often dictates a limiting of various types of activity in youngsters. In fact, asthma is the primary reason cited for school absence in children (Creer, Renne & Christian, 1976).

Youngsters may experience embarrassment and fear after an asthmatic attack. If the episodes are extremely serious or frequent, hospitalization may be required. Absence from peers, school involvement, and family due to hospitalization can have a marked impact on juvenile asthmatics. They may begin to regard themselves as being different, weak, sick, and of little value either to themselves or to others. Extended school absences without appropriate homebound or hospitalized teaching assistance make it difficult for the asthmatic student to remain current or to perform at grade level in terms of achievement.

Causation and Prevalence. The body produces **antibodies** in response to certain antigens, such as pollen. Individuals with asthma produce a surplus of these antibodies. When the antigens become responsible for allergic reactions they are identified as allergens. The intolerance of an asthmatic to these allergens is immense. Allergic antibodies do not insulate the body from an attack. As they react to offending allergens, harmful chemical substances known as histamines are produced or released. The histamines cause swelling in various affected areas, such as the bronchi (airways) (see Figure 11-3). The number of potential allergens is limitless. Certain foods, molds, drugs, insect stings, and bacteria can cause severe reactions. Several researchers are convinced that the house mite plays an important role in the presence of asthma and hay fever (Pepys, Chan & Hargreave, 1968; Smith, Disney, Williams & Goels, 1969).

There also appears to be a strong relationship between psychological wellbeing and the presence of asthmatic conditions. Children with asthma tend to have more emotional difficulties than children who do not have asthma (Graham, Rutter, Yule & Pless, 1967). Frequently asthmatic episodes are preceded by psychologically stressful events (McLean & Ching, 1973). Family factors also seem to play a role in the emergence of asthma. Between 50 and 75 percent of individuals who develop asthma have a family history of allergic reactions to various allergens (Kuzemko, 1980). However, the exact nature of the genetic and inheritance factors responsible for the emergence of asthma remains unknown.

Many children develop asthma after respiratory infections. Although the relationship between the infections and the development of asthma remains unclear, viral infections in particular seem to act as provocative agents for eventual onset of the condition. Exercise also often induces acute episodes as do changes in temperature and season.

The actual prevalence of asthma remains somewhat elusive. For children under ten years old, the prevalence in the United States is about 6.9 percent (Rhyne, 1974). This figure is relatively high compared to other countries. Ac-

Figure 11-3/ The Lungs, Trachea, and Bronchi, with Examples of Open and Closed Airways

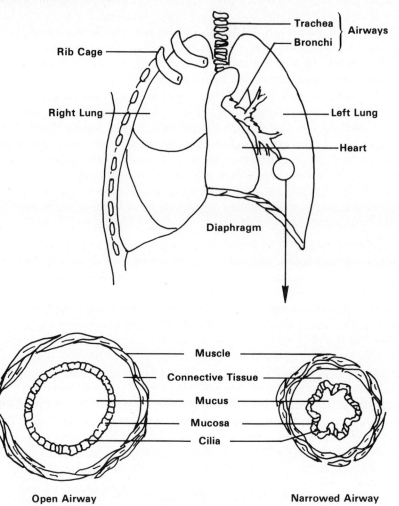

cording to Kuzemko (1980), the prevalence of asthma in children up to age fifteen is about 4 percent. Some researchers investigating the growth in new cases of asthma have found that the incidence of asthma in children appears to be increasing (Fireman, 1971; Morrison-Smith, 1974).

Intervention. The treatment of asthma requires a comprehensive diagnosis prior to intervention. Differentiating asthma from certain other conditions can be very challenging at times. Some children whose wheezing appears to be asthmatic may actually be suffering from other problems (e.g., cystic fibrosis, congenital heart disease, chronic adenoidal infection). A skilled physician who conducts a comprehensive diagnostic examination can successfully identify the asthmatic. Diagnosis typically includes skin-sensitivity tests, nasal and bronchial provocation tests, pulmonary function tests, a review of family medical history related to allergies, and an investigation of the nature and precipitating causes of the asthmatic episodes.

Drugs play a significant role in relieving children from the effects of an attack. Medication may be administered as injections or suppositories. If an attack occurs at home, the parents may be responsible for rendering the first phases of treatment. A portable air compressor, which can provide a combination of inhalation and drug therapy (i.e., antihistamine medication can be administered through the breathing apparatus), may be utilized by parents.

Hospital treatment of asthma also involves extensive use of drugs and oxygen therapy. Long-term treatment of asthma may include a variety of therapies. The family and the affected child are encouraged to maintain accurate records of the peak expiratory flow rates so that the effects of various treatments may be evaluated. A treatment plan is initiated, and monitored within two to four weeks following its implementation. Thereafter, monitoring varies according to the severity of the asthma and treatment success. Treatment is both medically and psychologically oriented. Drug treatments include bronchodilators, steroid aerosols, and corticosteroids. Psychotherapy, family therapy, and hypnosis are also used to aid the individual suffering from asthma. If personal or familial problems are aggravating the asthma, a psychiatrist or family therapist may be helpful in lessening personal or family tensions and problems. Behaviorally oriented therapies for asthma have recently received attention in the research literature. A number of operant and other behavior therapy techniques have been investigated and seem to be promising (Creer, Renne & Christian, 1976; Khan, 1973; Weiss, 1973).

Many families are unable to respond adequately to all the demands (exceptionally clean home environments, diet modification, limitation of vigorous exercise) that must be met for the asthmatic child or adolescent. In some instances the juvenile asthmatic must be removed from the family for a time and live in a specialized residential treatment center in order for successful treatment to occur.

The majority of individuals with asthma who receive appropriate medical and psychological support will successfully complete their schooling and lead normal lives. Teachers and others who must assist the person with asthma should work cooperatively with parents and attending medical personnel. Such cooperation will lessen many of the negative side effects of hospitalization, absence from school, and reduced physical activity.

Peptic Ulcers

Jonathan was a bright boy, but he was ineffective in performing many tasks because of his high-strung nature. He frequently had a gnawing pain in his stomach just prior to eating. The pain typically diminished after he ate. The pain occurred repeatedly one to four times daily, usually two to three hours after Jonathan ate. He was also awakened during the night with sharp pains in the lower abdominal area.

After prolonged struggling with this condition, Jonathan's mother decided to take him to their physician. After completing an initial evaluation, the physician sent Jonathan to see a gastroenterologist. Based on X-rays and other diagnostic information, it was determined that Jonathan had an ulcer.

Definitions and Concepts. Ulcers in children used to be relatively rare. The rarity was partially a function of the symptoms and lack of sophisticated diagnostic instruments and procedures. Most ulcer symptoms are nonspecific in children, which complicates the diagnosis. With the advent of fiberoptic endoscopy and improved X-ray techniques, however, the diagnosis of peptic ulcers in children has become less difficult.

Peptic ulcers are simply areas within the stomach in which the mucous membrane has eroded. The ulcer may also be found in the pylorus, duodenum, or any portion of the gastrointestinal tract where the enzyme pepsin and acid come in contact with mucosa (a membrane with many mucous glands).

The digestive system (also known as the peptic system) is responsible for changing food into amino acids for use in the body. These amino acids are essential for the growth and maintenance of the body. As food is consumed and chewed in the mouth, the salivary glands secrete enzymes, which begin to break down the food. Food then passes down through the pharnyx into the esophagus and eventually reaches the stomach. The stomach is lined with a mucous membrane that secretes the enzyme pepsin. By virtue of the action of pepsin and hydrochloric acid, food is gradually prepared for passage through the pylorus into the first portion of the small intestine, or duodenum. Ducts from the liver and pancreas provide further digestive juices that prepare the now-altered food for entry into the mucous membrane. From this membrane in the small intestine, the food, which is now in the form of amino acids, passes into the lymph and blood systems of the body. Remaining by-products of digestion, together with bacteria and other intestinal secretions, move through the large intestine to be expelled later.

Symptoms of ulcers may be manifested at any time and vary according to the age of the child. During the neonatal period, peptic ulcers present themselves in two manners: hemorrhaging and perforation. Toddlers manifest the condition in feeding problems or vomiting. Bleeding typically follows during the next several weeks, evidenced by blood in the stool of the toddler. In younger school-age children, pain may be the presenting symptom. The child may report such pain as being mild or severe, and the pain is often poorly localized. In older children, the symptoms are similar to those adults experience. Gnawing pain just prior to meals and vomiting are some of the more common symptoms.

Causation and Prevalence. Ulcers in **neonates** are primarily related to acute gastric erosions associated with such other conditions as prematurity, infections, burns, or other trauma. This is also true for children up to two years old. The lesions occurring during this period are associated with serious illnesses such as encephalitis, meningitis, and brain tumors. From two to fifteen years of age, emergence of the condition continues to be caused by acute gastric erosions of the mucosa (Menguy, 1976), but the reasons for excessive presence of these digestive substances remain unclear.

No reliable prevalence or incidence figures are available for peptic ulcers in children (Ament, 1978), but it is estimated that 3.4 children in 10,000 hospital admissions are treated for peptic ulcers. Peptic ulcers occur primarily in children from the ages of twelve to eighteen. The ratio of boys to girls suffering from peptic ulcers is about 2 to 1. There is also a strong relationship between ulcer problems and a family history of the condition. In addition, personality factors coupled with stress or other forms of psychological pressure seem to play a role in the initiation or aggravation of certain ulcer conditions (Pillitteri, 1977).

Intervention. Peptic ulcers in very young children tend to heal spontaneously without further recurrences. Surgery is rarely performed unless the infant or child is hemorrhaging severely or has a perforation of the stomach or duodenum. Perforation is rare. Ament (1978) identified three goals for peptic ulcer therapy: relieving ulcer pain through medications, hastening the healing process, and preventing recurrences and complications. Surgical treatment of peptic ulcers occurs only if other treatment techniques have been unsuccessful, but surgery is the treatment of choice if there is uncontrolled hemorrhaging, gastric outlet obstruction, intractability of abdominal pain, recurring bleeding, or perforation.

Once appropriate medical steps have been taken, the person with peptic ulcers may return to school or work. In the case of a child, the teacher may play a critial role in supporting therapeutic procedures already established by the medical personnel and parents. Helping the child cope with pressures of school and peers can be a challenge for teachers and counselors. For the youth or adult, a stress-management course may be beneficial. In some cases, psychiatric or psychological consultation may be necessary.

LIFE-ENDANGERING DISEASES

Cystic Fibrosis

Sally appeared normal when she was born, although her stools were abnormal. Her feces had a greenish tint at first and then became paler than normal. After the first few weeks of life, Sally's stools became soft, crumbly, and bulky, increased in frequency, and had a pungent, penetrating odor. Sally's mother said, "You could smell them a mile away."

Sally's mother and the pediatrician became concerned when Sally failed to make minimal weight gains, even though she seemed "to eat like a champ." Sally also had recurring bronchitis. As all factors were considered, Sally's pediatrician believed that cystic fibrosis was a definite possibility. Subsequent testing was undertaken at a regional children's hospital, and the diagnosis of cystic fibrosis was confirmed.

Definition and Concepts. **Cystic fibrosis** (CF) is a generalized disorder of the secretory (exocrine) glands. It is caused by thickened mucous secretions in the lungs, pancreas, liver, and intestines. These mucous secretions obstruct the functions of lungs and other vital organs and heighten the susceptibility of the lung to infection. With repeated infections, the lungs are gradually destroyed. As lung deterioration occurs, the heart is also burdened, and heart failure is a common by-product of this condition. Excessive mucous secretions also prevent or interfere with digestion and other intestinal processes.

Prognosis for an individual with cystic fibrosis depends on a number of factors. The two most critical factors relate to early diagnosis of the condition and the quality of care provided from the time of diagnosis. If diagnosis occurs late, preliminary damage, which is irreversible, may have already occurred. With an early diagnosis and appropriate medical treatment, most individuals with CF can achieve weight and growth gains similar to those of their normal peers. With the advent of increased early diagnosis and improved treatment strategies, the average life span of a person who has cystic fibrosis has increased from 11.2 years in 1966 to 19.4 years in 1974 (U.S. Department of Health, Education, and Welfare, 1978).

There are a number of variations of this condition and the severity of symptoms varies considerably as well. Cystic fibrosis can be present in the first weeks of life or occur as late as adolescence. Early symptoms of the disease may be mistakenly identified as those of asthma.

Causation and Prevalence. Causation of cystic fibrosis is unclear, and there are many theories about its origin. The theories fall into two groups. The first perspective views CF as a generalized disorder of the exocrine glands. The second view supports a notion that the primary disease involves an obstruction of the pancreatic ducts and that excessive secretions are all secondary (Spiro, 1970). Several factors have hampered the investigation of causation. For example, little basic research has been conducted regarding the normal composition, production, and expulsion of exocrine gland secretions. It is known, however, that cystic fibrosis is an inherited disease (Danks, Allan & Anderson, 1965)

Cystic fibrosis is primarily a Caucasian phenomenon. Studies conducted in the United States have demonstrated a minimum prevalence of the disease to range from 1 in 1,800 to 1 in 2,500 live births; it is extremely rare in black children. Spiro (1970) indicated that CF is the most common lethal genetic disease of childhood in Caucasians.

Intervention. The diagnosis of cystic fibrosis is based on a number of symptoms related to the gastrointestinal and respiratory systems. Since the disease may emerge at nearly any age, there is great variability in the ways the condition presents itself. Thus a number of different diagnostic techniques are useful. Infants with CF may fail to thrive, have soft and greasy stools, and exhibit respiratory symptoms. School-age children may have recurrent abdominal pain, heat exhaustion following exercise on hot days, and chest infection. Diagnosis of adolescents and adults with CF occurs less frequently than diagnosis during the younger years (Anderson & Goodchild, 1976).

Intervention for cystic fibrosis is varied and complex. Afflicted individuals must receive treatment throughout their lives. Consistent and appropriate application of medical, social, educational, and psychological aspects of the treatment process will allow these individuals to live longer with less discomfort and fewer complications. Treatment of CF is designed to accomplish a number of goals. The first goal is to diagnose the condition before any severe symptoms are exhibited. Other goals include control of chest infection, maintenance of adequate nutrition, education of the family regarding the condition, and provision of a suitable education for the child.

Management of respiratory disease caused by cystic fibrosis is critical. If respiratory insufficiency can be prevented or minimized, the youngster's life will be greatly enhanced and prolonged. Vital components of treatment for respiratory disease include the regular administration of antibiotics, intermittent inhalation therapy, chest physiotherapy, and postural drainage.

Various regimens of drug therapy have been suggested for treatment of cystic fibrosis, but at this point controlled research regarding effectiveness has not been conducted. Many youngsters with CF ingest as many as one hundred pills a day to treat their condition.

Physical therapy is absolutely crucial to the individual with cystic fibrosis. This intervention aids in preventing chronic lung infection and promotes the eradication of infection with antibiotics. It is both therapeutic and preventative. Exercises such as swimming and jumping on a trampoline are particularly helpful in loosening bronchial secretions and clearing the airways.

Inhalation therapy is also used as a means of treating respiratory disease. Aerosols may be employed to medicate and loosen bronchial secretions, moisturize the bronchi, and administer bronchodilators and mucolytic agents.

Diet management is also essential for the child with cystic fibrosis. Generally, individuals with this condition require more caloric intake than comparable normal peers. Fats must be carefully monitored. The diet should be high in protein and adjusted appropriately if the child fails to grow and/or make appropriate weight gains.

Management of cystic fibrosis in the family is challenging. Parents are often overwhelmed when informed of the diagnosis and the consequences of the condition. With training and support, however, parents and other family members can learn to provide the care, structure, and support necessary for the affected youngster.

The major social and psychological problems of CF children relate to chronic coughing, small stature, offensive stools, gas, delayed onset of puberty and secondary sex characteristics, and impaired social relationships because of the condition. Support provided by counseling or psychiatric personnel and a sensitive teacher may be helpful to the youngster who is burdened with these problems.

Education for the child with cystic fibrosis should occur, in most instances, in a regular school setting. Particularly children with well-controlled CF have few if any problems participating in the activities of a regular school program. In fact, school for these children can be therapeutic.

The prognosis for individuals with cystic fibrosis remains elusive. If we look only at the extension of life without measuring the quality of life, we are missing some vital facts. Warwick and Monson (1967) indicated that approximately 60 percent of those with CF live beyond the age of fifteen. These data should be treated with some caution, however, as the quality of life for many CF patients may be poor. For example, many teenagers with cystic fibrosis fail to maintain their treatment regimens. Gradually the consequences of such behavior emerge. Depression is common, and the quality of life for such adolescents wanes immensely. Nevertheless, future research related to promising diagnostic and treatment techniques may alleviate many of these problems.

Sickle Cell Anemia

Raymond seemed to have a lot of problems. At age sixteen he was constantly complaining and blaming others for his misfortunes. He was an angry young man, angry about being black, angry because the school system had unreasonable rules (e.g., assignment deadlines, attendance, and punctuality), and particularly angry at his family for their expectations.

Ray had been diagnosed as having sickle cell anemia when he was ten years old. He exhibited none of the more severe signs of the condition, but he had experienced frequent stomach pains and periodic hospitalization, where blood transfusions and medication were administered. Neither Ray nor his family viewed him as being seriously ill. His mother and father both thought Ray was lazy and moody. They argued with him a great deal and pressured him to "behave."

At seventeen Raymond was dead. His last complaints had fallen on the deaf ears both of his parents and of his teachers. They had become accustomed to his complaints and largely discounted them as representing an objectionable personality.

Definitions and Concepts. **Sickle cell anemia** (SCA) is a chronic hemolytic disorder, that is, the disease has a profound impact on the function and structure of red blood cells. Specifically, the hemoglobin molecules (of which there are millions in each red cell) release excessive amounts of oxygen. This release occurs as the cells supply oxygen and other nutrients to body cells. As the cells are deoxygenated, they become distorted into bizarre shapes. This distortion process is known as sickling. Cells that normally have a donut-like appearance now appear as microscopic sickle blades. The cells also become more rigid and fragile. This rigidity of the cells interferes with their passage through narrow blood capillaries. As a result, microvascular channels become blocked (local circulation is reduced or terminated) and tissues and cells die.

People affected by sickle cell anemia experience unrelenting **anemia**. In some cases this anemia is tolerated well, although in others the condition is quite debilitating. Another aspect of this condition involves periodic vascular blockage crises. These crises are characterized by pain in the extremities, abdomen, and back. A fever may also accompany these conditions. The crises may last for hours or even days. Actual pain and tenderness may appear to be that of appendicitis or another serious condition.

Diagnosis of sickle cell anemia is usually made before a child reaches the age of two. Clinical symptoms are infrequent during the first six months of life. The early childhood period is a particularly dangerous time for affected children. In the past, many children died of this condition before the age of seven. Bacterial infection was the cause of most of the deaths.

Clinical manifestations of sickle cell anemia are highly variable in adults. A significant number of adults with SCA experience relatively normal lives with only occasional episodes of illness. With others, the disease may be severe, involving frequent hospitalization and debilitation.

The primary manifestations of sickle cell anemia are observed most clearly in children. These symptoms are produced by vascular blockages and anemia.

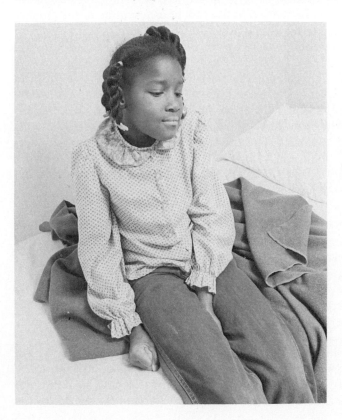

Swelling and tenderness in the hands and feet are two of the characteristic symptoms of SCA.

The anemia is ever present and is unrelated to symptoms. A number of secondary manifestations accompany sickle cell anemia. For example, children with this condition are much more likely to develop ankle ulcers and **osteomyelitis**. They are also much more susceptible to infections, particularly those that occur suddenly or progress rapidly. In addition, organ dysfunction is more common in these children. They may experience strokes as a result of infarctions to the brain. In contrast, afflicted adults experience seizures and deformities. The deformities usually take place as a function of circulatory blockages that occur in various glands and organs of the body. The lungs, heart, spleen, liver, kidneys, bones, skin, reproductive organs, and nervous system can all be affected as the individual ages. Eventually, permanent damage can occur as the disease takes its natural course.

Causation and Prevalence. Sickle cell anemia (SCA) and sickle cell trait (SCT) are caused by various combinations of genes which are inherited by the child. A child who receives a mutant S hemoglobin gene from *each* parent exhibits SCA to one degree or another. The child receiving a mutant S hemoglobin gene from only one parent and a normal hemoglobin gene from the other parent exhibits SCT.

The actual mechanisms responsible for onset of the primary and secondary clinical manifestations of sickle cell anemia are still unclear. The increased susceptibility to infection is likely due to the loss of functioning of the spleen, since the spleen is thought to be responsible for clearing microorganisms from the blood and providing antibody defense for incoming antigens. (deGruchy, 1978).

The prevalence of sickle cell anemia varies, depending on the geographic location in which one resides. Studies conducted during the 1950s and 1960s identified specific populations with high prevalence rates of SCT. These populations were found in a broad belt of tropical Africa. High prevalence rates of SCT were also found in Sicily, southern Italy, Greece, Turkey, Arabia, and southern India (Conley, 1980). SCA occurs in about 0.1 to 1.3 percent of the American black population (deGruchy, 1980). Neel (1973) estimated that 2.7 infants in 1,000 live births have SCA.

Intervention. Diagnosis of sickle cell anemia is based on various hemoglobin tests that confirm the presence of sickled cells. The individual's health history is also reviewed, with scrutiny of the characteristics of crises that may have preceded the diagnostic interview. The spleen may also be examined to determine if it is enlarged, has become atrophied, or is otherwise affected. The diagnosis is particularly critical for infants, since one in ten black babies who have SCA die before they reach ten years of age. After the age of ten, less then 5 percent experience death in the succeeding decade (deGruchy, 1978).

A number of treatments are employed to deal with the problems and pain caused by sickle cell anemia. In fact, much of the morbidity and mortality experienced by people with this condition in the past has been reduced through improved health care and living conditions in many parts of the world. In the main, most individuals learn to adapt to their anemia and lead relatively normal lives. When their lives are interrupted by crises, a variety of treatment approaches may be utilized. Medication may be helpful to those with severe anemia (Alexanian & Nadell, 1975). Other medical procedures may be aimed at improving the hemoglobin level of the blood.

Several factors predispose an individual to SCA crisis. They include dehydration from fevers and reduced liquid intake, and hypoxia (air which is poor in oxygen content). Stress, fatigue, and exposure to cold temperatures should be avoided by those who have a history of crisis associated with SCA. Treatment of crises is generally directed at keeping the individual warm, increasing liquid intake, and administering medication for infection. Support can also be provided for crisis periods by partial exchange transfusions with fresh normal red cells. Transfusions may also be necessary for individuals with SCA who are preparing for surgery or who are pregnant.

Children with sickle cell anemia require special attention and care on the part of school personnel. Teachers should be alert to signs of anemia and other conditions that may precipitate a crisis. These children have less energy because of their condition and consequently tire easily. Strenuous activities should generally be avoided by such youngsters. Sensitivity and careful management on the part of a teacher may prevent a crisis. If a crisis does occur, the teacher will need to take immediate action and secure prompt medical attention for the ailing child. Teachers and other school staff also play a critical role in helping the SCA child to adjust psychologically and physcially to the challenges associated with this condition.

Cancer

Steve had recently recovered from a case of bronchitis. He was just beginning to feel better, although his parents noticed that he did not have the same vitality he had before. His sixth birthday came, and Steve and his friends had a great day at the zoo. As time passed, Steve became less and less active; it seemed as though he had no energy at all.

Shortly after his sixth birthday, Steve went to the dentist to have his teeth examined and cleaned. During the week prior to his appointment he had a severe nose-bleeding episode. While at the dentist, Steve had a tooth removed, and he again experienced persistent bleeding at the site of the tooth removal. The dentist was also concerned about small ulcers in Steve's mouth and the slight swelling in the gum tissue. He recommended that Steve's mother make an immediate appointment with the family pediatrician.

The next day, Steve and his mother met with Dr. Fletcher, their pediatrician. She gave Steve a routine physical and found that his sternum was very tender. Slight bruises were also evident on his legs and arms. His liver and spleen also appeared to be enlarged. Dr. Fletcher gave Steve a blood test, which she sent off to the laboratory for analysis.

On receiving results from the blood test, Dr. Fletcher promptly called Steve's parents. She asked them to take Steve to the university medical school for further tests. A bone marrow biopsy was performed, as well as other blood tests. The bone marrow biopsy was examined by Dr. Pierson, a pathologist. Gradually the diagnosis became complete. The blood test revealed low hemoglobin and low white cell levels. Blast cells were also present in the blood. Steve had acute lymphocytic leukemia.

Definitions and Concepts. The principal type of leukemia which affects children is acute lymphocytic leukemia (ALL). ALL is a disorder of blood cell production in which abnormal white blood cells accumulate in the blood and the bone marrow. There are, however, two types of hematologic (of or relating to blood) cancer: the leukemias and the lymphomas. The leukemias are found throughout the body; their impact is primarily on the blood-forming organs (the bone marrow, liver, spleen, and lymph nodes). As these organs are affected, the blood is also changed. The lymphomas are localized. They are evidenced by swelling of the lymph nodes. The various leukemias are classified according to the types of cells predominantly affected (whether erythrocytes, granulocytes, or lymphocytes) and the clinical nature or course that the disease takes (whether acute or chronic).

Individuals may develop leukemia at any age, although the peak period for emergence is from birth through the first six years of life. The actual onset of leukemia may be either insidious or abrupt. The condition in children usually occurs abruptly. Symptoms of leukemia include anemia, pallor, bruises, and infective lesions in the mouth and pharynx. Frequently a series of respiratory infections precede the apparent onset of leukemia (deGruchy, 1978).

Because different types of leukemia affect the various blood cell groups in the body, natural defenses of the body are impaired, and the individual becomes more susceptible to infection. Anemia occurs as a function of the reduced number of red blood cells that transport the life-giving oxygen to all cells of the body. Hemorrhaging occurs as a function of reduced platelet production. The loss of these vital cell functions produces a child who is extremely ill.

Causation and Prevalence. Causation of the various leukemias remains obscure. Leukemias never rise from a single cause. Several factors interact together or in sequence to produce leukemia, and there are a variety of elements that contribute to the production of leukemic cells. These include a genetic predisposition for the condition, virus activity, and a variety of physical and chemical agents. Such factors have been collectively identified as triggering mechanisms. Other sources for the emergence of leukemia have been identified, including ionizing radiation, gamma rays, and atomic radiation.

The prevalence of leukemia is highest during the first six years of life (deGruchy, 1978). Some 20 percent of all leukemias appear in children. Of these children, the greatest mortality rate occurs between the ages of two and five (Grunz, 1980). Approximately 37 in 100,000 children under age fifteen develop some form of leukemia (Young, Heise, Silverberg & Meyers, 1978). Slightly more boys than girls are affected by this disease. Black children appear to be at less risk for developing acute lymphocytic leukemia than their Caucasian counterparts. Siblings of leukemic patients have a greater risk of eventually developing leukemia than the general pediatric population. The average American at birth has a 1 in 200 chance of developing leukemia in his or her lifetime (Grunz, 1980).

Intervention. Initially, a diagnosis of leukemia is made based on the clinical manifestations of the condition, blood tests, and bone marrow biopsy. Once a leukemic condition is confirmed, treatment proceeds in a twofold fashion. The first step of the intervention process is to treat the conditions that the leukemia has instigated: anemia, bleeding, infections, and metabolic complications. Transfusions of packed red cells may be administered for anemia, or the child may gradually self-correct an anemic condition. Bleeding may be handled with platelet transfusions.

A second step in the intervention process is antileukemic therapy. The goals of therapy are to decrease the number of leukemic cells that are burdening the blood and to foster the repopulation of stem cells in bone marrow. A variety of chemical agents are typically successful in achieving these goals. Adequate

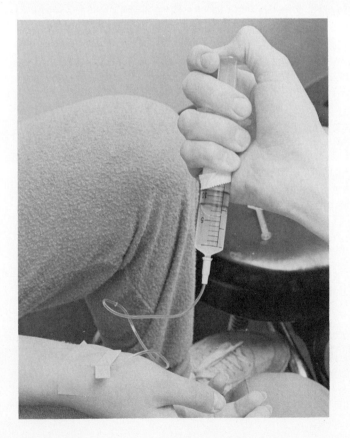

Chemotherapy is frequently used in the treatment of leukemia.

treatment of the predominant form of childhood leukemia (ALL) results in significant decreases in the number of leukemic cells in the body.

The major causes of death in leukemic children are infection and bleeding. The control and management of fever is of critical importance in dealing with infections. Fever and responsible bacteria are treated with a variety of broad-spectrum antibiotics.

Approximately 90 percent of the children with ALL experience substantial remissions, and approximately 50 percent of these children live five years or longer. In effect, some may be deemed cured of the disease. Children between the ages of three and seven are most likely to respond favorably to treatment (Klemperer, Rubins & Lichtman, 1978). For those not so fortunate, death may occur in only a few weeks or months.

Research is currently investigating immunology and bone marrow transplants as means for treating the leukemias. Grunz (1980) believes that new approaches must be sought for the cures of leukemia. Current thinking in medical research focuses predominantly on the development of new types of drugs and methods of administration. According to Grunz, leukemic cells do not grow more rapidly, nor do they grow excessively, as has long been assumed. It is Grunz's view that these cells simply never mature. Research related to the factors that make normal cells grow may ultimately provide the key to promoting maturity of leukemic cells.

Children with leukemia and their families need a great deal of social and emotional support. This can often be provided by the "Candlelighters," an organization of parents of young cancer patients. On the patient's release from the hospital, parents should discuss with their physician the nature and types of activities in which the child should be involved. The child should be allowed to pursue life as normally as possible. The same holds true with regard to the school environment. As a leukemic child returns to school, he or she may still be easily fatigued and susceptible to infection. Teachers should take these and other factors into account. If death of the child is expected soon or even likely, appropriate action should be taken to prepare the students for this eventuality. In a similar fashion, parents, siblings, and others who are potentially at risk emotionally may require help in coping with their feelings and behaviors. As with other life-endangering diseases previously discussed, there are materials and aids available. The Candlelighters may be particularly helpful in the case of leukemia. In addition, friends, psychiatric personnel, and clergy may play a critical role in the adjustment process.

MISCELLANEOUS CONDITIONS

Adolescent pregnancy and child abuse are seldom addressed in the context of health disorders. However, professionals from a variety of disciplines must increasingly deal with these conditions as they work with youths and their families. Moreover, adolescent pregnancy and child abuse are frequently related to other exceptionalities (behavioral disorders, mental retardation, and learning disabilities) that emerge in children and youths.

Tina's Family

The Sullivans, a white suburban family, have four children, aged ten to eighteen. Two of their three daughters became pregnant while attending high school. Tina, the second oldest, became pregnant when she was sixteen. She suspected both parents would be upset, but her father simply "hit the roof." One night he smashed their new hi-fi equipment in a rage; he then went into a depression for two months, going into his bedroom every night and not talking to anyone. The tension at home was felt by everyone. Tina told her mother that she thought she should leave home. Her mother encouraged her to have a talk with her father, which she did, and it was very emotional for them both.

After that, things changed for the better, and the whole family became involved in helping Tina with her pregnancy and caring for the new baby. The baby has changed many things for the family.

Tina's father is now a proud grandfather. So that Tina could continue in school, her mother has quit her part-time job to look after the baby. Her brother, Jimmy, who had been the baby of the family until then, feels displaced; his grades have started dropping in school. However, both he and his sister Arlene take turns caring for the baby.

Tina's older sister, Annie, who had been living across town and with her girlfriends, came home one day to announce that she, too, was pregnant. Annie has now moved back home for a while but thinks that maybe one day she will marry the baby's father and move out on her own.*

Gloria's Family

Mrs. Williams, a divorced black woman, suspected that her very attractive and somewhat rebellious sixteen-year-old daughter, Gloria, was having sex when she stayed out late. She told Gloria that she must not get into "trouble," and was pleased that Gloria followed her advice and went to a family planning clinic and got birth control pills. Mrs. Williams was very angry, but not surprised, when Gloria told her she thought she was pregnant. After all, Gloria could never remember to do anything every day. She thought the solution was obvious—she would help Gloria to get an abortion.

But Gloria was not so sure. The school counselor told her it was Gloria's decision, not her mother's. The doctor at the clinic said the same.

---

*Source: Reprinted by permission, from T. Ooms, Teenage Pregnancy in a Family Context: Indications for Policy, Philadelphia: Temple University Press, 1981, pp. 3-4.

Her boyfriend didn't want her to have an abortion either. She was confused, upset, and angry at her mother.

Gloria and her mother had some bad scenes. Mrs. Williams wanted to know who would take care of the baby. She couldn't help because she had a chronic illness that required frequent hospitalizations and left her tired and weak. The school counselor and the clinic social worker suggested a foster home. Mrs. Williams wouldn't hear of such a thing. She had known too many bad ones and wouldn't have a stranger taking care of her grandchild. But she added that Gloria was too young to take care of the baby and needed to finish school. Mrs. Williams pointed out that neither Gloria's boyfriend nor her boyfriend's family had offered any help beyond paying for the crib.

Finally Gloria agreed to an abortion. But by this time it was too late. The doctor confirmed it would no longer be safe.

Mrs. Williams and Gloria then went through a honeymoon period, becoming much closer during the pregnancy and early months of the baby's life as they shared in the care of Tommy. Then Gloria tired of being a mother and wanted to "party" again. She did not want to return to school. She left home from time to time, returning to shower Tommy with love, but never staying around for long. Mrs. Williams managed by first asking her eighty-year-old mother to move in with her. Then when her mother had to return to other responsibilities, Mrs. Williams luckily found a neighbor to care for Tommy when she could not. She wonders what would happen to Tommy if her health seriously deteriorated. She now realizes that her dream of Gloria going to college will never come true.*

Definition and Concepts. Adolescent pregnancy is a serious social problem. The emotional and physical reactions portrayed in the vignette involving Tina and Gloria represent a very small portion of the ramifications of adolescent pregnancy. For those involved, the disruption of life activities is much more profound than can be illustrated in such brief scenarios. Adolescents undergo a number of developmental changes: the development of self-identity; a clarification and emergence of personal relationships and responsibilities; the gradual preparation for vocational or professional work through education; an emancipation from parents; and adjustments to a complex society. Many if not all of these processes are affected by pregnancy.

For the pregnant adolescent, it is difficult to think about becoming a mother when she is really not sure who she is or what she wants to become. Such youngsters may be forced into parenthood before they are ready. For many, the education process is altered and may eventually be interrupted. In fact, many girls choose not to return to school following their deliveries, and thus terminate their education (Card & Wise, 1978).

**Source:* Reprinted by permission, from T. Ooms, *Teenage Pregnancy in a Family Context: Indications for Policy,* Philadelphia: Temple University Press, 1981, pp. 6-7.

Emancipation from parents is often postponed and/or the process may be aggravated. Just as the adolescent is beginning to feel independent, the pregnancy may put her back into a very dependent state. Dependency often breeds hostility, and this is often the case with a pregnant teenager. When one couples dependency with the natural inclination of some adolescents to rebel, the result may be a very disturbed household.

For adolescents who marry because of their pregnancy, the levels of stress may also be great. Furstenberg (1976) studied adolescent marriages and found that 20 percent of the mothers were divorced within one year of the marriage, 33 percent within two years, 50 percent within four years, and 60 percent within six years. The major impediments to success in adolescent marriages appear to be the financial and employment restrictions that beset the couples. These restrictions occur for a number of reasons, but the major factor is probably a lack of education, training, and/or experience. The ability to earn money and the employment choices may be severely limited because of premature termination of schooling.

Risks in adolescent pregnancy are substantial for the unborn child. Children born to adolescent mothers experience (1) higher rates of infant mortality, (2) higher rates of birth defects, (3) greater rates of mental retardation, (4) increased rates of central nervous system dysfunction, and (5) increased potential for a reduction in intelligence (Bolton, 1980). The child also becomes a likely target for mistreatment and abuse.

The adolescent father often becomes a father in absentia. Few adolescent fathers truly assume the role of parent. It is the adolescent mother and her immediate family who shoulder most of the burden of caring for and supporting

Adolescent pregnancy is a serious social problem.

the child. Lorenzi (1977) reported that as few as 23 percent of the adolescent mothers had married the fathers of their children. Furstenberg (1976) found that only 25 percent of the adolescent mothers who expected to marry the fathers of their offspring actually did so. Some 25 percent of *these* mothers had completely lost contact with the fathers within one year following their deliveries. At the conclusion of five years of mothering, 37 percent of the mothers had not seen or heard from the biological fathers within the immediate past year. With these factors in mind, it becomes clear that the majority of adolescent mothers must plan for a family existence that does not include participation by the actual fathers of their children.

Causation and Prevalence. A variety of studies have been conducted relative to the rates of adolescent pregnancy. The rates reported regarding births are probably quite accurate. In contrast, the figures cited relative to adolescent pregnancy rates may not be precise. This lack of accuracy is attributable to several sources. Many adolescents are reluctant to discuss a condition for which so much negative sentiment exists. Also, many adolescent pregnancies are terminated by abortion or may be lost in statistical summaries because they marry and are thus not reported. Therefore the figures reported may fluctuate depending on the sampling procedures employed, the source of the data, and the type of data collected.

Birth rates or prevalence figures for unmarried adolescent females have changed dramatically since 1940. From 1940 to 1973, the birth rate for female teenagers changed from 7.4 to 22.9 out of 1,000. This is an increase of almost 300 percent (Reiss, 1976). Since that time, the birth rates for this group have continued to rise gradually. In 1975, the birth rate per 1,000 unmarried adolescent females was 24.2 (Chilman, 1979). For unwed females ages 15 to 19, the birth rate per 1,000 in 1980 was 27.6 (U.S. Department of Health and Human Services, 1982). These figures may be balanced by other results that indicate that as many as 35 percent of the female adolescents who are sexually active become pregnant during the course of their adolescence (Zelnick, Kim & Kantner, 1979).

Adolescent sexual activity has increased substantially, as indicated by the prevalence figures. The latter half of the 1960s and the entire 1970s period culminated in major attitudinal and behavioral changes regarding sexual relationships. Participation in sexual activities came to be viewed as a matter of personal choice rather than as a violation of moral tradition. At present, it is estimated that about 50 percent of the adolescents in the United States engage in sexual intercourse. This results in nearly one million adolescent pregnancies (Bolton, 1980).

The theories related to adolescent pregnancy are relatively new. Moreover, they are rich with ideas and perspectives regarding the causes of increased sexuality and pregnancy among adolescent females. Bolton (1980) identified several theoretical categories: the majority view, the psychological view, the sociological perspective, and the practical view. The majority point of view holds that adolescent pregnancy, particularly in lower socioeconomic groups, is a self-selected approach to qualifying for welfare benefits. The psychological view deals primarily with a youngster's unmet needs or unresolved issues. From this perspective, adolescent pregnancy is an attempt to fill unmet needs or to respond to parental or family rejection. The sociological perspective identifies the agents of control as residing outside the adolescent. From this view the adolescent is influenced by peer pressure, changing societal values, the media, prolonged postponement of marriage because of extended educational training, lack of sex education, and a host of other variables. The practical view is straightforward. From this perspective, pregnancy is a function of sexual intercourse. Regardless of psychological or social factors, the problem from this view is one of responsible decision-making and behavior. Proponents of this theory do not deny the existence of other causal factors. They simply believe that many adolescents become pregnant because they are gradually eased into situations and behaviors that are commonplace in current society.

Intervention. The goals of treatment for the pregnant adolescent can be many and varied. The initial important goal for the prospective adolescent mother is to help her cope with the discovery that she is actually pregnant. What emerges from this discovery is a crisis—a crisis for her, for the father, and for the families of both individuals (as we saw briefly and partially with Tina and Gloria). Parents often react to the pregnancy announcement with anger. Affected adolescents may respond with denial, disbelief, bitterness, disillusionment, or a variety of other feelings. Anger in parents is often followed by shame and guilt. "What did we do wrong?" is a question pondered by many.

Treatment during this period is focused on reducing the intrapersonal and interpersonal strain and tension. A wise caseworker or counselor will involve the family or families in crisis intervention. This is achieved through careful mediation and problem-solving. Once some crisis issues have been resolved, goals and plans are established which are directly tied to the survival and subsequent life of the infant and its parents.

The group process has been extensively used in rehabilitation and treatment for pregnant adolescents. It provides adolescents with an opportunity to develop some friendships based on mutual needs. Communication that takes place in such group settings is often uniquely suited to the needs and perspectives of the adolescents involved. Members of the group likewise provide a form of psychological support for each other. As relationships and friendships grow, other types of support also emerge.

Many group process techniques are integral parts of school-based programs. School systems across the United States now allow the majority of pregnant students to continue their involvement in the regular school setting with their peers. Some modifications must be made to accommodate these students, but they are usually limited to such adjustments as allowing for appropriate rest periods and reducing their physical education activities.

Unfortunately, many services rendered to pregnant adolescents fade after the delivery of the child. This is most unfortunate, for the problem is one that requires ongoing attention and follow-up. Problems do not cease with the delivery. The development of functional life skills for independent living is a long-term educational and rehabilitation process. If adolescents are not assisted in developing these survival skills, they are likely to return to the decision-making processes and behaviors of the past. It is possible that some of the children born into these circumstances become the victims of abuse and mistreatment (Bolton, 1980). The problem then becomes one that may be intergenerational in nature and even more complex.

Child Abuse

Charles was born on Christmas Eve in 1968. Hospital records indicate his mother to be Mary H., age sixteen, and father unknown. He left the hospital with his mother after three days and went home—the home of his grandparents, Mr. and Mrs. Stanley H. It was a nice home with lots of brightly colored objects to play with. Charles matured rapidly, was active, and loved to play with all the little colored statues on the coffee table and end tables. They were great fun, but Charles was very confused. When his grandmother caught him playing with these little toys, she would scream at him and slap him very hard on the side of his head. One time it really hurt and his ear started to sound funny.

When Charles was four he was helping Grandma cook in the kitchen. He liked helping. Charles pushed a chair over to the stove. All of a sudden Grandma screamed at him: "What do you think you are doing? That is hot." Instinctively Charles put his hands over his ears to protect himself from the blow that always came. "Damn you, listen to me or else," his grandmother shouted. "If you won't listen to me then I'll show you what hot means." She grabbed his right hand away from his head and jerked him up on the chair. She pushed his palm down on the burner of the stove. "There you little bastard, now do you know what hot is?"

At the hospital the physicians were huddled in conference. The story regarding Charles' "accident" was disturbing, mainly because of the physical evidence. Charles' hand had second and third-degree burns. It was unlikely that he would ever regain functional use of his right hand. "It seems to me that a little kid would pull his hand back before it was burned that badly," said a young resident. "I think we have a lot more here than an accident," noted another. "No question about it, the kid is completely deaf in his left ear, has a hearing loss on the right side, and is bruised around the neck." "The bruises could be due to his fall. You know his grandmother said . . . ." "Nonsense. Call protective social services."

Definitions and Concepts. **Child abuse** and neglect are social problems that have recently received considerable public and professional attention. Numerous articles and books have been published on the subject. The interest in child abuse and neglect stands in stark contrast to earlier times, when children were considered little more than economic units utilized to generate income (Fraser, 1976).

Child abuse and neglect can be regarded as a means of coping. Parents (or grandparents, as in our vignette) are confronted with many personal and family challenges. Some are able to cope with adaptive behaviors that are not detrimental to their children, while others respond with maladaptive behaviors that are harmful to their children. Still others choose to deal with the pressures and strains of living by neglecting or abandoning their children. Nagi (1977) attempted to isolate the various epidemiological aspects of child mistreatment but found no clearly defined patterns. Child abusers come from all walks of life, all ethnic groups, and all socioeconomic strata.

Child abuse and neglect can be defined according to a variety of legal and social frameworks. Each approach has its advantages and disadvantages. The legal approach to defining abuse and neglect often has limited utility. The task of writing a truly legitimate and operational legal definition is challenging. Typically, state laws define abuse as inflicted, nonaccidental trauma or injury. Ample proof must be presented in order to substantiate that the parent has deliberately inflicted the child with serious physical injury.

The social definition of abuse and neglect is broader in nature. It is more likely to embrace aspects of neglect and the impact of the socioemotional climate of the home on the child. In this regard, it is generally more difficult to provide evidence for child neglect than for child abuse. In presenting a case for neglect, there must be evidence demonstrating that the child has been left

Figure 11-4/ A Reported Case of Child Abuse

CHILD ABUSE, a second degree felony, in Salt Lake County, on or between August 29, 1982 and November 10, 1982, in violation of Title 76, Chapter 5, Section 109 (2)   (a), Utah Code Annotated, 1953 as amended in that the defendant,   did intentionally or knowingly inflict serious physical injury upon an infant male child, born 29, August, 1981:

PROBABLE CAUSE STATEMENT: Your affiant is a detective with the Salt Lake City P. D., bases the information upon the following:
1) Statement to affiant by   M.D., that   , an infant male, is in intensive care at Primary Children's Medical Center, that the child is suffering cordigal atrophy, that the damage appears to be permanent, and that the injury created a substantial risk of death.
2) Statement to affiant by   that she is the mother of   , who was born August 29, 1982, that defendant who is the natural father of the child, has admitted that he hates   that she has seen the defendant shake the child vigorously several times, that on the evening of October 15th, 1982, she saw defendant shake the child after which the child appeared to stop breathing, that the child was taken to the hospital, treated, then released, that on the 1st of November, 1982, she left the child with the defendant, that when she returned, the child was in serious condition and taken to the hospital where the child now is and that she has never hit the baby or shaken the child.
3) Admission by defendant to Officer   that he has shaken the baby, that he had not meant to hurt the child, that he had a bad temper, and that when the child cried it made him angry.
4) Statement to affiant by   M.D., that the injury to the child has been caused by abuse.

Affiant

alone or unsupervised for long periods of time, has been abandoned, or has had an inadequate supply of food, clothing, or shelter.

Another perplexing form of child mistreatment is sexual abuse (incest, assault, and sexual exploitation). Sexual mistreatment is present in all strata of society. A large proportion (75 percent) of sexual abusers are parents or members of the recipient's family, relatives, neighbors, or other close acquaintances of the family (DeFrancis, 1969). MacFarlane (1978) referred to sexual abuse as a "psychological time bomb" that would eventually explode and have profound psychological effects on children and youths as they became adults. A variety of factors seem to influence the immediate impact and long-term effects of the explosion of the "psychological time bomb." They include the youngster's age and developmental status, the relationship of the abuser to the victim, the intensity of the violence or force used by the abuser, the nature of the responses made by the parents and professionals relative to the abuse incident(s), and the degree of guilt expressed by the abused child or youth.

Other forms of abuse are much more elusive to the investigator or health specialist than those already cited. The psychological and emotional abuse that some children experience is viewed by some to be the most serious kind. Effects of verbal abuse in the form of put-downs and sarcasm can have a profound impact on a child's self-esteem and overall personality development. In contrast to the broken bones and bruises of a physically abused child, psychological and emotional injuries may never heal or disappear (Costa & Nelson, 1978).

Causation and Incidence. An immense number of variables may cause a parent to be abusive. In fact, some have suggested that the abuse phenomenon is, in reality, the product of several constellations of interacting factors. Some research indicates that many abusive parents were mistreated by their own mothers and fathers (Bakan, 1971; Blumberg, 1974; Fontana & Besharov, 1977; Kempe & Helfer, 1972). Green, Gaines, and Sandgrund (1974) studied family interactions in sixty cases of child abuse and found that many of the mothers in these families described their own mothers as being critical, rejecting, and physically punitive. The intergenerational nature of child abuse is an etiological factor we cannot easily disregard. When abuse does occur, it is generally not a premeditated event, but a response to stress. The injury is inflicted in a moment of misdirected anger.

Other factors that seem to be correlated with child abuse and neglect include crises caused by unemployment, unwanted pregnancy, and economic difficulties (Gelles, 1973). The unwanted child often becomes a source of stress. "If we didn't have you, we wouldn't have all these problems" is a common rationalization of an adolescent parent. Parents who grew up in homes where physical force was an acceptable approach to handling child-related problems often employ the same approach with their own children. The process repeats itself. Such cyclic patterns of mistreatment have been identified across as many as five generations (Oliver & Taylor, 1971).

The incidence estimate for child abuse and neglect is approximately five hundred new cases for each one million people in the United States. Mandatory reporting laws (e.g., Senate Bill 1191) may greatly increase the number of cases identified. Some 85 percent of the child abuse cases are attributed to physical abuse. Some 10 percent of the cases are traced to sexual abuse, and 5 percent are ascribed to nutritional deprivation. Cases dealing with emotional abuse are often not reported because it is difficult to prove emotional abuse in court. Approximately two thousand children in the United States die as a result of physical abuse each year. This figure represents a major cause of childhood death. The overall mortality rate traced to child abuse is approximately 3 percent.

Girls are the primary recipients of sexual abuse, and half this abuse occurs before the girls reach the age of twelve. With regard to the perpetrators of abuse, 90 percent are related caretakers of the child, 5 percent are boyfriends of the mother, 4 percent are unrelated baby-sitters, and 1 percent are siblings. Abuse of children seems to be equally distributed between adult males and females (Schmitt, 1978).

Intervention. Treatment of child abuse and neglect can assume many forms. Diagnosis of the various forms of mistreatment can be formidable and trying. At the heart of diagnosis are some of these questions: When does discipline become abuse? What constitutes an accidental injury as opposed to an induced injury? Isn't child-rearing and the way parents treat their children a personal affair? How can I determine if this child has been sexually abused? None of these questions is easily answered.

With regard to physical abuse, the presence of bruises that cannot be attributed to accidents may be grounds for taking immediate protective action. Bruises are generally caused by unrestrained hitting. Other signs of physical abuse are burns, head injuries, fractures, abdominal injuries, and poisoning. Neglect, including nutritional neglect, failure to provide medical care, or failure to protect a child from physical or social danger, is often difficult to detect because many families do not maintain regular contact with a physician or nurse. Gauntness, a lack of fat padding on the cheeks and buttocks, and a voracious appetite are some of the characteristics of a child who fails to thrive. Diagnosis of sexual abuse or sexual exploitation is extremely perplexing and painful for the physician or counselor who must pursue the possibilities of this type of abuse. Complaints by children about their parents' fondling or exhibitionism must be taken seriously. Children who report being sexually assaulted or becoming incestuously involved should be handled delicately.

Sexual abuse in young children often results in fears, sleeping difficulties (e.g., nightmares, night terrors), clinging behavior, and developmental regression. The school-age child may exhibit other clinical symptoms, such as depression, insomnia, hysteria, anxiety, fear, sudden weight loss, sudden school failure, running away, or truancy. A variety of symptoms can surface in adolescents: serious rebellion against parents, serious delinquency, loss of self-esteem, chronic depression, social isolation, and running away.

Treatment of child abuse is a multifaceted process. The children, parents, siblings—the total family—must be involved in treatment. A first goal of treatment for abused children is to treat them for any serious injuries and prevent further harm or damage. Hospitalization may be necessary to deal with immediate physical injuries or complications thereof. During such hospitalization, an intervention plan may be devised by the child protection and treatment team. This team may be composed of a variety of medical and social service specialists. These specialists, in conjunction with the family, develop a comprehensive treatment plan. An emergency receiving home may be used as an alternative to hospital placement. We must remember that treatment can be provided only if a report is made and a diagnosis of abuse is confirmed. If there is a failure to report concerns, many children and youths will continue to be injured and damaged. The purpose of reporting is to protect the child and help the parents.

Once the child's immediate medical needs have been met, a variety of treatment options may be employed: individual play therapy, therapeutic play school, regular preschool, foster care, residential care (e.g., institutionalization), hospitalization, and group treatment (Kempe & Kempe, 1978). Individual play therapy is particularly well suited to children who have been severely disturbed as a result of abuse. This therapy is especially applicable to hyperactive or aggressive children. The intent of such play therapy is to provide these children with a stable, reliable, and understanding relationship with an adult.

The therapeutic play school serves as a temporary island of reprieve for abused children and their families. Within this predictable school environment, children gradually learn to trust themselves and others, particularly adults. They learn new information about themselves and how others behave and think. Their teachers or teacher-therapists serve as prototype parents. Many children referred to these play schools or centers are developmentally delayed, especially in areas of language and motor development. Therefore, special instruction may be provided which helps such children build confidence and strength in these areas.

Foster care used to be the predominant treatment for neglected or abused children, but this option is employed less frequently now. Foster-care placement is used as a temporary means of care while the family is experiencing a crisis or potentially volatile situation. It may also be employed to deal with cases of neglect wherein the child must be removed immediately to prevent further damage or injury.

A recent innovative but expensive option is the residential treatment center. Rather than placing the child in a foster home, the child, the child and mother, or the entire family enter a residential center for treatment. A comprehensive treatment program is implemented by a variety of specialists, based on the nature of the abuse problems.

Hospitalization and institutional care are provided for children in need of extensive long-term health or psychiatric care. Children with severe depression or other serious mental conditions may be best assisted in a hospital or specialized treatment facility.

Group treatment approaches have been particularly helpful to preadolescents and adolescents. Within the context of a group setting, they are able to share feelings and seek solutions to their problems. Group meetings may be structured and focused according to the needs of the individuals in the group.

This approach to treatment is much less expensive than the individual therapy procedure.

Treatment for parents and families of abused children is similar to that provided for the children themselves. According to Kempe and Kempe (1978), 80 percent of the parents receiving treatment in their programs improve sufficiently to be reunited with their children without further injury. The treatment options identified by Beezley (1978) included individual psychotherapy, lay therapy, marital and family therapy, group therapy, crisis hot lines, crisis nurseries, family therapy, and family residential treatment. Individual psychotherapy has not proven to be very effective for abusive parents. They are generally distrustful of such therapy and are reluctant to spend the time required.

Lay therapy is provided by nonprofessionals who may come from the same ethnic group or socioeconomic background of the abused parent. They qualify for the role of therapist because of their maturity, understanding of child abuse, and willingness to help. They serve as a link between the parents and other professional staff and often become the ally of the mother or father.

Marital and family therapy is designed to assist parents in removing barriers that interfere with their ongoing relationship with each other and their children. Sources of frustration and problems are identified, and communication skills are taught or enhanced. The parents and family members learn how to express feelings, to listen to one another, and to solve problems without physical and/or verbal combat.

Treatment groups also seem effective in remedying the problems associated with abuse. Couples are brought together to discuss various aspects of child-rearing, problems they experienced as children, and current child-related problems. This type of treatment is particularly appealing to many fathers in that they often feel less threatened or defensive in a group situation. They are also able to express views that represent a father's perspective of the various problems. Parents Anonymous is a particularly effective approach to assisting families. This organization is uniquely helpful for parents who distrust community agency personnel.

The crisis hot line is a twenty-four-hour emergency treatment approach. Frequently parents with known histories of abuse need immediate help in the form of some direction, counseling, or reassurance. The telephone hot line service may be operated by volunteer or paid staff who have been trained in crisis management. They are supervised by a trained social worker or other comparable professional. In responding to calls, they attempt to provide assistance that is truly tailored to the demands of the crisis.

Crisis nurseries are designed to provide services to parents, particularly mothers, who cannot cope with their child's behavior and need a reprieve. Crisis nurseries are open twenty-four hours a day with care facilities for newborns, toddlers, and preschoolers. Seventy-two hours is usually the maximum stay for a child placed in this type of nursery. During the child's stay, parents are given an opportunity to deal with their feelings, to gain control, and to seek solutions to the problems that precipitated the crisis. Crisis nurseries are much more suitable than the foster placement approaches of the past.

Family therapy and family residential treatment are interrelated. The latter treatment, however, is relatively new. The goal of these treatment approaches is to assist families as units, to help them learn new methods of communicating and solving problems. Family therapy may be preceded by individual therapy in certain cases.

SUMMARY

Some health disorders may be viewed as disorders in a literal sense, while others are really health conditions that result from societal problems. In all cases the conditions have a considerable impact on the affected individuals as well as on those around them. Medical and other technological advances now permit effective treatment and management of many health disorders. In some cases, however, treatment effectiveness is still disappointing and the prognosis remains dismal.

Four general categories of health conditions were discussed in this chapter: systemic disorders, stress-related disorders, life-endangering diseases, and miscellaneous conditions. Diabetes and cardiac disorders were examined under systemic conditions. Asthma and peptic ulcers were discussed as types of stress-related disorders. Three conditions were covered under the category of life-endangering diseases: cystic fibrosis, sickle cell anemia, and cancer. Under miscellaneous conditions, the focus was on two serious societal problems that have a significant impact on the people involved, adolescent pregnancy and child abuse, both of which present complex problems for those affected.

REVIEW QUESTIONS

1. Why is diabetes in youngsters often more serious than in adults?
2. Describe how intervention might be undertaken for congenital heart problems.
3. How does asthma influence the lifestyle of youngsters?
4. Why is early diagnosis important in cystic fibrosis?
5. Describe how sickle cell anemia influences the lifestyle of people with the disease.
6. How are adolescent pregnancy and child abuse similar to and different from other health disorders?

SECTION V

The Gifted, Creative and Talented

This section focuses on exceptional individuals who are very different from those discussed in most of the text: the gifted, creative, and talented. Here we are examining people who are exceptional by virtue of their intelligence, creativity, or artistic ability. A number of different interventions may be important if gifted and talented individuals are to maximize the development of their talents. Chapter 12 discusses definitions and concepts, and Chapter 13 examines intervention strategies. The following are topical guidelines for Section V:

1. Several definitions of giftedness have been presented over the years.

2. A broadening of definitions has led to the use of multiple criteria for identifying the exceptionally able.

3. A variety of characteristics are associated with the gifted, creative, and talented.

4. Several influences have been associated with the origins of intelligence, creativity, and talent.

5. Various intervention strategies have been used to enhance development in the gifted, creative, and talented.

6. Evidence regarding the effectiveness of differing interventions varies substantially.

CHAPTER TWELVE

The Gifted, Creative, and Talented: Definitions and Concepts

Historical Perspectives
Current Definitions of Giftedness
Characteristics

Origins of Giftedness
Prevalence of Giftedness
Identification of Giftedness

Gifted, *creative,* and *talented* are terms associated with a special group of people who have more ability in some areas than most of us. In many cases, we admire such individuals and occasionally are a little envious of their talent. This type of reaction is natural as we labor at what often seem to be mediocre achievements. Such perspectives have led to gifted populations being largely ignored in terms of extra assistance. This relative lack of attention has resulted in one of our most valuable resources being unexploited and improperly utilized.

Dwight spends most of his time in a variety of musical endeavors. It is his business. At the age of twenty-seven he is currently working as the musical director for an internationally popular singing group that performs frequently on television and for live audiences around the world. Dwight plays a number of instruments with great skill, including the bass viol, the fender bass, the guitar, the drums, and the piano. In addition, he has perfect pitch and sings well. Moreover, Dwight excels in a variety of nonmusical activities.

As a youngster, Dwight's brothers and sisters taunted him and referred to him as "the little professor" or "Doc." (Now Dwight makes a great deal more money than one of those brothers, who actually is a professor.) Throughout his education, Dwight had little difficulty in mastering the content in classes. His interests were broad and school was sheer pleasure. Dwight's teachers were receptive to his unquenchable thirst for all types of knowledge. They gave him the time and freedom necessary to explore well beyond the usual levels of investigation and instruction. Thus his schooling was, for the most part, engaging and exciting.

As a senior in high school, Dwight composed and arranged all types of musical scores. One example of his tremendous talent involved an audio tape that he created when he was seventeen years old. The tape included fifteen contemporary songs, recorded using the instruments Dwight played. First he recorded the piano on one tape track, then drums on another track, and so on. The product was a musical presentation that many professional producers would have appreciated and enjoyed.

Following his high school graduation, Dwight enrolled in a nationally recognized private university on a music scholarship. He soon discovered that his knowledge of musical composition equaled that of many of his music professors. Although his scholarship was funded through the college of fine arts, Dwight was actually more interested in preparing himself for law school. Consequently he enrolled in all the pre-law courses available.

Midway through Dwight's second year of college, he had an opportunity to audition for a singing group that performed all over the United States (not his current employers). He was very well received and was hired to travel with this group for the next year. When that tour concluded, he became a musical staff member for his current employers, where his future has become increasingly promising. Dwight is a remarkable young man.

For many years behavioral scientists described children with extraordinarily high intelligence as being gifted. Only recently have scientists included the adjectives *creative* and *talented* in their descriptions of individuals with ex-

365

The Gifted,
Creative, and
Talented:
Definitions and
Concepts

Dwight

ceptional skills and abilities. These terms are typically employed to suggest domains of performance other than those measured by intelligence tests. The young man described in the preceding vignette is one of those individuals who is probably gifted, creative, and talented. Not only did he excel in intellectual (traditional academic) endeavors, but he also exhibits tremendous prowess with regard to producing and performing music. Certainly each of the factors associated with these terms interacts with the others. Some individuals soar to exceptional heights in the talent domain, others in the intellectual area, and still others in creative endeavors. Furthermore, a select few exhibit remarkable levels of behavior and aptitude across several domains or areas. Unfortunately, some individuals who are gifted fail to achieve even though they have the potential to do so (Whitmore, 1980).

HISTORICAL PERSPECTIVES

Definitions describing the unusually able in terms of intelligence quotients and creativity measures are recent phenomena. Until the beginning of the twentieth century, no one had devised a suitable method for quantifying or measuring the human attribute of intelligence. The breakthrough occurred in Europe. Alfred Binet, a French psychologist, constructed the first developmental assessment scale for children during the early 1900s. The scale was created by observing children at various ages, which permitted identification of specific tasks that ordinary children were able to perform at each age level. These tasks were then sequenced according to age-appropriate levels. Children who could perform tasks well above that which was normal for their chronological age were identified as being developmentally advanced.

Gradually the notion of **mental age** emerged. The mental age of the child was derived by corresponding the tasks the child was able to perform to the age scale (i.e., typical performance of children at various ages) that had been carefully developed by Binet and Simon (1905; 1908). Although this scale was developed and used initially to identify mentally retarded children in the Parisian schools, it eventually became an important means for identifying those who had higher-than-average intelligence.

Lewis M. Terman, an American educator and psychologist, expanded the concepts and procedures developed by Binet (Gowan, 1977). He was convinced that Binet and his colleague, Simon, had developed an approach for measuring intellectual progress in all children, those who were extremely able as well as those who were retarded. This belief prompted him to revise the Binet instrument. In 1916, Terman published the Stanford-Binet Individual Intelligence Scale in conjunction with Stanford University. During this period, Terman developed the term *intelligence quotient*, or IQ. The IQ score was obtained by dividing a child's mental age by his or her chronological age and multiplying that figure by 100

$$\frac{\text{MA}}{\text{CA}} \times 100 = \text{IQ}.$$

Shortly after the publication of the Stanford-Binet Individual Intelligence Scale, Terman in 1922 was funded to inaugurate his intriguing *Genetic Studies of Genius*. His initial group of subjects included more than 1,500 students who had obtained IQ scores at or above 140 on the Stanford-Binet. The subjects were drawn from both elementary and secondary classroom settings. A number of research reports were published by Terman and his associates as the subjects reached average ages of twenty, thirty-five, and so on.

Terman and his followers aroused great interest in the gifted and their education. They also had a profound effect on the criteria and manner in which giftedness was initially defined. The intelligence quotient of an individual became the major gauge for determining one's eligibility for the designation of being gifted.

Gradually other researchers became interested in studying the nature and assessment of intelligence (e.g., Spearman, 1927a & b; Wechsler, 1950; 1958). These researchers tended to view intelligence as a unitary structure (Laycock, 1979). An individual's intelligence was seen as an underlying ability or capacity that expressed itself in a variety of ways. The unitary IQ scores that were derived from the Binet and Stanford-Binet tests were representative of and contributed to this notion. Over time, however, other researchers came to believe that the intellect of a person was represented by a variety of distinct capacities and abilities (e.g., Cattell, 1971; Guilford, 1959; Thorndike, 1927; 1940; Thurstone, 1938). This line of thinking suggested that each distinct, intellectual capacity

367

The Gifted,
Creative, and
Talented:
Definitions and
Concepts

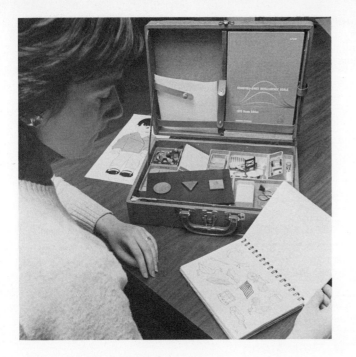

Intelligence tests
provide one
means for evalu-
ating a student's
performance and
potential.

could be identified and assessed. Several mental abilities then received attention in research, including memory capacity, divergent thinking, vocabulary
usage, and reasoning ability. Gradually the multiple-ability approach became
more popular than the unitary intelligence notion. Its proponents were convinced that the universe of intellectual functions was far-reaching and extensive. Moreover, they believed that the intelligence assessment instruments
utilized at that time measured a very small portion of an individual's true
intellectual capacities.

One of the key contributors to the multidimensional theory regarding
intelligence was Guilford (1950; 1959). He developed a model that included
many different types of intellectual abilities (see Figure 12-1). The model contained three dimensions: operations, contents, and products. This model warrants discussion because its development and dissemination had a profound
impact on the manner in which intelligence was viewed.

The first dimension of Guilford's model, operations, involves the processes by which individuals deal with information. They include (1) cognition,
the ability to perceive and comprehend incoming information; (2) memory, the
ability to store and retrieve information; (3) divergent production, the ability
to generate new ideas; (4) convergent production, the ability to utilize stored
information for problem-solving; and (5) evaluation, the ability to reach decisions and make suitable judgments.

According to Guilford, "information is anything that we know" (1977,
p. 14). He suggested that we develop our understanding of the world around
us by processing various types of information or content. We process infor-

Figure 12-1/ Guilford's Structure of Intellect Model

In the structure of intellect model, each little cube represents a unique combination of one kind of operation, one kind of content, and one kind of product, and hence a distinctly different intellectual ability or function.

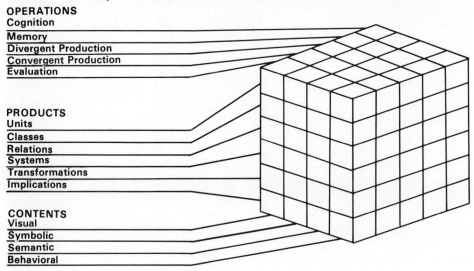

OPERATIONS
Cognition
Memory
Divergent Production
Convergent Production
Evaluation

PRODUCTS
Units
Classes
Relations
Systems
Transformations
Implications

CONTENTS
Visual
Symbolic
Semantic
Behavioral

Source: Guilford, 1977, p. 151.

mation through content categories that, in turn, enable us to create various products. The second dimension, known as contents, is divided into four sub-areas: (1) figural, information derived through our senses from tangible objects; (2) symbolic, information derived from symbols such as numerals, letter configurations, and formulas; (3) semantic, information derived from a code known as language; and (4) behavioral, information acquired from observing and responding to the behavior of others.

Guilford's third dimension, products, refers to the form and structure that is given to the information created by an individual. There are six kinds of products, according to Guilford: (1) units, objects or items that are independent of other things; (2) classes, objects that share some common attribute; (3) relations, units that are connected in some meaningful fashion (e.g., the words *ball, racket,* and *net* are integrally related to the game known as tennis); (4) systems, complex products such as a television or a computerized camera; (5) transformations, any unit, relation, or system that has been changed or altered; and (6) implications, products of the mind that may be expressed as predictions, deductions, or conclusions.

Guilford's work led many researchers to consider intelligence as more than a broad unitary ability, as a diverse range of intellectual and creative abilities. Furthermore, Guilford's theoretical contributions prompted many researchers to focus their scientific efforts on the emerging field of creativity and its various subcomponents (e.g., divergent thinking, problem-solving, decision-making). Gradually, tests or measures of creativity were developed using the constructs drawn from models created by Guilford and others. Scientists such as Getzels and Jackson (1958) began to conduct comparative studies of the creative, the academically advanced, and the intellectually gifted. Programs and materials were also developed to teach and foster creativity (Osborn, 1963; Parnes & Harding, 1962; Taylor, 1964). Although much effort has been expended in refining definitions, developing tests to measure creative potential, and studying creative individuals, problems related to explicating accurately the essence of creative potential, thought, and behavior continue to challenge social scientists.

In summary, conceptions of giftedness during the early 1920s were inextricably intertwined with the score that one obtained on an intelligence test. Thus a single score, an IQ, was the index by which one was identified as being gifted. Terman & Oden (1959), for example, selected subjects for his longitudinal studies based on their performance on the Stanford-Binet Individual Test of Intelligence. Those who had IQs equal to or greater than 140 were considered gifted. Commencing with the work of Guilford (1950; 1959) and Torrance (1961; 1965; 1968), notions regarding giftedness were greatly expanded. Giftedness began to refer not only to those with high measured IQs but also to those who demonstrated high aptitude on creativity measures. More recently the term *talented* has been added to the descriptors associated with giftedness. As a result, individuals who demonstrate remarkable skills in the visual or performing arts, or who excel in other areas of performance, may be designated as being among the gifted.

CURRENT DEFINITIONS OF GIFTEDNESS

Definitions of giftedness have been influenced by a variety of innovative and knowledgeable individuals. One definition that characterizes the changes that have occurred over time is that provided by the U.S. Office of Education (Marland, 1972, p. 2):

> Gifted and talented children are those identified by professionally qualified persons who, by virtue of outstanding abilities, are capable of high performance. These are children who require differentiated educational programs in order to realize their contribution to self and society.

Children capable of high performance include those with demonstrated achievement and/or potential ability in any of the following areas, singly or in combination.

1. General intellectual ability
2. Specific academic aptitude
3. Creative or productive thinking
4. Leadership ability
5. Visual and performing arts
6. Psychomotor ability

A significant number of states adopted this definition or amended it for their use (Karnes & Collins, 1978). However, this definition was revised by those drafting the Gifted and Talented Children's Act of 1978. The new definition continued to be multidimensional in nature, although the area of psychomotor performance was deleted. The new definition emphasized the importance of early identification and the necessity of providing differential education above and beyond that available in the regular school curriculum. The new definition reads as follows:

> For the purpose of this part, the term "gifted and talented children" means children and, whenever applicable, youth who are identified at the preschool, elementary, or secondary level as possessing demonstrated or potential abilities that give evidence of high performance capability in areas such as intellectual, creative, specific academic, or leadership ability, or in the performing and visual arts, and who by reason thereof require services or activities not ordinarily provided by the school. (P.L. 95-561)

Both definitions are very inclusive and broad. Many of the definitional terms discussed earlier may be found, in one form or another, in each definition.

Capturing the essence of any human condition in a definition can be very perplexing. This is certainly the case in defining the human attributes, abilities, and potentialities that constitute giftedness. However, definitions serve a number of important purposes. For example, definitions may have a profound influence on the following: (1) the number of students that are ultimately selected; (2) the types of instruments and selection procedures utilized; (3) the scores one must obtain in order to qualify for specialized instruction; (4) the types of differentiated education provided; (5) the amount of funding required to provide services; and (6) the types of training individuals need to teach the gifted and talented. Thus definitions are important in both practical and theoretical senses.

Many professionals have encountered confusion in attempting to identify the gifted and provide programs for them in accordance with the old and/or new definitions of giftedness presented by the U.S. Office of Education (Clark, 1979; Gallagher, 1979; Renzulli, 1978). Such confusion arises in several areas. One problem relates to identification of gifted students. Part of the identification difficulty occurs because of the number of areas to be assessed. Just selecting appropriate tests or procedures is a monumental challenge. Once the tests and procedures have been chosen, they must be administered and scored, which is no small undertaking. The entire identification process can be very expensive and time-consuming. Many school districts do not have adequate personnel or funding resources to implement such comprehensive screening and identification procedures.

Related to the identification of outstanding performers is the problem of those individuals who have not been able to distinguish themselves by their present performance but who may have the potential to do so. Many students who may be gifted have not been given adequate opportunities to develop their unusual talents. This may be particularly true for children who are culturally, ethnically, linguistically, socially, or economically different from the core culture. In addition, cultural bias inherent in most tests make the identification very difficult. Steps have been taken to circumvent such difficulty with assessment approaches. The development of the System of Multicultural Pluralistic Assessment (SOMPA) represents such an effort (Mercer, 1979). The SOMPA provides a unique approach to assessing culturally different children. Other promising approaches for identifying the underachiever and culturally different, creative child have been reviewed by Rim, Davis, and Bien (1982). Utilizing a variety of self-report and parent-report measures, these researchers appear to have found an effective means for identifying creativity in a broad range of children and youths; however, more research must be done before these measures can be validly used on a broader scale.

The definition of the U.S. Office of Education is not the only source of difficulty. If we were to examine other definitions of giftedness, we would find that each contains a host of terms. Often the terms are confusing, vague, and even contradictory. For example, we may encounter such terms as high general intellectual ability, cognitive superiority, high creativity, exceptionally high leadership ability, and inordinately talented. Intelligence may be defined narrowly or broadly, as we have seen earlier. Creativity may be seen by some as being distinctively different from intellectual capacity, whereas others may view them as being closely related. Superior talent in one school district may not be so viewed in another. Objectifying each of the definitional components is an extremely complex task. Martinson (1973), defined gifted students as follows:

> Students with superior cognitive abilities include approximately the top three percent of the general school population in measured general intelligence and/or in creative abilities or other talents that promise to make lasting contributions of merit to society. These students are so able that they require special provisions if appropriate educational opportunities are to be provided for them. (P. 193)

Although this definition has many of the problems inherent in the previous definitions, it also has several advantages. One advantage is its restrictiveness. This statement limits the number of students who can be identified as gifted to the *top 3 percent of the general school population*. It further limits the number who can be selected to those who can make *lasting contributions of merit to society*. This latter definitional component addresses the motivational aspect of individual performance that is critical. Even though one may have remarkable abilities, without proper motivation they may never be fully utilized.

Martinson (1973) provided other amplifications regarding her definition that warrant mention. First, she believed that a careful approach should be taken in locating the gifted. Particular concern in this regard was evident in terms of identifying the bright and potentially talented individuals from ethnic and racial minorities as well as from the socially and economically disadvantaged. Also, she believed that the gifted should be those "who function at unusually high levels of ideational production, generalization, and application and/or give evidence and promise of uniquely outstanding and original performance" (p. 194).

Renzulli (1978) provided another definition that is characterized by three clusters of behavior traits. His "three-ring conception" of giftedness has influenced the thinking and procedures employed by many practitioners. He pioneered the notion that giftedness was a combination of interacting clusters of behavior, that one could not be identified as being gifted based on only one cluster of behavior. Renzulli's definition stated:

> Giftedness consists of an interaction among three basic clusters of human traits—these clusters being above-average general abilities, high levels of task commitment, and high levels of creativity. Gifted and talented children are those possessing or capable of developing this composite set of traits and applying them to any potentially valuable area of human performance. Children who manifest or are capable of developing an interaction among the three clusters require a wide variety of educational opportunities and services that are not ordinarily provided through regular instructional programs. (1978, p. 261)

The clusters emphasized in this definition were drawn from research dealing with individuals who, as adults or youths, had distinguished themselves by their remarkable achievement and/or creative contributions.

Renzulli (1978) claimed that his definition was an operational one because it met several important criteria. First, as noted earlier, he developed the definition based on research on gifted individuals and their characteristics. Second, Renzulli asserted that it provided direction for selecting or developing instruments and procedures that could be used to devise defensible identification plans. In addition, he believed that such a definition directed practitioners to focus their programs on the essential characteristics of giftedness that really lead to future achievements and contributions. There are some inherent problems in Renzulli's definition that are common to others. However, his conceptualizations and their applicability have not gone unnoticed.

Each of the various definitions presented reveals the complexity associated with defining the nature of giftedness, a difficulty that is common to definitions in the behavioral sciences. The problems of definition and description are not easily resolved, and yet such efforts are vital to both research and practice.

CHARACTERISTICS

Accurately identifying the characteristics of the gifted is an enormous task and might very well be deleterious to many gifted youths because of the heterogeneity of the group. Many characteristics attributed to the gifted have been generated from different types of studies (Cox, 1926; Goertzel & Goertzel, 1962; Hollingsworth, 1942; MacKinnon, 1962; Terman, 1925). Frequently these studies served as catalysts for the production of lists of distinctive characteristics. Gradually what emerged from the studies was a stereotypical view of giftedness. The problems related to identifying accurately the characteristics of the gifted are directly related to (1) the populations that have been sampled and studied; (2) the changes that have occurred in definitions; and (3) the variant selection criteria that have been employed.

Unfortunately, much of the initial research relating to the characteristics of the gifted has been conducted with restricted population samples. Generally the studies did not include adequate samples of females, or individuals from various ethnic and cultural groups; nor did the researchers carefully control for the factors directly related to socioeconomic status (Callahan, 1981). Therefore the characteristics generated from these studies may not be representative of the gifted population as a whole, but rather a reflection of a select group of gifted individuals from advantaged environments.

The definitions of giftedness and the selection criteria that emerge from them have also had a profound effect on the results researchers obtain in studying the gifted. For many of the studies regarding the characteristics of the gifted, the major basis for inclusion in a study was an exceptionally high IQ score. The results therefore reflected little information regarding the characteristics of the creative person. The same is true of studies that were exclusively devoted to studying the remarkable achievement in adults. Such studies provide us with an incomplete understanding of the characteristics of the creative or intellectually able as youngsters.

Given the present multifaceted definitions of giftedness, we must conclude as Callahan (1981) did that the gifted are members of a heterogeneous population of individuals. Consequently, research findings of past and present must be interpreted with great caution as practitioners assess a particular youth's behavior and attributes.

In 1925 Terman commenced the first longitudinal study of gifted individuals. In conjunction with other associates, he investigated their physical characteristics, personality attributes, psychological and marital adjustment, educational attainment, and career achievement (see Table 12-1). Terman's work provided the impetus for the systematic study of gifted individuals. Since 1929, other researchers have sought to add to the knowledge base about the characteristics of gifted populations. For instance, Laycock and Caylor (1964) found no significant differences between the intellectually gifted and their siblings in measures of physical stature. The above-average stature findings of Terman were probably a function of his sampling procedures. However, Terman's other findings regarding the intellectually able have been generally affirmed by more current investigators (Boehm, 1962; Gallagher, 1975; Hitchfield, 1973; Ketcham & Snyder, 1977; Martinson, 1972; McGinn, 1976; Milgram & Milgram, 1976).

Recently, Clark (1979) has synthesized the work of past investigators and developed a comprehensive listing of differential characteristics of the gifted, their needs, and their possible problems. These characteristics have been organized according to five domains: cognitive, affective, physical, intuitive, and societal (see Tables 12-2, 12-3, 12-4, 12-5, 12-6).

TABLE 12-1/ Terman's Findings in the Study of the Gifted

Domains	Characteristics of the Gifted
Physical characteristics	• Robust and in good health. • Above average in physical stature.
Personality attributes and psychological adjustment	• Above average in willpower, popularity, perseverance, emotional maturity, aesthetic perceptivity, and moral reasoning. • Keen sense of humor and high levels of self-confidence. • Equal to their peers in marital adjustment. • Well adjusted as adults and had fewer problems with substance abuse, suicide, and mental health.
Educational attainment	• Generally read before school entrance. • Were frequently promoted. • Excelled in reading and mathematical reasoning. • Consistently scored in the top 10 percent of achievement tests.
Career achievement	• Mates were primarily involved in professional and managerial positions. • Women were teachers or homemakers (probably due to cultural expectations at the time). • Individuals at age 40 had completed 67 books, 1,400 scientific and professional papers, 700 short stories, and a variety of other creative and scholarly works. • Adult achievers came primarily from en couraging home environments.

TABLE 12-2/ Differential Cognitive (Thinking) Characteristics of the Gifted

Differentiating Characteristics	Examples of Related Needs	Possible Concomitant Problems
Extraordinary quanitity of information, unusal retentiveness	To be exposed to new and challenging information of the environment and the culture, including aesthetic, economic, political, educational, and social aspects; to acquire early mastery of foundation skill	Boredom with regular curriculum; impatience with "waiting for the group"
Advanced comprehension	Access to challenging curriculum and Intellectual peers	Poor interpersonal relationships with less able children of the same age; adults considering child "sassy" or "smart aleck"; a dislike for repetition of already understood concepts

Table 12-2/ (Continued)

375

The Gifted,
Creative, and
Talented:
Definitions and
Concepts

Differentiating Characteristics	Examples of Related Needs	Possible Concomitant Problems
Unusually varied interests and curiosity	To be exposed to varied subjects and concerns; to be allowed to pursue individual ideas as far as interest takes them	Difficulty in conforming to group tasks; overextending energy levels, taking on too many projects at one time
High level of language development	To encounter uses for increasingly difficult vocabulary and concepts	Perceived as a "showoff" by children of the same age
Ability to generate original ideas and solutions	To build skills in problem-solving and productive thinking; opportunity to contribute to solution of meaningful problems	Difficulty with rigid conformity; may be penalized for not following directions; may deal with rejection by becoming rebellious
Early differential patterns for thought processing (e.g., thinking in alternatives, abstract terms, sensing consequences, making generalizations)	To be exposed to alternatives, abstractions, consequences of choices, and opportunities for drawing generalizations and testing them	Rejection or omission of detail; questions generalizations of others which may be perceived as disrespectful behavior
Early ability to use and form conceptual frameworks	To use and design conceptual frameworks in information-gathering and problem-solving; to seek order and consistency; to develop a tolerance for ambiguity	Frustration with inability of others to understand or appreciate original organizations or insights; personally devised systems or structure may conflict with procedures of systems later taught
An evaluative approach to themselves and others	To be exposed to individuals of varying ability and talent, and to varying ways of seeing and solving problems; to set realistic, achievable short-term goals; to develop skills in data evaluation and decision-making	Perceived by others as elitist, conceited, superior, too critical; may become discouraged from self-criticism, can inhibit attempting new areas if fear of failure is too great; seen by others as too demanding, compulsive; can affect interpersonal relationships as others fail to live up to standards set by gifted individual; intolerant of stupidity
Persistent, goal-directed behavior	To pursue inquiries beyond allotted time spans; to set and evaluate priorities	Perceived as stubborn, willful, uncooperative
High level of verbal ability	To share ideas verbally in depth	Dominates discussions with information and questions deemed negative by teachers and fellow students; use

Table 12-2/ (Continued)

Differentiating Characteristics	Examples of Related Needs	Possible Concomitant Problems
		of verbalism to avoid difficult thinking tasks
Unusual capacity for processing information	To be exposed to ideas at many levles and in large variety	Resents being interrupted; perceived as too serious; dislike for routine and drill
Accelerated pace of thought processes	To be exposed to ideas at rates appropriate to individual pace of learning	Frustration with inactivity and absence of progress
Flexible thought processes	To be allowed to solve problems in diverse ways	Seen as disruptive and disrespectful to authority and tradition
Comprehensive synthesis	To be allowed a longer incubation time for ideas	Frustration with demands for deadlines and for completion of each level prior to starting new inquiry
Early ability to delay closure	To be allowed to pursue ideas and integrate new ideas without forced closure or products demanded	If products are demanded as proof of learning, will refuse to pursue an otherwise interesting subject or line of inquiry
Heightened capacity for seeing unusual and diverse relationships	To mess around with varieties of materials and ideas	Frustration at being considered "off the subject" or irrelevant in pursuing inquiry in areas other than subject being considered; considered odd or weird by others

Source: Reprinted, by permission of the publisher, from Barbara Clark, *Growing up Gifted* (Columbus, Ohio: Charles E. Merrill Publishing Co., 1979), pp. 91-93.

TABLE 12-3/ Differential Affective (Feeling) Characteristics of the Gifted

Differentiating Characteristics	Examples of Related Needs	Possible Concomitant Problems
Large accumulation of information about emotions that has not been brought to awareness	To process cognitively the emotional meaning of experience, to name one's own emotions, to identify one's own and other's perceptual filters and defense systems, to expand and clarify awareness of the physical environment, to clarify awareness of the needs and feelings of others	Information misinterpreted affecting the individual negatively
Unusual sensitivity to the expectations and feelings of	To learn to clarify the feelings and expectations of	Unusually vulnerable to criticism of others, high level of

Table 12-3/ (Continued)

377

The Gifted,
Creative, and
Talented:
Definitions and
Concepts

Differentiating Characteristics	Examples of Related Needs	Possible Concomitant Problems
others	others	need for success and recognition
Keen sense of humor—may be gentle or hostile	To learn how behaviors affect the feelings and behaviors of others	Use of humor for critical attack on others, resulting in damage to interpersonal relationships
Heightened self-awareness, accompanied by feelings of being different	To learn to assert own needs and feelings nondefensively, to share self with others, for self-clarification	Isolates self, resulting in being considered aloof, feeling rejected; perceive difference as a negative attribute resulting in low self-esteem and inhibited growth emotionally and socially
Idealism and sense of justice which appear at an early age	To transcend negative reactions by finding values to which he or she can be committed	Attempt unrealistic reforms and goals with resulting intense frustration (suicides result from intense depression over issues of this nature)
Earlier development of an inner focus of control and satisfaction	To clarify personal priorities among conflicting values To confront and interact with the value systems of others	Difficulty conforming; reject external validation and choose to live by personal values which may be seen as a challenge to authority or tradition
Unusual emotional depth and intensity	To find purpose and direction from personal value system To translate commitment into action in daily life	Unusual vulnerability; problem focusing on realistic goals for life's work
High expectations of self and others, often leading to high levels of frustration with self, others, and situations	To learn to set realistic goals and to accept setbacks as part of the learning process	Discouragement and frustration from high levels of self-criticism; problems maintaining good interpersonal relations as others fail to maintain high standards imposed by gifted individual; immobilization of action due to high levels of frustration resulting from situations which do not meet expectations of excellence
Strong need for consistency between abstract values and	To find a vocation that provides opportunity for ac-	Frustration with self and others leading to inhibited

Table 12-3/ (Continued)

Differentiating Characteristics	Examples of Related Needs	Possible Concomitant Problems
personal actions	tualization of student's personal value system, as well as an avenue for his or her talents and abilities	actualization of self and interpersonal relationships
Advanced levels of moral judgment	To receive validation for nonaverage morality	Intolerance of and lack of understanding from peer group, leading to rejection and possible isolation

Source: Reprinted, by permission of the publisher, from Barbara Clark, *Growing up Gifted* (Columbus, Ohio: Charles E. Merril Publishing Co., 1979), pp. 94-95.

TABLE 12-4/ Differential Physical (Sensation) Characteristics of the Gifted

Differentiating Characteristics	Examples of Related Needs	Possible Concomitant Problems
Unusual quantity of input from the environment through a heightened sensory awareness	To engage in activities that will allow integration and assimilation of sensory data	Attention moving diffusely toward many areas of interest; overexpenditure of energy due to lack of integration; seeming disconnectedness
Unusual discrepancy between physical and intellectual development	To appreciate their physical capacities	Result in gifted adults who function with a mind/body dichotomy; gifted children who are comfortable expressing themselves only in mental activity, resulting in a limited development both physically and mentally
Low tolerance for the lag between their standards and their athletic skills	To discover physical activities as a source of pleasure; to find satisfaction in small increments of improvement; to engage in noncompetitive physical activities	Refusal to take part in any activities where they do not excel; limiting their experience with otherwise pleasurable, constructive physical activities
"Cartesian split"—can include neglect of physical well-being and avoidance of physical activity	To engage in activities leading to mind/body integration; to develop a commitment to own physical well-being; to exend this concern to the social and political realm	Detrimental to full mental and physical health, inhibiting to the development of potential for the individual

Source: Reprinted, by permission of the publisher, from Barbara Clark, *Growing up Gifted* (Columbus, Ohio: Charles E. Merrill Publishing Co., 1979), p. 96.

379

The Gifted,
Creative, and
Talented:
Definitions and
Concepts

TABLE 12-5/ Differential Intuitive Characteristics of the Gifted

Differentiating Characteristics	Examples of Related Needs	Possible Concomitant Problems
Early involvement and concern for intuitive knowing and metaphysical ideas and phenomena	Opportunities to engage in meaningful dialogue with philosophers and others concerned with these ideas; to become aware of own intuitive energy and ability; guidance in developing and using intuitive energy and ability	Ridiculed by peers; not taken seriously by elders; considered weird or strange
Open to experiences in this area; will experiment with psychic and metaphysical phenomena	Guidance in becoming familiar with, analyzing, and evaluating such phenomena; should be provided a historical approach	Can become narrowly focused toward ungrounded belief systems
Creativity apparent in all areas of endeavor	Guidance in evaluating appropriate uses of creative efforts; encouragement for continued development of creative abilities	Seen as deviant; becomes bored with more mundane tasks; may be viewed as troublemaker

Source: Reprinted, by permission of the publisher, from Barbara Clark, *Growing up Gifted* (Columbus, Ohio: Charles E. Merrill Publishing Co., 1979), p. 97.

TABLE 12-6/ Differential Societal Characteristics of the Gifted

Differentiating Characteristics	Examples of Related Needs	Possible Concomitant Problems
Differential Societal Characteristics of the Gifted		
Strongly motivated by self-actualization needs	Opportunities to follow divergent paths, pursue strong interests, help in understanding the demands of self-actualization	Frustration of not feeling challenged; loss of unrealized talents
Advanced cognitive and affective capacity for conceptualizing and solving societal problems	Encounters with social problems, awareness of the complexity of problems facing society, conceptual frameworks for problem-solving procedures	Tendency for "quick" solutions not taking into account the complexity of the problem: young age of gifted person often makes usable alternatives suspect; older, more experienced decision makers may not take the gifted person seriously
Differential Social Expectations for the Gifted		

Table 12-6/ (Continued)

Differentiating Characteristics	Examples of Related Needs	Possible Concomitant Problems
Leadership	Understanding of various leadership steps and practice in leadership skills	Lack of opportunity to use this ability constructively may result in its disappearance from child's repertoire or its being turned into a negative characteristic, e.g., gang leadership
Solutions to social and environmental problems	Meaningful involvement in real problems	Loss to society if these traits are not allowed to develop with guidance and opportunity for meaningful involvement
Involvement with the meta-needs of society (e.g., justice, beauty, truth)	Exploration of the highest levels of human thought; application of this knowledge to today's problems	

Source: Reprinted, by permission of the publisher, from Barbara Clark, *Growing up Gifted* (Columbus, Ohio: Charles E. Merrill Publishing Co., 1979), pp. 99.

More recently, Walberg, Tsai, Weinstein, Gabriel, Rasher, Rosencrans, Rovai, Ide, Trujillo, and Vukosavich (1981) studied the childhood traits and environmental conditions of more than two hundred eminent men. Applying different research techniques, they were able to identify a variety of distinct traits for the group as a whole and select subgroups (e.g., statesmen, generals, religious leaders, essayists, historians, poets). Moreover, they attempted to describe environmental conditions associated with eminence. Tables 12-7 and 12-8 portray many of the results of their intensive investigation. As a group, the trait of intelligence was the most distinctive characteristic. Some 97 percent of the individuals were rated as highly intelligent. The group as a whole also exhibited exceptional abilities in divergent and convergent thinking. As children, they appeared to have been inordinately gifted in communication skills. The majority of the sample evidenced a variety of positive affective traits (e.g., popular, sensitive, magnetic, ethical, optimistic). Some, about one-quarter to one-third of the sample, exhibited neuroses, introversion, and illness. Slightly more than one-third (38 percent) were rated as tall, and 62 percent were rated as handsome. The aforementioned traits and others identified by these investigators provide us with a truly unique look at the characteristics and possible origins of eminence.

Terman initiated the first longitudinal study of giftedness. His work and that of his colleagues dispelled many of the prevailing but erroneous beliefs regarding brilliant individuals. Researchers and theorists since Terman have helped us achieve a more comprehensive picture of the gifted and their characteristics. The performance and attributes of the gifted, as a group, are out-

TABLE 12-7/ Samples of Eminent and/or Intelligent Persons and Group Characteristics

381

The Gifted,
Creative, and
Talented:
Definitions and
Concepts

Group and Sample Names	IQ	Eminence Percentile	Group Higher On:	Group Lower On:
32 Statesmen				
Franklin, Benjamin	160	88	Persuasive, economic, firm, magnetic, optimistic, popular, handsome, tall, liked by siblings, successful in school, cultural media in field of eminence restricted to privileged classes	Made analogies, concentrated, introverted, neurotic, single-minded, absence of father, only child, school problems, cultural emphasis on immediate gratification, strong external incentives and support of work in field of eminence
Grotius, Hugo	197	62		
Jefferson, Thomas	160	89		
Lincoln, Abraham	147	91		
17 Generals				
Bolivar, Simon	145	54	Questioning, tall, vitality, strong external incentives and support in field of eminence	Made analogies, skill in writing, scholarly, handsome, encouragement of others, encouragement of teacher, exposed to many adults at an early age, presence of significant persons working in concert in field of eminence
Jackson, Thomas Jonathan	132	80		
Bonaparte, Napoleon	142	99		
Washington, George	135	93		
21 Religious Leaders				
Bossuet, Jacques B.	177	60	Concentrated, joy in work, scholarly, precocious, ethical, philosophical, religious, sensitive, encouragement of mother, encouragement of others, exposed to many adults at an early age, early exposure to eminent persons, strong external incentives and support for work in field of eminence	Versatile, impatient, permitted to explore, openness and receptivity to varied cultures and ideas
Calvin, John	165	92		
Luther, Martin	157	97		
Melanchthon, Philipp	180	68		
23 Essayists, Historians, Critics and Sociologists				
John, Samuel	165	87	Fluid, made analogies, persevering, intelligent, precocious, religious, sensitive, solid, challenging, absence of father, encouragement of mother, clear parental expectations of conduct, cultural stimuli or materials related to	Economic, empirical, and opportunistic
Macaulay, Thomas	180	57		
Rousseau, J.J.	150	91		
Sarpi, Paolo	187	10		

Table 12-7/ (Continued)

Group and Sample Names	IQ	Eminence Percentile	Group Higher On:	Group Lower On:
			field of eminence available, cultural emphasis on immediate gratification, strict social class structure with little mobility, openness and receptivity to varied cultures and ideas	
43 Poets, Novelists and Dramatists				
Goethe, J.W.	200	96	Concentrated, challenging, neurotic, absence of father, only child, liked school	Persuasive, questioning, persevering, scholarly, competent, empirical, intelligent, philosophical, religious, magnetic, optimistic, popular, handsome, tall, encouragement of mother, liked by siblings, permitted to explore, clear parental expectations of conduct, cultural stimuli or materials related to field of eminence available, revolutionary period in field of eminence, openness and receptivity to varied cultures and ideas
Leopardi, Giacoma	185	13		
Milton, John	167	88		
Voltaire, Arouet de	185	92		
21 Musicians				
Bach, J. Sebastian	152	77	Competent, opportunistic, single-minded, popular, encouragement of father, encouragement of teacher, cultural emphasis on immediate gratification	Questioning, skill in speaking, empirical, intelligent, precocious, ethical, solid optimistic, absence of father, absence of mother
Beethoven, Ludwig van	157	92		
Mendelssohn, Felix	162	56		
Mozart, W.A.	162	88		
18 Artists				
Dürer, Albrecht	150	86	Fluid, competent, empirical, ethical, wholesome, challenging, optimistic, popular, handsome, vitality, liked by siblings, revolutionary period in field of eminence, openness and receptivity to varied cultures and ideas, presence of significant people working	Sensitive, single-minded, successful in school, cultural media in field of eminence restricted to privileged classes
Buonarroti, Michelangelo	170	94		
Rubens, Peter Paul	155	87		
Vinci, Leonardo da	167	94		

Table 12-7/ (Continued)

Group and Sample Names	IQ	Eminence Percentile	Group Higher On:	Group Lower On:
			in concert in field of eminence, strong external incentives and support of work in field of eminence	
19 Philosophers				
Bacon, Francis	172	94	Questioning, empirical, intelligent, versatile, philosophical, challenging, clear parental expectations of conduct, permitted to explore	Concentrated, economic, religious, sensitive, opportunistic, popular, handsome, sickly, tall, vitality, encouragement of father, encouragement of mother, encouragement of teacher, only child, liked school, successful in school, cultural emphasis on immediate gratification, strong external incentives and support of work in field of eminence.
Descartes, René	175	93		
Leibnitz, Gottfried Wilhelm von	200	92		
Spinoza, Baruch	172	84		
22 Scientists				
Darwin, Charles R.	160	89	Opportunistic, single-minded, absence of mother	Fluid, sensitive, clear parental expectation of conduct
Haller, Albrecht	185	33		
Newton, Sir Isaac	170	92		
Pascal, Blaise	192	81		

Source: From Walberg et al., "Childhood Traits and Environmental Conditions of Highly Eminent Adults," *Gifted Child Quarterly,* 1981, *25*(3), 105-6. Reprinted by permission of the *Gifted Child Quarterly.*

TABLE 12-8/ Traits and Environmental Conditions of 221 Eminent Men

Traits		Environments	
Cognitive		*Family and Educational Conditions*	
Fluid	91	Absence of father	29
Made analogies	74	Asence of mother	22
Persuasive	75	Encouragement of father	60
Questioning	91	Encouragement of mother	55
Skill in speaking	79	Encouragement of others	78
Skill in writing	82	Encouragement of teacher	70
Concentrated	77	Exposed to many adults at an early stage	80
Joy in work	87	Early exposure to eminent people	60
Persevering	91	Firstborn	36
Scholarly	77	Only child	13
Competent	79	Liked by siblings	77
Economic	38	Clear parental expectations of conduct	70
Empirical	93	Permitted to explore	82
Intelligent	97	Liked school	67

Table 12-8/ (Continued)

Traits		Environments	
Precocious	79	School problems	23
Versatile	86	Successful in school	79
Affective and Physical		*Social and Cultural Conditions*	
Ethical	85	Cultural stimuli or materials relatd to field of	
Philosophical	73	eminence available	77
Religious	67	Cultural emphasis on immediate gratification	30
Sensitive	68	Revolutionary period in field of eminence	51
Solid	84	Strict social-class structure with little mobility	62
Wholesome	70	Cultural media in field of eminence restricted to	
Challenging	54	privilged classes	46
Impatient	44	Openness and receptivity to varied cultures and ideas	46
Introverted	36	Presence of significant people working in concert	
Neurotic	26	in field of eminence	57
Opportunistic	56	Strong external incentives and support of work	
Single-minded	60	in field of eminence	57
Firm	81		
Magnetic	64		
Optimistic	77		
Popular	73		
Handsome	62		
Sickly	29		
Tall	38		
Vitality	61		

Source: From Walberg et al., "Childhood Traits and Environmental Conditions of Highly Eminent Adults," *Gifted Child Quarterly*, 1981, *25*(3), 107. Reprinted by permission.

standing, but we must remember that gifted and creative individuals vary considerably in the degrees to which they manifest the various capacities, personality characteristics, and achievements described above.

ORIGINS OF GIFTEDNESS

Scientists have been interested in identifying the sources of intelligence for centuries. Conclusions have varied greatly. For years many scientists adhered to a hereditary explanation of intelligence—that people inherited their intellectual capacity at conception. Thus intelligence was viewed as an innate capacity that remained relatively fixed during an individual's lifetime. The prevailing belief then was that little could be done to enhance one's intellectual ability.

During the 1920s and 1930s, scientists such as John Watson (1924) began to explore such new notions as behavioral psychology or behaviorism. Like other behaviorists who followed him, Watson believed that the environment played an important role in the development of intelligence as well as in a variety of personality traits. Initially Watson largely discounted the role of heredity and its importance in intellectual development. Later, however, he moderated his views, moving somewhat toward a theoretical perspective, where both heredity and environment contributed to an individual's intellectual ability.

During the 1930s many investigators sought to determine the proportional influence of heredity and environment on intellectual development (Laycock, 1979). Some genetic proponents asserted that as much as 70 to 80 percent of an individual's capacity was determined by heredity, and the remainder by environmental influences. Environmentalists believed otherwise. They countered such percentages with research like that conducted by Skodak and Skeels (1949). These investigators studied the intellectual development of infants who had been removed from institutions for the retarded as opposed to those who were not removed. Their results indicated that retarded infants who had been removed from their institutional environments and placed in more homelike settings evidenced remarkably positive changes in IQ as measured by individual intelligence tests. This study was widely criticized at the time because of research design problems. Critics rightly claimed that the results were inconclusive. Despite the appropriateness of these criticisms, results of further investigation are interesting. Skeels (1966) conducted a follow-up study on the two groups of infants thirty years later. He found that the individuals who had been removed from institutional settings continued to exhibit higher intellectual functioning than the other group (in some cases, near average). The other group, whose members had been institutionalized or otherwise understimulated throughout their lives, continued to exhibit lower and generally subaverage intelligence. Again, conclusions regarding the importance of the environment on intellectual growth must be kept in proper perspective, because there were design weaknesses in the initial study.

The controversy regarding heredity and environmental influence on intelligence (known as the nature-nurture controversy) is likely to continue for some time. During the history of this argument, several important theories have emerged which have shaped the nature of the controversy substantially. One of those includes the work of Piaget (e.g., 1950; 1952). Piaget was keenly aware of the relationships between organisms and their environments because of his early training in biology. Consequently, he became interested in the ecology of cognitive growth as he conducted his studies of children's intellectual development. Piaget attempted to examine how environmental and biological or inherited aspects of a child's world interacted in producing changes in cognitive functioning (rather than viewing one to the exclusion of the other). Although Piaget was not interested in specifically giftedness, his findings influenced the thinking of many behavioral scientists who were interested in the development of exceptional intelligence. Piaget's work, as well as that of those who followed him, contributed significantly to a more refined and balanced view regarding the interaction between innate human potential and environmental experience.

Thus far we have focused our attention on the origins of intelligence rather than giftedness per se. Many of the theories regarding the emergence or essence of giftedness have been derived from the study of general intelligence. Few authors have focused directly on the origins of giftedness (e.g., Callahan, 1981; Eisenstadt, 1978; Eysenck, 1979; Feldman, 1979; Laycock, 1979; Pressey, 1964).

Moreover, the continual changing of definitions regarding giftedness have further complicated the precise investigation of its antecedents.

Recent research continues to provide varying answers in terms of the inheritability of high intellectual capacity, creativity, and other exceptional talents. After studying "extreme giftedness," Feldman (1979) concluded that precocity was a function of complex interactions between environment and genetic endowment.

Other researchers believe that as much as 70 percent of an individual's intelligence can be attributed to genetic factors (Eysenck, 1979). However, Freeman (1979) concluded that "little real evidence for genetic transmission of IQ has been found in the work carried out to date" (pp. 109–110). She reached this conclusion based largely on the work of McAskie and Clarke (1976), psychologists who undertook a comprehensive review of the literature pertaining to intelligence and its sources. They concluded that the present evidence regarding environmental and genetic determinants of intelligence is inconclusive and unclear.

Intellectually gifted students come from all ethnic groups and socioeconomic classes, although not in equal proportions. Vernon, Adamson, and Vernon (1977) noted that middle-class families seem to produce proportionately more gifted children than the other socioeconomic classes. Martinson (1961) studied a group of California children with an average IQ of 140. The results of this investigation indicated that 2 percent of the children came from lower-income families, 45 percent from middle-income families, and 40 percent from families where the parents had professional-managerial backgrounds. Similar results have been found in youngsters at the secondary school level (Havighurst, 1961). Some have attributed these differences to the advantaged environments in which some children are reared (Laycock, 1979). Others attribute such findings to biased identification procedures often employed in selecting gifted subjects. The evidence available does not provide us with a clear picture, and a certain amount of controversy remains.

The nature/nurture issue is also present in the literature pertaining to the origins of creativity. For example, Gowan, Khatena, and Torrance (1979), utilizing Gowan's (1972) work, defined creativity as "an emergent characteristic of the escalation of developmental process when the requisite degrees of mental ability and environmental stimulation are present" (p. 276). The latter part of this definition illustrates the nature/nurture interactionalist point of view, namely, creativity in children cannot emerge without the *requisite degrees of mental ability and environmental stimulation*. In this regard, Gowan et al. (1979) have identified three major theories regarding the origins of creativity. The first theory is directly related to mental ability as conceptualized by Guilford (1959) in his "structure of intellect" model. In particular, individuals endowed with unusually high levels of ability in the divergent production "slice" of Guilford's model have an excellent chance of becoming very creative. The second theory posits that creativity is an outcome of good mental health or progress toward self-actualization (full utilization of one's potential). The third theory is directly related to environmental aspects of an individual's upbringing. Individuals who are reared in democratic family environments that foster risk-taking, openness, and spontaneity are more likely to be creative as youths and adults. Another source of creativity may lie in the encouragement of imagery through experiences designed to stimulate the functions of the right hemisphere of the brain (Khatena, 1982). A variety of studies reinforce the view that the right hemisphere is associated with independently specialized functions that are related to problem-solving and other aspects of creative behavior (Gazzaniga & LeDoux, 1978; Rubenzer, 1979).

The research pertaining to the origins of exceptional talent is limited. This is in part a function of the imprecise definitions that have emerged regarding the nature of remarkable talents. Pressey (1955, 1964) believed that parents and educators could actually create exceptional levels of talent. He studied a variety of eminent musicians and unusually able athletes and concluded that the development of exceptional talent was a function of (1) early opportunities for talent development, (2) encouragement of talents by friends and peers, (3) consistent and continuous practice, (4) challenging instruction and superb guidance, (5) opportunities for close association with similarly talented individuals, (6) favorable occasions for performing and demonstrating one's emergent talent, and (7) provision for regular recognition for growth and achievement in the talent domain. These factors are similar to findings of Walberg et al. (1981), who studied the family, educational, social, and cultural conditions of 221 eminent men as children.

The precise origins of giftedness are yet to be determined. Current thinking favors an interaction of natural endowment and appropriate environmental stimulation. As Laycock stated, "Neither heredity nor environment alone is sufficient [as an explanation]" (1979, p. 153). In this regard, each child who is capable of becoming gifted should have the opportunity to do so. It is hoped that future researchers will enhance our abilities to provide this opportunity for all children, regardless of their ethnic group, social-class standing, or geographical location.

PREVALENCE OF GIFTEDNESS

Determining the number of children who are gifted is a challenging task. The complexity of the task is directly related to problems inherent in determining who the gifted are and what is involved in giftedness. As we know, giftedness has been defined in several ways. Some definitions are quite restrictive in terms of the number of children to which they apply, others are very inclusive and broad. Consequently, there is tremendous variability in prevalence estimates.

Prevalence figures prior to the 1950s were primarily related to the intellectually gifted. At that time 2 to 3 percent of the general population was considered to be gifted. During the 1950s a number of writers advocated an expanded view of giftedness (e.g., Conant, 1959; DeHann & Havighurst, 1957). Such work had a substantial effect on the prevalence figures suggested for program-planning. Terms such as *academically talented* were used to refer to the upper 15 to 20 percent of the general school population. As noted before, the work of Getzels and Jackson (1958) also fostered the idea that students other than those who were intellectually gifted should be identified under the general term *gifted*. Following this line of thinking, Taylor (1964) asserted that many very creative individuals were not necessarily intellectually gifted. Taylor's work and that of others interested in creativity led many to believe that the prevalence of giftedness was much greater than had been previously suggested.

Thus prevalence estimates have fluctuated depending on the views of researchers and professionals working during each of the various periods. Currently 3 to 5 percent of the students in the school population may be identified as gifted, according to the U.S. Office of Education (Marland, 1972). However, regulations governing the number of students that can be identified and served vary from state to state. Thomason (1981) recently reviewed gifted programs in the United States and indicated that many potentially gifted students still are unidentified and unserved. The gifted continue to be the exceptional population that is least likely to receive appropriate services and support in our educational systems (Zettel, 1980).

IDENTIFICATION OF GIFTEDNESS

Gifted students are identified in a variety of ways. The first step in the identification process is generally known as screening. During the screening phase, teachers, psychologists, and other school personnel attempt to select all students who may be potentially gifted. A number of procedures are employed in the screening process. Historically, information obtained from group intelligence tests and teacher nominations was used to select the initial pool of students. However, many other measures and data-collection techniques have been used since the perspective of giftedness changed from unidimensional to multidimensional. They may include achievement tests, creativity tests, motivation assessment, teacher nominations, and evaluation of student projects. We will briefly highlight some of the findings related to teacher nomination, intelligence tests, achievement tests, and assessment of creativity.

Teacher nominations have been an integral part of many screening approaches. At the time of the Marland (1972) report to the U.S. Congress, teacher nomination was the most frequently used technique for identifying gifted students. However, some research has led many to conclude that the teacher nomination approach is not an efficient or effective means for identifying the gifted (e.g., Jacobs, 1971; Pegnato & Birch, 1959; Pohl, 1970). Often teachers were given few if any specific criteria for nominating such students. Another problem was related to the restriction on the number of students they were allowed to nominate. Fortunately some of these problems have been addressed. There are now several scales to aid teachers and others responsible for making nominations (Borland, 1978; Renzulli, Smith, White, Callahan & Hartman, 1976).

Intelligence testing has and continues to be a major approach to identifying the gifted. Research related to intelligence assessment, however, reveals some interesting findings. Wallach (1976) analyzed a series of studies on the relationship between future professional achievement and scores obtained earlier on academic aptitude tests or intelligence tests. He found that performance scores in the upper ranges, particularly those frequently used to screen and identify gifted students, served as poor criteria for predicting future creative and productive achievement. Similar results have also been obtained in other studies (Holland & Astin, 1962; Munday & Davis, 1974).

389
The Gifted,
Creative, and
Talented:
Definitions and
Concepts

Other criticisms have been aimed at intelligence tests and their uses. We discussed some of these in the introductory materials presented earlier in this chapter. One of the major criticisms relates to the restrictiveness of such instruments. Many of the higher mental processes that characterize the functioning of gifted individuals are not adequately measured, and some are not assessed at all (Gallagher, 1975; Guilford, 1967). Another criticism involves the limitations inherent in using the typical achievement tests with culturally different individuals. As noted earlier, few of the instruments currently available are suitably designed to assess the abilities of those who are substantially different from the core culture.

Similar problems are inherent in achievement tests. For example, achievement tests are not generally designed to measure the true achievement of potentially gifted children. Such youngsters are often prevented from demonstrating their unusual prowess because of the restricted range of test items. These **ceiling effects,** as they are known, prevent the gifted from demonstrating their achievement at higher levels.

There remains a great deal of debate regarding creativity, its assessment, and its relationship to intelligence as measured by traditional IQ instruments. Hudson (1966) argued that one cannot separate creativity from "general" intelligence. Burt (1962) also believed that general intelligence is the undergirding force that makes creativity meaningful. The relationship between creativity and intelligence has yet to be fully clarified. Moreover, the use of creativity measures to identify those who are highly imaginative and innovative continues to be controversial (Crackenberg, 1972). Freeman (1979) claimed that the tests for creativity were fraught with problems of subjectivity and unreliability. She also contended that the concepts associated with creativity are so broad and variable in nature that they have no meaning. In contrast, Khatena (1982) affirms that "the measurement of creativity like other facets of intellectual functioning will always be a challenge. We can manage this problem by realizing that available measures have established certain parameters of measurable creativity found to be of great importance to school learning. We can take advantage of those instruments whose psychometric and practical soundness has been evidenced" (p. 23).

The second step in the evaluation process is the identification phase. During this phase, each of the previously screened students is carefully evaluated again using more individualized procedures and assessment tools. Ideally these techniques should be closely related to the definition used by the district or school system and the nature of the program envisioned for the students. In addition, such procedures should have adequate levels of validity and reliability as well as be suited for use with the individuals being assessed. Moreover, information from these tests should be used in accordance with the purposes for which each instrument was designed. For example, one would not want to assume that a child was intellectually gifted based on his or her performance on a test of creativity. Nor would one establish a youngster's level of academic achievement based on IQ test performance. Instruments that have been standardized and normed on one population should not be casually employed to evaluate other populations.

Tests should be employed for the purposes and on the populations for which they were designed and intended. Although this is self-evident, it is not always the case. Alvino, McDonnel, and Richert (1981) conducted a national survey of identification practices in gifted education in the United States. They reported a number of alarming but persistent trends and concluded:

> Apparently, the state of the art of identification of gifted and talented youth is in some disarray. It is common practice in the field to use test instruments in a manner which does not conform to what is intended and described in the published test manuals of those instruments. In many cases such use betrays an indiscriminate conflation of categories of the federal definition of giftedness; in other cases it reflects confusion, if not ignorance, concerning the diversity and distinctness of identifiably different sets of abilities. There is a flagrant use of tests/ instruments with populations on which they were not normed and for which they were never intended. Beyond the intellectual and academic categories there is a relative paucity of formal, not to mention validated, measures being used to identify gifted students.
>
> In many respects, the decade since the appearance of the Marland Report (1972), the first national study on the state of the art of gifted education, has not seen significant progress in correcting problems of identification cited in that report. Indeed, with the multipart federal definition the problems have become more complex and intensified. (P. 131)

Thus there still seems to be a tremendous need to educate practitioners who have responsibilities for screening and identifying the gifted. Moreover, additional research and development effort must be devoted to refining our assessment procedures and/or developing new ones. It is hoped that such efforts will provide techniques that will allow practitioners to identify the gifted more accurately and effectively, regardless of their cultural, economic, ethnic, or other distinguishing characteristics. For instance, headway is now being made with regard to identifying the gifted who are disabled or impaired in some fashion (Ford & Ford, 1981; Whitmore, 1981). Only through such efforts will we be able to observe progress in working with the gifted.

SUMMARY

A variety of definitions of giftedness have been set forth over the years. Many are very restrictive in terms of their criteria and consequently in the number of individuals they identify. Others are very open or broad-based in that they provide multidimensional criteria and apply to greater numbers of individuals. The expanded definitions have provided some challenging problems for practitioners who are responsible for identifying and educating the gifted. Progress has been evident in attempts to operationalize definitions, identification instruments, and procedures. However, a great deal remains to be accomplished.

REVIEW QUESTIONS

1. Why were the terms *creative* and *talented* added as descriptors to the gifted population?
2. How did Guilford's conception of intelligence differ from earlier perspectives?
3. How does Renzulli's definition of giftedness differ from other perspectives?
4. Desribe how research problems have presented difficulties in accurately identifying the characteristics of the gifted.
5. Describe how views regarding the origins of giftedness have changed over the years.
6. How does one proceed with respect to identifying the gifted?

CHAPTER THIRTEEN

The Gifted, Creative, and Talented: Intervention Strategies

Intervention strategies with the gifted, creative, and talented have received little attention compared to programs for other exceptional populations. Because the unusually able may develop a tremendous capacity for learning, thinking, and solving problems, such individuals are valuable to a society that badly needs resources for problem-solving. There are many ways in which such talent may be promoted.

Joseph's high school grades indicate below-average achievement. He does not seem to be motivated to achieve at all. However, Joseph has an unusual number of interests and hobbies and makes unique contributions to classroom discussions. In outside activities he frequently emerges as a leader among his peers. It is obvious by his class contributions that he possesses a fund of knowledge which he is always willing to share. He expects to go to college, but writes extremely poorly. His teachers can't seem to convince him of the relationship between his high school achievement and his admission to college. It appears that although Joseph has excellent intellectual and creative potential, he is not likely to be admitted to college.

Mary is unusually artistic. Her paintings have been judged excellent by art teachers since elementary school. She contributes artwork to school newspapers and other publications, but she refuses to enter her work in art contests. She is not interested in pursuing an art-related education or career after high school because she thinks "My stuff isn't that good."

Marge is a uniquely creative and intellectually talented young lady. Her IQ is in the 150 range. Her poetry is mature and perceptive and has been accepted for publication in several English journals. Her grades are almost all A's though she puts forth little effort. She is very pretty and appears very independent. Since tenth grade her parents (upper middle class and very strict) have found her unmanageable. She drinks excessively and appears to be involved with several young men. She is presently a senior in high school but has no intention of going on to college. . . . Her only goal is to get married.

Elizabeth is a shy fifth-grader. She has a high IQ and is a good student. Although her teacher finds her to be a delightful child, Elizabeth tells her mother that she really hates school. Upon further questioning, she shows her mother a secret drawer stuffed full of stories she has written. She shows her mom her favorite one, which has just been returned from her teacher. Written across the top of the page is the following: "Elizabeth, you have copied this story from a book and that is dishonest. Be sure never to do that again." Elizabeth has been sick frequently and indicates that she likes staying in bed until she is "completely better."

David is a very active third-grader. His schoolwork is frequently not completed and his handwriting is illegible. Kids like David, but teachers don't. His main problem seems to be his outspoken sense of humor. His jokes and comments, which always send the class into hysterics, usually appear at the most inappropriate times—during lessons, when guests are in the room, or in the middle of a serious class discussion. David seems to be a capable child, but his school activities are domi-

395

The Gifted,
Creative, and
Talented:
Intervention
Strategies

*nated by practical jokes, humorous remarks, and poorly done assign-
ments. Parents and teachers are searching for a way to get David
motivated to apply himself to schoolwork.*

*Bobby is a second-grader who is an excellent reader. His reading skills
and interests far exceed those of his classmates. He has a high energy
level and a vivid imagination. He easily becomes impatient with
school routines. He finds mathematics boring and incomprehensible.
During math class, Bobby has been observed to covertly read a book
instead of listening to his math lesson. He does not hear many of his
assignments and failures in math seem not to disturb him. His parents
and teachers, however, are concerned about his "non-balanced" education.* (Davis & Rimm, 1979) pp. 227-28.*

The preceding vignettes typify some of the problems gifted children and youths
have. In some instances, the problems are family related. In other instances,
the school environment is causing the problems, and of course many of the
problems are caused by both family and school factors. Can some of these
problems be resolved with appropriate interventions or specialized programs?
What can parents do to aid their gifted children? What types of school programs
are available for students? Are they effective? Are they deleterious to students
socially or emotionally? Does specialized programming for the gifted make a
difference?

Gifted children may develop a tremendous capacity for learning, thinking,
performing, and producing. They have the potential for outstanding achievement. What makes this possible? Based on information related in the preceding
chapter, we know that there may be several answers to this question. We side
with the interactionalists, who believe that both factors of the gifted equation
are extremely important. Inherited capacity, strengthened by ongoing environmental experience and encouragement, provides the basis for the emergence
of giftedness. The encouragement and stimulation optimally begins in the home
prior to the child's entry into preschool or public school activities. Once the
child has entered the formal school years, the responsibility for providing
appropriate environmental conditions is jointly shared by family, school personnel, and community.

EARLY INTERVENTIONS FOR THE GIFTED

Identifying Young Gifted Children

The first obligation of parents and other care providers is to be aware of the behaviors that may signal giftedness in their child or children. Given the heter-

---

**Source:* Reprinted, by permission, from G. A. Davis and S. Rimm, "Identification and Counsel-
ing of the Creatively Gifted," in N. Colangelo and R. T. Zaffrann, eds., *New Voices in Counseling the Gifted* (Dubuque, Iowa: Kendall Hunt Publishing Company, 1979).

Early environ-
mental experi-
ences may
provide the
basis for the
emergence of
giftedness.

ogeneous nature of the gifted, this can be a challenging task. There are vast differences in the ways gifted children develop. Some may read, walk, and talk quite early, while others may be slow in development in these areas. Aspects of giftedness may emerge early in a child's development or later on as the child matures. Consequently, the identification process is ongoing and continuous throughout a youth's developmental growth years.

Rimm, Davis, and Bien (1982) previewed elements of a preschool screening instrument, the "PRIDE Preschool Interest Descriptor." This instrument was developed to help parents and teachers identify potentially gifted preschoolers and kindergarten students (see Table 13-1). The parent inventory items were developed using the characteristics generated from studies of creative preschool and gifted children. Although the scale has not been validated, the items identified in Table 13-1 give us an idea of what behaviors parents might be looking for in a potentially gifted child.

Hall and Skinner (1980) have also developed some interesting assessment approaches for parents interested in evaluating their children. They include a series of "developmental guidelines" related to general motor ability, fine motor ability, and cognitive language (see Table 13-2). Parents are encouraged to use these guidelines carefully in assessing their child's development. "For example, if an average child sits up alone at seven months, a child '30 percent more advanced' would do so 2.10 months earlier (7 months × .30 = 2.10 months) or at 4.9 months of age (7 months − 2.1 months = 4.9 months)" (Hall & Skinner, 1980, p. 2). They suggest that a child who meets or exceeds most of the "30

TABLE 13-1/ Sample Items from PRIDE Preschool Interest Descriptor

Item	Trait
My child gets interested in things for a long time.	Wide interests, task commitment
My child has a make-believe friend.	Imagination
My child likes to make up jokes.	Sense of humor
*My child usually does whatever other children do.	Independence
My child seems to do things differently from other children.	Independence
My child likes to take things apart to see how they work.	Curiosity
My child is quite reflective, rather than impulsive.	Reflectiveness
My child often does two things at the same time that aren't usually done together.	Unusual interests, attraction to complexity
My child can do some things that seem very difficult.	Attraction to complexity
My child likes to take walks alone.	Independence
I enjoy make-believe play with my child.	Biographical
My child has many interests.	Wide interests

* Negatively related to creativity.
Source: From S. Rimm, G. A. Davis, and Y. Bien, "Identifying Creativity: A Characteristics Approach," *Gifted Child Quarterly,* 1982, *26*(4), 165–71. Reprinted by permission of the *Gifted Child Quarterly.*

TABLE 13-2/ Hall & Skinner's Developmental Guidelines for Assessing a Child's Development

	Normal Months	30% More Advanced
General Motor Ability		
Lifts chin up when lying stomach down	1	0.7
Holds up both head and chest	2	1.4
Rolls over	3	2.1
Sits up with support	4	2.8
Sits alone	7	4.9
Stands with help	8	5.6
Stands holding on	9	6.3
Creeps	11	7.7
Stands alone well	11	7.7
Walks alone	12.5	8.75
Walks, creeping is discarded	15	10.5
Creeps up stairs	15	10.5
Walks up stairs	18	12.6
Seats self in chair	18	12.6
Turns pages of book	18	12.6
Walks down stairs one hand held	21	14.7
Walks up stairs holds rail	21	14.7
Runs well, no falling	24	16.8
Walks up and down stairs alone	24	16.8
Walks on tiptoe	30	21.0
Jumps with both feet	30	21.0
Alternates feet when walking up stairs	36	25.2
Fine Motor Ability		
Grasps handle of spoon but lets go quickly	1	0.7
Vertical eye coordination	1	0.7
Plays with rattle	3	2.1

Table 13-2 (Continued)

	Normal Months	30% More Advanced
Manipulates a ball, is interested in detail	6	4.2
Pulls string adaptively	7	4.9
Shows hand preference	8	5.6
Holds objects between fingers and thumb	9	6.3
Holds crayon adaptively	11	7.7
Pushes car alone	11	7.7
Scribbles spontaneously	13	9.1
Drawing imitates stroke	15	10.5
Folds paper once imitatively	21	14.7
Drawing imitates V stroke and circular stroke	24	16.8
Imitates V and H strokes	30	21.0
Imitates bridge with blocks	36	25.2
Draws person with two parts	48	33.6
Draws unmistakable person with body	60	42.0
Copies triangle	60	42.0
Draws person with neck, hands, clothes	72	50.4
Cognitive Language		
Social smile at people	1.5	1.05
Vocalizes four times or more	1.6	1.12
Visually recognizes mother	2	1.4
Searches with eyes for sound	2.2	1.54
Vocalizes two different sounds	2.3	1.61
Vocalizes four different syllables	7	4.9
Says "da-da" or equivalent	7.9	5.53
Responds to name, no-no	9	6.3
Looks at pictures in book	10	7.0
Jabbers expressively	12	8.4
Imitates words	12.5	8.75
Has speaking vocabulary of three words (other than ma-ma and da-da)	14	9.8
Has vocabulary of 4-6 words including names	15	10.5
Points to one named body part	17	11.9
Names one object (What is this?)	17.8	12.46
Follows direction to put object in chair	17.8	12.46
Has vocabulary of 10 words	18	12.6
Has vocabulary of 20 words	21	14.7
Combines two or three words spontaneously	21	14.7
Jargon is discarded, 3 word sentences	24	16.8
Uses I, me, you	24	16.8
Names three or more objects on a picture	24	16.8
Is able to identify 5 or more objects	24	16.8
Gives full name	30	21.0
Names 5 objects on a picture	30	21.0
Identifies 7 objects	30	21.0
Is able to tell what various objects are used for	30	21.0
Counts (enumerates) objects to three	36	25.2
Identifies the sexes	36	25.2

Source: Reprinted, by permission of the publisher, from Eleanor G. Hall and Nancy Skinner, *Somewhere to Turn: Strategies for Parents of the Gifted and Talented* (New York: Teachers College Press, © 1980 by Teachers College, Columbia University. All rights reserved), pp. 2–4.

percent more advanced" criteria in any one area may be gifted or talented. The other approach recommended by Hall and Skinner is that of keeping a journal in which parents record specific features of the child's development (e.g. "At 12 months and 15 days, Amy was able to follow the direction "Put the little horse on the chair, please"). A variety of assessment techniques can be utilized by parents and teachers in identifying the gifted. The more sophisticated and standardized types of measures (IQ tests, infant assessment scales) are generally used by trained preschool personnel as they become involved in the identification process.

Careful observation of parents and teachers provides the basis for the types of interventions employed in fostering the development of young gifted children. Through these observations the interests, potential talents, present strengths, and weaknesses of each child are identified. Steps are then taken to create a home or school environment sensitive to each child's distinguishing characteristics. Clark (1979) has referred to this environment as the "responsive" environment. It is responsive in the sense that it is designed to react in a positive fashion to the gifted child's interests, questions, and needs for meaningful learning activities. An essential component of the responsive environment is the parent and/or teacher. They are responsible for preparing the environment so that it is rich with attractive learning materials, "hands on" or manipulative experiences, explorative activities, language adventures, and social interactions. In addition, they are responsible for establishing an atmosphere of inquiry in which children are encouraged to ask questions and seek solutions to problems that are of interest to them.

Parent Interventions

Parents can promote the early learning and development of their gifted children in a number of ways. During the first eighteen months of life, 90 percent of all social interactions with children take place during such activities as feeding, bathing, changing diapers, and dressing (Clark, 1979). Parents who are interested in advancing their child's mental and social development will use these occasions for talking to their children, providing varied sensory experiences (e.g., bare-skin cuddling, tickling), smiling, and conveying a sense of trust. As gifted children gradually progress through their infancy, toddler, and preschool periods, the experiences provided become more varied and uniquely suited to their emerging interests. Language and cognitive development are encouraged by means of stories read and told to them. They are also urged to make up their own stories for telling. Brief periods are also reserved for discussions or spontaneous conversations that may arise from events that have momentarily captured their attention. Requests for help in saying or printing a word are promptly fulfilled. Thus many gifted children learn to read before they enter kindergarten or first grade.

During the school years, parents continue to advance their children's development by providing opportunities that correspond to the children's strengths and interests. The simple identification games that were played during the preschool period now become more complex. Discussions more frequently take place with peers and other interesting adults rather than parents. The nature of the discussions and the types of questions asked become more sophisticated. Parents assist their children in moving to higher levels of learning by asking questions that involve analysis (comparing and contrasting ideas), synthesis (integrating and combining ideas into new and novel forms), and evaluation (judging and disputing books, newspaper articles, etc.). Other ways in which parents can be helpful include (1) furnishing books and reading materials on a broad range of topics; (2) providing appropriate equipment as various interests surface (microscopes, telescopes, chemistry sets, etc.); (3) encouraging regular trips to the public library and other learning-resource centers; (4) providing opportunities for participation in cultural events, lectures, and exhibits of various kinds; (5) encouraging participation in extracurricular and community activities outside the home; and (6) fostering relationships with potential mentors and other resource people in the community.

Preschool Interventions

A variety of preschool programs have been developed for gifted children (Roedell, Jackson & Robinson, 1980). Some children are involved in traditional programs, which are characterized by activities and curricula that are devoted primarily to the development of academic skills. Many of the traditional programs emphasize affective and social development as well. The entry criteria for these programs is varied, but the primary consideration is usually the child's IQ and social maturity. Moreover, the child must be skilled in following directions, attending to tasks of some duration, and controlling impulsive behavior.

Creativity programs are designed to help children develop their natural endowments in a number of artistic or creative domains. Another purpose of such programs is to help the children discover their personal areas of promise. Children in these programs are also prepared for eventual involvement in the traditional academic areas of schooling.

Gifted and talented preschoolers with disabilities are now served in several programs in the United States (Karnes, 1978, 1979; Blacher-Dixon, 1977; Blacher-Dixon & Turnbull, 1979). Each program pursues the education and development process in varied ways. Some programs use Bloom's (1969) *Taxonomy of Education Objectives,* while others employ Guilford's (1956) "structure of intellect model" as the basis for advancing the children's thinking processes. Individualization is a key component in the entire process and is mandated by recent federal legislation (P.L. 94-142). Programs also vary according to the amount of structure present in the preschool environment. The RAPYHT Program (Retrieval and Acceleration of Promising Young Handicapped and Talented) provides children with open-classroom as well as structured-classroom experiences. The open-classroom experiences provide children with opportunities to initiate their own learning activities. They also select the pace at which they will accomplish their goals. Teachers in this classroom environment serve as facilitators. In contrast, the structured classroom is teacher directed. Learning activities are selected by the teacher, and the sequence of learning experiences is tightly structured (Karnes & Berschi, 1978).

Evaluating Preschool Programs for the Young Gifted

The evaluation of preschool programs for the gifted is fraught with two major difficulties (Roedell, Jackson & Robinson, 1980).

> The first problem lies in the difficulty of showing a positive change for children whose pretest scores are already far above the mean of the rest of the population. IQ gains, for example, can hardly be expected from a group of children whose mean IQ is already at the 99th percentile. Evaluation of academic achievement poses the same problem with the added difficulty that academic achievement tests normed for preschool-aged children do not allow them to demonstrate academic skills of which they are capable. The second problem is a more philosophical one, when children score below average levels on tests of intelligence or academic skill, the obvious goal of a program is to raise their scores toward the mean of the general population. When children score far above the mean, however, the program goal is less clear. How much improvement in areas such as academic skill should be expected of children who are already advanced? (P. 76)

Another factor that complicates the evaluation of programs for the young gifted is the paucity of data regarding the development and achievement of gifted young children who are not enrolled in special programs. Without these types of data, evaluators are unable to make any comparative statements regarding the overall effectiveness of present preschool interventions and programs for the young gifted. The same is true of programs for the gifted disabled.

Another issue tied closely to preschool education for the gifted is that of early school entrance. Should gifted children who are of preschool age and are ready and prepared for kindergarten and first-grade learning experiences be permitted to enroll early? Braga (1969; 1971) evaluated the progress and performance of three types of school entrants. The first group was composed of mentally able children who were admitted early. The second group was comprised of randomly selected, average children who were admitted at the normal time of entrance. The last group consisted of normal entrants who had IQs similar to those of the early entrants but who were approximately one year older chronologically. These groups were evaluated in grades one, three, or seven. No significant differences were found among the entrant groups on achievement tests, parent and teacher surveys, teacher ratings of classroom behaviors (work habits, motivation, etc.), or other school records. Studies completed since Braga's with similar populations reinforce his findings (Gallagher, 1975; Getzels & Dillon, 1973).

Intervention Programs for Elementary and Secondary Students

Giftedness in elementary and secondary students may be nurtured in a variety of ways. Various service-delivery systems and approaches have been employed in responding to the needs of the gifted. Frequently the nurturing process has been referred to as **differentiated education,** that is, an education uniquely and predominately suited to the capacities and interests of gifted individuals.

Selection of intervention approaches and organizational structures occurs as a function of variety of factors. First, a school system must determine what types of giftedness it is capable of serving. In this regard, it must also select identification criteria and measures that will allow it to fairly select qualified students. If the system is primarily interested in advancing creativity, measures and indices of creativity should be utilized. If the focus of the program is devoted to accelerating math achievement and understanding, instruments measuring mathematical aptitude and achievement should be employed. With regard to identifying giftedness in the culturally different, progress in instrumentation and measurement development has been made (Khatena, 1982). A variety of formal and informal approaches have been developed that allow practitioners to measure potential giftedness in the culturally divergent (Meeker, 1978; Mercer & Lewis, 1978; Taylor & Ellison, 1966; Torrance, 1971; 1977).

Second, the school system must select the organizational structures through which the gifted will receive their differentiated education. Third, the school personnel must select the intervention approaches that will be utilized within each program setting to foster the development of the gifted students who will be selected. Fourth, the school personnel and clientele must select evaluation procedures and techniques that will help them assess the overall effectiveness of the program. Data generated from the program evaluation efforts will serve as a catalyst for appropriate changes and maintenance activities.

Service Delivery Systems

Once the types of giftedness to be emphasized have been selected and appropriate identification procedures have been selected, planning must be directed at selecting suitable service delivery systems. Organizational structures for the gifted are similar to those found in other areas of special education. Clark (1979) has identified a "continuum model" that has been employed in developing services for the gifted (see Figure 13-1). Each of the learning environments in the model has its inherent advantages and disadvantages, as Clark indicated:

> *Regular classroom and regular classroom with cluster.* Not adequate for gifted education. These classrooms rely on instruction and a set curriculum. The instruction is by subject, with similar experiences for everyone.
>
> *Regular classroom with pullout.* Advantages: Gifted students may have an opportunity to work at their level of ability and in their area of interest and to interact with other gifted students for at least part of their

Figure 13-1/ Clark's Continuum Model for Ability Grouping

403

The Gifted,
Creative, and
Talented:
Intervention
Strategies

├─ **Regular classroom**

├─ **Regular class with cluster**

├─ **Regular class with pullout**

├─ **Regular class with cluster and pullout**

├─ **Individualized classroom**

├─ **Individualized classroom with cluster**

├─ **Individualized classroom with pullout**

├─ **Individualized classroom with cluster and pullout**

├─ **Special class with some integrated classes**

├─ **Special class**

└─ **Special school**

Source: Barbara Clark, *Growing up Gifted* (Columbus, Ohio: Charles E. Merrill Publishing Co., 1979), pp. 140-142.

school time. Upon leaving the regular program, the student may experience a seminar, a resource room, a special class, a field trip, or other unique learning situations. *Disadvantages:* The major part of the school week is still not an appropriate learning experience. Often gifted students are asked to do the regular classroom work missed when pulled out, in addition to the special class work. Also, the special class has little time for meeting all of the gifted needs; teachers may resent interruption of their program; other students in the regular classroom may envy and isolate the gifted child because of the special class. Teachers in pullout programs must establish good working relations with the regular class teachers if this plan is to benefit the gifted learner.

Regular classroom with cluster and pullout. The same advantages and disadvantages as above except for the additional advantage of having the possibility for more interaction with gifted peers and better follow-through with the gifted program. The quality of this program will depend on the pullout teacher and class.

Individualized classrooms Make use of individual, team, and flexible small group instruction. Assessments are used to determine the curriculum and materials for each student. The classroom is decentralized and gives access to many types of learning. In most cases such classes are ungraded, with students from several age levels.

Advantages: In this setting, gifted students are more likely to work at their own level and pace. The learning experience is continuous. *Disadvantages:* If there are only one or two gifted students, they may feel isolated and have no one with whom to share ideas. This type of classroom requires a highly competent teacher or it can become unstructured or only partially individualized. The teacher may not have enough resources available to keep up with a gifted learner and thirty-five others.

Individualized classrooms with cluster Same advantages and disadvantages as above without the disadvantage of the isolation of being the only gifted learner.

Individualized classrooms with cluster and pullout Same advantages as above with the additional advantage of more resources available to both the gifted learner and the teacher. In this situation, the problems created by the pullout program in number 2 will not be evidenced. If all students are valued and allowed to meet their needs, no one will feel that they must do what every other person does. The gifted can meet their needs without envy from others. Such a program has continuity and allows each student's needs to be met through the week.

Special class with some integrated classes Especially appropriate to intermediate and secondary schools that are organized by subject. *Advantages:* Programs and environments can be designed to meet gifted needs. By moving into integrated (gifted and nongifted) classes for subjects that stress talent rather than giftedness, the students can learn to appreciate other students for their abilities. The mildly and moderately gifted would find this helpful.

An example of this type of structure for meeting the needs of gifted students at the secondary level is the Teacher/Advisor model. Students are allowed to ask any faculty member to serve as their gifted advisor. They then sign up for one period of gifted program time and arrange with their advisor how this period will be used. This is a highly individualized model wherein the gifted students may do directed independent study, cooperatively design seminars with their advisor conducted by either the student or the advisor, and/or take regular classes. Having a small area set aside as a gifted center helps to make this a socially, as well as academically, successful modification. Teacher acceptance of this plan is unusually high, and it provides for a wide choice of curriculum.

Classes on college and university campuses are used successfully by many secondary schools. The assessment for such placement is the responsibility of the school district where the student is enrolled. This is frequently overlooked in programs that have limited offerings. Not all gifted students can benefit by attendance in such classes. Such a provision should not constitute the entire gifted program at the secondary level for all gifted students in that district. Placing students in advanced classes should be only part of a secondary gifted program.

Disadvantages: Such a class requires a specially trained teacher, or it can be just as inhibiting as no program. Often these classes are different only in the population attending them and in the added quantity of assignments. It is important to individualize in this setting, for the gifted are quite different from each other. Although gifted students are not highly advanced in every discipline, many secondary schools use tracking across all areas.

One often used practice that needs to be examined is the establishment of one or two advanced classes into which all gifted students are tracked regardless of their needs and abilities. Many high schools use special mathematics or science classes for this purpose. Such classes comprise the entire gifted program and, if students do not do well in mathematics or science, their identification as gifted comes under suspicion. We must offer the widest range of qualitatively different experiences we can devise, for this population is the most diverse in ability.

Special class.   Has the advantages and disadvantages of number 7 without the involvement with other groups that may be talented in other areas. This special class is most appropriate for the highly gifted.

Special schools.   Used most often for highly gifted or talented students, this plan has the advantages and disadvantages of numbers 7 and 8 in more intensified form.* (Clark, 1979, pp. 140-42)

Gifted students as well as their parents and teachers prefer organizational structures that are flexible and not totally segregated (Marland, 1972). Specialized grouping does not in itself account for the significant academic achievement results between grouped and ungrouped students (Findley & Bryan, 1971). Exceptional achievement in gifted students is, however, positively correlated with the amount of time they spend in special seminars or classes. Special classes also tend to provide very able students with greater opportunities for in-depth involvement with a content or topical area, the free exchange of ideas with comparable gifted peers, and acceleration that would not be possible in the normal class environment. Another outcome of specialized grouping is that of enhanced self-esteem. Many gifted students experience growth in this important personality dimension as a result of their association and instruction with bright peers.

Other similar service-delivery systems have been identified. Kaplan (1975) referred to her systems as the "intra-classroom" approach and the "extra-classroom" approach. The effectiveness of the first approach relies heavily on the

Table13-3/ Kaplan's Intra-classroom Approach to Service Delivery for the Gifted

1. Cluster grouping (gifted students temporarily grouped within grades or departments)
2. Supplemental activities brought to the classroom (e.g., community speakers)
3. Independent study (with the regular classroom)
4. Gifted students as tutors
5. Tutors for the gifted
6. Ungraded classes
7. Correspondence courses
8. Teacher provisions (teachers with specialties share their expertise)

Source: Reprinted, by permission of the publisher, from Harry J. Morgan, Carolyn G. Tennant, and Milton J. Gold, *Elementary and Secondary Level Programs for the Gifted and Talented* (New York: Teachers College Press, © 1980 by Teachers College, Columbia University. All rights reserved), p. 16.

* Reprinted, by permission of the publisher, from Barbara Clark, *Growing up Gifted* (Columbus, Ohio: Charles E. Merrill Publishing Co., 1979).

Table 13-4/ Kaplan's Extra-Classroom Approach to Service Delivery for the Gifted

1. Special interest groups (before, during, and after school)
2. Seminars
3. Mentorship programs
4. Community resources
5. Internship programs
6. Special classes (e.g., advanced placement, honors, special day classes)
7. Resource centers
8. Outside independent study
9. Off-campus enrollment

Source: Reprinted, by permission of the publisher, from Harry J. Morgan, Carolyn G. Tennant, and Milton J. Gold, *Elementary and Secondary Level Programs for the Gifted and Talented.* (New York: Teachers College Press, © 1980 by Teachers College, Columbia University. All rights reserved), p. 17.

skills of the regular classroom teacher. The latter approach is dependent on the quality of resources found within the community. The attendant advantages and disadvantages of each of these approaches are comparable to those identified earlier by Clark relative to her continuum.

The selection of the service-delivery systems is a function of the available financing and human resources (trained personnel, gifted specialists, mentors, etc.), as well as local community values and conditions. Optimally the delivery systems should facilitate the achievement of the program goals. Furthermore, the selection of delivery systems should interface well with the types of giftedness being nurtured.

DIFFERENTIAL EDUCATIONAL
APPROACHES FOR THE GIFTED

Traditionally, programs for the gifted have emphasized practices associated with acceleration and enrichment. **Acceleration** is a process whereby students are allowed to achieve at a rate consonant with their capacity. Acceleration approaches provide for one or many of the following options: grade-skipping, telescoped programs, rapid progress through subject matter, and early entry to college or advanced placement. Grade-skipping used to be a common administrative practice in providing for the needs of gifted learners, but it takes place much less frequently now (Solano & George, 1976). The decline in this practice is attributed to the convictions of some individuals that acceleration of this nature may heighten a gifted student's likelihood of becoming socially maladjusted. Others believe that accelerated students would experience significant gaps in their learning because of grade-skipping. Acceleration is generally limited to two years in the typical elementary school program.

Another practice related to grade-skipping is telescoped or condensed schooling, which makes it possible for students to progress through the content of several grades in a significantly reduced time span. An allied practice is that of allowing students to progress rapidly through a particular course or content offering. Acceleration of this nature provides students with the sequential basic learning that is so important at a pace commensurate with their ability. School programs that are ungraded in their orientation are particularly suitable for telescoping activities. Because of their very nature, students regardless of their chronological ages may progress through a learning or curriculum sequence that is not constricted by artificial grade boundaries.

Other forms of condensed programming occur at the high school level. They may include earning credit by examination, enrolling in extra courses for early graduation, reducing or eliminating certain coursework, enrolling in intensive summer programs, and completing university requirements while taking approved high school courses. Many of these options make it possible for students to enter college early or to begin their bachelor's programs with advanced students. According to Solano & George (1976), many gifted students are ready for college-level coursework at age fourteen, fifteen, or sixteen. Some unusually gifted students are prepared for college-level experiences prior to age fourteen.

Research relative to acceleration and its impact on gifted students suggests that carefully selected gifted students profit greatly from such experiences (Braga, 1969; Pressy 1949; Reynolds, 1962; Stanley, 1977; Terman & Oden, 1959). The major outcome of accelerated educational experiences is outstanding academic achievement. Whether acceleration actually fosters eventual high professional productivity is yet to be determined.

Enrichment can be thought of as experiences that extend or broaden a person's knowledge in a vertical or horizontal fashion (Newland, 1976). Horizontal enrichment refers to courses of study (e.g., music appreciation, foreign language instruction, mythology) that are added to a student's curriculum. These courses are usually not any more difficult than other classes in which the student is involved. By contrast, vertical enrichment involves experiences in which the student develops sophisticated thinking skills (synthesis, analysis interpretation, evaluation) or opportunities to develop and master advanced concepts in a subject area. Some forms of enrichment are actually types of acceleration. A student whose enrichment involves having an opportunity to fully pursue mathematical concepts that are well beyond his present grade level is experiencing a form of acceleration. Obviously the two approaches are interrelated.

The enrichment approach is the most common administrative provision utilized in serving the gifted. It is also the most abused approach in that it is often applied in name only and in a sporadic fashion without well-delineated objectives or rationale. There are also other problems. The enrichment approach is the least expensive service-delivery system option; consequently it is often utilized by school systems in a superficial fashion as a token response to the demands of parents of gifted children. Many enrichment activities are viewed by some professionals as periods devoted to educational trivia or instruction that is heavy in student assignments but light in content (Copley, 1961; Gallagher, 1975). Quality enrichment programs are characterized by well-trained teaching personnel; exciting and engaging content; well-sequenced learning activities, modules, or units; challenging but not overwhelming assignments; and evaluations that are rigorous and yet fair.

There is a paucity of systematic experimental research regarding enrichment programs for gifted students. Despite many of the limitations of current and past research, there is some evidence that supports the effectiveness of enrichment approaches (Callahan, 1981). Long-term experimental research addressing the effectiveness of enrichment programs is, however, particularly sparse. Cross (1975), in a follow-up study of very able students, found no differences in measures of financial accomplishments and educational attainment between gifted students who had and had not been enrolled in enrichment programs. Nonexperimental evaluations of enrichment programs indicate that gifted students, teachers, and parents are generally satisfied with the nature and content of enrichment programs. Enrichment activities do not appear to detract from the success gifted students experience on regularly administered achievement tests. Sociometric data regarding the gifted who are pulled out of their regular classrooms for enrichment activities are also positive. Gifted students do not appear to suffer socially from their involvement in enrichment programs that take place outside normal classrooms.

Enrichment models have been developed to respond to the learning needs of gifted students. Creators of these models have described a variety of approaches that can be utilized in promoting the development of the gifted (Renzulli, 1977; Taylor, 1967; Williams, 1970). For example, Renzulli's (1977) "enrichment triad model" is composed of three types of activities (see Figure 13-2). Type I, "general exploratory activities," encompasses a broad range of learning activities that encourage students to explore various disciplines, their structure, and their methods of inquiry. Explorations in the Type I domain provide the foundations for "individual and small group investigations of real problems" (Type III). The selection of problems for study occurs only after students have had ample opportunity to explore a number of topics and content areas. The "group training activities" (Type II) include experiences in problem-solving, critical thinking, predictive thinking, and other cognitive skills. All these training experiences are provided in context with the ongoing Type I exploratory ventures. These ventures for the most part have been chosen by students themselves. Through a series of various discussions and interest inventories, they select areas of interest and investigation. Because the Type I probes and ventures evolve from the student's interests, motivation is generally high.

Type III enrichment activities emphasize the production of knowledge and information rather than the mastering of information already available. Type II activities are designed to give students opportunities to work on real problems and generate or produce solutions or information that cannot be derived by the usual means of inquiry and thought. According to Renzulli, gifted learners evidence their unique abilities in Type III learning activities by being (1) producers rather than consumers of knowledge (2) investigators rather than reporters of phenomena, and (3) creators rather than reproducers of products. Gifted learners also exhibit a remarkable degree of persistence and commitment in solving the problems they have selected for inquiry.

The three types of learning activities, Type I, Type II, and Type III, complement, supplement, and interact with one another. The model is not restricted

409

The Gifted,
Creative, and
Talented:
Intervention
Strategies

Figure 13-2/ The Enrichment Triad Model.

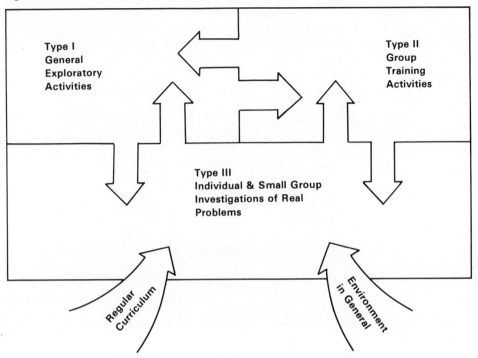

Type I
General
Exploratory
Activities

Type II
Group
Training
Activities

Type III
Individual & Small Group
Investigations of Real
Problems

Regular
Curriculum

Environment
in General

Source: Reprinted, by permission, from Joseph S. Renzulli, *The Enrichment Triad Model: A Guide for Developing Defensible Programs for the Gifted and Talented* (1977), p. 14, Creative Learning Press, Inc., P.O. Box 320, Mansfield Center, CT 06250.

by content, but can be applied across all disciplines and content areas. As such, Renzulli's model can be used flexibly throughout an able student's educational career.

Taylor's (1967) "multiple talent model" is another enrichment model designed for gifted students. The model was developed employing many of the notions and constructs that emanated from Guilford's (1956) research. In fact, three of the subcomponents found within the *operations* dimension of Guilford's "structure of intellect model" are employed in Taylor's model. A good deal of time is spent exposing students to activities designed to foster or enhance divergent, convergent, and evaluative thinking. The talent areas are briefly defined in Table 13-5. A variety of teaching materials have been developed to aid teachers and others in implementing Taylor's model (*Igniting Creative Potential*, Bella Vista Elementary School, 1971; *Talent Activity Packet* (2d ed.), Mobile County Public Schools, 1974). Although this model relies heavily on the basic knowledge of students, its major emphasis is on processing or utilizing the knowledge that can be used to create new products, to solve unique problems, or to make new uses of basic information.

Programs designed to advance the talents of gifted individuals in nonacademic areas such as the visual and performing arts have grown rapidly in

The enrichment
approach is the
most common
administrative
provision for
serving the
gifted.

Table 13-5/ Taylor's Multiple Talent Areas

Academic talent:	Ability as measure by valid and reliable achievement tests.
Creative talent:	The ability to go beyond; putting together seemingly unrelated information to come up with new solutions, new ways of expressing ideas, creative production (p. 63).
Planning talent:	Effective planning involves elaboration which considers details concerning operation; sensitivity to problems which need consideration; and organization of materials, time, and manpower (p. 79).
Decision-making talent:	Decision-making involves experimental evaluation, logical evaluation, and judgment (p. 125).
Forecasting talent:	Forecasting events, in the next instant or in the distant future requires conceptual foresight penetration or minute analyzation of related criteria, and social awareness (p. 111).
Communication talent:	Communication is the cornerstone of human interaction. Effective communication involves word fluency, expressional fluency, and associational fluency (p. 95).

Source: From *Igniting Creative Potential,* Project Implode, Bella Vista Elementary School, 1971.

recent years. Gold (1980) reports that at least fourteen states maintain arts programs at the secondary level. Students involved in these programs frequently spend half their school day working in academic subjects and the other half in arts studies. Often the arts instruction is provided by an independent institution but some school systems maintain their own separate schools. Most programs provide training in the visual and performing arts, but few emphasize instruction in creative writing, motion picture and television production, and/or photography.

"Governor's schools" in various states also provide valuable opportunities for the talented and academically gifted (Gold, 1980). These state-sponsored schools are in session during the summer months and are generally held on college campuses. Competitively selected students are provided with curricular experiences that are closely tailored to their individual aptitudes and interests (Khatena, 1982). Faculties for these schools are meticulously selected for competence in various areas and for ability to stimulate and motivate students. In Pennsylvania, the "governor's school" focuses solely on the visual and performing arts (Gold, 1980).

411
The Gifted,
Creative, and
Talented:
Intervention
Strategies

CAREER EDUCATION AND CAREER GUIDANCE FOR THE GIFTED

Career education and career guidance are essential components of a comprehensive program for the gifted. Ultimately, career education activities and experiences are designed to help gifted students make educational and occupational decisions. Unfortunately only a few functioning career education programs have been specifically designed for the gifted (Hoyt & Hebeler, 1974). Milne (1979) developed a list of the needs of gifted students as they relate to career

Career guidance is essential in helping the gifted student select appropriate career options.

education. He also described some of the important elements of career education for the gifted:

1. The interests, abilities, needs, and occupational or career aspirations arise at a much earlier age than in the regular student.
2. Gifted students need individualization and differentiation in career awareness, orientation, exploration, and preparation at a time commensurate with the growth and development of that giftedness.
3. The gifted are aware of a broad range of career alternatives earlier in life; as further awareness of careers occurs, there is an increased difficulty in making decisions about occupations and careers.
4. Gifted students tend to think beyond the known scope of career information and project themselves into nonexistent but highly potential careers.
5. Career selection, leading toward career satisfaction, takes into account the unique characteristics of the gifted individual, including personal, emotional, physical, and psychological traits.
6. Purposeful activity (work) and random activity (play) are essential enrichment experiences in the narrowing of alternatives for a satisfying career.
7. The student's gifts and talents may or may not directly relate to a career, but some gifts and talents can be translated into a wide range of careers.
8. Satisfactory career development for the gifted takes into account a harmonious balance among the physical, emotional, and intellectual drains on energy in one's total life, not merely in one's productive world of work.
9. Life satisfaction is total and complete at any point in the process of growth and development if there is an emerging realization of the potential contributions of the student's gifts and talents.
10. Career education, for the gifted, is part of the total process of becoming and should be continuous in all stages of growth and development.*(Milne, 1979, pp. 253-54)

Differentiated learning experiences provide gifted elementary and middle school students with opportunities to investigate and explore. Many of these investigations and explorations are career related and designed to help the gifted understand what it might be like to be a zoologist, a neurosurgeon, or a filmmaker. They also become familiar with the training and effort necessary for work in these fields. In groups they may discuss the factors that influence scientists to pursue a given problem, or experiments that led to his or her eminence. As gifted students grow and mature both cognitively and physically,

*Reprinted, by permission, from Bruce G. Milne, "Career Education," in *The Gifted and the Talented: Their Education and Development*, ed. A. Harry Passow, Seventy-eighth Yearbook of the National Society for the Study of Education (Chicago: University of Chicago Press, 1979), pp. 253-54.

the nature and scope of their career education activities become more sophisticated and varied.

Some students are provided opportunities to work directly with research scientists or other professionals who are conducting studies and investigations. They may spend as many as two days a week, three or four working hours a day, in laboratory facilities. Other students rely on intensive workshops or summer programs in which they are exposed to specialized careers through internships and individually tailored instruction.

As one might surmise, there is a broad array of career choices and problems that gifted students must contend with in selecting a career. By virtue of their multifaceted abilities and interests, they are often perplexed about what direction they should take in pursuing their studies and interests. The following statements exemplify the dilemmas that are theirs in dealing with their multipotentiality.

> I have found that if I apply myself I can do almost anything. I don't seem to have a serious lack of aptitude in any field. I find an English assignment equally as difficult as a physics problem. I find them also to be equally as challenging and equally as interesting. The same goes for math, social studies, music, speech, or any other subject area. . . . Nothing is so simple for me that I can do a perfect job without effort, but nothing is so hard that I cannot do it. This is why it is so difficult to decide my place in the future. Many people wouldn't consider this much of a problem; but to me, this lack of one area to stand out in is a very grave problem indeed.

> When I look for a career in my future, the clouds really thicken. There are so many things I'd like to do and be, and I'd like to try them all; where to start is the problem. Sometimes there is so much happiness and loneliness and passion and joy and despair in me that I practically take off over the trees, and when I get like that I love to write poetry. Sometimes I go for months without writing any, and then it kind of bursts out of me like spontaneous combustion. I'll probably always be like this, but I would also like to be able to discipline myself enough to write more short stories or novels. I'd like to be a physical therapist, a foreign correspondent, a psychiatrist, an anthropologist, a linguist, a folk singer, an espionage agent, and a social worker.*
> (Sanborn, 1979, p. 285)

There are other problems with which the gifted must deal (Sanborn, 1979). One such problem is directly related to the expectations the gifted have for themselves and those that have been explicitly and implicitly imposed by parents, teachers, and others. Gifted students frequently feel an inordinate

* Reprinted, by permission, from M. P. Sanborn, "Career Development: Problems of Gifted and Talented Students," in N. Colangelo and R. T. Zaffrann, eds., *New Voices in Counseling the Gifted* (Dubuque, Iowa: Kendall Hunt Publishing Co., 1974).

amount of pressure to achieve high grades or to select a particular profession. They often feel they are obligated or duty bound to achieve and contribute with excellence in every area. Such pressure often fosters a kind of conformity that prevents students from selecting avenues of endeavor that truly fit them and their personal interests.

Gifted students may also suffer from a certain amount of social isolation (Herr & Watanabe, 1979). Gifted students often tend to be more oriented in their interests than their peers. Thus they may spend more of their time interacting with adults rather than with their peers. Their age-mates may be interested in topics and things that are of little concern to a gifted student. Peers may also be intimidated by the unusual abilities of a gifted peer. Teachers and parents, who do not understand the nature of giftedness, may also alienate the gifted child or student (Witty & Grotberg, 1970).

Zaffrann & Colangelo (1977) found that gifted students have access to relatively few adult role-models who have interests and abilities that parallel theirs. This is particularly true for able students who grow up and receive their schooling in rural and remote areas. They complete their public schooling without the benefit of having a mentor or professional person with whom they can talk or discuss various educational and career-related problems. Societal expectations have and are changing, however, and women are gradually becoming more numerous in professions that were traditionally selected by men only.

Gifted females experience other problems in addition to those identified above that are unique to them (Gowan & Demos, 1964). These problems include conflicts between marital and career aspirations, stress induced from traditional cultural and societal expectations, and self-imposed and/or culturally imposed restrictions related to educational and occupational choices. For instance, as many as 80 percent of the academically talented females in some regions choose not to engage in university training (Baer & Roeber, 1964). Although many of the problems are far from being resolved at this point, some progress is being made. Women in greater numbers are now choosing to enter professions traditionally selected primarily by men. Multiple role assignments are emerging in family units, wherein the usual tasks of mothers are shared by all members of the family or are completed by someone outside the family. Cultural expectations are changing and, as a result, options for gifted and nongifted women are expanding rapidly.

Career guidance and other forms of counseling play an important role in helping the gifted utilize their remarkable abilities and talents. Gifted students may have a difficult time making educational and career choices because of their multiple talents; may feel an inordinate amount of pressure to select a certain career or achieve in a certain manner because of the expectations of others; may experience social isolation as a result of their unique abilities and preferences; and may have problems selecting career options because of traditional cultural values and expectations. These problems can be addressed and perhaps solved if appropriate assistance is provided by a skilled school counselor. The techniques used by a school counselor will vary according to the nature of the problems and the student's characteristics. In some instances, gifted students will need help in resolving personal/social problems before they will be able to address issues regarding career development and career preparation. If the problem is one of social isolation, the counselor may help the gifted student by involving him or her in a social skills group or group counseling program that emphasizes self-understanding and positive peer feedback. Problems caused by excessive or inappropriate parental expectations may need to be addressed in a family context, wherein the counselor helps the parents develop realistic expectations that fit their child's abilities and true interests.

ŝ SUMMARY

Interventions for the gifted are based on the principle of differentiation, that is, gifted individuals profit considerably from learning activities and experiences that are uniquely suited to their abilities and needs. The purpose of differentiated education is to prepare gifted children and youths for roles and problems in our society that require remarkable skills and expertise. It is also designed to bring them personal fulfillment in using their exceptional abilities. A variety of service delivery systems as well as accelerative and enrichment approaches have been utilized to foster the development of the gifted.

Gifted students experience a variety of problems in preparing for and selecting their careers or career emphasis areas. One major problem is that of multipotentiality. Other problems include those that surface from parent and family expectations, social isolation, lack of role models for gifted female students, and investment that gifted students must make in pursuing a career that demands a lot of training and money. Career education programs provide gifted students with activities and experiences that provide a basis for making sound career decisions. School counselors in conjunction with students and their families play a significant role in orchestrating and coordinating the entire career education and preparation process.

ŝ REVIEW QUESTIONS

1. Describe several means of identifying young gifted children.
2. How may parents promote early learning and development of gifted youngsters?
3. Why is it difficult to evaluate preschool programs for the gifted?
4. Describe the advantages and disadvantages of different service delivery systems for gifted youngsters.
5. Compare and contrast the various approaches to accelerated education for the gifted.
6. What are the important elements of career education and guidance for the gifted?

SECTION VI

Social Issues

As we complete our study of human exceptionality, we turn our attention to areas that differ substantially from what has gone before. In this section we will focus on the impact of a disordered individual on other family members. In addition, we will examine factors related to adulthood and aging in exceptionality.

Chapter 14 explores family perspectives and the stress an exceptional child places on the family. The family is discussed as a social system, and the impact on this social unit is examined, as well as the effects on individual members within that unit. Chapter 15 focuses on the adult and advanced years of life. Comparisons are made between disordered and normal populations in terms of a variety of factors. The following are topical guidelines for Section VI:

1. The initial impact of an infant with exceptional characteristics on family members may be substantial and create considerable stress.

2. Parents experience several stages of reaction as they learn to cope with their exceptional child.

3. Both parents and siblings may be affected by the entrance and continued presence of an exceptional individual in the family unit.

4. Extended-family members, particularly grandparents, often experience a substantial impact as the result of an exceptional individual's entrance into the family.

5. There are a number of difficulties in studying the effects of aging, both in normal and exceptional populations.

6. Physiological differences between older normal individuals and older exceptional individuals are apparent in some cases but not in others.

7. Cognition and intellectual changes as a function of aging may not be as great as often thought.

8. Behavior and personality factors may be more stable as one grows older than we typically think.

9. Disordered adults do not fare well in terms of employment and income when compared with their normal counterparts.

10. Leisure activities and living arrangements for disordered adults may be controversial in some cases and require a great deal more research.

CHAPTER FOURTEEN

Family Impact

Nowhere is the impact of an exceptional individual so strongly felt as the family. The birth of a disordered infant is likely to alter the family as a social unit in a variety of ways. Parents and siblings may react with shock, disappointment, anger, depression, guilt, and/or confusion, to name only a few. Relationships between family members often change, in either a positive manner or a negative manner. The impact of such an event is great, and it is unlikely that the family unit will ever be the same.

I had been looking forward to this event all my life. I was about to give birth to my first child and had done everything imaginable to prepare for this momentous day. I had been eating the right foods. I had avoided taking any medication, as my obstetrician had suggested. I had even maintained a regular fitness program. My husband was amazed at the diligence that I had exhibited in pursuing my many regimens

Finally, the day came. At the end of my regular appointment with the obstetrician, he told me that I should call my husband and prepare to enter the hospital that evening. Prior to Bill's arrival home, I began to experience fairly regular labor pains. They were not intense, but I knew that they foreshadowed the real labor that was to come.

Bill managed to get off work early, and we both left for the hospital with great expectations and a few normal fears. About 9:15 P.M., my labor pains intensified. In a short time, I was moved into the delivery room. The actual birth of my son proceeded normally—but then it happened. The atmosphere in the delivery room changed from one of hope to concern and then gloom. Sometime during that brief period, I was informed by the obstetrician that my new little infant boy had a serious birth defect known as spina bifida. It all happened so quickly. I saw my son only briefly before he was whisked away to the special neonatal unit.

A million thoughts raced through my groggy mind. "Can I handle this? Why did this happen to us? What could I have done to have this happen to our family? Bill must be very disappointed in me! What are we going to do?" Just then I felt Bill squeezing my hand and trying to get my attention. He said, "We'll get through it somehow." The next few days were like a series of nightmares—fleeting images of people in white coats, constant fear, and the terrifying feeling of despair. There were so many things to consider and decisions to make. I felt helpless, unable to think clearly. Maybe he'll die, I thought to myself, but then I felt guilty—so guilty. Bill was there most of the time, but we didn't talk much. Needless to say, this day changed our lives forever.

A child with physical or behavioral problems will present unique and diverse challenges to the family unit. In one instance, the child may hurl the family into crises, resulting in major conflicts among its members. Family relationships may be weakened by the added and unexpected physical, emotional, and financial stress imposed on them. In another instance, family members may see this child as a source of unity that bonds them together and actually strengthens relationships. It is impossible in a text of this scope to address fully the range of individual reactions experienced by families who have a child with disorders. Many factors influence the reactions of family members: the emotional stability of each individual, religious values, socioeconomic status, the severity of the child's disorder, and the type of disorder, to name only a few.

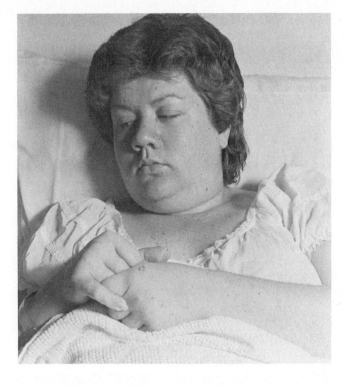

Mother who has given birth to a handicapped child

     In this chapter we will examine the family as a social system defined by a set of purposes, roles, and expectations. Each family member fulfills various roles that are consistent with expectations established by discussion, tradition, or other means. Each member functions in an interdependent manner with other members to pursue family goals. Utilizing a social-system framework, we can see how changes in one family member can have an effect on every other member and consequently the entire family system. If we accept the notions and concepts associated with this sociological view of a family, we can see how the birth and continued presence of a child with a disorder can significantly affect the family unit over time.

FAMILY CRISIS: THE INITIAL IMPACT

The birth of an infant with significant disorders will have a profound impact on the family. Some conditions are readily apparent at birth (Oglesby & Sterling, 1970; Volpe & Koenigsberger, 1981), while others are not detectable until later (Cruickshank, 1976; Haynes, 1977; Parmelee, 1962; Tjossem, 1976). Even if attending physicians suspect the presence of a disabling condition, they may be unable to give a confirmed diagnosis without the passage of some time and further testing. If the parents also suspect that something may be wrong, waiting for a diagnosis can be agonizing and anxiety-producing.

The most immediate predictable and common reaction to the birth of a child with a disorder is depression. Depression is often exhibited in the form of grief or mourning. Mothers whose abnormal babies survive frequently suffer more acute feelings of grief than mothers whose abnormal infants die. They also tend to mourn for a longer period before they recover (D'Arcy, 1968). Other reactions on the part of family members include shock, disappointment, anger, frustration, guilt, denial, fear, withdrawal, and rejection. The level of impact varies, but for most parents such an event creates a family crisis of considerable magnitude.

Shontz (1965) suggested that parental responses can be separated into four stages: shock, realization, defensive retreat, and acknowledgment. Unfortunately, families are seldom prepared to deal with the stages of such a crisis. However, parents must proceed through each stage successfully before they can become actively involved in the education and training of the child (Webster, 1977). Frequently it is the father who must inform other family members that the new infant is disordered. This is an extremely difficult task, and one for which the father has little preparation. The attitude in which such information is conveyed often determines the emotional tone of the reception that the mother and new infant receive when they come home from the hospital. But it is the mother's response to the infant which will have the greatest influence on family attitude over time (Buscaglia, 1975). If the mother is accepting and realistic in her responses to the child, other family members will probably adopt her method of responding.

The stage of *shock* is distinguished by feelings of anxiety, guilt, numbness, confusion, helplessness, anger, and despair. At this time, when many parents are most in need of assistance, the least amount of help may be available. The length of time it takes the family to move through this period depends on the parent's psychological makeup and the types of assistance rendered. During the initial shock period, parents may be unable to process and comprehend information provided by medical and other health-related personnel. For this reason, information provided the parents may need to be repeated on several occasions until they have fully grasped the concepts presented. It is also during this time that parents experience the greatest assaults on their self-worth and value systems. They may seriously question their positive perceptions of themselves. Likewise, they will be forced to reassess the meaning of life and the reasons for their present challenges.

Buscaglia (1975) surveyed parents of disabled children in an attempt to assess the level of psychological support rendered by the hospital staff at the time of their children's birth. He found that parents were generally given some knowledge of the child's special medical problems but that the information was viewed as inadequate. Moreover, parents indicated that psychological counseling was insufficient and that no formal or special counseling was provided during this period. Thus parents begin the child-rearing process with only a small amount of medical information and a significant number of apprehensions about the future of the child and the family.

The stage of *realization* is characterized by several types of parental behavior. Parents may be anxious or fearful about their ability to cope with the demands of caring for a child with unique needs. They may be easily irritated or upset. Considerable time may be spent in self-accusation, self-pity, or self-hate. Information provided by health-care professionals during this period may still be rejected or denied. However, during this stage parents come to understand the actual demands and constraints that will come with raising their exceptional child. This realization frequently overwhelms couples, and as a result they may remove themselves from family and social activities for a period of time.

The stage of *defensive retreat* is one in which the parents attempt to avoid dealing with the anxiety-producing realities of their child's condition. They may try to solve their dilemma by seeking placement for the child in a clinic, institution, or residential setting. Some parents respond by disappearing for a while or by retreating to a safer and less demanding environment. One mother, on returning home from the hospital, quickly packed her clothes and some belongings and left with the child in the family car, not knowing exactly what her destination was. She simply did not want to face her immediate family or relatives. After driving around for several hours, she decided to return home. Years later this child who prompted such panic is married and successfully working as an aide in a special school.

Acknowledgment is a stage in which parents are able to mobilize their strengths to confront the conditions created by having an exceptional child. At this stage, parents become capable of involving themselves in the intervention and treatment process. They are also better able to comprehend information or directions provided by a specialist concerning their child's condition and treatment. At this time some parents become interested in joining an organization that is suited to their child's condition and the needs of the family.

Parents of exceptional children have many other concerns. They especially want to know about what their child's future educational and social needs will be (Bice, 1952; Shelton, 1972). They want to know what their child will be capable of doing as he or she grows older and becomes an adult. They want to know how the presence of the child will affect other family members. Most important, they want to know how to maintain normal family functioning and minimize the stress associated with having an exceptional child.

THE IMPACT OF EXCEPTIONALITIES ON FAMILY FUNCTIONING

> My wife, Carol, has spent the majority of the last five weeks caring for our three-year-old son at St. Mark's Children's Hospital. He was born prematurely. Since that time he has needed constant attention from medical personnel and his mother. Our family has adjusted quite well to these circumstances, even though they complain now and then. All of us have had to assume some of my wife's usual tasks and responsibilities. I find this quite difficult, for Carol had really spoiled me prior to Dan's birth. I now fill the role of an overseer. I try to keep the laundry and dishes at manageable levels, in addition to doing the usual cleaning and vacuuming.

Rather than perform the tasks she once did, my wife spends most of her time caring for the physical and emotional needs of the youngest member of our family. Her constant involvement with Dan frequently taxes our patience, which makes us feel guilty when we know how much he needs her support and care.

I think our family has developed a greater closeness as a result of Dan's medical problems. At least we seem to be more united and loving toward each other. We do not necessarily get along better, we just seem to be a little more cognizant of our obligation to make things work out, and we try a little harder to be nice to each other.

I would be less than honest if I didn't say that I feel jealous of the time my wife spends with Dan. I sense the same feeling in my children. So far we are doing quite well, considering all the strain. At the end of July we are looking forward to taking a family vacation. We have made arrangements to have Carol's youngest sister take care of Dan while we are gone. We can hardly wait to spend time relaxing and talking with Mom.

The birth and continued presence of an exceptional child strongly influences the manner in which family members respond to one another. In most families it is the mother who experiences the greatest amount of trauma and role strain in responding to conditions created by the presence of an exceptional child. In caring for the child, she can no longer fulfill other roles that she once performed. Her time with the family is also greatly reduced because of time spent taking care of the child's unique needs. As a result of their care-giving role, many mothers may be drawn away from other tasks that they used to perform. When this occurs, other family members must often assume more responsibility. It may be difficult for family members to adjust to the new strains and routines that result from having an exceptional child in the family. Each family member may need to alter his or her personal routine in order to assist the mother as she cares for the exceptional child. Initially, the demands and needs of the exceptional child may be numerous and time-consuming. For families that are already experiencing serious emotional, financial, or other problems, the addition of an exceptional child may serve as the catalyst for dissolution.

As the child grows older, the mother is frequently faced with a unique dilemma. The dilemma revolves around striking a balance between the nurturing activities that the mother associates with her role as care-giver and the activities associated with fostering independence. It can be difficult for mothers to see their exceptional children struggle at new tasks and suffer some of the natural consequences of trying new behaviors. For many mothers, the "overprotectiveness syndrome" is extremely difficult to conquer, but it can be accomplished with help provided by others who have already experienced and mastered this syndrome. If the mother or other care providers continue to be overprotective, the results can be disastrous, particularly when the child reaches late adolescence and is unprepared for entry into adulthood or semi-independent living.

Each family exhibits a characteristic pattern of conveying information. The pattern and type of communication varies according to the size of the family, its age, and its cultural background. Generally, information conveyed to the family regarding the nature of a sibling's disorder is provided by the father, particularly if the exceptionality is diagnosed at birth. Once initial information regarding the sibling's condition has been conveyed, the older children frequently become responsible for providing additional clarification to younger siblings. At first, a new closeness occurs in families who discover that one of the children has a disorder. During this period, the mother frequently senses this closeness, and it serves to support her. Over time, however, this support may wane, and family members may gradually move away from the family unit to associate more closely with peers or friends. Questions children may want to ask parents regarding family issues may be posed to older siblings, or they may not be asked at all. Such behavior is probably a function of the strain that the children sense in their parents. It is a natural outcome and one that is to be expected in families in which parents must direct a great deal of their attention to an exceptional child.

As a rule, mothers develop a strong dyadic relationship with the exceptional child. Other dyadic relationships may also develop between various members of the family. Certain siblings may turn to each other for support and nurturing. Older siblings may serve as parent substitutes as a result of their new care-giving roles and responsibilities. Younger children, who come to be dependent on older siblings for care, tend to develop strong relationships with them.

Every family has its unique power structure. In some families, most of the power or control may be held by the father. In other families, the governance of the family may lie with the mother or the family at large. Power in the context of this discussion is defined as the amount of control or influence a family member or group of family members exerts in managing family decisions, assigning family tasks, and implementing family activities. Families will vary greatly in their membership and their organization. Some families have both parents living at home, while others may have only one parent. In a similar fashion, the power structure within each family varies according to the characteristics of each family member. Family power structure is often altered substantially by the arrival of an exceptional infant. It is not uncommon for older siblings to assume greater power than before as they also assume more responsibility.

The last area to be reviewed in this section is that of family unity. As illustrated in the vignette at the beginning of this section, the initial impact of crisis produces an increased level of family closeness over a short period of time. This closeness is characterized more by verbal comments than by any actual increase in behaviors representative of family harmony. After the initial period of shock has passed and the realities of having an exceptional child in the family have surfaced, siblings frequently seek support from peers outside the home to help them deal with the stress so prevalent within the family unit.

We were just beginning to get our feet on the ground when it happened. We had been in our new home for about two years. My job had been demanding and yet fulfilling. Our daughter, Julie, was doing well in the fifth grade, and everything about our family life and marriage was almost ideal. Sara was pregnant, and we were excited about having our last child. I was hoping for a boy and I think Sara was too.

Our boy, Steve, did arrive, but during the birth process he suffered extensive brain damage. From that point on, the tone of our marriage and family life went from optimism to pessimism and continual doubt. My wife spent so much time reading books about brain damage, keeping medical appointments, and caring for Steve that Julie and I have been forced to pursue other activities. We often avoid contact with my wife, since she has become demanding and domineering. I find it difficult to communicate with her. Somehow we have lost the affection and affinity we once had for each other.

Recently she took one of those assertiveness-training classes. Since then she has become almost unbearable. Often I view her assertiveness as a form of veiled anger. Moreover, I have become a little unsure of myself during the past six months. My boss is not as supportive as he once was, and I worry about being replaced by one of those confident, newly graduated college guys.

It is as if the birth of Steve and subsequent events have gradually removed the joy and contentment that Sara and I once knew. I don't want to leave my wife, but I have considered it more than a few times in the last two months.

Many families function and perform in a state of equilibrium prior to the birth of their exceptional child. From this perspective they have a well-defined set of roles and expectations. The goals for the family are typically clear, and various family members are striving to maintain the integrity of the system and each of its component parts. For families who are in a state of disequilibrium, their problems are often manifested in poor communication, poorly defined family roles, unclear expectations, general disorganization, and financial difficulty. For the family already experiencing major difficulties, the birth of an exceptional child may force them into further disarray, while the family that is on solid ground may temporarily be thrown into a period of reassessment and realignment of roles, tasks, and responsibilities.

According to Featherstone (1980), "A child's handicap attacks the fabric of a marriage in four ways. It excites powerful emotions in both parents. It acts as a dispiriting symbol of shared failure. It reshapes the organization of the family. It creates fertile ground for conflict" (p. 91). A disordered infant may require more immediate and prolonged attention from the mother for feeding,

Marital discord may increase with the presence of an exceptional child in the home.

treatment, and general care. Her attention becomes riveted on the life of the exceptional child. The balance once in effect between a mothering and wife relationship is now absent. The wife has become so involved with caring for the exceptional child that other relationships often lose their quality and intensity. It is not uncommon to hear such comments as "Jean spends so much time with Andy that she has little energy left for me. It is as if she has become consumed with his care." "You ask me to pay attention to Amy, but you rarely spend any time with me. When am I going to be a part of your life again?" "I am developing a resentment toward you and Petey. Who wants to come home when all your time is spent waiting on him?" One can sense from these comments the types of feelings a husband might have regarding a wife's involvement with the exceptional child.

Marital partners also have other types of feelings. Fear, anger, guilt, resentment, and other related feelings often interfere with a couple's capacity to communicate and seek realistic solutions. Fatigue will also have a profound effect on the ways in which couples function and communicate. All these feelings and conditions are exacerbated by the presence of an exceptional child in the home.

Other factors contribute to marital stress: unusually heavy financial burdens that must be incurred by the family to provide medical treatment or therapy; frequent visits to treatment facilities; a reduction of time spent together in couple-related activities. These factors, in conjunction with a host of others, account for the marital stress that many married couples experience in rearing an exceptional child.

Research related to marital stress and instability is limited. Farber (1959; 1962) investigated changes that took place in families with severely retarded children. Utilizing interview procedures, Farber evaluated the differences between families who had placed their children in institutions and families who chose to care for their children at home. Although the studies have some inherent methodological weaknesses, they provide valuable information regarding the effects of having a seriously retarded youngster remain in the home. Farber found that marriages were adversely affected by having a seriously retarded child remain at home. Koch and Dobson (1971), in their study of the impact of having a retarded child in the family, concluded that parents of such children tended to have more problems in personal and marital adjustment. This finding was particularly true for families of low socioeconomic status. Other studies suggested a more positive impact on the family. McAndrew (1976) studied 116 families with physically disabled children. He found that the majority of mothers surveyed reported a good marital relationship with their spouses. Of the remaining families, only seventeen wives believed that their marriages had worsened as a result of having a disabled child. After completing his extensive study of families with retarded children, Farber (1959) concluded that the best predictor of future family marital integration was simply the degree of integration present before a retarded child entered the family. If the family had marital problems before the birth of the retarded child, those problems were likely to continue.

Research related to the divorce rates of parents of retarded children provides an unclear picture. Love (1973) indicated that the divorce rate among parents of the retarded were three times higher than that of parents of normal children. In contrast, however, Davis and McKay (1973) indicated that there is no difference in the divorce rates of these two groups of parents.

Fowle (1968) assessed the level of marital integration of couples who chose to care for their retarded child at home versus those who chose to have their child cared for in an institution. He found no significant differences between the two groups as measured by Farber's "index of marital integration."It is important to note that children who did remain at home were served by a day-care center. Such services probably lessened the burden of the parents and family members in caring for the retarded child. In a related study, Fotheringham, Skelton, and Hoddinott (1971) evaluated families of severely retarded children prior to placement of the child in a community or institutional setting. One to three months before the children were placed in their various settings, a comprehensive evaluation was made of each family. The evaluation procedures were implemented again after the children had been served at least one year in their respective placements. Families whose children had been served in institutionalized settings showed greater improvement in family functioning than those families whose children were served in community programs. However, there are many variables involved in analyzing the efficacy of community placement as opposed to institutional placement, and it has been well over a decade since Farber and Fotheringham et al. conducted their investigations.

The availability of community support systems (e.g., mandated public education for exceptional children, availability of qualified family counselors, and respite-care opportunities) has changed dramatically during this period.

Cleveland (1980) studied the adaptations made by seventeen families where a youngster in the family had experienced traumatic spinal cord injury. She examined family adaptation to the injury shortly after the accident event and one year later. Changes in family functioning and specific intrafamilial relationships were the focus of the study. With regard to marital functioning, Cleveland identified several sources or types of spousal irritation and distress. As a rule, mothers in each of the families assumed the major role of caring for the injured youths. Husbands reported feeling angry toward their wives because of their involvement with the injured child. In a like manner, wives expressed hostility toward their husbands for a lack of empathy and understanding concerning the care they provided. In addition, overprotectiveness by the mothers was identified as a major source of tension for couples. Most husbands felt that their spouses were overly solicitous and shielding in their care-giving activities. Generally, couples reported that their marriages had been made neither better nor worse as a function of the injury to their child. They were, however, concerned about the prolonged period of parenthood that they would have to provide. They also felt they would have to alter some of the plans they had made for the postparenthood phase of their lives.

Tew, Lawrence, Payne, and Townsley (1977) investigated the impact of having a child with spina bifida on marital stability. They concluded that the divorce rate for such couples whose children survived the condition was nine times higher than that of average families. For those parents whose children died as a result of the condition, the divorce rate was three times higher.

In a comprehensive review of the effects of having a child with learning disabilities, Scagliotta (1974) found that parents generally reacted to their child's problems in one of two distinct ways. Some parents worked as a cooperative team. They perceived the child's behaviors from similar points of view. They usually agreed on the types of child-management techniques that they used to handle their child's problems. Their expectations for the child's behavior were also compatible. Other parents responded to their child's learning and behavior difficulties in a disjointed fashion. They had problems reaching agreement in selecting and implementing various discipline strategies. For instance, the mother may be the only adult family member actively involved in assisting the child, whereas the father may purposely separate himself from the child's treatment process. He may participate only as an observer or as an occasional critic of the intervention.

Parent counseling and training can be extremely helpful in ameliorating many of the problems encountered in attempting to cope with the exceptional child in the family system (Abrams & Kaslow, 1977; Baker, 1970; Friedman, 1978; Hetrick, 1979). Counseling may help parents work through such feelings as anger, resentment, and discouragement. Parent training may help parents develop appropriate expectations for their child's current and future achievement. In addition, parents may acquire specific skills to help them respond more effectively and therapeutically to their child's difficulties.

PARENT/CHILD RELATIONSHIPS

I had not always been at odds with Colette. The friction began when she reached adulthood. As she grew up, her father and I had worried about what would become of her when that time arrived, and because no one could tell us, our imaginations had run wild. We pictured her sitting in the dreary day-room of a state hospital drooling over a half-completed potholder, or we saw her following us around the house and becoming a burden to her younger sister and brother when we died.

But in the early 1960s, attitudes toward the retarded began to change. Gradually, owing to President Kennedy's particular interest and the civil rights movement in general, the concept of normalization evolved: The handicapped were to be helped to lead as normal lives as possible. In this climate our beliefs changed. We began to think that with careful preparation Colette could eventually live in a semisheltered arrangement.

Colette, however, had other ideas. By the time she was 20, her father and I realized we were rapidly losing control over her. While we struggled to instill money management practices and the wisdom of birth control, she continued to disappear overnight with her boyfriend and waste the wages from her part-time job on extravagances.

One day she abruptly announced that she had found a tiny apartment, and she moved out. Her stunned parents reacted with conflicting emotions. We were relieved to be finished with the stormy scenes that had exhausted us all and we were also proud of her determination. Yet by her sudden departure we felt she had surely sabotaged whatever chances she had for continuing independence. We predicted problems in her premature attempt to solo, and problems did occur with fatiguing regularity. During troubled times she would turn to us and we would bail her out, accompanying our rescue operation with interrogations and scoldings.

Months went by and we heard from her less and less frequently. When I phoned, she was reserved and distant. I was saddened. I did not want to lose my daughter. Yet when we did get together, I always reverted to my role as inquisitioner and judge, and she retreated further into lies and half-truths. We were locked into adversary positions.* (Kaufman, 1980, p. 18)

In this section, we will analyze the relationships that emerge between parents and their exceptional child. It must be understood that the types of relationships discussed are not characteristic of all exceptional individuals and

*From S. Z. Kaufman, "A Mentally Retarded Daughter Educates Her Mother," *The Exceptional Parent*, 1980, 10(6), 17–22. Reprinted with permission of *The Exceptional Parent* magazine. Copyright © 1982, Psy-ed Corporation, 296 Boylston Street, Boston, Massachusetts 02116.

their parents. They merely illustrate the findings derived from case studies, research, and literature pertaining to exceptional individuals.

The relationships between parents and their exceptional offspring are a function of many factors. Some of the more critical factors include the child's age (Seligman, 1979), the child's sex (Farber, 1959), the socioeconomic status of the family (Farber, 1959; 1962), the family's coping strength (Buscaglia, 1975), the nature and seriousness of the disability (Seligman, 1979), and the composition of the family—one-parent family, two-parent family, or reconstituted family (Balkwell & Halverson, 1980).

Seligman (1979) described a developmental cycle that families go through in responding to the needs and nuances of caring for an exceptional child. The cycle includes the following steps: (1) the time at which parents learn about or suspect a disability in their child, (2) the period in which the parents determine what action to take regarding the child's education, (3) the point at which the disabled individual has completed his or her education, and (4) the time when the parents become older and may be unable to care for their adult offspring. Gur (1976) identified similar periods of change through which families proceed. These events include (1) the time at which the impairment is suspected, (2) the final diagnosis period, (3) the time at which the child leaves the home for schooling, (4) the period of peer and sibling rejection, (5) the period during which the child may experience acute diseases or complications associated with the condition, (6) the pubescence period, in which the impaired youth must deal with issues related to sexuality, identity, and future employment, (7) the courtship and marriage period, (8) the career development or institutionalization periods, and (9) the period in which the exceptional individual leaves the nuclear family to live elsewhere. The cycle that each family experiences is different, and each of the phases within the cycle has a significant effect on the nature of relationships between parents and exceptional children. We will not review all these periods, but we will highlight some of the more common relationship patterns that appear over time in the life of an exceptional individual.

The first relationship pattern we will highlight is that between the mother and the exceptional child. If the child's impairment is congenital and readily apparent at birth, it is often the mother who becomes primarily responsible for relating to the child and his or her needs. If the infant is born prematurely or needs extensive early medical assistance, the relationship that emerges may be slow in coming. There are many reasons for this delayed emergence. The mother may be prevented from engaging in typical feeding and care-giving activities that most mothers would perform with a new infant. The child may need to spend many weeks in an isolette supported by sophisticated medical equipment. Some mothers come to question whether they really had a baby, because of the remoteness they experience in not being able to interact with their infant in a personally satisfying manner (Jogis, 1975). Many mothers report that, on discovering their infant had a serious birth defect, they were not adequately prepared for or instructed regarding what they could do to become involved with their disabled infants (Leigh, 1975). Without minimal levels of involvement and appropriate support from other adults or professionals, many mothers become estranged from their infants and find it difficult to begin the caring process. Physicians, nurses, and other health-related personnel responsible for providing parents with appropriate explanations, instructions, and expectations set the stage for the development of healthy and realistic parent/infant relationships. The mother's expectations are particularly important, for they shape the types of responses she will make in caring for and seeking assistance for her infant (Lavelle & Keogh, 1980).

The mother may be virtually forced into a close physical and emotional relationship with her injured offspring. The dyad that develops between mother and child is one that is strong and often impermeable. The mother becomes, according to Cleveland (1980), the "guardian of affective needs." She assumes the primary responsibility for fostering the child's emotional adjustment. She also frequently becomes the child's personal representative or interpreter. In this role, the mother has the responsibility of communicating the child's needs and desires to other family members. Because of the sheer weight of these responsibilities, other relationships often wane or even disappear. The mother who assumes this role and develops a very close relationship with her disabled offspring often walks a variety of tightropes. In her desire to protect her child, she often overprotects him or her, thus preventing the child from having optimal opportunities to practice the skills and participate in the activities that ultimately lead to independence. The mother may underestimate her child's capacities. She may be reluctant to allow her child to engage in challenging or risky ventures. In this regard, the mother might be described as being overprotective. On the other hand, some mothers may neglect their exceptional child and not provide the stimulation that may be so critical to the child's optimal development. Such neglect constitutes a severe form of child abuse that should receive the prompt attention of appropriate child-care workers.

Several investigators (Miller, 1958; Ross, 1964; Seligman, 1979) have suggested that it is the mildly disordered youngsters and their families who experience the most severe adjustment problems. In his research with parents of exceptional children, Barsh (1968) found that parents of the blind and deaf showed the greatest ease in rearing their children, compared to parents whose children had other impairments. There could be many reasons for this. One reason may be that diagnosis of blindness and deafness can occur earlier than that of other conditions, allowing the parents to begin the adjustment process earlier. Likewise, the services for these children may be more fully developed, thus removing some of the burdens parents experience in raising a blind or deaf child.

Balkwell and Halverson (1980) reviewed research on the sources of stress that families experience in rearing a hyperactive child. They found that mothers of hyperactive children interacted more frequently with their exceptional offspring than did mothers of normal children. In addition, these mothers used more controlling and negative statements when talking with their hyperactive children, in contrast to the way they talked to their normal children. In fact, it appeared as though many mothers anticipated misbehavior even when their hyperactive children were behaving appropriately. Such maternal expectations may interfere with the development of positive mother/child relationships.

There has not been much written about fathers and their relationships with exceptional children. The information available is primarily anecdotal in nature or appears in the form of case studies. As indicated earlier, it is the father who is often responsible for conveying the news that the mother has given birth to an exceptional child, and for a time the father may well be responsible for keeping the family aware of the mother's status and the child's condition. The father's reactions to the birth of an injured or damaged child are generally more reserved than those of other family members (Wunderlich, 1977). Fathers are more prone to respond with such coping mechanisms as withdrawal, sublimation, and intellectualization. They are more likely to internalize their feelings than express them openly. Although we do not know much about fathers' reactions to having an exceptional child, we must assume that, like their wives, they experience feelings of remorse, guilt, and disappointment.

The relationships that emerge between fathers and their exceptional children are a function of the same factors reviewed earlier in the section dealing with mother/child relationships. Of particular importance is the sex of the child. If the child is a male, and the father had idealized the role that he would eventually assume in interacting with a son, the adjustment for the father can be very difficult. The father may have had hopes of playing football with the child, having him eventually become a business partner, or participating with his son in a variety of activities. Many of these hopes may never be realized with a disabled child. Levine (1966) investigated parents' perceptions of social competence and the sex-role identification process that takes place in families with a retarded child. He concluded that fathers are affected more by the presence of a mentally retarded son than by a mentally retarded daughter. In a related study, Peck and Stephens (1960) found a high correlation between a father's rejection or acceptance of a retarded child and the family's response to the child.

Investigating the effect of traumatic spinal cord injury, Cleveland (1980) found that the initial response of fathers to injured sons was one of an increased feeling of closeness. Sons described their fathers as being more nurturing and supporting. With the passage of time, however, the father/son relationship became clouded with problems related to the meaning of maleness and manliness. Fathers did not know how to respond to a son who was unable to participate in activities traditionally associated with being a man. Sons faced the same dilemma. They too were at a loss as to what their new roles and activities would be in light of their physical limitations. We can easily see how perplexing such an injury can be to a father and a son who intended to go hunting, fishing, and camping together or who had participated actively in these pursuits prior to an injury. Certainly adjustments and modifications can be made for those who are unable to walk on their own or to utilize their arms and hands fully. Father and son can eventually be involved in the activities previously identified, but the period of transition is almost always traumatic and difficult. Expectations and goals must be modified. In conjunction with a variety of professionals, fathers must find new ways to help their sons manifest their masculinity and strengths. There are now many activities in which physically injured individuals can be involved both competitively and noncompetitively.

The intensity of the relationship between the mother and the child also has an impact on the father/child relationship. Many husbands resent the pronounced needs of their exceptional offspring. Although these feelings of resentment may never be expressed verbally, a child can often sense the father's irritation and displeasure.

SIBLING RELATIONSHIPS

I'll never forget the first time I saw my little brother, Frank. I can't say why I was so struck by his appearance, but there was something different about him. For reasons unknown to me, my mother on returning home from the hospital appeared to have been crying just before she entered the driveway. There weren't any tears, but her face was flushed, and even though she smiled I could sense that something was wrong.

A few days later my father informed us that little Frank was a Down's syndrome child. Naturally we were curious as to what was meant by this term. My dad said that this meant Frank would be very slow in learning to do the things that most children learn quite rapidly. That explanation satisfied our curiosity, and we other children returned to the activities we had been pursuing.

Not too long after that explanation, the word got out in our neighborhood that Frank was retarded. I can distinctly remember several of the neighborhood kids asking me, "Is it true? Do you have a retarded brother? What does he look like?" Responding to these questions was something I had not been prepared for. To this day, as I am completing my junior year in college, I have a difficult time talking about Frank, who is now ten. Although attitudes have changed, there is still a great deal of misunderstanding about people who are retarded.

As I look back on my years of schooling, I can remember the jealousy and resentment I often felt toward Frank and my parents. They always seemed to put Frank first, as if he were special. He was special, but I needed some of that intensive attention too. As I have matured and developed some perspective regarding Frank's problems, I can understand why my parents were so attentive to him. I just wish that they had talked to me and my other brothers and sisters a little more than they did. As it was, we were often left to develop our own explanations for my parents' behavior. These explanations were often inaccurate and ill conceived. This fall I took a class entitled "Families of Children with Disabilities." During this class I had my first opportunity to really explore my feelings and make sense of my earlier family experiences. Although I have not completely resolved all my feelings toward Frank and my parents, I am on the way to accomplishing just that.

Siblings respond to an exceptional member of the family in a variety of ways. These responses are subject to a number of variables, some of which appear to play a critical role in the types of responses that are made. Farber (1962) identified several factors that may be predictive of family and sibling adjustment to a retarded brother or sister. These include the quality of the interpersonal relationship between the child's parents, the retarded child's sex, the social class of the family, and interaction patterns of the family. Grossman (1972a; 1972b) found that families in the upper income brackets were more capable of relieving their normal children of some burdens associated with caring for a retarded sibling. By contrast, lower-income families often placed much of the burden for the retarded child's care on young female members of the family.

Siblings who learn that they have an exceptional brother or sister are frequently encumbered with many different kinds of concerns. Such questions as "Why did this happen?" "What am I going to say to my friends?" and "Am I going to have to take care of him all of my life?" are common. Like their parents, siblings want to know and understand as much as they can about the condition of their impaired sibling. They want to know how they should respond and how their lives might be different as a result of this event. If these concerns can be adequately addressed, the prognosis for positive sibling involvement with the impaired brother or sister is much better. Lamb (1980) has reviewed a number of books for children that may be used therapeutically to help children accept their exceptional siblings. Through these stories, children may become vicariously involved with the problems of having an exceptional sister or brother.

We would be remiss in our discussion of this topic if we were to leave the reader with the impression that all sibling problems can be handled through appropriate orientation, education, and counseling programs. Even with excellent extrafamilial support and assistance, having a disabled child in the family can be challenging and painful for both parents and siblings. In spite of assistance, many siblings may continue to disdain and resent their brother or sister. They may also develop emotional problems that surface because of the stresses inherent in having an exceptional sibling in the family.

One factor that can affect the attitudes of children toward an exceptional sibling is the attitude of the parents (Grossman, 1972a; Klein, 1972; Love, 1973). Children tend to mirror the attitudes and values of their parents. If parents are optimistic and realistic in their views toward the exceptional child, then the other children are likely to share these attitudes. If children are kindly disposed toward assisting the exceptional sibling, they can be a real source of nurturance and support (Koch & Dobson, 1971; Murphy, 1979). Many siblings play a critical role in fostering the intellectual, social, and affective development of an exceptional brother or sister.

Some children use the experiences gained from growing up with a disabled sibling as a basis for becoming members of various helping professions (Sullivan, 1979). In research dealing with college students who had grown up with a retarded sibling, Grossman (1972a; 1972b) found that a number of these individuals appeared to have benefited from the experience. They appeared to be more tolerant and less prejudiced in their outlook toward life and people in general. They also seemed more sure of themselves and of their vocational or professional futures than others. Because of the nature of the sample, Grossman could not cite the actual percentage of normal siblings who benefited from the process of growing up in a family with a retarded individual. However, these individuals tended to come from families who had moderate to high social economic standing. They also came from families where a positive attitude was a prominent feature of their parents' dispositions toward the exceptional child.

Siblings frequently experience a variety of problems as they interact with their parents, their exceptional brother or sister, and friends. Young siblings may fear that the disorder is a contagious disease that they may catch. Anger is one of many feelings that normal siblings may express or feel. Loneliness, anxiety, guilt, and envy are also common in normal siblings. Feelings of loneliness may surface in children who wanted a brother or sister with whom they could play. Anxiety may be present in a youth who wonders who will

Siblings may enhance the quality of life for an exceptional child.

care for the impaired sibling when the parents are no longer capable or present. Guilt may come from many sources. Normal siblings may feel that they are religiously or morally obligated to care for the disabled sibling. In their minds, failure to provide such care would make them "bad" or immoral. Similarly, they may feel guilty about the real thoughts and feelings they have about their sibling, for example, frustration, resentment, and even hate. Realizing that many parents would not respond positively to expression of such feelings, some siblings carry them inside only to express them later.

Many siblings resent the time and attention parents must devote to their sister or brother. This resentment may also take the form of jealously. Some siblings feel as if they have been emotionally neglected, that their parents are not responsive to their needs for attention and emotional support. For some siblings, the predominant feeling was one of bitter resentment or even rage. For others the predominant attitude toward the family experience of growing up with a disabled brother or sister was a feeling of deprivation, generally related to the notion that they felt as if their social, educational, and recreational pursuits had been seriously limited. The following statements are examples of such feelings of deprivation: "We never went on a family vacation because of my brother, Steven." "How could I invite a friend over? I never knew how my autistic brother would behave." "How do you explain to a date that you have a retarded sister?" "Many of my friends stopped coming to my house because they didn't know how to handle my deaf brother, Mike. They simply could not understand him." "I was always shackled with the responsibilities of tending my little brother. I didn't have time to have fun with my friends." "I want a real brother not a retarded one." Grossman (1972a) found that older female siblings from low-income families frequently had to assume responsibility for caring for the disabled family member. Many siblings resented having to assume the role of care-giver and felt they were deprived of some of the important opportunities that most young people want to have in growing up.

Siblings of exceptional children may also feel as if they must serve as compensators for their parents' disappointment about having a disabled child (Murphy, 1979). They may feel an undue amount of pressure to excel or to be successful in a particular academic or artistic pursuit. Such pressure can have a profound effect on the siblings' physical and mental health. In a similar vein, the expectations of parents can also serve as a source of pressure and emotional pain to siblings: "Why do I always feel as if I have to be the perfect child or the one who always does things right? I'm getting tired of constantly having to win my parents' admiration. Why can't I just be average for once?"

Sibling support groups for families with exceptional children are emerging and can be particularly helpful to adolescents. Within these groups, children and youths who are capable of benefiting from such involvement can be introduced to the important aspects of having an exceptional sibling in their family. Appropriate expectations can be established, and questions that children may be hesitant to ask in a family context may be freely discussed. These groups can also provide a therapeutic means by which these individuals can analyze family problems and identify practical solutions.

I can distinctly remember the tears of my father-in-law, and my mother-in-law's reluctance to visit me in the hospital, when they discovered that I had given birth to a child with an open spine (spina bifida). During my mother-in-law's first visit, all she could talk about was the dinner party she had held the night before and her upcoming vacation. All I could think about was my baby and whether he was going to make it through the night. At the time I was extremely angry and upset by her lack of sympathy and understanding. I could not figure out why she was so insensitive to my feelings and my son's condition.

Because of the seriousness of our son's defect, the consulting physicians recommended that Eric immediately undergo an operation. Shortly thereafter my mother-in-law asked me who had given permission for this operation, implying that it might have been better to have allowed Eric to survive or die on his own. Attempting to be stoic in spite of my heightened feelings of hostility, I remained silent. The silence was broken with another hurtful comment: "My son will be burdened for life." These and other similar comments were common during the first twenty-four months of Eric's life. It was as though I had burdened her.

As I reflect on this time period, I can see that I was simply too overwhelmed by my own feelings to give careful consideration to the comments made by my in-laws, neighbors, and friends. With the passage of time, however, I have come to understand my husband's parents and their responses to our exceptional son. They, in turn, have also developed an appreciation and understanding of our son and us. It took quite a bit of time, and we all had to adapt and change a great deal.

Eric is now ten. He loves both of his grandparents and looks forward to spending time with them on special weekend visits. It is during these weekends that my husband and I take time to renew our relationship and restore ourselves with recreational activities.

Extended family is a term frequently used to describe a household in which a nuclear family lives accompanied by a number of close relatives. For the purposes of this section, the term *extended family* is used to identify those individuals who are close relatives of the family and, while they may not be living with the family, have regular and frequent contacts with it. These individuals include such people as the grandparents and the parents' brothers and sisters and their children.

When a new child is born and becomes part of a family, he or she also becomes part of an extended family. Usually it is the grandparents who make the first official family visit or call to the hospital. This first visit from the grandparents can be extraordinarily taxing and difficult if it entails providing congratulations and support to a daughter who has given birth to a child with birth defects. In a very real fashion, grandparents perceive grandchildren as an extension of themselves (Berns, 1980). They look forward to babying, bragging about, and showing snapshots of their grandchildren without worrying about the burdens of responsibility that parents must assume. When a grandchild is born with an impairment, the joy of the occasion is almost absent. Like the biological parents, grandparents are hurled into a crisis that necessitates re-evaluation and reorientation (Pieper, 1976). They too must decide not only how they will respond to their child, who now is a parent, but also how they will relate to the child that has been born. Many grandparents grew up in a time when deviancy of almost any variety was barely tolerated, much less under-stood. Therefore they enter the crisis process without much understanding. In their day such a birth may have signified the presence of "bad blood" within a family. As a result of this attitude and other similar perceptions, the mother or the father of the newborn child may be selected as the scapegoat. But blaming only provides a temporary form of release and relief. It does little to promote the optimal family functioning that becomes so necessary in the weeks and months to come.

Little research is available regarding the impact of grandparents on the functioning of a family with an exceptional child. Davis (1967) contrasted the support maternal grandmothers gave their daughters who had given birth to a retarded child with the support provided by maternal grandmothers to daugh-ters who gave birth to normal children. Less than half the families with a retarded child received "effective" support from maternal grandmothers. By contrast, the normal families received "effective" support from three-quarters of the maternal grandmothers. In a related study, McAndrew (1976) found that 33 percent of 116 parents interviewed believed that their relationships with grandparents and friends were adversely affected by the birth of a disabled child.

Grandparents can, however, contribute much help to the primary family unit (Howard, 1978). If they live near to the family, they can become an integral part of a resource network. They may also be able to provide support before the energies of their children are so severely depleted that they need additional costly help. In order to be of assistance they must be prepared and informed. This can be achieved in a variety of ways. They must have an opportunity to voice their questions, feelings, and concerns about the disorder and its com-plications. They must have means by which they can become informed. Parents can aid in this informing process by sharing with their parents the pamphlets, materials, and books suggested by health and educational personnel. They can also encourge their parents to become involved in parent discussion groups. In such informal meetings they learn about the struggles and feelings of their own children. These meetings are also catalysts for frank and open conversa-tion. Grandparents need positive feedback regarding their efforts and support. When these conditions are met, grandparents can be an important part of the total treatment process.

According to Pieper (1976), grandparents can be helpful in several ways. They may be able to give parents a weekend reprieve from the pressures of maintaining the household. They can also assist with transportation or baby-sitting. Grandparents can also often serve as third-party evaluators, providing solutions to seemingly unresolvable problems. The grandchild with an impairment profits from the unique attention that only grandparents can provide. This attention can be a natural part of such special occasions as birthdays, vacations, fishing trips, or other traditional family activities.

Other close relatives of the family can fulfill roles similar to those of the grandparents. They too may be an important part of a resource network and may provide much valuable assistance. Like grandparents, their efforts are enhanced when they are well informed about the child's condition and receive feedback regarding the value of their assistance. Because of the mobile nature of our culture, however, many relatives are unable to provide a great deal of direct assistance to each other because of geographical distance.

We have highlighted the positive ways in which extended-family members can assist the primary family unit, but the types of assistance and support described may be difficult to find. For instance, few families freely volunteer to tend a hyperactive child. Baby-sitting exchanges and other similar arrangements are also much more difficult to set up when the tending involves a difficult child. Such is the case with many family activities. The exceptional child is not as likely to be invited to participate in recreational activities such as sleeping overnight at a friend's or cousin's house, eating dinner with neighbor's, or going with a neighborhood family on a weekend camping trip. Relatives and neighbors may also be critical of management procedures that the parents

Grandparents may provide an occasional reprieve from the demands of caring for an exceptional child.

have been encouraged to employ. Procedures associated with social isolation and various forms of punishment may be viewed as abusive parental behavior by close friends and relatives. Other types of treatment may also be viewed with a jaundiced eye if they include the use of stimulant drugs, very controlled diets, or various point systems. Parents who must administer these home-based interventions often feel they are completely alone. On the other hand, the support provided by extended-family members, if properly applied, can have a positive effect on the physical and social/emotional well-being of the primary family.

THE FAMILY'S DILEMMA: LEARNING TO WORK WITH PROFESSIONALS

I waited eagerly for the news that our obstetrician was about to bring regarding the birth of our first child. As I thought about my life and the birth of our child, I had strong feelings of anticipation. These feelings were mixed with other emotions of excitement, anxiety, and fear.

My wife and I were new at this enterprise, but we felt as if we were ready for the new arrival. Many pleasant pictures passed through my mind as I waited. Daydreaming about the future of our family, Dr. Stephens, our obstetrician, entered the small waiting-room area and immediately informed me that I had a new daughter and that my wife was perfectly fine. As he delivered this joyful news to me, his voice was flat. He did not appear to be either particularly happy or sad about the occasion. We quickly went to the viewing area, where I would have the first opportunity to see my daughter. She looked just like other babies I had seen, but I could sense that the nurses and Dr. Stephens were much more interested in my responses to my daughter than I had expected. As we stood there, Dr. Stephens asked how she looked, to which I responded, "I think she looks just fine!" It was as though he thought my child's impairment would be readily apparent to me. I saw nothing different in my child's appearance.

After viewing my daughter for the first time, I immediately went to the recovery room, where my wife was waiting to be taken to her own hospital room. She was in good spirits even though the anesthesia was still having its effect. I could tell that she was excited about our new daughter. She too asked me similar questions. "How does she look? Is she okay? Do you like her?" Although her speech was slightly slurred, she asked the questions in rapid succession. Again I responded as I had to Dr. Stephens, "Yes, she looks just fine and I think her name should be Melinda."

In the days that followed, Melinda lost quite a bit of weight, and it seemed as if she were already very sleepy and difficult to arouse. Our pediatrician was concerned, but not overly so, with the rapid weight loss. During this period, we felt as if we were in the dark. Little was said about Melinda except that she was making adequate progress. The nursing staff remained distant. They communicated only information that was essential. We began to sense that something might be wrong with our daughter. We felt that they knew something about our child that we were expected to discover by ourselves.

On the fourth day, after discussing the situation in some depth, we demanded a consultation with our pediatrician. He agreed to see us. Early the next morning we were told of the diagnosis: Down's syndrome. We were simply told that Melinda would be retarded and that her condition was stable at the present time. Our pediatrician also briefly talked about one of his relatives, who had a Down's syndrome child. He described the child as being quite happy, but such comments failed to provide us with any comfort or hope for Melinda's future. Our discussion, which was very brief, ended within fifteen minutes. We were still very much in the dark and wondering how we were to care for our new baby.

The interaction that occurs between professionals and parents is often marked with confusion, dissatisfaction, disappointment, and anger. Several writers have documented the pronounced presence of these and other negative feelings in parents (Buscaglia, 1975; Dougan, Isbell & Vyas, 1979; Fox, 1975; Turnbull & Turnbull, 1978). What are the sources of these feelings? Are they to be expected? A certain amount of dissatisfaction is present in even the best relationships. However, the research information available would lead many observers to believe that the relationship between parents and professionals could and should be significantly improved.

Many professionals are inadequately prepared to deal with the challenges of informing parents of their child's exceptionality. In a similar vein, many professionals do not have the counseling skills necessary for the development of satisfactory relationships. These and other factors frequently cause parents to shop around for an understanding physician, counselor, therapist, or educator. In discussing these relationship problems, Seligman and Seligman (1980) identified three types of professional understanding essential to establishing positive working relationships with families. First, professionals need to understand the impact they have on parents. Second, they need to understand the impact the exceptional individual has on the family over time. Third, they need to understand the impact the exceptional child and family have on the professional.

Medical and other health-related personnel have a profound impact on the ways parents respond to the birth or injury of a child. They cannot prevent the shock felt by parents as they learn of the child's impairment, but they can lessen its impact. They can also provide parents with perspective and direction as they gradually attempt to adjust their lives and make room for the child. Durham (1979), a pediatrician who examined his daughter at birth, provides

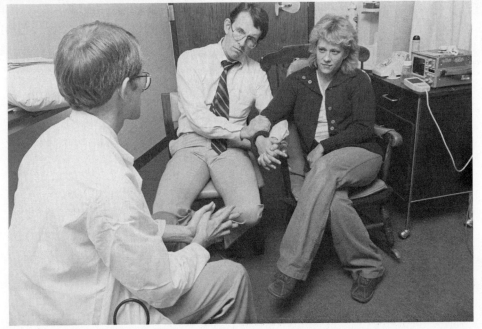

Medical personnel have a profound impact on the perceptions and feelings of parents of an exceptional infant.

insight with an account of his emotions felt as he discovered his own child's exceptionality:

> The delivery was blessedly brief. . . . The obstetrician quickly covered the infant's lower half and asked me to guess the sex. We had both expected a daughter . . . and it was.
>
> The next five minutes were among the most difficult I have ever spent. I not only confronted "surviving what the doctor has just told you," but I was the pediatrician on the scene.
>
> Our friend-nurse handed me the baby for her newborn evaluation. The obstetrician had noted a twisted left foot which I examined first. My usual routine was to examine newborns from the feet up and I soon recognized a talipes equinovarus, better known as a variety of club foot. By professional instinct I remembered the dictum "Where there is one anomaly, look for others." I did . . . and they were there.
>
> I examined her palms and discovered the frequently described simian crease and the less well-known but common hypoplastic midphalangeal sections of her petite fifth fingers. I now hoped that looking at her face and neck would dispel my fears, but there classic findings only confirmed the diagnosis. Christine and I had become the parents of a baby with Down's syndrome.
>
> Christine knew something was wrong and I tried—inadequately and gently—to describe our daughter's many signs, cataloguing them aloud

as if to help me become accustomed to the reality. Christine sensed my pain and with a gentle acceptance spoke the words I could not yet say, "Does she have Down's syndrome?" The physician in me knew but the husband/father did not want to say he was absolutely sure, so I quickly left the room to call one of my pediatric associates.

As I walked away from my wife and newborn daughter I was a valley of complicated feelings. The obstetrician and our nurse said virtually nothing to us for the next twenty-four hours. Moreover, I felt as though I had abandoned my wife and my daughter in the delivery room as I sought desperately to phone a colleague as if he could come and tell me I had erred in my diagnosis.

How to survive? It was nearly midnight. I made three calls—one to my partner, one to my parents, and one to Christine's parents. Within thirty minutes we had a family reunion in the hall just off of the labor and delivery suite. My colleague, of course, only confirmed the diagnosis and kindly began the introduction of mental retardation and the other special problems of Down's Syndrome to the assembled relatives. I concentrated on giving support to Christine.

Early the next morning, after a restless night, I called a neighbor in the next block whom I knew to be the father of a Down's daughter. I needed to talk to him. In retrospect, one of the very meaningful experiences of Melinda's birth was my realization of my need to reach out for support and understanding. Our neighbors were marvelous. Within hours they were at Christine's bedside sharing very real and human feelings. At this same time many of my professional colleagues with whom I had trained and shared so many experiences in the lives and deaths of others found difficulty in confronting us in our "new situation," whereas others who had gone through what we were now experiencing gave the needed support our friends and family could not extend.* (Durham, 1979, pp. 33–35)

Based on this vignette, one might assume that those who have personally experienced the trauma of dealing with exceptionalities in a family context are best suited to provide counsel and assistance during the initial crisis period. Such an assumption is probably valid. In reality, however, it is generally the treating physician and other health personnel who shoulder the initial responsibility for providing appropriate direction to the parents and family.

They set the stage and prepare the family for the next few days, weeks, and months. Unfortunately, many physicians are not adequately prepared to counsel with parents regarding the steps to take. In fact, many medical personnel are unaware of the resources and services available for exceptional infants and children (Gorham, 1975; Gorham, DesJardins, Page, Pettis & Schei-

**From *We Have Been There* by Terrell Dougan, Lyn Isbell, and Pat Vyas. Copyright © 1979 by Dougan, Isbell & Vyas Assoc. Used by permission of the publisher, Abingdon Press.*

ber, 1975). They are also unprepared to deal with the parents' present situation and feelings. Therefore, parents frequently leave the hospital or clinic confused and disoriented, not knowing exactly what their options are or how they should proceed. Wunderlich (1977) aptly captured many parents' sentiments when he indicated that the physician's role includes more than just providing a diagnosis.

In a comprehensive review of research related to counseling the disabled and their parents, Leigh (1975) concluded:

1. Parents are often dissatisfied with the information or lack of information provided by professionals regarding their children's problems.
2. ''Shopping'' parents are generally seeking valid assistance regarding new problem behaviors of their children rather than a new diagnosis.
3. The amount of meaningful information gained during the initial consultation is generally a function of the quality of the interactions that occur between the counselor and the parents.
4. Parents are much more likely to carry out the recommendations of the counselor or physician if they concur with the diagnosis.
5. Professionals often devalue the importance of the parents' attitudes in communicating and attempting to assist them in caring for their children.

Gorham (1975), who is a parent of a profoundly retarded child, provided some helpful suggestions for professionals interested in enhancing the positive impact they have on parents. Her suggestions include such practices as using appropriate key language in report-writing and in informal conversations, providing realistic management plans for the family that outline procedures to be taken during the next several weeks and months, emphasizing the children's assets and abilities as well as their weaknesses and deficits, referring parents to appropriate community agencies and parent organizations, and helping parents realize that their exceptional child will provide them with a series of problem-solving opportunities that they will not have to meet alone.

Little has been written about the impact the exceptional child and his or her family have on the lives of educational and health personnel. The information available is primarily anecdotal in nature. Like parents, professionals too are subject to emotional exhaustion (Maslach, 1978). Emotional exhaustion may exhibit itself in numerous ways. Professionals may become apathetic, pessimistic, or cynical about their work and involvement with patients, students, or clients. They may focus on the negative aspects of their work and feel their perceptions have become constricted. Depression is also a common characteristic of emotional exhaustion. Personnel affected this way may feel they have no power to enact meaningful changes in their work environments (Pagel & Price, 1980).

Emotional and physical exhaustion cannot be attributed entirely to the actions of families and children, but they do play an important role. As physicians, educators, and therapists interact with impaired children and their families, there are problems that frequently arise. Caring for an exceptional individual in a medical or educational setting can be very challenging. Progress may be exceedingly slow. Interventions may be unsuccessful. The exceptional individual may not be making the progress anticipated. Parents may be disappointed with the quality of services and may complain or even threaten to sue. Medication prescribed may be ineffective. These conditions can have an immense impact on the physical and mental well-being of helping professionals who feel responsible for exceptional individuals and their families. The recurring frustration, tedium, pressure, and dissatisfaction that characterize the work of helping professionals can at times be overwhelming and debilitating.

Because of the stress inherent in working with exceptional persons, many professionals experience a phenomenon known as burn-out (Freudenberger, 1977; Maslach, 1978). Child-care workers in a variety of settings leave their professional pursuits because of the excessive demands they confront. Smith and Cline (1980) evaluated the sources of stress for special education personnel. In order of importance, the following teacher tasks were identified causing stress: (1) completing individual educational programs and due-process paperwork, (2) coping with parents, (3) taking care of school-related work after the usual hours, (4) dealing with excessive student loads, (5) diagnosing and assessing, and (6) working with other teachers. It is interesting to note that the second item in order of magnitude was that of dealing with parents. In a related study, Pagel and Price (1980) reported similar findings. They found that teachers were frequently bothered by "disruptive and unmotivated students" as well as by "uncooperative parents" (p. 46).

Kraft and Snell (1980) have discussed parent-teacher conflicts. In their discussion, they include the "blame-oriented parent" and the "pseudoexpert parent." Each type of parent provides not only the teachers but also the physicians and other care providers with some unique challenges and problems. However, communication and understanding must prevail if parents and professionals are to share in the task of helping exceptional individuals achieve their fullest potential. There is still much work to be done. Both parents and professionals need to become more sensitive to one another and their respective needs. Schools that prepare people for the helping professions must provide better training for those who will be responsible for helping and counseling parents. In a similar vein, these schools should also provide their students with healthy means for coping with the stresses inherent in working with exceptional individuals and their families.

SERVICES FOR EXCEPTIONAL INDIVIDUALS AND THEIR FAMILIES

We had been to several doctors and had innumerable tests done to diagnose the cause of Diana's profound retardation. None of them had been able to pinpoint any reason for her deficits. My own conclusion was that somehow I was to blame. We were depressed mostly because we felt singled out and, frankly, I felt unable to cope.

One of the doctors suggested finding a day-care center and at least getting her on a waiting list to be admitted. (She was not yet able to walk at the time, although she was nearly three.) We did a lot of phoning and were invited to visit a day-care center which was then in an old house which had been condemned by the state and would shortly be demolished to make way for the new interstate freeway system. The staff told us of plans for a new day-care center nearby, and warmly invited us to join the parent group which met monthly to discuss common problems.

We joined the parent group and eventually Diana was admitted to the day-care program after she learned to walk. The meetings with the other parents were informative and as the parents discussed problems and how they had solved them, I found that these sessions were good therapy. But mostly we found we weren't the only ones who had been singled out to have a retarded child. And in the process we met so many people who have become our friends and who are still working hard for benefits for the retarded.* (Neeley, 1979, pp. 15–16)

A variety of services are available for exceptional individuals and their families. Many of these services are guaranteed by federal and state laws. Disabled people are eligible for medical, educational, financial, and other social services that are provided through a broad network of national, state, and community agencies and associations. Now more than ever, exceptional individuals have been granted greater access to education, employment, and health care. In this section we will review some types of assistance currently available for exceptional individuals and their families.

Parent Groups

Almost every type of disabling condition is represented by some parent or advocacy group (see p. 452). The importance of these groups and organizations cannot be underestimated. Parents of exceptional children who belong to such groups play a significant therapeutic role in helping other families cope with the stages of adjustment. These parents possess a unique type of understanding and sensitivity because they have been through the crisis periods. They know of the challenges, setbacks, and feelings that are so frequently a part of family experiences.

Parent groups serve many functions other than just providing moral support or an empathic ear. They are often responsible for promoting many types of programs for children. These may include sponsorship and support of a sheltered workshop, development of specialized group home facilities, provision of recreational and leisure-time activities, and ongoing parent education through annual local and state conferences. In addition, parent associations provide parents with access to the latest lay literature regarding various disabling conditions. Most associations publish a monthly newsletter or magazine

---

*From *We Have Been There* by Terrell Dougan, Lyn Isbell, and Pat Vyas. Copyright © 1979 by Dougan, Isbell & Vyas Assoc. Used by permission of the publisher, Abingdon Press.

for their membership. Several monthly and quarterly magazines have been developed solely for families with exceptional children.

Parent organizations also play a role in helping families unravel the bureaucratic red tape in identifying and securing appropriate services for their children. Moreover, parent organizations provide advocacy for exceptional individuals in a number of areas. They may assist these individuals directly by helping them obtain or maintain employment. They may help obtain legal assistance. During school breaks or summer vacations when school programs are not available, parent organizations frequently secure the funding and resources for such recreational activities as camping, skiing, river-running, and backpacking.

During legislative sessions, these organizations play an active role in lobbying for monies and legislation that have a direct impact on social and educational services available to the disabled. The power and impact of parent organizations is significant. In the remaining sections in this chapter, we will discuss the types of services families often become aware of through their involvement with parent and other professional groups.

Health Services

One of the most valuable resources for families is their state department of health. This agency provides a broad array of services often specifically tailored to exceptional populations. One such division is the Handicapped Children's Services (HCS) or Crippled Children's Services (CCS). Any child who is younger than twenty-one years of age and is suspected of having a disabling condition is eligible for HCS or CCS. Although funding patterns may change the nature and scope of the services provided, families who qualify may receive the diagnosis and treatment cost-free. This agency also serves as a referral resource for helping families obtain appropriate care and service for their impaired children. Almost all severe, chronic, or disabling forms of disorders (orthopedic, heart and kidney diseases, cerebral palsy, birth defects, serious eye and ear conditions) can be treated directly by HCS or CCS or by agencies with whom they have contracts for health care.

In addition to Handicapped Children's Services, state health departments also provide assistance in the following areas: (1) family planning, (2) genetic counseling, (3) infant stimulation, (4) maternal and infant care, (5) nutrition counseling, (6) early periodic screening and treatment, and (7) provision of supplemental foods. Some state departments provide these services in regional offices, while others utilize traveling clinics that regularly rotate through a given geographical area. As a rule, the services provided are free of charge or rendered on a sliding-fee scale.

Social Services

State social service agencies also provide assistance to families who have exceptional children. Child welfare services are designed to (1) prevent or remediate problems related to neglect, abuse, exploitation, or delinquency of children; (2) protect and care for homeless, dependent, or neglected children; and (3) protect and promote the welfare of children. Title IV-B of the Social Security Act provides state social service agencies with funds for referral or provision for special care to mentally retarded and physically disabled children, assistance to children discharged from institutions, respite care, foster care, day care, homemaker services, and adoptive placements of children.

Other federal legislation provides funding for case management, child development, alternative community living, and other social/developmental services for the disabled. This funding came into being as a result of subsequent amendments to the Developmental Disabilities Assistance and Bill of Rights Act. This act makes it possible for state social service or other related departments to secure funds to ameliorate service gaps or deficiencies in current social service programs for the disabled.

A *developmental disability*, as defined in the act, refers to an individual who has a severe, chronic, or physical impairment that (1) began at birth or emerged during childhood, (2) is expected to continue indefinitely, and (3) substantially restricts the individual's capacity to perform many functional life skills. The funds that come from the federal government are generally administered through the social services department of each state. However, the actual selection of programs to be funded through developmental disabilities monies is made by a state Departmental Disabilities Planning Council (DDPC). Parents may become aware of services available to them and their children by contacting their state DDPC. There are numerous programs administered through state social service departments which have a direct impact on disabled children and their families. However, the impact may be minimal for families that are unaware of the types of assistance available.

Financial Services

There are a variety of sources from which families may secure financial assistance. The major source of financial assistance is provided through Social Security Disability (SSD) benefits. Monthly cash payments are made to eligible disabled persons who have passed a statutory test of disability or blindness. In order to qualify for SSD benefits, a recipient must be unable to engage in any gainful employment as a result of some severe physical or mental impairment. Surviving children of a disabled parent are also eligible for assistance if the child developed a permanent disability prior to the age of twenty-two.

Applicants and recipients are processed through state vocational rehabilitation agencies. These agencies also provide other valuable services, such as counseling, health and restoration services, training, job placement, postemployment services, and transportation and maintenance allowances. Any individual sixteen or older who is eligible for employment may apply for vocational rehabilitation services.

Other types of financial assistance are also available to disabled individuals who need support in obtaining, maintaining, or repairing housing. Through a series of housing acts passed from 1937 to the present, disabled individuals may receive aid in the form of rent subsidies; funding for conjugate housing

(housing that includes residential shelter and social services such as the provision of meals, housekeeping assistance, and help with personal hygiene and grooming); insured loans for purchasing or repairing housing; and insured loans for building conjugate housing, sheltered workshop facilities, and group homes. For example, a family of a youngster who has experienced spinal cord injury as a result of a severe automobile accident may receive funds to make their home more accessible to their son by installing a ramp and modifying certain interior features of their home.

Educational Services

Educational opportunities for children and youths with handicapping conditions have expanded greatly in recent years. The right to a free and appropriate education in the public schools has been reaffirmed by the courts as well as by state and federal legislation. The Education of All Handicapped Children Act (P.L. 94-142), in conjunction with state mandatory special education laws, clearly established society's intent to provide for the educational needs of the exceptional individual. A discussion of the litigation leading to the passage of P.L. 94-142, as well as the major constructs of this law, may be found in Chapter 2, page 53.

The federal government has also provided funding incentives for libraries, colleges and universities, technical schools, and other related institutions to make their physical facilities and curriculum offerings more available to handicapped individuals. Federal vocational education funding requires that 10 percent of the state allotment must be utilized to provide vocational training to the disabled. An important national resource for parents and guardians is an organization known as Closer Look, The National Information Center for the Handicapped. It specializes in assisting families as they seek to find appropriate services for their children.

Employment Services

Training and education are crucial to disabled individuals. Without appropriate preparation, many will find it practically impossible to secure a job. Fortunately, most postsecondary educational institutions provide instruction and training for exceptional people. The state vocational rehabilitation division is responsible for assisting the disabled in acquiring occupational training and eventually securing employment. Personnel in this agency will also be aware of sheltered workshop employment available to the more severely impaired.

Sections 501, 503, and 504 of the Rehabilitation Act and Section 402 of the Vietnam Era Veterans Readjustment Assistance Act ensure that physically and mentally disabled individuals will have access to employment with employers who have contracts with the government that exceed ten thousand dollars (U.S. Department of Education, 1980). These affirmative-action programs cover more than just the hiring of the disabled, they include such employment related actions as job assignments, promotions, transfers, working conditions, training, and termination. Affirmative-action programs are primarily intended to encourage employers to hire qualified disabled individuals. They also encourage disabled people to enter the labor market and demonstrate their work skills.

̂ SUMMARY

The birth of an exceptional infant often has an immediate and shocking impact on the family. Those first affected are the parents, who pass through several stages of reaction as they attempt to adjust. The initial effect may be one of severe crisis in terms of the parents' personal functioning, thought structure, and view of themselves. Considerable stress may also be placed on the marital relationship. The relationships of parents to the disabled child are often different. Mothers frequently become quite attached to the child, even to the point of being overprotective. Fathers may play a very different role, and it is not uncommon for them to experience feelings of rejection by their wife as she becomes involved with the youngster.

Siblings are also greatly affected by the entrance of a disabled youngster into the family. Often they experience difficulty responding to questions from their peers regarding their brother or sister. They may also feel left out and deprived because of the attention given to their exceptional sibling. In certain cases they also have an unusual burden in that they are expected to baby-sit or provide other care for the exceptional youngster.

Several types of assistance are available to families encountering the trauma of a disabled relative. Parent and advocacy groups have recently come to provide a moving force for such help. In addition, many agencies and other organizations are committed to helping exceptional individuals and their families.

̂ REVIEW QUESTIONS

1. Think carefully about your family and its members during the time you were living at home. What do you think would have been their reaction if a disabled infant had been born into the family? What might your reaction have been? How might the family unit have been altered?
2. How are marital relations typically affected by an exceptional child?
3. Describe the factors influencing parents' relationships with their exceptional child.
4. Describe the factors influencing siblings' responses to their exceptional brothers or sisters.
5. What type of impact might the birth of an exceptional infant have on extended-family members?
6. What are important factors involved in the interactions between professionals and parents of exceptional youngsters?
7. Where might one find information regarding services for exceptional individuals and their families?

PARENT, PROFESSIONAL, AND
ADVOCACY ORGANIZATIONS

Learning and Behavioral Disorders

American Association of Psychiatric Services for Children, 250 West 57th Street, New York, New York 10019.

American Orthopsychiatric Association, Inc., 1790 Broadway, New York, New York 10019.

American Psychiatric Association, 1700 18th Street, N.W., Washington, D.C. 20009.

Group for the Advancement of Psychiatry, 419 Park Avenue South, New York, New York 10016.

National Association for Mental Health, 1800 North Kent Street, Arlington, Virginia 22209.

National Council of Community Mental Health Centers, 2233 Wisconsin Avenue, N.W., Washington, D.C. 20007.

Learning Disabilities

American Academy of Neurology, 4005 West 69th Street, Minneapolis, Minnesota, 55435.

Association for Children with Learning Disabilities, 5225 Grace Street, Pittsburgh, Pennsylvania 15236.

California Association for Neurologically Handicapped Children, P.O. Box 4088, Los Angeles, California 90051.

International Reading Association, 6 Tyre Avenue, Newark, Delaware 19711.

New York Association for Brain Injured Children, Richardson Hall, Room 272, State University of New York at Albany, Albany, New York 12222.

Orton Society, 8415 Bellona Lane, Towson, Maryland 21204.

Texas Association for Children with Learning Disabilities, 12610 East Shadowlake, Cypress, Texas 77429.

Mental Retardation

American Association on Mental Deficiency, 5201 Connecticut Avenue, N.W., Washington, D.C. 20015.

American Psychiatric Association, 1700 18th Street, N.W., Washington, D.C. 20009.

Association for the Help of Retarded Children, 200 Park Avenue South, New York, New York 10003.

Down's Syndrome Congress, 529 South Kenilworth, Oak Park, Illinois 60304.

Institute for the Study of Mental Retardation and Related Disabilities, 130 South First, University of Michigan, Ann Arbor, Michigan 48108.

International Association for the Scientific Study of Mental Deficiency, Ellen Horn, AAMD, 5201 Connecticut Avenue, N.W., Washington, D.C. 20015.

International League of Societies for the Mentally Handicapped, rue Forestiere 12, B-1050, Brussels, Belgium.

National Association of Sheltered Workshops and Homebound Programs, 1522 K Street N.W., Washington, D.C. 20005.

National Apostolate for the Mentally Retarded, P.O. Box 4588, Trinity College, Washington, D.C. 20017.

National Association for Retarded Citizens, 2709 Avenue E East, Arlington, Texas 76011.

National Association of Private Residential Facilities for the Mentally Retarded, 6269 Leesburg Pike, Falls Church, Virginia 22044.

National Institute on Mental Retardation, Kinsman NIMR Building, York University Campus, 4700 Keele Street, Downsview (Toronto), Ontario, Canada M3J 1P3.

President's Committee on Mental Retardation, Washington, D.C. 20201.

Severe and Profound/Multiple Disorders

American Academy of Child Psychiatry, 1800 R Street, N.W., Washington, D.C. 20009.

American Academy of Neurology, 4005 West 69th Street, Minneapolis, Minnesota 55435.

American Association for the Education of the Severely and Profoundly Handicapped, P.O. Box 15287, Seattle, Washington 98115.

American Association of Psychiatric Services for Children, 250 West 57th Street, New York, New York 10019.

American Association on Mental Deficiency, 5201 Connecticut Avenue, N.W., Washington, D.C. 20015.

American Genetic Association, 1028 Connecticut Avenue, N.W., Washington, D.C. 20036.

American Orthotic and Prosthetic Association, 1440 N Street, N.W., Washington, D.C. 20005.

American Psychiatric Association, 1700 18th Street, N.W., Washington, D.C. 20009.

American Schizophrenia Association, Huxley Institute, 1114 First Avenue, New York, New York 10021.

Group for the Advancement of Psychiatry, 419 Park Avenue South, New York, New York 10016.

International League of Societies for the Mentally Handicapped, rue Forestiere 12, B-1050, Brussels, Belgium.

National Association for Mental Health, 1800 North Kent Street, Arlington, Virginia 22209.

National Association of Private Residential Facilities for the Mentally Retarded, 6269 Leesburg Pike, Falls Church, Virginia 22044.

National Association for Retarded Citizens, 2709 Avenue E East, Arlington, Texas 76011.

National Committee for Multi-Handicapped Children, 239 14th Street, Niagara Falls, New York 14303.

National Genetics Foundation, 250 West 57th Street, New York, New York 10019.

National Information and Referral Service for Autistic and Autistic-like Persons, 306 31st Street, Huntington, West Virginia 25702.

National Institute on Mental Retardation, Kinsman NIMR Building, York University Campus, 4700 Keele Street, Downsview (Toronto), Ontario, Canada M3J 1P3.

National Society for Autistic Children, 169 Tampa Avenue, Albany, New York 12208.

New York Association for Brain Injured Children, Richardson Hall, Room 272, State University of New York at Albany, Albany, New York 12222.

President's Committee on Mental Retardation, Washington, D.C. 20201.

Speech and Language Disorders

American Speech and Hearing Association, 9030 Old Georgetown Road, Bethesda, Maryland 20014.

Speech Foundation of America, 152 Lombardy Road, Memphis, Tennessee 38111.

Vision Disorders

American Association of Opthalmology, 1100 17th Street, N.W., Washington, D.C. 20036.

American Foundation for the Blind, 15 West 16th Street, New York, New York 10011.

American Optometric Association, 7000 Chippewa Street, St. Louis, Missouri 63119.

American Printing House for the Blind, 1839 Frankfort Avenue, Louisville, Kentucky 40206.

Association for Education of the Visually Handicapped, 919 Walnut Street, Philadelphia, Pennsylvania 19107.

Association for the Visually Handicapped, 1839 Frankfort Avenue, Louisville, Kentucky 40206.

Library of Congress, Division for the Blind and Physically Handicapped, Washington, D.C. 20542.

National Aid to the Visually Handicapped, 3201 Balboa Street, San Francisco, California 94121.

National Association for the Visually Handicapped, 3201 Balboa Street, San Francisco, California 94121.

National Federation of the Blind, 218 Randolph Hotel, Des Moines, Iowa 50309.

United Cerebral Palsy Association, 66 East 34th Street, New York, New York 10016.

Hearing Disorders

Alexander Graham Bell Association for the Deaf, 3417 Volta Place, N.W., Washington, D.C. 20007.

American Speech and Hearing Association, 9030 Old Georgetown Road, Bethesda, Maryland 20014.

International Association of Parents of the Deaf, 814 Thayer Avenue, Silver Spring, Maryland 20910.

National Association of the Deaf, 814 Thayer Avenue, Silver Spring, Maryland 20910.

Volta Speech Association for the Deaf, 1537 35th Street, N.W., Washington, D.C. 20007.

Physical Disorders

American Academy for Cerebral Palsy, 1255 New Hampshire Avenue, N.W., Washington, D.C. 20036.

American Academy of Pediatrics, 1801 Hinman Avenue, Evanston, Illinois 60204.

American Epilepsy Society, Department of Neurology, University of Minnesota, Box 341, Mayo Building, Minneapolis, Minnesota 55455.

American Medical Association, 535 North Dearborn Street, Chicago, Illinois 60610.

American Occupational Therapy Foundation, 6000 Executive Boulevard, Rockville, Maryland 20852.

Arthritis Foundation, 1212 Avenue of the Americas, New York, New York 10036.

Association for the Aid of Crippled Children, 345 East 46th Street, New York, New York 10017.

American Orthotic and Prosthetic Association, 1440 N Street, N.W., Washington, D.C. 20005.

American Physical Therapy Association, 1156 15th Street, N.W., Washington, D.C. 20005.

Arthritis Foundation, 1212 Avenue of the Americas, New York, New York 10036.

Epilepsy Foundation of America, 1828 L Street, N.W., Washington, D.C. 20036.

Friedreich's Ataxia Group in America, P.O. Box 1116, Oakland, California 94611.

Library of Congress, Division for the Blind and Physically Handicapped, Washington, D.C. 20542.

Muscular Dystrophy Associations of America, 810 7th Avenue, New York, New York 10019.
National Amputee Foundation, 12-45 150th Street, Whitestone, New York 11357.
National Ataxia Foundation, 4225 Bolden Valley Road, Minneapolis, Minnesota 55422.
National Easter Seal Society for Crippled Children and Adults, 2023 West Ogden Avenue, Chicago, Illinois 60612.
National Epilepsy League, 116 South Michigan Avenue, Chicago, Illinois 60603.
National Paraplegia Foundation, 333 North Michigan Avenue, Chicago, Illinois 60601.
Spastics Society, 12 Part Crescent, London, WIN, 4EQ, England.
Spina Bifida Association of America, P.O. Box G-1974, Elmhurst, Illinois 60126.
United Cerebral Palsy Association, 66 East 34th Street, New York, New York 10016.

Health Disorders

Allergy Foundation of America, 801 Second Avenue, New York, New York 10017.
America Academy of Neurology, 4005 West 69th Street, Minneapolis, Minnesota 55435.
America Academy of Pediatrics, 1801 Hinman Avenue, Evanston, Illinois 60204.
American Diabetes Association, 18 East 48th Street, New York, New York 10017.
American Heart Association, 44 East 23rd Street, New York, New York 10016.
American Lung Association, 1790 Broadway, New York, New York 10019.
American Medical Association, 535 North Dearborn Street, Chicago, Illinois 60610.
Arthritis Foundation, 1212 Avenue of the Americas, New York, New York 10036.
Center for Sickle Cell Anemia, College of Medicine, Howard University, 520 W Street N.W., Washington, D.C. 20001.
National Cancer Foundation, 1 Park Avenue, New York, New York 10016.
National Cystic Fibrosis Research Foundation, 3379 Peachtree Road N.E., Atlanta, Georgia 30326.
National Heart Institute, 9600 Rockville Pike, Building 31, Room 5A50, Bethesda, Maryland 20014.
National Institute of Arthritis and Metabolic Disease, Bethesda, Maryland 20014.

Noncategorical Advocacy and Information Organizations and Agencies

American Alliance for Health, Physical Education, and Recreation, 1201 16th Street, N.W., Washington, D.C. 20036.
American Civil Liberties Union, 85 Fifth Avenue, New York, New York 10011.
American Coalition for Citizens with Disabilities, 1346 Connecticut Avenue, N.W., Washington, D.C. 20036.
American Psychological Association, 1200 17th Street, N.W., Washington, D.C. 20036.
Association for the Advancement of Behavior Therapy, 305 East 45th Street, New York, New York 10017.
Center for Law and Social Policy, 1751 N. Street, N.W., Washington, D.C. 20009.
Center on Human Policy, Syracuse University, Syracuse, New York 13210.
Child Study Association of America, 50 Madison Avenue, New York, New York 10010.
Child Welfare League of America, 67 Irving Place, New York, New York 10003.
Children's Defense Fund, 1763 R Street, N.W., Washington, D.C. 20009.

Children's Foundation, 1028 Connecticut Avenue, N.W., Suite 1112, Washington, D.C. 20036.

Committee for the Handicapped, People to People Program, 1028 Connecticut Avenue, N.W., Washington, D.C. 20036.

Council for Exceptional Children, 1920 Association Drive, Reston, Virginia 22091.

Council of National Organizations for Children and Youth, 1910 K Street, N.W., Washington, D.C. 20005.

Education Commission of the States, Handicapped Children's Education Project, 300 Lincoln Tower, 1860 Lincoln Street, Denver, Colorado 80203.

Goodwill Industries of America, 9200 Wisconsin Avenue, Washington, D.C. 20014.

International Society for Rehabilitation of the Disabled, 219 East 44th Street, New York, New York 10017.

Joseph P. Kennedy, Jr., Foundation, 1701 K Street, N.W., Suite 205, Washington, D.C. 20006.

Mental Health Law Project, 1751 N Street, N.W., Washington, D.C. 20036.

National Association for Music Therapy, P.O. Box 610, Lawrence, Kansas 66044.

National Association of Private Schools for Exceptional Children, P.O. Box 928, Lake Wales, Florida 33853.

National Association of Social Workers, 2 Park Avenue, New York, New York 10016.

National Association of Superintendents of Public Residential Facilities, c/o J. Iverson Riddle, M.D., Superintendent, West Carolina Center, Morganton, North Carolina 28655.

National Catholic Education Association, 1 Dupont Circle, N.W., Washington, D.C. 20036.

National Center for Child Advocacy, U.S. Department of Health, Education, and Welfare, Office of Child Development, P.O. Box 1182, Washington, D.C. 20013.

National Center for Law and the Handicapped, 1236 North Eddy Street, South Bend, Indiana 46617.

National Center for Voluntary Action, 1735 I Street, N.W., Washington, D.C. 20006.

National Center on Educational Media and Materials for the Handicapped, Ohio State University, 220 West 12th Avenue, Columbus, Ohio 43210.

National Committee for Citizens in Education, 410 Wilde Lake Village Green, Columbia, Maryland 21044.

National Education Association, 1201 16th Street, N.W., Washington, D.C. 20036.

National Foundation/March of Dimes, Box 2000, White Plains, New York 10602.

National Genetics Foundation, 250 West 57th Street, New York, New York 10019.

National Legal Aid and Defender Association, 2100 M Street, N.W., Washington, D.C. 20037.

National Recreation and Park Association, 1601 North Kent Street, Arlington, Virginia 22209.

National Rehabilitation Association, 1522 K Street, N.W., Washington, D.C. 20005.

Parenting Materials Information Center, Southwest Educational Development Laboratory, 211 East 7th Street, Austin, Texas 78701.

Physical Education and Recreation for the Handicapped: Information and Research Utilization Center, 1201 16th Street, N.W., Washington, D.C. 20036.

President's Committee on Employment of the Handicapped, Washington, D.C. 20210.

SIECUS (Sex Information and Education Council of the U.S.), 72 Fifth Avenue, New York, New York 10011.

Therapeutic Recreation Information Center, University of Oregon, 1597 Agate Street, Eugene, Oregon 97403.

United States Department of Health, Education, and Welfare, Health Services Administration, Bureau of Community Health Services, 5600 Fishers Lane, Rockville, Maryland 20857.

National Institutes of Health:

National Institute of Child Health and Human Developmnent, Office of Research Reporting, Landow Building, Room B-806, Bethesda, Maryland 20014.

National Institute of Mental Health, 5600 Fishers Lane, Rockville, Maryland 20857.

National Clearinghouse of Mental Health Information, Public Inquiries Section, 11400 Rockville Pike, Rockville, Maryland 20852.

Gifted and Talented

American Association for Gifted Children, 15 Gramercy Park, New York, New York 10003.

National Association for Gifted Children, 8080 Spring Valley Drive, Cincinnati, Ohio 45236.

National Council for the Gifted, 700 Prospect Avenue, West Orange, New Jersey 07052.

CHAPTER FIFTEEN

Adult and Aging Factors in Exceptionality

Research on Aging
Defining Adulthood and Aging
Characteristics
    Physiological Factors

Cognition/Intellectual Factors
Behavioral and Personality Factors
Employment and Economics
Leisure and Living

Most of the attention given to exceptional populations in the past has focused on youngsters, but more recent work has begun to address the status of and problems encountered by exceptional adults. This new emphasis has altered the overall perspective of exceptionality and broadened the views of many professionals working in the area. The needs and services required by exceptional children and youths and by exceptional adults vary greatly. Study of adult exceptionality has great potential for professionals entering the field.

Gerry was thirty-one years old when he came to what may have been the most startling realization of his life. He was learning disabled! Gerry was uncertain what the label meant, but at least he now had a term for what had mostly been a difficult life. The label came from a clinical psychologist who had administered a number of tests to him. Gerry had been referred to the psychologist by his counselor, whom he had been seeing since his divorce a year ago. The past year had been particularly rough, although most of Gerry's life had been troublesome.

As a young child, Gerry was often left out of the group by others. He was not very adept at sports, was uncoordinated, and could not catch or hit a baseball no matter how hard he tried. School was worse. Gerry had a difficult time completing assignments, and he often forgot what was supposed to be done. Paying attention in class was difficult, and it often seemed as though there were more interesting activities than the assignments. Gerry finally gave up on school when he was a junior and took a job in a local service station. That employment did not last long, for he was terminated because of the frequent errors he committed in billing. The owners said they could not afford to lose so much money because of "stupid mistakes on credit card invoices."

The loss of that job did not bother Gerry much. He was an enterprising young man and had already found employment in the post office which paid much more and seemed to have greater respectability. Sorting letters presented a problem, however, and loss of that job troubled Gerry. He began to doubt his mental ability further and sought comfort in his girlfriend, whom he had met recently at a YMCA dance. They married quickly when she became pregnant, but things did not become easier. After twelve years of marriage, two children, a divorce, and five jobs, we find Gerry labeled as learning disabled.

Roberta celebrated her fifty-fourth birthday with her dearest friends, Spencer, Ernie, and Josephine. They had a cake brought from the kitchen, with a single candle on top. Roberta's elderly friends seemed like family although none of her actual family were present—they had not visited Roberta for several years. Roberta lived in a nursing home just outside of Bend. She had not always lived there, in fact, she was a new resident compared to many. Five years earlier she had moved to the Willamette Manor Nursing Home from Riverview State Hospital, a residential institution for the mentally retarded. At Willamette Manor, Roberta was content with her friends, even though they were not similar with respect to age. Her best friend, Ernie, was seventy-six, while Spencer and Josephine were both in their early eighties.

Roberta has spent thirty-eight years living in residential institutions of one type or another. She was committed at the age of sixteen and had *a measured IQ of sixty-two at that time. Ruth has not been retested since she was forty years old, at which time her IQ was measured to be 51.*

Many questions face us regarding these case studies. Could Gerry's life as an adult be improved if intervention had occurred when he was younger? What can be done at this point? Is Roberta an elderly person and therefore appropriately placed in the Willamette Manor Nursing Home? Do retarded individuals age differently from their normal counterparts? Are older exceptional individuals more or less happy with their lot in life, even if we are speaking of residential care? These questions and others will receive attention in this chapter, although you should not expect precise answers. Adult life for exceptional individuals presents some perplexing issues.

This book has already shown that many different conditions are evident as one views human characteristics from a broad perspective. These conditions range from those representing serious physiological disease states to minor and transient emotional disruptions. However, what may be the most broadly dreaded condition in American culture has not been addressed—growing older. During the past few decades, our society has placed great emphasis on youth. Whether we admit it or not, many of us do not look forward to—we may even fear—becoming older.

Our population in general has become older over the years as the demands of mere survival have diminished and technology has progressed. Kaplan (1979) noted, "Geriatric psychiatry stands on the threshold of a period of great expansion, both in research and in clinical practice. It is estimated that there will be about 50 million Americans age 65 or over in the year 2030" (p. 1). Beyond the sheer increase in numbers of older people, there has also been a heightened interest and concern about the problems and welfare of this population. This interest has emerged only recently for exceptional individuals. With rare exceptions, most of the clinical attention and writing related to exceptional populations has focused on youths and children. However, the exceptional individual often grows up and frequently grows old, as illustrated by Table

Table 15-1/ U.S. Disability Rate Between Ages 16 and 65 by Sex and Age, 1970 Census. (Percent Disabled 6 Months or More)

	Total	*Male*	*Female*
Total	9.3	10.1	8.5
Age			
16-24	4.5	5.9	3.1
25-34	5.0	5.7	4.4
35-44	7.6	8.1	7.2
45-55	12.7	13.4	12.0
55-65	21.0	22.1	20.0

Source: From the U.S. Bureau of the Census. Used by permission.

15-1, which is derived from the 1970 census. Thus the topic is one that cannot be ignored.

The increased attention to adult and elderly populations also requires reflection on some fundamental questions if research is to progress effectively. For example, the notions of *adult, aging,* and *old* need serious examination, particularly as we view populations with exceptional characteristics. Most of us have some idea about the meaning of such terms, but our concepts are often quite personal and very fluid. As children, we typically thought of our parents as being old even though they may have been in their early forties, an age most adults do not view as old and some think is rather young. Is Gerry an adult? Most of us would say yes, but few would consider him to be "old." Is Roberta an elderly person? Certainly fifty-four is not young—by some people it may be viewed as being close, but not many would classify fifty-four years of age as "old." Yet Roberta lives in a nursing home with friends that most would say are elderly.

Living conditions and lifestyles for adult exceptional populations vary greatly. Many with mild disorders will have rather normal lives (though perhaps marginal) in that they may reside in the normal mainstream, perhaps marry, and be mostly self-supporting. Others, with more severe disorders, may reach adulthood, grow older, and die in residential institutions. The range of services varies greatly, and models of service delivery for such populations have been discussed in Chapter 2. Questions regarding the quality of life are complex and

Many more exceptional adults would be self-supporting, given the opportunity.

defy simple solutions (issues also examined in Chapter 2). Thus, as we begin
to explore the adult and advanced years for exceptional people, it is obvious
that precise answers will be infrequent. The lack of clear distinctions stems
from the conceptual problems noted above and the difficulties in conducting
solid research on aging.

RESEARCH ON AGING

Research on aging in general is a relatively recent phenomenon in the overall
field of behavioral science, and even more recent with exceptional populations.
In fact, empirical evidence regarding the aging process in exceptional individuals is "so limited that it might be characterized as nearly nonexistent" (Chinn,
Drew & Logan, 1979, p. 333). As suggested by our introductory comments, the
topic of aging is not clearly defined, probably because of the paucity of studies
in the area. However, other factors pertaining to problems in research methodology also seem relevant.

Research on aging faces some difficult complexities that have been com-
prehensively examined by Schaie and Gribbin (1975). These complexities have
greatly deterred the accumulation of evidence about aging. The study of aging
has typically employed one of two approaches, the cross-sectional design or
the longitudinal design. Both have certain strengths and limitations.

Investigations on the aging process necessarily study individuals across
varying age levels. The fundamental operating assumption is that as one observes behavioral and psychological status across ages one can draw conclusions regarding the effects of aging. Cross-sectional designs approach this by
sampling subjects from several age levels. For example, a cross-sectional investigation may select subjects from five groupings, those that are between 20
and 29, 30, and 39, 40 and 49, 50 and 59, and 60 and 69 years of age. Such a
study would then obtain measures that were thought important (e.g., IQ, annual
income, response time, job satisfaction) and compare groups. Differences between
groups might then be attributed to aging.

Longitudinal investigations use a quite different approach. Studies employing a longitudinal design select only one sample of subjects and then follow
these individuals as they grow older. Such investigations may measure individuals' behavioral or psychological status at age 25, 35, 45, 55, and 65. Once
again, significant differences between measures at different ages might be attributed to the aging process.

Both cross-sectional and longitudinal approaches have certain limitations
and strengths. Cross-sectional investigations are more convenient to execute
than longitudinal studies, because the researcher can gather all the data in a
short period of time. However, attributing differences to aging in cross-sectional
designs is more difficult than with longitudinal research. Since various age-
groups are used (e.g., 20 to 29, 60 to 69), differences may be the result of
sociocultural differences instead of aging. With nearly half a century between
the example groups, it is likely that the younger group was educated differently

and grew up in different social environments than the older group. Longitudinal designs also encounter certain difficulties. Interested readers may wish to consult volumes focusing on such research (e.g., Achenbach, 1978; Nesselroade & Baltes, 1979; Schaie & Gribbin, 1975).

We have already mentioned that aging is a fluid concept. There is considerable variation in terms of what chronological age is considered to represent adulthood or elderly status. Certainly there are rules of thumb; some are derived from legislation (e.g., eighteen years of age may be viewed as reaching adult status because one can then vote), while others have a historic tradition derived from other sources (e.g., sixty-five years old being viewed as retirement age by agencies or companies providing retirement benefits). We all know of many exceptions to such rules, however, and these exceptions seem to be particularly problematic as we examine certain types of exceptional individuals. For example, Dickerson, Hamilton, Huber, and Segal (1974) suggested that a mentally retarded individual between the ages of forty-five and fifty might be considered old. "Such conjecture is striking primarily because a chronological age of 45 to 50, or even 55, would not typically be thought of as old in the general population" (Chinn et al., 1979, p. 335). Such problems in defining age are not new to research on aging and have led some authors to consider the idea of **functional age** as an appropriate concept for investigating the aging process (e.g., Birren, 1959; Nuttall, 1972). Functional age reflects a person's level of functioning or ability to perform a task relative to the average age of those who can perform the task. Although such an idea has certain intuitive appeal, assumptions underlying the concept have a number of potential problems, and some data have not supported the notion (Schaie & Gribbin, 1975) and "the status of functional age as a concept, and as an index, is still uncertain" (Birren & Renner, 1977, p. 16). The definition of age has presented considerable difficulty for researchers working in the area of aging (Siegel, 1980).

The study of aging is not new, although its visibility has grown recently. Problems associated with studying the process have been evident for years. For example, Cowdry (1942) noted that "a general theory of aging is very difficult, if not impossible to formulate at the present time" (p. xv). There have been advances in theory and research procedures since Cowdry's statement, but considerable confusion still exists regarding the appropriate way to view aging processes. Birren and Renner (1977) described the conceptual base for aging research: "While there is much to be optimistic about our advancement in understanding the processes of aging, . . . there is [little] in the way of systematic theory to help us organize the information that exists" (p. 35).

DEFINING ADULTHOOD AND AGING

Our earlier discussion illustrated the fluid nature of the concepts of adulthood and elderly status. As individuals we all hold different perceptions, and those views change from time to time and between types of individuals. As we continue our examination, however, it is essential that we have a common referent. Consequently we will use chronological age as our definitional reference.

We do not intend this choice to discount other perspectives, such as biological age, psychological age, social age (Birren & Renner, 1977), or functional age (Birren, 1959; Nuttall, 1972). These views may have a great deal of validity, but to date they have not proven themselves as preeminent concepts in the study of aging. Chronological age is a measure that has a common reference point both for professionals and for the lay public. Imperfect and imprecise as it may be, chronological age (CA) provides a means for comparing biological, psychological, social, and functional status between populations.

Dividing the life span into periods is clearly arbitrary, as evidenced by the differing perspectives of aging. Our scheme is based on a composite review of several author's work (e.g., Bromley, 1974; Gould, 1972; Havighurst, 1972; Levinson, Darrow, Klein, Levinson & McKee, 1974; Neugarten, 1974). For our purposes, adulthood falls between CAs of 20 to 60. Early adulthood ("young adults") is between 20 and 35 years of age, and the middle-age category is applied to those between the ages of 35 and 60. Such gross categories raise many questions for most of us, probably because of the terminology and our respective ages or views. There is little question that these categories are imprecise to some degree, but the research is imprecise and variable too. As we continue our discussion, it will become clear that these age limits are fluid, partly because of definitional differences and partly because of the research that is available.

CHARACTERISTICS

Adulthood represents the major portion of most people's life, although it may be the least studied of all the stages in the life cycle. Less scientific information is available concerning changes during the adult years than during prenatal development, childhood, adolescence, and the time when one is considered to be elderly (Lugo & Hershey, 1979). Traditional developmental views, particularly in the behavioral sciences, have focused largely on children and youths (Reinert, 1980). In fact, a review of the literature shows that there is an inverse relationship between age and the amount of research evidence available (i.e., a great deal on exceptional children, less on adolescents, and even less on adults). As we continue this chapter, the paucity of information about adult exceptional populations will become even more evident. In many cases our discussion of this population will have to be in terms of traditional categories of exceptionality (mental retardation, learning disabilities, etc.), because that is the manner in which the literature exists. Each area of discussion begins with an examination of the normal adult in order to provide the reader with a referent from which to view the exceptional adult. Readers interested in more comprehensive information regarding normal adults may wish to consult any of a number of volumes focusing solely on life-span development (e.g., Baltes, 1978; Baltes & Brim, 1979; Baltes & Brim, 1980).

In discussing the exceptional adult, we will be examining individuals in the same age range mentioned as representing adulthood for normal populations. This group, however, is in many respects different from their normal counterparts. As we address this adult population, we are speaking of individuals who, by this time or during this period, have been diagnosed, evaluated, or otherwise identified as exceptional individuals. They have learning, behavior, health, physical, communication, or sensory disorders of sufficient magnitude to classify them in one of the categories presented in the previous chapters.

There is a general perception of the exceptional adult that does not present a pleasant picture. For example, Heward and Orlansky (1980) cited evidence regarding how physically handicapped young adults eighteen to twenty-two years of age felt about their lives. They noted that a vast majority of these young people "felt their lives were unsuccessful in *all* areas. Most . . . were unemployed . . . few had any friends, most were almost completely dependent on their parents" and had poor self-concepts (p. 385). Other authors have written about employment and economic discrimination related to those with learning, behavior, and health disorders (e.g., Gliedman & Roth, 1980). Our task here is to examine the status of exceptional adults in several areas. In some cases inferences must be drawn from data available on exceptional children or adolescents because similar evidence regarding exceptional adults is so scarce.

Physiological Factors

From a biological or physical perspective, humans generally reach their peak during early adulthood. Most people are in their best physical condition between the ages of twenty and twenty-five (Stevens-Long, 1979). Several factors are involved as we speak of physical status: general health, endurance, height, speed, coordination, strength, and speed of response. There is considerable variability regarding the development, peak status, and decline of these factors. For example, people often grow slightly in terms of height between nineteen and twenty-eight years of age (Hammar & Owens, 1973). Physical strength of the striped muscles is typically greatest between the ages of twenty-three and twenty-seven, whereas one's ability to work at a maximum rate without fatigue does not begin to decline until about age thirty-five (Hershey, 1974). It should be noted that decline in physical status during the early adult years is gradual, in fact, "so gradual as to make them seem like a long plateau" (Troll, 1975, p. 16).

Prior to about 1970, there was little research interest in the middle-aged population. This was probably a function of several factors. Certainly societal values were inclined to characterize the middle adult years as rather stable and less exciting developmentally than those of youths. In addition, psychologists and physiologists tended to view this period as one of little change and consequently not an area for fruitful investigation. This perspective has undergone certain changes, and more attention is being focused on the middle-aged group in recent years (e.g., Binstock & Shanas, 1977; Birren & Schaie, 1977; Finch & Hayflick, 1977; Knox, 1977).

Physiological factors may be the most obvious changes in the middle-aged population. One of the first physical signs typically relates to "increasing body weight and change in body girth. Most people weigh the most they ever do in their lives between thirty-five and fifty-nine" (Stevens-Long, 1979, p. 215). The changes during this period are not limited to a simple increase in weight—they also involve a redistribution of body fat in certain unflattering ways. Significant changes occur in bone and connective tissue, and the skin loses a great deal of its elasticity. There is a continued decline of vitality and endurance capability. The deterioration of general physiological status is noticeable as one enters the middle-aged population.

In certain cases the physiological status of exceptional adults is, by definition, different from that of their normal counterparts. We refer to circumstances where the characteristics of the disorder directly involve the individual's physical condition. In this category we include such exceptionalities as physical disabilities and health disorders that have a direct impact on physiological development, vitality, and physical status of the individual. For example, in earlier chapters we examined such health problems as diabetes, asthma, and cardiac abnormalities. In many cases the nature of the problem results in slower growth or restricted activity levels. These differences often continue into adulthood and may even result in early death. Such factors have been discussed earlier and will not be repeated here, but the reader should keep them in mind.

Other disorders, such as mental retardation, learning disabilities, and behavior disorders, do not necessarily involve characteristics that are centrally physiological in nature. For example, questions have been raised regarding the physical status (e.g., diminshed stature) of the mentally retarded when compared with those of normal intelligence (Marshall, 1968). Evidence in terms of this notion is not necessarily straightforward and clear (Hardman & Drew, 1977). Some early research has indicated that the mentally retarded have a generally stunted physical stature (e.g., height, weight) and that in this population a positive relationship exists between size and intelligence (Goddard, 1912; Mosier, Grossman & Dingman, 1965). It should be noted that these data were collected on institutionalized individuals. Other findings obtained on retarded outpatients from a psychiatric research institute indicated that there were "classes of mentally defective children . . . in which no stunting of linear or skeletal development is associated with mental deficiency" (Pozsonyi & Lobb, 1967, p. 867).

These results become more understandable as one views other evidence. The relationship between physical stature and intelligence does not seem to be a simple one, and interpretations probably should not be attempted in that fashion. Some research has indicated that stunting is evident in those retarded individuals where causation involves physiological pathology or deviance of some type, whereas those with nonpathological etiology seem to have normal or near-normal growth (Dutton, 1959). Thus causation and/or other influences may be more predictive of physical stature than intelligence level per se (Hardman & Drew, 1977).

Much of the evidence cited above was gathered either on younger mentally retarded individuals or on undifferentiated groups with aggregated data being reported. Although specific information regarding the adult retarded has not been focused on in the literature, certain inferences about this group may be cautiously drawn. There is little reason to believe that the complexity of the relationship changes substantially in adulthood. Until further data are forthcoming, one must consider that physical stunting will be most evident when physiological factors are involved in the causation. Otherwise, one may assume that the physical development of the mentally retarded will be normal or near normal in the adult years. This assertion will be altered to the degree that such individuals lead different lifestyles because of their reduced intellectual functioning (e.g., exercise and activity).

Evidence regarding the physiological status of adults with other disorders is extremely scarce, although in some cases there are limited data. In the general area of learning disabilities, Wender, Reimherr, and Wood (1981) studied adults' motor ability and found their subjects scoring "below the fifth percentile for their respective sexes" (p. 451). Such results should be interpreted cautiously because of the infrequency of the studies and questionable measurement procedures (Wender et al., 1981). Physical "pathology" may affect these individuals much as it seems to affect mentally retarded persons. Similarly, environmental contingencies, like extreme malnutrition associated with poverty, may contribute to a disorder. In such cases physiological differences may result (Hallahan & Cruickshank, 1973) which are likely to have an influence in adulthood as they do in the younger years.

Cognition/Intellectual Factors

Much of the research and thinking about adult cognitive behavior seems to be plagued with certain *a priori* assumptions that involve the idea that aging erodes cognitive ability (Baltes & Labouvie, 1973; Labouvie-Vief, 1977; Reigel, 1973; Schaie & Gribbin, 1975). While that might be true, the argument is simply that such assumptions may unduly guide research and the interpretation of results. Labouvie-Vief discussed such assumptions and noted that "although in accord with much of the empirical evidence available [the assumptions] are not necessarily *derived* from empirical research, but nevertheless *determine* the range of hypotheses, methodologies, and interpretations accepted as valid. Rather than refining theory in the light of accumulating evidence, the process appears to operate in the opposite direction" (1977, p. 228; emphasis in the original). This argument does not contend that a decrement in cognitive performance does *not* occur as a function of age. Instead, the contention is that we should be more cautious with respect to how much our assumptions influence our research questions, methods, and *particularly* interpretations of data.

Cognitive functioning during the adult years has received some attention, but it is also an area that is undergoing a transition in thinking regarding evidence about the influence of aging. As noted above, much of the research has been approached from a theoretical view of somewhat stable or slightly declining cognitive performance during adulthood. Research has typically supported such a perspective, although interpretations seem to have been simplistic in terms of the decrement theory of functioning (Labouvie-Vief, 1977).

A more analytical examination of the data suggests that there is the least amount of change in tasks measuring information stored. On the other hand, tasks requiring perception of relationships, abstract reasoning, and time-restricted memory (e.g., timed tests) seem to show substantial performance decrements across age levels (Baltes & Labouvie, 1973; Botwinick, 1967; 1973; Horn, 1976). Thus there would seem to be considerable variation in the areas of cognitive functioning across ages. Clearly the effect of aging on intellectual functioning cannot be accurately interpreted in a simple "single variable" fashion. The general health status of an individual also seems to interact substantially with age in terms of cognitive performance. Jarvik (1975) noted a *lack* of declining intellectual status for *healthy* older people. This observation may have considerable importance as further research explores aging and cognition in exceptional populations.

The answers regarding cognition and aging seem unsatisfactory. Is there a decline in cognitive and intellectual functioning as a result of aging? Answers to this question remain elusive and must be tempered with a number of qualifiers. The answer seemed apparent fifteen years ago, when it was an affirmative one, but it is not so clear today. Perhaps an apparent decline in intellectual functioning is due to slowed response times or health status and is, in fact, greatly dependent on the type of function assessed. The picture has become less clear as the research and thinking on this topic have become more analytical and sophisticated.

In discussing the cognitive and intellectual factors of exceptional adults, we are faced with problems similar to those encountered earlier. Solid data are often unavailable or obscured by data aggregation. Once again, we will be specific where possible, but we will often have to rely on inferences based on the literature available.

The Mentally Retarded. Intellectual functioning is a central topic of study for professionals working with the mentally retarded. Consequently, as we discuss this group in the context of aging, the question naturally arises whether any changes occur in intellectual functioning as age increases. The question was characterized by Goodman (1977a) in the following manner: "It is commonly supposed that the intelligence gap between retarded and normal individuals widens with age" (p. 199). The underlying assumption of this statement was that the question relates to how rapidly intellectual functioning *declines*, although the sentence speaks only to a widening of the gap. It should be noted that Goodman's research (1977a, b) does not support "more rapid" decline of intelligence for the mentally retarded. The question is not simple and the answers are even less so, but the question persists despite the fact that the precise nature of intellectual change in normal individuals remains unclear and controversial (e.g., Baltes & Schaie, 1976; Horn & Donaldson, 1976).

Many elements are involved in the notion of intellectual functioning. Fisher and Zeaman (1970) studied mental age (MA) and measured intelligence (IQ) as well as other factors in 1,159 institutionalized subjects and reached several conclusions. They noted that "the growth of MA of retardates is roughly linear between 5 and 16 years" (p. 175). This linear (straight-line) growth seemed evident regardless of the level of retardation, although the *rate* of growth (slope of the line) differed depending on the level of retardation. Fisher and Zeaman concluded their paper with several other statements:

> High level retardates continue to grow (although not linearly) in MA for longer periods of their life (at least until the late 30s). The MA growth functions for lower level subjects flatten off earlier.

> MAs for all levels show a tendency to decline with advancing age (after chronological age 60).

> Between 5 and 16 years, IQs of retardates fall precipitously despite their linear increase in MA. This is true for measurements made semi-longitudinally or cross-sectionally. . . .

> Between 16 and 60 years, retardate IQ is relatively stable, with higher levels showing some tendency to gain IQ points with age.

> The subject variables of sex and diagnostic category had little effect on the growth of intelligence, when level was controlled. (1970, p. 175).

Goodman (1977a) criticized research on institutionalized subjects and stated that much of it "is methodologically suspect. At the most obvious level, the measuring instruments, usually the Stanford-Binet, were never standardized on institutional populations and thus take no account of the probability that institutional living depresses many aspects of intelligence, particularly language. An even more critical, and equally neglected, source of bias is the factor of sample attrition" (p. 199). Goodman conducted two studies (1977a, b) that seem to pursue the same questions and augment the findings of Fisher and Zeaman (1970). She noted that "when the IQ data are viewed cross-sectionally there is the appearance of decline, but when the same population is studied semi-longitudinally, not only is there no decrease in IQ with age but there are regular increments, particularly in performance scores" (1977a, p. 203). In the second study, Goodman stated, "Contrary to studies of normal adults, the older retarded subjects did somewhat better than the younger ones. . . . The results raise the possibility that fluid mental abilities show a later decline in the mentally retarded than in the non-retarded" (1977b, p. 255).

The results from these studies have a number of similarities as well as certain differences. What is clearly evident, however, is that the "conventional wisdom" cited by Goodman (1977a, p. 199) should not be accepted at face value. It is *not* clear what the precise nature of changes in intellectual functioning in the retarded may be, although certain trends may be suspected from the evidence discussed above. In addition, a number of factors, such as methodological flaws and testing situations, may significantly contaminate research results (Chinn et al., 1979; Goodman, 1977a). Thus the answers to our questions are currently unclear, clouded by many influences.

The Learning Disabled. Cognition and intellectual functioning also presents some interesting questions regarding learning-disabled adults. Unfortunately, little attention has been given to this population in the scientific literature, probably because of the emphasis on problems evident during the school years in terms of learning disabilities. Only in the last decade have professionals begun to express concern for the learning disabled beyond the elementary school years. Miller (1973) referred to a U.S. Department of Health, Education, and Welfare pamphlet that characterized the focus on learning disabilities in this way:

(P. 47; emphasis in the original)

It is true that professionals have largely ignored the adult with this type of problem, which has "long been considered a disorder limited to childhood" (Wood, Reimherr, Wender & Johnson, 1976).

Once again we have encountered differing terms being employed with this population (e.g., learning disabilities, minimal brain dysfunction). As noted earlier in this volume, the term *learning disabilities* is a general (and broad educational) label that includes many different specific disorders (Gelfand, Jenson & Drew, 1982; Rosenthal & Allen, 1978). Even certain narrowly defined disorders within the general term *learning disabilities* (e.g., dyslexia) have been described as involving several different syndromes (Benton & Pearl, 1978). The multiplicity of specific disorders in learning disabilities has received more attention in the recent literature, but some noted this situation in the context of adults earlier than the sweep of current thinking about learning disabilities in general. For example, Anderson (1974) stated:

> In adults, as among children, there is no rigid or characteristic pattern which is invariably present. There are perhaps *even more* variations in the symptoms and signs displayed by adults with minimal brain dysfunction than there are in children because adults have had a lifetime to develop compensatory or collateral patterns to help them cope with their problems. (P. 217; emphasis added)

Thus when we discuss learning disabilities during adulthood, we are compelled to use a variety of terminologies. Given the status of the field, this lack of precision is unavoidable.

There is currently little question among researchers and professionals that specific learning disabilities (or symptoms thereof) exist among adults and may cause serious problems for those affected (Anderson, 1974; Cox, 1977; Lynn, Gluckin, & Kripke, 1979; Miller, 1973; Wallace & McLoughlin, 1979; Wender, Reimherr & Wood, 1981; Wood et al., 1976). However, solid evidence regarding the characteristics and functioning of such individuals remains fragmentary, often involving case reports, anecdotal commentaries, limited studies, or general descriptions in textbooks. Wender et al. (1981) noted that there is a strong indication that "ADD [**attention deficit disorder**] in childhood is associated with an increased frequency of psychopathology in later life, but its nature and the degree of increased risk is uncertain" (p. 449). ADD represents new terminology in the American Psychiatric Association's latest edition of the *Diagnostic and Statistical Manual* (DSM III) (1980). ADD replaces minimal brain dysfunction (MBD) in the DSM III classification system. Evidence of symptoms persisting "into adult life is formally recognized as 'ADD, residual type' " (Wender et al., 1981, p. 449).

Wender and his associates (1981) found that their adult subjects exhibited certain cognitive and intellectual characteristics often associated with learning-disabled children. Their sample was described as follows:

> "WAIS [Wechsler Adult Intelligence Scale] full-scale IQ, 110 ± 10 (verbal IQ, 110; performance IQ, 113); this patient population is in about the 75th percentile of intelligence. The WRAT [Wide Range Achievement Test] levels were below those that would be anticipated on the basis of the subjects' IQ and education. Both the men and the women read at expected levels. However, the men were in the 23rd percentile in spelling and arithmetic; the women were average or above, as would be anticipated on the basis of their intelligence. (P. 451)

Solid evidence is not now available. That which is available suggests that some learning-disability characteristics persist into adulthood, a notion that clinicians have held for some time.

Behavioral and Personality Factors

Unfortunately, the study of **personality** and aging is not clearly organized and coherent, a matter noted by many over the years (Chown, 1968; Kuhlen, 1945; 1959; Neugarten, 1977; Reigel, 1959; Riley & Foner, 1968; Schaie & Marquette, 1972). There are a variety of theories regarding what personality entails, and consequently differing views about whether personality changes during the life span (let alone during the adult years). There is even some question whether traditional notions of personality can be combined successfully with theory and research approaches from developmental psychology (Stevens-Long, 1979). In fact, it is difficult to find a generic but succinct definition of personality that satisfies a broad spectrum of disciplines or professionals.

For definitional purposes we will accept the general idea that personality represents "the characteristic way we behave and respond to our environment" (Birren, Kinney, Schaie & Woodruff, 1981, p. G-8). Because this is a general definition, the varying theoretical views of personality probably could not all agree that it is a complete or appropriate definition. For our purposes, however, we need a general backdrop that can incorporate the variety of factors involved. Personality and behavior are inextricably intertwined in different definitions and theoretical perspectives of this topic. This will be confirmed as we further explore the area of personality and aging.

Part of the difficulty with studying personality changes during adulthood is related to an apparent point of incompatibility between developmental theory

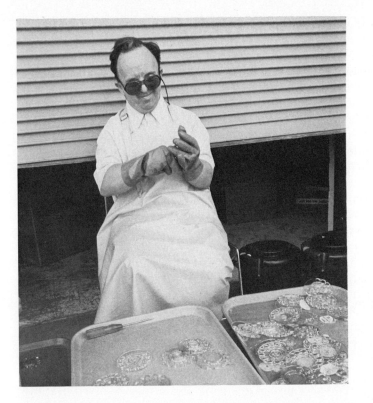

Very little re-
search has been
done on excep-
tional individuals
beyond
adolescence.

and personality theory. Developmental scientists are basically observing, de-scribing, and explaining changes that occur as individuals mature. Thus we have a study of change. On the other hand, personality theorists are interested in discovering and describing stable attributes of human emotions and behav-iors. Thus the marriage of these two theoretical perspectives has not been a harmonious one. The future of the study of personality and aging remains uncertain (Neugarten, 1977), but a discussion of our current knowledge base is important for this volume.

At a general level, it seems that many aspects of personality remain stable during the adult years (Birren et al., 1981; Stevens-Long, 1979), but certain factors seem to show some change. For example, introversion is a feature that seems to increase with age, particularly during the latter portion of adulthood (Neugarten, 1977). Another factor that seems to change has to do with cau-tiousness. People appear to become more cautious in the way they respond to tasks as they grow older (Botwinick, 1978). This finding has been consistent and may have a substantial impact on a variety of apparent performance dec-rements in other areas (e.g., intelligence tests, response-time tests).

On a general level, one can wonder about the happiness of the adult years. The adolescent period is known as a period of crisis, but many popular beliefs also focus on crisis periods during adulthood (the "mid-life crisis"). A variety of sources seem to support the "crisis" idea associated with middle adulthood. Marital problems seem to often surface at this time (Pineo, 1961). Likewise, mental health problems (Weintraub & Aronson, 1968), substance abuse and health problems (Rosenberg & Farrell, 1976), and suicide rates are disturbingly high for this period (Stevens-Long, 1979). All these difficulties seem to point to a period of relative unhappiness during adulthood. This may be only a surface view, however. For example, the experience of menopause for women is often characterized as a time of physical change and mental stress. While this view is widespread, it may be more myth than fact (at least in terms of degree of crisis). Younger women seem to have more negative perceptions in anticipation of the event than older women who are actually undergoing this change. In fact, many women experiencing menopause see it as an inconvenience and may not regret (or even be relieved about) the loss of reproductive ability (Datan, 1971; Neugarten & Datan, 1974; Neugarten, Wood, Kraines & Loomis, 1963).

The data regarding mid-life crisis are inconclusive for both men and women. For example, some research indicates no evidence of a midlife crisis for either men or women (Stevens-Long, 1979, p. 259). There are some individuals who do experience difficulties and unhappiness during the adult years, but there is no clear link to the aging process. Many problems are associated with specific events (e.g., divorce, poor health, family death). We can conclude that in general the adult years do not bring any predictable unhappiness and that they may even be relatively happy years.

Behavioral and personality characteristics in exceptional adults must be examined with the same qualifiers articulated for their normal counterparts. Definitions of personality factors and the terminology employed remains fluid, perhaps even more variable because of the many disciplines involved in studying exceptionality.

Adults who might be considered learning disabled are often described in terms of behavioral and/or personality disturbances in the literature available. For example, such problems were prominently mentioned by Mendelson, Johnson, and Stewart (1971), who studied hyperactivity among adolescents labeled MBD (minimal brain dysfunction) as children. (Once again, inferences regarding adults must be drawn from data on younger populations.) These investigators found that 74 percent of their subjects were "impulsive," 77 percent encountered "concentration difficulties," and 71 percent were "overactive." While these terms are vague, the high percentages involved and the constellation of behavior differences are substantial. It should also be mentioned that the notion of "overactivity" (viewed as a *general* excess of activity) has been seriously questioned. Research suggests that hyperactivity might be more appropriately viewed as an excess of activity *in certain settings* (Gelfand et al., 1982).

Supportive evidence regarding behavioral/personality disturbance among learning-disabled adults has included a number of other symptoms. Impulsivity seems to continue, as well as severe alcoholism, "explosive" personalities, irritability, depression, anxiety, and a general increased frequency of psychopathology (Borland & Heckman, 1976; Hartocollis, 1968; Mann & Greenspan, 1976; Menkes, Rowe & Menkes, 1967; Morris, Escool & Wexler, 1956; Morrison & Minkoff, 1975; O'Neal & Robins, 1958; Quitkin & Klein, 1969; Shelly & Riester, 1972; Tarter, McBride, Buonpane, et al., 1977). Recent research has further supported serious behavioral problems, such as those noted above, for adults who might be labeled learning disabled (Wender et al., 1981). These researchers reported another finding that is interesting because it differs from learning disabilities in children. In two studies (Wender et al., 1981; Wood et al., 1976) they found more adult females had a learning disability than males (whereas in children, boys labeled as learning disabled substantially outnumber girls). Although it is interesting, this finding must be interpreted with great caution because of sample bias. Wender et al. (1981) noted:

> A partial explanation may be that while children with ADD are brought to psychiatric attention because their behavior causes trouble for others, most of our patients came because they had personal discomfort, giving us an obviously skewed sample of 'children with ADD grown up.' If one of the developmental outcomes for boys with ADD is alcoholism and/or antisocial personality, the underrepresentation of men in the sample could be a simple consequence of the fact that few alcoholic or antisocial males seek psychiatric care in our mental health clinics. (P. 451)

Thus far this section has focused on *disturbances* of behavior in adults who may be labeled as learning disabled. This is not unusual as one studies exceptional individuals and their behavior, but it is important to balance this focus with the positive side. Adults with learning disabilities do not have an easy life—progress and positive achievement are difficult. In a number of cases, however, the accomplishments of learning-disabled adults have been remarkable. For example, in the political arena, the late Nelson Rockefeller, who had a severe learning disability (dyslexia), stands out. Roa Lynn found a label for her problems at thirty-eight years of age. Few would say she has been unsuccessful, although her career has been a series of difficult struggles. Ms. Lynn has worked as a reporter on such widely known publications as *Time* and *Newsweek* and served on the staffs of the late Senator Hubert H. Humphrey and the Japanese Mission to the United Nations, despite the fact that she has a learning disability. She has also studied learning disabilities and published in the area (e.g., Lynn, Gluckin & Kripke, 1979). These people do not achieve at such levels without difficulty, but they are examples of what can be accomplished by some adults with learning disabilities.

Mental retardation, like certain other disorders, has most often been studied and thought of in terms of younger individuals—children and adolescents. The adult and elderly retarded have been relatively ignored. Frequently mentally retarded adults are thought of as individuals who are institutionalized and out of the societal mainstream, as we saw in Roberta's case (perhaps an "out of sight, out of mind" mentality). The lay public often has a generalized fear of grown adults who are not institutionalized but who are unable to live within the rules of society.

The concern about living within the rules of society cannot be ignored, although it also should not be magnified out of proportion. Certain early studies indicated that a disproportionately high number of mentally retarded were

criminals or involved in similar antisocial activity (e.g., Goddard, 1914; Kvaraceus, 1946; Moore, 1911; Peterson & Smith, 1960). Even more recent work
has suggested that there is a higher percentage of mentally retarded individuals
in correctional institutions than in the general population (Allen, 1969). It is
important to note, however, that these early studies have serious methodological flaws that make interpretation of results difficult and possibly erroneous.
Some of the investigations have basic design weaknesses; in other cases inferences must be tempered by imperfections in the operation of the judicial system.
To be incarcerated as a criminal, an individual must be convicted in a trial.
Allen (1969) noted that the trial process for the mentally retarded may often
be little more than a formality. Concern about such problems has led to a greater
analytical focus on the mentally retarded and legal processes (e.g., Kindred,
Cohen, Penrod & Shaffer, 1976) which will, it is hoped, lead to more rigorous
research and cautious interpretations in this area.

Nihira (1976) studied several dimensions of adaptive behavior in the mentally retarded from a developmental perspective. This investigation employed
a cross-sectional design and assessed behavior in 3,354 institutionalized subjects ranging from four to sixty-nine years old. Three major factors pertinent
to this section emerged from the analysis and were charted across age levels.
These included personal self-sufficiency (defined primarily by the variables of
eating, toilet use, cleanliness, dressing and undressing and motor development),
community self-sufficiency (defined primarily by the variables of travel, shopping skills, expression, comprehension, social language development, numbers
and time, cleaning, kitchen duties, and other domestic activities), and personal-
social responsibility (defined primarily by the variables of initiative, perseverance, leisure time, responsibility, socialization, vocational activity, appearance, and care of clothing). Readers interested in further descriptions of these
variables may wish to consult Nihira (1976, pp. 218-20). Subjects' performances
were plotted across age-groups by level of retardation. These data are graphed
in Figure 15-1. Review of the data in Figure 15-1 indicates a substantial growth
in all three factors for most groups (except the lowest level of retardation) and
some decline for certain groups in the older age periods. Equally interesting is
that the growth and decline (rates and levels) vary considerably depending on
the level of retardation. These data may be viewed from another perspective
in Figure 15-2, which includes five separate graphs, one for each level of retardation included in the study.

Kleban, Lawton, Brody, and Moss (1976) also studied the status of behavioral functioning in aged mentally retarded individuals who were institutionalized. These investigators utilized a longitudinal design in making
behavioral observations over a two-year period. Subjects for this study were
limited in age range from 70 to 94 with the mean being 83 years. Although
sixty-seven subjects began the study, only forty-three were used in final analyses, because of deaths in the sample. Several categories of behavior were
observed, as summarized in Table 15-2. Results indicated that approximately
37 percent of the subjects evidenced a deterioration in functioning. However,
"an equal number of subjects gave evidence of stability. They maintained their

plateau over the 2 years of observation. Finally, a smaller number showed behavioral improvements" (Kleban et al., 1976, p. 337). Subjects who declined in functioning seemed to be those who "evidenced more psychopathology or more serious medical conditions at the beginning [of the study] and less comprehension of their living conditions" (p. 339).

Learned helplessness is a concept initially described in animal research (Overmier & Seligman, 1967; Seligman & Maier, 1967). However, interest in human learned helplessness has been growing at a phenomenal rate (Abramson, Seligman & Teasdale, 1978). Helplessness (passivity or an inability to respond) may be learned when individuals are repeatedly confronted with situations where their responses (whatever they are) seem ineffective in resolving a problem. When we repeatedly make responses that are ineffective, we come to feel helpless and no longer respond, or do so only in a random fashion. Thus such individuals may learn that responding has little or no effect on outcomes. Such behavioral patterns have been frequently associated with personality disturbances like depression (e.g., Abramson et al., 1978; Depue & Monroe, 1978).

Despite the growing interest in learned helplessness, little attention has been given to this phenomenon with exceptional populations such as the mentally retarded. This is interesting, because researchers in the area suggest "intriguing analogies to clinically observed phenomena among retarded persons" (Floor & Rosen, 1975, p. 566). Floor and Rosen (1975) did investigate learned helplessness in one study, using retarded adults as subjects. They compared

Figure 15-1/ Behavioral Functioning in the Mentally Retarded by Age and Level of Retardation

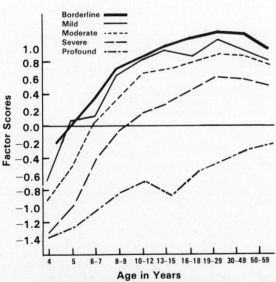

Personal Self-Sufficiency. Mean factor scores for ten-age groups. Each line represents a specific level of measured intelligence.

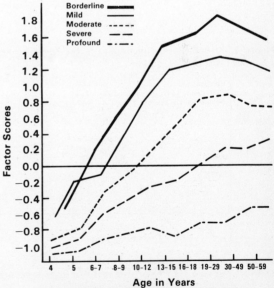

Community Self-Sufficiency. Mean factor scores for ten-age groups. Each line represents a specific level of measured intelligence.

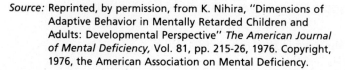

Personal-Social Responsibility. Mean factor
scores for ten-age groups. Each line represents
a specific level of measured intelligence.

Source: Reprinted, by permission, from K. Nihira, "Dimensions of
Adaptive Behavior in Mentally Retarded Children and
Adults: Developmental Perspective" *The American Journal
of Mental Deficiency,* Vol. 81, pp. 215-26, 1976. Copyright,
1976, the American Association on Mental Deficiency.

**Figure 15-2/ Behavioral Functioning in the Mentally Retarded by
Age and Level of Retardation**

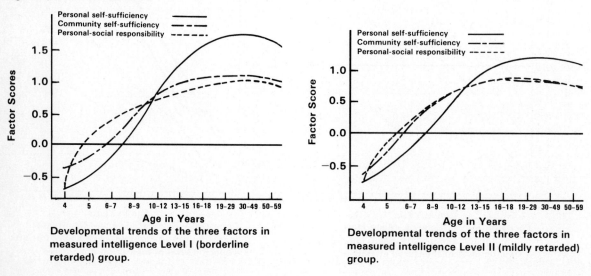

Developmental trends of the three factors in
measured intelligence Level I (borderline
retarded) group.

Developmental trends of the three factors in
measured intelligence Level II (mildly retarded)
group.

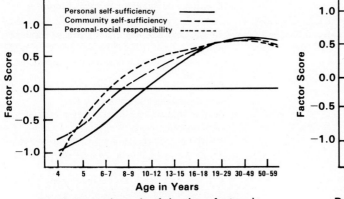

Developmental trends of the three factors in measured intelligence Level III (moderately retarded) group.

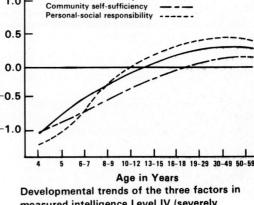

Developmental trends of the three factors in measured intelligence Level IV (severely retarded) group.

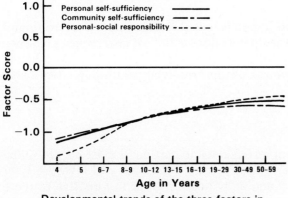

Developmental trends of the three factors in measured intelligence Level V (profoundly retarded) group.

Source: Reprinted, by permission, from K. Nihira, "Dimensions of Adaptive Behavior in Mentally Retarded Children and Adults: Developmental Perspective," *The American Journal of Mental Deficiency,* Vol. 81, pp. 215-26, 1976. Copyright, 1976, the American Association on Mental Deficiency.

two groups of retarded individuals (one group being institutional residents, the second living at home but attending the institutional training programs on a daily basis) with nonretarded controls and found no differences between the retarded groups; however, the control group differed significantly . . . in a non-helpless direction" (p. 568). Other measures in this study indicated behaviors that have been used to characterize learned helplessness in the retarded groups to a greater degree than the control subjects. Floor and Rosen noted that "in

Table 15-2/ Behavioral Observations of Institutionalized Mentally Impaired, Ages 70 to 94.

Category of Behavior	*Examples of Behavior Within Categories*
Passive nonfunctional, nonsocial	Sitting, lying, sleeping, staring, aimless casting of looks
Active nonfunctional, nonsocial	Standing, purposeless object manipulation, talking to self
Passive functional, nonsocial	Waiting for doctor, off-the-floor medical attention, taking medications on the floor
Active functional, nonsocial	Self-locomotion, functional object manipulation, personal care, chores
Involvement in group activities	Watching ongoing activities, watching TV, listening to radio with others, planned floor activity
Involvement in individual activities	Reading, writing, knitting
Involvement in institutional activities	Off-floor activities, occupational therapy, physical therapy, sewing, workshop
Social functioning	Talking, social activities

Source: Abridged and adapted from M.H. Kleban, M.P. Lawton, E.M. Brody, & M. Moss, "Behavioral Observations of Mentally Impaired Aged: Those Who Decline and Those Who Do Not," *Journal of Gerontology,* 1976, *31,* 333-39. By permission of *The Gerontologist* / the *Journal of Gerontology.*

general, the data supported the hypothesis that helplessness is a meaningful personality variable among retarded populations and . . . it discriminates between retarded and nonretarded groups of the same age" (1975, p. 571). Unfortunately the concept of learned helplessness has not received continuing attention in mental retardation research.

Employment and Economics

Employment activities represent a considerable portion of most people's time and effort during the adult years. Typically an individual will invest forty or more hours a week in work-related activities for thirty to forty-five or more years during his or her life (Kimmel, 1974, p. 241). For many men and women, their occupation represents much more than a source of revenue; it also plays an important role in their sense of identity. Consequently, employment warrants a certain amount of attention as we study humans in general and exceptional populations in particular.

Employment represents a significant part of the ongoing activity in the United States. Figure 15-3 illustrates the number of individuals that were employed and unemployed, and the unemployment rates, from 1968 to 1979. According to the U.S. Bureau of the Census (1979) there are some variations across age-groups and between the sexes with regard to employment status. Table 15-3 summarizes the employment rates by sex and age for the year 1978. In reviewing this table, certain definitions need to be kept in mind. Footnotes b and c are the definitions employed by the Census Bureau regarding employed and unemployed persons.

One of the reasons for being employed is to receive income. Income changes dramatically across the age span, typically peaking during the middle-age period

A job can mean
more than
money.

and declining rapidly thereafter. Figure 15-4 illustrates the relative income across age-groups for heads of households. The reader should be cautious in interpreting Figure 15-4 with regard to *absolute* income level. Because of incredible changes in the economy (part of which is inflation), this graph is intended to present only *relative* changes across ages. Note also that the income levels are presented in 1977 dollars.

Issues regarding employment in exceptional populations are both imprecise and clear. Matters are clear in that employment among those with disorders seems to be at a considerably lower level than employment of their nonimpaired counterparts. Imprecision emerges from the inconsistent estimates and data collection regarding employment. Data have not been systematically recorded at any level. For example, the U.S. Bureau of Labor Statistics discontinued data collection on employment of exceptional individuals about ten years ago (Hippolitus, 1981).

There *are* available limited data that provide us with a general notion regarding employment in exceptional populations. Some researchers have reported that about 40 percent of all exceptional adults are employed, which is far below that recorded for the general population (Levitan & Taggart, 1977). Such figures are cause for concern, but the underemployment of the disabled is also a serious situation. Disabled workers seem to be channeled into lower skill-level jobs, which leads to their receiving wages lower than the nondisabled earn. Biklen and Bogdan (1976) indicated that 85 percent of those with disorders

Figure 15-3/ Numbers of Individuals Employed, United States,
1968–1979

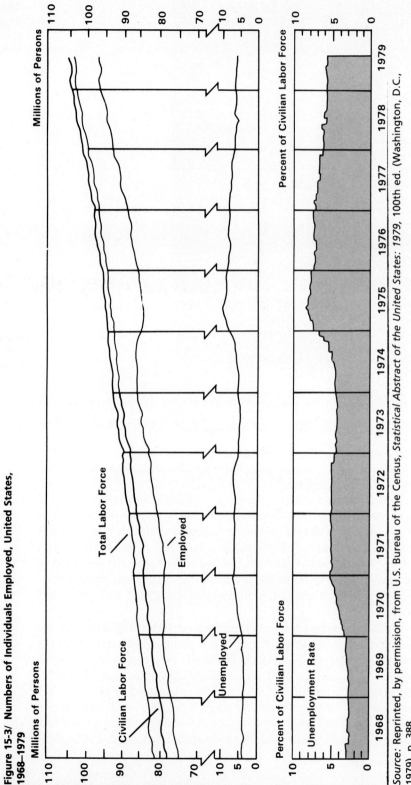

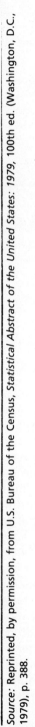

Source: Reprinted, by permission, from U.S. Bureau of the Census, *Statistical Abstract of the United States: 1979*, 100th ed. (Washington, D.C., 1979), p. 388.

Table 15-3/ Employment Status of General U.S. Population by Sex and Age, 1978[a]

| | Male | | Female | |
| | Percent Employed[b] | Percent Unemployed[c] | Percent Employed[b] | Percent Unemployed[c] |
Age				
16-19	84.3	15.7	83.0	17.0
20-24	90.9	9.1	89.9	10.1
25-34	95.7	4.3	93.3	6.7
35-44	97.2	2.8	95.0	5.0
45-54	97.2	2.8	96.0	4.0
55-64	97.3	2.7	96.8	3.2
65 +	95.8	4.2	96.2	3.8

[a]Percent of total labor force for respective sex and age-groups.
[b]*Employed persons* comprise (1) all civilians who, during the reference week, did any work for pay or profit (minimum of an hour's work) or worked fifteen hours or more as unpaid workers in a family enterprise, and (2) all persons who were not working but who had jobs or businesses from which they were temporarily absent for noneconomic reasons (illness, bad weather, vacation, labor-management dispute, etc.).
[c]*Unemployed persons* comprise all civilians who had no employment during the reference week, who had made specific efforts to find a job within the previous four weeks (such as applying directly to an employer or to a public employment service or checking with friends), and who were available for work during that week. Persons laid off or waiting to report to a new job within thirty days are also classified as unemployed. All other persons, sixteen years old and over, are "not in the labor force" (U.S. Bureau of the Census, 1979, p. 390).
Source: Adapted from U.S. Bureau of Census, *Statistical Abstract of the United States: 1979*, 100th ed. (Washington, D.C., 1979), table 650, p. 396. Used by permission.

have an annual income of less than $7,000 and that 52 percent of these make less than $2,000 a year.

Such figures do not provide much of a descriptive picture regarding employment and unemployment among exceptional individuals. Different disorders and the varying severity of those disorders are likely to involve differing levels of unemployment. Adults with disorders resulting from Vietnam-era military conflicts illustrate this well. The 1977–1978 edition of the *Yearbook of Special Education* summarized data from impaired Vietnam veterans in terms of disorder severity. Figure 15-5 illustrates this information with regard to (1) unemployment rate, (2) those who become discouraged and stopped seeking employment, and (3) those who work in jobs with low pay. Even within this group, certain *types* of disorders vary with regard to their impact on employment. "Compared to other disabled veterans, those with neuropsychiatric conditions have more trouble finding work and work at lower paying jobs" (*Yearbook of Special Education*, 1977–1978, p. 337). Figure 15-6 summarizes this information.

Employment rates for mentally retarded adults compared to their normal counterparts are also disappointing. Bluhm (1977) cited evidence indicating a 55.6 percent employment figure for noninstitutionalized retarded individuals from twenty to sixty-four years of age. Bluhm also reported a substantial difference in employment between the male retarded and the female retarded (81.2 percent vs. 30.4 percent respectively).

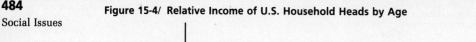

Figure 15-4/ Relative Income of U.S. Household Heads by Age

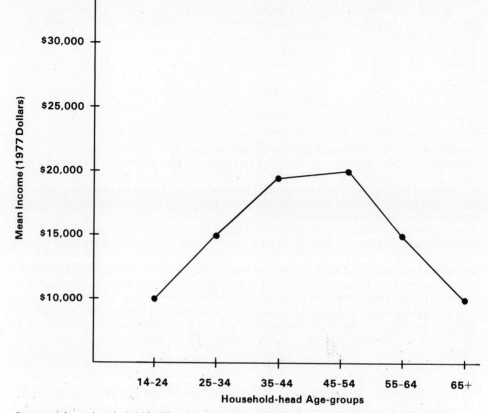

Source: Adapted and abridged from U.S. Bureau of the Census, *Statistical Abstract of the United States: 1979,* 100th ed. (Washington, D.C., 1979), table 752, p. 459. Used by permission.

Although, as we noted earlier, estimates of employment among exceptional populations vary, it is clear that the level of gainful employment is somewhat low compared to the general population. Despite this dismal picture, some have suggested a more positive outlook and implicated a number of factors other than impairment status which may be operative. For example, Brolin (1976) recounted several cases where favorable vocational adjustment and performance were evident in retarded workers. In addition, low employment may be linked to negative social stereotypes associated with persons who have a disorder as well as continuing economic fluctuations (e.g., Gliedman & Roth, 1980). And the legal issues regarding rights to adequate income and employment for the disabled have been examined (e.g., Bernstein, 1976). Such issues, however, remain unresolved at present and become increasingly complex as society changes.

Figure 15-5/ Employment Factors in Vietnam Veterans with Disorders by Degree of Impairment

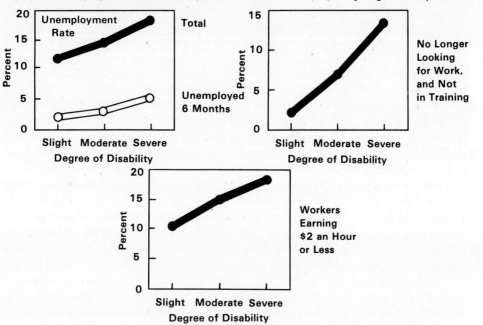

Source: Reprinted from Therlow R. Wilson and John A. Richards, *Wanted: Jobs with Fair Pay for Veterans with Disabilities.* (Alexandria, Va.: Human Resources Research Organization, 1974), p. 11.

Figure 15-6/ Employment Information for Vietnam Veterans with Neuropsychiatric Disorders

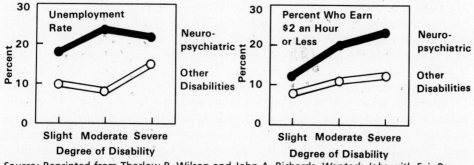

Source: Reprinted from Therlow R. Wilson and John A. Richards, *Wanted: Jobs with Fair Pay for Veterans with Disabilities.* (Alexandria, Va.: Human Resources Research Organization, 1974), p. 11.

Leisure and Living

Leisure is a concept that has different meanings for different people. We can speak of leisure time, leisure activities, recreation, and many other such notions. Many would agree that we are addressing the same *general* matters. However, specific ideas regarding what is being discussed will be as varied as the number of people we talk to. Consequently, we will be examining a generalized notion in this section, but one that is recently receiving growing attention.

Neulinger (1974) defined *leisure* as "doing what we don't have to do" (p. 186), but he also noted that leisure is "a state of mind, . . . a way of being, of being at peace with oneself and what one is doing" (p. 120). Thus, even in terms of definition, leisure is an imprecise concept. Rogers (1979) stated, "Free time is not equivalent to leisure, but it does make leisure possible. . . . The way in which we determine how to use free time can be called the leisure style" (p. 269). It is already evident that many influences other than increasing chronological age enter into the study of aging. This is also very much the case with leisure—it is difficult to determine the effects of age on leisure. "At least two, and probably three, minimal conditions must exist before leisure activities are viewed by the elderly as appropriate and valuable" (Stevens-Long, 1979, p. 419). These conditions include adequate financial resources, acceptance of a view that leisure activities are valuable, and teaching individuals how to utilize free time in fulfilling ways. Some of these factors become impediments to leisure for older people (e.g., note the income levels for older individuals portrayed in Figure 15-4).

There has long been a stereotype that suggests changes in leisure interests and activities as people grow older. It should be clear from our earlier discussion that attributing change solely to aging is difficult if not impossible. Other factors correlated with aging seem to have a substantial impact. From a broad perspective, leisure activities do seem to become less complex and more sedate as one grows older (Birren et al., 1981; Rogers, 1979). However, some leisure interests are much more stable across age-groups than generally thought (Birren et al., 1981). Some authors have been quite assertive in their statements regarding the latter point. For example, Chown (1977) cited research indicating that "leisure roles do not appear to be aged-related and (contrary to the stereotype) individual interests seem to be remarkably stable over time . . . although activities may become slightly fewer with age" (p. 677). As research on aging progresses, it will be important to isolate the factors influencing leisure interests, activities, and potential changes over time.

Leisure among disabled adults remains unexplored in any systematic fashion. Most often one finds only anecdotal notations of leisure interests in case studies focusing on the problems of symptoms (e.g., Webb, 1974). However, some investigations have included attention to leisure in these populations. For example, in certain ways, retarded adults living in a community setting do not differ substantially from the general population with regard to leisure activity (Edgerton, 1967; Edgerton & Bercovici, 1976). Watching television, and other sedentary activities, is often a major source of entertainment for such individuals (Edgerton, 1967; Stanfield, 1973). More recent data suggest that active involvement may also be a part of leisure interest for this population (Edgerton & Bercovici, 1976). Nevertheless, the information in this area remains limited and "the retarded adult is . . . often left with a lonely, inactive life (Chinn et al., 1979, p. 313). For all exceptional adults, leisure is likely to be limited to the degree that their problems inhibit activity. As research continues to explore the lives of these individuals, leisure will certainly be a topic of interest.

Leisure should be
part of every
person's life.

Where and under what conditions people live have been of interest in social science for many years. Such topics are also of concern to the lay public, often on some type of personal basis. As young adults, most people strive to live in pleasant surroundings, whether that means owning a home or renting an apartment that meets their needs. For older adults, living arrangements often seem to be an obsession. Most of us can recount stories regarding our parents, grandparents, or other elderly adults being concerned about where they will spend the rest of their lives.

Living arrangements are no less of a concern for adult and elderly exceptional populations. In some cases, however, the considerations are substantially different. For example, some individuals with more severe mental, behavioral, or physical disorders may spend their adult and later years in some sort of residential institution. Such situations may include residential institutions for the mentally retarded or mentally ill, prisons, or nursing homes. Institutionalized living arrangements were once more common for all disorder-severity levels than they are today. Currently there is a philosophy that disordered individuals can profit substantially by living in community settings that are as near normal as possible. This line of thinking emerges from the "least restrictive environment" concept (see Chapter 2). Community living arrangements for the disabled have received a great deal of attention in terms of the mentally retarded (Baker, Seltzer & Seltzer, 1977; Bank-Mikkelsen, 1969; Nirje, 1969; Wolfensberger, 1969; 1972). Partial community living in terms of convicted criminals (halfway houses) has also been advocated for prison rehabilitation programs.

Community living arrangements have resulted in considerable controversy, to a greater degree for some exceptional populations than others. Many adults with disorders live rather normal lives in community settings with little difficulty from those around them. However, serious mental disturbance or behavior disorders frequently result in concern on the part of neighborhood residents. Often such concerns involve neighbors' fear for their physical well-being. In other cases, there is a belief that their property values will be reduced by the presence of such living arrangements. These controversies will continue to test our society's commitment to those with differences.

♪ SUMMARY AND COMMENT

This chapter has examined a number of factors in the adult and elderly populations. The normal population was discussed in order to provide a referent with regard to the behavior and functioning of those who may be labeled exceptional. In many cases such comparisons are not possible because of incompatible or nonexistent data. In other areas, however, comparisons can be made and provide interesting information.

A variety of difficulties have plagued research on adult and aged populations. There have been continuing conceptual problems concerning what defines *adult* and *elderly*. These difficulties have been particularly problematic with exceptional individuals. In addition, the basic research designs employed in studying the effects of aging (longitudinal and cross-sectional) present interpretation problems.

One set of characteristics examined in this chapter involved physiological factors. Physiologically, humans generally reach their peak status during early adulthood and exhibit what appears to be a long plateau for a good number of years. The middle-age years typically mark the beginning of deterioration of general physiological status. Certain exceptional populations are, by definition, different from their normal counterparts in terms of physiological status. Evidence regarding the physiological status of those with other disorders is scarce and provides conflicting information. In some cases physical differences are apparent, whereas in others they seem nonexistent.

Cognition and intellectual factors were also discussed in this chapter. Recent research and writing in this area seriously challenges popularly held notions that there is a decline in intellectual functioning due to aging. This area is receiving increased attention in light of such theories. Information regarding exceptional adults in terms of intellectual performance seems to be following that of normal populations, and research interest is increasing.

Behavior and personality factors seem to include an unusual abundance of poorly defined concepts, making solid research even more difficult. Current interpretations of existing information suggest that some personality dimensions *seem* to change during the adult years whereas others do not. The same may be said with regard to exceptional adults, although there may also be variations between types of disorders.

Employment and economic factors represent an important part of the adult years. Income for adults in the general population tends to increase considerably, usually peaking during the middle-age period and declining thereafter. Exceptional adults do not seem to fare as well in terms of employment. Societal stereotypes, economic fluctuations, and employer ignorance are conditions that may have an impact on this population more than on the general adult population.

Popular stereotypes regarding leisure interests have been challenged in recent literature; such interests may be more stable than often thought. Leisure activities among adult exceptional populations remain largely unexplored. Limited information on certain types of disorders (e.g., mental retardation) suggests that leisure time often involves sedentary activities. Living arrangements continue to be of great concern for some exceptional adult populations (e.g., mentally retarded, mentally ill, behavior disordered). Controversy regarding institutionalization as opposed to community placement continues.

In this volume we have examined many aspects of the lives of exceptional individuals. The severity of disorders has varied from those with extremely serious impairments to those with only mild problems. The life span has been discussed, with this final chapter probing the later years. It is hoped that many questions have been answered for the reader, although certainly many more may have been raised. As students of human behavior, the continual asking of questions will represent a way of life. For example, there are still many areas regarding exceptional adults where the information base is sorely lacking. It is our hope that this volume has stimulated you to pursue further knowledge regarding exceptional populations.

♪ REVIEW QUESTIONS

1. Think carefully about how you view the concepts of aging, adulthood, and elderly. Describe the basis or bases on which you view such labels (e.g., chronological age, behavior, combinations).
2. Discuss the problems involved in conducting research on aging, both in general and with respect to exceptional populations.
3. What difficulties are encountered in interpreting results of cross-sectional studies in terms of aging?
4. Compare the physiological status and changes of normal adults and exceptional adults.
5. Compare the cognitive/intellectual factors of normal adults and exceptional adults.
6. Do behavioral and personality factors of normal adults and exceptional adults seem different? If so, how? If not, where are the similarities?
7. Compare the employment and economic status of normal adults and exceptional adults.
8. How are leisure and living factors similar and different for normal adults and exceptional adults?

GLOSSARY

Aberration: Deviation from what is common or normal.

ABIC: The Adaptive Behavior Inventory for Children, a part of SOMPA.

Acceleration: A process whereby students are allowed to achieve at a rate that is consonant with their capacity.

Adaptive behavior: A parameter of classification that refers to one's ability to be socially appropriate and personally responsible.

Akinetic seizure: A seizure that is evidenced by an absence or poverty of repetitive or clonic movements.

Amblyopia: Loss of vision due to an imbalance of eye muscles.

Ameslan: Nickname for American Sign Language.

Anemia: A condition in which the blood is deficient in red blood cells.

Anopthalmos: An absence of the eyeball.

Anoxia: A lack of oxygen.

Antibodies: Proteins formed in the blood stream to fight infection.

Aphasia: An acquired language disorder caused by brain damage that is characterized by complete or partial impairment of language comprehension, formulation, and use.

Arthritis: A disease involving inflammation of the joints due to infections or metabolic or constitutional (genetic) causes.

Articulation disabilities: Speech problems such as omissions, substitutions, additions, and distortions.

Articulation disorder: An abnormality in the speech-sound production process resulting in inaccurate or otherwise inappropriate execution of speaking.

Asthma: A condition often of allergic origin that is characterized by continuous labored breathing accompanied by wheezing, a sense of constriction in the chest, and attacks of coughing and gasping.

Astigmatism: A refractive problem that occurs when the surface of the cornea is uneven or structurally defective, preventing the light rays from converging at one point.

Ataxia: A condition wherein the individual experiences extreme difficulties in controlling fine and gross motor movements.

Athetosis: A condition characterized by constant, contorted twisting motions in the wrists and fingers.

Atonia: A condition evidenced by lack of muscle tone.

Atropinization: A treatment for cataracts that involves washing the eye with atropine, which will permanently dilate the pupil.

Attention deficit disorder (ADD): A diagnostic label used by the American Psychiatric Association to signify a condition in which a child exhibits signs of developmentally inappropriate hyperactivity, impulsivity, and inattention.

Audiometer: An electronic device used to detect a person's response to sound stimuli.

Audition: The act or sense of hearing.

Auditory association: The ability to associate verbally persented ideas or information.

Auditory blending: The act of blending the parts of a word into an integrated whole when speaking.

Auditory discrimination: The act of distinguishing between different sounds.

Auditory memory: The ability to recall verbally presented material.

Aura: A subjective sensation experienced by some individuals before the onset of a grand mal seizure.

Autism: A severe behavior disorder, with onset in early childhood, that is characterized by extreme withdrawal and self-stimulation.

Behavior disordered: A term applied to people who cannot care for themselves, are unable to function in society, and/or are a threat to themselves or others because of behavioral excesses or deficits.

Behavioral manifestations: A parameter of classification that focuses on a description of behavior.

Breech presentation: A situation in which the fetus is positioned with buttocks toward the cervix at delivery.

Bupthalmos: An abnormal distention and enlargement of the eyeball.

Cardiac disorders: Diseases of the heart that affect its functioning and output.

Cataract: A clouding of the eye lens, which becomes opaque, resulting in visual problems.

Ceiling effects: A restricted range of test questions or problems that does not permit students to demonstrate their true capacity of achievement.

Central nervous system disorders: Diseases and/or conditions that affect the brain and/or spinal cord.

Cerebral palsy: A neurological disorder characterized by motor problems, general physical weakness, lack of coordination, and perceptual difficulties.

Child abuse: Inflicted, nonaccidental, sexual, physical, and/or psychological trauma and/or injury to a child.

Choroid: A vascular membrane in the eye containing pigment cells that lies between the retina and sclera.

Choroidoretinal degeneration: Deterioration of the choroid and retina.

Cleft palate: A gap in the soft palate and roof of the mouth, sometimes extending through the upper lip.

Clonic: The phase of a grand mal seizure that is characterized by rhythmic contractions of all extremities.

Cochlea: A structure in the inner ear that converts sound coming from the middle ear into electrical signals that are transmitted to the brain.

Conditioning: The process in which new objects or situations elicit responses that were previously elicited by other stimuli.

Conduct disorders: Behavior disorders in which an individual exhibits antisocial behavior that may include both verbal and physical aggression.

Conductive hearing loss: A hearing loss resulting from poor conduction of sound along the passages leading to the sense organ.

Congenital: A condition existing at birth.

Congenital aural atresia: A condition that results when the external auditory canal is either malformed or completely absent at birth.

Congenital heart diseases: Conditions that ensue for inborn anomalies in heart structure or functioning.

Cornea: The external covering of the eye.

Cultural relativity: An approach to labeling that defines normalcy relative to standards established by a particular social structure.

Cystic fibrosis: A hereditary disease that usually appears during early childhood. It involves a generalized disorder of exocrine glands and is evidenced by respiratory problems and excessive loss of salt in perspiration.

Deaf: A term used to categorize individuals who have hearing losses greater than 75 to 80 dB, have vision as their primary input, and cannot understand speech through the ear.

Decibel (dB): A unit used to measure sound intensity.

Delayed speech: A deficit in speaking proficiency where the individual performs like someone much younger.

Diabetes mellitus: A familial constitutional disease characterized by inadequate utilization of insulin resulting in disordered metabolism of carbohydrates, fats, and proteins.

Differentiated education: Instruction and learning activities that are uniquely and predominantly suited to the capacities and interests of gifted students.

Disability: More specific than a disorder. Results from a loss of physical functioning or difficulties in learning and social adjustment that significantly interfere with normal growth and development.

Disorder: A disturbance in normal functioning (mental, physical, or psychological).

Disorders associated with immaturity and inadequacy: Behavior disorders in which an individual may be exceptionally clumsy, socially inadequate, or easily flustered.

Diplegia: Paralysis that affects the legs more than the arms.

Double hemiplegia: Paralysis that involves both sides of the body, with one side being more greatly affected.

Down's syndrome: Sometimes called mongolism. A condition resulting from a chromosomal abnormality that results in varying degrees of mental retardation.

Due process: A legal term referring to the regular administration of the law wherein no person may be denied his or her legal rights.

Dyslexia: An impairment of the ability to read.

Echolalia: A meaningless repetition or imitation of words that are heard.

Educability expectation: A parameter of classification that represents a prediction of expected educational achievement.

Elective mutism: A disorder of childhood where the youngster has speaking abilities but chooses not to use them.

Emotionally disturbed: See **Behavior disordered.**

Encopresis: Lack of bowel control.

Enrichment: Educational experiences for gifted students that enhance their thinking skills and extend their knowledge regarding various areas.

Enuresis: Lack of bladder control.

Environmental bias: A subjective point of view based on the environment (culture and social structure).

Epilepsy: A syndrome characterized by differing types of recurrent seizures.

Ethnocentrism: The belief that one's own group or culture is superior.

Etiology: The cause(s) of a condition. Also used as a parameter of classification.

Eugenics: The science of improving offspring through careful selection of parents.

Eustachian tube: A structure that extends from the throat to the middle ear cavity and controls air flow into the middle ear cavity.

Exceptional: Refers to any individual whose physical, mental, or behavioral performance deviates so substantially from the average (higher or lower) that additional services are necessary to meet the individual's needs.

Expressive language disorders: Difficulties in language production.

Extended family: Close relatives to a family who visit or interact with the family on a regular basis.

Figure-ground discrimination: The process of distinguishing an object from its background.

Fluency disabilities: Speech problems such as repetitions, prolongation of sound, hesitations, and impediments in speech flow.

Focal motor seizure: A seizure that emanates from a particular area of the brain that governs or controls various motor functions.

Focal seizures: Seizures that affect specific motor, sensory, and psychomotor functions.

Functional age: An individual's level of ability to perform various tasks relative to the average age of others who can perform the tasks.

Galactosemia: A metabolic disorder where the infant has difficulty processing lactose. May cause mental retardation and other problems.

Genealogical: Refers to a record or account of a person's family and ancestry.

Genetic screening: A search in a population for persons possessing certain genotypes (genes transmitted from parents to offspring) that are (1) already associated with disease or predisposed to disease, (2) may lead to disease in their descendants, or (3) produce other variations not known to be associated with disease.

Gifted and talented: Terms applied to those with extraordinary cognitive abilities and capable of superior performance.

Grand mal seizures: Seizures that involve a sudden loss of consciousness followed immediately by a generalized convulsion.

Habilitation: The process of making fit, often referring to training.

Handicap: A limitation imposed on an individual by the environment and the person's capacity to cope with that limitation.

Haptic: Refers to touch sensation and information transmitted through body movement and/or position.

Hard-of-hearing: A term used to categorize individuals with a sense of hearing that is defective but somewhat functional.

Health disorders: Conditions or diseases that interfere with an individual's functioning but do not necessarily or initially have an impact on their ability to move about independently in various settings.

Hearing disorder: Pertaining to the loss of hearing, the term includes both persons who are hard-of-hearing and persons who are deaf.

Hertz (Hz): A unit used to measure the frequency of sound in terms of the number of cycles that vibrating molecules complete per second.

Hemiplegia: Paralysis that involves one side of the body in a lateral fashion.

Hydrocephalus: An excess of cerebrospinal fluid, often resulting in enlargement of the head with pressure on the brain, which may cause mental retardation.

Hyperactivity: See **Hyperkinetic.**

Hyperkinetic: Refers to an excess of behavior in inappropriate circumstances.

Hyperopia: Farsightedness. A refractive problem wherein the eyeball is excessively short, focusing light rays behind the retina.

IEP: See **Individualized education program.**

Impairment: A physical deviation or defect that is either acquired or congenital (e.g., spina bifida, cerebral palsy, spinal cord injury).

Incidence: The number of new cases of a condition that have been identified within a specific period of time (e.g., one year).

Individual relativity: See **Internal relativity.**

Individualized education program: An educational plan tailored to an individual student's needs. Required by Public Law 94-142 for exceptional students.

Individualized language plan (ILP): Language-training program tailored to an individual's needs in terms of strengths and limitations.

Infantile spasms: Seizures that infants (three months to two years of age) experience characterized by flexor spasms of the arms, legs, and head. Also known as ''jacknife'' seizures.

Interindividual: Refers to comparisons of an individual's performance with that of others.

Internal relativity: Labeling that occurs when an individual imposes a label on himself or herself.

Intraindividual: Refers to comparisons of an individual's different areas of performance.

Iris: The colored portion of the eye.

Juvenile rheumatoid arthritis: A childhood viral disease characterized by inflammation and swelling of joint structures.

Kinesthetic: Pertaining to sensations derived from muscles or movement.

Language: The intended messages contained in the speaker's utterances.

Language disorder: See **Speech and language disorders.**

Laryngeal: Pertaining to the larynx.

Learning disability: A disorder in one or more of the basic psychological processes in understanding or using language.

Learning disordered: A term applied to people who are significantly below average in learning performance when compared to others of a comparable chronological age.

Least restrictive environment (LRE): The most normal environment possible for instruction, treatment, and/or living. Also referred to as the least restrictive alternative.

LRE: See **Least restrictive environment.**

Mainstreaming: The temporal, instructional, and social integration of exceptional children and youth with their regular education peers in the school setting.

MBD: See **Minimal brain dysfunction.**

Meningitis: An inflammation of the membranes covering the brain and spinal cord.

Mental retardation: Significantly subaverage general intellectual functioning existing concurrently with deficits in adaptive behavior and manifested during the developmental period. (Grossman, 1977, p. 11)

Micropthalmos: An abnormally small eyeball.

Mild learning and behavior disorders: A generic classification of disorders that involve academic and/or social-interpersonal performance deficits that generally become evident in a school-related setting and make it necessary for the individuals to receive additional support services beyond those typically offered in a regular education setting. However, it is assumed that a mildly disordered student would remain in the regular education setting for the majority of the school day. The severity of the performance deficit for this population ranges from one to two standard deviations below the interindividual and/or intraindividual mean on the measure(s) being recorded.

Minor motor seizures: Seizures that have been identified as myoclonic (shock-like contractions in muscles or muscle groups), akinetic (sudden loss of muscle tone), and infantile spasms ("jack-nife" seizures).

Minimal brain dysfunction: The condition in which an individual exhibits behavioral signs of brain injury.

Mixed hearing loss: A hearing loss resulting from a combination of conductive and sensorineural problems.

Moderate learning and behavior disorders: A generic classification of disorders that involve intellectual, academic, and/or social-interpersonal performance deficits that range between two and three standard deviations below the interindividual and/or intraindividual mean on the measure(s) being recorded. These performance deficits are not limited to any given setting but are typically evident in the broad spectrum of environmental settings. Etiology of the problem(s) may be identified in some cases but typically cannot be precisely pinpointed. Individuals with functional disorders at this level will require substantially altered patterns of service and treatment, and may need modified environmental accommodations.

Monoplegia: Paralysis that involves one limb.

Morphology: The form and internal structure of words. The transformation of words in such areas as tense and number.

Mosaicism: A type of Down's syndrome in which the chromosomal accident occurs after fertilization.

Muscular dystrophy: A group of inherited, chronic disorders that are characterized by gradual wasting and weakening of the voluntary skeletal muscles.

Myoclonic seizure: A seizure that is characterized by shock-like contractions involving parts of a muscle, an entire muscle, or groups of related muscles.

Myopia: Nearsightedness. A refractive problem wherein the eyeball is excessively long, focusing light in front of the retina.

Neonatal seizures: Seizures evidenced by alternating contractions of various muscle groups in newborns.

Neonates: Newborn children or children of less than one month of age.

Neurofibromatosis: An inherited disorder resulting in tumors of the skin and other tissue (e.g., the brain).

Neurological: Pertaining to the nervous system.

Neuroses: Behavior that involves a partial disorganization characterized by combinations of anxieties, compulsions, obsessions, and phobias.

Nondisjunction: A type of Down's syndrome in which the chromosomal pairs do not separate properly as the sperm or egg cells are formed.

Normalization: Making an individual's life and surroundings as culturally normal as possible.

Norm-referenced: Refers to assessment where a person's performance is compared with the average of a larger group.

Nystagmus: Uncontrolled rapid eye movements.

Occlusion: The closing and fitting together of dental structures.

Optic atrophy: A degenerative disease that results from deteriorating nerve fibers connecting the retina to the brain.

Optic nerve: The nerve that connects the eye to the visual center of the brain.

Ossicular chain: The three small bones (malleus, incus, and stapes, or hammer, anvil, and stirrup) that transmit vibrations through the middle ear cavity to the inner ear.

Osteomyelitis: An infectious inflammatory disease of the bone evidenced by local death and separation of the tissue.

Otitis media: An inflammation of the middle ear.

Otologist: One who is involved in the study of the ear and its diseases.

Otosclerosis: A condition associated with disease of the inner ear that is characterized by destruction of the capsular bone in the middle ear and growth of a web-like bone that attaches to the stapes. May result in hearing disorders.

Ototoxic drugs: Drugs that can be poisonous to or have a deleterious effect on the eighth nerve or on the organs of hearing and balance.

Parameters of classification: The basis used for classification.

Paraplegia: Paralysis that involves the legs only.

Perceptual abnormality: An abnormality in one's ability to interpret the stimuli around him or her.

Personality: The characteristic way in which individuals behave and respond to various environments.

Personality disorders: Behavior disorders in which an individual may be overly anxious, extremely shy, or unusually sad much of the time.

Petit mal seizures: Seizures characterized by brief periods of inattention with rapid eye-blinking or head-twitching.

Phenylketonuria (PKU): A genetic disorder that may cause mental retardation if left untreated.

Phonology: The system of speech sounds that an individual utters.

Physical disorders: Bodily impairments that interfere with an individual's mobility, coordination, communication, learning, and/or personal adjustment.

PKU: See **Phenylketonuria.**

Precipitous birth: A delivery wherein the time between the onset of labor and birth is unusually short (generally less than two hours).

Proprioceptive: Pertaining to stimuli receptors located in tissue that is under the skin, such as muscles.

Prevalence: The number of persons in any given population who exhibit a condition or problem at a specific point in time.

Pseudoglioma: A nonmalignant intraocular disturbance resulting from the detachment of the retina.

Psychomotor seizure: A seizure evidenced by inappropriate, purposeless behavior such as lip smacking, chewing, or other automatic reactions.

Psychosis: A serious disorder resulting in loss of contact with reality, characterized by delusions, hallucinations, or illusions.

Pupil: The opening in the iris of the eye that expands and contracts to control the amount of light entering the eye.

Quadraplegia: Paralysis that involves all four limbs.

Receptive language disorders: Difficulties in comprehending what others say.

Refractive problems: Visual problems that occur when the refractive structures of the eye fail to properly focus light rays on the retina.

Replicate: To repeat. In research, to duplicate an experiment.

Retina: The light sensitive cells in the eye that transmit images to the brain via the optic nerve.

Retinal detachment: A condition that occurs when the retina is separated from the choroid and sclera.

Retinitis pigmentosa: A hereditary condition resulting from a break in the choroid.

Retinoblastoma: A malignant tumor in the retina.

Retrolental fibroplasia (RLF): Scar tissue formation behind the lens of the eye, preventing light rays from reaching the retina. The result of administering excessive oxygen to premature infants.

Rh incompatibility: A situation in which the mother has Rh-negative blood and the fetus has Rh-positive blood. May result in birth defects.

Rheumatic heart disease: A condition that ensues from rheumatic fever wherein the muscles, valves, or lining of the heart may become inflamed and then permanently damaged.

Rigidity: A condition that is characterized by continuous and diffuse tension as the limbs are extended.

Schizophrenia: A severe behavior disorder involving a misconception or loss of contact with reality and distorted thought processes.

School phobia: An extreme fear of school and matters related to school.

Self-fulfilling prophecy: Refers to the theory that someone will become what they are labeled.

Semantics: The component of language most concerned with the meaning and understanding of language.

Sensorineural hearing loss: A hearing loss resulting from an abnormal sense organ (inner ear) and a damaged auditory nerve.

Sensory disorders: Differences in vision and hearing affecting performance.

Sensory seizure: A seizure that is primarily characterized by visual, auditory, gustatory, olfactory, or emotional sensations.

Severe and profound multiple disorders: A generic classification of disorders that involve physical, sensory, intellectual, and/or social-interpersonal performance deficits ranging beyond three standard deviations below the interindividual and/or intraindividual mean on the measures being recorded. These deficits are not limited to any given setting but are evident in all environmental settings and often involve deficits in several areas of performance. Etiologies are more identifiable at this level of functioning, but exact cause(s) may be unknown in a large number of cases. Individuals with functional disorders at this level require significantly altered environments with regard to care, treatment, and accommodation.

Sickle-cell anemia (SCA): An inherited disease that has a profound effect on the function and structure of red blood cells.

Snellen test: A test of visual acuity.

Spasticity: A condition that involves involuntary contractions of various muscle groups.

Speech: The audible production of language.

Speech and language disorders: Difficulties in communicating effectively.

Sociopathic: A severe behavior disorder in which the individual is aggressively antisocial and shows no remorse.

SOMPA: The System of Multicultural Pluralistic Assessment developed by Mercer and Lewis (1977).

Speech disorders: Speech behavior that is sufficiently deviant from normal or accepted speaking patterns to attract attention, interfere with communication, and adversely affect communication for either the speaker or the listener.

Spina bifida: A developmental defect of the spinal column.

Spina bifida cystica: A malformation of the spinal column in which a tumor-like sack is produced on the infant's back.

Spina bifida meningocele: A cystic swelling or tumor-like sack that contains spinal fluid but no nerve tissue.

Spina bifida myelomeningocele: A cystic swelling or tumor-like sack that contains both spinal fluid and nerve tissue.

Spina bifida occulta: A very mild condition of spina bifida in which an oblique slit is present in one or several of the vertebral structures.

Spinal cord injury: An injury in which the spinal cord is traumatized or transected.

Spondylitis of adolescence: A form of rheumatoid arthritis that affects the entire body rather than isolated joints or areas.

Standard deviation: A statistical measure of the amount an individual score deviates from the average.

Statistical relativity: A method of labeling that defines deviance based on the frequency of a behavior or characteristic. An average frequency is calculated, and a person's status is compared with that average.

Strabismus: Crossed eyes (internal) or eyes that look outward (external).

Stuttering: A speech disorder involving abnormal repetitions, prolongations, and hesitations as one speaks.

Symptom severity: A parameter of classification that refers to the degree of deviation from the norm.

Syndrome description: A parameter of classification that often describes exceptionalities in technical or medical terms.

Syntax: The order and way in which words and sequences or words are combined into phrases, clauses, and sentences.

System of Multicultural Pluralistic Assessment: See **SOMPA**.

Tonic: The phase of a grand mal seizure that is marked by prolonged muscular contraction (rigidity).

Toxoplasmosis: An infection caused by protozoa carried in raw meat and fecal material.

Translocation: A type of Down's syndrome in which a portion of the twenty-first chromosome pair breaks of and fuses with another pair.

Transverse presentation: A situation in which the fetus lies across the birth canal.

Tremor: A motion or movement that occurs in a limb that is constant, involuntary, and uncontrollable.

Triplegia: Paralysis that involves three appendages, usually both legs and one arm.

Vestibular mechanism: A structure in the inner ear containing three semicircular canals filled with fluid. It is sensitive to movement and assists the body in maintaining equilibrium.

Visual acuity: The sharpness or clearness of vision.

Visual discrimination: The act of distinguishing one visual stimulus from another.

Visual disorder: Pertaining to the loss of seeing or sight, the term includes both persons who are partially-sighted and those who are blind.

Voice disorder: A condition in which an individual habitually speaks with a voice that differs in pitch, loudness, or quality from the voices of others of the same sex and age in the cultural group.

Voice disorders: Abnormal acoustical qualities in one's speech.

REFERENCES

CHAPTER ONE

Avoiding handicapist stereotypes. *Interracial Books for Children Bulletin*, 1977, *8*(6,7), 1.

Becker, H. S. Labeling theory reconsidered. In P. Rock & M. McIntosh (Eds.), *Deviance and social control*. London: Tavistock Publications, 1974 (distributed in the U.S. by Harper & Row).

Benedict, R. *Patterns of culture*. Boston: Houghton Mifflin Co., 1934.

von Bertalanffy, L. Some biological considerations of the problem of mental illness. In L. Appleby, J. Scher & J. Cumming (Eds.), *Chronic schizophrenia*. Glencoe, Ill.: The Free Press, 1960.

Clark, R. S. *Edison: The man who made the future*. New York: G. P. Putnam's Sons, 1977.

Collins, J. J. *Anthropology: Culture, society, and evolution*. Englewood Cliffs, N. J.: Prentice-Hall, 1975.

Connor, F. P. Hoover, R., Horton, K., Sands, H., Sternfeld, L., & Wolinsky, G. F. Physical and sensory handicaps. In N. Hobbs (Ed.), *Issues in the classification of children* (Vol. 1). San Francisco: Jossey-Bass, 1975.

Cowen, E. Social and community interventions. In P. H. Mussen & M. R. Rosenzweig (Eds.). *Annual review of psychology* (Vol. 24). Palo Alto, Calif.: Annual Reviews, 1973.

Dinitz, S., Dynes, R. R., & Clarke, A. C. *Deviance: Studies in definition, management, and treatment* (2d ed.). New York: Oxford University Press, 1975.

Edgerton, R. B. *Deviance: A cross-cultural perspective*. Menlo Park, Calif.: Cummings Publishing Co., 1976.

Feldman, D. D. *Deciphering deviance*. Boston: Little, Brown & Co., 1978.

Foster, G. G., Ysseldyke, J. E., & Reese, J. H. I wouldn't have seen it if I hadn't believed it. *Exceptional Children*, 1975, *41*(7), 469-73.

Frost, L. A. *The Thomas Edison album*. Seattle: Superior Publishing Co., 1969.

Goldenberg, H. *Abnormal psychology: A social/community approach*. Monterey, Calif.: Brooks/Cole Publishing Co., 1977.

Gould, L. Who defines delinquency? A comparison of self-reported and officially reported indices for three racial groups. *Social Problems*, 1969, *16*, 335.

Greenberg, J. An interview with David Rosenhan. *APA Monitor*, 1981, *12*(6-7), 4-5, 35.

Grossman, H. J. (Ed.). *Manual on terminology and classification in mental retardation*. Washington, D. C.: American Association on Mental Deficiency, 1977.

Keogh, B. K., & Levitt, M. L. Special education in the mainstream: A confrontation of limitations. *Focus on Exceptional Children*, 1976, *8*, 1-11.

Laing, R. D. *The politics of experience*. New York: Pantheon Books, 1967.

McConnell, J. V. *Understanding human behavior* (2d ed.). New York: Holt, Rinehart & Winston, 1977.

MacMillan, D. L., & Becker, L. D. Mainstreaming the mildy handicapped learner. In R. D. Kneedler & S. G. Tarver (Eds.), *Changing perspectives in special education*. Columbus, Ohio: Charles E. Merrill Publishing Co., 1977.

MacMillan, D. L., Jones, R. J., & Aloia, G. G. The mentally retarded label: A theoretical analysis and review of research. *American Journal of Mental Deficiency*, 1974, *79*, 241-61.

Mercer, J. *SOMPA technical manual*. New York: Psychological Corp., 1979.

Merton, R. K. The self-fulfilling prophecy. In R. A. Farrell & V. L. Swigort (Eds.), *Social deviance* (2d ed.). Philadelphia: J. B. Lippincott Co., 1978.

Meyen, E. L. *Exceptional children and youth: An introduction*. Denver, Colo.: Love Publishing Co., 1978.

National Society for the Prevention of Blindness. *Estimated statistics on blindness and vision problems*. New York: National Society for the Prevention of Blindness, 1966.

Renzulli, J. S. What makes giftedness? Re-examining a definition. *Phi Delta Kappan*, 1978, *60*(3), 180-84, 261.

Report of the Ad Hoc Committee to Define Deaf and Hard-of-Hearing. *American Annals of the Deaf*, 1975, *120*, 509-12.

Rogers, J., & Buffalo, M. D. Fighting back: Nine modes of adaptation to a deviant label. *Social Problems*, 1974, *22*, 101-18.

Roos, P. Special trends and issues. In P. T. Cegelka & H. J. Prehm (Eds.), *Mental retardation: From categories to people*. Columbus, Ohio: Charles E. Merrill Publishing Co., 1982.

Rosenhan, D. L. On being sane in insane places. *Science*, 1973, *179*, 250-58.

Rosenthal, R., & Jacobsen, L. *Pygmalion in the classroom*. New York: Holt, Rinehart & Winston, 1968.

Scheff, T. J. The role of the mentally ill and the dynamics of mental disorder: A research framework. In S. Dinitz, R. R. Dynes & A. C. Clarke, *Deviance: Studies in definition, management, and treatment*. New York: Oxford University Press, 1975.

Sheils, M. A portrait of America. *Newsweek*, January 17, 1983, p. 26.

Schur, E. M. *Labeling deviant behavior*. New York: Harper & Row, 1971.

Snow, R. E. Unfinished pygmalion. *Contemporary Psychology*, 1969, *14*, 197-99.

Szasz, T. S. *The myth of mental illness*. New York: Hoeber-Harper, 1961.

Thorndike, R. L. Review of *Pygmalion in the classroom* by R. Rosenthal and L. Jacobsen, *American Educational Research Journal*, 1968, *5*, 708-11.

Thorsell, B., & Klemke, L. The labeling process: Reinforcement or deterrent? *Law and Society Review*, 1971, *6*, 401-2.

U. S. Department of Health, Education, and Welfare. Education of Handicapped Children (Implementation of Part B of the Education of the Handicapped Act), *Federal Register*, August 23, 1977.

Wald, J. R. Crippled and other health impaired and their education. In F. P. Connor, J. R. Wald & M. J. Cohen (Eds.), *Professional preparation for educators of crippled children*. New York: Teachers College Press, 1971.

Wyne, M. D., & O'Connor, P. D. *Exceptional children: A developmental view*. Lexington, Mass.: D. C. Heath & Co., 1979.

Ysseldyke, J. E., & Foster, G. G. Bias in teachers' observations of emotionally disturbed and learning disabled children. *Exceptional Children*, 1978, *44*(8), 613-15.

CHAPTER TWO

Abeson, A., & Weintraub, F. Understanding the individualized education program. In S. Torres (Ed.), *A primer on individualized education programs for handicapped children*. Reston, Va.: Council for Exceptional Children, 1977.

Ainsworth, S. H. *An exploratory study of educational, social, and emotional factors in the education of mentally retarded children in Georgia Public Schools*. Athens, Ga.: University of Georgia, 1959.

Baldwin, W. K. The social position of mentally handicapped children in the regular classes in the public school. *Exceptional Children*, 1958, *25*, 106-8.

Balla, D. Relationship of institution size to quality of care: A review of the literature. *American Journal of Mental Deficiency*, 1976, 81, 117-24.

Barr, M. W. The prevention of mental defect, the duty of the hour. *Proceedings of the National Conference on Charities and Corrections*, 1915, 361-67.

Binet, A., & Simon, T. Methodes nouvelles pour le diagnostic du niveau intellectual des anormaux. *L'Année Psychologique*, 1905, 11, 191-244.

Blatt, B., & Kaplan, F. *Christmas in purgatory: A photographic essay on mental retardation.* Boston: Allyn & Bacon, 1966.

Blatt, B., Ozolins, A., & McNally, J. *The family papers: A return to purgatory.* New York: Longman, 1979.

Brown v. Topeka, Kansas, Board of Education, 347 U.S. 483 (1954).

Butterfield, E. C. The role of environmental factors in the treatment of institutionalized mental retardates. In A. A. Baumeister (Ed.), *Mental retardation: Appraisal, education, and rehabilitation.* Chicago: Aldine Publishing Co., 1967.

Cassidy, V. M., & Stanton, J. E. *An investigation of factors involved in the educational placement of mentally retarded children: A study of differences between children in special and regular classes in Ohio.* U.S. Office of Education Cooperative Research Program, Project no. 043. Columbus, Ohio: Ohio State University, 1959.

Deno, E. Special education as developmental capital. *Exceptional Children*, 1970, 37, 229-37.

Dunn, L. M. Special education for the mildly retarded—Is much of it justifiable? *Exceptional Children*, 1968, 35, 5-22.

Fernald, W. E. What is practical in the way of prevention of mental defect. *Proceedings of the National Conference on Charities and Correction*, 1915, 289-97.

Gearheart, B. R. *Special education for the 80s.* St. Louis: C. V. Mosby Co., 1980.

Goddard, H. H. *The Kallikak family: A study in the heredity of feeblemindedness.* New York: Macmillan Co., 1912.

Goddard, H. H. *Feeblemindedness: Its causes and consequences.* New York: Macmillan Co., 1914.

Goffman, E. Characteristics of total institutions. In S. Dinitz, R. R. Dynes & A. C. Clarke (Eds.), *Deviance: Studies in definition, management, and treatment.* New York: Oxford University Press, 1975.

Goldenberg, H. *Abnormal psychology: A social/community approach.* Monterey, Calif.: Brooks/Cole Publishing Co., 1977.

Halderman v. Pennhurst State School and Hospital, No. 74-1345 (U.S. Dist. Ct., E.D. Pa.), filed May 30, 1974.

Hardman, M. L., & Drew, C. J. Parent consent and the withholding of treatment from the severely defective newborn. *Mental Retardation*, 1980, 18(4)165-69.

Itard, J. [*The wild boy of Aveyron*] (G. Humphrey & Muriel Humphrey, Eds. and trans.) Englewood Cliffs, N.J.: Prentice-Hall, 1962. (Originally published, 1801 and 1806.)

Johnson, A. Custodial care. *Proceedings of the National Conference on Charities and Corrections*, 1908, 333-36.

Johnson, G. O. *A comparative study of the personal and social adjustment of mentally handicapped children placed in special classes with mentally handicapped children who remain in regular classes.* Syracuse: Syracuse University Research Institute, Office of Research in Special Education and Rehabilitation, 1961.

Johnson, G.O. Special education for the mentally handicapped—A paradox. *Exceptional Children*, 1962, 29, 62-69.

Jordan, A. M. Personal-social traits of mentally handicapped children. In T. G. Thurstone (Ed.), *An evaluation of educating mentally handicapped children in special classes and regular classes.* Chapel Hill: School of Education, University of North Carolina, 1959.

Karier, C. J. Testing for order and control in the corporate liberal state. In C. J. Karier, P. Violas & J. Spring (Eds.) *Roots of crisis: American education in the twentieth century.* Chicago: Rand McNally & Co., 1973.

Kenowitz, L. A., Gallaher, J., & Edgar, E. Generic services for the severely handicapped and their families: Are they available? In E. Sontage (Ed.), *Educational programming for the severely and profoundly handicapped.* Reston, Va.: Council for Exceptional Children, 1977.

MacMillan, D. L., & Becker, L. D. Mainstreaming the mildly handicapped learner. In R. D. Kneedler & S. G. Tarver (Eds.) *Changing perspectives in special education.* Columbus, Ohio: Charles E. Merrill Publishing Co., 1977.

Menolascino, F. J., McGee, J. J., & Casey, K. Affirmation of the rights of institutionalized retarded citizens (implications of Youngberg vs. Romeo). *TASH Journal,* 1982, *8,* 63-72.

Mills v. District of Columbia Board of Education, 348 F. Supp. 866 (D.D.C. 1972).

O'Connor v. Donaldsen, 493 F.2d 507 (5th Cir. 1974), vacated and remanded on the issue of immunity, 95 U.S. 2486 (1975).

Pennhurst State School and Hospital v. Halderman, 451 U.S. 1 (1981).

Pennsylvania Association for Retarded Citizens v. Commonwealth of Pennsylvania, 334 F. Supp. 1257 (E.D. Pa. 1971).

Residential services: Postiton statements of the National Association for Retarded Citizens. Austin, Tex.: National Association for Retarded Citizens, 1976.

Robinson, N. M., & Robinson, H. B. *The mentally retarded child* (2d ed.). New York: McGraw-Hill Book Co., 1976.

Samelson, F. J. B. Watson's little Albert, Cyril Burt's twins, and the need for a critical science. *American Psychologist,* 1980, *35*(7), 619-25.

Skinner, B. F. *The behavior of organisms.* New York: Appleton-Century-Crofts, 1938.

Skinner, B. F. *Science and human behavior.* New York: Macmillan Co., 1953.

Suchar, C. S. *Social deviance: Perspectives and prospects.* New York: Holt, Rinehart & Winston, 1978.

Thurstone, T. G. *An evaluation of educating mentally handicapped children in special classes and regular classes.* U.S. Office of Education, Cooperative Research Project No. OE-SAE 6452. Chapel Hill: University of North Carolina, 1959.

U.S. Congress. Section 504 of the Vocational Rehabilitation Act, Public Law 93-112, 1973.

U.S. Congress. Education of All Handicapped Children Act, Public Law 94-142, 1975.

Watson, J. B. *Behaviorism.* New York: Norton, 1925.

Watson, J. B., & Rayner, R. Conditioned emotional reactions. *Journal of Experimental Psychology,* 1920, *3,* 1-14.

Wolfensberger, W. *The origin and nature of our institutional models.* Syracuse, N.Y.: Human Policy Press, 1975.

Wolfensberger, W. The principle of normalization. In B. Blatt (Ed.), *An alternative textbook in special education.* Denver, Colo. Love Publishing Co., 1977.

Wyatt v. Stickney, 344 F. Supp. 387, 344 F. Supp. 373 (M.D. Ala. 1972).

Wyne, M. D., & O'Connor, P. D. *Exceptional children: A developmental view.* Lexington, Mass.: D. C. Heath & Co., 1979.

Youngberg v. Romeo, No. 80-1429 U.S. (1982).

Zigler, E. The retarded child as a whole person. In D. K. Routh (Ed.), *The experimental psychology of mental retardation.* Chicago: Aldine Publishing Co., 1973.

CHAPTER THREE

Bateman, B. D. An educator's view of a diagnostic approach to learning disorders. In J. Hellmuth (Ed.), *Learning disorders* (Vol. 1). Seattle: Special Child Publications, 1965.

Becker, L. D. Learning characteristics of educationally handicapped and retarded children. *Exceptional Children,* 1978, *44,* 502-11.

Carter, C. H. *Handbook of mental retardation syndromes* (3d ed.). Springfield, Ill.: Charles C. Thomas, 1975.

Carter, C. H. *Medical aspects of mental retardation.* Springfield, Ill.: Charles C. Thomas, 1978.

Chinn, P. C., Drew, C. J., & Logan, D. R. *Mental retardation: A life cycle approach* (2d ed.). St. Louis: C. V. Mosby Co., 1979.

Clarizio, H. F., & McCoy, G. *Behavior disorders in children* (2d ed.). New York: Thomas Y. Crowell Co., 1976.

Clements, S. D. (Ed.). *Minimal brain dysfunction in children: Terminology and identification.* (NINDS Monograph No. 3, U.S. Public Health Service Publication No. 1415.) Washington, D.C.: U.S. Government Printing Office, 1966.

Diagnostic and statistical manual of mental disorders (DSM III). Washington, D.C.: American Psychiatric Association, 1980.

Drew, C. J., Freston, C. W., & Logan, D. R. Criteria and reference in evaluation. *Focus on Exceptional Children*, 1972, 4(1), 1-10.

Gelfand, D. M., Jenson, W. R., & Drew, C. J. *Understanding child behavior disorders*. New York: Holt, Rinehart & Winston, 1982.

Gellis, S. S., & Feingold, M. *Atlas of mental retardation syndromes*. Washington, D.C.: U.S. Government Printing Office, 1968.

Grossman, H. J. (Ed.). *Manual on terminology and classification in mental retardation*. Washington, D. C.: American Association on Mental Deficiency, 1977.

Hallahan, D. P., & Kauffman, J. M. *Introduction to learning disabilities: A pyscho-behavioral approach*. Englewood Cliffs, N.J.: Prentice-Hall, 1976.

Hardman, M. L. Learner characteristics of students with mild learning and behavior differences. In M. L. Hardman, M. W. Egan & E. D. Landau, *The exceptional student in the regular classroom*. Dubuque, Iowa: William C. Brown Co., 1981.

Kauffman, J. M. *Characteristics of children's behavior disorders* (2d ed.). Columbus, Ohio: Charles E. Merrill Publishing Co., 1981.

Keogh, B., Becker, L., Kukic, S., & Kukic, M. *Programs for EH and EMR pupils: Review and recommendations* (technical report). Los Angeles: University of California, 1972.

Kirk, S. A. Behavioral diagnosis and remediation of learning disabilities. *Proceedings, Conference on Exploration into the Problems of the Perceptually Handicapped Child*, First Annual Meeting, Chicago, April 6, 1963, Vol. 1.

Kirk, S. A. *Educating exceptional children (2d ed.)*. Boston: Houghton Mifflin Co., 1972.

Laycock, V. P. Environmental alternatives for the mildly and moderately handicapped. In J. W. Schifani, R. M. Anderson & S. J. Odle (Eds.), *Implementing learning in the least restrictive environment*. Baltimore: University Park Press, 1980.

Lemeshow, S. *The handbook of clinical types in mental retardation*. Boston: Allyn & Bacon, 1982.

Lilly, M. S. Special education: Emerging issues. In M. S. Lilly (Ed.), *Children with exceptional needs*. New York: Holt, Rinehart & Winston, 1979.

MacMillan, D. L., Meyers, C. E., & Morrison, G. M. System-identification of mildly mentally retarded children: Implications for interpreting and conducting research. *American Journal of Mental Deficiency*, 1980, 85, 108-15.

National Advisory Committee on Handicapped Children. *First Annual Report*. Washington, D.C.: U.S. Office of Education, 1968.

President's Committee on Mental Retardation and Bureau of Education for the Handicapped. *The Six-Hour Retarded Child*. Washington, D.C.: U.S. Government Printing Office, 1969.

Rhodes, W. C. The disturbing child: A problem of ecological management. *Exceptional Children*, 1967, 33, 449-55.

Strauss, A. A., & Lehtinen, L. E. *Psychopathology and education of the brain-injured child* (Vol. 1). New York: Grune & Stratton, 1947.

U.S. Congress, Education of All Handicapped Children Act (Public Law 94-142), 1975, Section 5(b)(4).

U.S. Department of Health, Education, and Welfare. Education of Handicapped Children (implementation of Part B of the Education of the Handicapped Act), *Federal Register*, August 23, 1977.

CHAPTER FOUR

Balow, B. Definitional and prevalence problems in behavior disorders of children. *School Psychology Digest*, 1979, 8(4), 348-54.

Binet, A., & Simon, T. New methods for the diagnosis of the intellectual level of subnormals. *L'Année Psychologique*, 1905. Translated and reprinted in A. Binet & T. Simon, *The development of intelligence in children*. Baltimore: Williams & Wilkins, 1916.

Bower, E. *Early identification of emotionally handicapped children in school*. Springfield, Ill.: Charles C. Thomas, 1960.

Buchanan, M., & Wolf, J. Academic strategies. In M. L. Hardman, M. W. Egan & E. D. Landau, *The exceptional student in the regular classroom.* Dubuque, Iowa: William C. Brown Co., 1981.

Cantor, G. N., & Ryan, T. J. Retention of verbal paired associates in normals and retardates. *American Journal of Mental Deficiency,* 1962, *66,* 861-65.

Cassell, T. Z. A social-ecological model of adaptive functioning: A contextual developmental perspective. In N. A. Carson (Ed.), *Final report: The contexts of life: A socioecological model of adaptive behavior and functioning.* East Lansing, Mich.: Institute for Family and Child Study, Michigan State University, 1976.

Commission on Emotional and Learning Disorders in Children. *One million children.* Toronto, Ont.: Leonard Crainford, 1970.

Deloach, T. F., Earl, J. M., Brown, B. S., Poplin, M. S., & Warner, M. M. LD teachers' perceptions of severely learning disabled students. *Learning Disability Quarterly,* 1981, 4(4), 343-58.

Drew, C. J. Associative learning as a function of material associative strength. *American Journal of Mental Deficiency,* 1969, *74,* 369-72.

Drew, C. J. Research on social adjustment and the mentally retarded: Functioning and training. *Mental Retardation,* 1971, 9(4), 26-29.

Dunn, L. M. Children with mild general learning disabilities. In L. M. Dunn (Ed.), *Exceptional children in the schools: Special education in transition* (2d ed.). New York: Holt, Rinehart & Winston, 1973.

Englemann, S. E. Sequencing cognitive and academic tasks. In R. D. Kneedler & S. G. Tarver (Eds.), *Changing perspectives in special education.* Columbus, Ohio: Charles E. Merrill Publishing Co., 1977.

Eyman, R. K., & Call, T. Maladaptive behavior and community placement of mentally retarded persons. *American Journal of Mental Deficiency,* 1977, *82,* 137-44.

Gelfand, D. M., Jensen, W. R., & Drew, C. J. *Understanding child behavior disorders.* New York: Holt, Rinehart & Winston, 1982.

Girardeau, F. L., & Ellis, N. R. Rote verbal learning by normal and mentally retarded children. *American Journal of Mental Deficiency,* 1962, 66, 861-65.

Glidewell, J., & Swallow, C. *The prevalence of maladjustment in elementary schools.* Chicago: University Park Press, 1968.

Grossman, H. J. (Ed.). *Manual on terminology and classification in mental retardation.* Washington, D.C.: American Association on Mental Deficiency, 1977.

Hallahan, D. P., & Kauffman, J. P. *Introduction to learning disabilities: A psycho-behavioral approach.* Englewood Cliffs, N. J.: Prentice-Hall, 1976.

Hammill, D. D. Defining learning disabilities for programmatic purposes. *Academic Therapy,* 1976, *12,* 29-37.

Hammill, D. D., Leigh, J. E., McNutt, G., & Larsen, S. C. A new definition of learning disabilities. *Learning Disability Quarterly,* 4(4), 1981, 336-42.

Hansen, C. L., & Eaton, M. D. Reading. In N. G. Haring, T. C. Lovitt, M. D. Eaton & C. L. Hansen (Eds.), *The fourth R: Research in the classroom.* Columbus, Ohio: Charles E. Merrill Publishing Co., 1978.

Harber, J. R. Learning disability research: How far have we progressed? *Learning Disability Quarterly,* 1981, 4(4), 372-81.

Hardman, M. L. Learner characteristics of students with mild learning and behavior differences. In M. L. Hardman, M. W. Egan & E. D. Landau, *The exceptional student in the regular classroom.* Dubuque, Iowa: William C. Brown Co., 1981.

Haring, N. Research in the classroom: Problems and procedures. In N. G. Haring, T. C. Lovitt, M. D. Eaton & C. L. Hansen (Eds.), *The fourth R: Research in the classroom.* Columbus, Ohio: Charles E. Merrill Publishing Co., 1978.

Heber, R. A manual on terminology and classification in mental retardation (2d ed.). *American Journal of Mental Deficiency, Monograph Supplement,* 1961.

Idol-Maestas, L., Lloyd, S., & Lilly, S. A noncategorical approach to direct service and teacher education. *Exceptional Children,* 1981, *48,* 213-20.

Jenkins, J. R., & Mayhall, W.F. Describing resource teacher programs. *Exceptional Children,* 1977, *40,* 35-36.

Johnson, S. W., & Morasky, R. L. *Learning disabilities*. Boston: Allyn & Bacon, 1977.

Jordan, J. B. On the educability of intelligence and related issues—A conversation with Burton Blatt. *Education and Training of the Mentally Retarded*, 1973, 8, 219-27.

Kass, C., & Myklebust, H. Learning disabilities: An educational definition. *Journal of Learning Disabilities*, 1969, 2, 377-79.

Kauffman, J. M. *Characteristics of children's behavior disorders*. Columbus, Ohio: Charles E. Merrill Publishing Co., 1977.

Kavale, K., & Nye, C. Identification criteria for learning disabilities: A survey of the research literature. *Learning Disability Quarterly*, 1981 4(4), 383-88.

Kelly, T. K., Bullock, L. M., & Dykes, M. K. Behavior disorders: Teachers' perceptions. *Exceptional Children*, 1977, 43(5), 316-317.

L'Abate, L., & Curtis, L. T. *Teaching the exceptional child*. Philadephia: W. B. Saunders Co., 1975.

Larsen, S. Learning disabilities and the professional educator. *Learning Disability Quarterly*, 1978, 1(1), 5-12.

Laycock, V. P. Environmental alternatives for the mildly and moderately handicapped. In J. W. Schifani, R. M. Anderson & S. J. Odle (Eds.), *Implementing learning in the least restrictive environment*. Baltimore: University Park Press, 1980.

Lerner, J. W. *Children with learning disabilities* (2d ed.). Boston: Houghton Mifflin Co., 1976.

Lilly, M. S. Special education: Emerging Issues. In M. S. Lilly (Ed.), *Children with exceptional needs*. New York: Holt, Rinehart & Winston, 1979.

Lovitt, T. C. The learning disabled. In N. G. Haring (Ed.), *Behavior of exceptional children* (2d ed.). Columbus, Ohio: Charles E. Merrill Publishing Co., 1978.

Marozas, D. S., May, D. C., & Lehman, L. C. Incidence and prevalence: Confusion in need of clarification. *Mental Retardation*, 1980, 18(5), 229-30.

Marsh, G. E., Gearheart, C. K., & Gearheart, B. R. *The learning disabled adolescent: Program alternatives in the secondary school*. St. Louis: C. V. Mosby Co., 1978.

Meier, J. H. Prevalence and characteristics of learning disabilities found in second grade children. *Journal of Learning Disabilities*, 1971, 4, 6021.

Mercer, J. R., & Lewis, J. F. *System of multicultural pluralistic assessment*. New York: The Psychological Corporation, 1979.

Myklebust, H., & Boshes, B. *Minimal brain damage in children* (Final report, U.S. Public Health Service contract 108-65-142, U.S. Department of Health, Education, and Welfare). Evanston, Ill.: Northwestern University Publication, June 1969.

National Advisory Committee on Handicapped Children. *First annual report*. Washington, D.C.: U.S. Office of Education, 1968.

National Advisory Council on Education Professions Development. *Mainstreaming: Helping teachers meet the challenge*. Washington, D.C.: Author, 1976.

Newbrough, J. R., & Kelly, J. G. A study of reading achievement in a population of school children. In J. Money (Ed.), *Reading disability: Progress and research needs in dyslexia*. Baltimore: Johns Hopkins Press, 1962.

O'Grady, D. J. Psycholinguistic abilities in learning disabled, emotionally disturbed, and normal children. *Journal of Special Education*, 1974, 8, 157-65.

Pate, J. E. Emotionally disturbed and social maladjusted children. In L. M. Dunn (Ed.), *Exceptional children in the schools*. New York: Holt, Rinehart & Winston, 1963.

Reinert, H. R. *Children in conflict*. St. Louis: C. V. Mosby Co., 1976.

Reynolds, M. C., & Birch, J. W. *Teaching exceptional children in all America's schools*. Reston, Va.: Council for Exceptional Children, 1982.

Richardson, S. Careers of mentally retarded young persons: Services, jobs, and interpersonal relations. *American Journal of Mental Deficiency*, 1978, 82, 349-58.

Ring, E. M., & Palermo, D. S. Paired associate learning of retarded and normal children. *American Journal of Mental Deficiency*, 1969, 66, 100-107.

Rogers, C. R. Mental health findings in three elementary schools. *Educational Research Bul-*

letin, Ohio State University Education Research Bureau, 1942, *21*(3), 69-70.

Sitlington, P. L. Vocational assessment and training of the handicapped. *Focus on Exceptional Children*, 1979, *12*(4), 1-11.

Stennett, R. G. Emotional handicaps in the elementary years: Phase or disease? *American Journal of Orthopsychiatry*, 1966, *36*, 444-49.

Swanson, B. M., & Willis, D. J. *Understanding exceptional children and youth.* Chicago: Rand McNally & Co., 1979.

Terman, L. *The measurement of intelligence.* Boston: Houghton Mifflin Co., 1916.

Torgesen, J., & Dice, C. Characteristics of research on learning disabilities. *Journal of Learning Disabilities*, 13(10), 531-35.

Wallace, G., & McLoughlin, J. A. *Learning disabilities: Concepts and characteristics.* Columbus, Ohio: Charles E. Merrill Publishing Co., 1975.

Wang, M. C. Mainstreaming exceptional children: Some instructional design and implementation considerations. *Elementary School Journal*, 1981, *81*(4), 195-221.

Wechsler, D. *The measurement and appraisal of adult intelligence* (4th ed.). Baltimore: Williams & Wilkins, 1958.

Weller, C. Discrepancy and severity in the learning disabled: A consolidated perspective. *Learning Disability Quarterly*, 1980, *3*, 84-89.

Wickman, E. K. *Children's behavior and teachers' attitudes.* New York: Commonwealth Fund, 1928.

Wiederholt, J. L., Hammill, D. D., & Brown, V. *The resource teacher: A guide to effective practice.* Boston: Allyn & Bacon, 1978.

Ysseldyke, J., & Algozzine, B. Perspectives on assessment of learning disabled students. *Learning Disability Quarterly*, 1979, *4*, 3-13.

CHAPTER FIVE

Ackerson, L. *Children's behavior problems.* Chicago: University of Chicago Press, 1942.

Adelman, H. S. Diagnostic classification of LD: Research and ethical perspectives as related to practice. *Learning Disability Quarterly*, 1979, *2*(3), 5–16.

Algozzine, B., Forgnone, C., Mercer, C. Trifiletti, J. Toward defining discrepancies for specific learning disabilities: An analysis and alternatives. *Learning Disability Quarterly*, 1979, *2*(3), 25–31.

Ayres, A. J. Sensorimotor foundations of academic ability. In W. M. Cruickshank & D. P. Hallahan (Eds.), *Perceptual and learning disabilities in children: Research and theory* (Vol. 2). Syracuse, N.Y.: Syracuse University Press, 1975.

Bauer, R. H. Memory processes in children with learning disabilities: Evidence for deficient rehearsal. *Journal of Experimental Child Psychology*, 1977, *24*, 415–30.

Baxley, G. B., & LeBlanc, J. M. The hyperactive child: Characteristics, treatment, and evaluation of research design. In H. Reese (Ed.), *Advances in child development and behavior* (Vol. 11). New York: Academic Press, 1976.

Benton, A. L., & Pearl, D. (Eds). *Dyslexia: An appraisal of current knowledge.* New York: Oxford University Press, 1978.

Bower, E. M. *Early identification of emotionally handicapped children in the school* (2d ed.). Springfield, Ill.: Charles C. Thomas, 1969.

Bower, E. M., & Lambert, N. M. *A Process for in-school screening of children with emotional handicaps.* Princeton, N.J.: Educational Testing Service, 1962.

Bruininks, R. H., Glaman, G. H. & Clark, C. R. *Prevalence of learning disabilities: Findings, issues, and recommendations.* Washington, D.C.: Department of Health, Education, and Welfare, U.S. Office of Education, 1971. (Project No. 332189)

Bryan, T. H. Learning disabilities: A new stereotype. *Journal of Learning Disabilities*, 1974, *7*, 304–9.

Burks, H. F. *Burk's behavior rating scales, preschool and kindergarten edition, Administration booklet.* Los Angeles: Western Psychological Services, 1977.

Carter J. L. Intelligence and reading achievement of EMR children in three educational settings. *Mental Retardation*, 1975, *13*(5), 26–27.

Clarizio, H. F., & McCoy, G. *Behavior disorders in children* (2d ed.). New York: Thomas Y. Crowell Co. 1976.

Coleman, J. *Abnormal psychology and modern life.* Glenview, Ill.: Scott Foresman, 1972.

Cone T. E., & Wilson, L. R. Quantifying a severe discrepancy: A critical analysis. *Learning Disability Quarterly,* 1981, 4(4), 359–71.

Cruickshank, W. M. Some issues facing the field of learning disability. *Journal of Learning Disabilities,* 1972, 5, 380–88.

Cruickshank, W. M. Myths and realities in learning disabilities. *Journal of Learning Disabilities,* 1977, 10, 51–58.

Denny, M. R. Research in learning and performance. In H. A. Stevens & R. Heber (Eds.), *Mental retardation: A review of research.* Chicago: University of Chicago Press, 1964.

Diagnostic and statistical manual of mental disorders (DSM III), Washington, D.C.: American Psychiatric Association, 1980.

Federal Bureau of Investigation. FBI Uniform Crime Reports, Crime in the United States, 1978. Washington, D.C.: U.S. Government Printing Office, 1979.

Frank, H. S. & Rabinovitch, M. S. Auditory short-term memory: Developmental changes in rehearsal. *Child Development,* 1974, 45, 397–407.

Gaddes, W. H. *Learning disabilities and brain function: A neuropsychological approach.* New York: Springer-Verlag, 1980.

Gelfand, D. M., Jenson, W. R. & Drew, C. J. *Understanding child behavior disorders.* New York: Holt, Rinehart & Winston, 1982.

Gibson, E. J., Gibson, J. J., Pick, A. D. & Osser, H. A developmental study of the discrimination of letter-like forms. *Journal of Comparative and Physiological Psychology,* 1962, 55, 897–906.

Goldstein, K. The modifications of behavior consequent to cerebral lesions. *Psychiatric Quarterly,* 1936, 10, 586–610.

Goldstein, K. *The organism.* New York: American Book, 1939.

Gottlieb, J. Mainstreaming: Fulfilling the promise? *American Journal of Mental Deficiency,* 1981, 86(2), 115–26.

Gropper, G., Kress, G., Hughes, R., & Pekich, J. Training teachers to recognize and manage social and emotional problems in the classroom. *Journal of Teacher Education,* 1968, 19, 477–85.

Grossman, H. J. (Ed.). *Manual on terminology and classification in mental retardation.* Washington, D.C.: American Association on Mental Deficiency, 1977.

Hallahan, D. P., & Cruickshank, W. M. *Psycho-educational foundations of learning disabilities.* Englewood Cliffs, N.J.: Prentice-Hall, 1973.

Hallahan, D. P., & Kauffman, J. M. *Introduction to learning disabilities: A psycho-behavioral approach.* Englewood Cliffs, N.J.: Prentice-Hall, 1976.

Hallahan, D. P., Kauffman, J. M., & Ball, D. W. Selective attention and cognitive tempo of low achieving and high achieving sixth grade males. *Perceptual and Motor Skills,* 1973, 36, 579–83.

Hallgren, B. Specific dyslexia ("congenital word blindness"): A clinical and genetic study. *Acta Psychiatrica et Neurologica,* 1950, 65, 1–279.

Hammill, D. D. Learning disabilities: A problem in definition. *Division for Children with Learning Disabilities Newsletter,* 1974, 4, 28–31.

Hammill, D. D., & Larsen, S. C. The effectiveness of psycholinguistic training. *Exceptional Children,* 1974, 41, 5–14.

Hammill, D. D., Leigh, J. E., McNutt, G., & Larsen, S. C. A new definition of learning disabilities, *Learning Disability Quarterly,* 1981, 4(4), 336–42.

Harber, J. R. Learning disability research: How far have we progressed? *Learning Disability Quarterly,* 1981, 4(4), 372–381.

Hardman, M. L., & Drew, C. J. Incidental learning in the mentally retarded: A review. *Education and Training of the Mentally Retarded,* 1975, 10(1), 3–9.

Harris, A. *How to increase reading abilities* (5th ed.). New York: David McKay Co., 1970.

Hermann, K. *Reading disability: A medical study of word-blindness and related handicaps.* Springfield, Ill.: Charles C. Thomas, 1959.

Hewitt, L. E., & Jenkins, R. L. *Fundamental patterns of maladjustment: The dynamics of their origin.* Springfield: State of Illinois, 1946.

International classification of diseases (8th rev. ed.) (Vol. 1). Geneva: World Health Organization, 1967.

Kaluger, G., & Kolson, C. *Reading and learning disabilities.* Columbus, Ohio: Charles E. Merrill Publishing Co., 1969.

Kauffman, J. M. *Characteristics of children's behavior disorders.* Columbus, Ohio: Charles E. Merrill Publishing Co. 1977.

Kavale, K., & Nye, C. Identification criteria for learning disabilities: A survey of the reserch literature. *Learning Disability Quarterly,* 1981, 4(4), 383–88.

Kelly, T. K., Bullock, L. M., & Dykes, M. K. Behavioral disorders: Teachers' perceptions. *Exceptional Children,* 1977, 43(5) 316–317.

Kirk, S. A. *Teaching reading to slow-learning children.* Boston: Houghton Mifflin Co., 1940.

Kirk, S. A. *Educating exceptional children* (2d ed.). Boston: Houghton Mifflin Co., 1972.

Kirk, S., McCarthy, J., & Kirk, W. *Illinois test of psycholinguistic abilities* (rev. ed.). Examiners manual. Urbana: University of Illinois Press, 1968.

Kvaraceus, W. C. Problems of early identification and prevention of delinquency. In W.W. Wattenberg (Ed.), *Social Deviancy Among Youth: Yearbook of the National Society of the Study of Education,* 1966, 65, Part 1, 189–220.

Lerner, J. W. *Children with learning disabilities* (3d. ed.). Boston: Houghton Mifflin Co., 1981.

Linsjö, A. Down's syndrome in Sweden: An epidemiological study of a three-year material. *Acta Paediatrica Scandinavia,* 1974, 63, 571–76.

Logan, D. R., & Rose, E. Characteristics of the mildly mentally retarded. In P. T. Cegelka & H. J. Prehm (Eds.), *Mental retardation: From categories to people.* Columbus, Ohio: Charles E. Merrill Publishing Co., 1982.

Long, N. J., Fagen, S., & Stevens, D. *Psychoeducational screening system for identifying resourceful, marginal, and vulnerable pupils in the primary grades.* Washington, D.C.: Psychoeducational Resources, 1971.

MacMillan, D. L. *Mental retardation in school and society* (2d ed.). Boston: Little, Brown & Co., 1982.

MacMillan, D. L., & Borthwick, S. The new educable mentally retarded population: Can they be mainstreamed? *Mental Retardation,* 1980, 18, 155–58.

MacMillan, D. L., Meyers, C. E. & Morrison, G. M. System-identification of mildly mentally retarded children: Implications for interpret-ing and conducting research. *American Journal of Mental Deficiency,* 1980, 85, 108–15.

Meier, J. H. Prevalence and characteristics of learning disabilities found in second grade children. *Journal of Learning Disabilities,* 1971, 4, 6–21.

Mercer, C. D. *Children and adolescents with learning disabilities.* Columbus, Ohio: Charles E. Merrill Publishing Co., 1979.

Mercer, C. D., & Snell, M. E. *Learning theory research in mental retardation.* Columbus, Ohio: Charles E. Merrill Publishing Co. 1977.

Mercer, J. R., & Lewis, J. F. *System of multicultural pluralistic assessment.* New York: The Psychological Corporation, 1977.

Morse, W. C., Cutler, R. L., & Fink, A. H. *Public school classes for the emotionally handicapped: A research analysis.* Washington, D.C.: Council for Exceptional Children, 1964.

Myers, J. K. The efficacy of the special day school. *Mental Retardation,* 1976, 14(4), 3–11.

Myklebust, H. R. Learning disabilities: Definition and overview. In H. R. Myklebust (Ed.), *Progress in learning disabilities* (Vol. 1). New York: Grune & Stratton, 1968.

Myklebust, H. R., Bannochie, M. N., & Killen, J. R. Learning disabilities and cognitive processes. In H. R. Myklebust (Ed.), *Progress in learning disabilities* (Vol. 2). New York: Grune & Stratton, 1971.

Myklebust, H. R., & Boshes, B. *Minimal brain damage in children* (Final Report, Contract 108-65-142, Neurological and Sensory Disease Control Program). Washington, D.C.: U.S. Department of Health, Education, and Welfare, 1969.

National Advisory Committee on Handicapped Children. *Special education for handicapped children: First annual report.* Washington, D.C.: U.S. Department of Health, Education, and Welfare, January 31, 1968.

National Joint Committee for Learning Disabilities. *Learning disabilities: Issues on definition.* Unpublished manuscript, 1981.

Newcomer, P. L. *Understanding and teaching emotionally disturbed children.* Boston: Allyn & Bacon, 1980.

Newcomer, P., & Hammill, D. D. ITPA and academic achievement: A Survey. *The Reading Teacher*, 1975, *28*, 731–41.

Paraskevopoulos, J. N., & Kirk, S. A. *The development and psycholinguistic abilities*. Urbana: University of Illinois Press, 1969.

Pelham, W. E., & Ross, A. O. Selective attention in children with reading problems: A developmental study of incidental learning. *Journal of Abnormal Child Psychology*, 1977, *5*, 1–8.

Quay, H. C. Patterns of aggression, withdrawal, and immaturity. In H. C. Quay & J. S. Werry (Eds.), *Psychopathological disorders of childhood*. New York: John Wiley & Sons, 1972.

Quay, H. C. Classification in the treatment of delinquency and antisocial behavior. In N. Hobbs (Ed.), *Issues in the classification of children* (Vol. 1). San Francisco: Jossey-Bass, 1975.

Rarick, G. L., & Dobbins, D. *Basic components in the motor performance of educable mentally retarded children: Implications for curriculum development*. Washington, D.C. U.S. Office of Education, 1972.

Redick, R. *Utilization of psychiatric facilities by persons under 18 years of age*. Washington, D.C.: U.S. Department of Health, Education, and Welfare, 1973.

Reid, D. K., & Hresko, W. P. *A cognitive approach to learning disabilities*. New York: McGraw-Hill Book Co., 1981.

Richmond, J., & Walzer, S. The central task of childhood learning: The physician's role. In F. De La Cruz, B. Box & R. Roberts (Eds.), *Minimal Brain Dysfunction: Annals of the New York Academy of Sciences*, 1973, *205*, 390–94.

Rie, H. E., Rie, E. D., Stewart, S., & Ambuel, J. P. Effects of methylphenidate on underachieving children. *Journal of Consulting and Clinical Psychology*, 1976, *44*, 250-60 (a).

Rie, H. E., Rie, E. D., Stewart, S., & Ambuel, J. P. Effects of Ritalin on underachieving children: A replication. *American Journal of Ortho-psychiatry*, 1976, *46*, 313–22 (b).

Rosenthal, R. H., & Allen, T. W. An examination of attention, arousal, and learning dysfunctions of hyperkinetic children. *Psychological Bulletin*, 1978, *85*, 689–715.

Salvia, J., & Ysseldyke, J. E. *Assessment in special and remedial education*. Boston: Houghton Mifflin Co., 1978.

Satterfield, J. H., & Dawson, M. E. Electrodermal correlates of hyperactivity in children. *Psychophysiology*, 1971, *8*, 191–97.

Schultz, E. W., Hirshoren, A., Manton, A. B., & Henderson, R. A. Special education for the emotionally disturbed. *Exceptional Children*, 1971, *38*, 313–19.

Silverstein, A. B. Note on the construct validity of the ITPA. *Psychology in the Schools*, 1978, *15*, 371–72.

Spivack, G., & Spotts, J. *Devereaux Child Behavior (DCB) Rating Scale*. Devon, Pa.: Devereaux Foundation, 1966.

Spivack, G., Spotts, J., & Haimes, P. E. *Devereaux Adolescent Behavior (DAB) Rating Scale*. Devon, PA.: Devereaux Foundation, 1967.

Spivack, G., & Swift, M. *Devereaux Elementary School Behavior Rating Scale*. Devon, Pa.: Devereaux Foundation, 1967.

Stager, S. F., & Young, R. D. Intergroup contact and social outcomes for mainstreamed EMR adolescents. *American Journal of Mental Deficiency*, 1981, *85*, 497–503.

Stephens, W. E. Equivalence formation by retarded and nonretarded children at different mental ages. *American Journal of Mental Deficiency*, 1972, *77*, 226–73.

Swanson, H. L. Developmental recall lag in learning-disabled children: Perceptual deficit or verbal mediation deficiency? *Journal of Abnormal Child Psychology*, 1979, *7*, 199–210.

Sykes, D. H., Douglas, V. I., & Morgenstern, G. Sustained attention in hyperactive children. *Journal of Child Psychology and Psychiatry*, 1973, *14*, 213–20.

Tarver, S. G., Hallahan, D. P., Kauffman, J. M., & Ball, D. W. Verbal rehearsal and selective attention in children with learning disabilities: A developmental lag. *Journal of Experimental Child Psychology*, 1976, *22*, 375–85.

U.S. Office of Education. *Estimated number of handicapped children in the United States, 1974–75*. Washington, D.C.: U.S. Office of Education, 1975.

Wacker, J. A. How long do we wait? *ACLD Newsletter*, 1982, *144*, 10.

Walker, H. M. *Walker problem behavior identification checklist.* Los Angeles: Western Psychological Services, 1976.

Wallace, G., & McLoughlin, J. A. *Learning disabilities: Concepts and characteristics* (2d ed.). Columbus, Ohio: Charles E. Merrill Publishing Co., 1979.

Wedell, K. L. *Learning and perceptuo-motor disabilities in children.* New York: John Wiley & Sons, 1973.

Wender, P. H. *The hyperactive child: A handbook for parents.* New York: Crown Publishers, 1973.

Werner, H., & Strauss, A. A. Types of visuo-motor activity in their relation to low and high performance ages. *Proceedings of the American Association on Mental Deficiency*, 1939, *44*, 163–68.

Werner, H., & Strauss, A. A. Pathology of figure-background relation in the child. *Journal of Abnormal and Social Psychology*, 1941, *36*, 236–48.

Whalen, C. K., & Henker, B. Psychostimulants and children: A review and analysis. *Psychological Bulletin*, 1976, *83*, 1113–30.

Wolfgang, M. E., Figlio, R. E., & Sellin, T. *Delinquency in a birth cohort.* Chicago: University of Chicago Press, 1972.

Zentall, S. Optimal stimulation as a theoretical basis of hyperactivity. *American Journal of Orthopsychiatry*, 1975, *45*, 549–61.

Zigler, E. National crisis in mental retardation. *American Journal of Mental Deficiency*, 1978, *83*, 1–8.

Zigler, E., & Balla, D. Issues in personality and motivation mentally retarded persons. In M. J. Begab, H. C. Haywood & H. L. Garber (Eds.), *Psychosocial influences in retarded performance: Vol. 1, Issues and theories in development.* Baltimore: University Park Press, 1981.

Zigler, E., Balla, D., & Watson, N. Developmental and experimental determinants of self-image disparity in institutionalized and noninstitutionalized retarded and normal children. *Journal of Personality and Social Psychology*, 1972, *23*, 81–87.

CHAPTER SIX

Abroms, K. I., & Bennett, J. W. Current genetic and demographic findings in Down's syndrome: How are they presented in college textbooks on exceptionality. *Mental Retardation*, 1980, *18*, 101–7.

Bartak, L., & Rutter, M. Special educational treatment of autistic children: A comparative study—I. Design of study and characteristics of units. *Journal of Child Psychology and Psychiatry*, 1973, *14*, 161–79.

Bleuler, E. *Dementia praecox or the group of schizophrenias.* (J. Zinkin, Trans.). New York: International University Press, 1950. (Originally published, Leipzig: Deutiche, 1911.)

Blue, C. M. Trainable mentally retarded in sheltered workshops. *Mental Retardation*, 1964, *2*, 97–104.

Brown, L., & York, R. Developing programs for severely handicapped students: Teacher training and classroom instruction. *Focus on Exceptional Children*, 1974, *6*(2), 1–11.

Bunker, L. K. Motor skills. In M. E. Snell (Ed.) *Systematic instruction of the moderately and severely handicapped.* Columbus, Ohio: Charles E. Merrill Publishing Co., 1978.

Burt, R. A. Authorizing death for anomalous newborns. In A. Milunsky & G. J. Annas (Eds.), *Genetics and the law.* New York: Plenum Publishing Corporation, 1976.

Carter, C. H. *Handbook of mental retardation syndromes* (3d. ed.). Springfield, Ill.: Charles C. Thomas, 1975.

Chinn, P. C., Drew, C. J., & Logan, D. R. *Mental retardation: Life cycle approach* (2d ed.). St. Louis: C. V. Mosby Co., 1979.

Cooper, L. Z., & Krugman, S. Diagnosis and management: Congenital rubella. *Pediatrics*, 1966, *37*, 335–38.

Diagnostic and statistical manual of mental disorders (DSM III). Washington, D.C.: American Psychiatric Association, 1980.

Diamond, E. F. The deformed child's right to life. In D. J. Horan & D. Mall (Eds.), *Death, dying, and euthanasia.* Washington, D.C.: University Publications of America, 1977.

Duff, R., & Campbell, A. Moral and ethical dilemmas in the special-care nursery. *New England Journal of Medicine*, 1973, *289*, 890–94.

Erickson, J. D. Down's syndrome, paternal age, maternal age, and birth order. *Annals of Human Genetics* (London), 1978, *41*, 289–98.

Fletcher, G. P. Legal aspects of the decision not to prolong life. *Journal of the American Medical Association*, 1968, *203*, 119–122.

Fletcher, J. Abortion, euthanasia, and care of defective newborns. *New England Journal of Medicine*, 1975, *292*, 75–78.

Gold, M. W. Vocational training. In J. Wortis (Ed.), *Mental retardation and developmental disabilities: An annual review* (Vol. 7). New York: Brunner/Mazel, 1975.

Grossman, H. J. (Ed.). *Manual on terminology and classification in mental retardation.* Washington, D.C.: American Association on Mental Deficiency, 1977.

Hardman, M. L., & Drew, C. J. The physically handicapped retarded individual. *Mental Retardation*, 1977, *15*(5), 43–48.

Hardman, M. L., & Drew, C. J. Life management practices with the profoundly retarded: Issues of euthanasia and withholding treatment. *Mental Retardation*, 1978, *16*(6), 390–96.

Hardman, M. L. & Drew, C.J. Parent consent and the practice of withholding treatment from the severely defective newborn. *Mental Retardation*, 1980, *18*, 165–69.

Haring, N. G. The severely handicapped. In N. G. Haring (Ed.), *Behavior of exceptional children.* Columbus, Ohio: Charles E. Merrill Publishing Co., 1978.

Hart, V. The use of many disciplines with the severely and profoundly handicapped. In E. Sontage (Ed.), *Educational programming for the severely and profoundly handicapped.* Reston, Va.: Council for Exceptional Children, 1977.

Hayden, A. H., & McGinness, G. D. Bases for early intervention. In E. Sontag (Ed.), *Educational programming for the severely and profoundly handicapped.* Reston, Va.: Council for Exceptional Children, 1977.

Heath, R. G., Krupp, I., Byers L.W., & Liljekvist, J. I. Schizophrenia as an immunologic disorder. *Archives of General Psychiatry*, 1967, *16*, 1–33.

Hoffer, A., Osmond, H., & Smythies, J. Schizophrenia, a new approach: II. Results of a year's research. *Journal of Mental Science*, 1954, *100*, 29–45.

Horan, D. J., & Mall, D. (Eds.). *Death, dying, and euthanasia.* Washington, D.C.: University Publications of America, 1977.

Justen, J. E., & Brown, G. E. Definitions of severely handicapped: A survey of state departments of education. *AAESPH Review*, 1977, *2*, 8–14.

Kanner, L. Autistic disturbances of affective contact. *Nervous Child*, 1943, *2*, 217–50.

Kanter, F. J. *Heredity in mental health and mental disorder.* New York: W. W. Norton & Co., 1953.

Kauffman, J. M. *Characteristics of children's behavior disorders.* Columbus, Ohio: Charles E. Merrill Publishing Co., 1977.

Linsjö, A. Down's syndrome in Sweden: An epidemiological study of a three-year material. *Acta Paediatrica Scandinavia*, 1974, *63*, 571–76.

Lovaas, O. I., Koegel, R. L., Simmons, J. Q., & Long, J. S. Some generalizations and follow-up measures on autistic children in behavior therapy. *Journal of Applied Behavior Analysis*, 1973, *6*, 131–66.

Matsunaga, E., Tonomura, A., Oishi, H., & Kikuchi, Y. Reexamination of paternal age effect in Down's syndrome. *Human Genetics*, 1978, *40*, 259–69.

Mikkelsen, M., & Stene, J. Genetic counseling in Down's syndrome. *Human Heredity*, 1970, *20*, 457–64.

Miller, W. A., & Erbe, R. W. Prenatal diagnosis of genetic disorders. *Southern Medical Journal*, 1978, *71*, 201–7.

Mori, A. A., & Masters, L. F. *Teaching the severely mentally retarded.* Rockville, Md.: Aspen Systems Corporation, 1980.

National Academy of Sciences. *Genetic screening: Programs, principles and research.* Washington, D.C.: National Academy of Sciences, 1975.

National Joint Committee for Learning Disabilities. *Learning disabilities: Issues on definition.* Unpublished manuscript, 1981.

Olson, J., Algozzine, B., & Schmid, R. E. Mild, moderate, and severe: An empty distinction. *Behavior Disorders*, 1980, 5(2), 96–101.

Orelove, F. P., & Hanley, C. D. *School accessibility survey.* Unpublished manuscript. Department of Special Education, University of Illinois, 1977.

Peck, C. A., Apolloni, T., & Cooke, T. P. Rehabilitation services for Americans with mental retardation: A summary of accomplishments in research and program development. In E. L. Pan, T. E. Backer & C. L. Vash (Eds.), *Annual Review of Rehabilitation* (Vol. 2). New York: Springer-Verlag, 1981.

Pomerantz, D., & Marholin, D. Vocational habilitation: A time for change. In E. Sontag (Ed.), *Educational programming for the severely and profoundly handicapped.* Reston, Va.: Council for Exceptional Children, Division on Mental Retardation, 1977.

Ramsey, P. Abortion. *Thomist*, 1973, 37, 174–226.

Robertson, J. A. Involuntary euthanasia of defective newborns: A legal analysis. *Stanford Law Review*, 1975, 27, 213–69.

Robinson, N. M. & Robinson, H. B. *The mentally retarded child: A psychological approach.* (2d ed.). New York: McGraw-Hill Book Co., 1976.

Rutter, M., & Bartak, L. Special educational treatment of autistic children: A comparative study—II. Follow-up findings and implications for services. *Journal of Child Psychology and Psychiatry*, 1973, 14, 241–70.

Sever, J. L. Infectious agents and fetal disease. In H. A. Waisman & G. R. Kerr (Eds.), *Fetal growth and development.* New York: McGraw-Hill Book Co., 1970.

Shaw, A. Dilemmas of "informed consent" in children. In D. J. Horan & D. Mall (Eds.), *Death, dying, and euthanasia.* Washington, D.C.:University Publications of America,1977.

Slater, E. A review of earlier evidence on genetic factors in schizophrenia. In D. Rosenthal & S. S. Kety (Eds.), *The transmission of schizo—phrenia.* New York: Pergamon Press, 1968.

Smith, D. W., & Wilson, A. A. *The child with Down's Syndrome.* Philadelphia: W. B. Saunders Co., 1973.

Snell, M. E. (Ed.). *Systematic instruction of the moderately and severely handicapped.* Columbus, Ohio: Charles E. Merrill Publishing Co., 1978.

Sontag, E., Burke, P., & York, R. Considerations for serving the severely handicapped in the public schools. *Education and Training of the Mentally Retarded*, 1973, 8, 20–26.

Stainback, S., & Stainback, W. *Educating children with severe maladaptive behaviors.* New York: Grune & Stratton, 1980.

Stene, J., Fischer, G., Stene, E., Mikkelsen, M., & Peterson, E. Parental age effect in Down's syndrome. *Annals of Human Genetics* (London), 1977, 40, 299–306.

Swanson, D. M., & Willis, D. J. *Understanding exceptional children and youth.* Chicago: Rand McNally & Co., 1979.

U.S. Congress, Education of All Handicapped Children Act, Public Law 94-142, 1975.

U.S. Office of Education (USOE), Bureau for the Education of the Handicapped. *Definition of severely handicapped children.* Code of Federal Regulations, 1974, Title 45, Section 121.2.

Van Etten, G. V., Arkell, C., & Van Etten, C. *The severely and profoundly handicapped.* St. Louis: C. V. Mosby Co., 1980.

Wilcox, B. Severe/profound handicapping conditions: administrative considerations. In M. S. Lilly (Ed.), *Children with exceptional needs.* New York: Holt, Rinehart & Winston, 1979.

Williams, G. L. Euthanasia and abortion. *University of Colorado Law Review*, 1966, 38, 181–87.

CHAPTER SEVEN

Azrin, N. H., & Nunn, R. G. A rapid method of eliminating stuttering by a regulated breathing approach. *Behaviour Research and Therapy*, 1974, 12, 279–86.

Bauermeister, J. J., & Jemail, J. A. Modification of "elective mutism" in the classroom setting: A case study. *Behavior Therapy*, 1975, 6, 246–50.

Bloodstein, O., Alper, J., & Zisk, P. Stuttering as an outgrowth of normal disfluency. In D. A. Barbara (Ed.), *New directions in stuttering:*

Theory and practice. Springfield, Ill.: Charles C. Thomas, 1965.

Bloomer, H. H. Speech defects associated with dental malocclusions and related abnormalities. In L. E. Travis (Ed.), *Handbook of speech pathology and audiology.* New York: Appleton-Century-Crofts, 1971.

Brady, J. P., & Berson, J. Stuttering, dichotic listening, and cerebral dominance. *Archives of General Psychiatry,* 1975, *32,* 1449–52.

Brewer, D. W., Sr. Early diagnostic signs and symptoms of laryngeal disease. *Laryngoscope,* 1975, *85,* 499–515.

Bricker, W. A., & Bricker, D. D. An early language training strategy. In R. L. Schiefelbusch & L. L. Lloyd (Eds.), *Language perspectives— acquisition, retardation, and intervention.* Baltimore: University Park Press, 1974, 431–468.

Cohen, M. S., & Hanson, M. L. Intersensory processing efficiency of fluent speakers and stutterers. *British Journal of Disorders of Communication,* 1975, *10,* 111–22.

Cole, M. L., & Cole, J. T. *Effective intervention with the language impaired child.* Rockville, Maryland: Aspen Systems Corporation, 1981.

Colligan, R. W., Colligan, R. C., & Dilliard, M. K. Contingency management in the classroom treatment of long-term mutism: A case report. *Journal of School Psychology,* 1977, *15,* 9–17.

Converse, J. The techniques of cleft palate surgery. *Proceedings of the Conference: Communicative Problems in Cleft Palate* (ASHA Reports), 1965, *1,* 55–82.

Cooper, J. M., & Griffiths, P. Treatment and prognosis. In M. A. Wyke (Ed.), *Developmental dysphasia.* New York: Academic Press, 1978.

Cromer, R. F. Reconceptualizing language acquisition and cognitive development. In R. L. Schiefelbusch & D. D. Bricker (Eds.), *Early language acquisition and intervention.* Baltimore: University Park Press, 1981.

Eisenson, J. Aphasia in adults: Basic considerations. In L. E. Travis (Ed.), *Handbook of speech pathology and audiology.* New York: Appleton-Century-Crofts, 1971 (a).

Eisenson, J. Therapeutic problems and approaches with aphasic adults. In L. E. Travis (Ed.), *Handbook of speech pathology and audiology.* New York: Appleton-Century-Crofts, 1971 (b).

Emerick, L. L., & Hatten, J. T. *Diagnosis and evaluation in speech pathology* (2nd ed.). Englewood Cliffs, N.J.: Prentice-Hall, 1979.

Friedman, R., & Kargan, N. Characteristics and management of elective mutism in children. *Psychology in the Schools,* 1973, *10,* 249–52.

Gelfand, D. M., Jenson, W. R., & Drew, C. J. *Understanding children's behavior disorders.* New York: Holt, Rinehart & Winston, 1982.

Geschwind, N. Human brain: Left-right asymmetrics in temporal speech region. *Science,* 1968, *161,* 186–87.

Gray, B. B. *Some effects of Anxiety Deconditioning upon stuttering behavior.* Monterey, Calif.: Monterey Institute for Speech and Hearing, 1968.

Griffith, E. E., Schnell, J. F., McNees, M. P., Bissinger, C., & Huff, T. M. Elective mutism in a first grader: The remediation of a complex behavioral problem. *Journal of Abnormal Child Psychology,* 1975, *3,* 127–34.

Gruber, L., & Powell, R. L. Responses of stuttering and nonstuttering children to a dichotic listening task. *Perceptual and Motor Skills,* 1974, *38,* 263–64.

Helm, N., Butler, R. B., & Benson, D. F. Acquired stuttering. *Neurology,* 1977, *27,* 349–50.

Hurt, H. T., Scott, M. D., & McCrosky, J. C. *Communication in the classroom.* Reading, Mass.: Addison-Wesley Publishing Co., 1978.

Hutchinson, B. B., Hanson, M. L., & Mecham, M. J. *Diagnostic handbook of speech pathology.* Baltimore: Williams & Wilkins, 1979.

Johnston, J. M., & Johnston, G. T. Modification of consonant speech-sound articulation in young children. *Journal of Applied Behavior Analysis,* 1972, *5,* 233–46.

Knepflar, K. J. *Report writing in the field of communication disorders.* Danville, Ill.: Interstate Printers & Publishers, 1976.

Kretschmer, R. R., & Kretschmer, L. W. *Language development and intervention with the hearing impaired.* Baltimore: University Park Press, 1978.

Lucas, E. V. *Semantic and pragmatic language disorders: Assessment and remediation.* Rockville, Md.: Aspen Systems Corporation, 1980.

Mecham, M. J., & Willbrand, M. L. *Language disorders in children: A resource book for speech/language pathologists.* Springfield, Ill.: Charles C. Thomas, 1979.

Milisen, R. The incidence of speech disorders. In L. E. Travis (Ed.), *Handbook of speech pathology and audiology.* New York: Appleton-Century-Crofts, 1971.

Moore, G. P. Voice disorders organically based. In L. E. Travis (Ed.), *Handbook of speech pathology and audiology.* New York: Appleton-Century-Crofts, 1971.

Moore, W. H., Jr., & Lang, M. K. Alpha asymmetry over the right and left hemispheres of stutterers and control subjects preceding massed oral readings: A preliminary investigation. *Perceptual and Motor Skills,* 1977, *44*, 223–30.

Morley, M., Court, D., Miller, H., & Garside, R. Delayed speech and developmental aphasia. *British Medical Journal,* 1955, *4937* (2), 463–67.

Morris, A., & Greulich, R. Dental research: The past two decades. *Science,* 1968, *160*, 1081–88.

Mowrer, D. E., Baker, R. L., & Schutz, R. E. Operant procedures in the control of speech articulation. In H. N. Sloane, & B. D. MacAulay (Eds.), *Operant procedures in remedial speech and language training.* Boston: Houghton Mifflin Co., 1968, 296–321.

Mykelbust, H. R. Childhood aphasia: Identification, diagnosis, remediation. In L. E. Travis (Ed.), *Handbook of speech pathology and audiology.* New York: Appleton-Century-Crofts, 1971.

National Institute of Dental Research. *Research News from NIDR,* No. 45, 1967.

Newport, E. L., Gleitman, H., & Gleitman, L. R. Mother, I'd rather do it myself: Some effects and non-effects of maternal speech style. In C. E. Snow & C. A. Ferguson (Eds.) *Talking to children: Language input and acquisition.* Cambridge: Cambridge University Press, 1977.

Perkins, W. H. *Speech pathology: An applied behavioral science.* St. Louis: C. V. Mosby Co., 1971.

Perkins, W., Rudas, J., Johnson, L., & Bell, J. Stuttering: Discoordination of phonation with articulation and respiration. *Journal of Speech and Hearing Research,* 1976, *19*, 509–22.

Powers, M. H. Functional disorders of articulation—symptomology and etiology. In L. E. Travis (Ed.), *Handbook of speech pathology and audiology.* New York: Appleton-Century-Crofts, 1971.

Ryan, B. P. A study of the effectiveness of the S-Pack program in the elimination of frontal lisping behavior in third-grade children. *Journal of Speech and Hearing Disorders,* 1971, *36*, 390–96.

Sheehan, J. G., & Costly, M. S. A reexamination of the role of heredity in stuttering. *Journal of Speech and Hearing Disorders,* 1977, *42*, 47–59.

Sloane, H. N., Jr., Johnston, M. K., & Harris, F. R. Remedial procedures for teaching verbal behavior to speech deficient or defective children. In H. N. Sloane & B. D. MacAulay (Eds.), *Operant procedures in remedial speech and language training.* Boston: Houghton Mifflin Co., 1968.

Slorach, N., & Noeher, B. Dichotic listening in stuttering and dyslalic children. *Cortex,* 1973, *9*, 295–300.

Sommers, R. K., Brady, W. A., & Moore, W. H., Jr. Dichotic ear preferences of stuttering children and adults. *Perceptual and Motor Skills,* 1975, *41*, 931–38.

Travis, L. E. (Ed.), *Handbook of speech pathology and audiology.* New York: Appleton-Century-Crofts, 1971.

Van Der Kooy, D., & Webster, C. D. A rapidly effective behavior modification program for an electively mute child. *Journal of Behavior Therapy and Expermental Psychiatry,* 1975, *6*, 149–52.

Van Riper, C. *Speech correction: Principles and methods* (5th ed.). Englewood Cliffs, N.J.: Prentice-Hall, 1972.

Waldo, A. L. *Sacajawea.* New York: Avon Books, 1978.

Weiss, C. E., & Lillywhite, H. S. *A handbook for prevention and early intervention: Commu-*

nicative disorders. St. Louis: C. V. Mosby Co., 1976.

Wiig, E. H., & Semel, E. M. *Language assessment and intervention for the learning disabled.* Columbus, Ohio: Charles E. Merrill Publishing Co., 1980.

Wintz, H. *Articulatory acquisition and behavior.* New York: Appleton-Century-Crofts, 1969.

Wohl, M. T. The electric metronome—an evaluative study. *British Journal of Disorders of Communication,* 1968, *3,* 89–98.

Wolfe, V. I., & Irwin, R. B. Feedback modification in instrumental conditioning of articulation. *Perceptual and Motor Skills,* 1975, *40,* 770.

Wood, K. S. Terminology and nomenclature. In L. E. Travis (Ed.), *Handbook of speech pathology and audiology.* New York: Appleton-Century-Crofts, 1971.

CHAPTER EIGHT

Abroms, I. F. Nongenetic hearing loss. In B. F. Jaffe (Ed.), *Hearing loss in children.* Baltimore: University Park Press, 1977.

Advisory Committee on the Education of the Deaf. The handicap of deafness. In R. L. Jones (Ed.), *Problems and issues in the education of exceptional children.* Boston: Houghton Mifflin Co., 1971.

Altshuler, K. Z. Personality traits and depressive symptoms in the deaf. In J. Wortis (Ed.), *Recent advances in biological psychiatry* (Vol. 6). New York: Plenum Press, 1964.

Annual survey of hearing impaired children and youth. Washington, D.C.: Office of Demographic Studies, Gallaudet College, 1977–1978.

Berg, F. S. *Educational audiology: hearing and speech management.* New York: Grune & Stratton, 1976.

Bitter, G. B. Identification and educational management of hearing loss. In *Utah skills project.* Salt Lake City: Utah State Board of Education, 1981.

Boothroyd, A. *Some aspects of language function in a group of lower school children* (Sensory Aids Research Project Report No. 6) Northampton, Mass.: C. V. Hudgins Diagnostic and Research Center, Clarke School for the Deaf, 1971.

Boulton, B., Cull, J. G., & Hardy, R. E. Psychological adjustment to hearing loss and deafness. In R. E. Hardy & J. G. Cull (Eds.), *Educational and psychosocial aspects of deafness.* Springfield, Ill.: Charles C. Thomas Publishing Co., 1974.

Brooks, P. H. Some speculations concerning deafness and learning to read. In L. S. Liben (Ed.), *Deaf children: Developmental perspectives.* New York: Academic Press, 1978.

Butler, M. J. Teaching students with a hearing impairment. In M. L. Hardman, M. W. Egan, & E. D. Landau (Eds.), *What will we do in the morning? The exceptional student in the regular classroom.* Dubuque, Iowa: William C. Brown Co., 1981.

Caldwell, D. C. Closed-captioned television: Educational and sociological implications for hearing-impaired learners. *American Annals of the Deaf,* September 1981, 627–30.

Craig, W., & Craig, H. (Eds.). Directory of services for the deaf. *American Annals of the Deaf,* April 1975, 120.

Davis, H. Abnormal hearing and deafness. In H. Davis and S. R. Silverman (Eds.), *Hearing and deafness* (4th ed.). New York: Holt, Rinehart & Winston, 1978 (a).

Davis, H. Audiometry: Pure-tone and simple speech tests. In H. Davis and S. Richard Silverman (Eds.), *Hearing and deafness* (4th ed.). New York: Holt, Rinehart & Winston, 1978 (b).

Davis, J. Personnel and services. In J. Davis (Ed.), *Our forgotten children: Hard-of-hearing pupils in the schools.* Minneapolis: University of Minnesota, 1977.

Delk, J. H. *Comprehensive dictionary of audiology.* Sioux City, Iowa: Hearing Aid Journal, 1973.

Dipietro, L. J., Knight, C. H., & Sams, J. S. Health care delivery for deaf patients: The provider's role. *American Annals of the Deaf,* April 1981, 106–12.

Downs, M. P. Goals and methods of communication. In B. F. Jaffe (Ed.), *Hearing loss in children.* Baltimore: University Park Press, 1977.

Eichenwald, H. F. *Human toxoplasmosis: Proceedings of the conference on clinical*

aspects and diagnostic problems of toxoplasmosis in pediatrics. Baltimore:
Williams & Wilkins, 1956.

Fant, L. J. Ameslan: An introduction to the American Sign Language. Silver Springs, Md.:
National Association of the Deaf, 1972.

Fellendorf, G. W. The Alexander Graham Bell
Association for the Deaf. In L. J. Bradford &
W. G. Hardy (Eds.), Hearing and hearing
impairment. New York: Grune & Stratton,
1979.

Gentile, A., & McCarthy, B. Additional handicapping conditions among hearing impaired
students, United States: 1971–72. Series D,
No. 14. Washington, D.C.: Office of Demographic Studies, Gallaudet College, 1973.

Glorig, A. Thunderation. Hearing and Speech
News, 1972, 40(1), 6–7, 23–26.

Hanshaw, J. B. Cytomegalovirus infection and cerebral dysfunction. Hospital Practice, 1970,
5, 111–20.

Heider, F., & Heider, G. M. Studies in the psychology of the deaf, no. 1. Psychological
Division, Clarke School for the Deaf.
Psychological Monographs, 1940, 52,
no. 242.

Hicks, D. E. Comparison profiles of rubella and
nonrubella children. American Annals
of the Deaf, 1970, 115, 86–92.

Higgins, P. C. Outsiders in a hearing world: A sociology of deafness. Beverly Hills, Calif.:
Sage Publications, 1980.

Hoemann, H. W., & Briga, J. S. Hearing impairments. In J. M. Kauffman & D. P. Hallahan
(Eds.), Handbook of special education. Englewood Cliffs, N.J.: Prentice-Hall, 1981.

Jaffe, B. F. History and physical examination for
evaluating hearing loss in children. In B. F.
Jaffe (Ed.), Hearing loss in children. Baltimore: University Park Press, 1977.

Jensema, C. J., Karchmer, M. A., & Trybus, R. J.
The rated speech intelligibility of hearing
impaired children: Basic relationships and
a detailed analysis. Series R, no. 6. Washington, D.C.: Office of Demographic Studies,
Gallaudet College, 1978.

Karchmer, M., & Kirwin, L. The use of hearing
aids by hearing impaired children in the
United States. Series S, no. 2, Washington,
D.C.: Office of Demographic Studies,
Gallaudet College, 1977.

Karchmer, M. A., Milone, M. N., & Wolk, S. Educational significance of hearing loss at three
levels of severity.American Annals of the
Deaf, April 1979, 97–109.

Kodman, F. Educational status of hard of hearing
children in the classroom. Journal of
Speech and Hearing Disorders, 1963, 28,
297–99.

Konigsmark, B. W. Genetic hearing loss with no
associated abnormalities: A review. Journal
of Speech and Hearing Disorders, 1972, 37,
89–99.

Lim, D. J. Histology of the developing inner ear:
Normal anatomy and developmental anomalies. In B. F. Jaffe (Ed.), Hearing loss in
children. Baltimore: University Park Press,
1977.

Ling, D. Rehabilitation of cases with deafness sec-
ondary to Otitis Media. In A. Glorig & K. S.
Gerwin (Eds.), Otitis Media. Springfield, Ill.:
Charles C. Thomas Publishing Co., 1972.

Ling, D., & Ling, A. H. Aural rehabilitation:
Foundations of verbal learning in hearing-
impaired children. Washington, D.C.: Alexander Graham Bell Association for the Deaf,
1978.

Lovrinic, J. H. Pure tone and speech audiometry.
In R. W. Keith (Ed.), Audiology for the physician. Baltimore: Williams & Wilkins, 1980.

Mandell, C. J., & Fiscus, E. Understanding exceptional people. St. Paul, Minn.: West Publishing Co., 1981.

Mayberry, R. I. Manual communication. In H.
Davis & S. R. Silverman (Eds.), Hearing and
deafness. New York: Holt, Rinehart &
Winston, 1978.

McConnell, F. Children with hearing disabilities.
In L. M. Dunn (Ed.), Exceptional children
in the schools (2d ed.). New York: Holt,
Rinehart & Winston, 1973.

Meadow, K. P. Personality and social development for deaf persons. In B. Bolton (Ed.),
Psychology of deafness for rehabilitation
counselors. Baltimore: University Park
Press, 1976.

Meadow, K. P. Deafness and child development.
Berkeley, Calif.: University of California
Press, 1980.

Mental Health Needs of Deaf Americans: Task
panel reports submitted to the President's
Commission on Mental Health, Vol. 3.

Washington, D.C.: U.S. Government Printing Office, 1978.

Moores, D. F. *Educating the deaf: Psychology, principles, and practices.* Boston: Houghton Mifflin Co., 1978.

Myklebust, H. *The psychology of deafness.* New York: Grune & Stratton, 1960.

Nance, W. E. Studies of hereditary deafness: Present, past, and future. *The Volta Review,* 1976, *78,* 6–11.

Niemoeller, A. F. *Hearing aids.* In H. Davis & S. R. Silverman (Eds.), *Hearing and deafness* (4th ed.). New York: Holt, Rinehart & Winston, 1978.

Olmstead, R. W., Alvarez, M. C., Moroney, J. D., & Eversden, M. The pattern of hearing following acute otitis media. *Journal of Pediatrics,* 1964, *65,* 252–55.

O'Neill, J. J. *The hard of hearing.* Englewood Cliffs, N.J.: Prentice-Hall, 1964.

Oyers, H. J., & Frankmann, J. P. *The aural rehabilitation process: A conceptual framework analysis.* New York: Holt, Rinehart & Winston, 1975.

Pahz, J. A., & Pahz, C. S. *Total communication.* Springfield, Ill.: Charles C. Thomas Publishing Co., 1978.

Paparella, M. M., & Davis, H. Medical and surgical treatment of hearing loss. In H. Davis & S. R. Silverman (Eds.) *Hearing and deafness* (4th ed.). New York: Holt, Rinehart & Winston, 1978.

Pinter, R., Eisenson, J., & Stanton, M. *The psychology of the physically handicapped.* New York: F. S. Crofts & Co., 1941.

Proctor, C., & Proctor, B. Understanding hereditary nerve deafness. *Archives of Otolaryngology,* 1967, *85,* 23–40.

Report of the Ad Hoc Committee to Define Deaf and Hard-of-Hearing. *American Annals of the Deaf,* 1975, *120,* 509–12.

Ries, P. *Reported causes of hearing loss for hearing impaired students: 1970–1971.* Series D, No. 11, Annual Survey of Hearing Impaired Children and Youth. Office of Demographic Studies, Gallaudet College, 1973.

Ross, M. Definitions and descriptions. In J. David (Ed.), *Our forgotten children: Hard-of-hearing pupils in the schools.* Minneapolis: Audio-Visual Library Service, University of Minnesota, 1977.

Sanders, D. A. Psychological implications of hearing impairments. In W. M. Cruickshank (Ed.), *Psychology of exceptional children* (4th ed.). Englewood Cliffs, N.J.: Prentice-Hall, 1980.

Schein, J. D. Society and culture of hearing-impaired people. In L. J. Bradford & W. G. Hardy (Eds.), *Hearing and hearing impairment.* New York: Grune & Stratton, 1979.

Schein, J. D., & Delk, M. T. *The deaf population in the United States.* Silver Springs, Md.: National Association of the Deaf, 1974.

Schlesinger, H. S. The effects of deafness on childhood development: An Eriksonian perspective. In L. S. Liben (Ed.), *Deaf children: Developmental perspectives.* New York: Academic Press, 1978.

Schlesinger, H. S., & Meadow, K. P. Emotional support for parents. In D. L. Lillie, P. L. Trohanis & K. W. Goin (Eds.), *Teaching parents to teach.* New York: Walker & Co., 1976.

Schreiber, F. C. *National Association for the Deaf.* In L. J. Bradford & W. G. Hardy (Eds.), *Hearing and hearing impairment.* New York: Grune & Stratton, 1979.

Silverman, S. R., Lane, H. S., & Calvert, D. R. Early and elementary education. In H. Davis & S. R. Silverman (Eds.), *Hearing and deafness* (4th ed.). New York: Holt, Rinehart & Winston, 1978.

Trybus, R. J., & Karchmer, M. A. School achievement scores of hearing impaired children: National data on achievement status and growth patterns. *American Annals of the Deaf,* 1977, *122,* 62–69.

Tucker, B. P. Mental health services for hearing-impaired persons. *The Volta Review,* May 1981, 223–35.

Vernon, M. Current etiological factors in deafness. *American Annals of the Deaf,* 1968, *113,* 106–15.

Vernon, M. Sociological and psychological factors associated with hearing loss. *Journal of Speech and Hearing Research,* 1969, *12,* 541–63.

Vernon, M., & Brown, B. A guide to psychological tests and testing procedures in the evaluation of deaf and hard-of-hearing children. *Journal of Speech and Hearing Disorders,* 1964, *29,* 414–23.

Wrightstone, J. W., Aronow, M. S., & Moskowitz, S. Developing reading test norms for deaf children. *American Annals of the Deaf*, 1963, *108*, 311–16.

Yater, V. V. *Mainstreaming of children with a hearing loss*. Springfield, Ill.: Charles C. Thomas Publishing Co., 1977.

CHAPTER NINE

American Printing House for the Blind. *Distribution of January 6, 1979, Quota registrations by school, grades, and reading media*. Author, 1979.

Ashcroft, S. C. Blind and partially-seeing children. In L. M. Dunn (Ed.), *Exceptional children in the schools*. New York: Holt, Rinehart & Winston, 1963.

Ashcroft, S. C. Delineating the possible for the multihandicapped adult with visual impairment. *Sight-Saving Review*, 1966, *36*, 90–94.

Barraga, N. C. *Increased visual behavior in low vision children*. Research Series No. 13. New York: American Foundation for the Blind, 1964.

Barraga, N. C. Utilization of sensory-perceptual abilities. In B. Lowenfeld (Ed.), *The visually handicapped child in school*. London: Constable, 1974.

Barraga, N. C. *Visual handicaps and learning: A developmental approach*. Belmont, Calif.: Wadsworth Publishing Co., 1976.

Bateman, B. *Sighted children's perceptions of blind children's abilities*. Research Bulletin No. 8. New York: American Foundation for the Blind, 1965.

Blank, H. R. Dreams of the blind. *The Psychoanalytic Quarterly*, 1958, *27*, 158–174.

Chapman, E. K. *Visually handicapped children and young people*. London: Routledge & Kegan Paul, 1978.

Connor, F. P., Hoover, R., Horton, K., Sands, H., Sternfeld, L., & Wolinsky, G. F. Physical and sensory handicaps. In N. Hobbs (Ed.), *Issues in the classification of children* (Vol. 1). San Francisco: Jossey-Bass, 1975.

Craig, R. H., & Howard, C. Teaching students with visual impairments. In M. L. Hardman, M. W. Egan, & E. D. Landau (Eds.), *What will we do in the morning? The exceptional student in the regular classroom*, Dubuque, Iowa: William C. Brown Co., 1981.

Fraser, G. R., & Friedman, A. I. *The causes of blindness in children*. Baltimore: Johns Hopkins University Press, 1967.

Frisby, J. P. *Seeing: Illusion, brain, and mind*. New York: Oxford University Press, 1979.

Getman, G. N. The visuomotor complex in the acquisition of learning skills. In J. Hellmuth (Ed.), *Learning disorders* (Vol. 1). Seattle: Special Child Publications, 1965.

Ginsberg, E. Preventive health: No easy answers. *The Sight-Saving Review*, 1973–1974, *43*, 187–95.

Gregg, J. R., & Heath, G. G. *The eye*. Lexington, Mass.: D. C. Heath & Co., 1964.

Halliday, C., & Kurzhals, I. W. *Stimulating environments for children who are visually impaired*. Springfield, Ill.: Charles C. Thomas Publishing Co., 1976.

Harley, R. K., Henderson, F. M., & Truan, M. B. *The teaching of braille reading*, Springfield, Ill.: Charles C. Thomas Publishing Co., 1979.

Jones, R. L., Gottfried, N. W., & Owens, A. The social distance of the exceptional child: A study at the high school level. *Exceptional Children*, 1966, *32*, 551–56.

Kirtley, D. D. *The psychology of blindness*. Chicago: Nelson-Hall, 1975.

Koestler, F. A. *The unseen minority: A social history of blindness in America*. New York: David McKay Co., 1976.

Lowenfeld, B. Psychological considerations. In B. Lowenfeld (Ed.), *The visually handicapped child in school*. London: Constable, 1974.

Lowenfeld, B. *The changing status of the blind: From separation to integration*. Springfield, Ill.: Charles C. Thomas Publishing Co., 1975.

Lowenfeld, B. Psychological problems of children with severely impaired vision. In W. M. Cruickshank (Ed.), *Psychology of exceptional children and youth* (4th ed.). Englewood Cliffs, N.J.: Prentice-Hall, 1980.

National Society for the Prevention of Blindness. *Estimated statistics on blindness and vision problems*. New York: National Society for the Prevention of Blindness, 1966.

National Society to Prevent Blindness. *Vision problems in the U. S.* New York: National Society to Prevent Blindness, 1980.

Raikes, A. Preliminary visual screening. In V. Smith & J. Keen (Eds.), *Visual handicap in children.* London: William Heinemann Medical Books, 1979.

Reynolds, M. C., & Birch, J. W. *Teaching exceptional children in all America's schools* (2d ed.). Reston, Va.: Council for Exceptional Children, 1982.

Schlaegel, T. F. The dominant method of imagery in blind as compared to sighted adolescents. *Journal of Genetic Psychology*, 1953, *83*, 265–77.

Scholl, G. T. Understanding and meeting development needs. In B. Lowenfeld (Ed.), *The visually handicapped child in school.* London: Constable, 1974.

Schrock, R. E. Research relating to vision and learning. In R. M. Wold (Ed.), *Vision: Its impact on learning.* Seattle: Special Child Publications, 1978.

Suran, B. G., & Rizzo, J. V. *Special children: An integrative approach.* Glenview, Ill.: Scott, Foresman & Co., 1979.

Taylor, J. L. Educational programs. In B. Lowenfeld (Ed.), *The visually handicapped child in the schools.* New York: John Daly, 1973.

Telford, C. W., & Sawrey, J. M. *The exceptional individual* (4th ed.). Englewood Cliffs, N.J.: Prentice-Hall, 1981.

Terry, T. L. Extreme prematurity and fibroblastic overgrowth of persistent vascular sheath behind each crystalline lens, I: Preliminary report. *American Journal of Ophthalmology*, 1942, *25*, 203.

Tobin, M. J., & James R. K. Evaluating the optacon: General reflections on reading machines for the blind. *Research Bulletin: American Foundation for the Blind.* 1974, *28*, 145–57.

Toth, Z. *Die vorstellunswelt der blinden.* Leipzig: Johann Ambrosius Barth, 1938.

Warren, D. H. *Blindness and early childhood development.* New York: American Foundation for the Blind, 1977.

Willis, D. J., Groves, C., & Fuhrman, W. Visually disabled children and youth. In B. M. Swanson & D. J. Willis (Eds.), *Understand-ing exceptional children and youth: An introduction to special education.* Chicago: Rand McNally & Co., 1979.

Zinkin, P. M. The effect of visual handicap on early development. In V. Smith & J. Keen (Eds.), *Visual handicap in children.* Philadelphia: J. B. Lippincott Co., 1979.

CHAPTER TEN

Albrecht, G. L. Socialization and the disability process. In G. L. Albrecht (Ed.), *The sociology of physical disability and rehabilitation.* Pittsburgh: University of Pittsburgh Press, 1976.

Arthritis Foundation. *Arthritis, the basic facts.* New York: Arthritis Foundation, 1974.

Barton, D. *Dying and death.* Baltimore: Williams & Wilkins, 1977.

Batshaw, M. L., and Perret, Y. M. *Children with handicaps: A medical primer.* Baltimore, Maryland: P. H. Brookes, 1981.

Calhoun, M. L., & Hawisher, M. *Teaching and learning strategies for physically handicapped students.* Baltimore: University Park Press, 1979.

Cruickshank, W. M. The problem and its scope. In W. M. Cruickshank (Ed.), *Cerebral palsy: A developmental disability* (3d ed.). Syracuse, N.Y.: Syracuse University Press, 1976.

Dikmen, S., Matthews, C. G., & Harley, J. P. The effect of early versus late onset of major motor epilepsy upon cognitive-intellectual performance. *Epilepsia*, 1975, *16*, 73–81.

Dunham, C. S. Amputations. In R. M. Goldenson, J. R. Dunham & C. S. Dunham (Eds.), *Disability and rehabilitation handbook.* New York: McGraw-Hill Book Co., 1978.

Education Development Center. *No two alike: helping children with special needs.* Cambridge, Mass.: Education Development Center, 1975.

Epilepsy Foundation of America. *Answers to the most frequent questions people asked about epilepsy.* Washington, D.C.: Epilepsy Foundation of America, 1973.

Ferguson, A. B. *Orthopedic surgery in infancy and childhood* (4th ed.). Baltimore: Williams & Wilkins, 1975.

Friedman, L. W. *The psychological rehabilitation of the amputee.* Springfield, Ill.: Charles C Thomas, 1978(a).

Friedmann, L. W. *The Surgical rehabilitation of the amputee.* Springfield, Ill.: Charles C Thomas, 1978(b).

Friedman, R. J., & MacQueen, J. C. Psycho-educational considerations of physically handicapped conditions in children. *Exceptional Children,* 1971, *37,* 538–39.

Gastaut, H. Clinical and electroencephalographical classification of epileptic seizures. *Epilepsia,* 1970, *11,* 102–113.

Green, M. *Pediatric diagnosis.* Philadelphia: W. B. Saunders Co., 1980.

Gyulay, J. *The dying child.* New York: McGraw-Hill Book Co., 1978.

Haeussermann, E. *Evaluating the developmental level of preschool children handicapped by cerebral palsy.* New York: United Cerebral Palsy Association, 1952.

Hall, C. B., Rosenfelder, R., & Tablada, C. The juvenile amputee with a scarred stump. In G. T. Aitken (Ed.), *The child with an acquired amputation.* Washington, D.C.: National Academy of Sciences, 1970.

Heilman, A. Intelligence in cerebral palsy. *The Crippled Child,* 1952, *30,* 11–13.

Howell, L. Spinal cord injury. In R. M. Goldenson, J. R. Dunham & C. S. Dunham (Eds.), *Disability and rehabilitation handbook.* New York: McGraw-Hill Book Co., 1978.

Kübler-Ross, E. *Death, the final stage of growth.* Englewood Cliffs, N.J.: Prentice-Hall, 1975.

Kurland, L. T., Kurtzke, J. F., & Goldberg, I. D. *Epidemiology of neurologic and sense organ disorders.* Cambridge, Mass.: Harvard University Press, 1973.

Lewandowski, L. J., & Cruickshank, W. M. Psychological development of crippled children and youth. In W. M. Cruickshank (Ed.), *Psychology of exceptional children and youth.* Englewood Cliffs, N.J.: Prentice-Hall, 1980.

Mullins, J. B. *A teacher's guide to management of the physically handicapped.* Springfield, Ill.: Charles C Thomas, 1979.

Parker, H. J. Children and youth with physical and health disabilities. In B. M. Swanson & D. J. Willis (Eds.), *Understanding exceptional children and youth.* Chicago: Rand-McNally Co., 1979.

Peters, D. M. Developmental and conceptual components of the normal child: A comparative study with the cerebral palsy child. *Cerebral Palsy Review,* 1964, *25,* 3–7.

Rodin, E. A. Medical considerations. In G. N. Wright (Ed.), *Epilepsy rehabilitation.* Boston: Little, Brown, & Co., 1975.

Solomon, G. E., & Plum, F. *Clinical management of seizures.* Philadelphia: W. B. Saunders Co., 1976.

Stark, G. D. *Spina bifida.* London: Blackwell Scientific Publications, 1977.

Svoboda, W. B. *Learning about epilepsy.* Baltimore: University Park Press, 1979.

U.S. Department of Health and Human Services. *Muscular dystrophy and other neuromuscular disorders.* Bethesda, Md.: Office of Scientific and Health Reports, National Institute of Neurological and Communicative Disorders and Stroke, National Institute of Health, 1980. (NIH Publication No. 80-1615).

U.S. Department of Health and Human Services. *The NINDS research program, spina bifida and neural tube defects.* Washington, D.C.: U.S. Government Printing Office, 1981(a).

U.S. Department of Health and Human Services. *The NINDS research program: Spinal cord injury and nervous system trauma.* Washington, D.C.: U.S. Government Printing Office, 1981(b).

CHAPTER ELEVEN

Alexanian, R., & Nadell, J. Oxymetholene treatment for sickle cell anemia. *Blood,* 1975, *45,* 769–77.

Ament, M. E. Peptic ulcer disease. In E. Lebenthal (Ed.), *Digestive diseases in children.* New York: Grune & Stratton, 1978.

Anderson, C. M., & Goodchild, M. C. *Cystic fibrosis: Manual of diagnosis and management.* Philadelphia: J. B. Lippincott Co., 1976.

Armington, C. S., & Creighton, H. *Nursing of people with cardiovascular problems.* Boston: Little, Brown & Co., 1971.

Bakan, D. *Slaughter of the innocents.* San Francisco: Jossey-Bass, 1971.

Beezley, P. J. Modern treatment options. In B. D. Schmitt (Ed.), *The child protection team handbook. New York: Garland STPM Press, 1978.*

Blumberg, M. L. Psychopathology of the abusing parent. *American Journal of Psychotherapy,* 1974, *28,* 21–29.

Bolton, F. G. *The pregnant adolescent.* Beverly Hills, Calif.: Sage Publications, 1980.

Card, J. J., & Wise, L. L. Teenage mothers and teenage fathers: The impact of early child rearing on the parents' personal and professional lives. *Family Planning Perspectives,* 1978, *10,* 199–205.

Chilman, C. *Adolescent sexuality in a changing American society: Social and psychological perspectives.* Bethesda, Md.: National Institute of Health, 1979. (DHEW No. [NIH] 79-1426)

Conley, C. L. Sickle-cell anemia: The first molecular disease. In M. W. Wintrobe (Ed.), *Blood, pure and eloquent.* New York: McGraw-Hill Book Co., 1980.

Costa, J. J., & Nelson, G. K. *Child abuse and neglect: Legislation, reporting, and prevention.* Lexington, Mass.: Lexington Books, 1978.

Creer, T. L., Renne, C. M., & Christian, W. P. Behavioral contributions to rehabilitation and childhood asthma. *Rehabilitation Literature,* 1976, *37,* 226–32.

Danks, D. M., Allan, J., & Anderson, C. M. A genetic study of fibrocystic disease of the pancreas. *Annals of Human Genetics,* 1965, *28,* 323–56.

Davidson, M. B. *Diabetes mellitus: Diagnosis and Treatment* (Vol. 2). New York: John Wiley & Sons, 1981.

DeFrancis, V. *Protecting the child victim of sex crimes by adults.* Denver: American Humane Association, 1969.

deGruchy, G. C. Disorders of hemoglobin structure and synthesis. In D. Penington, B. Rush & P. Castaldi (Eds.), *Clinical hematology in medical practice.* Oxford: Blackwell Scientific Publications, 1978.

Ellenburg, M. Diabetes mellitus. In R. M. Goldenson, J. R. Dunham & C. S. Dunham (Eds.), *Disability and rehabilitation handbook.* New York: McGraw-Hill Book Co. 1978.

Fireman, P. A review of asthma admissions and deaths at the Children's Hospital of Pittsburgh from 1935 to 1968. *Journal of Allergy,* 1971, *46,* 257–69.

Fontana, V. J., and Besharov, D. J. *The maltreated child: The maltreatment syndrome in children, a medical, legal and social guide.* Springfield, Ill.: Charles C. Thomas Publishing Co., 1977.

Fraser, B. G. The child and his parents: A delicate balance of rights. In R. E. Helfer & C. H. Kempe (Eds.), *Child abuse and neglect.* Cambridge, Mass.: Ballinger Publishing Co., 1976.

Furstenberg, F. F. *Unplanned parenthood: The social consequences of teenage child bearing.* New York: Free Press, 1976.

Gelles, R. J. Child abuse as psychopathology: A sociological critique and reformulation. *American Journal of Orthopsychiatry,* 1973, *43,* 611–21.

Ghory, J. E. The adolescent in an asthmatic rehabilitation program. *Journal of Asthma Research,* 1972, *16,* 55–60.

Gorwitz, K., Howen, G., & Thompson, T. Prevalence of diabetes in Michigan school-age children. *Diabetes,* 1976, *25,* 122–27.

Graham, P. J., Rutter, M. L., Yule, W., & Pless, I. B. Childhood asthma: A psychosomatic disorder? Some epidemiological considerations. *British Journal of Preventative and Social Medicine,* 1967, *21,* 78–85.

Green, A. H., Gaines, R. W., & Sandgrund, A. Child abuse: Pathological syndrome of family interaction. *American Journal of Psychiatry,* 1974, *131,* 882–86.

Grunz, F. W. The dread leukemias and lymphomas: Their nature and their prospects. In M. W. Wintrobe (Ed.), *Blood, pure and eloquent.* New York: McGraw-Hill Book Co., 1980.

Kempe, R. S., & Kempe, C. H. *Child abuse.* Cambridge, Mass.: Harvard University Press, 1978.

Kempe, C. H., & Helfer, R. E. *Helping the battered child and his family.* Philadelphia: J. B. Lippincott Co., 1972.

Khan, A. U. Present status of psychosomatic aspects of asthma. *Psychosomatics,* 1973, *14,* 192–200.

Klemperer, M. R., Rubins, J. M., & Lichtman, M. A. Lymphocytosis. In M. A. Lichtman (Ed.), *Hematology for practitioners,* Boston: Little, Brown & Co., 1978.

Kuzemko, J. A. Incidence, prognosis, and mortality. In J. A. Kuzemko (Ed.), *Asthma in children* (2d ed.). Baltimore, Md: University Park Press, 1980.

Lincoln, R., & Landman, L. Fertility rise in 1977 not sustained, teenage rates continue decline. *Family Planning Perspectives,* 1979, *11*(2), 126–27.

Lorenzi, M. Marital outcomes of adolescent pregnancy. *Adolescence,* 1977, *12*, 13–22.

MacFarlane, K. Sexual abuse of children. In J. Chapman & M. Gates (Eds.), *The victimization of women.* Beverly Hills, Calif.: Sage Publications, 1978.

McLean, J. A., & Ching, A. Y. T. Follow-up study of relationships between family situations and bronchial asthma in children. *Journal of the American Academy of Child Psychiatry,* 1975, *12*(1), 142–61.

Menguy, R. *Surgery of peptic ulcer.* Philadelphia: W. B. Saunders Co., 1976.

Morrison-Smith, J. Studies of the prevalence of asthma in childhood (abstract). In M. E. Ganderton and A. W. Frankland (Eds.), *9th European Congress of Allergology and Clinical Immunology.* London: Pitman Medical, 1974.

Nagi, S. Z. *Child maltreatment in the United States: A challenge to social institutions.* New York, Columbia University Press, 1977.

National Commission on Diabetes. Diabetes forecast. *Diabetes* (Supplement No. 1, Special Education), 1975, *28*, 1–60.

Neel, J. V. Sickle cell disease: A worldwide problem. In H. Abramson, J. F. Bertles & D. L. Wethers (Eds.), *Sickle cell disease: Diagnosis, management, education, and research.* St. Louis: C. V. Mosby Co., 1973.

Oliver, J. E., & Taylor, A. Five generations of ill-treated children in one family pedigree. *British Journal of Psychiatry,* 1971, *119*, 473–80.

Ooms, T. *Teenage pregnancy in a family context: Indications for policy.* Philadelphia: Temple University Press, 1981.

Pepys, J., Chan, M., & Hargreave, F. F. Mites and house dust allergy. *Lancet,* 1968, *1*, 1270–72.

Phibbs, B. *The human heart: A guide to heart disease.* St. Louis: C. V. Mosby Co., 1979.

Pillitteri, A. *Nursing care of the growing family: A child health text.* Boston: Little, Brown & Co., 1977.

Pinkerton, P. The enigma of asthma. *Psychosomatic medicine,* 1973, *35*, 401–63.

Pinkerton, P., & Weaver, C. M. Childhood asthma. In C. H. Hill (Ed.), *Modern trends in psychosomatic medicine.* London: Butterworths, 1970.

Pless, I. B. Epidemiology of chronic disease. In M. Green & R. J. Haggerty (Eds.), *Ambulatory pediatrics.* Philadelphia: W. B. Saunders Co., 1968.

Podolsky, S., Krall, L. P., & Bradley, R. F. Treatment of diabetes with oral hypoglycemic agents. In S. Podolsky (Ed.), *Clinical diabetes: Modern management.* New York: Appleton-Century-Crofts, 1980.

Reiss, I. L. *Family systems in America.* Hinsdale, Ill.: Dryden Press, 1976.

Resh, M. G. Asthma of unknown origin as a psychological group. *Journal of Consulting and Clinical Psychology,* 1970, *35*, 429.

Rhyne, M. B. Incidence of atopic disease. *Medical Clinics of North America,* 1974, *58*(1), 3–24.

Schmitt, B. D. Introduction: Basic information and assumptions regarding child abuse and neglect. In B. D. Schmitt (Ed.), *The child protection team handbook.* New York: Garland STPM Press, 1978.

Smith, J. M., Disney, M. E., Williams, J. D. & Goels, Z. A. Clinical Significance of skin reactions to mites in children with asthma. *British Medical Journal,* 1969, *2*, 723–26.

Smith, L. Personal communication. December 28, 1982.

Spiro, H. M. *Clinical gastroenterology.* London: Macmillan Co., Collier-Macmillan, 1970.

Steinhauer, P. D., Mushin, D. N., & Rae-Grant, Q. Psychological aspects of chronic illness. *Pediatric Clinics of North America,* 1974, *21*, 825–40.

Storr, A. Introduction: Asthma as a personal experience. In D. J. Lane & A. Storr (Ed.), *Asthma: The facts.* New York: Oxford University Press, 1979.

Straker, N., & Tamerin, J. Aggression and childhood asthma: A study in a natural setting. *Journal of Psychosomatic Research*, 1974, *18*, 131–35.

Sultz, H. A., Schlesinger, E. R., Mosher, W. E., & Feldman, J. G. *Long-term childhood illness*. Pittsburgh: University of Pittsburgh Press, 1972.

U.S. Department of Health and Human Services. Monthly Vital Statistics Report, 1982, *31*(8), 1–40.

U.S. Department of Health, Education, and Welfare. *Cystic fibrosis: State of the art and directions for future research efforts*. Bethesda, Md.: National Institute of Health, 1978. (DHEW No. [NIH] 78-1642).

Walker, C. H. M. Congenital heart malformations. In B. Phibbs (Ed.), *The human heart*. St. Louis: C. V. Mosby Co., 1979.

Warwick, W. J., & Monson, S. Life table studies of mortality. *Modern Problems in Pediatrics*, 1967, *10*, 353–67.

Weiss, J. H. Letter to the editor. *Psychosomatic Medicine*, 1973, *35*, 461–63.

Williams, H. E., & McNicol, K. N. The spectrum of asthma in children. *The Pediatric Clinics of North America*, 1975, *22*, 43–52.

Young, J. L., Heise, H. W., Silverberg, E., & Myers, M. H. *Cancer incidence, survival, and mortality for children under 15 years of age*. American Cancer Society, Inc., 1978.

Zelnick, M., & Kantner, J. F. Contraceptive patterns and premarital pregnancy among women aged 15–19 in 1976. *Family Planning Perspectives*, 1978, *10*, 135–42.

Zelnick, M., Kim, Y. J., & Kantner, J. F. Probabilities of intercourse and conception among U.S. teenage women, 1971–1976. *Family Planning Perspectives*, 1979, *13*(3), 177–83.

CHAPTER TWELVE

Alvino, J., McDonnel, R. C., & Richert, S. National survey of identification practices in gifted and talented education. *Exceptional Children*, 1981, *48*, 124–32.

Barron, F. The disposition toward originality. *Journal of Abnormal and Social Psychology*, 1955, *51*, 478–85.

Binet, A., & Simon, T. Methodes nouvelles pour le diagnostique du niveau intellectuel des anomaux. *L'Anée Psychologique*, 1905, *11*, 196–98.

Binet, A., & Simon, T. Le development de intelligence chez les enfants. *L'Anée Psychologique*, 1908, *14*, 1–94.

Boehm, L. The development of conscience: A comparison of American children of different mental and socioeconomic levels. *Child Development*, 1962, *33*, 575–90.

Bonsall, M., & Stefflre, B. The temperament of gifted children. *California Journal of Educational Research*, 1955, *6*, 162–65.

Borland, J. Teacher identification of the gifted. *Journal for the Education of the Gifted*, 1978, *2*, 22–31.

Burt, C. The gifted child. In G. Z. F. Bereday & J. A. Lauwerys (Eds.), *The gifted child: The yearbook of education*. New York: Harcourt Brace & Jovanovich, 1962.

Callahan, C. M. The gifted and talented woman. In A. H. Passow (Ed.), *The 78th yearbook of the National Society for the Study of Education: The gifted and the talented, their education and development*. Chicago: University of Chicago Press, 1979.

Callahan, C. M. Superior abilities. In J. M. Kauffman & D. P. Hallahan (Eds.), *Handbook of special education*. Englewood Cliffs, N.J.: Prentice-Hall, 1981.

Cattell, R. B. *Abilities: Their structure, growth, and action*. Boston: Houghton Mifflin Co., 1971.

Clark, B. *Growing up gifted*. Columbus, Ohio: Charles E. Merrill Publishing Co., 1979.

Conant, J. B. *The American high school today*. New York: McGraw-Hill Book Co., 1959.

Cox, C. M. *The early traits of three hundred geniuses: Genetic studies of genius* (Vol. 2). Stanford, Calif.: Stanford University Press, 1926.

Crackenberg, S. B. Creativity tests: A boon or boondoggle for education. *Review of Educational Research*, 1972, *42*, 27–45.

Dehann, R., & Havighurst, R. J. *Educating gifted children*. Chicago: University of Chicago Press, 1957.

Eisenstadt, J. M. Parental loss and genius. *American Psychologist*, 1978, *33*, 211–23.

Eysenck, H. J. *The structure and measurement of intelligence*. New York: Springer-Verlag, 1979.

Feldman, D. The mysterious case of extreme gift-edness. In A. H. Passow (Ed.), *The 78th yearbook of the National Society for the Study of Education: The gifted and talented, their education and development.* Chicago: University of Chicago Press, 1979.

Ford, B. G., & Ford, R. D. Identifying creative potential in handicapped children. *Exceptional Children*, 1981, 48, 115-22.

Freeman, J. *Gifted children.* Baltimore: University Park Press, 1979.

Gallagher, J. J. *Teaching the gifted child* (2d ed.). Boston: Allyn & Bacon, 1975.

Gallagher, J. J. Issues in education for the gifted. In A. H. Passow (Ed.), *The 78th yearbook of the National Society for the Study of Education: The gifted and talented, their education and development.* Chicago: University of Chicago Press, 1979.

Gallagher, J. J., & Crowder, T. The adjustment of gifted children in the regular classroom. *Exceptional Children*, 1957, 23, 306–7, 317–19.

Gazzaniga, M. S., & LeDoux, J. E. *The integrated mind.* New York: Plenum Press, 1978.

Getzels, J. W., & Jackson, P. W. The meaning of giftedness: An examination of an expanding concept. *Phi Delta Kappan*, 1958, 40, 75–77.

Getzels, J. W. & Jackson, P. W. *Creativity and intelligence: Explorations with gifted students.* New York: John Wiley & Sons, 1962.

Gilchrist, M. *The psychology of creativity.* Melbourne: Melbourne University Press, 1972.

Goertzel, H. G., & Goertzel, M. C. *Cradles of eminence.* Boston: Little, Brown, 1962.

Gowan, J. C. *Development of the creative individual.* San Diego: Robert P. Knapp, 1972.

Gowan, J. C. Background and history of the gifted-child movement. In J. C. Stanley, W. C. George & C. H. Solano (Eds.), *The gifted and the creative: A fifty-year perspective.* Baltimore: Johns Hopkins University Press, 1977.

Gowan, J. C. Khatena, J., & Torrance, E. P. *Educating the ablest.* Itasca, Ill.: F. E. Peacock Publishers, 1979.

Guilford, J. P. Creativity. *American Psychologist*, 1950, 5, 444–54.

Guilford, J. P. Three faces of intellect. *American Psychologist*, 1959, 14, 469–79.

Guilford, J. P. *The nature of human intelligence.* New York: McGraw-Hill Book Co., 1967.

Guilford, J. P. *Way beyond the IQ.* Buffalo: Creative Education Foundation, 1977.

Havighurst, R. J. Conditions productive of superior children. *Teachers College Record*, 1961, 62, 524–31.

Hitchfield, E. M. *In search of promise.* London: Longman, 1973.

Holland, J. L. & Astin, A. W. The prediction of the academic, artistic, scientific, and social achievement of undergraduates of superior scholastic aptitude. *Journal of Educational Psychology*, 1962, 53, 132–33.

Hollingsworth, L. M. *Children with above 180 I.Q.* Yonkers-on-Hudson, N.Y.: World Book, 1942.

Hudson, L. *Contrary imaginations.* New York: Schocken Books, 1966.

Jacobs, J. C. Effectiveness of teacher and parent identification of gifted children as a function of school level. *Psychology in the Schools*, 1971, 8, 140–42.

Kahl, J.A. Educational and occupational aspirations of "common man" boys. *Harvard Educational Review*, 1953, 23(3), 186–203.

Karnes, F. A., & Collins, E. C. State definitions of the gifted and talented. *Journal for the Education of the Gifted*, 1978, 3, 157–72.

Ketcham, B., & Snyder, R. T. Self-attitudes of the intellectually and socially advantaged students. *Psychological Reports*, 1977, 40, 111–16.

Khatena, J. Myth: Creativity is too difficult to measure. *Gifted Child Quarterly*, 1982, 26(1), 21–23.

King, E. J. (Ed.). *Post-compulsory education: A new analysis in Western Europe.* Beverly Hills, Calif.: Sage Publications, 1974.

Laycock, F. *Gifted children.* Glenview, Ill.: Scott, Foresman & Co., 1979.

Laycock, F., & Caylor, J. S. Physiques of gifted children and their siblings. *Child Development*, 1964, 35, 63–74.

MacKinnon, D. W. The nature and nurture of creative talent. *American Psychologist*, 1962, 17(7), 484–495.

MacKinnon, D. W. Personality and the realization of creative potential. *American Psychologist*, 1965, 20, 273–281.

Marland, S., Jr. *Education of the gifted and talented.* Report to the Congress of the United States by the U.S. Commissioner of Education. Washington, D.C.: U.S. Government Printing Office, 1972.

Martinson, R. A. *Educational programs for gifted pupils.* Sacramento: California State Department of Education, 1961.

Martinson, R. A. Research on the gifted and talented: Its implications for education. In S. Marland, Jr. (Ed.), *Education of the gifted and talented.* Report to the Congress of the United States by the U.S. Commissioner of Education. Washington, D.C.: U.S. Government Printing Office, 1972.

Martinson, R. A. Children with superior cognitive abilities. In L. M. Dunn (Ed.), *Exceptional children in the schools.* New York: Holt, Rinehart & Winston, 1973.

McAskie, M., & Clarke, A. M. Parent-offspring resemblances in intelligence: Theories and evidence. *British Journal of Psychology,* 1976, *67,* 243–73.

McCurdy, H. G. The childhood pattern of genius. *Horizon, 1960, 2,* 33–38.

McGinn, P. V. Verbally gifted youth: Section and description. In D. P. Keating (Ed.), *Intellectual talent: Research and development.* Baltimore: Johns Hopkins University Press, 1976.

Mercer, J. R. *System of multicultural pluralistic assessment, technical manual.* New York: The Psychological Corporation, 1979.

Milgram, R. M., & Milgram, N. A. Personality characteristics of gifted Israeli children. *Journal of Genetic Psychology,* 1976, *129,* 185–94.

Munday, L. A., & Davis, J. C. *Varieties of accomplishment after college: Perspectives on the meaning of academic talent* (Research Report No. 62). Iowa City, Iowa: American College Testing Program, 1974.

Nason, L. J. *Academic achievement of gifted high school students: Patterns of circumstances related to educational achievement of high school pupils of superior ability.* Los Angeles: University of Southern California Press, 1958.

Nicholls, J. C. Creativity in the person who will never produce anything original and useful: The concept of creativity as a normally distributed trait. *American Psychologist,* 1972, *27,* 717–27.

Osborn, A. F. *Applied imagination: Principles and procedures of creative problem solving* (3rd ed.). New York: Charles Scribner's Sons, 1963.

Parkyn, G. W. *Children of high intelligence: A New Zealand study.* Wellington, N.Z.: Council for Educational Research, 1948.

Parnes, S. J., & Harding, H. R. *A sourcebook for creative thinking.* New York: Charles Scribner's Sons, 1962.

Pegnato, C. W., & Birch, J. W. Locating gifted children in junior high schools: A comparison of methods. *Exceptional Children,* 1959, *25,* 300–304.

Piaget, J. *Psychology of intelligence.* London: Routledge & Kegan Paul, 1950.

Piaget, J. *Origin of intelligence.* New York: International Universities Press, 1952.

Pohl, R. *Teacher nomination of intellectually gifted children in primary grades.* Unpublished doctoral dissertation, University of Illinois, 1970.

Pressy, S. Concerning the nature and nurture of genius. *Science,* 1955, *31,* 123–29.

Pressy, S. The nature and nurture of genius. In J. French (Ed.), *Educating the gifted child.* New York: Holt, Rinehart & Winston, 1964.

Renzulli, J. S. What makes giftedness? Reexamining a definition. *Phi Delta Kappan,* 1978, *60*(3), 180–84, 261.

Renzulli, J. S., Smith, L. H., White, A. J., Callahan, C. M., & Hartman, R. K. *Scales for rating the behavioral characteristics of superior students.* Wethersfield, Conn.: Creative Learning Press, 1976.

Rim, S., Davis, G. A., & Bien, Y. Identifying creativity: A characteristics approach. *Gifted Child Quarterly,* 1982, *26*(4), 165–71.

Roe, A. *The making of a scientist.* New York: Dodd, Mead & Co., 1952.

Rubenzer, R. The role of the right hemisphere in learning and creativity implications for enhancing problem solving ability. *Gifted Child Quarterly,* 1979, *13*(1), 78–100.

Skeels, H. M. Adult status of children with contrasting early life experiences: A follow-up study. *Monographs of the Society for Re-*

search in *Child Development*, 1966, 31(105), 1–11, 13, 54–59.

Skodak, M., & Skeels, H. M. A final follow-up study of one hundred adopted children. *Journal of Genetic Psychology*, 1949, 75, 85–125.

Spearman, C. S. *The nature of intelligence and the principles of cognition.* New York: Macmillan Co., 1927. (a)

Spearman, C. S. *The abilities of man.* London: Macmillan Co., 1927. (b)

Stanley, J. C. Background and history of the gifted child movement. In J. C. Stanley, W. C. George & C. H. Solano (Eds.), *The gifted and the creative: A fifty-year perspective.* Baltimore: Johns Hopkins University Press, 1977.

Taylor, C. W. (Ed.). *Creativity: Progress and potential.* New York: McGraw-Hill Book Co., 1964.

Terman, L. M. *Genetic studies of genius, Vol. 1: Mental and physical traits of a thousand gifted children.* Stanford, Calif.: Stanford University Press, 1925.

Terman, L. M. The discovery and encouragement of exceptional talent. *American Psychologist*, 1954, 9, 221–30.

Terman, L. M., & Oden, M. *Genetic studies of genius, Vol. 5: The gifted group at mid-life.* Stanford, Calif.: Stanford University Press, 1959.

Thomason, J. Education of the gifted. A challenge and a promise. *Exceptional Children*, 1981, 48, 101-3.

Thorndike, E. L. *The measurement of intelligence.* New York: Columbia University, Teachers College Bureau of Publications, 1927.

Thorndike, E. L. *Human nature and the social order.* New York: Macmillan Co., 1940.

Thurstone, L. L. *Primary mental abilities.* Chicago: University of Chicago Press, 1938.

Torrance, E. P. Problems of highly creative children. *Gifted Child Quarterly*, 1961, 5, 31–34.

Torrance, E. P. *Guiding creative talent.* Englewood Cliffs, N.J.: Prentice-Hall, 1962.

Torrance, E. P. *Gifted children in the classroom.* New York: Macmillan Co., 1965.

Torrance, E. P. Finding hidden talent among disadvantaged children. *Gifted and Talented Quarterly*, 1968, 12,131–37.

Vernon, P. E., Adamson, G., & Vernon, D. F. *The psychology and education of gifted children.* New York: Methuen, 1977.

Walberg, H. J., Tsai, S., Weinstein, T., Gabriel, C. L., Rasher, S. P., Rosecrans, T., Rovai, E., Ide, J., Trujillo, M., & Vukosavich, P. Childhood traits and environmental conditions of highly eminent adults. *Gifted Child Quarterly*, 1981, 25(3), 103–7.

Wallach, M. A. Tests tell us little about talent. *American Scientist*, 1976, 64, 57.

Watson, J. B. *Behaviorism.* New York: W.W. Norton & Co., 1924.

Wechsler, D. Cognitive, conative, and non-intellective intelligence. *American Psychologist*, 1950, 5(3), 78–83.

Wechsler, D. *The measurement and appraisal of adult intelligence.* Baltimore: Williams & Wilkins, 1958.

Whitmore, J. R. *Giftedness, conflict, and underachievement.* Boston: Allyn & Bacon, 1980.

Whitmore, J. R. Gifted children with handicapping conditions: A new frontier. *Exceptional Children*, 1981, 48, 106–14.

Witty, P. A. A genetic study of fifty gifted children. In G. M. Whipple (Ed.), *39th yearbook of the National Society for the Study of Education*, Part II. Chicago: University of Chicago Press, 1940.

Zettel, J. J. *Gifted and talented education from a nationwide perspective.* Reston, Va.: Council for Exceptional Children, 1980.

CHAPTER THIRTEEN

Baer, M. F., & Roeber, E. C. *Occupational information.* Chicago: Science Research Associates, 1964.

Barbe, W. Evaluation of special classes for gifted. *Exceptional Children*, 1955, 22, 60–62.

Belle Vista Elementary School. *Igniting creative potential.* Salt Lake City: Bella Vista Elementary School, 1971.

Blacher-Dixon, J. *Preschool for the gifted-handicapped: Is it untimely, or about time?* Paper presented at the 55th Annual International

Convention of the Council for Exceptional Children, Atlanta, April 11–15, 1977.

Blacher-Dixon, J., & Turnbull, A. P. A preschool program for gifted-handicapped children. *Journal for the Education of the Gifted,* 1979, *1(2),* 15–23.

Bloom, B. *Taxonomy of educational objectives.* New York: David McKay Co., 1969.

Bloom, B. S. (Ed.). *Taxonomy of educational objectives. Handbook I: Cognitive domain.* New York: David McKay Co., 1956.

Borg, W. *An evaluation of ability grouping* (U.S. Department of Health, Education, and Welfare, Office of Education, Cooperative Research Project No. 577). Logan, Utah: Utah State University, 1964.

Braga, J. L. Analysis and evaluation of early admission to school for mentally advanced children. *Journal of Educational Research,* 1969, *63,* 103–6.

Braga, J. L. Early admission: opinion vs. evidence. *Elementary School Journal,* 1971, *72,* 35–46.

Callahan, C. M. Superior abilities. In J. M. Kauffman & D. P. Hallahan (Eds.), *Handbook of special education.* Englewood Cliffs, N.J.: Prentice-Hall, 1981.

Callaway, W. R. Modes of biological adaptation and their role in intellectual development. *Galton Institute Monograph Series,* 1970, *1(1),* 1–34.

Clark, B. *Growing up gifted.* Columbus, Ohio: Charles E. Merrill Publishing Co., 1979.

Copley, F. O. *The American high school student and the talented student.* Ann Arbor: University of Michigan Press, 1961.

Cox, C. M. The early mental traits of three thousand geniuses. *Genetic studies of genius* (Vol. 2). Stanford, Calif.: Stanford University Press, 1926.

Cross, M. A. *An evaluation of the program for the academically talented in Kansas City, Missouri, public schools.* Unpublished doctoral dissertation, University of Missouri, 1975.

Davis, G. A., & Rimm, S. Identification and counseling of the creatively gifted. In N. Colangelo & R. T. Zaffrann (Eds.), *New voices in counseling the gifted.* Dubuque, Iowa: Kendall/Hunt Publishing Co., 1979.

Dubos, R. Biological individuality. *Columbia Forum,* 1969, *12(1),* 5–9.

Fantz, R. The origin of form perception. *Scientific American,* 1961, *204,* 66–72.

Fantz, R. Visual perception from birth as shown by pattern selectivity. *New Issues in Infant Development, New York Academy of Sciences Annals,* 1965, *118(21),* 793–814.

Feldhusen, J. F., & Kolloff, M. B. A three stage model for gifted education. *Gifted/Creative/Talented,* 1978, *4,* 3–5, 53–57.

Feldhusen, J. F., & Treffinger, D. J. *Teaching creative thinking and problem solving.* Dubuque, Iowa: Kendall/Hunt Publishing Co., 1977.

Findley, W., & Bryan, M. *Ability grouping 1970: Status, import, and alternatives.* Athens, Ga.: Center for Educational Improvement, University of Georgia, 1971.

Fox, L. H. Programs for the gifted and talented: An overview. In A. H. Passow (Ed.), *The gifted and the talented: Their education and development.* The 78th yearbook of the National Society for the Study of Education. Chicago: University of Chicago Press, 1979.

Fredrickson, R. H. Career development and the gifted. In N. Colangelo & R. T. Zaffrann (Eds.), *New voices in counseling the gifted.* Dubuque, Iowa: Kendall/Hunt Publishing Co., 1979.

Gallagher, J. *Teaching the gifted child* (2d ed.). Boston: Allyn & Bacon, 1975.

Getzels, J. W., & Dillon, J. T. The nature of giftedness and the education of the gifted child. In R. M. W. Travers (Ed.), *Second handbook of research on teaching.* Chicago: Rand McNally & Co., 1973.

Goertzel, V., & Goertzel, M. *Cradles of eminence.* Boston: Little, Brown & Co., 1962.

Gold, M. J. Secondary level programs for the gifted and talented. In H. J. Morgan, C. G. Tennant & M. J. Gold (Eds.), *Elementary and secondary level programs for the gifted and talented.* New York: Teachers College Press, 1980.

Goldberg, M., & Passow, A. H. A study of underachieving gifted. *Educational Leadership,* 1959, *16,* 121–25.

Goldberg, M., Passow, A., Justman, J., & Hage, G. *The effects of ability grouping.* New York:

Bureau of Publications, Columbia University, 1965.

Gowan, J. C. Background and history of the gifted-child movement. In J. C. Stanley, W. C. George & C. H. Solano (Eds.), *The gifted and the creative, a fifty-year perspective.* Baltimore: Johns Hopkins University Press, 1977.

Gowan, J. C., & Demos, G. D. *The education and guidance of the ablest.* Springfield, Ill.: Charles C. Thomas, 1964.

Guilford, J. P. Structure of intellect. *Psychological Bulletin,* 1956, *53,* 267–93.

Hall, E. G., & Skinner, N. *Somewhere to turn: Strategies for parents of the gifted and talented.* New York: Teachers College Press, 1980.

Haynes, H., White, B., & Held, R. Visual accommodation in the human infant. *Science,* 1965, *148, 528*–30.

Herr, E. L., & Watanabe, A. Counseling the gifted about career development. In N. Colangelo & R. T. Zaffrann (Eds.), *New voices in counseling the gifted.* Dubuque, Iowa: Kendall/Hall Publishing Co., 1979.

Hollingsworth, L. S. *Children above 180 IQ Stanford-Binet: Origin and development.* Yonkers-on-the-Hudson, N.Y.: World Book Co., 1942.

Hoyt, K. B., & Hebeler, J. R. (Eds.). *Career education for gifted and talented students.* Salt Lake City: Olympus Publishing Co., 1974.

Kagan, J. *Change and continuity in infancy.* New York: John Wiley & Sons, 1971.

Kaplan, S. *Providing programs for the gifted and talented: A handbook.* Reston, Virginia: Council for Exceptional Children, 1975.

Karnes, M. B. Identifying and programming for young gifted/talented handicapped children. In A. Fink (Ed.), *International perspectives on future special education.* Reston, Va.: Council for Exceptional Children, 1978.

Karnes, M. B. Young handicapped children can be gifted and talented. *Journal for the Education of the Gifted,* 1979, *2*(3), 157–72.

Karnes, M. B., & Bertschi, J. D. Identifying and educating gifted/talented nonhandicapped and handicapped preschoolers. *Teaching Exceptional Children,* 1978, *10,* 114–19.

Keating, D. P. (Ed.). *Intellectual talent: Research and development.* Baltimore: John Hopkins University Press, 1976.

Khatena, J. *Educational psychology of the gifted.* New York: John Wiley & Sons, 1982.

Laycock, F. *Gifted children.* Glenview, Ill.: Scott, Foresman & Co., 1979.

Lenneberg, E. *Biological foundations of language.* New York: John Wiley & Sons, 1967.

Marland, S. P., Jr. *Education of the gifted and talented, Vol. 1, Report to the Congress of the U.S. by the U.S. Commissioner of Education.* Washington, D.C.: U.S. Government Printing Office, 1972.

Martinson, R. A. *Educational programs for gifted pupils.* Sacramento: California Department of Education, 1961.

McCurdy, H. The childhood pattern of genius. *Journal of Elisha Mitchell Scientific Society,* 1957, *73,* 448–62.

Meeker, M. N. Nondiscriminatory testing procedures to assess giftedness in black, Chicano, Navajo, and Anglo children. In A. Y. Baldwin, G. H. Gear & L. J. Lucito (Eds.), *Educational planning for the gifted.* Reston, Va.: Council for Exceptional Children, 1978.

Mercer, J. R., & Lewis, J. F. Using the system of multicultural pluralistic assessment (SOMPA) to identify gifted minority child. In A. Y. Baldwin, G. H. Gear & L. J. Lucito (Eds.), *Educational planning for the gifted.* Reston, Va.: Council for Exceptional Children, 1978.

Milne, B. G. Career education. In A. H. Passow (Ed.), *The gifted and the talented: Their education and development.* The 78th yearbook of the National Society for the Study of Education. Chicago: University of Chicago Press, 1979.

Mobile County Public Schools. *Talent activity packet* (2d ed.). Mobile, Ala.: Mobile County Public Schools, 1974.

Morgan, H. J., & Tennant, C. G. Elementary level programs for the gifted and talented. In H. J. Morgan, C. G. Tennant & M. G. Gold (Eds.), *Elementary and secondary level programs for the gifted and talented.* New York: Teachers College Press, 1980.

Newland, T. E. *The gifted in socio-educational perspective.* Englewood Cliffs, New Jersey: Prentice-Hall, 1976.

Pressey, S. L. Educational acceleration: Appraisal and basic problems. *Ohio State University Bureau of Educational Research Monographs,* 1949, No. 13.

Pressey, S. L. Concerning the nature and nurture of genius. *Scientific Monthly*, 1955, *81,*

Project Implode, Bella Vista Elementary School. *Igniting creative potential.* Salt Lake City, Utah: Bella Vista Elementary School, 1971.

Provence, S., & Lipton, R. *Infants in institutions: A comparison of their development with family-reared infants during the first year of life.* New York: International Universities Press, 1962.

Renzulli, J. S. *The enrichment triad model.* Mansfield Center, Conn.: Creative Learning Press, 1977.

Reynolds, M. (Ed.). *Early school admission for mentally advanced children.* Reston, Va.: Council for Exceptional Children, 1962.

Rimm, S., Davis, G. A., & Bien, Y. Identifying creativity: A characteristics approach. *Gifted Child Quarterly,* 1982, *26*(4), 165–71.

Robinson, H. B., Roedell, W. C., & Jackson, N. E. Early identification and intervention. In A. H. Passow (Ed.), *The gifted and the tal-Their education and development.* The 78th yearbook for the study of education. Chicago: University of Chicago Press, 1979.

Roedell, W. C., Jackson, N. E., & Robinson, H. B. *Gifted young children.* New York: Teachers College Press, 1980.

Sanborn, M. P. Career development: Problems of gifted and talented students. In N. Colangelo & R. T. Zaffrann (Eds.), *New voices in counseling the gifted.* Dubuque, Iowa: Kendall/Hunt Publishing Co., 1979.

Schlichter, C. L. The multiple talent approach to the world of work. *Roeper Review,* 1979, *2*(2), 17–20.

Schlichter, C. L. The multiple talent approach in mainstream and gifted programs. *Exceptional Children,* 1981, *48*(2), 144–50.

Simpson, R., & Martinson, R. *Educational programs for gifted pupils.* Sacramento: California State Department of Education, 1961.

Solano, D. H., & George, W. L. College courses for the gifted. *Gifted Child Quarterly,* 1976, *20*(3), 274–85.

Stanley, J. C. Rationale of the study of mathematically precocious youth (SMPY) during its first five years of promoting educational acceleration. In J. C. Stanley, W. C. George & C. H. Solano (Eds.), *The gifted and the creative: A fifty-year perspective.* Baltimore: Johns Hopkins University Press, 1977.

Stanley, J., Keating, D., & Fox, L. (Eds.). *Mathematical talent: Discovery, description, and development.* Baltimore: Johns Hopkins University Press, 1974.

Sutherland, A., & Goldschmid, M. L. Negative teacher expectation and change in children with superior intellectual potential. *Child Development,* 1974, *45,* 852–56.

Taylor, C. W. Questioning and creating: A model for curriculum reform. *Journal of Creative Behavior,* 1967, *1,* 22–33.

Taylor, C. W., & Ellison, R. L. *Manual for alpha biographical inventory.* Salt Lake City, Utah: Institute for Behavioral Research in Creativity, 1966.

Terman, L. M., & Oden, M. *Genetic studies of genius, Vol. 5, The gifted group at midlife.* Stanford, Calif.: Stanford University Press, 1959.

Thomason, J. Education of the gifted: A challenge and a promise. *Exceptional Children,* 1981, *48*(2), 101–3.

Torrance, E. P. Are the Torrance tests of creative thinking biased against or in favor of disadvantaged groups? *Gifted Child Quarterly,* 1971, *15*(2), 75–80.

Torrance, E. P. Creatively gifted and disadvantaged gifted. In J. C. Stanley, W. C. George & C. H. Solano (Eds.), *The gifted and the creative: A fifty-year perspective.* Baltimore: Johns Hopkins University Press, 1977.

Ward, V. S. Basic concepts. In W. B. Barbe & J. S. Renzulli (Eds.), *Psychology and education of the gifted* (2d ed.). New York: Irvington Publishers, 1975.

Williams, F. *Classroom ideas for encouraging thinking and feeling.* Buffalo, N.Y.: Dissemination of Knowledge Publishers, 1970.

Witty, P. A., & Grotberg, E. H. *Helping the gifted child.* Chicago: Science Research Associates, 1970.

Zaffrann, R. T., & Colangelo, N. Counseling with gifted and talented students. *Gifted Child Quarterly,* 1977, *21,* 305–20.

CHAPTER FOURTEEN

Abrams, J. C., & Kaslow, F. Family systems and the learning disabled child: Intervention and treatment. *Journal of Learning Disabilities,* 1977, *10,* 86–90.

Baker, B. E. The effectiveness of parent modalities in the treatment of children with learning disabilities. *Dissertation Abstracts International*, 1970, *31*, 1929A–2541A (p. 2166A).

Barsh, R. H. *The parent of the handicapped child: The study of child rearing practices.* Springfield, Ill.: Charles C. Thomas, 1968.

Berns, J. H. Grandparents of handicapped children. *Social Work*, 1980, *15*(3), 238–39.

Bice, H. *Group counseling with mothers of cerebral palsied.* Chicago: National Society for Crippled Children and Adults, 1952.

Balkwell, C., & Halverson, C. F. The hyperactive child as a source of stress in the family: Consequences and suggestions for intervention. *Family Relations*, 1980, *29*(4), 550–57.

Buscaglia, L. *The disabled and their parents: A counseling challenge.* Thorofare, N.J.: Charles B. Slack, 1975.

Cleveland, M. Family adaptation to traumatic spinal cord injury: Response to crisis. *Family Therapy*, 1980, *29*(4), 558–65.

Cruickshank, W. M. *Cerebral palsy: A developmental disability* (3d ed.) Syracuse, N.Y.: Syracuse University Press, 1976.

D'Arcy, E. Congenital defects: Mothers' reactions to first information. *British Medical Journal*, 1968, *3*, 796–98.

Davis, R. D. Family processes in mental retardation. *American Journal of Psychiatry*, 1967, *124*(3), 340–350.

Davis, M. & MacKay, D. N. Mentally subnormal children and their families. *The Lancet*, 1973, *2*, (7832), 974–75.

Dougan, T., Isbell, L., & Vyas, P. *We have been there: A guide book for parents of people with mental retardation.* Nashville, Tenn.: Abingdon Press, 1979.

Durham, G. H. What if you are the doctor? In T. Dougan, L. Isbell & P. Vyas (Eds.), *We have been there: A guide book for parents of people with mental retardation.* Nashville, Tenn.: Abingdon Press, 1979.

Farber, B. Effects of a severely retarded child on family integration. *Monographs of the Society for Research in Child Development*, 1959, *24*(2).

Farber, B. Effects of a severely retarded child on the family. In E. P. Trapp & P. Himelskin (Eds.), *Readings on the exceptional child.* New York: Appleton-Century-Crofts, 1962.

Featherstone, H. *A difference in the family: Living with a disabled child.* New York: Penguin Books, 1980.

Fotheringham, J. B., Skelton, M., & Hoddinott, B. A. *The retarded child and his family: The effects of home and institution.* Toronto, Canada: Ontario Institute for Studies in Education, 1971. (Monograph Series No. 11)

Fowle, C. M. The effect of the severely mentally retarded child on his family. *American Journal of Mental Deficiency*, 1968, *73*, 468–73.

Fox, M. A. The handicapped family. *Lancet*, 1975, *2*, 400–401.

Freudenberger, J. J. Burn-out: Occupational hazard of the child care worker. *Child Care Quarterly*, 1977, *6*, 90–98.

Friedman, R. Using the family and school in the treatment of learning disabilities. *Journal of Learning Disabilities*, 1978, *11*, 378–82.

Gorham, K. A. A lost generation of parents. *Exceptional Children*, 1975, *41*, 521–25.

Gorham, K. A, DesJardins, C., Page, R., Pettis, E., & Scheiber, B. Effect on parents. In N. Hobbs (Ed.), *Issues in the classification of children.* San Francisco: Jossay-Bass, 1975.

Grossman, F. K. *Brothers and sisters of retarded children.* Syracuse, N.Y.: Syracuse University Press, 1972. (a)

Grossman, F. K. Brothers and sisters of retarded children. *Psychology Today*, 1972, *5*, 82–84, 102–4. (b)

Haynes, U. *A developmental approach to case finding.* Rockville, Md.: U.S. Department of Health, Education, and Welfare, 1977.

Hetrick, E. W. Training of parents of learning disabled children in facilitative communication skills. *Journal of Learning Disabilities*, 1979, *12*, 275–77.

Howard, J. The influence of children's developmental dysfunctions on marital quality and family interaction. In R. M. Lerner & G. B. Spanier (Eds.), *Child influences on marital and family interaction: A life-span perspective.* New York: Academic Press, 1978.

Jogis, J. L. To be spoken sadly. In L. Buscaglia (Ed.), *The disabled and their parents: A counseling challenge.* Thorofare, N.J.: Charles B. Slack, 1975.

Kaufman, S. Z. A mentally retarded daughter educates her mother. *The Exceptional Parent*, 1980, *10*(6), 17–22.

Klein, S. D. Brother to sister, Sister to brother. *Exceptional Parent*, 1972, *2*, 10–15, 26–27.

Koch, R. C., & Dobson, J. C. *The mentally retarded child and his family*. New York: Brunner/Mazel, 1971.

Kraft, S. P., & Snell, M. A. Parent-teacher conflict: Coping with parental stress. *The Pointer*, 1980, *24*,(2), 29–37.

Lamb, C. B. Fostering acceptance of a disabled sibling through books. *The Exceptional Parent*, 1980, *10*(1), 12–13.

Lavelle, N., & Keogh, B. K. Expectations and attributions of parents of handicapped children. In J. J. Gallagher (Ed.), *New directions for exceptional children, parents, and families of handicapped children*. San Francisco: Jossey-Bass, 1980.

Leigh, J. What we know about counseling the disabled and their parents: A review of the literature. In L. Buscaglia (Ed.), *The disabled and their parents: A counseling challenge*. Thorofare, N.J.: Charles B. Slack, 1975.

Levine, S. Sex-role identification and parental perceptions of social competence. *American Journal of Mental Deficiency*, 1966, *70*, 907–12.

Love, H. *The mentally retarded child and his family*, Springfield, Ill.: Charles C. Thomas, 1973.

Maslach, C. Job Burnout: How people cope. *Public Welfare*, 1978, *36*, 56–58.

McAndrew, I. Children with a handicap and their families. *Child: Care, Health, and Development*, 1976, *2*(4), 213–38.

Miller, E. A. Cerebral palsied children and their parents. *Exceptional Children*, 1958, *24*, 298–302.

Murphy, A. T. The families of handicapped children: Context for disability. *Volta Review*, 1979, *81*, 265–79.

Neeley, B. Join a parent group! In T. Dougan, L. Isbell, & P. Vyas (Eds.), *We have been there: A guide book for parents of people with mental retardation*. Nashville, Tenn.: Abingdon Press, 1979.

Oglesby, A., & Sterling, H. *Proceedings: Bi-regional institute on earlier recognition of handicapping conditions in childhood*. Berkeley, Calif.: School of Public Health, 1970.

Pagel, S., & Price J. Strategies to alleviate teacher stress. *Pointer*, 1980, *24*(2), 45–53.

Parmelee, A. The doctor and the handicapped child. *Children*, September–October, 1962, pp. 190–93.

Peck, J. R., & Stephens, W. B. A study of the relationship between the attitudes and behaviors of parents and that of their mentally defective child. *American Journal of Mental Deficiency*, 1960, *64*, 839–43.

Pieper, E. Grandparents can help. *The Exceptional Parent*, 1976, *6*(2), 7–10.

Ross, A. O. *The exceptional child in the family*. New York: Grune & Stratton, 1964.

Scagliotta, E. G. Contributions of the learning disabled child to family life. In D. Kronick (Ed.), *Learning disabilities: Its implications to a responsible society*. San Rafael, Calif.: Academy Therapy Publications, 1974.

Seligman, M. *Strategies for helping parents of handicapped children*. New York: The Free Press, 1979.

Seligman, M., & Seligman, D. A. The professional's dilemma: Learning to work with parents. *The Exceptional Parent*, 1980, *10*(5), 511–13.

Shelton, M. Areas of parental concern about retarded children. *Mental Retardation*, 1972, *2*, 38–41.

Shontz, F. Reactions to crisis. *Volta Review*, 1965, *67*, 364–70.

Smith, J., & Cline, D. Quality Programs, *The Pointer*, 1980, *24*(2), 80–87.

Sullivan, R. Siblings of autistic children. *Journal of Autism and Developmental Disorders*, 1979, *9*(3), 287–98.

Tew, B. F., Lawrence, M., Payne, H., & Townsley, K. Marital stability following the birth of a child with spina bifida. *British Journal of Psychiatry*, 1977, *131*, 77–82.

Tjossem, T. D. *Intervention strategies for high risk infants and young children*. Baltimore: University Park Press, 1976.

Turnbull, A. P., & Turnbull, H. R., III. *Parents Speak Out*. Columbus, Ohio: Charles E. Merrill Publishing Co., 1978.

U.S. Department of Education. *Summary of existing legislation relating to the handicapped*. Washington, D.C.: U.S. Department of Education, Office of Special Education and Rehabilitative Services, Office for Handicapped Individuals, Publication No. E–80–22014, 1980.

Volpe, J. J., & Koenigsberger, R. Neurologic disorders. In G. B. Avery (Ed.), *Neonatology, pathophysiology, and management of the newborn* (2d ed.). Philadelphia: J. B. Lippincott Co., 1981.

Webster, E. J. *Counseling with parents of handicapped children: Guidelines for improving communications.* New York: Grune & Stratton, 1977.

Wunderlich, C. *The mongoloid child: Recognition and care.* Tucson: University of Arizona Press, 1977.

CHAPTER FIFTEEN

Abramson, L. Y., Seligman, M. E. P., & Teasdale, J. D. Learned helplessness in humans: Critique and reformation. *Journal of Abnormal Psychology*, 1978, 87, 49–74.

Achenback, T. M. *Research in developmental psychology: Concepts, strategies, methods.* New York: The Free Press, 1978.

Allen, R. C. *The retarded citizen: Victim of mental and legal deficiency.* Unpublished paper. Washington, D.C.: George Washington University, Institute of Law, Psychiatry, and Criminology. Portions of this paper were published in *Legal rights of the disadvantaged.* Washington, D.C.: U.S. Department of Health, Education, and Welfare, 1969.

Anderson, C. M. The brain-injured adult: An overlooked problem. In Weber, R. E. (Ed.), *Handbook on learning disabilities: The prognosis for the child, the adolescent, the adult.* Englewood Cliffs, N.J.: Prentice-Hall, 1974.

Baker, B. L., Seltzer, G. B., & Seltzer, M. M. *As close as possible: Community residences for retarded adults.* Boston: Little, Brown & Co., 1977.

Baltes, P. B. (Ed.). *Life-span development and behavior* (Vol. 1). New York: Academic Press, 1978.

Baltes, P. B., & Labouvie, G. V. Adult development of intellectual performance: Description, explanation, and modification. In C.

Eisdorfer & M. P. Lawton (Eds.), *The psychology of adult development and aging.* Washington, D.C.: American Psychological Association, 1973.

Baltes, P. B., & Brim, O. G., Jr. (Eds.). *Life-span development and behavior* (Vol. 2). New York: Academic Press, 1979.

Baltes, P. B., & Brim, O. G., Jr. (Eds.). *Life-span development and behavior* (Vol. 3). New York: Academic Press, 1980.

Baltes, P. B., & Schaie, K. W. On the plasticity of intelligence in adulthood and old age: Where Horn and Donaldson fail. *American Psychologist*, 1976, 31, 720–25.

Bank-Mikkelsen, N. E. A metropolitan area in Denmark: Copenhagen. In R. B. Kugel & W. Wolfensberger (Eds.), *Changing patterns in residential services for the mentally retarded.* Washington, D.C.: President's Committee on Mental Retardation, 1969.

Benton, A. L., & Pearl, D. (Eds.). *Dyslexia: An appraisal of current knowledge.* New York: Oxford University Press, 1978.

Bernstein, M. C. The right to an adequate income and employment. In M. Kindred, J. Cohen, D. Penrod & T. Shaffer (Eds.), *The mentally retarded citizen and the law.* New York: The Free Press, 1976.

Biklin, D., & Bogden, R. Handicapism in America. *WIN*, 1976.

Binstock, R. H., & Shanas, E. (Eds.). *Handbook of aging and the social sciences.* New York: Van Nostrand Reinhold Co., 1977.

Birren, J. E. Principles of research on aging. In J. E. Birren (Ed.), *Handbook of aging and the individual.* Chicago: University of Chicago Press, 1959.

Birren, J. E., Kinney, D. K., Schaie, K. W., & Woodruff, D. S. *Developmental psychology: A life-span approach.* Boston: Houghton Mifflin Co., 1981.

Birren, J. E., & Renner, V. J. Research on the Psychology of Aging: Principles and Experimentation. In J. E. Birren & K. W. Schaie (Eds.), *Handbook of the psychology of aging.* New York: Van Nostrand Reinhold Co., 1977.

Birren, J. E., & Schaie, K. W., (Eds.). *Handbook of the psychology of aging.* New York: Van Nostrand Reinhold Co., 1977.

Bluhm, H. P. The right to work: Employers, employability, and retardation. In C. J. Drew, M. L. Hardman & H. P. Bluhm (Eds.), *Mental retardation: Social and educational perspectives.* St. Louis: C. V. Mosby Co., 1977.

Borland, B. L., & Heckman, H. K. Hyperactive boys and their brothers: A 25-year follow-up study. *Archives of General Psychiatry,* 1976, *33,* 669–75.

Botwinick, J. *Cognitive processes in maturity and old age.* New York: Springer Publishing Co., 1967.

Botwinick, J. *Aging and behavior.* New York: Springer Publishing Co., 1973.

Botwinick, J. *Aging and behavior: A comprehensive integration of research findings* (2d ed.). New York: Springer Publishing Co., 1978.

Brolin, D. E. *Vocational preparation of retarded citizens.* Columbus, Ohio: Charles E. Merrill Publishing Co., 1976.

Bromley, D. B. *The psychology of human aging* (2d ed.). Baltimore: Penguin Books, 1974.

Chinn, P. C., Drew, C. J., & Logan, D. R. *Mental retardation: A life cycle approach* (2d ed.). St Louis: C. V. Mosby Co., 1979.

Chown, S. M. Personality and aging. In K. W. Schaie (Ed.), *Theory and methods of research on aging.* Morgantown: West Virginia University Library, 1968.

Chown, S. M. Morale, careers, and personal potentials. In J. E. Birren & K. W. Schaie (Eds.), *Handbook of the psychology of Aging.* New York: Van Nostrand Reinhold Co., 1977.

Cowdry, E. V. *Problems of aging.* Baltimore: Williams & Wilkins, 1942.

Cox, S. The learning-disabled adult. *Academic Therapy,* 1977, *13,* 79–86.

Datan, N. *Women's attitudes toward the climacteric in five Israeli subcultures.* Unpublished doctoral dissertation, University of Chicago, 1971.

Depue, R. A., & Monroe, S. M. Learned helplessness in the perspective of the depressive disorders: Conceptual and definitional issues. *Journal of Abnormal Psychology.* 1978, *87,* 3–20.

Diagnostic and statistical manual: Mental disorders (DSM III). Washington, D.C.: American Psychiatric Association, 1980.

Dickerson, M., Hamilton, J., Huber, R., & Segal, R. The aged mentally retarded: The invisible client—a challenge to the community. Paper presented at the annual meeting of the American Association on Mental Deficiency, Toronto, May, 1974.

Dutton, L. The physical development of mongols. *Archives of the Diseases of Childhood,* 1959, *34,* 46–50.

Edgerton, R. B. *The cloak of competence.* Berkeley: University of California Press, 1967.

Edgerton, R. B., & Bercovici, S. M. The cloak of competence years later. *American Journal of Mental Deficiency,* 1976, *80,* 485–97.

Finch, C. E., & Hayflick, L. (Eds.). *Handbook of the biology of aging.* Van Nostrand Reinhold Co., 1977.

Fisher, M. A., & Zeaman, D. Growth and decline of retardate intelligence. In N. R. Ellis (Ed.), *International review of research in mental retardation* (Vol. 4). New York: Academic Press, 1970.

Floor, L., & Rosen, M. Investigating the phenomenon of helplessness in mentally retarded adults. *American Journal of Mental Deficiency,* 1975, *79,* 565–72.

Gelfand, D. M., Jenson, W. R., & Drew, C. J. *Understanding child behavior disorders.* New York: Holt, Rinehart & Winston, 1982.

Gliedman, J., & Roth, W. *The unexpected minority: Handicapped children of America.* New York: Harcourt Brace Jovanovich, 1980.

Goddard, H. H. The height and weight of feeble minded children in American institutions. *Journal of Nervous and Mental Disorders,* 1912, *39,* 217.

Goddard, H. H. *Feeblemindedness: Its causes and consequences.* New York: Macmillan Co., 1914.

Goodman, J. F. IQ decline in mentally retarded adults: A matter of fact or methodological flaw. *Journal of Mental Deficiency Research,* 1977, *21,* 199–203. (a)

Goodman, J. F. Aging and intelligence in young retarded adults: A cross-sectional study of fluid abilities in three samples. *Psychological Reports,* 1977, *41,* 255–63. (b)

Gould, R. L. The phases of adult life: A study in developmental psychology. *American Journal of Psychiatry,* 1972, *129,* 521–31.

Hallahan, D., & Cruickshank, W. *Psychoeduca-tional foundations of learning disabilities.* Englewood Cliffs, N.J.: Prentice-Hall, 1973.

Hammar, S. L., & Owens, J. W. M. Adolescence. In D. Smith & E. Bierman (Eds.), *The biologic ages of man.* Philadelphia: W. B. Saunders Co., 1973.

Hardman, M. L., & Drew, C. J. The physically handicapped retarded individual: A review. *Mental Retardation.* 1977, *15*(5), 43–48.

Hartocollis, P. The syndrome of minimal brain dysfunction in young adult patients. *Bulletin of the Menninger Clinic,* 1968, *32,* 102–14.

Havighurst, R. J. *Developmental tasks and education.* New York: David McKay Co., 1972.

Hershey, D. *Life span and factors affecting it.* Springfield, Ill.: Charles C. Thomas, 1974.

Heward, W. L., & Orlansky, M. D. *Exceptional children: An introductory survey to special education.* Columbus, Ohio: Charles E. Merrill Publishing Co., 1980.

Hippolitus, P. (President's Commission on Employment of the Handicapped, Washington, D.C.). Personal communication, December 10, 1981.

Horn, J. L. Human abilities: A review of research and theory in the early 1970's. *Annual Review of Psychology,* 1976, *27.*

Horn, J. L., & Donaldson, G. On the myth of intellectual decline in adulthood. *American Psychologist,* 1976, *31,* 701–19.

Jarvik, L. F. Thoughts on the psychology of aging. *American Psychologist,* 1975, *30,* 576–83.

Kaplan, O. J. Introduction. In O. J. Kaplan (Ed.), *Psychopathology of aging.* New York: Academic Press, 1979.

Kimmel, D. C. *Adulthood and aging: An interdisciplinary, developmental view.* New York: John Wiley & Sons, 1974.

Kindred, M., Cohen, J., Penrod, D., & Shaffer, T. (Eds.). *The mentally retarded citizen and the law.* New York: The Free Press, 1976.

Kleban, M. H., Lawton, M. P., Brody, E. M., & Moss, M. Behavioral observations of mentally impaired aged: Those who decline and those who do not. *Journal of Gerontology,* 1976, *31,* 333–39.

Knox, A. B. *Adult development and learning.* San Francisco: Jossey-Bass, 1977.

Kvaraceus, W. C. *Juvenile delinquency and the school.* Yonkers-on-the-Hudson, N.Y.: World Publishing Co., 1945.

Kuhlen, R. G. Age differences in personality during adult years. *Psychological Bulletin,* 1945, *42,* 333–58.

Kuhlen, R. G. Aging and adjustment. In J. E. Birren (Ed.), *Handbook of aging and the individual.* Chicago: University of Chicago Press, 1959.

Labouvie-Vief, G. Adult cognitive development: In search of alternative interpretations. *Merrill-Palmer Quarterly,* 1977, *23,* 227–63.

Levinson, D. J., Darrow, C. M., Klein, E. G., Levinson, M. H., & McKee, B. The psychological development of men in early adulthood and the midlife transition. In D. F. Ricks, A. Thomas & M. Roff (Eds.), *Life history research in psychopathology* (Vol. 3). Minneapolis: University of Minnesota Press, 1974.

Levitan, S. A, & Taggart, R. *Jobs for the disabled.* Baltimore: Johns Hopkins University Press, 1977.

Lugo, J. O., & Hershey, G. L. *Human development: A physiological, biological, and sociological approach to the life span* (2d ed.) New York: Macmillan Co., 1979.

Lynn, R., Gluckin, N. D., & Kripke, B. *Learning disabilities: An overview of theories, approaches, and politics.* New York: The Free Press, 1979.

Mann, H. B., & Greenspan, S. I. The identification and treatment of adult brain dysfunction. *American Journal of Psychiatry,* 1976, *133,* 1013–17.

Marshall, W. A. Growth in mentally retarded children. *Developmental medicine and child neurology,* 1968, *10,* 390–91.

Mendelson, W., Johnson, N., & Stewart, M. A. Hyperactive children as adolescents: A follow-up study. *Journal of Nervous and Mental Disorders,* 1971, *153,* 273–79.

Menkes, M. H., Rowe, J. S., & Menkes, J. H. A 25-year follow-up study on the hyperkinetic child with MBD. *Pediatrics,* 1967, *39,* 393–99.

Miller, J. What happened to those that got away? *Academic Therapy,* 1973, *9*(1), 47–55.

Moore, F. Mentally defective delinquents. In I. C. Burrows (Ed.), *Proceedings of the National*

Conference on Charities Correction. Boston: George H. Ellis, 1911.

Morris, H. H., Escoll, P. J., & Wexler, R. Aggressive behaviors of childhood: A follow-up study. *American Journal of Psychiatry,* 1956, *112,* 991–97.

Morrison, J. R., & Minkoff, K. Explosive personality as a sequel to the hyperactive child syndrome. *Comparative Psychiatry,* 1975, *16,* 343–48.

Mosier, H. D., Grossman, H. J., & Dingman, H. F. Physical growth in mental defectives. *Pediatrics,* 1965, *36,* 465–519.

Nesselroade, J. R., & Baltes, P. B. (Eds.). *Longitudinal research in the study of behavior and development.* New York: Academic Press, 1979.

Neugarten, B. L. Age groups in American society and the rise of the young old. *Annals of American Academy of Science,* September 1974.

Neugarten, B. L. Personality and aging. In J. E. Birren & K. W. Schaie (Eds.), *Handbook of the psychology of aging.* New York: Van Nostrand Reinhold Co., 1977.

Neugarten, B. L., & Datan, N. Sociological perspectives of the life cycle. In P. B. Baltes & K. W. Schaie (Eds.), *Life-span developmental psychology: personality and socialization.* New York: Academic Press, 1974.

Neugarten, B. L., Wood, V., Kraines, R. J., & Loomis, B. Women's attitudes toward the menopause. *Vita Humana,* 1963, *6,* 140–51.

Neulinger, J. On leisure. *Behavior Today,* 1974.

Nihira, K. Dimensions of adaptive behavior in institutionalized mentally retarded children and adults: Developmental perspective. *American Journal of Mental Deficiency,* 1976, *81,* 215–26.

Nirje, B. The normalization principle and its human management implications. In R. B. Kugel and W. Wolfensberger (Eds.), *Changing patterns in residential services for the mentally retarded.* Washington, D.C.: President's Committee on Mental Retardation, 1969.

Nuttall, R. L. The strategy of functional age research. *Aging and Human Development,* 1972, *3,* 149–52.

O'Neal, P., & Robins, L. M. The relation of childhood behavior problems to adult psychiatric status: A 30-year follow-up study of 150 patients. *American Journal of Psychiatry,* 1958, *114,* 961–69.

Overmier, J. B., & Seligman, M. E. P. Effects of inescapable shock upon subsequent escape and avoidance learning. *Journal of Comparative and Physiological Psychology,* 1967, *74,* 1–9.

Peterson, L., & Smith, L. L. A comparison of postschool adjustment of educable mentally retarded adults with that of adults of normal intelligence. *Exceptional Children,* 1960, *26,* 404–8.

Pineo, P. C. Disenchantment in the later years of marriage. *Marriage and Family Living,* 1961, *23,* 3–11.

Pozsonyi, J., & Lobb, H. Growth in mentally retarded children. *Journal of Pediatrics,* 1967, *71,* 865–68.

Quitkin, F., & Klein, D. F. Two behavioral syndromes in young adults related to possible minimal brain dysfunction. *Journal of Psychiatric Research,* 1969, *7,* 131–42.

Reinert, G. Educational psychology in the context of the human life span. In P. B. Baltes & O. G. Brim, Jr. (Eds.), *Life-span development and behavior* (Vol. 3). New York: Academic Press, 1980.

Riegel, K. F. Personality theory and aging. In J. E. Birren (Ed.), *Handbook of aging and the individual.* Chicago: University of Chicago Press, 1959.

Riegel, K. F. An epitaph for a paradigm. *Human Development,* 1973, *16,* 1–7.

Riley, M. W., & Foner, A. *Aging and society* (Vol. 1). New York: Russell Sage Foundation, 1968.

Rogers, D. *The adult years: An introduction to aging,* Englewood Cliffs, N.J.: Prentice-Hall, 1979.

Rosenberg, S. D., & Farrell, M. P. Identity and crisis in middle-aged men. *International Journal of Aging and Human Development,* 1976, *3,* 45–62.

Rosenthal, R. H., & Allen, T. W. An examination of attention, arousal, and learning dysfunctions of hyperkinetic children. *Psychological Bulletin,* 1978, *85,* 689–715.

Schaie, K. W., & Gribbin, K. Adult development and aging. *Annual Review of Psychology,* 1975, *26,* 65–96.

Schaie, K. W., & Marquette, B. Personality in maturity and old age. In R. M. Dreger (Ed.), *Multivariate personality research: Contributions to the understanding of personality in honor of Raymond B. Cattell.* Baton Rouge: Claitors Publishing Division, 1972.

Seligman, M. E. P., & Maier, S. F. Failure to escape traumatic shock. *Journal of Experimental Psychology,* 1967, *74,* 1–9.

Shelly, E. M., & Riester, A. Syndrome of MBD in young adults. *Diseases of the Nervous System,* 1972, *33,* 335–39.

Siegel, J. S. On the demography of aging. *Demography,* 1980, *17,* 345–64.

Stanfield, J. S. Graduation: What happens to the retarded child when he grows up? *Exceptional Children,* 1973, *39,* 548–52.

Stevens-Long, J. *Adult life development processes.* Palo Alto, Calif.: Mayfield Publishing Co., 1979.

Tarter, R. E., McBride, H., Buonpane, N., et al. Differentiation of alcholics: Childhood history of minimal brain dysfunction, family history, and drinking pattern. *Archives of General Psychiatry,* 1977, *34,* 761–68.

Troll, L. E. *Early and middle adulthood.* Monterey, Calif.: Brooks/Cole Publishing Co., 1975.

U.S. Bureau of the Census, *Statistical abstract of the United States: 1979* (100th ed.). Washington, D.C., 1979.

Wallace, G., & McLoughlin, J. A. *Learning disabilities: Concepts and characteristics* (2d ed.) Columbus, Ohio: Charles E. Merrill Publishing Co., 1979.

Webb, G. M. The neurologically impaired youth goes to college. In R. E. Weber (Ed.), *Handbook on learning disabilities: A prognosis for the child, the adolescent, the adult.* Englewood Cliffs, N.J.: Prentice-Hall, 1974.

Weintraub, W., & Aronson, H. A survey of patients in classical psychoanalysis: Some vital statistics. *Journal of Nervous and Mental Disorders,* 1968, *146,* 98–102.

Wender, P. H., Reimherr, F. W., & Wood, D. R. Attention deficit disorder ("minimal brain dysfunction") in adults: A replication study of diagnosis and drug treatment. *Archives of General Psychiatry,* 1981, *38,* 449–56.

Wolfensberger, W. Twenty predictions about the future of residential services in mental retardation. *Mental Retardation,* 1969, *7*(6), 51–54.

Wolfensberger, W. Will there always be an institution? II: The impact of new service models: Residential alternatives to institutions. *Mental Retardation,* 1972, *9*(6), 31–38.

Wood, D. R., Reimherr, F. W., Wender, P. H. & Johnson, G. E. Diagnosis and treatment of minimal brain dysfunction in adults: A preliminary report. *Archives of General Psychiatry,* 1976, *33,* 1453–60.

Yearbook of special education (3d ed.). Chicago: Marquis Who's Who, 1977.

AUTHOR INDEX

SUBJECT INDEX